The Economy of Goodness

Rey-Sheng Her

The Economy
of Goodness

Rey-Sheng Her
Tzu Chi Charity Foundation
Hualien, Taiwan

ISBN 978-981-97-6362-7 ISBN 978-981-97-6363-4 (eBook)
https://doi.org/10.1007/978-981-97-6363-4

ACKNOWLEDGMENTS

I would like to express my sincere gratitude to the Dunhe Foundation for their generous sponsorship of my research for Economy of Goodness. I am also grateful to the Faculty of Asian and Middle Eastern Studies (FAMES) at the University of Cambridge and the Oxford Centre for Buddhist Studies (OCBS) at the University of Oxford for providing invaluable access to reference materials. Finally, I would like to thank the Tzu Chi Foundation for its inspiration, resources, and the wealth of information they provided on case examples.

CONTENTS

1   **The Author's Preface to *The Economy of Goodness***   1
Happiness Through Altruism   4
Goodness Across Various Economic Civilizations   5
Business Once as the Highest Good   8
Altruism as a Great Distributor of Resources   8
The Economy of Goodness that Cherishes Material Life   9
An Ideal of Harmonious Unification and Common Goodness   10

2   **Introduction: The Origin of Economy of Goodness**   11
Value-Based Philosophy and Economic Prosperity   11
From Economy of Charity to Economy of Goodness   13
Take Faith as the Core Foundation   14
The Theoretical Origination of the Economy of Goodness   15
A Discussion of Perceptions of Goodness   16
   Goodness in the West   16
   Goodness in the East is to Benefit All People and Things   21
   The Motivation of Goodness Leads to Central Harmony   25
   The Means of Goodness: Preserving Harmony,
   Compassion, and Humility   29
   The Fruit of Goodness: Supreme Harmony   35
   Supreme Goodness that Aims for Truth   46
   Harmonious Goodness that Encompasses Oneself
   and Others   47
   Common Goodness with Unification of All Laws   49

3   Reflections on the Contemporary Capitalist Economy   51

Section 1: The Historical Construction of Individualism   52

   Marine Trade and Capitalism: A Historical Examination   52

   Commerce as the Great Equalizer   53

   Business Development and Political Equality   54

Section 2: Individuals in Traditional Western Society   55

   The Fundamental Ignorance of Individualism   56

Section 3: Outlook on Life as a Whole   57

   The Taoist View of the Individual   58

Section 4: The Buddhist View on Life and Capitalism   62

Section 5: Altruism and Harmonious Unification as the Core   67

Section 6: Economy of Goodness Based on All-Connected Things   70

   Taoist Altruism of Supreme Goodness   71

   The All-Inclusive and All-Shared Confucian Economy of Goodness   72

   The Four Sufficiencies in the Buddhist Economy of Goodness   73

   Altruistic and Self-Interested Economies of Goodness with Spiritual and Material Abundance   74

4   The Origin of Altruism: The Key to Group Survival   77

Section 1: Exploring the Possibility of Human Altruism   77

   Altruistic Groups and Natural Selection   78

Section 2: Altruism: Nature and Reality for Humans   80

Section 3: An Ideological Discussion of Altruism   81

   Voluntary Altruism   81

   Altruism Begins with the Self   82

   Deficiencies in Calculating Self-interest   84

Section 4: Starvation Dilemma   85

   Mutual Love Between the Self and Others   85

Section 5: Integrating Altruism and Self-Interest in the Economic System   88

   Pareto Optimality Enabled by Altruism   89

Section 6: Altruism May Generate Self-Interests   91

   Complete Altruism Seeks No Self-Interest   92

   Altruism Should Not Be the Sole Motivation   93

Altruism that Combines Motivation and Result   94
Section 7: Altruism Transcending the Human Self   95
Section 8: The Altruistic Philosophy That All Things Are One   98
Altruism Provides the Root for Individuals to Find
Belonging   98

5   **The Economy of Goodness in Feudal Society**   101
Section 1: Sumer Civilization: A Symbiotic Choice Between
Mechanical Urban Economy and Nature   101
Section 2: Greek Civilization: Dialectic Between Idealism
and Materialism   105
The Value of Use and Exchange   106
Spiritual Abundance and Money Transaction   108
Support for the Community Brings Happiness   109
Happiness is Synonymous with Goodness; Goodness Brings
Forth Happiness   110
Section 3: Chinese Civilization: The Economic Life
of the Individual and the Group   111
Clan Inheritance and Economic Development in China   115
The Equal Affluence of Both Individuals and Country   116
Economic Inequality and Political Disturbance
in Ancient China   118
Monarchy and Economic Development   119
Section 4: The Transnational Economy of the Roman Empire   121
The Beginning of the Transnational Industrial Division
of Labor   121
The Pioneer of Government Expanding Domestic Demand   122
The Predatory Economy Ends in Pillage   124
Section 5: Economic Thought in Western Feudalism   124
The Economic Views of the Church Fathers   124
The Medieval Church and the Genesis of Modern
Capital Entrepreneurs   127

6   **Philosophical and Cultural Beliefs and the Economy**
of Goodness   129
Section 1: Hebrew Jewish Economic Philosophy: The
Harmonious Unification of Abstinence and Pleasure   129
The God that Assumes No Image and Pragmatic Jews   130
Prophets Are All Wealthy and Influential   131
Unlimited Wealth from Limited Resources   131

Man Is the Master of All Creatures on Earth   132
The Jewish Outlook on Interest and Good Deeds   133
Follow the Commandments and Make Good Results
Through Good Deeds   135
Pure Goodness in Jewish Thought   136
The Reward for Doing Good Is Goodness   137
Section 2: Economic Justice in Christian Civilization:
Balance Between Material and Mind   139
Humankind as God's Agent and Governor on Earth   139
Anti-slave Economy and the Commercialization
of Humanity   139
Christ's Compassion for the Poor   141
Christ's Concern with Both Matter and Mind   142
The Affluent People's Extended Love for Humanity   143
Interest and Economic Equality   144
The Goodness in the Christian Economy   146
Section 3: Economic Thought of Islamic Civilization   148
Section 4: Economic Thought and Practice of Confucianism
in China   152
The Economy of Goodness Is Consistent with the Way
of Heaven   152
The Justification of Personal Desire   154
The Enterprise Rooted in Virtues   156
The Economic Thought of the King's Way   157
The Economy of Goodness and China's Historical Cycle
of Governing Social Chaos   157
The Economy of Goodness Is Rooted in Prosperity
and Harmony and the Shared Responsibility
of Government and the Public   162
The Economy of Goodness with Virtue-Based Governance   165
Entrepreneurs of Internal Sage and External King   170
Section 5: Economic Thought in Early Buddhist Civilization   171
Economic Life During the Time of the Buddha   171
The Buddha's Views on Worldly Possessions   173
The Bodhisattva of Wealth, Purity, and Tranquility   175
The Buddha's Views on Business Development   176
The Buddha's Teachings on Wealth Management   182
The Buddha's Views on Business Principles   185
The Buddha on Economic Responsibility   193

The Buddha's Ideal Bodhisattva Businessmen   195
The Lonely Elder: A Good Business Model   197
Section 6: Economic Thought and Practice in Traditional
Chinese Buddhism   200
    The Entry Period of Buddhism in China   200
    Exploring Buddhist Economics at the Dunhuang Grottoes   202
    An Inexhaustible Store of Teaching Across Three Levels
    and an Altruistic Economy   203
    Zen Master Baizhang's Temple Economic Reform   205
    The Good Economic Ideal of Chinese Buddhism   208
Section 7: A Modern Look at Confucian and Buddhist
Views on the Economy of Goodness   209
    Master Taixu's Reform of Temple Teaching and Property
    Management   209
    Jing Si Abode's Self-Reliance Through Independent
    Farming   211
    Practicing Monetary Purity   211
    Diligence, Self-Restraint, and Extending to All People   213

7   **Economic Goodness Before the Industrial Revolution**   215
Section 1: Economic Mutual Trust Structure in Medieval
Commercial Society   215
    The Ascension of Medieval Towns   215
    The Origin of Capital   216
    The Rise of Free People   218
    The Establishment of the Medieval Chamber of Commerce   218
    The Formation of the Joint Stock Company   219
    A Business System of Fraternity and Mutual Aid   220
    The Rise of Citizen Economy and the Establishment
    of Mutual Aid   221
Section 2: Historical Dialectic of Altruism and Egoism
in Commerce Development   223
Section 3: Historical Dialectics of Self-Interested
and Altruistic Economy   225
    Economic Exploitation and Fair Distribution   226
    Self-Interest Leading to Structural Global Exploitation   227
Section 4: Deviation from Mutual Assistance in Commerce   229

8   The Evolution of Self-Interested and Altruistic Economic Thought   231
  Section 1: The Beginning of Self-Interested Economy   231
  Section 2: Free Market and Overall Interests   234
    The Free Market and Exploitation of Workers   234
    The End of the Free Market Is Freedom   237
  Section 3: Bureaucratic Morality and Good and Evil Economy   241
  Section 4: Goodness and Morality of Social Enterprise   243
    Leading the Historical Development of Economic Fairness and Justice 244
    Micro-Credit and Social Enterprise   245
    The Actualization and Case Example of Economy of Goodness and Public Welfare 247
    Non-profit Social Enterprise with Revenue   251
    Concrete Contributions of Social Enterprises to the Economy 253
  Section 5: A Capitalist Market with the Motives of Goodness and Morality 254

9   Goodness as the Foundation: The Motivation of Goodness in Economic Activities   257
  Section 1: Altruistic Motivation and Economic Activities   257
    Motivation and Objectives in the Economy   258
    The Human Pursuit of Infinity   261
    Altruistic Practices in the Economy   262
  Section 2: Nature of Production and Consumption   266
    The Source of Product Creation Is Altruism   266
    The Motive of Production Should Be for Human Welfare   267
    Creation Comes from the Individual's Pure Nature   268
    Choosing Does Not Equal Freedom   269
    Money Cannot Buy Happiness   270
    A Global Organization Built with Goodness   271
    Altruism Not for Self-Gain   272
    Educate People with Goodness After Enriching Them   274
    Businessmen Can Be Sages   276
    The Economy of Goodness: Rooted in Compassionate Giving   278
  Section 3: Cultivation of the Motivation of Goodness   280
    How Can We Foster a Rising Spirit of Altruism?   280

      Heuristic Altruistic Practices   283

      Introspective Transformation into Altruism   284

      Section 4: The Construction of an Altruistic System   287

**10 Goodness in Use: The Means of the Economy
of Goodness**   289

      *Section 1: The Method of Goodness, Its Value
and Significance to Human Beings*   289

        Expand Necessary Goodness   291

        Expanding Good Is Not Fighting the Evil   292

      Section 2: The Means and Results of Goodness   294

      Section 3: Goodness in Trade   298

      Section 4: Financial Goodness   300

        Altruism Made Micro-Banks Successful   303

        From Poverty Alleviation to Local Economic Incubator   304

        *Intelligent Poverty Alleviation Through Production
and Marketing*   305

        *A Harmonious Symbiosis of Commercial Revenue,
Poverty Alleviation, and Public Welfare*   306

        Impact Investing for Public Welfare and Good Enterprises 306

        Impact Investing in China   308

        The Shutdown of Hainan Development Bank   309

        *Ma's Dealing with Two Major Crises upon Entering
China Merchants Bank*   310

        *Development of Internet Banking and Electronic
Commerce*   310

        *Strengthening the Bank's System and Accumulating
Funds*   311

        *Taking Hong Kong as a Pilot to Move Toward
Internationalization*   312

        Capital to Goodness   313

      Section 5: Production of Goodness   315

        The Economy of Goodness that Cherishes Material Life 319

      Section 6: The Consumption of Goodness   321

        Consumption in Cognition of Material Life   323

        Consumption that Cares for One's Mind   324

        Consumption for the Protection of Lives   326

**11   Goodness as Reality: The Result of Economy
      of Goodness**   329
Section 1: Achieving Equal Wealth Through Love   329
   The Exquisite Happiness of the Majority   329
   Equal Wealth Should Be Both Material and Spiritual 330
   Love as the Key to Achieving Equal Wealth   332
   There Is No Competition in EOG   334
Section 2: Benevolence as Happiness   336
Section 3: Altruistic Innovation   340
Section 4: Sustainable and Common Prosperity   342
   Full Employment   342
   Work as Self-Cultivation   345
   Live in Abundant Prosperity with All Beings   347

12   Thoughts and Practice of Good Enterprises   351
Section 1: Faith as the Core   351
   Faith Is Better than Strategy   354
   Fostering Corporate Culture for Exponential Growth 355
   Change the World with Faith   356
   *Practicing the New Wangdao: Stan Shih, the Pioneer
      of Taiwan's IT Industry*   357
   *The Key to Operating a Business of Goodness Is Subtlety,
      Invisibility, and Future*   358
   Customer-Oriented Branding   359
   *Altruism: A Force that Promotes Harmonious Balance
      of Multi-Party Interests*   360
   Run a Marathon with Chinese-Western Philosophy   361
   *One of the World's Largest Faith-Based Charity
      Organizations*   361
Section 2: Value-Oriented Leadership   362
   Value-Oriented Leadership in Corporate Management 362
   Lend Life to Enterprises with Value   364
   Consolidate a Country's Culture with Value   365
   Value-Oriented and Spiritual Leadership   368
   Mind-Power Unleashes Material Power   371
   Values are Better at Creating Wisdom than Strategies 376
   Mobilize People with Value   378
   Universal Equality in Value Practice   379
   Value in Work   380

The Hospital of Love Built with Love 382
Section 3: Management with Love 384
People-Centered Polycentric System 387
Family-Like Management 388
Loving Employees Means Guiding Them to Love Others 391
How to Love an Unfit Employee 393
The Power of Leading by Example 396
Employees' Autonomy and Entrepreneurship 397
Section 4: Governance with Principles 398
Integrity-Based Business 400
Section 5: Innovation with Compassion 403
Innovate with Compassion 403
The Practice of Compassion 405
Innovation with Concentration 406
Innovation with Equality 407
Section 6: Round Organization 408
Always on the Frontline 409
Holacratic Organizational Model 410
Pluralistic and Round Organizational Structure 411
Section 7: Altruism as a System 412
Wealth Through a System of Benefiting the Public 413
Structural Altruism and the Refresh of Microsoft 415
Systematic and Structural Thinking and Altruism 416
Section 8: Establishing Role Models for Sustainable Development 418
Commercial Sustainability with Role Models 418
The Sustainability of Commandments Over Time 419
All Are Successors 420
Role Model in Enterprises 421
Section 9: Coexist with Planet Earth 423
Cherish the Material Life 423
Dedicated to Environmental Protection and Love for the Earth. 425
The Earth Is Our Home 427
Section 10: Co-Prosperity for All Things 428
Good Enterprises with a Philosophy of All Things Connected 428
The Enterprise of Goodness, Compassion, and Equality 432
Good Enterprises that Benefit All Things 435

Spiritual Cultivation for Good Enterprises   438
Six Practices of Good Enterprises   439

Economic System for Common Goodness   445

References   461

Index   471

CHAPTER 1

The Author's Preface to *The Economy of Goodness*

In Spring 2018 I came to the University of Cambridge as a visiting scholar and began writing my book, *The Economy of Goodness*. I had rented an apartment facing the river and from my second-floor window, I could admire the river's tranquil beauty. It was April and the air and the water both felt crisp and cool. The house was surrounded by a large expanse of grass and beyond, a peaceful town snuggled up against rolling woods. The River Cam, beloved of many weeping willows, meandered through these woods and through Cambridge without making a sound.

The River Cam is an immortal soul and eternal lover of Cambridge. It captivated the romantic poet Xu Zhimo in the 1920s, who was renowned for his poetic verses. He used to wander around the grass beside the river rather than study in the library. Rather than following Xu's steps, I had my work to do here in Cambridge. Every morning, I would ride my bicycle through the ancient buildings, over cobblestone streets, and past a church that had existed for 800 years. The church carried a plaque that said, "The Saints, sinners, rich, poor, mansion owner or homeless are all welcome to dine in the church." This conveys the principle of Christian charity inherent in Cambridge's humanitarian traditions.

The University of Cambridge Library is situated in the woods, providing a tranquil and secluded atmosphere that suits my needs perfectly. I devoted much of my time to the library of the Faculty of Asian and Middle Eastern Studies (FAMES). This library contains a profusion of books on culture and religion. Additionally, I had the opportunity to compare research with other academics.

A day would pass in the blink of an eye with my reading and writing. At dusk, I'd sit peacefully beside the River Cam or stand on the grass to sense the vitality and elation of the earth. I'd let my musings rest in the final glints of the sunset. This is Cambridge.

Nothing is better than such a serene setting for brainstorming. My goal at Cambridge was to research the concept of goodness through various economic systems in human history. I had served with the Tzu Chi Foundation for 18 years, pondering how goodness in charity can be solidified and incorporated into an economy.

FAMES stands in contrast to the Faculty of Economics, which is where Keynes advanced his planned economy that aided in relieving the Great Depression in America. This was accomplished through President Roosevelt's "New Deal," which increased local demand and restored the US economy. Propelled by Keynes' financial reasoning, Chiang Ching-Kuo implemented ten construction projects in Taiwan, boosting consumer demand as well as government control, thus making Taiwan one of the Four Little Dragons (i.e., New Industrial Economies) in Asia. With the same principle of Four Modernizations, Deng Xiaoping also succeeded in turning China into one of the world's most successful economic entities.

Keynes' economic ideal aimed at national and individual wealth. However, wealth is not the ultimate aim of an economy; it does not equate to happiness. Happiness lies in the relationship of love, spiritual enrichment, and contribution to public welfare. Thus, a blueprint of social wealth and individual happiness can be labeled "Goodness" and the economic system centered around it, the "Economy of Goodness."

Goodness has always been a central theme in both Eastern and Western civilizations. Generally, it implies truth in the West, whereas in China it encompasses the benefit of all things and all people.

When Confucius heard Wu's music, he said, "It's beautiful, but lacks goodness." He also heard Shao's music and commented, "It's beautiful, and is full of goodness." The meaning is that simply being beautiful is not enough; goodness is also necessary. Beauty aims not to ignite desire but to purify the human spirit. Therefore, beauty cannot be separated from goodness, and beauty must strive toward goodness in order to be complete.

An important Confucian classic, *The Book of Rites*, recorded: "…however perfect the course may be, if one does not learn it, he does not know its goodness."[1] This indicates that the truth must be of goodness. "Learn" should be understood as "practice." One must practice the truth to know its benefits. Goodness carries the meaning of "to benefit." Goodness is not some truth that sets up rules for everybody but creates happiness for everybody. An ultimate truth, if not able to benefit people, is not of goodness. In short, the truth must be of goodness. Considering the completeness of life, goodness is more ultimate than truth.

Goodness (善 shan) in Chinese implies itself by its word form. It consists of a Person's Mouth and a Sheep, suggesting that everyone should have an equal share of a Sheep. To create an inclusive, equitable, and prosperous society, it is fitting that everyone is benevolent.

Plato, a luminary of Western philosophy, spoke of the Summum Bonum and attached great importance to the ultimate truth. Nevertheless, the Chinese do not pursue the ultimate truth, and they do not measure everything in the world against it. In ancient China, goodness means allowing everybody to have their own goodness and beauty. As Mencius said: "What everybody wants is goodness," "When everybody has goodness, it is called beauty."[2] Meeting people's needs is goodness; true beauty arises only when everybody is happy. Hence, "when everybody has goodness, it is called beauty."[3]

Even Lao Tzu, who advocates for life to return to "nothingness," emphasizes that "The highest goodness resembles water. Water greatly benefits myriad things without contention. It stays in places that people dislike. Therefore, it is similar to the Tao."[4] It benefits all things, even approaching and helping that which is disliked by others. Therefore, it is not about striking down evil, but about educating and transforming it. Only when all evil in the world is transformed into good can it be considered true goodness. Therefore, it is not about striking down evil, but about educating and transforming it.

[1] Confucius. (2013). *The Book of Rites (Li Ji): English-Chinese Version* (D. Sheng, Ed., J. Legge, Trans.). CreateSpace Independent Publishing Platform. p. 167.

[2] Mencius. (2019). *The Works of Mencius* (Sun Jiaqi ed.). New Taipei City: Jen Jen Publishing Co., Ltd. p. 339.

[3] M. & Legge, J. (2011). *The Works of Mencius*. New York: Dover Publications. p. 490.

[4] Tzu, L., Lin, D., & Das, L. S. (2006). *Tao Te Ching: Annotated & Explained* (SkyLight Illuminations) (1st ed.). SkyLight Paths.

Therefore, goodness is ultimately altruism; a benefit to all people and all things.

The ultimate ideal of goodness is that all things and laws unite to form one common good.

To practice such an ideal is to foster a loving relationship with all people and things.

Goodness means altruism. The Economy of Goodness encompasses altruistic economic activities, making altruism the primary purpose of an economy."

HAPPINESS THROUGH ALTRUISM

This book argues that in economic activities, self-interest can only be realized through altruism and that profits come only from benefiting all people.[5] The purpose of altruism is neither to gain an advantage for oneself nor to imply suffering losses; instead, it involves creating mutual benefits between the giver and the recipient, ultimately proving more effective than self-interest.

However, we have long accepted that altruism stems from self-interest, as Adam Smith said. He convinced people who seemed selfish that, through pursuing our own interests, the "invisible hand" would distribute these for equal wealth and the collective good of society. Sadly, however, this prediction has never materialized. The gap between the wealthy and the impoverished has never leveled off and instead become enlarged.

Today, about 800 million people are still living in extreme poverty, as defined by the United Nations as those living on less than $2.15 per day. Professor Angus Deaton from Fitzwilliam College at the University of Cambridge notes that, if every person in the US donated just 15 cents, it would lift the 800 million people out of extreme poverty. However, not everyone is so generous, and donations often don't reach those in need, due to misuse and exploitation. This makes it impossible for charities to effectively tackle global poverty.

So, how can we make it? We cannot achieve our goal of helping 800 million poor people if we take an Adam Smith viewpoint that the self-interested pursue benefits for themselves and not for all.

---

[5] A viewpoint by Bai Yansong (白岩松), a senior host with CCTV (China Central Television) of China.

The mind of a self-interested person is insatiable, their desires are bottomless. The Law of Diminishing Marginal Utility tells us that a person will be happy to get their first million, but they are not as excited about the second million, because two million is only twice as much as one million.

So, a person may be pleased to acquire their first million dollars, but may not be as ecstatic for the second million. To get from one dollar to one million dollars, they require one million times the money. But what is one million times of one million dollars? Marginal benefits are diminishing, and that kind of happiness requires earning one trillion dollars. But how many people can earn one trillion? After one trillion, the marginal benefit will be diminished again for the next one trillion. In this way, one can never be truly satisfied or happy.

People will not find happiness through desire.

Humans tend to pursue infinite satisfaction. A mind filled with desires can never be satisfied, and happiness will always be out of reach. On the other hand, a mind that pursues infinity will learn to give, and to give infinitely brings infinite happiness.

Psychologically, it is easier to find happiness by benefiting others than by benefiting oneself.

Darwin proposed natural selection and concluded that altruistic races are more competitive than selfish ones; all still-existing races on Earth feature the ingrained mechanism of altruism.

Scientists have found that animals possess a "temporal cortex" responsible for altruism and mercy. This cortex enlarges in a mouse when seeing one of its kind slaughtered, as humans do when witnessing charitable deeds or suffering. This implies that altruism and mercy can be stimulated and augmented. When we come to understand that altruism can promote our growth, we will be more proactive in practicing it on a greater scale.

GOODNESS ACROSS VARIOUS ECONOMIC CIVILIZATIONS

In the context of *The Economy of Goodness*, I will examine the concepts of goodness and altruism across various civilizations. Instead of discussing evils, my focus will be on identifying models of goodness within multiple civilizations and exploring how each can play an active role in economic development.

The ancient Sumerian civilization dates back 8,000 years. *The Epic of Gilgamesh* reveals the fear of people toward urbanization and mechanization; the former increasing the divide between the haves and have-nots and the latter worsening the tension between humans and nature. This Epic is a representation of the Economy of Goodness in ancient Sumer.

"Works and Days," a didactic poem from Greece, highlighted industry, and temperance in an economy. Greed eventually leads to one's downfall. Aristotle believed that the aim of economic activity shouldn't be money, as chasing it without restraint removes chances for true happiness. Happiness instead comes from loving connections with people, public service, philosophical thought, and spiritual bliss.

Jews are believed to have the sharpest business aptitude in humanity. They think what God may grant them is in the everyday, rather than the afterlife. Jews invest all their energy into their current life; still, they keep the Sabbath and realize people should labor under certain limits. Work time and financial resources are finite, but humans should aim for maximum financial gain and contentment.

In the Confucian viewpoint within Chinese culture, the ideal approach to wealth includes not only material prosperity but also the presence of benevolence and virtue. Additionally, true wealth is reflected in the ability to foster harmony and reconciliation through one's prosperity. Consequently, Confucius advised his disciples: "He possesses the wealth of the whole world, yet no one complains about him; he who could spread his wealth to the world without worrying about being poor can be called a man of virtue."[6] Beyond wealth, Confucianism focuses on fostering social harmony. It upholds wealth based on the harmony between people and between humans and nature. The economic philosophy in Confucianism is known as Harmonious Goodness.

Following the idea that "everything unified into one," Buddhism believes that all economic activities should seek to bring the greatest amount of happiness and harmony to the world. Its economic ideal is "Common Goodness."

The rise of ocean trade and urban living in recent centuries has been pivotal in the emergence of Capitalism. This saw the proliferation of mutual-aid systems of ocean trade and chambers of commerce and craftspeople supporting each other through their networks.

---

[6] Xianqian, W. (1994). *Collected Annotations of Xunzi*. Shandong: Shandong Friendship Publishing House. pp. 853–854.

In the eighteenth century, the world was rife with wars and religious disputes. The Catholic Church and Protestantism were fiercely opposed, and commerce was the only reliable sphere. Voltaire proclaimed that

> Come into the London Exchange, a place more respectable than many a court. You will see assembled representatives of every nation for the benefit of mankind. Here the Jew, the Mohametan, and the Christian deal with one another as if they were of the same religion, and reserve the name "infidel" for those who go bankrupt. Here the Presbyterian puts his trust in the Anabaptist, and the Anglican accepts the Quaker's promissory note. Upon leaving these peaceful and free assemblies, one goes to the synagogue, the other for a drink; yet another goes to have himself baptized in a large tub in the name of the Father through the Son to the Holy Ghost; another has his son circumcised, and over the infant, he has muttered some Jewish words that he doesn't understand at all: Some others go to their church to await divine inspiration with their hat on their head. And all are content.[7]

Voltaire's description precisely reflects the commercial justice of that era, during times filled with political and religious conflicts, commerce provided a harmonious and mutually beneficial domain. Commerce, in the various realms of the world during that time, was the greatest good.

Here is what we find when we look at the thoughts and actions of goodness in history.

Every strong economy must have a strong philosophy behind it.

Each economic entity must base its sustainable development on a strong philosophy, or else the economy could stagnate or even decline.

So, what should the philosophy be? I'd say it's goodness and altruism.

Goodness is not about establishing the ultimate truth, but about pursuing the best benefits for all people and all things.

As long as a few control an economy, its progress is unlikely to be seamless. When a culture fails to offer values that benefit the majority, and an ideology controlled by a few allows a monopoly, the economy will reach its limit, leading to eventual decline.

---

[7] Muller, J. Z. (2007). *The Mind and the Market: Capitalism in Western Thought.* United Kingdom: Knopf Doubleday Publishing Group. p. 29.

BUSINESS ONCE AS THE HIGHEST GOOD

In the eighteenth century, self-interest was acknowledged by all religions and peoples, even they were opposed to or against each other in many perspectives. Commerce occurred in harmony, with everyone treating each other equally and without ideological conflicts.

Today, however, the economic issue is that self-interest is viewed as the highest good; thus, it has become the greatest common denominator in the world.

Conflicts in the world today are largely driven by the widening gap between the rich and poor, and the struggle for control of economic resources. Those who are disadvantaged may try to use religious or racial reasons to further aggravate such disputes and overthrow those who are advantaged.

Samuel Huntington argued the greatest danger to humankind is the clash of civilizations. He foresaw that those consuming American Coca-Cola and watching Hollywood films could, due to the absence of civilization affiliation, bomb American buildings. I think this clashing should be attributed to cultural rifts resulting from economic imbalances.

Statistics suggest that terrorism is more likely to originate from cities with populations of 100,000 to 200,000. Individuals from these regions have witnessed significant disparities in wealth and exploitation of the less fortunate. Compared to those who struggle below the poverty line, these people are better informed and equipped to pose terrorist threats.

In an overly self-interested global economy, the wealthy become wealthier; the disadvantaged become poorer, and the influential become more powerful. Only by shifting our values and no longer solely pursuing our individual benefit but instead striving for a shared world of mutual benefit, shared prosperity, and shared welfare can humans end the conflicts in the world.

Isn't it because of humans' selfishness that there are conflicts not only between people but also between humans and nature?

ALTRUISM AS A GREAT DISTRIBUTOR OF RESOURCES

Self-interest leads to no beneficial allocation of resources. The Prisoner's Dilemma demonstrated that when two prisoners only focus on themselves, neither will gain any reward. They are only able to obtain benefits when both take their mutual interests into account.

Economically, self-interest does not lead to "Pareto optimality." Pareto optimality is when no other arrangement would make some better off without making others worse off, which can only be achieved through altruism.

Altruism is like water that naturally flows into low places.

As long as an altruistic attitude arises, individuals will care for those in need in their own ways. Giving the example of Tzu Chi, which is one of the largest charitable foundations in the world, and wherever disasters occur, Tzu Chi volunteers are there.[8] This spontaneity results from having cultivated compassionate minds of altruism.

THE ECONOMY OF GOODNESS THAT CHERISHES MATERIAL LIFE

The Economy of Goodness that cherishes material life seeks to create a more equitable balance between consumerism and sustainability. It seeks to restore the balance between nature and humanity by using renewable resources, ensuring environmental protection, and promoting economic development. It also seeks to reduce the negative impacts of human activities and create a better, more ethical economy which rejects the idea of mass production, mass consumption and then mass wasting.

Manufacturing should be driven by altruism. Adam Smith suggested that a baker or brewer has no consideration for consumers, only providing for their own family. But if this is the case, how can they make their products attractive to buyers?

Behind commercial self-interest lies altruism, and for a business to succeed it must be altruistic.

The Economy of Goodness promotes "self-interest through altruism" as the means to solve conflicts. Altruism that is motivated by compassion

---

[8] The Tzu Chi Foundation was founded in 1966 in Hualien County, on the east coast of Taiwan. Its founder, Dharma Master Cheng Yen, embraces the spirit of Buddhist compassion and altruism to promote its four missions of Charity, Medicine, Education, and Humanistic Culture. Tzu Chi has provided humanitarian aid to over 130 countries and regions around the world. It has been written about as a case study in the Harvard Business Review by Professor Herman B. (Dutch) Leonard, who describes it as one of the most efficient humanitarian organizations in the world. Master Cheng Yen has also been honored by Time Magazine and the BBC as one of the most influential people and charity leaders of our time.

and recognizes the mutual benefit of humans can create harmony in the world while supporting the planet from destruction.

Altruism advocates all-win and all-prosperous paths for humans.

People are born with both self-interest and altruism; growing more altruistic and reducing self-interest is the key to inspiring goodness in the economy of kindness. Helping those in need cultivates altruism, leading to a transformation from self-interest to selflessness.

AN IDEAL OF HARMONIOUS UNIFICATION AND COMMON GOODNESS

Goodness is motivated by altruism and achieved through harmonious unification.

In China, harmony is split into three levels. The first—"Central Harmony"—Advocates "holding steadfast to the golden mean" and emphasizes finding common ground between opposing forces and interests. The second level, "Preserving Harmony," aims to secure a place for everyone to pursue their interests and build a righteous life of well-being. The third and highest level is "Supreme Harmony," referring to an everlasting social state of common goodness. The ancient Forbidden City of China houses three halls—the Hall of Central Harmony, the Hall of Preserving Harmony, and the Hall of Supreme Harmony—as symbols of the ideals and wisdom of China's ancient rulers.

Harmony is goodness. The ideal of goodness is to "be in harmony with all things" and to have a common benefit of being "in harmony with all laws."

To unite with all things means to love all people and things. To unite with all laws means to embrace all truths.

Altruism as the foundation and harmony which promotes the common good is the ultimate ideal of the Economy of Goodness.

The Economy of Goodness seeks a prosperous and harmonious society both financially and spiritually. It strives to achieve material prosperity while also searching for a path to mental peace. It desires to usher in universal wealth and secure a sustainable future. It wishes to implement acts of goodness, matters of righteousness, and benevolent minds in the world.

CHAPTER 2

Introduction: The Origin of Economy of Goodness

VALUE-BASED PHILOSOPHY AND ECONOMIC PROSPERITY

Through human civilizations, it is evident that a strong economy requires an entrenched system of philosophical thoughts and values.

Jews believe that God honors them in the worldly realm, not in the hereafter or Heaven. All the Jewish prophets were wealthy. Abraham had a large number of cattle and sheep and lived a long life. King David was wise and Jacob was an aristocrat; Joseph was Egypt's premier. Moses was royalty. Jews gather fortunes, believing in God's laws and laboring hard. Additionally, they keep the Sabbath, when even God relaxes. The Sabbath instructed Jews that they ought to make the most of their wealth under restricted circumstances.

Greek rationalism is the source of modern scientific civilization. Socrates emphasized the power of human reason, while Plato championed its eternity—the "ideal." He gave more importance to concepts than to matter. Aristotle, Plato's student, revised his teacher's philosophy by advocating the fusion of reason and matter, and of mind and matter; the concept of an apple, he asserted, could only be realized in an apple. Aristotle was instrumental in ushering in the most flourishing and prosperous period of Greek antiquity, by emphasizing both practical issues and philosophical ideas. Alexander the Great, his pupil, further spread Greek civilization across Europe, Asia, and Africa through a vast empire spanning these three continents.

© The Author(s), under exclusive license to Springer Nature Singapore Pte Ltd. 2024
R.-S. Her, *The Economy of Goodness*,
https://doi.org/10.1007/978-981-97-6363-4_2

The Protestant ethic of Christianity states that success in the current world is demonstrating the honor God has granted an individual. Protestants trust that whether God selects someone is decided not by the Catholic church, but by their accomplishments and compliance with God's laws. Protestants believe that if they create great goals and stick to the virtues of diligence and frugality, they can prove that they are chosen by God.

Such belief has motivated numerous capitalists in Western countries, such as John D. Rockefeller, Henry Ford, Bill Gates, and Warren Buffett, to build cross-international enterprises while adhering to a simple lifestyle and a highly disciplined work ethic.

Historically, there have been few times more frenzied than modern capitalism, which has ceaselessly sought expansion of its territory. No matter how much success is achieved in honoring God, it appears never to be enough. Such Protestant ethics drive capitalists to expand their capital globally, leading to the growth of huge corporations and an ever-widening gulf between the rich and the developing countries as well as between their people.

Confucianism favors agriculture and disdains commerce; it promotes the official career and discourages commerce. Thus, Chinese merchants traditionally strove for success to bring honor to their clans.

Though many Confucian merchants conducted business across China, they often returned to fulfill their responsibilities to their clan and home-town growth. This is why China does not have capital markets, as occurs in the West, even with its greatest wealth in history. It was a traditional Chinese merchant's greatest wish to honor their homes and clans.

Under the teachings of Buddha, Buddhism stresses the Four Noble Truths: the truth of suffering, the truth of causation, the truth of cessation, and the truth of the Path. Buddhists are encouraged to abstain from desires and practice compassion to end suffering and attain Nirvana. Thus, they do not concern themselves with worldly pursuits.

The Buddha instructed His disciples to follow the Bodhisattva Path, entering the mundane world to benefit people. In Buddhism's history, however, the focus remains on escaping suffering. In India and Nepal, the place of its origin, large-scale poverty and suffering remains a major issue. Lumbini (now Nepal) saw the birth of the Buddha over 2,500 years ago. To this day, many peasants in the area live in the same cow dung houses.

Mahayana Buddhism underwent a shift toward the mundane world after it entered and rose in China. It was still mainly focused on preaching

Buddhism and charitable acts by temples, with little attention given to its economic thought. This gave the impression of evasion from the world, centering around suffering and emptiness, in disinterest of worldly wealth or success.

The Buddhists' ultimate goal is to aim for the afterlife rather than this life, and to strive for the "Western Pure Land" rather than this mundane world.

Throughout history, Buddhist countries have not had robust and enduring economies. This must be linked to Buddhist thought.

This book investigated the philosophical and values systems across various human civilizations and concluded that strong economic systems must be underpinned by such systems for an orderly economic society.

As all countries strive for material prosperity and an equitable economic system, the debates on the philosophy and values underlying the economy have become increasingly pressing for achieving wealth equality.

This book endeavors to sharpen altruistic ideas and moral values in economic matters and examine their influence on an economy's prosperity, fairness, and rationality. It looks to construct a prosperous, equitable, and perfect world by utilizing the Economy of Goodness as its foundation.

FROM ECONOMY OF CHARITY TO ECONOMY OF GOODNESS

The Economy of Goodness stems from my twenty-plus years of charity work with Tzu Chi Foundation. I have been blessed with the privilege to follow Master Cheng Yen, founder of Tzu Chi, for numerous years and have seen remarkable transformations in entrepreneurs' entities through their involvement with Tzu Chi's charity.

I have seen entrepreneurs go from being self-centered to caring, from self-interested to altruistic, from growing their businesses to understanding the importance of giving to the public.

The entrepreneurs' devotion to charity is not motivated by a desire for accolades; they experience joy and satisfaction from giving without expecting anything in return, which pushes them to continue their philanthropic pursuits.

I have observed substantial alterations in the way these entrepreneurs managed their businesses. They adopted Tzu Chi's humanistic values, particularly gratitude, into their jobs. They showed increased appreciation to their staff, family, and contacts. Master Cheng Yen has affirmed that gratitude is the fundamental element and has been instrumental in the entrepreneurs' attainment of interpersonal harmony.

Both bosses and employees are grateful to be part of a loving family, something Tzu Chi actively encourages: Management with Love.

Therefore, success for entrepreneurs lies not only in their devotion to charity but in running their businesses efficiently. The practice of good business fosters wealth and well-being for employees, society, and the environment.

Practicing altruism in business is good. Any business or industry that benefits all people and things can be deemed good. This is how my experiences with charity work have been led to the Economy of Goodness.

Take Faith as the Core Foundation

My determination to study the theory and practice of the Economy of Goodness began in 2011 when I presented a speech at Harvard Business School. In 2009, Professor Herman Leonard of Harvard University interviewed Master Cheng Yen, and concluded that she leads through faith and value.

In 2010, he completed the Tzu Chi case study and asked me to review it. In 2011, he formally invited me to address Harvard Business School's class on Tzu Chi's Values-Oriented Leadership and Management with Love—the essence of Master Cheng Yen's success in spreading Tzu Chi to 136 countries and regions around the world. My speech was welcomed with keenness by Harvard's faculty and students, leaving them to ponder if similar NGO organizational principles could be applied to their business ventures.

After the address, Professor Herman Leonard told me that Harvard Business School students had heard little of core concepts such as "Value-Oriented Leadership," "Take Faith as the Core," and "Management with Love." These students will all become future key figures of businesses. "I want them to learn values apart from those based on competition and interests," Professor Herman Leonard said. He recorded my speech to form teaching material for the Tzu Chi case study taught every semester so that Harvard Business School students, prospective business leaders, can discover the significance of values, love, and faith in business growth.

THE THEORETICAL ORIGINATION
OF THE ECONOMY OF GOODNESS

In 2013, I proposed the concept of "Economy of Goodness" and completed a 10,000-word paper published at the Third Tzu Chi Forum.[1] It begins with Western capitalist thinking, from Adam Smith's Wealth of Nations to Marx's communism, and considers Weber's Protestant ethics, Schumpeter's bureaucratic hierarchy, Hayek's free market, and Keynes's planned economy as well as Dennis Bell, who propagated and anticipated the appearance of social enterprises. It also explains how human economic society has progressed from a self-interested economy to an altruistic one.

At the Fourth Tzu Chi Forum in 2016, I invited Professor Herman Leonard to give a keynote speech in Taiwan, titled "The Importance of Tzu Chi as a Model for Organizational Management and Leadership"[2] He attributed Tzu Chi's relief work success to the establishment of its core convictions. Despite the uncertainty of disaster situations, the extent of the damage, and the effectiveness of the local relief system, Tzu Chi volunteers have faith in their convictions to go wherever disasters strike. This is the reason for Tzu Chi's success in its disaster relief efforts.

Professor Leonard highlighted that the economic, political, and social environment for today's enterprises is not unlike what Tzu Chi has to contend with. Global conflicts can be unpredictable, the advancement of science and technology unforeseen, and disasters resulting from environmental shifts cannot be predicted. Such uncertainties are growing. In the face of precarious situations, businesses may find themselves in a quandary without any core convictions. Thus, enterprises must build their core conviction and values to rise above uncertainties and guarantee a flourishing and sustainable future.

This is how Professor Leonard views the value of faith-based businesses in today's society.

A Good Enterprise takes faith as its cornerstone and values as its guiding principle.

---

[1] Her, R. S. (2016). *Shan jingji—lun ziben shichang de shan xing yu daode* [Economy of Goodness: On the Virtue and Ethics of Capital Markets]. *Shandong: Shandong Normal University Journal*, Vol. 3.

[2] Lou, Y., & Leonard, H. D. (2017). *Ciji zong men de pushi jiazhi* [The Universal Values of Tzu Chi]. Taipei: Tzu Chi Culture and Communication Foundation. pp. 86–108.

The Economy of Goodness seeks to bring goodness to fruition, using altruism as its core. Goodness provides both motivation and a way to benefit everyone and everything.

The Economy of Goodness strives for common and equal wealth and prosperity for all humans through altruism and the perfecting of individuals and communities. It seeks to create an ideal world in which people can enjoy health, wealth, and mental clarity in harmonious societies.

The core of the Economy of Goodness is the motivation, means, and result of goodness.

A DISCUSSION OF PERCEPTIONS OF GOODNESS

What is goodness? How can it be defined? What links goodness to the world around us?

This book initially examines philosophical ideas on goodness, followed by an analysis of the "Economy of Goodness." I will evaluate and contrast Eastern and Western theories and practices of goodness.

Goodness in the West

The Goodness of Knowledge

From Socrates onward, the West viewed the pursuit of goodness as a virtue. Socrates believed virtues required knowledge, and that acts of goodness depend on one's understanding. He argued that no one would strive for evil but would see it as goodness. In a nutshell, only accurate awareness leads to the virtues of goodness.

Virtues stem from knowledge and are indications of supreme goodness; without it, evils will manifest.

Knowledge leads to supreme goodness and virtues.

Knowledge, as Socrates said, is being aware of the world. People can reach their goals and find contentment if they are aware of what is beneficial to them.

Socrates believed that the ultimate goal of humanity should be to strive for supreme goodness. Although humans enjoy their senses, they are rational and should prioritize rationality, as this is the route to supreme goodness.

Socrates believed that humans cannot truly comprehend this ultimate goodness; only gods can. In Socrates' view, these gods are not the creators of religion but rational forces beyond the worldly realm. These gods are capable of acting in accordance with reason and pursuing the ultimate good as their purpose.

To sum up, Socrates saw goodness as rational behavior. He believed humans had the capacity to be rational, which set us apart from animals. Being rational signifies being honest and being truly good.

Ideals of Goodness

Plato, a student of Socrates, saw Supreme Goodness as the quest for truth. He defined Summum Bonum as Supreme Goodness, which was equivalent to the "Ideal" or "Form."

All things have ideals; visible ones are subject to birth and death, yet the concept behind them is eternal. As Husserl advocated, only one perfect triangle exists in the world; all visible ones, subject to harm, are imperfect, while the concept of a triangle is perfect and immortal. This echoes Plato's concepts of perfect ideals.

Plato viewed supreme goodness as the highest ideal and ultimate measure of morality. He argued that the world must be guided by it and that an ideal city-state could be constructed on it, thus enabling people to achieve true contentment.

In his book *The Republic*,[3] Plato wrote that individuals have certain characteristics that are innate and unique to them, such as slaves being born into slavery, artisans being born artisans, and rulers being born rulers. Thus, in Plato's ideal state, the country would be best ruled by a philosopher who is wise and good and possesses virtue, called the "Philosopher King."

In this regard, Plato's thought is akin to the "Internal Sage and External King" philosophy in ancient China.

In ancient Chinese philosophy, the concepts of "saints," "kings," and "heaven" are inseparable. Saints are attuned to heaven, and kings can only rule because they follow the way of heaven.[4] A king who follows the way of heaven is naturally a saint.

Greater Odes of the Kingdom in *The Book of Poetry* praises King Wen of Zhou:

---

[3] Plato. (2018). *Lixiangguo* [The Republic] (Wu, S. L. Trans.). Taipei: Huazhi wenhua chubanshe.

[4] The definition of Heaven in ancient China means neither the paradise in the sense of Christianity nor the eternal place of well-being or the Creator-God, but rather the Way of universal truth and virtue. It also conveys non-personalized strength.

"Profound was King Wen;
Oh! Continuous and bright was his feeling of reverence.
Great is the appointment of Heaven!
There were the descendants of the sovereigns of Shang to follow him."[5]

The Greater Odes of the Kingdom from *The Book of Poetry* praises the great King Wen of Zhou. These odes celebrate his profound wisdom and continuous reverence for the divine. The people of Zhou believed that King Wen's appointment as their leader was a testament to the will of Heaven, which recognized his great virtue and wisdom. The Odes also suggest that the descendants of the Shang dynasty, which preceded the Zhou, recognized King Wen's greatness and were eager to follow his leadership. Nonetheless, Heaven observes King Wen's performance continuously, and hence "The illustration of illustrious [virtue] is required below,

And the dread majesty is on a high.
Heaven is not steadily to be relied on.
It is not easy to be king."[6]

Heaven entrusted this mission, watching over the shoulder of its steward, so "it is not an easy task being king." We must always honor and embolden ourselves, and live according to the will of Heaven.

"*The Book of Poetry*" says:

"This King Wen,
Watchfully and reverently,
With entire intelligence serving God,
And so secured the great blessing.
His virtue was without deflection;
And in consequence, he received [the allegiance of] the States from all quarters."[7]

---

[5] Legge, J. (1967). *The Book of Poetry* (Vol. 1). Taiwan: Paragon Book Reprint Corporation.

[6] Legge, J. (1967). *The Book of Poetry* (Vol. 1). Taiwan: Paragon Book Reprint Corporation.

[7] Legge, J. (1967). *The Book of Poetry* (Vol. 1). Taiwan: Paragon Book Reprint Corporation.

Confucius, the saint who inherited the ideals of King Wen (文王) and Zhou Gong(周公),[8] aimed to establish an ideal world order that abided by benevolence (仁ren) and propriety (禮 li) in a world of chaos. The virtues of King Wen were inherited from Heaven and established by virtue of Heaven, and so were the sages.

According to *The Biography of Confucius* in The Records of the Grand Historian, during the Warring States period, Huan Gui, Minister of the Song State, attempted to have him assassinated. Confucius then stated, "Heaven produced the virtue that is in me. Huan Tui, what can he do to me?"[9] Confucius pondered how someone like Huan Tui could effortlessly inflict harm when his virtues were granted by Heaven. While Confucius acknowledged the divine origin of his virtues, he emphasized that being a sage didn't exempt him from the necessity of personal effort and diligence.

Ordinary people could not be saints through only their efforts; it is a gift from heaven. As the saying goes, "The kingdom has long been without the principles of truth and right; Heaven is going to use your master as a bell with its wooden tongue."[10] That is to say, the mandate of Heaven marks the awakening of Confucius in pursuit of completing his life's virtues. Thus, in Confucianism, saints are the great men who received the decrees of heaven and practiced them by the Way of Heaven.

The Qian Hexagram in *The I Ching (The Book of Changes)* said:

> The great man is he who is in harmony in his attributes with heaven and earth; in his brightness with the sun and moon; in his orderly procedure with the four seasons; and in his relation to what is fortunate and what is calamitous with the spiritual agents. He may precede Heaven, and Heaven will not act in opposition to him; he may follow Heaven but will act only

[8] Zhou Gong (周公) was a saint and a great Prime Minister in the Zhou dynasty of ancient China. He brought prosperity to the dynasty after King Wen's passing, around 1042–1035 BCE.

[9] Legge, J. (1971). *Confucian Analects: The Great Learning, and The Doctrine of the Mean*. New York: Dover Publications. p. 202.

[10] Legge, J. (1971). *Confucian Analects: The Great Learning, and The Doctrine of the Mean*. New York: Dover Publications. p. 164.

as Heaven at the time would do. If Heaven will not act in opposition to him, how much less will men![11]

The explanations of ideals and Heaven may differ, yet they both point to the highest goodness and truth.

Goodness that Unites Mind and Matter

Plato inherited Socrates' thoughts and echoed them with ideals of reason. On the other hand, Aristotle revised Plato's concept, believing pure reason was unattainable and that the concept of an apple couldn't be separated from the physical apple. This mirrors what Buddhism proclaims: "Form is Emptiness, Emptiness is Form. Emptiness is an invisible, formless, and intangible concept." However, a concept cannot be found in emptiness. We can only apprehend it concretely in the real world.

We see the triangle in triangular tools, the circle in round balls, and the apple in an apple.

Aristotle brought back pure idealism and goodness-reason to the real world. Applying this supreme goodness to business, Aristotle believed that the supreme goodness of business was the pursuit of happiness. However, happiness is not merely chasing money, which deviates from happiness. Happiness comes from the pursuit of Theoria and Philosophia.[12] Supreme happiness in life means leading a moral life, establishing a relationship of love with others, and devotion to public affairs.

Aristotle's idea is similar to Chinese philosophy, which emphasizes contentment and moral fulfillment in real life.

Western Platonic goodness pursues the highest truth, whereas Chinese goodness seeks to create the most happiness. Plato sought the Ideal as the ultimate truth, while Christianity claims God is the only true deity and the ultimate truth. This notion of the highest and only truth implies I am right, and you are wrong, which can cause religious disputes and fighting between good and evil—me and you, right and wrong, pitting us against each other.

Wars in China's history were mainly caused by hunger and conflicting interests, rather than ideological divisions. Throughout history, Western

---

[11] Legge, J. (1963). *The I Ching: The Book of Changes.* United Kingdom: Dover Publications. p. 47.

[12] Pearce, Colin D. (2013). *Aristotle and Business: An Inescapable Tension, Handbook of the Philosophical Foundations of Business Ethics* (Vol. 1). Springer Publishing. pp. 34–35.

countries have been confronted with various ideologies and religious beliefs due to their pursuit of the absolute and supreme truth.

Goodness in the East is to Benefit All People and Things

In Chinese culture, goodness is defined as benefiting all people and all things. As Lao Tzu said, "The highest goodness is like (that of) water. The goodness of water appears in its benefiting all things, and in its occupying, without striving (to the contrary), the low place which all men dislike. Hence (its way) is near to (that of) the Tao."[13]

The highest good is akin to water; it benefits all creatures and beings. It does not defeat evil but takes a low-key stance, cleanses and instructs badness, and even changes it into righteousness.

Goodness does not merely oppose evil; it seeks to transform it and teach it.

In the West, truth often denigrates what is not considered true, leading to conflicts. Acts of goodness, often done in the name of truth, have been known to involve the slaughter and extinction of other ethnic groups and religions. In Chinese culture, goodness involves benefiting others and benefiting all people. That's why Lao Tzu said, "When everyone recognizes beauty as beautiful, ugliness is already there. When everyone recognizes goodness as goodness, evil is already there."[14] Good and evil thus exist together—Chinese culture then emphasizes not the destruction of one by the other, but the finding of a civil, reasonable, and inclusive way of integration.

China's goodness, in contrast to the pursuit of supreme truth in the West, strives for the benefit of all people and all things. The West aspires to an absolute truth by which to order the world. The Chinese, however, believe that goodness surpasses any absolute truth and that the highest order is derived from mutual benefit, perfect completion, and harmony in all relations.

Goodness is deemed of greater importance than truth because truth is not accepted unless it is also good. In Eastern philosophy, truth is not considered valid if it doesn't bring benefit to all living beings; it must be

---

[13] Tzu, L. (Eds.). (2021). *Tao Te Ching* (J. Legge, Trans.). Standard Ebooks. Retrieved from https://standardebooks.org/ebooks/laozi/tao-te-ching/james-legge.

[14] Bangxiong, W. (2010). *A Modern Interpretation of Dao De Jing*. Taipei: Yuan-Liou Publishing Co., Ltd., p. 20.

beneficial in order to be viewed as beautiful. On the other hand, Western philosophy tends to focus more on concepts rather than practical, beneficial outcomes. If a society of goodness is to be created, truth needs to be aligned with goodness, which is the underlying foundation.

These are the basic values of Confucianism. As Mencius said, "What everybody wants is goodness...when everybody has goodness, it is called beauty."[15] When everyone obtains what they want, it is called goodness, and the result is beauty. This is the real happiness of life. China's concept of goodness does not oppose material wealth, but instead takes it as a basis. The material alone is not enough; we must be educated in virtues in order to have a complete and fulfilled life. Thus, that is why Confucius said, "Make them rich and then educate them, teach them with the virtues of benevolence, righteousness, filial piety, and fraternal love."

According to Xunzi, fostering individuals' desires and meeting their necessities is essential for propriety.[16] This is the essence of propriety. Providing people with what they desire and need is virtuous. However, Xunzi emphasizes the importance of moderation. Moderation depends on the power of education. Desire shall not exhaust things; things will not be subject to desires. The two can coexist and prosper, which is the starting point of propriety. Therefore, propriety is nurturing.[17] Desire cannot exhaust all things, and things are not generated to satisfy endless desires, but rather based on the needs of life. Therefore, it is important to understand the importance of moderation. Moderation is based on self-cultivation.

As stated in the *Book of Rites*, "The Way of greater learning lies in manifesting the original brightness of innate virtue; it lies in restoring the original brightness of that virtue in the people generally; it lies in coming to rest in the utmost goodness."[18] The way of great learning and the way of the sage lies in self-cultivation, achieving moral integrity, and then through caring for the people, one can attain the utmost goodness. What

[15] Mencius. (2019). *The Works of Mencius* (Sun Jiaqi ed.). New Taipei City: Jen Publishing Co., Ltd. p. 339.

[16] Wang, X. Q. (1994). *Xunzi ji jie* [Collected Annotations of Xunzi]. Shandong: Shandong Friendship Publishing House. p. 593.

[17] Wang, X. Q. (1994). *Xunzi ji jie* [Collected Annotations of Xunzi]. Shandong: Shandong Friendship Publishing House. p. 593.

[18] Legge, J. (1971). *Confucian Analects: The Great Learning, and The Doctrine of the Mean*. New York: Dover Publications. p. 356.

is the ultimate path of goodness? It is not only recognizing and practicing the path of righteousness but also benefiting all people and cherishing all things.

Confucius' view on goodness also focuses on benefiting all people. In Yongye of *The Analects of Confucius*, Zi Gong, a disciple, asked Confucius, "Suppose the case of a man extensively conferring benefits on the people, and able to assist all, what would you say of him? Is that called being benevolent?" Confucius replied, "What does benevolence have to do with it? It must be said that they are sages! Even Emperor Yao and Shun[19] were afraid that they could not reach the level of being extremely generous to the people. The benevolent person wants to establish themselves and others; they want to achieve themselves and help others achieve. If we can practice this virtue from something close at hand, we can say that this is an aspect of the benevolent way."[20]

Confucius believed that saints were benefactors to all people, not just those who were aware of the truth. Even Yao and Shun felt overwhelmed at the prospect of emulating the saint's ability to aid everyone.

A benevolent person can aid those in need within their reach. Saints bring well-being to all people. China's goodness is based upon the well-being of daily life.

The fulfillment of life in terms of economics is based on the premise of equal wealth distribution. As Confucius said, "Not troubled lest their people should be few, but are troubled lest they should not keep their several places."[21] The wealth gap has always been a source of social unrest in China and an important factor in dynastic changes. Therefore, unlike the feudal society of medieval Europe, where aristocrats inherited their titles and most farmers were tenants, ancient China's equal land allocation system granted every farmer equal land ownership. This is the Chinese standard of goodness. Equal opportunities for wealth and prosperity for all are the ideal economic goals in China.

In the book of *Xunzi*, Confucius expressed the idea that possessing vast wealth without causing discontent among others, and being able to

---

[19] Yao and Shun were two great sage-kings in ancient China. They founded the Xia dynasty in ancient China around 2070-1600 BCE.

[20] Legge, J. (1971). *Confucian Analects: The Great Learning, and The Doctrine of the Mean*. New York: Dover Publications. p. 194.

[21] Legge, J. (1971). *Confucian Analects: The Great Learning, and The Doctrine of the Mean*. New York: Dover Publications. p. 308.

generously share that wealth without fearing personal poverty, exemplifies virtuous conduct.[22] The acquisition of wealth through righteousness and propriety is allowed in Confucian thought. For example, during the late Spring and Autumn period (770–221 BCE) of ancient China, Fan Li (536–448 BCE) served as a general and prime minister to assist Goujian, benefiting countless people. Later, he retired and became rich three times, but gave away his wealth three times without any complaints. With this generosity, He and his family enjoyed wealth for generations. He is a representative of the Confucian virtue of being a wealthy benefactor.

The goodness of Taoism, as Lao Tzu said, "The highest goodness is like (that of) water. The goodness of water appears in it benefiting all things, and in its occupying, without striving (to the contrary), the low place which all men dislike. Hence (its way) is near to (that of) the Tao."[23] True goodness is like water, not bound by form, and can benefit all beings and things.

Dealing with evil is not about striking it down, but educating it. Dealing with the evil of the masses is almost like following the Tao, which means saving the evil through close to the evil. It is approaching evil and transforming it without destroying it. Just as I stated in my book, *The Essential Studies of Tzu Chi Buddhism*, "eliminating evil is not about striking it down, but increasing good. Eliminating poverty is not about striking down the wealthy but extending great love."[24]

The Taoist belief in eliminating evil by doing good is similar to the compassionate vow of the Buddhist Bodhisattva Ksitigarbha, "If I do not go to hell, who will go to hell? If hell is not empty, I will never become a Buddha." This is very different from the Western struggle between good and evil, which ultimately leads to the extinction of the opposing force. When Christianity and Islam both claim to be the only true believers of God and the only true religion, conflicts, and wars inevitably arise.

Therefore, China demonstrates shared and equitable prosperity. This is to benefit all people and all things, culminating in supreme goodness.

[22] Wang, X. Q. (1994). *Xunzi ji jie* [Collected Annotations of Xunzi]. Shandong: Shandong Friendship Publishing House. pp. 853–854.

[23] Tzu, L. (Eds.). (2021). *Tao Te Ching* (J. Legge, Trans.). Standard Ebooks. Retrieved from https://standardebooks.org/ebooks/laozi/tao-te-ching/james-legge.

[24] Her, R. S. (2022). *Ciji xue gailun* [The Essential Studies of Tzu Chi Buddhism], Linking Publishing Ltd.

Goodness is the motivation, means, and result; the only way it can be complete is with all three.

The motivation of goodness is to benefit all people, not to pursue pure truth; this is the foundation of goodness in Chinese culture.

I conclude that goodness entails altruism. The Result of Goodness must be obtained through the Motivation of Goodness and the Means of Goodness.

The Motivation of Goodness Leads to Central Harmony

The motivation of goodness involves doing things with altruistic motives.

In traditional Chinese cultural thought, "achieving central harmony" is a virtue that encompasses motive, method, and outcome. "central" refers to the state of mind with the middle way, "achieving" refers to the approach one takes, and "harmony" refers to the ultimate result. The Doctrine of the Mean states, "While there are no stirrings of pleasure, anger, sorrow, or joy, the mind may be said to be in the state of Equilibrium. When those feelings have been stirred, and they act in their due degree, there ensues what may be called the state of Harmony."[25] By keeping one's emotions properly and maintaining sincerity, harmony can be achieved in all situations.

The *Book of Changes (The I Ching)* states, "...and (thereafter the conditions of) great harmony are preserved in union. The result is 'what is advantageous, and correct and firm.'"[26] Harmony means constantly practicing goodness, maintaining concord and altruistic relationships with others, in order to achieve ultimate harmony, which is the highest result of goodness.

To attain Central Harmony, we must seize both sides and go forward with the centrality.[27] We ought to be aware of the polarizing values, outlooks, and objectives to maintain the middle way. That implies there

[25] Legge, J. (1971). *Confucian Analects: The Great Learning, and The Doctrine of the Mean*. New York: Dover Publications. p. 384.

[26] Legge, J. (1963). *The I Ching: The Book of Changes*. United Kingdom: Dover Publications. p. 213.

[27] Centrality in the context of Chinese culture, represents the way to be modest, reasonable, selfless, inclusive and wise in dealing with all conflicts and all things.

would be no discrepancies in values and objectives, which takes both fore-sight and altruism. Whether it is a selfish person or a selfish emperor, they will be unable to remain in the middle way.

Centrality (middle way) is superior to the right as implies impartiality. Only centrality leads to justice and selflessness, and everyone is following their own way. It is evident that centrality encompasses all perspectives and stances. In China, centrality takes precedence over the right, since adhering to each individual's right leads to no mutual understanding and interests. Thus, centrality signifies the merging of interests and the forming of bonds.

Mind and motivation are key. Not being driven by personal or organizational interests and values is the true measure of one's worth. Setting aside personal emotions and interests and being sympathetic to polarized opinions is the true meaning of centrality.

How can one be unselfish? Start with empathy. Show genuine concern for others and their paths, values, and needs. Show kindness to all with a selfless attitude and be mindful of how others may be feeling.

Be grateful for all involved.

Moreover, inclusiveness is essential for Central Harmony.

Inclusiveness is paramount. The Chinese Dragon totem stems from ancient Chinese tribal wars and amalgamations. The Chinese regard themselves as descendants of Emperors Yan and Huang. Yan clashed with Huang, but Huang eventually beat Yan—yet instead of destroying Yan's tribe, Chiyou, Huang formed a union with him and then established China. Emperor Yan (炎帝) became the co-founder of China along with Emperor Huang (黃帝). Huang even put the Yan's tribe before his own. This is why the Chinese always say they are the descendants of Emperors Yan and Huang.

The dragon totem emerged when the tribe that worshiped Snakes and the one that worshiped Deers merged after wars. They then fought and merged with the Fish tribe, and the dragon grew scales. Following another war with the Bird tribe, the dragon became a flying totem. The dragon symbolizes an inclusive, prosperous, and shared society in China.

Therefore, goodness leads to inclusivity, unlike in Western thought where the pursuit of absolute truth often leads to conflict and war.

The meaning of inclusiveness is harmony. According to *The I Ching*: "The changes of Heaven (乾) make everything on its correct nature, maintain in Preserve Harmony to reach Supreme Harmony then eternal well-being."[28] Everything stems from the changes of Heaven, so when they are all in accordance with their nature, it is the centrality.

The I Ching said, "Yin and Yang constitute the Way of Heaven, and people inherited goodness from it and develop it by true nature."[29] In other words, "The successive movement of the inactive and active operations constitutes what is called the course (of things). That which ensues as the result (of their movement) is goodness; that which shows it in its completeness is the natures (of men and things)."[30] So, goodness must be able to include Yin and Yang[31] in itself at once. Yao, a great ruler in ancient China, counseled his follower Shun to grasp the two ends and use the means to reach Central Harmony.

Preserving Harmony is letting everything take their own righteous paths while maintaining their differences to achieve collaborative harmony. From the long-term sustaining of correct nature and preservation of harmony, supreme harmony emerges. Supreme Harmony implies that everything joins together for everlasting contentment, according to eternal good (利貞 Li Zhen). This necessitates being altruistic.

Before elucidating the utmost ideal that everything unites in one, we should first comprehend how all distinct elements can be ideologically reconciled.

Originally, Heaven produces various things, but how can different things, values, beliefs, and interests be reconciled to maintain harmony?

The key is that everyone is in their own place, living out their nature and beliefs without clashing with their core beliefs.

Liberals advocate absolute individual freedom; communitarians believe that establishing the well-being of the group ensures individual well-being; monarchism governs the people based on its own ideas. So long

---

[28] Chang, J. (2002). *The Book of Change: A New Translation* (Guo Jianxun, Trans & Ed.). Taipei: San Min Books. p. 7.

[29] Chang, J. (2002). *The Book of Change: A New Translation* (Guo Jianxun, Trans & Ed.). Taipei: San Min Books. p. 504.

[30] Legge, J. (1963). *The I Ching: The Book of Changes.* United Kingdom: Dover Publications. pp. 355–356.

[31] Yin and Yang in the context of Chinese culture constitute two opposite forms of energy or force, like dark and bright, sun and moon, male and female, positive and negative. It is believed that composing, employing, balancing, or harmonizing these two opposite forces altogether is the way of Tao (the universal true wisdom).

as the monarch is capable of caring for the people, he, taking both heavenly and earthly matters into account, can ensure a benefit for all. No single ideology is absolutely correct. As long as it can effectively express the values it promotes, it can truly "be in its own genuine nature" and bring the greatest good to individuals.

Conflicts arise from the dilution and erosion of one's own values, escalating a desire for control over others, seeking to make the masses conform to their own ideas rather than contemplating how those ideas can benefit the people. Therefore, Emperor Yao governed the world with the principle of harmony, which represents the true path. Every ideological system has its perfect vision, and the true embodiment of that vision lies in the consideration of the well-being of the people.

Therefore, we can discern high-quality and low-quality democracies. We have seen monarchies that oppressed the people as well as those that served them. This implies that every system can perform optimally, and different regimes coexist in mutual acceptance and harmony.

Religious beliefs, though varying, are essentially unified by love. Consequently, conflict can be avoided if each religion maintains its stance yet appreciates and cooperates with others. Through this way, harmony can be preserved, and collective social benefits can be created. This is how Preserving Harmony achieves eternal good for all people.

Tzu Chi is a Buddhist relief foundation with members from all religions—Buddhists, Christians, Catholics, and Muslims—embracing each other with great love. This shows an example of inter-religious harmony. In South Africa, Christian Tzu Chi volunteers see that they are doing God's work and feel closer to Him through it.

By returning to its true nature, each religion can regain its core missions and beliefs. This allows different religions to coexist harmoniously.

In terms of economic life, each industry and product are distinct. With hard work, attending to customer needs, and producing top-quality goods, all will flourish and live up to their particular capabilities, without feeling the pressure of intense competition.

Adam Smith was not wrong: aside from the baker and the brewer who make good bread and wine, respectively, an invisible hand ensures balanced distribution. When they make their own produce, they should think of the interests of their consumers instead of their own for each to be in its own true nature.

Altruism is the foundation for everyone to be in their true nature. When each producer upholds altruistic values, they can remain in their own place and reap the rewards in the long run.

The Buddhist Eightfold Path emphasizes Right Livelihood, which creates Right Action. Right Livelihood includes Right View, Right Speech, Right Thinking, Right Concentration, Right Mindfulness, and also requires the Right Effort to create Right Action.

In economic activities, enterprises must conduct production, creation, and management with a positive, altruistic frame of mind to attain the Right View and Right Thinking. Advertise products honestly and earnestly, leading to Right Concentration. Establishing the enterprise this way is Right Behavior, and sustained innovation could be deemed Right Effort.

Each individual keeps their true nature according to the principles of the *Book of Changes*, and in Buddhism, cultivating righteous actions creates positive karma. When everyone conducts themselves morally and for the benefit of others, conflicts will not arise. Without conflicts, people can harmonize with each other, promoting peace. By maintaining harmony, one can achieve prosperity and sustain mutual benefits in the long term.

Long-term inclusiveness and Preserving Harmony require sharing. The concept of sharing implies Central Harmony: temperance, wisdom, proper conduct, and benefiting all in Chinese culture.

The Means of Goodness: Preserving Harmony, Compassion, and Humility

After exploring the motivations of goodness, the methods and processes of goodness are crucial. In Chinese, the meaning of goodness includes wisdom and skillfulness. As an old saying in Chinese goes, "The mechanic, who wishes to do his work well, must first sharpen his tools."[32] Goodness means the ability to possess wisdom and intelligence.

Lao Tzu also said, "The goodness of a Residence is in the suitability of the place; that of the Mind is in abysmal stillness; that of Giving is in their being with the virtuous; that of Words is in their trustworthiness; that of Governance is in its securing good order; that of the Conduct

---

[32] Legge, J. (1971). *Confucian Analects: The Great Learning, and The Doctrine of the Mean*. New York: Dover Publications. p. 297.

of affairs is in its ability; and that of the Initiation of any movement is in its timeliness."[33] Goodness means wisdom. Without the wisdom of goodness, even with good motives, one cannot achieve good results.

China's goodness places great importance on wisdom and its accomplishments. Lao Tzu's Seven Standards of Goodness are all about wisdom.

The I Ching states, "The successive movement of the inactive and active operations constitutes what is called the course (of things). That which ensues as the result (of their movement) is goodness; that which shows it in its completeness is the natures (of men and things)."[34]

The Tao in heaven is Yin and Yang, on earth it is hardness and softness, and for humanity, it is benevolence and righteousness. The Tao between heaven and earth is a unity of Yin and Yang, where hardness and softness complement each other. Likewise, the human Tao is a matter of black and white, good and evil, which are interdependent and complementary. There is no absolute good or evil, black or white, or ugly or beautiful. The wise person can harmonize Yin and Yang, balance hardness and softness, and integrate benevolence and righteousness, harnessing the paradoxical power of opposites to realize the great Tao. Those with this ability are considered virtuous, as they continue the legacy of goodness.

The person who can understand the Great Way and inherit it with wisdom is one of goodness.

So, where does goodness come from? It is a natural occurrence.

"Nature determines one's character," returning to one's inherent nature that they bring with them in life.

Goodness is wisdom, which comes from one's inherent nature. The inherent nature is in harmony with the Tao. As the *Doctrine of the Mean* states, "What Heaven has conferred is called The Nature; an accordance with this nature is called The Path of duty; the regulation of this path is called Instruction."[35] Goodness is not just intelligence, but also a symbol of a complete personality and spirit. Therefore, Chinese sages equate intelligence with personality and equate the saint with the king. The inner saint is also the outer king and the outer king must also be a saint.

[33] Tzu, L. (Eds.). (2021). *Tao Te Ching* (J. Legge, Trans.). Standard Ebooks. Retrieved from https://standardebooks.org/ebooks/laozi/tao-te-ching/james-legge.

[34] Legge, J. (1963). *The I Ching: The Book of Changes.* United Kingdom: Dover Publications. pp. 355–356.

[35] Legge, J. (1971). *Confucian Analects: The Great Learning, and The Doctrine of the Mean.* New York: Dover Publications. p. 383.

A king who possesses wisdom and can rule a country must also be a saint. It has always been a Chinese ideal to combine wisdom and virtue. The result of goodness is inseparable from the means of it. A true king must possess true virtue to guide and perfect their wisdom for governing.

Goodness from Goodness

Only the means of good can lead to the result of good: this is the essence of traditional Chinese thought. No evil is necessary, as some Western thinkers suggest that self-interest serves to achieve altruism. Adam Smith's famous statement that public goodness is achieved through self-interest, which implies that good is derived from evil; and selflessness is achieved through selfishness; It is akin to adding fuel to a fire in an attempt to quench it.

To realize good through good was an important belief in ancient China.

In The Analects of Confucius, Confucius noted, "Zhou conferred great gifts, and the good were enriched (周有大賚,善人是富)."[36] Lai (賚) in the original Chinese denotes granting something. The Zhou Dynasty lavished benefits on the virtuous, thereby making them wealthy.

Wealth through goodness is traditional Chinese economic thought.

The Motivation of Goodness and the Means of Goodness bring about the Result of Goodness. This is the value that Chinese philosophy firmly believes in.

I realized this for the first time when Master Cheng Yen, the founder of Tzu Chi, decided that Tzu Chi's Taipei Hospital should be built with love. Its purpose is to express love, the construction must also be done in such a way.

Workers who built Tzu Chi hospitals abstained from smoking, drinking, and chewing betel nuts. Instead, they followed a vegetarian diet, guided by the loving care of Tzu Chi volunteers. The volunteers went as far as to tidy the site, providing the workers with more comfortable conditions.

The fruits of love should be borne of love, as the outcome of goodness should be formed by goodness.

As of today, Taipei Tzu Chi Hospital has grown into a large-scale institution with highly acclaimed humanistic medical services, and its business

---

[36] Legge, J. (1971). *Confucian Analects: The Great Learning, and The Doctrine of the Mean*. New York: Dover Publications. p. 351.

operations are also in excellent condition. The connection between charity and prosperity, from the charitable organization's philosophy of doing good to promote good, to the economic domain's idea of doing good to achieve prosperity, is desirable. Economic life is not solely aimed at self-interest but follows a method of benefiting others to achieve mutual benefit. This is the essence of the philosophy of economy of goodness.

The Economic Means of Goodness
Goodness means altruism.

Altruism in the Economy of Goodness should be voluntary, not compelled by coercion.

Altruism is a belief that people are willing to follow and a value of which people are truly convinced. If altruism becomes a hard and fast rule, it will lose vitality and creativity.

Altruism is not for the self; altruism does not harm the self; altruism is better than the self.

Altruism is based on the idea that everything is connected, all dharmas are one, and is a noble life ideal. It should be practiced with enthusiasm, liberty, and creativity. Charity, economics, science, and technology, as well as politics, should be reassessed and reconstructed in an altruistic light.

Altruism does not always harm the self. Anything that does harm the self is not genuine or sustainable. If life is of equal value, how can one be sacrificed for the benefit of the other?

Altruism will not hurt one's self; this is how it continues and will not be transformed into immoral consequences. This calls for more wisdom.

Altruism does not pursue self-interest in economic activities but instead benefits consumers, business partners, staff, and the environment.

Contemporary Capitalism aims to reach maximum production with the lowest cost to meet market demands, making it ideal for free competition. Yet this cannot be achieved via self-interest; when entrepreneurs pursue the highest production with the least cost, they will not consider the market's maximal demand, instead only trying to maximize their gains, which Schumpeter deemed as a market monopoly.

When every manufacturer strives for the greatest market share, the result is overproduction at reduced costs. Low prices are not beneficial to small producers, but advantageous for large manufacturers with bigger production and greater absolute value of profits. Big companies possess big capital, they are able to compete at low costs. Hence, small businesses ultimately quit the market as they cannot keep up. Major companies then acquire a market monopoly. This is what is known as Natural Monopoly. As Schumpeter predicted, unrestricted competition eventually turns into an oligopoly or monopoly.

For the past 50 years, the US newspaper industry has seen the trend of capitalist natural monopolies. Free competition leads to oligopolies because desire and self-interest lie at the heart of it. The issue is not with free competition but with the self-interested mindset.

Because every self-interested manufacturer focuses on maximizing their own output and minimizing costs, without considering the market's maximum demand, they always believe they can dominate the largest market. The result is overproduction, leading to a decrease in product prices. In order to maximize profits, manufacturers are forced to lower the quality of their products, ultimately harming consumers. As a consequence, they are either rejected by consumers or replaced by other higher-quality products. Small-scale businesses are eventually forced to leave the market because they cannot sustain the fierce price competition.

If based on altruism, each manufacturer first understands the maximum demand of the market and creates an appropriate production quantity required by the market within its existing cost basis. Manufacturers also act altruistically, considering the scale of the market collectively. As a result, every manufacturer can survive, and each product will not lower its quality due to price competition or be produced in a way that harms the environment.

With altruism, we will produce not inferior, but high-quality products.

With altruism, we will consider maximum supply and demand in the market, so each manufacturer will produce the appropriate quantity of goods.

With altruism, we are not expanding market share merely for personal or business gain.

With altruism, we will effectively manage the amount of goods and avoid sliding into aggressive cost rivalry, thereby safeguarding the quality of the product.

With altruism, we will not create demand beyond production, thus avoiding continual rises in product prices, resulting in a significant consumption disparity between the wealthy and the impoverished.

With altruism, every manufacturer can endure and make top-notch products. Altruism is more conducive to achieving the three perfect market principles: lowest cost, maximum output, and maximum market demand.

Altruism does not negate the free market but rather helps to promote it. The essence of the free market is free competition that, theoretically, yields benefits for consumers, yet history has shown this is not always the case. Free competition leads to the emergence of a natural monopoly or oligopoly since everyone is motivated by self-interest and seeks to outdo rivals.

Altruism won't impede innovation stemming from free competition but will bring about innovation with a focus on kindness and public good. By fostering qualities of goodness and selflessness, we can generate the greatest good for consumers.

Steve Jobs is a prime example. He created the revolutionary iPhone for what he saw to be the requirement for humankind—a smartphone that fuses science and tech with human nature, mechanics with art, and electronics with intelligence.

Steve Jobs was driven intrinsically and altruistically. In contrast, while self-interest appears fueled intrinsically, it is oriented externally and focused on out-maneuvering others, enticing consumers, and generating profits.

Admittedly, new technologies and innovative products will cause the disappearance or transformation of many manufacturers that cling to traditional technologies. Thus, in an altruistic market structure, the circulation and elimination of industries are inevitable, causing structural unemployment. This is beneficial to consumers, but not to some businesses and employees; it is beneficial to the public, yet not to some segments of the population.

However, in an altruistic market, winners don't seek to destroy their opponents; rather, they aim to find new solutions for them. This attitude of integration and adaptation goes back to the Chinese dragon's incorporation of totems. It's all about intermingling and coexistence.

For example, a successful new technology manufacturer can establish a consultancy to aid disadvantaged businesses with their transformation, from which both advantaged and disadvantaged enterprises could benefit. As an alternative, the winner could purchase some of the disadvantaged enterprise's shares or make it their downstream manufacturer, creating a mutually beneficial situation. This altruistic economic structure would turn a zero-sum game into a win–win one.

The winner does not take all. The winner can share all.

Therefore, an altruistic economic structure will not be subject to oligopoly or monopoly, avoiding the stifling of enterprise creativity and industry freedom that could occur in free competitive markets.

Cooperation and mutual benefit should be incorporated into economic growth in new ways.

In e-commerce, enterprises strive to outmaneuver competitors, yet Alibaba created an outstanding platform enabling small businesses and industries of all sizes to access the entire nation. Jack Ma's desire was to empower small business people to succeed, and he achieved it with the right motivation, the right method, and the right outcome.

The outcome of goodness comes from good means.

It should be noted that many companies initially rose on the principles of altruism, but failed when they became too focused on self-interests that were contrary to their original core beliefs. Henry Ford once declared his expectation for everyone to own a car. However, after decades, his successors shifted from altruism to profit-driven strategies, raising vehicle prices and neglecting the mass market. This resulted in significant losses as they struggled to compete with newcomers who produced more affordable cars for ordinary consumers.

Apple was founded on the democratization of technology when Steve Jobs introduced the Macintosh. Later, Apple shifted to a market-driven approach and faced a financial crisis. This continued until Jobs returned to Apple and reinstated the core value of being product-driven. Apple strives to produce the best and most innovative products for the public. As Steve Jobs said, "We believe people with passion can change the world for the better."

Altruism can lead a company to great success, but it is destined to fail once its core values are compromised.

The Fruit of Goodness: Supreme Harmony

The Outcome of Goodness leads to ultimate goodness in a harmonious, mutual, and all-thriving society.

Kant argued in his Groundwork of the *Metaphysics of Morals*[37] that the Motivation of Goodness should be the most important principle, namely "good will".

Goodwill follows the notion and idea of supreme goodness, even if the realization of it is not possible.

---

[37] Kant, I. (2012). *Kant: Groundwork of the Metaphysics of Morals* (M. J. Gregor & J. Timmermann, Ed. & Trans.). United Kingdom: Cambridge University Press (Original work published 1785).

Kant stated that one's goodness should not be judged by the results achieved, but rather by their good will.

> A good will is good not because of what it effects, or accomplishes, not because of its fitness to attain some intended end, but good just by its willing, i.e., in itself; and, considered by itself, it is to be esteemed beyond compare much higher than anything that could ever be brought about by it in favor of some inclination, and indeed, if you will, the sum of all inclinations. Even if by some particular disfavor of fate, or by the scanty endowment of a stepmotherly nature, this will should entirely lack the capacity to carry through its purpose; if despite its greatest striving it should still accomplish nothing, and only the good will were to remain (not, of course, as a mere wish, but as the summoning of all means that are within our control); then, like a jewel, it would still shine by itself, as something that has its full worth in itself.[38]

Kant's conception of a good will from the perspective of altruism should be seen as a non-utilitarian, non-consequentialist, motivational, or supra-rational moral ethical view. Kant believed that good will cannot be equated with its consequences. Even if the good will result in pain, it still remains good because its purpose is to do good.[39]

On May 5, 1992, a kindergarten bus caught fire in Taipei. The teacher, Jingjuan Lin, quickly rescued six children. However, hearing the cries of 20 still trapped, she hurriedly returned and aided eight out the window. Yet, she and over ten children were engulfed by the blaze.

From Kant's perspective, Lin's act can be considered Good Will and its value will not be diminished by any undesirable outcome. Furthermore, this act of altruism is voluntary.[40]

We emphasize not only Good Will and the Stimulus of Goodness but also the Outcome of Goodness. Although Lin failed to rescue all the students, it wasn't her fault. She had already saved 14, which was definitely a result of goodness.

[38] Kant, I. (2012). *Kant: Groundwork of the Metaphysics of Morals* (M. J. Gregor & J. Timmermann, Ed. & Trans.). United Kingdom: Cambridge University Press (Original work published 1785). p. 10.

[39] Kant, I. (1997). *Groundwork of the Metaphysics of Morals* (M. J. Gregor, Ed. & Trans.). Cambridge University Press (Original work published 1785). p. 62.

[40] Lin, H. W. (2013). *Jiben lunli xue* [The Basics of Ethics]. Taiwan: San Min Book Co. p. 109.

We cannot expect all motives and methods of goodness to yield 100% of what we anticipate, but they should produce positive outcomes. Lin did all she could. Further investigation ought to be conducted concerning whether the kindergarten bus' driver had taken all necessary steps to avoid the tragedy, or if the producer had provided the bus with effective emergency features. The consequence of non-goodness must be attributed to the lack of good intentions.

In this regard, the outcome of goodness is not merely a personal view, but the aim of collective social and communal endeavors.

What is the vision of good outcomes? It is to create an inclusive, shared, and prosperous world full of supreme goodness.

All-Shared Goodness
All Should Share the Result of Goodness.

Our sharing economy today emphasizes transparency in the production process—e.g., Facebook, WeChat, bike-sharing, and Uber.

Good results in Chinese philosophy are about sharing. The Great Harmony in *The Book of Rites* describes a united and harmonized world: "Thus men did not love their parents only, nor treat as children only their own sons." This is altruism and sharing.[41] It is about benefiting others, it is about sharing.

Confucianism's ideal is that the human world is in balance with the virtues of Heaven and Earth.

Confucius said, "Does Heaven speak? The four seasons pursue their courses, and all things are continually being produced, but does Heaven say anything?"[42] The virtue of heaven nurtures all things, and the unity of heaven and humanity means that humans should also nurture the growth and prosperity of all things, providing for the needs of the people like heaven does.

The Goodness that Combines Yi or Justice and Interests
Only through equitable sharing can we have long-term coexistence. Thus, harmony between justice and interests must be achieved.

---

[41] Confucius. (2013). *The Book of Rites (Li Ji): English-Chinese Version* (D. Sheng, Ed., J. Legge, Trans.). CreateSpace Independent Publishing Platform. p. 100.

[42] Legge, J. (1971). *Confucian Analects: The Great Learning, and The Doctrine of the Mean*. New York: Dover Publications. p. 326.

Xunzi thought that "It is when justice is employed that what is correct can be distinguished and people can settle disputes."

> How can people gather together? It is through division. How can division be effective? It is through righteousness. Therefore, with righteousness in division, there is harmony, with harmony there is unity, with unity there is greater strength, with greater strength one can overcome obstacles, and thus one can attain a place to dwell in peace and prosperity.[43]

Justice is key. Xunzi asserted that it looks out for the welfare of humanity, not just for individual gain. Xunzi went on and said:

> Thus, individuals have the ability to organize the cycles of the four seasons, oversee all aspects of the world, and ensure the welfare of all living beings. The only underlying factor for this is the equitable administration of justice.[44]

A person's life cannot be without a community. Without proper divisions within the community, there will be conflicts, leading to chaos and separation. This separation will lead to weakness, making one unable to overcome challenges. Therefore, one cannot live in a place without proper community, nor should one abandon etiquette and justice even for a moment.[45]

"Distribution of interests justly" is an appropriate, reasonable, and balanced practice. Otherwise, tensions will develop, potentially resulting in the weakening or downfall of groups. To successfully spread advantages to all parties is the duty of rulers. It is the highest standard for those in authority.

A competent ruler adeptly oversees the coordination of communities. By adhering to the path of collective harmony, every entity enjoys its rightful advantages: domestic animals prosper, vegetation thrives, and all life is sustained. Thus, in periods of nurturing and abundance, domestic animals flourish; in times of harvest and sacrifice, vegetation blooms; and

---

[43] Wang, X. Q. (1994). *Xunzi ji jie* [Collected Annotations of Xunzi]. Shandong: Shandong Friendship Publishing House. p. 335.

[44] Wang, X. Q. (1994). *Xunzi ji jie* [Collected Annotations of Xunzi]. Shandong: Shandong Friendship Publishing House. pp. 335–336.

[45] Wang, X. Q. (1994). *Xunzi ji jie* [Collected Annotations of Xunzi]. Shandong: Shandong Friendship Publishing House. p. 336.

in eras of governance and stability, people unite. This exemplifies the conduct of the virtuous and embodies the decree of the wise sovereign.[46]

Ensuring that everything finds its proper place, domestic animals thrive, and all living beings fulfill their destinies represents the profound responsibility and remarkable accomplishment of the sage ruler. This embodies a harmonious scene of coexistence and mutual sharing among all entities.

In the collected annotations of *Xunzi*, it is stated that conducting spring plowing, summer weeding, autumn harvesting, and winter storage in their appropriate seasons ensures that the five grains remain plentiful and that the people have an excess of food. Careful management of muddy pools, deep ponds, rivers, and swamps according to the season results in abundant fish and turtles, providing the people with surplus resources. By responsibly cutting and cultivating trees in a timely manner, the mountains and forests remain intact, and the people have an abundance of timber.[47]

Moreover, the responsibility of the sage king is to discern the changes in Heaven and orchestrate the progress of the human realm. Acting as a mediator between heaven and earth, the sage king serves the interests of all entities. Despite being enigmatic, their actions are apparent; they are concise yet far-reaching, focused yet comprehensive, and their influence is subtly pervasive, nurturing all existence. Hence, those who steadfastly adhere to their principles can be deemed saints.[48]

The saintly king's ideal world is to observe the timing and functioning of all things in the universe and properly nurture their growth and prosperity. Consequently, with everything thriving, humans will naturally live and work peacefully and contentedly.

The sage provides for what is lacking and brings abundance to what is deficient. Therefore, it is said: "Subtle yet clear, brief yet long-lasting, narrow yet expansive."

This resembles the three conditions proposed by John Rawls of Harvard University, a contemporary thinker, to address the economic

---

[46] Wang, X. Q. (1994). *Xunzi ji jie* [Collected Annotations of Xunzi]. Shandong: Shandong Friendship Publishing House. p. 336.

[47] Wang, X. Q. (1994). *Xunzi ji jie* [Collected Annotations of Xunzi]. Shandong: Shandong Friendship Publishing House. p. 336.

[48] Wang, X. Q. (1994). *Xunzi ji jie* [Collected Annotations of Xunzi]. Shandong: Shandong Friendship Publishing House. p. 336.

and social issues resulting from unequal distribution in free competition. These conditions are equal opportunity, toleration of differences, and providing the most disadvantaged with the greatest benefits which he wrote about in A Theory of Justice. In *A Theory of Justice*, he wrote:

> ...since inequalities of birth and natural endowment are undeserved, these inequalities are to be somehow compensated for. Thus, the principle holds that in order to treat all persons equally, to provide genuine equality of opportunity, society must give more attention to those with fewer native assets and to those born into the less favorable social positions. The idea is to redress the bias of contingencies in the direction of equality. In pursuit of this principle greater resources might be spent on the education of the less rather than the more intelligent, at least over a certain time of life, say the earlier years of school.[49]

Given the gap between rich and poor caused by free competition, John Rawls thought that equality was of paramount importance in a post-capitalistic society. Even though equal opportunities exist, people's abilities differ and lead to unequal wealth generation. Thus, tolerating differences is the only justifiable approach.

Xunzi conveyed the idea that complete equality does not necessarily equate to true equality.[50] Forcing everyone to be the same does not conform to the reality of life. "Each fulfilling their own destiny" means that all things are inherently different, and the goal of goodness is for diverse individuals to harmoniously benefit and share with one another. Therefore, John Rawls said to allow differences and give maximum benefits to the disadvantaged.

In Chinese philosophy, moderation is the foremost principle of central harmony, as stated in *The Doctrine of the Mean* in *The Book of Rites*:

> While there are no stirrings of pleasure, anger, sorrow, or joy, the mind may be said to be in the state of Equilibrium. When those feelings have been stirred, and they act in their due degree, there ensues what may be called the state of Harmony.[51]

---

[49] Rawls, J. (1999). *A Theory of Justice*. United Kingdom: Oxford University Press.

[50] Wang, X. Q. (1994). *Xunzi ji jie* [Collected Annotations of Xunzi]. Shandong: Shandong Friendship Publishing House. p. 318.

[51] Legge, J. (1971). *Confucian Analects: The Great Learning, and The Doctrine of the Mean*. New York: Dover Publications. p. 384.

> This Equilibrium is the great root from which grow all the human acting in the world, and this Harmony is the universal path which they all should pursue. Let the states of equilibrium and harmony exist in perfection, and a happy order will prevail throughout heaven and earth, and all things will be nourished and flourish.[52]

Central Harmony means acting and dealing with others and things in accordance with reasonable rules and measures that take into account the needs of others. It involves striving for a world of equality, in line with the Way of Heaven.

Confucius also said in *The Book of Rites*, "The way of the superior man may be found, in its simple elements, in the intercourse of common men and women; but in its utmost reaches, it shines brightly through heaven and earth."[53] The happiness of all couples and common people, even the nurturing of heaven and earth, are all objects of concern and accomplishment for a gentleman.

Confucius praised the holy emperor Shun as the paragon of the Central Way. He said:

> There was Shun: He indeed was greatly wise! Shun loved to question others, and to study their words, though they might be shallow. He concealed what was bad in them and displayed what was good. He took hold of their two extremes, determined the Mean, and employed it in his government of the people. It was by this that he was Shun![54]

Shun's greatness lies in his knowing everyone well without giving up on anyone. He hid evil and promoted goodness. He knew the two extremes and acted in a central (moderate) way.

Cheng Yi, a prestigious philosopher in the Song Dynasty, thought that practicing the right path of the world is what "Central" means. Central speaks of impartiality and spiritual mind, wisdom and views. As a Chinese Confucian ideal, cultivating people of virtue through Central Harmony is

[52] Legge, J. (1971). *Confucian Analects: The Great Learning, and The Doctrine of the Mean*. New York: Dover Publications. pp. 384–385.

[53] Legge, J. (1971). *Confucian Analects: The Great Learning, and The Doctrine of the Mean*. New York: Dover Publications. p. 393.

[54] Legge, J. (1971). *Confucian Analects: The Great Learning, and The Doctrine of the Mean*. New York: Dover Publications. p. 388.

the aim. A saintly king loves all people, good and evil, working to benefit them all for mutual prosperity.

Western philosophical thoughts about fairness and justice are usually described in concrete and practical terms, whereas Chinese philosophy emphasizes motivation and mentality. "Central" for example, refers to the self-improvement of life. The *Book of Documents* praises the greatness of Emperor Yao and Shun, "The mind of man is restless, prone (to err); its affinity to what is right is small. Be discriminating, be uniform (in the pursuit of what is right), that you may sincerely hold fast the Mean."[55]

This saying, composed of sixteen ancient Chinese characters, was the lesson Yao taught Shun, which was passed on to saints such as Yu, Tang, Wen, Wu, the Duke of Zhou, and Confucius. It means that when one stays focused, impartial, and continually refines their knowledge and wisdom, they follow the Central Way. When they keep this Way without being distracted by external influences, they are incessant (Yong 庸); when they keep the Central Way and further benefit the world, Harmony is achieved. To attain Central Harmony (中和) is to do one's part in contributing to the world's common happiness and prosperity through the right mindfulness.

Without altruistic motivation, we would not grant the most vulnerable the greatest advantages nor foster interdependence among diverse entities, to build a world of shared prosperity. The three conditions of justice, as proposed by John Rawls, must be backed by the benevolence and selflessness of humanity. Otherwise, equal opportunity, tolerance for diversity, and preferential treatment for the worst off would be almost impossible.

Chinese philosophy, premised on self-cultivation, stresses inner goodness to achieve goodness. For instance, Emperor Shun's inner goodness precipitated the prosperity, joy and harmony of the people in tandem with the mountains, rivers, and the Earth. This is an ideal society exhibiting wealth, balance, and purity.

Goodness in Common Prosperity
The Result of Goodness should be common prosperity. Only with common prosperity can true goodness be reached.

---

[55] Sturgeon, D. (2019). *Chinese Text Project: A Dynamic Digital Library of Premodern Chinese* (J. Legge, Trans.). Digital Scholarship in the Humanities. Retrieved from https://ctext.org.

Common prosperity for all people and things is the goal of supreme goodness, as well as being the highest guideline of a good economy.

The *I Ching* states:

> The great man is he who is in harmony in his attributes with heaven and earth; in his brightness with the sun and moon; in his orderly procedure with the four seasons; and in his relation to what is fortunate and what is calamitous with the spiritual agents. He may precede Heaven, and Heaven will not act in opposition to him; he may follow Heaven but will act only as Heaven at the time would do. If Heaven will not act in opposition to him, how much less will men![56]

Harmonious unification with all things is the highest form of goodness for shared and collective prosperity.

All laws are interconnected and endure eternally. According to the Buddhist conception of Interdependent Arising, everything is based on and correlates with each other, and so they merge as one. All are one, hence benefiting others is to benefit oneself.

All laws stem from interdependent arisings, hence salvation for sentient beings is derived from compassion. All is one, thus to aid others also benefits oneself.

Therefore, we should care for all sentient beings and regard them as part of ourselves; this is the essential ideology of Buddha's compassion: being benevolent to everyone and to be compassionate toward all.

Embracing all beings and all things with selfless great love is the ultimate state of altruistic enlightenment in Buddhism. The Buddha's fundamental principle of interdependent arising is the path to practicing altruism. Only through thorough altruism can the common flourishing of all beings be realized.

Goodness in Love for All Beings and Things

All things arise interpedently, so we cherish all affinities and practice altruism—an act of great love.

To love all people and all things with great compassion is the highest ideal of Buddhism, and it starts with good deeds. Behavior alters thoughts and emotions, as good deeds spark good ideas and love.

[56] Legge, J. (1963). *The I Ching: The Book of Changes*. United Kingdom: Dover Publications. p. 47.

Charity inspires entrepreneurs to love and cultivate their inner mercy, both of which are innate traits. I've seen Tzu Chi volunteer who are entrepreneurs, influenced by Master Cheng Yen, put great effort into philanthropy that they may not have initially comprehended. However, once they start to do good deeds, they quickly learn how to lead a selfless life and experience a newfound compassion.

Good deeds shape minds of goodness. Selfless charity and corporate governance infused with goodness and love, are at the core of the Economy of Goodness.

Selfless love embodies the highest emotions and thoughts that all laws unite as one, and all become one. This is the ultimate path of goodness.

As expressed in traditional Chinese philosophy, Supreme Goodness refers to Supreme Harmony—the highest harmony state in the Universe. Not just between people, but between people, nature, and all beings, living in shared prosperity.

Supreme Harmony, described in The *Book of Changes (The I Ching)*, represents the merging of Yin and Yang. According to *The History of the Han Dynasty*, all beings in the world originate from the same source, experiencing deep virtue and dwelling in tranquility and joy.[57] All Human beings and things coexist harmoniously and mutually benefit each other, thus fulfilling the foundation of Supreme Harmony. Its essence is altruism.

The *Book of Changes* said, "The method of Heaven (乾Qian) is to change and transform so that everything obtains its correct nature as appointed (by the mind of Heaven); and (thereafter the conditions of) great harmony are preserved in the union. The result is "what is advantageous, and correct and firm. (The sage) appears aloft, high above all things, and the myriad states all enjoy repose."[58]

The Qian diagram of the *Book of Changes* creates changes; all things follow their own paths, yet are ultimately working toward converging and reaching a harmonious state of Preserving Harmony.

Supreme Harmony means all things are inseparable from the power of the Qian diagram which created the world. This power is one, returning to one after the birth of all things—representing the harmony and unity

---

[57] Ban, G. & Yan, S. G. (1962). *Han shu* [Book of the Han Dynasty] (Vol. 12). Taipei: Chung hwa book co. ltd. p. 4228.

[58] Legge, J. (1963). *The I Ching: The Book of Changes*. United Kingdom: Dover Publications. p. 213.

of all and bringing peace and happiness. As a result, all countries enjoy peace.

This is as Lao Tzu said:

> The Tao produced One; One produced Two; Two produced Three; Three produced All things. All things leave behind them the Obscurity (out of which they have come), and go forward to embrace the Brightness (into which they have emerged), while they are harmonized by the Breath of Vacancy.[59]

The harmony between Yin and Yang creates all things and fills the world, each occupying its own position, thus creating harmony. All things are born according to the Tao, Lao Tzu's Tao ultimately returns to nature and returns to nothingness. This kind of creation and endpoint are no different, both are the harmony of all things, the unity of all laws. This harmony and unity are all based on benefiting others, with benefiting others as a prerequisite. Self-interest separates and each becomes different. Separation leads to chaos, as Xunzi said.

"The only way to help oneself is to help others." All must act altruistically, not just one person or thing. Achieving harmonic unity and shared success cannot be accomplished by any single entity and instead requires the combined strength of everyone.

Lu Cheng, a prominent Buddhist scholar, emphasized that in the pursuit of Nirvana, individual action is insufficient; collective effort is essential. Acting solely for oneself reflects self-interest, which is incompatible with the interconnectedness of existence. One should embrace self-interest alongside altruism, extending care to others as if they were one's own, and merging with the vast ocean of sentient beings. True altruism encompasses self-interest, affirming the interconnected nature of existence.[60]

Nirvana is the highest state of goodness in Buddhism. The Buddha realized, through deep understanding, that all laws are interconnected. All sentient beings possess the qualities of Nirvana, alongside sufficient wisdom and purity.

---

[59] Tzu, L. (Eds.). (2021). *Tao Te Ching* (J. Legge, Trans.). Standard Ebooks. Retrieved from https://standardebooks.org/ebooks/laozi/tao-te-ching/james-legge.

[60] Lu, C. (2000). *Yindu foxue yuanliu lue lun* [An Outline of the Origins of Indian Buddhism]. Taiwan: Darchen publisher. p. 182.

Supreme Goodness that Aims for Truth

In comparison with Eastern goodness, Western goodness unites with the supreme truth or ruler.

Western civilizations' reflections on goodness are grounded in the belief of a fixed truth, which serves as a foundation for creating all life ethics.

Saint Thomas Aquinas, a Church Father of Medieval Scholasticism, believed that real happiness lies in God's hands, and is the supreme good humans experience while under God's reign.

God created humans and gave them an inclination to seek supreme happiness. To attain it, one must constantly turn to God. Reuniting with God is humanity's ultimate good.

Greek philosophers Democritus and Epicurus argued that the highest good of human beings is the pursuit of happiness. This is closer to the pragmatic thinking found in the East; as Mencius said, "A man who commands our liking is what is called a good man... He whose goodness has been filled up is what is called a beautiful man."[61]

This thought is known as Hedonism, proposing that the goal of life is to be happy, which is of utmost importance.

However, happiness does not signify the accomplishment of desires, rather it implies spiritual peace and joy. The Stoics contend that the pinnacle of goodness rests in virtue, not the striving for happiness.

Emmanuel Kant attempted to settle the debate between virtue and happiness regarding supreme goodness in ancient Greek philosophy, as mentioned above.

Kant believed that both theories are one-sided, so he sought to reconcile their conflicts between idealist motivism and material utilitarianism, asceticism and happiness via the concept of the highest good.

Kant held that the supreme good is the combination of morality and happiness; he regarded virtue as the highest good, but argued that, alone, it could not fulfill all of human reason's aims, and so must be coupled with happiness.[62]

[61] M. & Legge, J. (2011). *The Works of Mencius*. New York: Dover Publications. p. 490.

[62] Kant, I. (2012). *Kant: Groundwork of the Metaphysics of Morals* (M. J. Gregor & J. Timmermann, Ed. & Trans.). United Kingdom: Cambridge University Press (Original work published 1785).

In Kant's view, people strive for virtue and happiness due to Good Will—the foundation of all morality.

In his book *Groundwork of the Metaphysics of Morals*, Kant stated that the establishment of morality must be a universal, natural, self-acting, absolute, purposeless, and unconditional law. He said, "It is impossible to think of anything at all in the world, or indeed even beyond it, that could be taken to be good without limitation, except a good will."[63]

Kant's interpretation of moral laws is metaphysical: they first existed there, and people act in accordance with them, even if reality does not offer a basis for their realization. Hence, moral practice is a tool for morals.

Kant contends that the highest good is to first establish Good Will and let all good deeds follow suit; this Will, he suggests, should be free from force. Through metaphysical laws, Kant endeavors to bridge the gap between theory and practice, manifesting the will in reality via free will.

John Rawls referred to Kant's goodness as Conception-dependent Desire; when fully aware of the highest moral principles stemming from their free will, people naturally wish to act in accordance.

John Hick, a religious scholar, asserts that Kant's highest good parallels the Buddha's idea, as Kant's highest good is inescapable, being truth, and thus is consistent with the Buddha's state of unity of consciousness and truth.

Harmonious Goodness that Encompasses Oneself and Others

Kant's highest good is based on reason, starting with concepts then emotions. Whereas, the Buddha's supreme goodness is perceptually derived, stemming from compassion to wisdom.

The harmony of emotions and wisdom is the highest good. The combination of virtue and happiness is the ultimate good. This is a common belief among Aristotle, Kant, and Eastern wise men, with different focuses. The West emphasizes rationality, while the East emphasizes sensibility, as in "all people have a sympathetic heart." Western philosophers say that humans are rational animals.

---

[63] Kant, I. (2012). *Kant: Groundwork of the Metaphysics of Morals* (M. J. Gregor & J. Timmermann, Ed. & Trans.). United Kingdom: Cambridge University Press (Original work published 1785). p. 9.

In China, pursuit of the highest good means the harmonious unification of rationality and sensibility, namely that of wisdom, thought, and emotion. This is the foundation of a soul. Only with this foundation can a Confucian man of virtue understand the cultivation of heaven and earth, coexist with all things, and even participate in creating all things between heaven and earth. As *The Doctrine of the Mean* states:

> It is only he who is possessed of the most complete sincerity that can exist under heaven, who can give its full development to his nature. Able to give its full development to his own nature, he can do the same to the nature of other men. Able to give its full development to the nature of other men, he can give their full development to the natures of animals and things. Able to give their full development to the natures of creatures and things, he can assist the transforming and nourishing powers of Heaven and Earth. Able to assist the transforming and nourishing powers of Heaven and Earth, he may with Heaven and Earth form a ternion.[64]

Goodness means wisdom, which comes from nature. Nature and Tao are interconnected. *The Doctrine of the Mean* says, "What Heaven has conferred is called The Nature; an accordance with this nature is called Dao-The Path of duty."[65] Goodness contains not only wisdom but symbolizes complete human character. Therefore, ancient Chinese philosophers equated wisdom with character and equated sages with kings. The internal sage means external kingship and vice versa.

What a great realm it is that human beings can create things just like heaven and earth when they give full development to their nature with sincerity.

The ultimate goal of fully utilizing human nature is to achieve harmony in all human relationships, such as a union of benevolence and justice, and to achieve equity and justice. Being benevolent entails empathizing and considering others' interests. Righteousness (義 yi) relates to ethics and human interactions. Perfect relationships, including between family members and between leaders and followers, refer to righteousness. In

---

[64] Legge, J. (1971). *Confucian Analects: The Great Learning, and The Doctrine of the Mean*. New York: Dover Publications. pp. 389–399.

[65] Legge, J. (1971). *Confucian Analects: The Great Learning, and The Doctrine of the Mean*. New York: Dover Publications. p. 383.

terms of economics, justice and interest must be balanced; this is giving full play to human nature.

Understanding the interconnectedness of fulfilling human nature and comprehending the nature of things, it becomes evident that human beings play a pivotal role in both comprehension and utilization. Xunzi advocated for a balanced approach to desires and material resources, emphasizing moderation to cultivate propriety, wherein neither excessive desires nor depleted resources hinder one another but instead harmoniously coexist and flourish.[66] Respecting human desires will not be hindered by a lack of material possessions, and things will not be exhausted by human desires. On the contrary, things flourish because of human beings, which is the growth of both. This is fulfilling the nature of things. All things and all people prosper together. Being able to do so can participate in the creation of heaven and earth.

Moderation of desires involves channeling people's urges to support the growth and well-being of all, as opposed to solely satisfying selfish yearnings. This is when propriety (禮 li) is activated and, ultimately, the convergence and balance of people and all things is the most recognizable display of Confucian propriety.

In Buddhism, such a realm entails caring for, enlightening, and completing the affinity of all things with a pure mind.

Approach everything with a pure heart, achieve and even transform all conditions, allowing all phenomena in the world (interdependent arising) to return to their pure essence, returning to the highest state of being able to create everything without attachment to anything. This is known as "dwelling nowhere and giving birth to the mind,"[67] giving rise to a joyful mind, a mind free of desires, a pure mind, and a mind capable of fostering all laws. This state is called Buddha, and it is known as Nirvana.

Common Goodness with Unification of All Laws

Goodness means that all things are prosperous and all laws unite into one.

We could unite under all laws via self-improvement, requiring selfless great love for all beings and people. Through cultivating wisdom in

---

[66] Wang, X. Q. (1994). *Xunzi ji jie* [Collected Annotations of Xunzi]. Shandong: Shandong Friendship Publishing House. p. 318.

[67] Hua, H. (Eds.). (1974). *The Diamond Sutra*. San Francisco: Sino-American Buddhist Association. https://www.buddhanet.net/pdf_file/prajparagen2.pdf.

this love, we could have our compassion enlightened to benefit all living creatures.

Goodness in a person is a combination of wisdom, compassion, and a pure mind.

Altruism leads to selfishness, so we should treat others as we wish to be treated until all living beings benefit and are transformed into goodness.

Goodness in economic activities implies equal wealth.

A society of equal wealth in which everyone lives and works peacefully and contentedly requires the upholding of altruistic values, not self-serving ones. The prevalence of self-interest only serves to aggravate disputes of interest, where the wealthy few obtain the bulk of the wealth while the majority suffer from deprivation.

The Economy of Goodness implies mutual benefit, not competition, leading to oligopolies and monopolies that do not favor the collective interests.

The Economy of Goodness is open to innovations driven by compassion and products that bring happiness to all human beings.

The Economy of Goodness is sustainable not only for businesses but also for the environment. It is devoted to the harmonious relationship between people and the planet.

The Economy of Goodness means shared prosperity. It paints a picture of a society in which all lives flourish mutually.

CHAPTER 3

Reflections on the Contemporary Capitalist Economy

The capitalist system is the most crucial force for building civilization in present-day times. It has generated unprecedented material wealth and joy for people, although not for all. Unfortunately, it has also resulted in poverty and environmental degradation for around half of the world's inhabitants.

The capitalist economy is unstoppable. Its social innovation and scientific development make humans appear to be in control of the world. Yet, excessive consumption of the earth's resources has put the very foundation of our existence at risk, raising the alarm for the environment's sustainability and creating an unprecedented crisis.

The reflections here on the capitalist economy do not aim to remove it, but to preserve and make it enduring so that it can confer long-term advantages to humanity and the planet.

To attain this objective, we must first examine and debate some essential issues in the Capitalist economic system.

Among many issues, justice in distribution and environmental matters are the most often discussed. These only scratch the surface of Capitalism's numerous drawbacks.

The true issues and dynamics of a capitalist economy are rooted in individualism.

R.-S. Her, *The Economy of Goodness*,
https://doi.org/10.1007/978-981-97-6363-4_3

This chapter first examines the mutual generation between individualism and Capitalism and how to find an acceptable solution for these two strongly connected forces.

SECTION 1: THE HISTORICAL CONSTRUCTION OF INDIVIDUALISM

To discuss Capitalism's structure, we must first reflect on its ideological basis. Since the eighteenth century, booming industrial science and tech propelled maximum and standardized production. Furthermore, it maximized consumption and caused people to seek material satisfaction as a way to fill their inner void.

Before capitalism, marine trade flourished from the fifteenth to sixteenth centuries, yet Western churches exerted a checking effect on people's material ambitions. Meanwhile, Islam's brotherly love served as a discouragement of too much capital and greed in Muslim countries. Muslims from the fifteenth to eighteenth centuries prospered economically with its emphasis on even income distribution, resulting in a small gap between the rich and poor, leading to a stable society.

By comparison, Western society and Muslim countries were equal in terms of wealth and power in the sixteenth and seventeenth centuries. However, capital had grown exponentially at the end of the eighteenth century, widening the economic gap between Muslims and the West, as well as the rich-poor divide in the West, due to maritime commerce.

Marine Trade and Capitalism: A Historical Examination

At the time, there were many Western financial investors and speculators in the maritime trade. The church disapproved of financial transactions and interest but did not object to oceanic trading ventures, believing it could spread the gospel. These investors and adventurers would come to an agreement on dividends, with one party investing and the other taking part at sea. This brought great profits and high risks for those involved, but despite that people eagerly invested immense amounts of money. Countries such as Italy, Holland, Spain, Britain, and France took enormous chances on the seas and reaped huge rewards as a result. Unfortunately, some never returned to their endeavors, but the risk was accepted by all.

However, Muslim countries at the time were staunchly opposed to business finance. Muslims could take out private loans to purchase the necessities of life, but discipline in the Muslim world would not permit transactions of capital involving interest. This is why Western Capitalism flourished during the eighteenth century. Even more significant is how it was the rise of commerce that enabled individualistic culture to develop. Looking at it from a cultural point of view, we can gain a better understanding of where Capitalism originated.

The rise of Capitalism was accompanied by the growth of individualism. In other words, early Capitalism encouraged individualism, which fueled Capitalism's ultimate success.

Between the sixteenth and seventeenth centuries, as sea trade gained momentum, many wealthy cities emerged on coasts, such as Venice and Amsterdam. This rise of new cities facilitated the establishment of a bourgeois class, thereby diminishing the control and dominance of the aristocracy and the Church. Having access to newfound freedoms in these cities, tenants sought their fortune in crafts and trades and could no longer be managed as before. Consequently, aristocrats and the Church were forced to sell their large tracts of land to the bourgeois class, who gradually replaced them as the wealthy class, providing a source of finance for the king and bringing with them job opportunities and free urban citizens (different from tenants).

Commerce as the Great Equalizer

In the fifteenth and sixteenth centuries, the Catholic Church was embroiled in internal struggles and the ongoing conflict between Muslim and Christian civilizations. Countries frequently waged wars in pursuit of maritime dominance. The business sphere, however, became the most neutral, tolerant, respectful, and equitable plane.

As the eighteenth-century French philosopher Voltaire once said, in the realm of commerce, Muslims, Christians, Protestants, Hindus, Jews, and Chinese people all sit together on equal footing, mutually pursuing interests and showing respect for one another. Perhaps only those who have faced bankruptcy are met with skepticism. In this domain, everyone engages in conversation, transactions, and laughter without distinction. Outside of these interactions, Jews may return home to perform circumcision rituals, Christians may head to church for baptisms, and Muslims may continue their five daily prayers. However, within the business sphere, everyone is treated equally, disregarding differences in religion or national borders. A borderless environment fosters greater freedom and equality.[1]

It was amidst this setting that commerce was seen as hallowed and admirable. Concurrently, commerce's growth brought about the emergence of contemporary individualism.

Business Development and Political Equality

Ocean trade spurred the rise of cities. Urban life demanded more craftsmen and entrepreneurs. People from rural areas flocked to the cities, exchanging tenantship for personal freedom and prosperity. The church and government consequently faced pushback. If the king wanted war, he had to negotiate taxes with established merchants, which was the start of business-swaying politics.

Faith-wise, Catholic Church rule wavered, and Protestantism gained strength and support, culminating in a new political thought outside Church control. Locke took the Protestant belief that all were God's people and extended it to the equality of all men and natural human rights. He argued that everyone has inherent rights, thus sealing the picture of individualism.

Locke argued that humans are equal in the eyes of God, and thus have basic rights. This gave rise to absolute individualism in the West, wherein one's relationship with God would be mirrored in their relationships with their country and nature. These, in turn, depend on individuals' decisions.

That individuals were paramount became a widely accepted value in the West. No legal, political, economic, or social system could contravene the rights and desires of individuals.

The hotbed of individualism facilitated the rapid growth of capitalism, with maximized production and ceaseless consumption.

In Locke's view, individuals were innately entitled to fundamental rights as a safeguard of life. Nonetheless, in the economic sphere, this right transformed into a "divine sanction" enabling them to strive for personal success. Consequently, people were spurred to search for the optimization of wealth, consumption, and even authority.[2]

---

[1] Muller, J. Z. (2007). *The Mind and the Market: Capitalism in Western Thought*. United Kingdom: Knopf Doubleday Publishing Group.

[2] In the eighteenth century, Napoleon advocated for freedom, equality, and universal love, yet he crowned himself emperor. Individual rights, once freed from the control of the

Adam Smith wasn't the first to legitimize seeking personal gain; he merely provided footnotes for the idea. His major contribution to Capitalism is the notion that pursuing self-interest will result in the most benefit for the public.

The perfection of the Western capitalist economy stems from the dominance of individualism and the collaboration and reinforcement between individualism and the legitimacy of self-interest.

Section 2: Individuals
in Traditional Western Society

Individuals stayed part of groups and families prior to the Middle Ages when the standing of families, groups, and countries far outstripped that of individuals.

As mentioned before, the division of individuals and communities was due to the alteration in the relationship between man and God; in tandem, the protracted battle among spiritual and political authority, as well as the church's sale of indulgences, in the Middle Ages resulted in the Reformation guided by Luther and Calvin. Luther argued that individuals could communicate directly to God bypassing the church's assessment. Following Weber's point, there was a significant spiritual bond between Protestantism and Capitalism in terms of whether mankind was God's elect.

The link between people and God was the crucial starting point for individualism.

It is through accomplishments that individuals show if they are God's chosen. The more significant the work, the bigger the glory as God's chosen. However, in keeping with Protestant ethics and Weber's theory, adhering to God's laws is still of utmost importance. Achievements and laws signify those selected by God.

God lost His position in the Middle Ages due to doubts among many Westerners, leaving individuals to their own, void of God's laws. This vacuum allowed Capitalism to gain space for material desires.

Individuals during the Reformation belonged to God, but from the Enlightenment in the eighteenth century, they belonged to themselves.

---

traditional church and the constraints of hereditary classes, found their greatest expression in his becoming an emperor. Napoleon was indeed a pioneer in the early modern Western world who thoroughly and fully demonstrated individualism.

Westerners who have lost God affirm themselves through personal achievements and replace God's laws with professionalism. Instead of relying on the religious promise of Heaven, they find satisfaction in material things, using them to create their version of Heaven on Earth.

As two significant capitalist subjects, material desires, and individualism mutually justify and reinforce one another; they become unshakeable.

It is not enough to merely reflect on Capitalist economic ethics issues concerning the pursuit of desire and the justice of allocation; Individualism should be examined as well.

The Fundamental Ignorance of Individualism

Individualism in the current era is widespread. However, the concept of individual dominance is misguided, although it is the basis of liberalism and Capitalism. To grasp Capitalism and liberalism one must consider individualism.

Individualism, as mentioned, is a product of modern times, originating from changes in the relationship between man and God, and man and group.

Individual existence is relative to God's. Without God, there is no individual, and absolute individualism is a reaction to God. Individuals first rebelled against the Church and then away from God.

In the West, after the fifteenth century, people first established a relationship with God, followed by one with their country. With the belief in individual supremacy, people hold a higher status than the state and their own faith surpasses that of the church. This creates opposition between individual and state and between individual and church.

If there is no oppression, the individual does not exist. Individuality is a reaction to church and state oppression.

Individuals are products of belief in God.

According to *the Bible*, God created man; however, man disobeyed and spawned the world we live in today. Adam and Eve's shame at being naked demonstrated the acknowledgment of individual consciousness. People became separated from the unified mass of nature, realizing they were distinguished from each other, and that individuals and God were distinct. This marked the start of Western individualism.

Individualism was a rejection of God. Without a divine being, individualism would be impossible. In the West, traditionally, rejecting God meant denying individuals, as they were thought to have been created by a higher power. Dependence on God's will presupposes that individuals should be part of the overall order, rather than isolated from it. Yet, in the modern era, separating individuals from God, in addition to other entities, is the source of ignorance of individualism.

Individuals cannot be placed above other entities, be they God or otherwise. Science has advanced far enough to possibly create artificial intelligence and robots more powerful than humans, but like mankind did with God, will it be uncontrollable and ultimately betray humans? Stephen Hawking warns of that possibility.

Under what framework must individuals be placed to achieve true happiness and fulfillment?

What model and thought do individuals need to follow to find the fundamental source of their lives? Western dualism has historically been a dichotomy between individuals and God, nature, or other forces.

Only when binary opposition is discarded can an individual's worth be fully revealed and life find harmony. As a tree needs a forest, the forest needs the earth, the earth needs the sky, and the sky must be in tune with the truth of the universe; all is intertwined and in synchronized creation. It is only in this way that individuals can find fulfillment.

We look to the East: why didn't individualism appear in its history? Not as a result of its being a collective society throughout since the West was too before the Middle Ages.

Instead, in the East there was no creator like God; so, there was no historical individualism, no tension between the whole and the individual, omnipotence, insignificance, and domination/submission.

SECTION 3: OUTLOOK ON LIFE AS A WHOLE

The concept of "individual" is relatively unfamiliar in the East, both to Confucianism and Buddhism. Confucius's benevolence (仁 ren) is about the relationship between two people. Confucian thought has never emphasized the individual, but rather places the individual in the context of family and community, emphasizing the individual's emotions and responsibilities toward family and country. Therefore, Confucius taught filial piety (孝 xiao) and loyalty as developing benevolence into propriety (禮 li)[3] and virtue (德 de), and practicing righteousness (義 yi) and equity

[3] Propriety in Chinese, pronounced Li (禮), denotes treating others with respect and courtesy.

through propriety. Virtue comes from filial piety, respect for elders (悌 ti), and justice.

On the other hand, benevolence, propriety, justice, respect for elders, and virtue all place the value and function of one's life in a relative order and relationship of human relations, rather than emphasizing the absoluteness of the individual self. Human existence is found in relationships, and human cognition of the self is achieved in the harmonious and good/ well handling of relationships. This is what it means to be a gentleman, and this is what it means to have virtue.

This three-dimensional and circular way of thinking, in contrast to the vertical Western way of thinking (the relationship between man and God is vertical), will not develop extreme individualism; nor will it develop a life value that emphasizes the satisfaction of one's own selfish desires, as is generally shown in capitalism today.

The Taoist View of the Individual

Taoism and Buddhism share a view of the individual as a being on a path to freedom and liberation. Freedom is freedom from the bondage of desire, and liberation is freedom from the limitations of the individual's small vessel. Taoists believe that it is possible for humans to transcend the body and become immortals, unifying, and disappearing into the unknown.

In Taoism, the perception of self is that true selfhood lies in the absence of self. The notion of self is considered perilous, and genuine selfhood must align and merge with the greater self. Lao Tzu said:

> And what is meant by saying that honor and great calamity are to be (similarly) regarded as personal conditions? What makes me liable to great calamity is my having the body (which I call myself); if I had not the body, what great calamity could come to me? Therefore, he who would administer the kingdom, honoring it as he honors his own person, may be employed to govern it, and he who would administer it with the love which he bears to his own person may be entrusted with it.[4]

Only through selflessness can one truly possess their greater self.

---

[4] Tzu, L. (Eds.). (2021). *Tao Te Ching* (J. Legge, Trans.). Standard Ebooks. Retrieved from https://standardebooks.org/ebooks/laozi/tao-te-ching/james-legge.

The bigger one's heart, the greater their establishment and achievements.

By relinquishing the self, one can attain this true self, their greater self. This self is characterized by universal love, serving as a vessel for the world.

However, achieving such a greater self requires the practice of "preserving stillness" and "returning to the mandate." Preserving stillness, as Lao Tzu teaches, involves shedding personal desires and eliminating self-centered thoughts, thereby gaining insight into the eternal mandate of life. Lao Tzu said:

> The (state of) vacancy should be brought to the utmost degree and that of stillness guarded with unwearyingly vigor. All things alike go through their processes of activity, and then we see them return to their original state. When things (in the plant world) have displayed their luxuriant growth, we see each of them return to its roots. This returning to their roots is what we call the state of stillness, and that stillness may be called a reporting that they have fulfilled their appointed end. The report of that fulfillment is the regular, unchanging rule. To know that unchanging rule is to be intelligent; not to know it leads to wild movements and evil issues. The knowledge of that unchanging rule produces a (grand) capacity and forbearance, and that capacity and forbearance lead to a community (of feeling with all things). From this community of feeling comes a kingliness of character, and he who is king-like goes on to be Heaven-like. In that likeness to heaven, he possesses the Tao. Possessed of the Tao, he endures long; to the end of his bodily life, he is exempt from all danger of decay.[5]

Tao is constant (unchanging); knowledge of it brings one back to their true nature. Through this, the world can be accommodated and one can become a king. The king follows paths of Heaven that are everlasting, and they remain wise forever.

Taoism regards humans as merely one form of life within the universe, obligated to harmonize and resonate with the greater cosmic order known as the Tao. The concept of Non-Action in Taoism entails aligning with the Tao and returning to a state of naturalness. Through this alignment and return to nature, individuals discover the essence of life. This is encapsulated in the saying, "Man takes his law from the Earth; the Earth takes

---

[5] Tzu, L. (Eds.). (2021). *Tao Te Ching* (J. Legge, Trans.). Standard Ebooks. Retrieved from https://standardebooks.org/ebooks/laozi/tao-te-ching/james-legge.

its law from Heaven; Heaven takes its law from the Tao. The law of the Tao is its nature of being what it is."[6]

Nature means that humans and all beings return to and adhere to their inherent nature.

Returning to nature is a core idea in Taoism. Reaching back to the state of Non-Being is a life goal. It is impossible to define or restrict life with worldly titles and forms. Lao Tzu objected to some Confucian scholars who placed too much emphasis on hierarchical titles and ceremonial practice. Yet, Lao Tzu thought that titles and forms don't conflict with nature, since both come from nature but with varying names. One can consider them the Cosmic Mystery: traversing into the mysterious depths is the entryway for life's secrets. Beyond titles, Tao is found within nature.

Nature is one integrated mass. According to Lao Tzu, the meaning of names denotes various forms of entities. Lao Tzu's nameless Tao is still attributed to diverse entities, but there is no name for it. Only nature is an integrated primal state to which life should return. Therefore, Zhuang Zi expressed the idea that everything and oneself are inseparable. Lao Tzu said:

> There was something undefined and complete, coming into existence before heaven and earth. How still it was and formless, standing alone and undergoing no change, reaching everywhere and in no danger (of being exhausted)! It may be regarded as the mother of all things. I do not know its name, and I give it the designation of the Tao (the Way). Making an effort (further) to give it a name, I call it The Great. Great, it passes on (in constant flow). Passing on, it becomes remote. Having become remote, it returns. Therefore, the Tao is great; Heaven is great; Earth is great, and the (sage) king[7] is also great.[8]

"Having become remote, it returns,"[9] means that the source and end of life are the same, and the group and the individual are also the same.

---

[6] Tzu, L. (Eds.). (2021). *Tao Te Ching* (J. Legge, Trans.). Standard Ebooks. Retrieved from https://standardebooks.org/ebooks/laozi/tao-te-ching/james-legge.

[7] The sage king may not refer to a king of kingdom but rather indicates a completeness of man.

[8] Tzu, L. (Eds.). (2021). *Tao Te Ching* (J. Legge, Trans.). Standard Ebooks. Retrieved from https://standardebooks.org/ebooks/laozi/tao-te-ching/james-legge.

[9] Tzu, L. (Eds.). (2021). *Tao Te Ching* (J. Legge, Trans.). Standard Ebooks. Retrieved from https://standardebooks.org/ebooks/laozi/tao-te-ching/james-legge.

Eastern thinking has no first cause and theory of occurrence, and all generations are endless. This is eternal Tao.

> The Tao is (like) the emptiness of a vessel; and in our employment of it, we must be on our guard against all fulness. How deep and unfathomable it is, as if it were the Honored Ancestor of all things! We should blunt our sharp points, and unravel the complications of things; we should temper our brightness, and bring ourselves into agreement with the obscurity of others. How pure and still the Tao is, as if it would ever so continue! I do not know whose son it is. It might appear to have been before God.[10],[11]

This Tao comes from Nature and is not created by any gods. Nature is spontaneous and not the result of anything else. It is, and not should be.

Individuals are part of the Tao and nature, and thus must be in harmony with them; as a result, they will become carefree.

The Taoist view of life is so free, easy, and unruly. It does not deny material but emphasizes Non-Attachment.

> They grow, and there is no claim made for their ownership; they go through their processes, and there is no expectation (of a reward for the results). The work is accomplished, and there is no resting in it (as an achievement). The work is done, but how no one can see; it is this that makes the power not cease to be.[12]

Fan Li is a quintessential economic virtuoso of Taoism. He helped Emperor Gou Jian reclaim his kingdom, Fan Li gave up his beloved Xi Shi (It is said that she was one of the most beautiful women in Chinese history) to Fu Cha (King of Yue State), Gou Jian's nemesis, and supported him clandestinely till the former re-established the State of Yue and overcame the State of Wu. Afterward, Fan Li retired with Xi Shi to modern-day Zhejiang Province, where he achieved immense fortune.[13]

---

[10] Lao Tzu's God does not equal the God in Christian or Muslim belief as a creator with will. The God mentioned by Lao Tzu refers to universal rules and truth.

[11] Tzu, L. (Eds.). (2021). *Tao Te Ching* (J. Legge, Trans.). Standard Ebooks. Retrieved from https://standardebooks.org/ebooks/laozi/tao-te-ching/james-legge.

[12] Tzu, L. (Eds.). (2021). *Tao Te Ching* (J. Legge, Trans.). Standard Ebooks. Retrieved from https://standardebooks.org/ebooks/laozi/tao-te-ching/james-legge.

[13] Fan Li was a legendary politician and businessman in Ancient China.

Fan Li served as Prime Minister in the Imperial Court and was a tycoon in the business world. He gave away his wealth three times, showing no care for it. Legend has it that he retreated to Lihu Lake with Xi Shi, sailing the rivers and lakes and disappearing into the mountains, his whereabouts unknown.

This is Fan Li's view of life and wealth; it is almost Taoist in nature.

Buddhism promotes selflessness and teaches that the perception of self is the cause of all suffering because it is limited and false. Instead, it poses that people should understand their oneness with the infinite and that the sense of "self" is misguided and therefore redundant. For this reason, the Buddha dedicated His life to showing people that all living beings share the same Buddha-nature, meaning that self and other are one and the same. By viewing this unity of the self and others, altruism ultimately serves one's own well-being. Through relinquishing the notion of "me," one discovers a wider understanding of the self, and when this sense of selflessness is realized, the so-called "self" is then united with the grandeur of the cosmos.

I believe Capitalism's extreme material strivings stem from individualism, which can only be circumvented by eliminating extreme individualism.

Therefore, drawing from the Eastern perspective, especially Buddhism, we can explore the relationship between individuals and groups, striving to not only acknowledge the positives of Capitalism's innovations and entrepreneurship, but to also reduce personal greed, lessen the detrimental effects of some Capitalist economic systems, such as exploitation of the environment and excessive consumption, and ultimately, to counter the loss of joy and lack of spiritual fulfillment.

Due to the rise of individualism and free competition in Capitalism, the gap between the rich and poor has widened, leading to social conflict and unrest.

SECTION 4: THE BUDDHIST VIEW ON LIFE AND CAPITALISM

The fundamental teachings of Buddhism are precisely a remedy for individualism. The Buddhist teaching of no-self and the greater self are a thorough subversion, reflection, and reconstruction of individualism.

According to the *Agama Sutra*, when the Buddha was born, he took seven steps, with a lotus flower blooming with each step. With one hand pointing to Heaven and the other to the earth, the Buddha said, "Throughout heaven and earth, I alone am the supreme one."

This "self" is the greater self. The Buddha explains that He and the truth are one, only the Buddha is supremely honored, that is, only the truth is supremely honored. The Buddha realized the truth of all things, His realization pervades the void, the void is finite and his vows are boundless.[14] To abide by the truth and to be one with the truth is the proclamation that the Buddha made to the world when he was born.

This is the manifestation of the greater self,[15] which is unified with all truths and all things. This is the Buddhist view of the self in life.

In this view of life, there is no distinction between self and others, between individuals and groups, between individuals and nature. As one life is created, so is another. This worldview, the central tenet of Buddhism, eschews the notion of capitalism wherein the individual reigns supreme, and individual desires reign paramount. It also rejects any system that focuses solely on the survival of humanity, disregarding other species.

Therefore, eliminating negative factors in capitalism hinges on how one handles individual life.

How to transform individualistic thinking while checking it, without eliminating it, and impacting group and individual survival?

Buddhism believes that all things arise from interconnectivity. Nothing is independent, and all life is interdependent and mutually created. Thus, if one existence exists, so too does another; if one is extinguished, then so too is the other.

According to the law of Interdependent Arising, all things are interconnected. Therefore, to benefit others is to benefit oneself.

Therefore, capitalist economic thought based on Buddhism is altruistic, not abolishing self-interest, but striving to create and share prosperity with all.

To be born from things, yet not bound by things. To be shaped by the world, yet also transcend it.

In traditional Buddhist thought, there is a tendency toward cultivating emptiness. However, emptiness is not truly empty and devoid of all things. It is an infinite capacity for containing all things, as Master

---

[14] Shih, Cheng Yen. (2014). *Jing Si Abode Morning Service*. Hualien: Jing Si Abode. August 31, 2014.

[15] The "greater self" in Buddhist definition does not equal God, but denotes awakening of self.

Huineng said, "The wondrous nature of people is originally empty; there is nothing that can be grasped. And the true emptiness of the essential nature is the same."[16]

True Buddhist emptiness encompasses all manifestations of things and creates them, without any fixation on anyone. It is, indeed, the Great Emptiness.

It is through the void of the greater self that all beings benefit. Altruism is what fills the void of the greater self.

Buddhism doesn't oppose material life, and the Buddha taught that holding onto things and desires won't bring lasting happiness and fulfillment. The mind can make all things, so why does it need to be tied to material desires?

Therefore, the Buddha said that if the mind does not enter the Five Aggregates,[17] one will be free. The Five Aggregates do exist, but the Buddha wanted people to be free from being bound by them, to be unencumbered by desires, and to not be deceived by their manifestations or shackled by their delusions.

The Five Aggregates do exist, but liberation can be achieved if the heart does not enter them, as stated in Samyukta-agama:

> At that time, the Blessed One said to the monks: '...If a monk does not delight in bodily form, does not commend bodily form, does not cling to bodily form, does not attach to bodily form, then by not delighting in bodily form, his mind attains liberation. In the same way [if he] does not delight in feeling... perception... formations... does not delight in consciousness, does not commend consciousness, does not cling to consciousness, does not attach to consciousness, then by not delighting in consciousness his mind attains liberation.' If a monk does not delight in bodily form. His mind has attained liberation; in the same way [if he] does not delight in feeling... perception... formations... consciousness and his

---

[16] Huineng, D. (Eds.). (2014). *The Sixth Patriarch's Dharma Jewel Platform Sutra*. Buddhist Text Translation Society. p. xlv.

[17] Five aggregates (skandhas), are five psycho-physical aggregates, which according to Buddhist philosophy are the basis for self-grasping. The five aggregates are essentially a method for understanding that every aspect of our lives is a collection of constantly changing experiences. There is no one aspect that is truly solid, permanent, or unique. Everything is in flux. Everything is dependent upon multiple causes and conditions. This footnote is from: Five skandhas. (2020 October 21). In *Wikipedia*. Retrieved from https://encyclopediaofbuddhism.org/wiki/Five_skandhas.

mind has attained liberation, [for him] there is no perishing and no [re-]arising, he is established in balanced equanimity, with right mindfulness and right comprehension.[18]

If one doesn't take pleasure in the Five Aggregates—Form, Feeling, Perception, Impulse, and Consciousness—they will free their mind.

There are five aggregates in the world. If the mind is not impacted by them, one will not experience suffering.

By not being subject to birth and death, forsaking avarice for all things, and with right thought and wisdom, the Buddha did not reject the Five Aggregates existing in the real world, instead advocating the right wisdom and thought in them leading to Tao.

The material world exists, yet one must not let their mind be consumed by it. Otherwise, they won't be able to generate or conceive new ideas independently.

In this context, Master Huineng declared:

> How unexpected! The essential nature is intrinsically pure.
> How unexpected! The essential nature is originally unborn and undying.
> How unexpected! The essential nature is complete in itself, lacking nothing.
> How unexpected! The essential nature is fundamentally still and unmoving.
> How unexpected! From the essential nature the myriad dharmas come to be.[19]

In a capitalist economy, the mind can generate all material possessions and wealth; however, in the realm of the infinite, the mind should not be restrained by finite material and wealth. It is only such an unrestricted mind that can stay undefiled and pure.

Self-nature is complete and sufficient, why, then, should it be tethered to material and wealth? The mind, unconstrained by birth and death, why submit to the vicissitudes of possessions? Most importantly, the mind's

---

[18] Anālayo, B. (2013). *On the Five Aggregates (3)—A Translation of Saṃyukta-āgama Discourses 59 to 87*. Dharma Drum Journal of Buddhist Studies. New Taipei City: Dharma Drum Buddhist College. pp. 5–6.

[19] Huineng, D. (Eds.). (2014). *The Sixth Patriarch's Dharma Jewel Platform Sutra*. Buddhist Text Translation Society. p. xvii.

potentiality for laws—how can it generate when enchained to material and wealth?

The mind can generate all kinds of laws and generate material and spiritual civilizations, reaching the ideal state portrayed by Buddha, where the rope is golden, the earth is glazed with colors, and the people have abundance with no worldly cravings. It is a luxuriant and radiant world that can create all laws and spiritual land with purified minds.

Material abundance and spiritual transcendence are embodied in the world of the Buddha, Amitabha, and Halo Buddha of the *Lotus Sutra*.

Therefore, Buddhism opposes material prosperity, as it emphasizes non-attachment and non-bondage with material possessions. It views the mind as able to produce all laws and prosperity, while preserving its purity and harmony with all things; this is its fundamental economic thought.

In Buddhism, the relationship between mind and environment emphasizes how Bodhisattvas can transform their minds to achieve the wisdom of non-discrimination, becoming Bodhisattvas of the Power of Freedom. As stated by Master Yin Shun, Bodhisattvas, through the practical application of concentration and wisdom within their minds, have the ability to transform or negate all phenomena.[20]

In Buddhism, Master Cheng Yen, the founder of the Tzu Chi Merit Society, also emphasizes the concept of "the three reams being created by the mind." She teaches that transcending the desire realm comes from having no desires in the mind, surpassing the form realm involves being free from attachment to colors in the mind, and entering the formless realm means having a mind free from delusions and attachments.[21]

Master Cheng Yen's teaching on "the three realms being created by the mind" illustrates that Buddhism is neither mere idealism nor a seeker of an illusory, fantastical unknown world, but rather pursues inward cultivation at the ethical level.

According to Master Cheng Yen, spiritual cultivation means transcending the three realms of the mind and transforming the suffering of the Five Aggregates into altruistic acts of compassion. Master Cheng Yen said:

[20] Shih, Yin Shun (1992). *Weishi xue tan yuan* [Exploring the Origins of the Consciousness-Only Theory]. Taipei: Zhengwen Publishing House. p. 31.

[21] Shih, Cheng Yen. (2013). *Jing Si Abode Morning Service*. Hualien: Jing Si Abode. Dec. 20, 2013.

Ordinary people are deluded by the Five Aggregates of Form, Feeling, Perception, Impulse, and Consciousness. Our sensory organs perceive things from the outside world, yet we must go beyond sound and form and listen for the cries of suffering; it is our responsibility to show compassion and take action to relieve the suffering of those in need. This is the Way.

Sounds and forms may tempt our greed, which we should overcome; in seeing suffering we must give rise to love and give with compassionate love. This is the purpose of "form." The actions we can take and the path we can walk is the path of kindness and compassion. This is the Way.

The Buddha explains that when we can transform the Five Aggregates of Form, Feeling, Perception, Impulse, and Consciousness from the ten evils to practicing the ten virtuous deeds, this is the path to righteousness.[22]

From Master Cheng Yen's perspective, when the mind enters the realm of the Five Aggregates, it not only remains unaffected by their binding influence but also has the potential to transform and benefit the sentient beings who suffer and are bound by the Five Aggregates.

The economic thought of Buddhism is to benefit all living beings and to practice the Bodhisattva Path. The Medicine Buddha too follows the Way of the Bodhisattva to bring benefit to all sentient beings.

Tzu Chi, as a practitioner of the Buddha's teachings, has entered the mundane world to alleviate suffering, purify souls, and contribute to social prosperity and harmony.

The Buddhist economic ideal is to free all sentient beings from suffering and evil and bring about a world of health, wealth, and harmony with purified minds; this is what the Medicine Buddha desires and the intention of Bodhisattvas and all Buddhas to bring salvation to all beings.

SECTION 5: ALTRUISM AND HARMONIOUS UNIFICATION AS THE CORE

Eastern philosophy does not espouse individualism nor curtail it. Rather, it guides individuals to attain genuine autonomy by contributing to others and aligning with the entirety of the universe.

---

[22] Shih, Cheng Yen. (2013). *Wisdom at Dawn*. Hualien: Jing Si Abode. July 3, 2013.

By comparison, modern Western individualistic thinking is fragmented, detached from the collective, and disconnected from a relationship with God. It is like a floating piece of fluff without roots in the universe. What remains is desire, the pursuit of fulfilling desires, becoming the fundamental basis for personal self-realization.

Aristotle guided individuals to contribute to the city-state, establish a relationship of love with others, and live a moral and spiritual life, which meant real happiness. Aristotle's business ethics are based on the happiness of the city-state as a whole, not on the pursuit of personal wealth.[23]

In the Middle Ages, Saint Thomas warned Christians that unity with God was the bedrock of life. However, modern times have seen all of these beliefs dismantled one by one. Individuals are granted God-like powers, enabling them to dominate nature and prioritize their interests over others. This was the reality of individualism in the early stages of Capitalism.

Marx is comparable to an Apostle of Christ, demanding fairness and justice in the world. He advocated violent revolution, similar to the God of the *Old Testament*, who afflicted Egypt with ten plagues and liberated the Israelites from their four-hundred-year enslavement.

Marx, at the core, was like a dedicated Christian. To him, it seemed that God had been employed by the Church to chain people up. His economic revolutions were an attempt to liberate workers, similar to Moses' Exodus and Jesus' liberation, where the spiritual freedom of the Jewish people was achieved away from the temple.

The predicted arrival of communism eventually led to the Soviet bureaucracy. Marx still could not move away from the idea of a supreme ruler in Western society, which meant that personal freedom would be hard to achieve. Consequently, communism, as Marx advocated, ended up becoming the ruling power of the privileged classes.

The fundamental essence of Eastern Confucianism, Buddhism, and Taoism lies in the absence of an ultimate, supreme ruler. In Confucianism, Heaven is not a ruler but a bestower, a benevolent force. It is a Heaven that benefits others. As Confucius said, "Does Heaven speak?

---

[23] Pearce, Colin D. (2013). *Aristotle and Business: An Inescapable Tension, Handbook of the Philosophical Foundations of Business Ethics* (Vol. 1). Springer Publishing.

The four seasons pursue their courses, and all things are continually being produced, but does Heaven say anything?".[24]

Taoism has no concept of a supreme ruler. It seeks to follow nature, not dominate, but rather to adapt in harmony. The ultimate aim is to attain Non-Being.

The ultimate way of nature is Non-Being, not domination or control. Individual life relies on Tao and Non-Being, which is true freedom.[25] Lao Tzu did not reject the physical but urged one to leave it behind, having pursued it, and go beyond it once they have acquired it.

The Buddhist perspective on the laws of Interdependent Arising counteracts the view of a creator and ruler, claiming instead that all things arise from affinity. There is no fixed essence; everything is in a state of generation and alteration, better known as Impermanence.

Buddhism promotes more thorough individualism, positing that each life can reach its completion. It declares all beings possess Buddha-nature and are equal to Buddha. Self-nature is self-sufficient and requires no external search; one must contemplate self-nature to attain liberation.

In accordance with the laws of Interdependent Arising, all things in the universe are interconnected and stem from one another. Consequently, the world is a single entity, and thus, the self and others are not two; Buddhism is the Dharma of Non-Dualism. Altruism, then, contains self-interest and is the only path to it.

Understanding the laws of karma leads to enlightenment. Silent and peaceful Nirvana is pure wisdom; free of desires and worries, one with wisdom can save all living beings without being upset by their ignorance.

Buddhism desires that everyone attain their utmost Buddha nature and accomplish personal fulfillment in harmony with everything and laws.

True self-nature unites all laws; this is the state that the Buddha attained. All laws, singly and collectively, fit together harmoniously. As opposed to Western concepts of disruptive individualism, this is entirely different.

---

[24] Legge, J. (1971). *Confucian Analects: The Great Learning, and The Doctrine of the Mean*. New York: Dover Publications. p. 326.

[25] Non-Being is not absolute nothingness; on the contrary, it accommodates all things. We can consider it as the empty part of a cup, which is substantially able to contain anything as long as it constantly keeps its function of emptiness without being occupied by a particular matter.

In the East, individuals and groups are intimately connected, and the belief is that "I" am well-off when others are, too. Altruism can lead to a beneficial self-interest.

Such philosophy does not lead to the pursuit of only desire and wealth. It does not condone individual supremacy. Rather, it stresses the self's peace and harmony in a shared, prosperous society that includes everyone.

Confucianism, Buddhism, and Taoism reveal that self-cognition, self-development, and self-actualization are integrated with a greater "I."

This could address individualism in the West as a supplement to the thought of the supreme ruler, evoking fear in contemporary liberal circles toward traditional Western religious thought

Confucianism, Buddhism, and Taoism of the East have fostered a combination of individual and collective liberty, dominance and subordination, others and self, and discord and harmony.

Therefore, I am certain that Eastern thought can achieve a harmonious and altruistic society featuring abundance, equality, and ultimate economic prosperity.

Section 6: Economy of Goodness Based on All-Connected Things

From the global perspective, economic thinking cannot be merely self-interested. As the world is interconnected, all existence and economic activities are interdependent; that is, altruism yields self-interest and is, ultimately, preserving self-interest. Thus, economic life needs to be altruistic.

The Economy of Goodness is an economic system based on altruism; it benefits oneself more through kindness. Those who create value for others gain more in return. Through selflessness to achieve self-interest, we can find joy and balance in the world.

What is goodness? It is altruism. Motivated by goodness, and using good means, one can produce the result of goodness, namely overall social happiness and prosperity.

The motivation of goodness means staying in a state of pure, unfiltered thought. Modeling goodness means wisdom, it is an indispensable element even if one has had the motivation of goodness.

Taoist Altruism of Supreme Goodness

Lao Tzu said, "The goodness of a residence is in (the suitability of) the place; that of the mind is in abysmal stillness; that of association (or giving) is in their being with the virtuous; that of words is in their trustworthiness; that of governance is in its securing good order; that of the conduct of affairs is in its ability; and that of the initiation of any movement is in its timeliness."[26] These are wise principles to live by in business. One must handle with great capability in managing an enterprise, move with great timing in making investments, give with great kindness in fulfilling customers' needs, dwell with the right location for their operating premises, speak with great integrity in business partnerships, feel with great depth to be inclusive of partners and staff and govern with great administration in leadership.

Goodness in Chinese culture entails both a good state of mind and complete intelligence. Through the motivation of goodness and wisdom, we can reach ultimate goodness wherein everyone is prosperous and in good health, with clear thoughts, living in harmony with the earth.

Lao Tzu's goodness is rooted in altruism. "The highest goodness is like (that of) water. The excellence of water appears in its benefiting all things."[27] "It is because he is thus free from striving that therefore no one in the world is able to strive with him."[28] As such, altruism displays immense wisdom and can be utilized to create wealth and joy in the economic sphere.

I oppose the self-interested economy not only from an ethical and moral standpoint but also from a practical perspective. Through altruistic economic activities, the interests of society, individuals, and also the public can all be maximized, resulting in a mutually beneficial situation for everyone.

[26] Tzu, L. (Eds.). (2021). *Tao Te Ching* (J. Legge, Trans.). Standard Ebooks. Retrieved from https://standardebooks.org/ebooks/laozi/tao-te-ching/james-legge.

[27] Tzu, L. (Eds.). (2021). *Tao Te Ching* (J. Legge, Trans.). Standard Ebooks. Retrieved from https://standardebooks.org/ebooks/laozi/tao-te-ching/james-legge.

[28] Tzu, L. (Eds.). (2021). *Tao Te Ching* (J. Legge, Trans.). Standard Ebooks. Retrieved from https://standardebooks.org/ebooks/laozi/tao-te-ching/james-legge.

The All-Inclusive and All-Shared Confucian Economy of Goodness

Confucianism reconciles opposites for common prosperity, as stated in *The I Ching*:

> The successive movement of the Yin (inactive) and yang (active) operations constitutes what is called the course (of things). That which ensues as the result (of their movement) is goodness; that which shows it in its completeness is the natures (of men and things). The benevolent see it and call it benevolence. The wise see it and call it wisdom. The common people, acting daily according to it, yet have no knowledge of it. Thus, it is that the course (of things), as seen by the superior man, is seen by few.[29]

Yin and Yang are opposites that give birth to one another. *The I Ching* posits that great people can take on "Tao"—a prominent, yet invisible and unknowable position, utmost in sincerity, concentration, and dedication. Combining Yin and Yang to create is goodness, which requires utmost sincerity.

Such sincerity is an unselfish motivation for combining one's own and others' interests—the Means of Goodness for the Result of Goodness. *The I Ching* states:

> It is manifested in the benevolence (of its operations), and (then again) it conceals and stores up its resources. It gives their stimulus to all things, without having the same anxieties that possess the sage. Complete is its abundant virtue and the greatness of its stores! Its rich possessions are what is intended by 'the greatness of its stores;' the daily renovation which it produces is what is meant by 'the abundance of its virtue.'[30]

Treating others with benevolence and virtue, abandoning cleverness and utilitarianism, and creating all things without stress are the great causes of great virtue. This means great wealth can be created and attained arbitrarily, hence its name of great virtue. With benevolent foresight,

---

[29] Legge, J. (1963). *The I Ching: The Book of Changes.* United Kingdom: Dover Publications. pp. 355–356.

[30] Legge, J. (1963). *The I Ching: The Book of Changes.* United Kingdom: Dover Publications. p. 356.

one can achieve great wealth, and be able to continuously innovate and generate. This is great wealth and great virtue.

This represents the ideal of the Chinese economy, which stems from the integration of two opposites—coexistence, sharing, and collective prosperity, thus achieving great virtue and significant accomplishments.

The Four Sufficiencies in the Buddhist Economy of Goodness

The *Agama Sutra* emphasizes four sufficiencies.
The Four Sufficiencies include:

Commercial professional ability, which is Expedient Sufficiency;
   Protection Sufficiency in safeguarding property;
   Good Knowledge Advisor (Kalyāṇa-Mitra) Sufficiency to ensure joyful life;
   and Right Livelihood Sufficiency to live reasonably within our means.

These Four Sufficiencies provide everything necessary for prosperity and contentment in the Economy of Goodness and Good Enterprises.

Buddhism sees "Expedient" as referring to worldly laws and the mastery of such rules as the root of Expedient Sufficiency. Economic actions need specialized knowledge and abilities; to gain the ability to aid any living thing is Expedient Sufficiency.

Protection Sufficiency requires the adoption of a moral life, as Aristotle held, as the foundation of economic life. The Buddha emphasized this with his Six Non-Tao: no speculation, refusing ill-gotten gains, abstaining from cheating, not associating with thieves or socially questionable individuals, avoiding overly indulgent behavior, and being industrious. This is the key to safeguarding property and one's economic assets.

The Six Non-Tao assist individuals to secure their assets for long-term prosperity. They urge all members of society to be hard-working and seek out Good Knowledge Advisors, to acquire property through lawful means, and to prevent cravings. This is the route toward a Good Economy, where everyone is wealthy, reliable, honest, industrious, and plain living, thus constituting a thriving society of goodness.

The Buddha encouraged people to approach Good Knowledge Advisors and be Good Knowledge Advisors to others. To enable others to live and work successfully, we should not only help others profit but inspire goodness in others. Only when employees, partners, and consumers obtain wisdom from products can Good Knowledge Advisor Sufficiency and Economy of Goodness be realized.

The economic activities one engages in should benefit others with wealth, and increase the lifetime value of oneself and others. This is referred to as Right Livelihood Sufficiency.

Altruistic and Self-Interested Economies of Goodness with Spiritual and Material Abundance

The Buddha summed up the four precepts of the Economy of Goodness for technology and management innovation: earning wealth without unjust methods, at no unjust times, with no desire, and no business that encourages others' desires. Economic activities should not only give others profit but should also inspire the life values of ourselves and others. This is the Right Livelihood Sufficiency and the ideal of an Economy of Goodness.

Aristotle argued against the mindless search for money, as he believed it would not bring true happiness. Instead, true joy was derived from philosophical contemplation and reflection on life (Theoria and Philosophia). Happiness can be gained by taking part in civic activities, forming loving relationships, and leading an ethical life.

If economic activities do not seek to promote individual happiness and the well-being of society, people will be left pursuing only wants and wealth. This could lead to moral degeneration and social decline, rather than happiness.

Therefore, Aristotle thought that while achieving economic success, one should be involved in civic affairs, assist citizens, nurture loving families, and abide by moral truth. These wholesome practices will lend favor to the Economy of Goodness.

The Economy of Goodness aspires to be founded on Good Enterprises, businesses that engage in economic activities with ethical practices and socially responsible actions. Their goal is not only to generate profits for themselves and others but also to foster a sense of community and interconnectedness among stakeholders. By doing so, they aim to create an Economy of Goodness that prioritizes not just material well-being but also individual growth and societal harmony.

The Economy of Goodness (EOG) seeks to create an all-inclusive, all-shared, all-prosperous world by promoting altruism so that everyone can benefit. Through self-interest achieved by altruism, people can learn life values, avoid indulging in desires, and enrich their lives.

Abundant resources, a healthy body, a clear mind, aiding others and oneself, realizing the value of everyone's life within society, and sharing prosperity with all, these are happiness and goodness!

This book will discuss the historical roots of the Economy of Goodness and how it can be applied in the modern era to create a better future for mankind.

The premise of the EOG is an altruistic economy.

Why should humans be altruistic? Are they always?

Humans are interdependent through evolution. Nature and humans are mutually dependent, and economic activities cannot be done in isolation. Humans may be self-interested yet can be altruistic simultaneously.

In the following chapter, we will delve into the origin and evolution of altruism in human history.

CHAPTER 4

The Origin of Altruism: The Key to Group Survival

SECTION 1: EXPLORING THE POSSIBILITY OF HUMAN ALTRUISM

Darwin's nineteenth-century theory of evolution revealed that human nature is altruistic, thereby saving us from extinction.

Darwin believed that altruism arose from evolution. He noted the competition among species and concluded that those with altruistic traits had a better chance of survival.

Scholars of Darwin's Theory of Evolution, e.g., Sober and Wilson, have concluded from experiments that moral altruism derives from evolution, aiding species continuation and the establishment of social norms.

Social norms transfer highly altruistic traits into individual selfish ones. Possessing altruistic psychological traits is a gradually emerging psychological behavior pattern in the process of evolution, i.e., the so-called "Proximate Mechanism."[1] The "Proximate Mechanism" has social and cultural meanings and the value of genetic propagation. It suggests that human society has developed huge communities, while other species such as chimpanzees do not have such mature and complicated social systems, due to the altruistic and helpful cultural mechanisms of human societies.

---

[1] Scott-Phillips, T. C., Dickins, T. E., & West, S. A. (2011). Evolutionary Theory and the Ultimate–Proximate Distinction in the Human Behavioral Sciences. *Perspectives on Psychological Science*, 6(1), 38–47. https://doi.org/10.1177/1745691610393528.

R.-S. Her, *The Economy of Goodness*, https://doi.org/10.1007/978-981-97-6363-4_4

Why have humans developed mutual aid and altruism whereas gorillas have not?

There exists a contrast in communal interaction between humans and gorillas. Ancient humans stuck together, discovering that aiding others promoted the benefit of themselves and their tribal communities. Group life necessitates the development of behavior models from one another. In close contact, humans learned that reciprocity and altruism allowed them and their groups to prevail in intense species rivalry. Therefore, from an evolutionary standpoint, altruism is both natural and real for humans.

Evolutionists have explained the emergence of altruism in human nature from both social and biological viewpoints: social culture and genetic inheritance.

According to the Proximate Mechanism, people's behavior and attitude are formed via learning from others.

As pointed out by the Russian psychologist Vygotsky in his "Zone of Proximal Distance" theory, children develop behavior patterns by learning from people they are close to. People learn through the behavior of others, and form concepts through that behavior.[2]

Psychological researchers of evolutionary theory believe that the power of social-cultural systems enables a community to communicate through language and behavioral means, from one to another and from one generation to the next. Gradually, selfish behavior with negative traits or behaviors becomes replaced in human societies by reciprocal and altruistic ones.[3]

Altruistic Groups and Natural Selection

Evolutionists explained this further in terms of genetic heredity. The epigenetic process has a hub that controls the expression and suppression of genes (DNA). It doesn't alter genes but can make some Express or Not Express. For example, if a young mouse is separated from its mother, its interactions with offspring as an adult will be limited, as was with its

---

[2] Vygotsky, L. S., & Davydov, V. V. (1992). *Educational Psychology* (S. Robert, Trans.). Florida: St. Lucie Press (Original work published 1926).

[3] Scott-Phillips, T. C., Dickins, T. E., & West, S. A. (2011). Evolutionary Theory and the Ultimate–Proximate Distinction in the Human Behavioral Sciences. *Perspectives on Psychological Science*, 6(1), 38–47. https://doi.org/10.1177/1745691610393528.

own mother. The behavior of living things is determined by their social and cultural context, which can shape biological characteristics.

The epigenetic process can inhibit the expression of some genes[4] while the Altruistic mechanism can become an instinct of offspring via gene transmission.

Altruism has become a part of human nature, but how can it be a moral reality?

Psychologists studying evolution contend that religion is the origin of morality, and fear of supernatural forces was integral to the survival of ethnic groups, with those fearing such forces having a greater chance of surviving natural selection.

Fear of the supernatural became religious rituals emphasizing the importance of selflessness and altruism to different ethnic groups. Worship and rituals in primitive religions likely originated from the belief that sacrifices would appease deities and ensure the survival of the group.

The research of Darwin, contemporary psychologists, and biologists shows that altruism is beneficial to the long-term development of ethnic groups. In social cultures, altruism has evolved into ethical thinking or religious rituals. This has discouraged people from acting out of self-interest or harming others and curbed selfish thoughts.

From an evolutionary standpoint, the emergence of this altruistic nature and phenomenon is a well-established fact. Marx's historical materialism asserts that it is the production mode and relationships that shape human nature in historical evolution. Toynbee's *A Study of History* further emphasizes this by commenting on how most human civilizations came into being by overcoming demanding external challenges.[5] It is not hard to envisage the vulnerability primitive humans had among all other species. Therefore, the necessity for them to bind together and turn to the power of the group in order to keep out threats from nature and other species resulted in the Proximate Mechanism.

However, in Earth's history, why couldn't many other equally vulnerable, or even more vulnerable, species survive by clustering in groups? I believe that specific characteristics and wisdom inherent in humans were

---

[4] Scott-Phillips, T. C., Dickins, T. E., & West, S. A. (2011). Evolutionary Theory and the Ultimate–Proximate Distinction in the Human Behavioral Sciences. *Perspectives on Psychological Science*, 6(1), 38–47. https://doi.org/10.1177/1745691610393528.

[5] Toynbee, A. J. & Somervell, D. C. (1987). *A Study of History: Volume I: Abridgement of Volumes I–VI*. United Kingdom: Oxford University Press.

critical to developing the Proximate Mechanism, and altruism is probably inherent in us.

Many species on Earth have not developed altruistic moral or ethical systems. Many that exist or existed have developed survival mechanisms that make them tighter-knit than humans. Bees and ants have immense non-individual consciousness, labor, and interaction and are instinctually altruistic (within the species). Still, they don't produce morally necessary ethical values. Altruism is a unique human mode of life; it doesn't come from the Proximate Mechanism, which can't convincingly explain the emergence of moral altruism.

Some inherent characteristics of humans, such as abstract thinking, moral tendency, and mutual affection, are essential for humans to develop altruistic thoughts and personalities. Inseparable from altruism is living in a group setting.

SECTION 2: ALTRUISM: NATURE AND REALITY FOR HUMANS

Purely self-interested lives cannot create organizations, and groups lacking in altruism cannot form altruistic moral codes. Therefore, altruism is an integral part of human nature, having become a moral necessity over time.

In Buddhism, altruism is considered to be the natural way of doing things. As the Samyukta-agama states, a bhikkhu should benefit others, help them accumulate merits, and make them happy.[6]

In Buddhism, happiness is not just about oneself. It flourishes when shared with others through merit-making. The Treatise on the Great Perfection of Wisdom emphasizes this by describing the Bodhisattva as both enlightened and selfless. Their wisdom guides them to save all living beings, and their practice embodies the highest form of enlightenment, earning them the praise of all sages. This is precisely why they are called Bodhisattvas.[7]

Bodhisattva's self-enlightenment and altruism come from understanding all laws and realities. Knowing that altruism is truth, people show their nature by practicing it. Altruism in Buddhism is both reality and as

---

[6] Za'a han jing [Samyukta-agama (Sect. 41)]. Dazheng xinxiu dazang jing [Taishō Tripiṭaka (Vol. 2)]. No. 0099.

[7] Nagarjuna. Da zhi du lun [The Treatise on the Great Perfection of Wisdom]. Dazheng xinxiu dazang jing [Taishō Tripiṭaka (Vol. 25)]. No. 1509.

it morally should be, as demonstrated by human nature. True self-interest lies in altruism.

The altruistic spirit should be voluntary, not obligatory. Master Cheng Yen stated that assisting others is a responsibility driven by one's inner nature. Moreover, a Bodhisattva should be an unsolicited teacher.

From Tzu Chi's viewpoint, altruism should be seen as a cultural value rather than a legal requirement. If it was made compulsory, it would be a requirement, not an impulse to help. The lesson taught by the Buddha is about natural laws, not imposed by outside forces. As for wrongdoings, Devadatta is accountable for its consequences and those monks who make mistakes may be silently rebuked in Buddhism. All spiritual and moral practices should be of free will. Bodhisattva's altruism in aiding sentient beings is even more voluntary, and it is an expression of love and mercy to save all living beings.

Section 3: An Ideological Discussion of Altruism

Voluntary Altruism

Altruism should not be attained through legislative or political means; it should be something people wholeheartedly embrace and practice.

If altruism is strictly adhered to, it will lose energy and innovation. Attaining a state of oneness with all beings and laws is a noble ideal. We should comprehend it, produce it, and express it freely in various forms. Whether it is philanthropy, commerce, science, tech, or even politics, we may redefine and create them with altruistic perspectives.

Altruism means the Economy of Goodness in economic terms. The economy should prioritize helping others over pursuing self-interest. Non-profit organizations, which have burgeoned recently, are a prime example of people with a shared goal, who give back to society.

Western political science assumes human nature is evil, necessitating checks and balances and oversight, which often leads to more distrust and opposition. To address this, the concept of altruism should be rethought in order to restore moral and value judgments to politics, thereby benefiting all citizens. Through this, the destruction of democratic and undemocratic political systems can be averted.

The discussion also holds true for science. Science and technology, being value-neutral, can be beneficial to society or potentially create disasters. It is essential for these to be developed with altruism and compassion, to foster good social morality, and to protect humanity from destruction or enslavement by machines.

However, these altruistic constructions must be conceptually understood so that people can choose to practice them, rather than being forced to comply by law. Promoting moral concepts may be difficult, but forcing it would destroy altruism.

Altruism Begins with the Self

Michael Sandel, a professor at Harvard University, famously posed the case of benefit maximization. A trolley car was hurtling down a slope, about to strike five workers. To save them, the driver needed to steer it and hit just one person on the opposite side. Would you sacrifice five or one?

This is a utilitarian proposition: Save one or sacrifice five?

We cannot decide who ought to die, nor do we have the right or capability to determine which life is more significant.

If life could be measured in quantity, General Marshall wouldn't have saved Private Ryan with a squad of soldiers during WWII. Ryan's mother had already lost three sons in the war, so General Marshall couldn't let her suffer the loss of another. But this meant other mothers' sons had to pay the price—was it worth it?

Human life can't be measured in numbers, yet economics quantifies life and death, poverty, and wealth.

In another instance, the average annual number of fatalities from car accidents on a steep highway incline is fifteen. Making improvements to the slope could reduce the fatalities, yet the plan would cost one billion dollars; unfortunately, the local government lacked the budget to save dozens of lives, implying human life is not worth a billion.

Professor Lin Quan, a Taiwanese economist (a former Chairperson of the Executive Yuan), told me about this case.

This is the same as Sandel's situation, where a policy benefits one group while causing detriment to another, like canceling children's nutritious lunches to increase policing expenditure for better law enforcement, or reducing subsidies for some critically ill patients in order to fund long-term care for another type of patient?

Once their nutrition lunches are canceled, malnourished children in remote areas may become more prone to various diseases. What matters more—the health of those children or improving police equipment for a safer city?

Utilitarianism specializes in solving problems, with a simple, effective model for calculating maximum benefit and formulating policies.

We tend to sacrifice a group of people for the larger good, but is this altruistic?

In Sandel's case, I believe that it is best to have the driver intervene and personally sacrifice in an attempt to stop the car to save all six people; this is the only true example of altruism.

Altruism must be spontaneous, not prompted by others' decisions to sacrifice oneself to save others or someone to save five.

Sacrifice yourself instead of deciding who should be sacrificed.

In real life, we must decide who will be sacrificed and saved. We must also know which product to buy. This decision could mean that those who make the product will earn less or could even lose their jobs tomorrow. These are unavoidable outcomes.

So, what is the Economy of Goodness?

Obviously, we can't buy all products to benefit the employees of every company; what we can do is reduce waste. We buy products that reduce environmental consumption, and we don't support products from companies that exploit workers or damage the environment.

Transform Sandel's fable into economics, and the conclusion is that one should give up part of their profits to benefit others without weighing who benefits most.

Spontaneous help is the moral of Sanders' fable. If everyone—government officials, businesses, professionals, and citizens—desired to assist others, poverty would be eliminated.

But we tend to wait for someone else to rise to the occasion, not considering that we could voluntarily sacrifice some of our interests for the benefit of more people.

Likewise, entrepreneurs should take care of their employees' welfare without waiting for labor laws to be implemented.

Entrepreneurs save various unnecessary expenses because "the rich have their fine wines and meats, while the poor freeze to death on the roadside." What they save can be used to help others. They voluntarily take care of the impoverished around them, without relying on government welfare.

Consumers who are capable can spend from their own pockets to back products that are eco-friendly, even if they may be pricier. This is the Economy of Goodness.

If everyone could benefit others spontaneously, the gap between the wealthy and the disadvantaged would naturally reduce, consumption would be evened out, and sustainability of the Earth would be attained.

The Economy of Goodness aims to spur good economic activities spontaneously.

Deficiencies in Calculating Self-interest

Western economics emphasizes that, beginning with self-interest, there is an invisible hand that will distribute interests best and maximize public benefit. According to Adam Smith, self-interest is in essence altruism.

However, in the East, economic thoughts are based on altruism. Confucius said that one who is to establish himself should first establish others; Lao Tzu said one should be able to benefit others while competing with none; the Buddha put forward Four Immeasurable States of Mind: Compassion, Mercy, Bliss, and Giving, which are all rooted in altruism.

To solve conflicts arising from human self-interest, contemporary economists have developed the model of reciprocity and altruism, such as game theory.

In game theory, only cooperation leads to mutually beneficial outcomes.

Prisoner's Dilemma[8] by William Poundstone and *Game Changer*[9] by David McAdams explore game theory and analyze that two prisoners can gain maximum benefit when they cooperate with each other. Interrogated separately, they won't confess, not due to affection or altruism, but through a deliberate self-seeking calculation. The prisoner's dilemma in game theory is applied to a variety of commercial negotiations, crisis management, and dispute settlement situations, from which all parties can benefit. This is self-interested altruism.

---

[8] Poundstone, W. (1993). *Prisoner's Dilemma: John von Neumann, Game Theory, and the Puzzle of the Bomb* (First Edition Thus ed.). Anchor.

[9] McAdams, D. (2014). *Game-Changer: Game Theory and the Art of Transforming Strategic Situations.* United States: W. W. Norton.

The Evolution of Cooperation by Robert Axelrod and Hamilton applies game theory to investigate how mutual benefit can benefit both sides most.

In other words, if the result is unfavorable to either party, this game theory, known as the prisoner's dilemma, is not sustainable.[10]

Reciprocity is based on self-interest, so this theory can only be effective if the outcomes are positive.

Game theory may fail when one cannot predict the other party's actions. For example, in an arms race, neither side may know the other's budget; and in an auction, with a price ceiling unknown, it would be difficult for a buyer to make an offer, thus confounding the game theory.

Therefore, when predicting another's interests or gathering info is uncertain, game theory fails and reciprocity is lost. This type of reciprocity is driven by self-interest calculations, under which altruistic behavior is to be motivated by expected results.

This model ensures that altruism does no harm to oneself. Altruism in game theory is based on the premise of not resulting in harm to oneself. However, if altruism is expected to harm oneself, will it still be altruistic? The answer is No.

Game theory cannot address the weaknesses of human nature; when faced with conflicts of interest, people are unlikely to be altruistic.

This flexing of human nature will not yield an altruistic state of mind; rather, altruism must originate from love, courage, and a willingness to forgo some of one's interests for the benefit of the collective. It must be a voluntary action, rather than something imposed on them. Ultimately, those with a proactively altruistic mindset will benefit all.

Next, I will use the Starvation Dilemma to explain why love and altruism can genuinely benefit others and ourselves.

SECTION 4: STARVATION DILEMMA

Mutual Love Between the Self and Others

Self and others can be in a relationship of love, competition, hostility, dependency, exploitation, and alienation.

---

[10] Poundstone, W. (1993). *Prisoner's Dilemma: John von Neumann, Game Theory, and the Puzzle of the Bomb* (First Edition Thus ed.). Anchor.

These relationships are inseparable from business, politics, religion, and human activities.

This chapter argues that a loving relationship stemming from altruism is more formidable than any other relationship, especially for economic activities.

In a world of two people, is there mutual aid or rivalry? Aggression or harmony? Giving or exploiting? Division of labor or dependency?

We assume the starving dilemma for ourselves and others.

Suppose there was a famine in a village. Two people, starving for two weeks and on the brink of death, desperately needed food. As they staggered along, they spotted a large loaf of bread, hanging from a tree across the river, where a crocodile was waiting for prey. Both the starving people hungrily desired the bread, with little hope of either one getting it.

Under such circumstances, should they cooperate or fight, or divide labor to get bread? Was it better to give or take advantage?

If they fought one another, neither would obtain the bread. It could only be procured through joint effort. Someone needs to lead the crocodile away, allowing the other to get the bread.

Who would distract the crocodile?

The person who attempts to draw off the crocodile risks being killed, and the other person risks their food being eaten. If neither is prepared to draw the reptile away, both will soon starve. However, if one is willing to take the risk, at least one can survive, or both can share the bread, thus avoiding starvation. What will the pair do?

Cooperation or Acting Alone: Exploring the Pros and Cons.

If two people fight for the bread, and one of them suffers injury or death, the other will not obtain the bread.

Besides, in conflict, they risk both falling into the water and becoming food for the crocodile.

Dependence on one's own effort may result in being exposed to the waiting crocodile and decreased odds of obtaining the bread.

The only way is mutual help, not mutual benefit, as one may have to sacrifice. Those who are willing to make the sacrifice are those who love.

Suppose what these two people would do if they were father and son, or husband and wife, with deep love for each other. Nine times out of ten, one would lead the crocodile away while the other fetched the bread; a relationship of love that sees one risking or sacrificing for the other's benefit, possibly affording them both respite from hunger.

In this case, there is no relationship other than mutual aid and love that could facilitate survival.

If two people are in a loving relationship, they can rationally work it out. A quick runner could distract the crocodile, while the other could climb a tree and get the bread. By working together, they can share the bread, or at least one can stay alive.

If this mutually beneficial mode is not necessarily a win–win, will they still do it?

This situation is not imaginary. Real-world economic and political activities now come with risks from external environments. There are opportunities at risk, and those brave and in love must take them to seize them.

However, what benefits can a brave person with love or a wise and rational person gain? The answer is to save others, as well as themselves.

Love is both rational and courageous.

Altruism implies rationality and courage, benefiting oneself and/or others while taking risks.

This differs greatly from game theory, which pursues win–win strategies, implying that one will only take action if they think they will be the sole victor.

In the economic and financial realm, banks lend mortgages to people because they are reluctant to take risks, only providing loans when they are confident of recouping the funds. This is a game of giving and taking for one's own benefit.

However, the philanthropist Yunus' micro-loans were unique. While loans to the poor may not require repayment, Yunus strongly advocated for and encouraged micro-loans through kindness and faith. The outcomes were uplifting. Yunus took the risk out of altruism, and it was incredibly successful; 95% of impoverished women repaid their loans punctually.

Micro-loans are now being implemented globally, not only by charities but also commercial entities and financial institutions. Small loans can be just as profitable as mortgages. Consider those who bravely obtain crocodiles: they wish to grant others with sustenance but also benefit from their risk-taking.

The Starvation Dilemma pushes human nature to its extremes; when no one is willing to take risks, no one can survive.

What attitude could save everyone, or at least one individual, in such a predicament? The solution is not self-centeredness but altruism.

Altruism is the ultimate power humans can depend on to prevent mutual destruction.

The Starvation Dilemma presents a moral and emotional challenge, as well as testing one's reasoning and wisdom. The only way for both, or either, of them to survive is by dividing labor and aiding each other, so each must take on their share of responsibility.

If one is adept at running and the other is good at climbing trees, they should each play to their strengths. Otherwise, they may find themselves in deep trouble when the crocodile turns its head.

Thus, aside from altruism, we should also look into the segmentation of responsibilities in the Starvation Dilemma. Altruism is based on trust, and the classification of functions is essential for endurance and victory.

In the Starvation Dilemma, compassionate love and rational wisdom must go hand in hand, as the Buddha dharma stresses having both.

SECTION 5: INTEGRATING ALTRUISM AND SELF-INTEREST IN THE ECONOMIC SYSTEM

From the prisoner's dilemma, we can see that acting for our own benefit won't ensure our interests. Both criminals will suffer losses if one shifts the blame to the other. Cross-interrogation may result in both losing even if one is selfish.

If both people are altruistic and don't disclose the truth, they can both gain. The less data available makes the decision more entangled. This must depend on mutual trust and a readiness to be altruistic, even when the two possess imbalanced information. The prisoner's dilemma indicates that only when both sides are aware they won't be betrayed by the other, they will be eager to work in their associate's best interest. If the facts are asymmetrical and obstructed, the prisoners will be self-centered, and this is altruism for guaranteed personal benefit.

Benefiting ourselves cannot guarantee our interests. In the prisoner's dilemma, both criminals can get the greatest benefit by covering for each other; otherwise, neither of them will.

Can altruism be established in economics when information is unclear and asymmetric?

The Prisoner's Dilemma can never attain Pareto Optimality. Self-interest in the prisoner's dilemma invariably results in win-lose or lose-lose scenarios.

Pareto Optimality takes its name from Italian economist Vilfredo Pareto, who was the first to employ the concept in his studies of economic efficiency and income distribution. It denotes a state of resource allocation where no individual or criterion can benefit from any further redistribution.

In a situation with a group of people, when the switch from resource allocation A to B won't worsen any individual's situation, yet makes it better for at least one person, it is Pareto Improvement.

Therefore, Pareto Optimality Theory posits that the result of resource allocation in a market equilibrium should be Pareto Optimal, due to full competition and prolonged trading. Pareto Optimal has three attributes:

First, Optimal Exchange. The substitution rates of the commodities between the two parties are equal and utility is maximized, so no further benefit can be gained by repeating the transaction.

Second, there is Optimal Production. With an equal production ratio, the marginal rate of technical substitution of one product to that of another can be determined. If this rate is not equal, the output of one product can be increased without reducing the other, and both products can be increased simultaneously. However, when the marginal rates of technical substitution are equal, and the output of both products is maximized, increasing the quantity of one product will replace the other, thereby attaining Pareto optimality of production.

Third, Optimal Exchange and Production. The product range must precisely reflect consumers' preferences. Currently, the marginal rate of technical substitution between any two commodities and the marginal rate of transformation between any producers must be identical.

Pareto Optimality Enabled by Altruism

Can Pareto optimality be achieved through altruism?

If each individual takes altruism as the basis of their economic behavior, would it be beneficial to each of them?

Production-wise, if enterprises focus on altruism, they will pay close attention to market needs and will not intentionally produce low-quality or harmful products. Furthermore, they will avoid aggressive competition and could make products not accessible or in short supply in the present market. In such a faith-centered economic market, business closures as a result of competition should decrease, and product quality should be enhanced. This is Optimal Production.

Likewise, optimal exchange can only be achieved through altruism. In an altruism-driven financial market, loans and interest must prioritize the interests of both parties. Each side has to make compensation for the other to reach optimal exchange. This can be realized through mutual openness and transparency in negotiation and communication, facilitated by altruism. If information is intentionally hidden or manipulated, and neither is altruistic during negotiations, it can lead to the prisoner's dilemma, with nobody emerging as a winner.

Optimal exchange and production can only be achieved through altruism. The advancement of science and technology drives the development of production, bringing about new business opportunities and industrial transformation, yet leading to structural failure of businesses or unemployment. If all products were to mix well, with no one being "kicked out" of the market (as the iPhone did to Nokia), technology sharing would have to be monetized, as nothing comes for free. However, if new technologies and innovations are given to others, they may not trust or adopt them, which would lead to competition and one side obtaining advantages while the other possibly endures great losses or even bankruptcy. Is this form of competition and elimination in line with the notion of altruism under the "Economy of Goodness"?

The Open Innovation Program at the Garwood Center for Corporate Innovation, University of California, Berkeley was established by Professor Henry Chesbrough. It advocates open innovation which encourages all parties of competitors to share knowledge and co-create new technologies. Steve Jobs employed open innovation and successfully innovated the iPod and many new technologies to shape lives in our world. In the last two decades, technology companies like Amazon, Dell, Siemens, Fuji, TSMC, and many others have become members of the Berkeley Innovation Forum. This is the altruistic model for technology experts to collaborate for the mutual benefit of human beings.

We observe that Japan's sustained economic development over the past two decades is related to its national unity and alliance. Frequent alliances between enterprises and industries rather than American competition and bankruptcy have helped the country. Inter-industry and inter-enterprise collaborations, including sharing new technologies and management models and exchanging unsuitable employees under industrial transformation, have enabled stable employment while promoting industrial prosperity.

China's government is driving continuous economic development. In the digital age, the post office has been transformed by the government and industrial associations into a savings bank and bulk package delivery service, with an emphasis on altruistic information transparency and exchange. This kind of shift is unlikely in a free market. China and Japan focus on collective altruism rather than self-serving individualism, a major asset to collective economic entities. This allows for Optimal Exchange and Production.

This is in line with China's Confucian view that one should own the wealth of the world without complaint, and that a person who is capable of sharing their wealth without worry of becoming poor can be considered virtuous. The greatest wealth is reached through a satisfied relationship between people, humankind, and nature, namely Pareto Optimality with altruism.

SECTION 6: ALTRUISM MAY GENERATE SELF-INTERESTS

For thousands of years, Western philosophy has debated altruism and self-interest. Logic implies that these ideas are at odds. Greek thought posited that only Reason could lead people to morality, whereas St. Thomas Aquinas suggested it was God who guided people toward goodness. Similarly, Freud argued that desires drive human behavior, and even altruism serves self-interest.

Before Auguste Comte proposed altruism in the nineteenth century, the question of why we want to help others in the West was answered in terms of compassion, charity, friendship, and benevolence.[11] Comte was the first Western philosopher to create the word Altruism, which comes from the Latin word alter, meaning other.

Comte discussed the difference between altruism and egoism. From Comte's point of view, altruism refers to one's motive to think for the highest welfare of others. The motivation is for others, resulting in the highest welfare for others.[12]

[11] Batson, C. D. (2014). *The Altruism Question: Toward A Social-Psychological Answer*. United States: Taylor & Francis. p. 5.

[12] Batson, C. D. (2014). *The Altruism Question: Toward A Social-Psychological Answer*. United States: Taylor & Francis. p. 5.

Psychological Altruism is the desire to benefit another's well-being. Psychologists consider motivation critical to understanding altruism; this motivation must be for the benefit of others, not one's self.

However, contemporary psychologists have suggested that altruism, potentially advantageous to the evolution of a group, may stem from self-serving aims. An example provided by Philip and Dickins is that of a woman seeking to marry someone of higher status, something that is more conducive to evolutionary fitness. Here, altruism and egoism are bestowed through psychological and evolutionary processes.

Psychological altruism is defined as the desire for others' well-being. Psychologists consider motivation a critical factor in defining altruism, which must come from others, not oneself.

I call this an empirical interpretation of psychology and evolution within Western Altruism geared toward Self-Interest. This Altruism for Self-Interest explains the existence of certain ethnic groups or people, but cannot satisfactorily explain why there are conflicts between tribes and tribes, nations and nations, and religions and religions over the interests of their self-interest groups from primitive society to contemporary human society. Scientific interpretations of altruism (such as evolutionary and psychological) are still limited to ethnic, national, and tribal realms. Generally speaking, humans still possess a certain degree of psychological mechanisms of self-interest.

Complete Altruism Seeks No Self-Interest

Altruism should not expect a return. As Master Cheng Yen said: "Give without expecting anything in return and giving with gratitude." Buddhism teaches that giving something out of self-interest makes us relapse into greed, anger, and ignorance. Altruism must broaden itself and inspire altruism in more people so that a recipient can also become a giver. There should be no difference between a giver and a recipient and even surpass the giving itself.

Furthermore, altruism underscores the collective rather than individual interests. If referring to individual endeavors, altruism isn't valid. All things, in the end, are equal and share no distinction. Therefore, assisting others is also helping oneself. I am no different from anyone else, and I am just like everyone else.

If altruism is not group-based, then it will not be Buddhist, but it borders on Christian salvation from God's grace that could be for the individual and not for all human beings. However, the Buddha would save all sentient beings and guide all sentient beings save all sentient beings. In Buddhism, one is all, and all are one. From one seed of goodness to ten, to a hundred and a thousand, till limitlessness.

According to Lu Cheng, a respected Buddhist scholar in the mid-twentieth century, it's impossible to solely pursue self-interest under the conditions of dependent origination. To truly benefit oneself, one must also benefit others and even consider their interests as one's own. This involves merging oneself into the vast ocean of sentient beings, where benefiting others becomes synonymous with benefiting oneself.[13]

However, altruism should not harm oneself either. When Tzu Chi's Bone Marrow Registry was established, Master Cheng Yen was concerned about the health of the bone marrow donors. She said, "We will never harm a healthy person to save a sick person." This is the middle way. If life is equally important, how can we sacrifice one person to save another? "Altruism without harming oneself" is the only way to sustain altruism and prevent it from becoming moral violence.

Some may wonder, "Does Buddhism not say to give all, even one's head and brain, to others?" Indeed, it is a sign of great giving to give away one's body. For instance, some Tzu Chi volunteers become Silent Mentors and offer their bodies after death for medical study. I don't consider my body as my personal property; instead, I would leave all my compassion to help create a better world. They also contribute to organ and bone marrow donation to assist leukemia patients. Despite giving away their bodies, Silent Mentors still achieve an eternal, wisdom-filled life. Body donation does not harm oneself; it is a great act of wisdom to turn something useless into something useful.

The doctrines of Buddhism and Tzu Chi do not demand a person to sacrifice themselves for others. It is impractical and could be seen as an unethical burden. Just like sacrificing one person to save the world, we do not know when such a sacrifice would end.

Altruism Should Not Be the Sole Motivation

Can altruistic motivations, that don't come to fruition, still be considered altruistic?

---

[13] Lu, C. (2000). *Yindu foxue yuanliu lue lun* [An Outline of the Origins of Indian Buddhism]. Taiwan: Darchen publisher. p. 182.

Kant's "good will" is independent of the outcome; he believed a person's good should not be diminished by their failure to make it a reality.

Kant's view within the theory of good will suggests that altruism should be considered a non-utilitarian, non-consequentialist, motive-based, or purely mental ethical perspective. Kant believed that good will cannot be equated with its results. Even if good will leads to suffering, it remains good because its intention is to do good.[14]

Altruism that Combines Motivation and Result

Compared to Kant's view on the motivation of altruistic goodness, Buddhist altruism is rooted in a moral view that combines motive and outcome. The Buddha articulated that giving need not be contingent on a reward, as Master Cheng Yen declared: "Giving without expectation of anything in return." Yet, such giving and refraining from seeking a return still involve consequences, which cannot be quantified solely by worldly standards.

According to *the Bālapaṇḍitasutta Sutra* (Sutra on the Wise and Foolish), the Buddha was once in hell during His long practice. However, with goodness in His heart, He ascended to Tushita (One of the Heavens in Buddhism), and eventually, He became the Buddha. In the *Bālapaṇḍitasutta Sutra*, the Buddha once suffered in hell for a lifetime of transmigration, and when He saw a sinner pulling a flaming iron cart, He mercifully helped the sinner drag the cart but was beaten to death by a jailer.

The Buddha, who was killed by the jailer, ultimately ascended to the Heaven of the Thirty-three Gods. After an untold number of eons, the Buddha emerged, teaching that compassion for all living beings is the key to his path. Imagine one life in which the Buddha was a sinner in hell, willingly carrying an iron cart for someone else, not for advancement, but out of compassion that could not bear the thought of seeing others suffer. This is in contrast with Kant's good will, since here the moral motivation isn't reason's will but that of compassion. The sinner doesn't know of the law of good will yet personifies it through their compassion.

---

[14] Kant, I. (1997). *Groundwork of the Metaphysics of Morals* (M. J. Gregor, Ed. & Trans.). Cambridge University Press (Original work published 1785). p. 62.

The jailer killed the sinner who had been carrying the cart for others. As a result, the sinner's altruistic actions brought salvation to him. Despite his death, he ascended to Heaven. Most importantly, his life marked the beginning; after countless eons of practice, he eventually became the Buddha. This story metaphorically conveys that altruism is a good starting point, leading to ultimate goodness. This is distinguishable from utilitarian altruism.

Tzu Chi holds the safety of volunteers in disaster relief in utmost regard. They will only send volunteers to places where their safety can be ensured, e.g., war zones. According to the Tzu Chi School of Buddhism, altruism should not be to the detriment of oneself, and if it risks that, it should be a personal will and shall not become a request of any organization.

Buddhist scriptures contain many stories about sacrificing oneself for others. As a bhikkhu, the Buddha saw a hungry tigress and her cub, so he sacrificed himself to provide them with sustenance. Despite dying in the process, the bhikkhu showed no regrets. This act of altruism showed that preventing evil and protecting life can be done through inner purity and practice. Through this story, altruism is presented as a way to achieve enlightenment and become a true Buddha.

SECTION 7: ALTRUISM TRANSCENDING THE HUMAN SELF

Altruism is the drive to surpass oneself. As Karl Jaspers said in *The Perennial Scope of Philosophy*: "He becomes for himself the greatest of all mysteries when he senses that despite his finite nature, his possibilities seem to extend into the infinite."[15]

Humans yearn for union with infinity, a cornerstone of religion's existence and continuation. Many religions consider limitation, differentiation, and separation as karma, pain, obliviousness, wickedness, transgression, or sin.

Take Christianity as an example. The sin in Christianity derives from Adam and Eve's disobedience to God by taking the forbidden fruit. This gave them knowledge of the distinction between men and women, as well as a sense of shame about nudity. Thus, human ancestors committed the sin of breaking away from the infinite unity of all things and becoming

---

[15] Jaspers, K. (1949). *The Perennial Scope of Philosophy* (R. Manheim, Trans.). United Kingdom: Philosophical Library. p. 49.

attached and differentiated, leading to the perception of such behavior as sinful.

When human civilization began to perceive that it was different from all other things, the laws of birth and death began. If all things were regarded as one, and the self's birth and death were part of the cycle of all things and laws of the universe, there would be no birth or death of individuals. Therefore, to return to God becomes the highest aspiration of limited human beings (Christians). Confucianism's harmony between man and nature, India's Brahma-I thought, and Taoism's humans follow earth, earth follows Heaven, Heaven follows Tao, and Tao follows nature. They all extend the existence of man to infinity. Humans and all other things were originally connected. Therefore, self-interest is limited, and combining it with infinity is the tendency and motivation of altruism.

Karl Jaspers' goal of self-return is to recognize the transcendence of being through the being of individual life. He described this transcendental being as the Encompassing, who does not fall into the subject-object, generality, and specialty opposition. Karl Jaspers does not regard God as the Encompassing but uses Lao Tzu's Tao to describe God. He said: "Tao...remains the Encompassing."[16]

John Hick also discussed ethical practice from the perspective of religious transcendence. He expounded his ideas in his works *An Interpretation of Religion: Human Responses to the Transcendent*[17] and *The Fifth Dimension.*[18] He advocated that all human beings have the fifth dimension, namely the spiritual dimension, which leads to Brahma, God, Buddha-nature, and Tao, depending upon various religious explanations under certain historical conditions. However, they all point to the common lives of human beings who tend to cooperate, love, and help each other in common existence and well-being.

Heidegger also discussed Being or Dasein from the perspective of transcendence.[19] The existence of human beings and all things are included

[16] Jaspers, K. (1962). *Kant: From the Great Philosophers* (Vol. 1). United Kingdom: Harcourt, Brace & World.

[17] Hick, J. (2005). *An Interpretation of Religion: Human Responses to the Transcendent* (Second ed.). United Kingdom: Yale University Press.

[18] Hick, J. (2013). *The Fifth Dimension: An Exploration of the Spiritual Realm* (Second ed.). Oneworld Publications.

[19] Heidegger, M., & Macquarrie, J. (2008). *Being and Time*. United Kingdom: HarperCollins.

in Being or Dasein. Lao Tzu's Tao profoundly influenced Heidegger, and his Dasein carries a note of Tao. Heidegger even said that Non-Being and Being coexist as one, which is the foundation of universal existence. However, Heidegger's Non-Being is not Lao Tzu's idea of Nothingness. The latter is considered the source of all things, while Heidegger's Dasein is a kind of being. Like a sheet of blank paper, the blank space is a being, just as space without light indicates darkness is still in existence.

From Heidegger and Karl Jaspers to John Hick, Western religious scholars and philosophers have sought to understand existence through Eastern concepts such as "the Way," "nothingness," "dharmakaya," "emptiness," and "Brahman," after removing the framework of God. They all point to a larger existence, and the goal for individuals is to understand and return to the path of this larger whole.

When Western philosophers tried to find a way out from the opposition between individual and whole, Eastern philosophers seemed to have understood the harmony and unity beyond the binary opposition. Lao Tzu attributed all things to Tao. Tao begets one, one begets two, and two begets three that, begets all things. All things are born from one and return to one. As stated in *Avatamsaka Sutra*, one is infinity, and infinity is one. Buddha-nature enlightens all sentient beings. As master Du Shun of the Tang Dynasty put it, Buddha-nature raised in every affinity, Dharma Nature was raised in every affinity, and the reality realm was raised in every affinity. Buddha-nature pervades all sentient beings and finally reaches a state of harmony and freedom all over the world. This is the boundless merit of Bodhisattva in rescuing all living beings.

Eastern philosophy has strong persistence and adaptability, relying on our interpretation and creation. In particular, Buddhist altruism is said to possess objectivity and practicality that carry a significant value and influence in understanding between Eastern and Western philosophies. For example, John Hick described Buddhism's compassion as that compassion without egoism, showing wisdom's objectivity and clarity.[20]

When Western philosophers increasingly recognized that compassion is a union of wisdom and self-integration with the greater self, Buddhist altruism became increasingly crucial for our modern studies.

---

[20] Hick, J. (2005). *An Interpretation of Religion: Human Responses to the Transcendent* (Second ed.). United Kingdom: Yale University Press.

Section 8: The Altruistic Philosophy
That All Things Are One

The Buddha's initial enlightenment was that all dharmas are one. The Bodhisattva's vow to serve all living beings stems from the interdependence of all things in the universe, that they are all one. This is the essence of Buddhist altruism, that I am one with others, one with all things, and one with all laws.

Mr. Lu Cheng articulated that from an understanding of dependent origination, it becomes clear that everything in the world is interconnected and interdependent. This extends to the relationships between individuals and between humans and other living beings. Rather than viewing individuals as isolated entities, they should be seen as integral parts of a unified whole. Consequently, the pursuit of enlightenment is not a solitary endeavor but a collective one. Seeking one's own enlightenment alone is inherently self-serving. In the intricate web of dependent origination, pursuing individual self-interest is implausible; instead, one must strive to benefit both oneself and others, even embracing the perspective that benefiting others is tantamount to benefiting oneself. Thus, by integrating oneself into the vast expanse of sentient beings, the act of benefiting others becomes synonymous with self-benefit.[21]

The Buddha's compassion and efforts to save all sentient beings are based on the law of Interdependent Arising, with everything depending on one another, preventing any from existing alone. To demonstrate kindness and compassion to all, recognizing our interconnectedness in the depths of life, is altruistic and self-interested.

Altruism Provides the Root for Individuals to Find Belonging

No one can survive alone in this world without relying on others and the natural and social conditions that produced them. Buddhism believes that the rules of interdependent arising are in everything and all living creatures are created and perish through affinity. Solitary and unified, single and multiple, single and environment, and single and solitary—these are all mutually reliant.

---

[21] Lu, C. (2000). *Yindu foxue yuanliu lue lun* [An Outline of the Origins of Indian Buddhism]. Taiwan: Darchen publisher. p. 182.

Nevertheless, modern people seek separation from groups, alienation from society, and opposition to the environment. Individuals are like rootless droplets, vulnerable to evaporation under the harsh sun and amidst swirling dust. However, a drop of water cannot dry up because it merges into the shining sea.[22]

Altruism encourages us to reconnect to mutual aid, love, and gain, which are critical for life. Without mutual help and affection, no being would survive.

Many people deeply believe in natural selection. Is it not based on objective causes and conditions? Some argue that life is simply a struggle, yet how can that struggle exist without resources and energy? It is the convergence of affinity that fuels everything—from the small to the great, the narrow-minded to the broad-minded—from selfishness to selflessness, from privilege to deprivation. Causes and effects come together to make it clear that no one lives and grows alone. Thus, we ought to be thankful for all the aid and power that brought us into existence. Altruism is born out of gratitude, providing boundless energy, much like the earth nurturing all.

When individuals begin to practice altruism, they combine with a source of strength which, according to As C. G. Jung, is the collective subconscious. Any great person will know how to use this collective subconscious.[23] Even visible and tangible collective consciousness is of great help to individuals. Altruism is a positive energy that leads individuals to groups and enables individuals to find their roots in nature and society, in which people become more complete and powerful.

Altruism is the salvation of individuals, returning them to the whole. It is the only way to achieve a broader self; and when the ego is constantly expanded to the unity of all things due to altruism, it reaches Buddha's nature.

---

[22] Shih, Cheng Yen. (2003). *Tzu Chi Bimonthly*: Issue 558. Taipei: Tzu Chi Culture & Communication Foundation. May 25, 2003. p. 125.

[23] Jung, C. G. (1969). *The Archetypes and the Collective Unconscious Collected Works of C.G. Jung* (Vol. 9) (Part 1) (R. F. C. Hull, Trans.). United Kingdom: Princeton University Press.

CHAPTER 5

The Economy of Goodness in Feudal Society

Section 1: Sumer Civilization: A Symbiotic Choice Between Mechanical Urban Economy and Nature

Sumerian culture had an economically organized, imperial community. The Sumerian people were part of a collective economy, with grain supply and demand regulated by the emperor.

Research shows that Sumerian homes were centered around the king, with individuals living under the directive of the emperor, who trusted the advice of his ministers.

There was no endless economic growth for individuals in Sumer, but a unified economy that discouraged excessive wealth or waste. This did not mean a total loss of individual identity; instead, the self was defined within collective life. In this way, excessive economic development for individuals or groups was automatically kept in check. Basic life needs were met by a collective system, except for the king, and any extra was prevented from occurring.

Notably, here collective refers to the system of sustaining family life and individuals' basic needs, as opposed to a modern, mechanized collective approach which slots people into a large system, thus breaking the bond between families and community.

However, in the later period of Sumer's civilization, people were deprived of traditional family life and neighborhood intimacy due to the crisis of over-mechanized bureaucracy.

The Epic of Gilgamesh reveals the Sumerians' anxiety about urbanization and industrialized existence. Thomas Sedrakic, a Czech economist, noted that *The Epic* portrays a conflict between customary economic society and urbanization. The king wished to create a mighty city, disallowing husband-and-wife reunions, and customary family life was stifled by mechanized organization. People's lives started to disintegrate, to fulfill the king's vision of gargantuan urbanization.

In *The Epic*, families were split, fathers and sons torn apart to erect a great city. Great suffering was endured by the people. *The Epic* is not just an ancient legend: it is also a presage of present-day society.

Modern society also sees a separation of fathers and sons, who would otherwise lose their natural connection, when they encounter the rapids of life. Urban life has largely isolated us and distanced us from family and community. Disconnected from nature and rural areas, many are now enslaved in urban life.

Gilgamesh's urbanization suggests a prioritizing of achievement over the happiness of others. Is this not a dilemma faced by contemporary tycoons, where business growth overrules the well-being of workers and people?

Gilgamesh only came to comprehend the toil of city-building when he encountered the savage Enkidu. He discerned that without nature and kin, genuine mirth was forfeited.

In the Sumerian epic, Enkidu was a beast sent by the gods to punish Gilgamesh. He had a body with fur as thick as barley. In the end, however, the two became friends.

Enkidu, was once a wild creature, but Gilgamesh schemed, bribing a harlot to seduce him with carnal pleasure for a week. After his desires were sated, Enkidu became a human, unable to revert to his feral, untamed life.

This story demonstrates that when we gratify our desires, we can lose our true nature. Even animals cannot escape this pitfall. The fable sends a warning of how humans can become estranged due to their indulgences.

At the end of *The Epic of Gilgamesh*, Enkidu's influence caused Gilgamesh to forsake the building of a great city and renounce exploiting his workforce for his own glory. He reverted to his human nature with Enkidu and ventured into the forest to battle Humbaba.

Humbaba was portrayed as the worst force of nature, meaning humans are battling against nature rather than constructing a huge, mechanized city that disrupts families and is far removed from nature.

Humans must strive to control their nature, but shouldn't lead robotic lives either. Isn't excessive discipline and rules designed to completely control human nature the same as having a robotic life?

To avoid nature's elements, the creation of a city far from the natural landscape has led to people embracing a mechanized lifestyle: an inadvertent, extreme development of human civilization.

Through Gilgamesh and Enkidu, *The Epic of Gilgamesh* reveals the fear that nature elicits in human civilization. Humans are both afraid of their own nature and of the natural world, yet they cannot live without either. Humans have a complex relationship with nature and human nature alike. The best solution may be to confront nature and come to harmony with it, rather than trying to control it or stay away from it.

Gilgamesh and Enkidu's victory over Humbaba symbolizes a human triumph over the fear of nature, and not giving in to fear to build a mechanized city. Gilgamesh's city-building denotes the human yearning to break away from nature. Nevertheless, the unsustainable and proliferating ambition to build the city makes many people forsake the joys of home and natural life.

Afraid of being dictated by the wildness in their nature, humans created disciplines and dogmas. Out of fear for the harshness of nature, they built settlements and cities. Ultimately, they locked themselves in the prison of moral dogma and a robotic economic life.

The Epic of Sumerian civilization illustrates the three middle ways.

The first point is that humans are inseparable from group life and norms in constructing a civilized economic life, and they yearn to return to nature.

The enlargement of any single aspiration, in the quest for grandness, especially those with authority, either economic or political, will ruin the peace of collective life.

The group's inclusivity and prosperity should not be undermined by individuals' limitless desires. This should serve as an ancient Sumerian warning to promote economic well-being.

The economic system set up by ancient Sumerian civilization was a shared one, granting people the ability to live and work peacefully, be independent, and aid the community. It was only when a powerful person appeared, trying to fulfill their "great dream," that the community started breaking apart.

The second middle way is that humans should conquer their fear of nature while staying within it.

In *The Epic*, we see people's eternal attachment to and alienation from nature. We can't be afraid of nature, yet not think we can tread a path completely divergent from nature. A mechanical urban system tends to sever people from nature and human nature.

The third middle way is that our human nature stems from nature, yet we must maintain our faith as humans.

Enkidu's transformation into a human symbolizes our capacity to convert our primitive nature. This savagery doesn't imply external features, but rather what is ingrained in our character. There are uncharted cravings, impulses, and scuffles inside us, yet in addition passionate delicacy, understanding, inventiveness, and affection.

We must oversee the erratic and unbridled parts of our being, yet do so carefully, so that it does not lead to a monotonous life, morally or financially.

The Economy of Goodness is about finding balance and harmony between human nature and life in a community.

Enkidu was transformed from tyrannical and violent to tamed and equipped with eagerness, agreeableness, loyalty, and trust. Meanwhile, Gilgamesh gave up striving for mechanical greatness, contrary to nature, and instead focused on conquering human fear of nature. As a result, he was his own master, uncontrolled by his impulses and desires and having conquered them.

The true happiness of humans lies not in constructing a mechanized, industrialized urban lifestyle that estranges them from nature, but in harnessing their natural selves, and replacing fear with trust, aiding each other—just as the peaceful merging of Enkidu and Gilgamesh tamed wild nature without resulting in a mechanical life.

In economic life, goodness denotes harmonization between original human nature and humanity; a legacy of the Sumerian civilization that is important.

SECTION 2: GREEK CIVILIZATION: DIALECTIC BETWEEN IDEALISM AND MATERIALISM

Greece's outlook on wealth and money is apparent in Hesiod's famed mythical poem "Works and Days,"[1] which highlights the importance of hard work via the story of his division of property with his brother Perses.

The brothers divided their father's estate equally, but Perses bribed the judge to get more. Hesiod then cautioned his brother that riches must be acquired through toil, citing their father, who had moved their family from poverty to affluence through farming.

Hesiod asked Perses if his inheritance was sufficient to be deemed wealth. He warned him not to bank on those bribable officers interceding for him. Zeus had bestowed humans with riches, which he had obscured so that they could be uncovered only after laboring persistently. Fearful that, should it be feasible to trudge through a year with a single day's effort, humans would cease working, leaving fields uncultivated.

Hesiod allegorized the work and worth of humanity, stating that one must opt between leisure and labor, with prosperity only achievable through diligence, integrity, and harmony.

Fearing human speculation, Zeus hid the tools for creating wealth and decreed that people must toil with their hands. Prometheus and Epimetheus, however, stole fire and thrust it into the human world. In retribution, Zeus chained Prometheus atop a mountain, where an eagle would feast on his liver daily; it grew back overnight. Just like Prometheus, people suffer day after day in their work and leisure, unless something of value—i.e., love—pushes them to labor.

However, to the gods, stealing fire for humans symbolized the indolence of mankind, so they made humans suffer labor work day after day, such as Prometheus.

Hesiod's mythical prophecy reveals two aspects of Greek economic thought. One is the virtue of diligence and hard work. The second is value, namely honesty and peace as the work ethic.

The most hazardous aspect mentioned in "Works and Days" is desire. The poem utilizes Pandora's box to illustrate the misfortunes of humanity.

Prometheus and his brother stole fire for humans, and humans accepted it. As punishment, Zeus created Pandora—whom Venus

---

[1] H. & Stallings, A. E. (2018). *Works and Days* (Reprint ed.). Penguin Classics.

bestowed with immense beauty, Apollo gifted her with musical talent, and Mercury gave her a vibrant tongue. Pandora: Gifts of All.

Zeus gave Pandora to Epimetheus, Prometheus's younger brother. Prometheus had warned his brother not to accept the gift, yet Epimetheus could not resist Pandora's allure. At the nuptials of Epimetheus and Pandora, Zeus asked each god to present them with a box of prized possessions, and he bestowed one full of unbeneficial occurrences, except for one blessing: hope.

Pandora gladly accepted all the boxes, but Epimetheus begged her not to open Zeus' treasure box, fearful of what could be inside. Nonetheless, Pandora could not restrain herself and opened it. Consequently, innumerable misfortunes, calamities, falsity, penury, illness, and death spread throughout the world.

Sensing the peril, Pandora swiftly shut the treasure chest, leaving only hope within.

This is the earliest economic thought in Greek mythology: the virtues of diligence and value being the core of the economy, with a prevention of the expansion of desires being necessary to avoid evil.

The Ancient Greeks, who were mostly reliant on agriculture, stressed balance between humans and nature. People worked for a living and to be prosperous; however, they had to be wary of how over-developed techniques and crafts could be detrimental to their hard work.

Prometheus was a craftsman in Heaven whose taking of fire was a metaphor for technology. His punishment symbolizes an agricultural society's fear of the over-development of skilled craftsmen. That the development of artisans cannot suffice for urban life implies a need for balance between economic and social life. Nevertheless, avarice for excessive expansion of assets and money should also be kept in check.

When asked how to define one's property, Aristotle replied that it should stay within the parameters of one's sight. That is, an excessive expansion of real estate or assets should be prevented.

The Value of Use and Exchange

The society that solely focused on money and technology was a central topic for Greek Philosophers.

The values of goods production and exchange for money were hotly discussed in ancient Greece. The argument centered around whether economic activities simply obeyed the law of supply and demand of goods, or if money could be pursued as an end in itself.

The first person to put forward the word economics in human history is the Greek philosopher Xenophon (430–355 BCE), who described human economic life with Oeconomicus. "Oikos" means house, and "nomos" means norm or law.

The laws and principles governing buildings and assets are, per Xenophon's original definition, the essence of economy. Assets and laws are both noted as the two key elements.

According to Xenophon, economics is concerned with the principles and laws of owning property.

In his book *Oeconomicus*,[2] Xenophon was the first to discuss the concepts of value in use and value in exchange in economic life.

Xenophon said in Socrates' words that the value in use varies from person to person. If a pair of shoes were not sold, it would have no property value. Therefore, commodity value came from the transaction (exchange). Otherwise, the commodity could not represent wealth. Socrates further explained that if a pair of shoes was sold to a person who did not need them, it was not a good deal. Therefore, in Socrates' words, Xenophon said that it was through the transaction that brought benefits that real property value is embodied.

The real issue behind Xenophon's metaphor is defining the satisfaction of human desires.

Xenophon thought that silver was different from the furniture. After a family has enough furniture, they will not continue to buy it, but no one does not want to have more silver. If a man has a considerable amount of silver, he will have as much joy in storing it as he has in spending it.[3]

Is the mere accumulation of money a legitimate source of happiness? Specific desires can be fulfilled, but abstract ones can never be, in Xenophon's eyes. Money is abstract and thus, the desire to accumulate it will never be satisfied.

---

[2] Xenophon, X. & Hayes, B. J. (2017). *Oeconomicus*. Andesite Press.

[3] Xenophon, X. & Hayes, B. J. (2017). *Oeconomicus*. Andesite Press.

Spiritual Abundance and Money Transaction

Aristotle believed that the objective of economic activities should be to promote people's happiness and spiritual well-being.

Any pursuit of money and wealth in economic activities purely for their own sake is immoral, and such a pursuit will not lead to Eudaimonia.

Aristotle referred to Eudaimonia as the ideal way of life, implying happiness and good conduct in a thriving society. Aristotle believed that commercial activities should give people what they need and bring them moral life and spiritual satisfaction. He called this Oikonomike, the economic activity of goodness.

Aristotle favored buying and selling of commodities, but abhorred purely monetary trade. He thought domestic commerce was limited, whereas the chase for money was endless, and would harm human souls.

Aristotle argues that any profession has its legitimate purpose. If a doctor's goal is to make money rather than to save people, they would lose their legitimacy. Similarly, if a war were to be pursued for monetary gain, it would lose its legitimacy. Likewise, if a business venture was initiated for the sole purpose of profiting, it too would lack legitimacy.

In his book *Politics*,[4] Aristotle points out that there were two commercial activities: the sale of goods for household use and purely monetary transactions. The latter was considered evil, as it was not a product of nature, and Usury was seen as even more repugnant since it profited from money rather than commodities.

Aristotle opposed the futile pursuit of money and transactions, as it would corrupt human morality. He thought commercial activities should not predominate over other human pursuits. Happiness isn't merely derived from material wealth; it also involves participating in civic life, following moral principles, and attaining spiritual fulfillment.

Another reason Aristotle objected to pursuing money was that it could lead to a widening gap between rich and poor, causing social tension and potentially political unrest. He believed that a generous person should prefer to give than receive, stressing the joy of donating.

It is more blessed to give than to receive, as taught in Christianity. Aristotle seemed to think that instead of pursuing money, it was better to participate in more civic activities and help more suffering people, which he called Eudaimonia, namely living well and doing well.

---

[4] A. & Ellis, W. A. M. (2015). *Politics*. CreateSpace Independent Publishing Platform.

The widening wealth gap caused political turmoil, a concern in ancient China. Dynasties there struggled to prevent annexations, exploitation of peasants, and usury by wealthy business people, compounded by natural disasters; leading to peasant uprisings that overthrew the regimes.

Aristotle also hoped that liberal men would take part in public affairs, as it was crucial for the optimal governance of city-states, establishing the stability of the regime.

Support for the Community Brings Happiness

Aristotle believed the virtue of citizens depended on their use of money. They gave generously, serving God, participating in city-state affairs, providing for the needy, funding wars, and even becoming city-state councilors to benefit the city. Those who did this were viewed as "magnificent," understanding the greater good and putting money to use for the city's gain, rather than for personal satisfaction. Conversely, liberality was seen as focusing on happiness for oneself.

Aristotle's view helps reduce the disparity between wealthy and poor in city-state life, unifying its citizens and stabilizing city-state growth.

However, Plato, Aristotle's teacher, held a divergent view. He believed all material existence was imperfect and illusory, whereas the Ideal was perfect.

In other words, there is no perfect circular object, but an outstanding concept of a circle.

To Plato, pursuing material things and satisfying desires is incorrect and not the ultimate goodness. "Bodily happiness," he said, "will only enslave us." Only when the mind is freed from bodily desires can we realize the highest goodness.

Plato proposed that the highest good be living according to the ideal, and advocated for strong elitism and the abolishment of a ruler's personal assets in city-state life. Furthermore, he argued that rulers should possess no personal wealth, remain unmarried, and dedicate themselves exclusively to sustaining philosophy and managing the city-state.

The ruler contemplates how to provide the citizens of the city-state with the best life possible, and their goal is to construct the strongest city-state.

The ruling elite in Plato's ideal should abstain, forgo owning property, and subdue their sexual desires. Satisfying such desires would jeopardize their loyalty to the city-state and dedication to their lovers could weaken loyalty to gods and city-states. Consequently, Plato proposed that philosophers should reign as kings.

The ruling class represents reason, followed by soldiers representing courage, and craftsmen representing sensory pleasure. Plato believed that the latter belonged to a lower level of human nature and that only proletarians could be the supreme rulers and philosophers.

Plato was the earliest idealist, emphasizing mind and reason while deemphasizing matter and desire. His student Aristotle seemingly countered Plato's idealism by taking the middle way.

Aristotle believed that the idea of an apple could not be separated from the apple itself; mind and matter must intertwine, and material desire is inherent to human nature and can motivate positive human goals.

This is manifested in his economic thinking, in which Aristotle emphasizes the satisfaction of "use value" of goods, but also curbs transactions for pure monetary gain, because the latter is an endless desire, and is detrimental to the moral order of society. He hopes that free citizens can engage in more public services and thereby attain true happiness in life.

In ancient China, there were similar viewpoints. The importance of thriving small farmers was crucial to the stability of the state. Excessive money transactions would widen the gap between rich and poor and cause social unrest. However, political participation in ancient China was by Confucian officials who did not engage in production. This is different, socially and culturally, from Aristotle's notion that free citizens should engage in civil duties and use their business successes to help the government and the vulnerable.

Even though there are differences, Greece's Economy of Goodness is still an important example. It showed that a person's happiness did not mean simply aiming for money; personal contentment was linked to collective joy; meeting individual needs was essential, but overindulgence ought to be prevented; wanting, particularly wanting money, was limitless. It would harm one's character and cause unfairness in society, leading to a nationwide crisis.

Happiness is Synonymous with Goodness; Goodness Brings Forth Happiness

According to Aristotle, Greeks' economic ideas on goodness show the significance of sustaining the Middle Way between self-interest and altruism and material and desire in economic existence.

The trade of commodities should be limited to meeting personal needs; it is wrong to seek and acquire wealth for its own sake. True happiness results from both material satisfaction and from doing good deeds for the benefit of society. Aristotle argued for a middle ground between idealism and materialism, and between individual ambition and being altruistic.

Aristotle argued that the pursuit of happiness should not be focused on pleasure, but rather on attaining goodness and beauty. Pleasure could arise from activities that reach the highest degree of goodness and beauty, but should not be sought in and of itself.

The aim of economic activities is achieving goodness, leading to happiness. Goodness may bring joy, but it is not the sole source of it; desires can also be a source of pleasure, albeit one that can lead to pain. Still, perfect happiness is derived from goodness.

This differs from Epicurean hedonism that derives pleasure from fulfilling desires. Rather, Aristotle highlighted the joy of being good and beautiful.

Later, Western Utilitarianism advocates maximizing benefits to attain the greatest happiness, which contrasts with Aristotle's view. Aristotle emphasizes the unification between body and soul, so individuals find happiness through morality and their social duty; not the utilitarian calculation of total social well-being.

SECTION 3: CHINESE CIVILIZATION: THE ECONOMIC LIFE OF THE INDIVIDUAL AND THE GROUP

China's economic ideology has always been based on agriculture and Heaven. For thousands of years, agriculture has been the foundation and legitimacy of China's ruling class. Harnessing the floods of the Yellow River was a concerted effort for the ancient central plain states to build a unified country, as irrigation was necessary for agriculture.

The war between Emperor Yan and Chiyou, opposed to Emperor Huang, was the only one between agrarian and primitive craftsmanship. Emperor Yan had lost the war, but not been defeated; he became the ancestor of China, alongside Emperor Huang. The totem of the dragon symbolizes their unity.

In Li Zehou's words, the tribe of snakes integrated with that of fish, so the snakes grew scales. Then it integrated the tribe of birds so that it could fly. Then it grew antlers after the integration with the tribe of moose.

China, therefore, is a symbol of tribal integration and a community of life.[5]

This is especially true when considering China's economy. For generations, the Yellow River has given sustenance to millions. In ancient times, controlling its flooding was seen as a huge achievement in China, one which led to unification.

In a life centered around agriculture, where stability relies on the land and economic sustenance hinges on the forces of nature, this reality shaped the philosophical concept of viewing Heaven as the ultimate path, or Tao. Confucius encapsulated this idea, saying, "Does Heaven speak? The four seasons pursue their courses, and all things are continually being produced, but does Heaven say anything?"[6] This sentiment reflects the reverence and admiration that agricultural life held toward Heaven.

When an emperor was wise and virtuous, Heaven would favor the country's peace and prosperity. Should they go against Heaven, disasters would befall them as punishment.

The emperor was unable to deal with natural disasters that could cause famine and incite widespread resentment. This would not be tolerated, leading to an uprising and requiring a new administration. Nevertheless, the new administration still had to address peasants' survival issues. After wars, land was often re-divided to enable people to live and be content.

Ancient Chinese regimes employed a policy of equal wealth among individuals and groups. The Zhou Dynasty (1046–256 BCE) instituted the well-field system, in which each person held a quarter of a field, while one portion was reserved for the public. In the Han Dynasty, ordinary citizens were subject to taxes and labor to fund the empire's military and administrative needs.

The relationship between emperors and civilians in ancient China was quite loose. As long as the people lived and worked in peace and contentment, they would not care much about the court and vice versa. Heaven was too high for ordinary people, and an emperor was so far away. That is why Lao Tzu said:

---

[5] Li, Z. H. (1996). *Mei de licheng* [Beautiful journey]. Taipei: Sanmin shuju. pp. 11–12.

[6] Legge, J. (1971). *Confucian Analects: The Great Learning, and The Doctrine of the Mean*. New York: Dover Publications. p. 326.

Heaven and earth do not set the ways of benevolence; they follow the ways of all beings, as worshiping the Straw Dogs.[7] The sages do not act from their ways of benevolence; they follow the ways of people as worshiping the Straw Dogs.[8]

Emperors who are not self-important think of ordinary people as sage emperors.

In ancient China's economic life, the common people enjoyed a peaceful and prosperous life during peacetime, as described by Tao Yuanming:

> I pluck chrysanthemums under the eastern hedge,
> And gaze afar towards the southern mountains.
> The mountain air is fine at evening of the day
> And flying birds return together homewards.
> Within these things there is a hint of Truth,
> But when I start to tell it, I cannot find the words.[9]

Such a pleasant life embodies a blueprint of happiness in ancient China's ideal economic life.

In this blueprint, people had no extravagant wants or consumption. Those with ambitions strove to be top candidates in the imperial examinations and serve in the government. It was plain how to become an official-through studying and taking tests. One's residence was where they worked, studied, and resided.

Self-cultivation, maintaining one's family, governing the state, and ensuring people enjoy a peaceful and prosperous existence all revolve around the family. The entire court was like a home, with the emperor and officers acting like fathers and sons, and the officials like brothers. Loyalty and filial piety were the underlying principles of the entire system.

Modern scholars have discussed why China did not develop Capitalism in its history. China has never encouraged self-interest or the expansion of individual desires; anyone wishing to take part in public life was expected

---

[7] Straw dogs were used in worshipping ceremonies by common people in ancient China before the Qin Dynasty (221 BCE).

[8] Tzu, L., & Legge, J. (2013). *Tao Te Ching (Legge): A New Translation and Commentary*. Start Publishing LLC.

[9] Birch, C. & Keene, D. L. (1965). *Anthology of Chinese Literature*. United States: Grove Press. p.184.

to take the well-being of the world as their duty, rather than their own. Throughout the changing fortunes of dynasties, the code of conduct for officials remained people-oriented and monarch-guided. Ancient Chinese culture can be defined by its Altruistic personalities, and commitment to moral standards.

Jin Guantao wrote that in the early dynasties, dividing land granted equal land rights and livelihoods. During poor harvests, people had to borrow from the wealthy, leading to eventual land loss, and becoming tenant farmers. Land seizure worsened in the later dynasties. When people fell sick and their children had to pay for examination fees, land seizure was commonplace.

The tenant peasant system perpetuates poverty among some peasants and deepens the gap between the rich and poor. In an unfavorable economic climate, peasants would have difficulty paying their debts. A concentration of such farms could give rise to uprisings and regime changes. The uprisings of Chen Sheng and Wu Guang[10] at the end of the Qin Dynasty serve as examples.

So, the War of Liberation to establish the People's Republic of China (PRC) prompted impoverished peasants to rebel against landowners.

The entire history of China is a story of peasants fighting for their living.

Agriculture has been a symbol of happiness in China throughout history. During peacetime, peasants were self-reliant and free; however, it couldn't last long. Nature significantly impacts the livelihood of peasants and affects changes of regime.

Therefore, to understand the prosperity of the ancient Chinese economy, we should focus on the small peasants. They lived and worked calmly and with satisfaction, without overly pursuing material possessions, capturing the typically serene economy of small Taoist countries, with minimal population and Confucian fulfillment.

Chinese regimes greatly emphasized agriculture and suppressed commerce due to their fear of wealth inequality caused by land annexation. The stability of a small-scale peasant economy was essential for preserving political power. If the government could not restrain the ambitions of businessmen nor prevent land annexation, the peasants would likely revolt.

---

[10] These two men were peasants who rose against the Qin emperor in 209 BCE.

We cannot say merchants in ancient China were not good, but the issue is their strong commercial power could endanger the economic system.

The small-scale, peasant-based economic system sustained families and clans, and, in turn, they maintained the Chinese cultural heritage from one generation to the next. This system of agriculture and clan life brought with it economic prosperity. In this clan-based farming economy, people worked for families, not just individuals. Because of Confucian filial piety, children put in their best effort in their work. Moreover, the practice of nepotism and strong interpersonal relations placed great social pressure on the idle and the wealthy to contribute to their families and villages.

China's economic reform in 1978 allowed peasants to cultivate their land and reap their harvests, which marked the first economic recovery in modern China and a critical measure for the Chinese government's political stability.

Developing the small-scale peasant economy meant re-establishing clan stability and social order. After a period of great disruption in modern China, economic reforms reconnected families that had been separated in the chaos, while family members aiding each other gradually reanimated the small-scale peasant economy. Recuperation of the small-scale peasant economy brought new economic success and a stable social structure, a critical key to the regime's approval from the public.

Clan Inheritance and Economic Development in China

The small-scale peasant economy reflects a vision of long-term economic growth. Kazimierz Poznanski, an expert on Confucian economics at the University of Washington, contends that continuity within Chinese families encourages them to prioritize the long-term implications of economic actions over short-term gratification.[11]

The Chinese dragon symbolizes an eternal lineage of clans. Professor Yulie Lou, a Peking University philosophy professor, remarked, "Continuing a clan is the most crucial religious belief in China." Within the family is the basis of their economy. Activities conducted in ancient China sought

---

[11] Poznanski, K. Z. (2015). *Confucian Economics: The World at Work*. World Review of Political Economy, 6(2), 208–251.

not to maximize personal gain, or based on Weber's Protestant business ethics—which seeks to glorify God—that underpins the inflationary Western Capitalism.

The economy in ancient China wasn't just for individuals, it shouldered responsibility for family inheritance.

The economic thinking in ancient China was not focused on hedonism. Although economic activities were not aimed at benefiting the society as a whole, they still aimed to benefit families and villages, and had a spirit of benefiting others. Like the ambition expressed by the Shanxi merchants in the fifteenth century, "If a man cannot achieve fame in the world, can he not establish a foundation for his family?" Scholars in Confucianism are renowned among lords, seeking fame for generations. In contrast, merchants aim to establish a family business. Both are aimed at benefiting society and individual prosperity.

Economic thought in Ancient China centered around the notion that the Earth's resources were plentiful and could be enjoyed freely as long as people followed the Way of Heaven. Violation of the Way of Heaven would be met with punishment from Heaven.

In economics, abundance is seen as inseparable from heaven and earth, with no opposition between humans and nature, or endless exploitation of the Earth. Ancient Chinese economy believed in mutual inclusion and prosperity of people and nature.

The Equal Affluence of Both Individuals and Country

As mentioned in this chapter, the economy in ancient China was based on the prosperity of small peasants. A regime's legitimacy was embedded in maintaining the prosperity and well-being of small farmers. Confucianism, Taoism, and Buddhism did not oppose economic prosperity and happiness. In *The Analects of Confucius*, Confucius said: "When a country is well governed, poverty and a mean condition are things to be ashamed of. When a country is ill governed, riches and noble are things to be ashamed of."[12] To realize the equal affluence of individuals and the country was an economic ideal in ancient China.

In the modern West, there was tension between a country's and an individual's wealth. Debates between economists on whether hefty taxes

---

[12] Legge, J. (1971). *Confucian Analects: The Great Learning, and The Doctrine of the Mean*. New York: Dover Publications. p. 212.

on the rich might limit economic progress or lower taxes which could increase the inequality between the affluent and the deprived have been constant. Confucian opinions on this have been moderate. If a country is impoverished despite being governed rightly, it's likely due to the people's lack of hard work; and if it has become wealthy in an improper fashion, it must have been accomplished by means of exploitation that goes against benevolence (仁 ren).

Confucius said:

> Riches and Nobles are what men desire. If it cannot be obtained in the proper way, they should not be held. Poverty and meanness are what men dislike. If it cannot be avoided in the proper way, they should not be avoided.[13]

Wealth, status, poverty, and humility depend on justice and Tao. They are all part of a happy life as long as they are based on justice and Tao. Therefore, what the ancient Chinese yearned for was not pure wealth, but wealth through a proper way, as Confucius said, "The superior man does not, even for the space of a single meal, act contrary to virtue. In moments of haste, he cleaves to it. In seasons of danger, he cleaves to it."[14]

In answering a question from his disciple Ran You, Confucius showed his pioneering vision in supporting wealth. "You said, 'Since they are thus numerous, what more shall be done for them?' 'Enrich them,' was the reply. 'And when they have been enriched, what more shall be done?' The Master said, 'Teach them.'"[15]

In ancient Chinese oracle bone inscriptions, "numerousness" refers to cooking, meaning that people had enough food. As Confucius explained, one should not only strive for abundance, but for knowledge and propriety, or moral discipline. Thus, economic thought in ancient China emphasized gaining wealth and enriching oneself with justice and propriety.

---

[13] Legge, J. (1971). *Confucian Analects: The Great Learning, and The Doctrine of the Mean*. New York: Dover Publications. p. 166.

[14] Legge, J. (1971). *Confucian Analects: The Great Learning, and The Doctrine of the Mean*. New York: Dover Publications. p. 166.

[15] Legge, J. (1971). *Confucian Analects: The great Learning, and The Doctrine of the Mean*. New York: Dover Publications. pp. 266–267.

Economic Inequality and Political Disturbance in Ancient China

As I stated, ancient China emphasized wealth and propriety, as well as benevolence. However, why did large-scale land mergers occur often in the middle and late dynasties and impoverish lower classes? Even in peaceful periods, despite unfavorable climates, governmental and private forces were able to cope with its effects on society. Overall, rebellions and social chaos in ancient China were mainly caused by humans.

Corruption may be a cause. Confucian scholars, upon gaining power through the imperial examination system, their families and clans may have been engaged in land annexation and usury, resulting in economic inequality and the breakdown of small-scale peasant economies.

No wonder Confucius said, "When a country is ill governed, riches and noble are things to be ashamed of."[16] A corrupt regime must involve the rich. Therefore, governmental integrity is the key to maintaining economic stability. A chaotic governance cycle always looms largest. With corruption being curbed, economic prosperity would continue.

In ancient China, the degradation of intellectuals was the impetus of commercial decline, not the other way around. Scholar-officials' decline mainly occurred in power struggles, which caused frequent factional conflict. Taoism and Buddhism, however, seemed relatively more reserved in Ancient China. Intellectuals might have resorted to Taoism and Buddhism when their political career was at a low point. For instance, the Buddhist beliefs of Su Shi (蘇軾), a renowned essayist and poet in Song Dynasty (960–1279 CE), and Tao Yuanming's Taoism illustrated their shift from Confucianism's ambition for social success to a more detached from life attitude.

However, some intellectuals failed in politics and turned to business. This is a positive shift toward engaging with the world. The next chapter will explore whether a businessman can be both an Internal Sage and an External King. Ancient China's political system heavily hindered economic activity, thus stifling the emergence of modern Capitalism in China.

---

[16] Legge, J. (1971). *Confucian Analects: The Great Learning, and The Doctrine of the Mean.* New York: Dover Publications. p. 212.

Monarchy and Economic Development

As Weber argued, free trade was generally easier to advance in a republican system, whereas in a monarchy it was frequently repressed. The latter tended to impede commerce progress on the basis of maintaining social order; this could explain why, despite the abundance of the Chinese economy and commerce in the past, there was no significant emergence of capitalists.[17]

This is surely not a deficit, as Western Capitalism can foster endless consumption and avarice. It is an unfair economy that amplifies the disparity between rich and poor and exacerbates depletion of the planet's resources.

Avoiding the amassing of too much wealth and focusing on the wealth of families, individuals, and political stability were important economic aspects in ancient China. This belief ensured that wealth would bring contentment, and economic growth would not deplete the earth, nor create vast differences in individual wealth, leading to inequality and unrest.

This economic concept of the amalgamation of individual and collective life should be re-examined in regard to present-day China's economic progress.

Personal wealth should not be for fulfilling individual desires and satisfying oneself, but for the benefit of families and society at large.

Personal economic life is essential for the harmony and progress of society. In ancient China's small-scale peasant economy, happiness was not determined by how much abundance one could have but rather the loving relationships one could have with family, clan, society, and bigger groups.

Applying the notion of Economy of Goodness in ancient China to today's economy, businessmen wouldn't pursue the endless expansion of enterprises as sanctioned by Western Protestant ethics. Instead, they'd consider the welfare of people, society, and the planet, as well as conforming to nature without violating its laws.

---

[17] In the third year of Emperor Xianping in the Northern Song Dynasty (1000), China's total GDP was US$26.55 billion, accounting for 22.7% of the world's total economy, and its per capita GDP was US$2,280. In 1820, during the Qing Dynasty, China's per capita GDP was US$600. At that time, the per capita GDP of Britain, after the first Industrial Revolution, was US$1,250.

As quoted earlier from The Qian Hexagram in *The I Ching* states:

> The great man is he who is in harmony in his attributes with heaven and
> earth; in his brightness with the sun and moon; in his orderly procedure
> with the four seasons; and in his relation to what is fortunate and what is
> calamitous with the spiritual agents. He may precede Heaven, and Heaven
> will not act in opposition to him; he may follow Heaven but will act only
> as Heaven at the time would do. If Heaven will not act in opposition to
> him, how much less will men![18]

Not only should the law of Heaven be respected and not violated by
people, but they should also adhere to the laws of heaven and earth and
foster the virtues of all things. For instance, in *The Rites by Daide*, it
is mentioned that the Great Way encompasses the laws observed in the
creation of all things.[19]

Duke Lu of the Lu State said to Confucius, "I venture to ask what it
is that the superior man values in the way of Heaven." Confucius replied:

> He values its unceasingness. There is, for instance, the succession and
> sequence of the sun and moon from the east and west - that is the way
> of Heaven. There is the long continuance of its progress without interrup-
> tion - that is the way of Heaven. There is its making (all) things complete
> without doing anything - that is the way of Heaven. There is their brilliancy
> when they have been completed - that is the way of Heaven.[20]

Just as Heaven and Earth achieve all without being seen, so too was the
ideal of a noble character and economic life in ancient China.

---

[18] Legge, J. (1963). *The I Ching: The Book of Changes*. United Kingdom: Dover
Publications. p. 47.

[19] Guo, J. X. (2002). *Xin yi jing duben* [New Translation of the Book of Change].
Taipei: Sanmin shuju. p. 20.

[20] Confucius. (2013). *The Book of Rites (Li Ji): English-Chinese Version* (D. Sheng, Ed.,
J. Legge, Trans.). CreateSpace Independent Publishing Platform. p. 242.

Section 4: The Transnational Economy of the Roman Empire

The Roman Empire was the wealthiest in human history, its national output surpassing that of any other country before Capitalism, surpassed only by medieval China.

The Roman Empire's economic prosperity stemmed from its early understanding of international division of industry, specialized production, and manufacturing.

As the pillar of Rome's economy, agriculture supported urban life and consumption. Rome, in Augustine's reign, had an estimated population of 700,000 to 1 million, similar to a large Chinese city of the Middle Ages. Rome's wealth stemmed from its ability to mediate supply and demand. Nobles and soldiers often gathered in the town. Aristocrats possessed expansive suburban agricultural lands, which served as their source of riches.

The Beginning of the Transnational Industrial Division of Labor

The Roman Empire controlled a large region, comprising Egypt, North Africa, Spain, and France (Gaul). These areas were agriculturally productive, supplying Rome with olive oil from North Africa, wine from Spain, and grain from Egypt. Without the contribution of these newly conquered areas, the Roman economy would have been in serious trouble.

Urban consumption versus countryside production aptly described Rome. Urban commerce, agriculture, factories, and craftsmanship formed the basis of Rome's economy. In its first three centuries, it produced 12 billion Sesterces (1 Sesterce = 2.25 USD).

The Roman aristocracy became wealthy by owning rural land, viewing it as a valuable asset they rarely sold. They used enslaved people or sharecroppers to be the primary producers, while Rome was well-developed in the manufacture of textiles and pottery. The elite landowners supplied their farms with raw cotton and wool, while the local farmers used their downtime to make and vend clothing in their own areas or in the bigger cities. Some of the farmers also used their ceramic-making skills to create and sell pottery in urban locations, allowing them to earn additional income away from their farming activities.

In terms of agricultural tech, a breakthrough in olive oil compression and refining occurred in the Roman Empire. This brought substantial income to Spain, North Africa, and France. Plus, the mining industry experienced remarkable technological progress during the Roman Empire.

Mining was highly developed during the Roman Empire; it had advanced enough to provide the Empire with gold and silver for minting coins. In Spain, the miners could produce sufficient iron, copper, and gold, while silver was mined in Africa. Refining of minerals by water flushing was a major technique used. To achieve this, large trenches were dug and water was released in large amounts, washing over the surrounding earth to reveal alluvial minerals. This process was known as Hushing.[21]

It is worth noting that these processes are conducted through large institutions in the civil sector. During Augustine's reign in the Roman Empire, there were already operations involving public and private enterprise, with private operators mining minerals through contracts granted by the government.

The Roman government did not monopolize mines; however, they did indirectly control them, as any new mining needed their approval. Meanwhile, trade was conducted in free markets, which contributed to early economic success due to the lack of government regulation.

The Roman government wasn't funded by state agencies, but primarily through taxation of the aristocracy and free farmers. Taxes on tenant farmers were kept low considering their limited incomes. The greatest burden was placed on the aristocracy, which was essential to maintain their social status.

The Pioneer of Government Expanding Domestic Demand

Julius Caesar was one of the most renowned political-military leaders in history. From birth, he was a soldier and later achieved the same level of military excellence as Pompey through his superior strategic ability. He conquered Gaul, an area corresponding to what is now France, thus extending the Roman Empire from the Mediterranean to the Atlantic and the English Channel. His strong political ambitions took him all the way

---

[21] Kehoe, D. P. (1992). *Management and Investment on Estates in Roman Egypt during the Early Empire* (Papyrologische Texte und Abhandlungen 40). Bonn: R. Habelt.

to becoming Emperor/Dictator of the Roman Empire. In addition, he strived to improve the lives of his people by growing domestic demand, having public works constructed such as libraries, and rebuilding ports and other infrastructure. In spite of his efforts, his actions incensed the Senators, who at that time wielded great economic power, and led to his assassination.

Nevertheless, the economic gains generated by Caesar's stimulated domestic consumption were always remembered fondly by the masses. It is an ironic twist of history that authoritarian rulers often serve to benefit the common folk, yet elites concentrate on upholding republican values while only looking out for their own interests.

In the centuries following Caesar, the Roman Empire continued to heavily spend its tax revenues on the construction of monumental structures, such as colosseums, which proved to be a costly investment. Relying on bricks from Egypt and North Africa, and marble blocks from quarries, the government employed private builders to supply the necessary materials.

The city-building materials of the Roman Empire were dominated by marble, with stone used for making roads. Rome's streets connected all corners of the Empire and government buildings were grand, solid, and detailed, equaling modern architectural standards. Private contractors provided the necessary materials and quality of construction. The BOT (Build-Operate-Transfer) Model adopted today by governments was already in practice in the Roman Empire.

Compared to Qin Shi Huang, the First Qin emperor of Ancient China, who began the construction of the Great Wall and conscripted many to the labor, the Roman Empire had much earlier implemented an economic model of government-expanded domestic demand and collaboration between the private sector and the government.

Apart from its government's large budget, the Roman Empire's most significant expenditure was its army. Accounting for around 40% of the country's yearly taxes, the army reached a peak of more than 400,000 troops, situated at various borders but with a luxurious way of living. All grains, olive oil, and meat were brought by Rome's transportation system from land to sea for distant war zones.

The Predatory Economy Ends in Pillage

Most of the Roman Empire's economy relied on war plunder and slavery. During a conflict, soldiers were rewarded with land and assets by the government. Thus, having property and land enabled them to partake in public affairs. Thus, though soldiering posed a great risk, it was also a means to gain riches.

Ordinary citizens didn't have this right. Enslaved people, those at the bottom of society, were the tools of their masters, often having been captives taken by the Roman Empire, bankrupt peasants, or servants. During its heyday, enslaved people were the primary producers while soldiers and nobles held hereditary wealth and status, assuming responsibility for the government and national security.

In the fourth century of the Roman Empire, Constantine the Great converted to Christianity, which had an impact on the economy of the Empire. By the fourth century, barbarian invasions had led to the destruction of the Western Roman Empire, while the Eastern Roman Empire continued to rely on Egyptian granaries until the fourteenth century.

SECTION 5: ECONOMIC THOUGHT IN WESTERN FEUDALISM

The Economic Views of the Church Fathers

Before the Roman Empire recognized Christianity, Christian economic ideas had little influence on Western society. But from the third century, that changed when Constantine the Great adopted Christianity as the state religion.

Next, I will discuss the economic impact of Church Fathers during the Godfather era.

The Church Fathers Period refers to the period from the first to eighth centuries, after the establishment of the Catholic Church system and before the Second Council of Nicaea. During this time, the Bishop of Rome had authority and Patristic Theology reached its peak. Prior to this, all European bishops were equal.

The Fathers touched every aspect of life. Their economic thought followed Jesus' example and saw unnecessary wealth accumulation as a lack of faith in God According to them, seeking wealth was a sin, yet having enough was permissible. Crafting and holding property was considered acceptable, but earning money without producing anything was wrong and led to sin.

The Fathers agreed that believers needed food and clothing, but they did not advocate the pursuit of profit. Thus, they condemned merchants who engaged in agriculture, trade, or interest in the pursuit of profit. The economy was primarily agriculture-based, and Father John Chrysostom[22] believed that women should maintain their households and weave while men were held responsible for farming.

The word "Economy" comes from the Greek word "oikonomia," which translates to "manage the household well." According to Ancient Western economies, people living in the countryside and being involved in agriculture were essential. Additionally, the Fathers of this era also believed that craftsmanship was necessary to achieve a livelihood, leading to a multitude of tasks such as weaving, embroidery, bronze-making, leather-making, and candy-making. While these activities provided abundance in life, the main purpose of them should be not to simply seek out profit.[23]

Father Jerome broadened the scope of craftsmanship to include philosophy, physics, rhetoric, geology, and music—all of which correlated with biblical teachings that were advantageous for human life.[24]

Christian priests of this period called for a life of communal ownership, believing humans shared a common nature and thus should collectively own everything in nature. They argued that God had provided humanity with sunlight, air, water, animals, and plants, and so the rich should not be allowed any more of these than the poor. After all, God's blessings were far greater than material possessions and therefore should be distributed equally across all people.

Opposing private ownership has been a consensus in the Patristic Period. Father Basil the Great, revered as one of the three Christian saints,

---

[22] John Chrysostom, the Bishop of Constantinople in the fourth century AD, was born in Greece. He had a great influence on Christian theology in later generations. John Chrysostom was canonized by the Holy See, the Orthodox Church, and the Catholic Church as a saint. John Chrysostom, Basil the Great, and Gregory of Nazianzus are honored as the Three Great Hierarchs by Christianity.

[23] Stander, H. (2014). *The Oxford Handbook of Christianity and Economics: Economics in the Church Fathers.* Oxford: Oxford University Press. p. 29.

[24] Stander, H. (2014). *The Oxford Handbook of Christianity and Economics: Economics in the Church Fathers.* Oxford: Oxford University Press. pp. 29–30.

interpreted that man had no possession of material goods; as he had come into the world naked and would leave it likewise, so man should not own anything on the Earth.[25] During this period, Christianity viewed communal or shared living as the ideal.

A century after Father Basil, Father Tertullian asserted that humankind was unified in mind and body, and ought not to be parsimonious with what we have.

Before Karl Marx advocated communism, the notion of social ownership had arisen in the Patristic Period. Noteworthy is that while the Fathers would state their opinion when many people owned property and land, they exhorted them to see it as a present from God, thus deepening their love for Him.

Although the Fathers did not encourage private property ownership, the Church had great amounts of real estate from the fourth century onward when Christianity was recognized in Rome and considerable amounts of land were bestowed upon the Church from the state and individuals. Augustine argued that since the lands belonged to God, possession of them by the Church was suitable. Furthermore, the Church donated possessions and money to the destitute, displaying God's love.

Augustine further explained that private possessions and property were acceptable, provided they were used correctly or for exemplary purposes.

The Church was strongly against interest. *The Old Testament* taught that one must not charge interest to their brother, but he must help them instead. Money that could gain interest was seen as immoral and against God's law.

By then, Christianity had become a Western world religion, encompassing all ethnic groups, so that the brotherly people portrayed in *The Old Testament* had expanded to include all believers. It was unfair to charge interest from one's brother.

Though not widespread in Europe before the Middle Ages, land and sea trading was already occurring. The Fathers saw trade work as evil: firstly, because it sought profit, and secondly, because it enabled deception. Poor people needing goods often faced high prices in trade.

[25] Stander, H. (2014). *The Oxford Handbook of Christianity and Economics: Economics in the Church Fathers*. Oxford: Oxford University Press. p. 26.

While opposed to trade, certain godfathers such as Gregory and Nazianzus[26] extolled the greatness of the sea trade. He said that the sea trade was good in the eyes of God and that transporting goods through it facilitated exchanges between people. It was for the benefit of all that ocean trade allowed the wealthy to profit and the needy to obtain their basic necessities.

From the Fathers, it is evident that Jesus' early teachings emphasized treating the poor as beloved. He further taught not to be concerned with material possessions, and instead concentrate on knowing God and practicing His law. As such, any business dealt purely for monetary benefit was disallowed.

At this time, economic prosperity was rooted in family wellness and geared toward furthering overall societal prosperity. Any overzealous business conduct or pursuit of profit was forbidden. However, the private property earned through proper means gained the approval of the Fathers.

Faith-wise, it is noteworthy that the Fathers had a favorable view of maritime trade that seemed intrinsically linked to the large-scale maritime adventures of Western countries such as Italy, Spain, the Netherlands, and England from the tenth to the thirteenth century. In his praise and prophecy of the sea, Father Gregory said that the sea was favored by God and connected the world, provided profits for the rich, and fed the poor.[27]

The Christian economic thought entrenched in ocean civilizations laid the groundwork for maritime conquests that reached their peak in the seventeenth and eighteenth centuries, materializing in economic, political, and religious hegemony of maritime cultures.

The Medieval Church and the Genesis of Modern Capital Entrepreneurs

After centuries of continuation, Patristic economic thought experienced a significant change in the Middle Ages. The hard work and austerity that

---

[26] Gregory of Nazianzus is the most important Christian philosopher of the fifth century CE and a theologian of the Patriarchal School. He established the ideological foundation of the early church, including some Greek ideas inherited by the Byzantine Empire. He is an influential theologian in the history of Christianity.

[27] Stander, H. (2014). *The Oxford Handbook of Christianity and Economics: Economics in the Church Fathers*. Oxford: Oxford University Press. pp. 31–32.

the Fathers demanded lessened in both Church and society. While this can be viewed as a moral decline, it was also the beginning of modern Capitalism.

After being established as the state religion of the Roman Empire, Christianity played a pivotal role in politics, economy, society, and culture—economically, especially. Like the nobility, the Church owned vast tracts of land, far removed from Augustine's argument that they belonged to God. Instead of using the land just to build churches, the Church leased it to tenant farmers, its hold then extending to their faith, economy, marriage, and political status.

The Medieval Church owned more than a quarter of the land in England, France, and Western Europe. In highland countries like Sweden, it constituted 40% of the nation's area, far more than any king or nobleman.

The Church opposed interest on capital transactions, yet charged interest on loans to the laity. For instance, the Cistercian Order in thirteenth-century England had many ranches and workers producing wool and, in competition with other churches, encouraged pilgrimage tourism.

The Catholic Church in the Middle Ages was said to be the first transnational enterprise in history, taking large sums of money from wealthy believers in exchange for spiritual services. It even went into business, competing with city merchants and the malls of the aristocracy.[28] The church held a powerful position in thirteenth-century England, and in some places, it had trading rights granted by the king.

The Church backed maritime ventures and commerce that started in Europe in the fourteenth and sixteenth centuries, believing it would foster mutual awareness of the world and propagate the gospel of Christ.

Though the church eventually fell into corruption and the Reformation began in the sixteenth century, Schumpeter argued that between the thirteenth and fifteenth centuries, church bishops and popes were the first capital entrepreneurs.[29]

---

[28] Casson, M., & Casson, C. (2014). *The History of Entrepreneurship: Medieval Origins of a Modern Phenomenon*. Cambridge: Business History, 56(8), pp. 1223–1242.

[29] Casson, M., & Casson, C. (2014). *The History of Entrepreneurship: Medieval Origins of a Modern Phenomenon*. Cambridge: Business History, 56(8), p. 1237.

CHAPTER 6

Philosophical and Cultural Beliefs and the Economy of Goodness

SECTION 1: HEBREW JEWISH ECONOMIC PHILOSOPHY: THE HARMONIOUS UNIFICATION OF ABSTINENCE AND PLEASURE

Jewish economic philosophy is based on present-day wealth and glory. According to Jewish doctrine, all of God's rewards are for this life.

The Jewish population totals only 14 million globally, yet they have remarkable economic strength as a single ethnicity. They dominate the diamond, banking, movie, watch industries, etc., around the world.

Why are Jews so economically powerful? Are Jews profit-minded? These doubts have been constantly discussed in recent centuries.

The Jewish people's beliefs affected their economic life. Believing that God gave all humanity glory in this lifetime, they reject the Hindu-Buddhist ideas of reincarnation and karma. They believe God's law governs all and thus in this life they have the responsibility to follow it.

The Jewish faith is closely connected to family. Mothers are key in Judaism, with their beliefs being passed on to their children, forming the core of their faith. Mothers' nurture of the faith's beliefs guides their children's beliefs.

For the past millennia, Jews have been cosmopolitan. Has their roaming lifestyle shaped their character, or has it been their character that led them to live globally?

Before World War II, Jews lacked a homeland; they had only faith and wealth.

Faith and wealth are two sides of the same coin, both supporting Jewish survival and growth.

The God that Assumes No Image and Pragmatic Jews

Jews have always been practical, and the Jewish religion calls for worshippers to not visualize God.

When I visited the Wailing Wall in Jerusalem, many Orthodox believers were praying, meditating, reading, and singing, and their bodies were occasionally trembling.

A lack of concrete images of God allows Jews to avoid the pursuit of abstract ideals.

"And Moses said unto God, Behold, when I come unto the children of Israel, and shall say unto them, The God of your fathers hath sent me unto you; and they shall say to me, What is his name? What shall I say unto them? And God said unto Moses, I AM THAT I AM." (*King James Bible*, 1769/2017, Exodus 3:13–14).[1]

No single thing, language, or image in the world can refer to Jehovah, the Almighty Lord.

In the *Old Testament*, God told the Jewish people:

> Therefore, take good heed unto yourselves; for ye saw no similitude on the day that the Lord spoke unto you in Horeb out of the midst of the fire: Lest ye corrupt yourselves, and make you a graven image, the similitude of any figure... (*King James Bible*, 1769/2017, Deuteronomy 4:15–16)

No form of the mundane world—be it an earthbound animal, a flying bird, a swimming fish, the sun, the moon, or the stars—can represent Jehovah.

Attention to reality of life is key to Jewish economic success; there is no Heaven, Paradise, Eden, Canaan, or Holy Land outside of the reality of life.

---

[1] *King James Bible*. (2017). King James Bible Online. https://www.kingjamesbibleonline.org/ (Original work published 1769). Note: Subsequent quotations of the Bible are all from this source.

The Garden of Eden is not beyond this life; historically, it is in Mesopotamia. The Holy Land of Canaan is too in the hearts of believers.

Dating to the third century AD, when foreigners occupied the ancient Jewish city of Canaan, the Jews began their thousand-year exile. By the seventh century AD, when Byzantium occupied it, the Byzantium emperor allowed them to return to their former homes. But only half returned home. The other half kept Canaan as their Holy Land in their minds.

It is like the Buddhist saying that the practice hall is where one's heart is.

The Jews do not pursue holy places and Heaven of the coming day; they commit to current accomplishments to honor God. This is where Jewish economic thought originates.

Prophets Are All Wealthy and Influential

The Jewish pursuit of material wealth is in line with their moral code. The prophets of the Jews were all wealthy—Abraham had thousands of cattle and sheep; Jacob was clothed and fed well; Job, a tribulation saint, had great wealth; David was king; and Solomon was a renowned sage king.

The Jewish saints were all affluent. Abundance was their moral and life standard.

Nevertheless, no perfect saint is found in the Jewish holy book. Noah became drunk and exposed himself in his later years. King David's adulterous affair with the spouse of his vassal. Abraham, too, was unfaithful at one point. Moses slew a Jew. All prophets had certain faults. This taught the Jews that their aim was not perfection, but that dwelling with God was their glory.

Unlimited Wealth from Limited Resources

Living in God entails abiding by the commandments, which bestow Jews with strong discipline and faithfulness. After sundown on Friday, there is no cooking or lighting, simply repose. Activities resume when darkness falls on Saturday.

The Sabbath and Talmud gives Jews an economic principle that everyone must work within constraints.

God even needed rest when creating Heaven and Earth, not to mention humans.

Working hours and economic resources are limited, yet we must still strive to maximize welfare under these restrictions.

The Sabbath symbolizes discipline. Greed and indulgence must be avoided in business, and Jews' early adherence to discipline enabled them to manage intricate business affairs more aptly.

Man Is the Master of All Creatures on Earth

According to *The Old Testament*, after God created Heaven and the Earth, He let humans name all species. Naming means giving meaning and value. God created all things, but man endowed their value. The Lord said:

> And out of the ground, the LORD God formed every beast of the field and every fowl of the air; and brought them unto Adam to see what he could call them; and whatsoever Adam called every living creature, that was the name thereof. (*King James Bible*, 1769/2017, Genesis 2:19)

"And he gave names to all cattle and all fowls in the air, and every beast of the field, but for Adam, there was not found a help meet for him." (*King James Bible*, 1769/2017, Genesis 2:20).

The man was Adam. God created him, taking one rib from him, and creating his spouse, whom He named Eve.

God gave Adam the power to name all things, thus enabling humans to become users and rulers of them all. This grants the Jewish people a significant mission, as they must make use of all God has given them in the present world and gain mastery over them in order to bring about their own happiness. God has bestowed humans with the authority to use all things.

Jews view this life as salvation, so it's no wonder they eagerly pursue careers and endeavors no matter where they are.

Toynbee, the historian, referred to Jews as an exemplary example of a "non-residential race," living throughout the world but not rooted in any land or nationality other than that which was shared through their faith and its commandments.

The Jewish Outlook on Interest and Good Deeds

Do Jews remain loyal to the country of their residence, or are they only making the most of local economic resources that have resulted in the exclusion of Jews? This has been a matter of debate throughout history.

Jews have been labeled as usury speculators since the late eighteenth century in Germany which resulted in a frenzy of criticism and expulsion. This was linked to the alienation of overly secularized Jews. Despite God allowing his people to live life on earth, it is necessary to follow his law.

The book of *Nehemiah* recorded that overtaxed people wept, because they could not repay their loans with interest. The Prophet Nehemiah said:

"I likewise, and my brethren, and my servants, might exact of them money and corn: I pray you, let us leave off this usury." (*King James Bible*, 1769/2017, Nehemiah 5:10).

> Restore, I pray you, to them, even this day, their lands, their vineyards, their olive yards, and their houses, also the hundredth part of the money, and of the corn, the wine, and the oil, that ye exact of them. (*King James Bible*, 1769/2017, Nehemiah 5:11)

> No interest was allowed to be charged to brothers, as detailed in The Book of Deuteronomy: Thou shalt not lend upon usury to thy brother; usury of money, usury of victuals, usury of anything that is lent upon usury. (*King James Bible*, 1769/2017, Deuteronomy 23:19)

So, Jews to this day still observe the tradition of absolving debts every 49 years. On the 50th anniversary, debts would be annulled and slaves released.

In the book of *Leviticus*, the Lord said to Moses on Mount Sinai.

> Speak unto the children of Israel, and say unto them, 'When ye come into the land which I give you, then shall the land keep a sabbath onto the LORD.'

> Six years thou shalt sow thy field, and six years thou shalt prune thy vineyard, and gather in the fruit thereof.

> But in the seventh year shall be a sabbath of rest unto the land, a sabbath for the LORD; thou shalt neither thy field, nor prune thy vineyard.

That which grown of its own accord of thy harvest thou shalt not reap, neither gather the grapes of thy vine undressed; for it is a year of rest unto the land.

And the sabbath of the land shall be meat for you; for thee, and for thy servant, and for thy maid, and for thy hired servant, and for thy stranger that sojourneth with thee.

And for the cattle. And for the beast that are in thy land, shall all the increase thereof be meat.

And thou shalt number seven sabbaths of years shall be unto thee forty and nine years. (*King James Bible*, 1769/2017, Leviticus 25:2–8)

This is the economist's reference that Jews experienced an upswing at an early stage. It is necessary to diminish, or even remove, the disparities in wealth every forty-nine years in order to enable the general populace a pause, thus averting an over-accumulation of wealth among a small few and a limited use of spending capability among most of the people, which can ultimately result in a production lull and economic downturn.

No interest or benefit should be taken from a brother in debt. But what about debts owed by Gentiles?

Thou that shall not lend usury to thy brother; usury of money, usury of victuals, usury of anything that is lent upon usury. (*King James Bible*, 1769/2017, Deuteronomy 23:19)

This suggests that Jews engaging in charging interest, and even usury, in Europe would not be against their beliefs as those people were Gentiles.

In Judaism, Jehovah is the tribal God of the Jews. Jesus introduced Him to the wider world, and Paul spread the gospel of Jesus abroad.

Unlike Peter, who preached the gospel of Jesus to the Jews, Paul vowed to take the gospel to all the world. He proposed that Gentiles, who followed justice and accepted the gospel, were also considered just people. This definition of just people was no longer exclusive to Jews who trusted in Jehovah, but to all who followed the law and believed in Jesus.

This is the most striking difference between Christianity and Judaism: Christianity broke free from the Jewish tribal gods and spread Jehovah to the world. This is the greatest spiritual difference between the *New Testament* and the *Old Testament*.

Because of the differences between Jews and Gentiles, Jews around the world held a criticism of being greedy and money-oriented, until World

War II. Academic studies have long considered the degree of Jewish integration in the nations in which they lived. Even before World War I many German Jews tried to publicly demonstrate their allegiance to Germany, downplaying their Jewish identity. Jewish society at that time was grappling with the question of loyalty to the state or to the tribe.

I'd like to argue that Jews' economic success was not rooted in being money-minded, but in adhering to and loving God's commands.

Follow the Commandments and Make Good Results Through Good Deeds

Is there a reward for loving God's commandments and practicing goodness?

As previously stated, the prophets of Israel were all wealthy. Nevertheless, they had all been tested in adhering to the laws and fulfilling good deeds.

According to *The Old Testament*, Abraham was the first prophet, with countless sheep and oxen, and he lived a peaceful family life. Nevertheless, how could Abraham have children when he had not given birth to his second son Isaac until he was a hundred years old, and his wife had been postmenopausal for decades? It was a reward from God to Abraham. However, years later, when Isaac grew up, as the only son of Abraham, God asked Abraham to sacrifice his son to Him. (*King James Bible*, 1769/2017, Genesis 22:13).

Abraham, in immense pain, took his son to the top of the mountain and was about to sacrifice his own son Isaac to God with a knife when the Lord called out to him from the sky, saying, "Abraham! Abraham!" And the Lord said: "Stop! Stop! I am here."

The angel of the Lord told him to halt and sacrifice a ram, entangled in a thicket nearby, instead of Isaac, as a burnt offering. God revealed to Abraham that He was aware of his love for Him, above all else.

This is the teaching of the *Bible*: to love God's law above all else.

From then on, Abraham was richly rewarded for his obedience to God, and his cattle multiplied. His Egyptian concubine, Hagar, bore him his other son, Ishmael, who was the ancestor of the Abelites.

The Old Testament story of Abraham reveals that good deeds result in a good reward.

Abiding by God's will and law, Abraham became a saint, according to *The Old Testament*. He lived to be 175 years old, was wealthy, and had a large family of sons and daughters.

Abraham's moral perseverance was a historical exemplar for the Jews and a model of virtuous entrepreneurship in the Economy of Goodness for them.

Pure Goodness in Jewish Thought

In Jewish thought, good rewards arise from good deeds, but are good deeds only for the purpose of acquiring good reward? Is utilitarianism the basis of Jewish culture?

The Book of Job tells of Job, a righteous, devout servant who sincerely trusted in God and joyfully lived a virtuous life. He was rewarded for his loving faithfulness by God, but then God tested him with tremendous suffering.

Job was engulfed in grief, fury, bafflement, and disbelief over the series of calamities that God inflicted on him until God gave him the complete solution.

According to *The Book of Job*, God had made a pact with the Devil, to test God's most faithful servant. Abruptly, someone rushed to Job and told him that his flock had been struck down by lightning on the hillside. Before the man could finish, another informed Job his daughter, at her son's house, had died. Not long after, a third man came running in to announce his house had been engulfed in flames. Misfortunes followed one another in succession.

Job fell to his knees, tore his clothes in pain, and cried out, "The Lord gave and the Lord hath taken away; blessed be the name of the Lord." (*King James Bible*, 1769/2017, Job 1:21) But in the ensuing days, Job stayed wondering and inflicted, "Even today is my complaint bitter: my stroke is heavier than my groaning." (*King James Bible*, 1769/2017, Job 23:2) I cry unto thee, and thou dost not hear me: I stand up, and thou regardest me not. Thou art become cruel to me: with thy strong hand thou opposest thyself against me. (*King James Bible*, 1769/2017, Job 30:20–21) Did not I weep for him that was in trouble? was not my soul grieved for the poor? When I looked for good, then evil came unto me: and when I waited for light, there came darkness. (*King James Bible*, 1769/2017, Job 30:25–26).

God did not answer him straight away. For many aching nights, Job speculated why a fair person should experience hard luck.

At last, God told Job that He is the sovereign and creator of all. God asked Job: "Where wast thou when I laid the foundations of the earth? Declare, if thou hast understanding." (*King James Bible*, 1769/2017, Job 38:4) "When the morning stars sang together, and all the sons of God shouted for joy?" (*King James Bible*, 1769/2017, Job 38:7) "Or who shut up the sea with doors, when it brake forth, as if it had issued out of the womb?" (*King James Bible*, 1769/2017, Job 38:8) "Then Job arose, and rent his mantle, and shaved his head, and fell down upon the ground, and worshipped." (*King James Bible*, 1769/2017, Job 1:20) "In all this Job sinned not, nor charged God foolishly." (*King James Bible*, 1769/ 2017, Job 1:22) Reward or calamity is all in God's hands.

This answer may be difficult to comprehend for those lacking deep faith. Nevertheless, those with a strong belief understand that being gifted by God is a great privilege, and thus feeling pain with composure and strength is the highest honor and glory.

The Reward for Doing Good Is Goodness

Doing good does not entail trading for blessings or rewards. It should be done out of human nature, not for wealth, fame, or fortune.

The reward for doing good is goodness itself, bringing the highest joy.

The reward of goodness does not come from material advantages, approval, or respect from others, but from the delight and spiritual fulfillment that comes from being good. Experiencing God's goodness is a reward in itself.

This is the Hebrews' view of ultimate goodness, akin to Kant's Good Will. Both point to the inherent goodness of thought and emotion.

For Kant, the Good Will should transcend all earthly purposes, being independent and thus supremely moral in metaphysics.

Altruism in Kant's Good Will is regardless of outcome. Kant maintained that the value of one's desire to do good should not be diminished, even if it could not be realized in practice.

Altruism in Kant's Good Will should be regarded as non-utilitarian, non-consequentialist, motivistic, or idealistic moral ethics.

Kant maintained that Good Will cannot be judged by its outcomes. Even if the Good Will leads to painful results, it is still good, as its intention is positive. The idea of Kant might be related to Job's testament.

The Book of Job depicted pure goodness. In the face of misfortune, those who do good persevere. Through God's trials, Job's life became more abundant, not asked for, but a reward from God.

This informed the Jews that even though good deeds may experience a brief period of misfortune, they will ultimately yield positive outcomes. The most profound concept is to do good, not with the intent of achieving a result, but as a core element of existence.

Jewish life joy seems to be gained through abstinence: a phenomenon hardly understandable in history. Abraham's reward for sacrificing his most beloved son was great, both materially, morally, and historically. Abraham is the ancestor of Jews and Arabs, and prophet Muhammad called him a prophet. Isaac and Ishmael, his sons, are ancestors of both Jews and Arabs. Few people in history have achieved a status as high as Abraham did.

After suffering and misery, Job stayed faithful and was rewarded in the end. His choices were not driven by a desire for material or life happiness, but rather his belief that goodness is more valuable than anything else. For Hebrews, godliness is the reward of abiding by God's law and will.

Good deed's reward is to be goodness.

Concerning good deeds and good rewards, Judaism and Buddhism have different doctrines but comparable ideas. Buddhism emphasizes giving detached from expectations, asserting that true joy can solely result from giving and performing good deeds without seeking recompense. It is not accurate to suggest that while we are doing good, our hearts are secretly expecting blessings.

Doing good is not about seeking a blessing; sometimes, however, it can bring one. Even if the reward has not yet come, it can keep misfortune at bay.

Buddhism holds a doctrine of karma. Good deeds done in this life may not absolve any karma accrued in previous lives, and it is possible for misfortunes in this life to be due to a large amount of karma from past lives.

The Buddhist Teaching of Consciousness-Only asserts that human destiny resides in Store Consciousness, which holds all the seeds. When evil seeds from our Store Consciousness encounter evil causes from the external world, adversity can ensue. Hence, it's essential to transform and clear out any bad seeds from our Store Consciousness, replacing them with seeds of goodness.

Thus, each moment is an opportunity to transform evil seeds into seeds of goodness, which is Right Mindfulness. This mindset can be applied in any situation, good or bad. We should never become excessively joyous or boastful when things are going well or frustrated when we hit a roadblock. Both can be seen as a chance for Enlightenment and to rid ourselves of the evil seeds rooted in our Store Consciousness. In all cases, a devoted Buddhist will say that we are simply balancing our karma by facing misfortune.

Good intentions will certainly lead to good results; this is the law of cause and effect in Buddhism.

The observance of God's goodness is good in itself, according to Judaism.

Goodness is both the aim of doing good and the drive to do it. The outcome, as written in the Scriptures, is good.

Section 2: Economic Justice in Christian Civilization: Balance Between Material and Mind

Humankind as God's Agent and Governor on Earth

Christian economics must begin with God's perspective of humanity.

God modeled humanity in His own image and gave humans the right to name and have dominion over all things. Thus, humanity has been provided with abundance on Earth. Yet, from a modern viewpoint, the planet's resources are seen as being limited.

As far as Christianity is concerned, God has bestowed humans with plentiful economic and material resources, yet they have been squandered in opposition to God's will. Representing God, humans must abide by His commands to make all things flourish.

M. Douglas Meeks said that the human understanding of God is composed of three elements: first, "love" because we are the caretakers of all things; "obedience" because we accept God's commandments; and "gratitude" because God has given us the ability to steward all things.

Anti-slave Economy and the Commercialization of Humanity

According to the *Bible*, God's purpose is to bring salvation to humanity who are oppressed.

As recorded in Exodus, God sent Moses to free the Jews from their 400 years of enslavement in Egypt.

God's economics forbids taking human labor as a commodity and views slavery as an iniquitous system. God declared:

> I have surely seen the affliction of my people which are in Egypt, and have heard their cry by reason of their taskmasters; for I know their sorrows. (*King James Bible*, 1769/2017, Exodus 3:7)

The freeing of slaves marked the beginning of God's economic system.

It implies that those at the bottom of society, who are oppressed, become liberated.

Christian economic thought is focused on providing a livelihood for the most vulnerable, thereby ensuring economic justice.

So, God's economics stresses not just equal justice for all, but the abolishment of structural economic oppression. God promises not just welfare for some, but for all of humanity.

God's economic view is a revolutionary world, with the liberated slave, the needy in Heaven and the wealthy in Hell, all under God's governance.

In the New Testament, Jesus told his disciples:

> Verily I Say unto you, Whosoever shall not receive the kingdom of God as a little child, he shall not enter therein. (*King James Bible*, 1769/2017, Mark 10:15)

It shows that everyone is a new and pure child to God, and that all economic injustices of the world will be overturned. God's kingdom will bring His economic justice just as the Jews left Egypt. His justice will arrive with the Judgment.

By then, God's justice will be revealed in each person who endures, which will be their ultimate redemption.

By then, the world will be free of poverty, economic exploitation, oppression, usury and greedy rich people—but only under God's law of justice, faithfully maintained.

Has salvation come, or is it coming? Different branches of Christianity disagree, but they all strive to attain economic justice in God's kingdom.

Christ's Compassion for the Poor

From the Old and New Testaments, it is clear that God and Jesus do not disregard earthly materials; instead, they pledge to feed the hungry and poor. *The Book of Isaiah* said:

> They shall not labor in vain, nor bring forth for trouble; for they are the seed of the blessed of the LORD, and their offspring with them. (*King James Bible*, 1769/2017, Isaiah 65:23)

God opposes poverty, and His people must not be poor: a promise written in the *Bible*.

As Jesus Said:

> The Spirit of the Lord is upon me, because he hath anointed me to preach the gospel to the poor; he hath sent me to heal the brokenhearted, to preach deliverance to the captives, and recovering of sight to blind, to set at liberty them that are bruised. (*King James Bible*, 1769/2017, Luke 4:18)

In Jesus' time, Jewish class consciousness persisted, and the temple was the path of salvation. Yet, Jesus blessed the poor in the baths and wilds for forgiveness of their sins, a strong reaction against the Jewish classes of the period. *The Old Testament* teaches to provide all with a life of abundance. Christ did not contradict Biblical doctrine, but countered the rabbinical class.

The Gospel of Jesus emphasizes spiritual connection with God and economic justice, so that the poor and oppressed can be equally respected and enriched. This is another clear statement against class oppression since Moses freed the Jews.

The most important economic principle in Christ's gospel is caring for the poor. *The Bible* states:

> ...Blessed be ye poor: for yours is the kingdom of God. (*King James Bible*, 1769/2017, Luke 6:20)

> Blessed are ye that hunger now: for ye shall be filled. Blessed are ye that weep now: for ye shall laugh. (*King James Bible*, 1769/2017, Luke 6:21)

For the Poor, Christ Is the Gospel.

Jesus tried to feed 5,000 people with just five loaves of bread and two fish, but the disciples said it wasn't enough. He had the crowd line up and said he would feed them; then he prayed. Suddenly, many fish appeared in the basket. The disciples had twelve baskets with bread, and the multitude was fed.

We can see that the gospel of Jesus was not only spiritual, but also meant to bring material abundance. Jesus' miracles in the Bible can be seen as examples of the wisdom of sharing, for when He fed the five thousand with five loaves and two fish, it taught that scarcity of resources isn't a problem if people share. The story shows the importance of equal economic justice, showing that if everyone is willing to do so, five loaves and two fish would be sufficient for everyone.

A sense of giving to the poor is essential in Christian economic thought. Giving, for Christians, is about redemption for the poor. In the Gospel of Luke, Jesus says again:

> Then said he also to him that bade him, When thou makest a dinner or a supper, call not thy friends, nor thy brethren, neither thy kinsmen, nor thy rich neighbors; lest they also bid thee again, and a recompence be made thee. (*King James Bible*, 1769/2017, Luke 14:12)

> But when thou makest a feast, call the poor, the maimed, the lame, the blind.... (*King James Bible*, 1769/2017, Luke 14:13)

These two sentences show Jesus' care for the poor, and his opposition to self-interest in relationships.

Giving asks for nothing in return, yet it can still bless the giver. Giving to the poor may not bring anything back, but it can be incredibly fulfilling.

In the Gospel of John, Lazarus, a poor man, suffered and died, yet Jesus resurrected him, and even had him sit beside Him at the honor-laden feast. Jesus set a model by inviting the weak and lowly to the banquet, offering them equal life dignity.

Christ's Concern with Both Matter and Mind

The salvation of Jesus has always been material and spiritual. His gospel is for disciples and the world to strive for God's faith.

Christianity is not opposed to material wealth, but insists it should be used for God's glory. Christ provided material support for His disciples as follows.

> Therefore, I say unto you, Take no thought for your life, what ye shall eat, or what ye shall drink; nor yet for your body, what ye shall put on. Is not the life more than meat, and the body than raiment? (*King James Bible*, 1769/2017, Matthew 6:25)

> Behold the fowls of the air: for they sow not, neither do they reap, nor gather into barns; yet your Heavenly Father feedeth them. Are ye not much better than they? (*King James Bible*, 1769/2017, Matthew 6:26)

The central teachings of Jesus are not to be distracted by material things, but to live for the sake of life.

Jesus believed mind to be more important than matter, as taught in the New Testament.

Jesus did not reject the material; instead, he encouraged his followers to trust that God would bless them if they put their faith in God, particularly to guard them from a lack of material.

Jesus wanted His disciples to trust the Lord with their hearts, be spiritual, and answer God's call to be righteous.

Christ did not want people to live in wealth and forget their faith. Instead, they should, through faith, gain wealth in the hands of God.

> And Jesus looked round about, and saith unto his disciples, "How hardly shall they that have riches enter into the kingdom of God!" (*King James Bible*, 1769/2017, Mark 10:23)

This portrays people as wealthy but without faith in what God taught them. What He taught them was to love their neighbors and all humans since to not love others is not to love God.

The Affluent People's Extended Love for Humanity

Thou shalt love thy neighbor as thyself (*King James Bible*, 1769/2017, Matthew 22:39) is an important part of the Christian economic thought. Christ's economic thinking is altruistic, as Jesus said:

> Look not every man on his things, but every man also on the things of others. (*King James Bible*, 1769/2017, Philippians 2:4)

In the eyes of Jesus, loving one's neighbor is as important as loving God. Both acts of affection demonstrate faith and obedience. Loving both God and neighbor is to love all humanity, which reflects true devotion to God.

It can be seen that Christ's economic views are to first give benefits to others, to love one's neighbor, and to give benefits to humanity. This spirit is similar to the Buddhist concept of benefiting all sentient beings and making a vow to not become a Buddha until all beings are saved. As Master Cheng Yen, the founder of Tzu Chi, said, "Bodhisattvas save others before themselves."

Protestant entrepreneurs, who, upon success, engage in charitable work for the benefit of others, exemplify a Christ-like attitude.

The Christian ethic, as Weber elaborated it, is to bring glory to God by extending their cause while humbling themselves and obeying God's law.

Many Western entrepreneurs are frugal, such as the president of IKEA who wears second-hand clothes and flies economy class. His dedication to charity is a demonstration of the Christian entrepreneurship which glorifies God through individual accomplishments and loves one's neighbor as oneself.

Warren Buffett, who is America's stock king and one of the world's wealthiest men, lives a frugal life. He jokingly refers to his daily spending as six dollars a day when stocks are up and three dollars a day when stocks are down. He eats burgers and drinks Cokes. He has over a hundred billion dollars in his eighties, but remains as frugal as ever.

Besides his wealth, Bill Gates is also renowned for his philanthropy, which focuses on providing medical assistance. In partnership with Rotary International, he has nearly eradicated the polio virus globally.

To love more people after a successful, wealthy career manifests Christian love; this is a model of Western Christian entrepreneurship.

To live in Christ is the Christian ideal of entrepreneurship.

Interest and Economic Equality

In the *Old Testament*, God forbids people from charging interest on loans to their brethren, as discussed in the Jewish economic thought. This is expressly stated in Exodus:

If thou lend money to any of my people that is poor by thee, thou shalt not be to him as a usurer, neither shalt thou lay upon him usury. (*King James Bible*, 1769/2017, Exodus 22:25)

If thou at all take thy neighbor's raiment to pledge, thou shalt deliver it unto him by that the sun goeth down.... (*King James Bible*, 1769/2017, Exodus 22:26)

Interest leads to poverty and poverty to slavery, extreme human commercialization, and Christianity's greatest economic injustice. Therefore, God overthrew the King of Egypt and liberated His people from slavery.

Interest is a financial accumulation and exchange that stirs up yearning, leading to moral deterioration and critical social problems such as wealth disparities.

The *Old Testament* mentioned remission of interest for brethren, but did not address it for all debtors. Charging interest for Gentiles was common in the Jewish world, however for Jesus Christ, Gentiles were neighbors, as well. Paul argued that those who adhere to God's law can be called just Christians, which took Christianity worldwide and away from tribes' deities. Jesus declared:

But I say unto you, Love your enemies, bless them that curse you, do good to them that hate you, and pray for them which despitefully use you, and persecute you; (*King James Bible*, 1769/2017, Matthew 5:44) that ye may be the children of your Father which is in Heaven: for he maketh his sun to rise on the evil and the good, and sendeth rain on the just and on the unjust. (*King James Bible*, 1769/2017, Matthew 5:45) For if ye love them which love you, what reward have ye? Do not even the publicans the same? And if ye salute your brethren only, what do ye more than others? Do not even the publicans so? (*King James Bible*, 1769/2017, Matthew 5:46–47)

Jesus expanded the love for brothers to all humanity, even enemies and Gentiles. Paul also advocated universal justice for believers in God. This is a broad and cosmopolitan religious outlook.

The early apostles of Jesus Christ such as Peter and Paul lived a frugal life of bread, water, and one garment. They did not receive money from believers, rather gave away their possessions. This is an act of loving one's neighbors and all and living in Christ.

By the fourth century AD, when the Roman regime stopped persecuting Christians, Constantine the Great declared Christianity the state religion, Churches were then established and Priests began to own property.

During the Patristic era, a church father's life was frugal, and their focus was on the faithful, their faith, and God rather than on economic matters. Though interest and usury were both widespread then, church fathers believed these activities were against God's and Jesus' will, yet they had no power to oppose it.

Christian churches during that period focused on people's relationship with God rather than on the structural problems of society. To address the economic inequality, they carried out charitable deeds in an attempt to bridge the divide between rich and poor, but they did not delve into structural inequality until the Renaissance.

The Goodness in the Christian Economy

The Goodness in the Christian Economy can be summed up in a few points, of which the foremost is: "Don't worry about material things".

As Jesus said, "Don't worry about tomorrow; there is tomorrow's worry." As stated before, birds do not labor nor store up provisions; yet God feeds them. Are humans not as valued as birds?

Jesus wanted the disciples to focus on faith in God and spiritual growth, not on material gain. To Jesus, living in the faith of God brings freedom from material hardship.

Faith comes first and materials will follow. This is the core of the Christian economy.

By believing in God's commandments with all your heart, material abundance is sure to come. As the *Book of Proverbs* states:

> Trust in the LORD with all thine heart; and lean not unto thine own understanding. In all thy ways acknowledge him, and he shall direct thy paths. (*King James Bible*, 1769/2017, Proverbs 3:5–6)

Being carefree is the most difficult thing for modern people. Not the troubled, but the successful ones are the ones who worry the most. They create plans to grow their businesses, and they monitor their competitors' movements each day. Extreme stress and anxiety is a sign of our present-day economic life.

Modern social-economic life is full of plans, competition, and interests. People who succeed live with anxiety every day, leading to psychological issues and addictions. It seems that Jesus' teaching about not worrying about physical things is a distant memory.

In his case study of the Buddhist Tzu Chi Foundation's global success, Professor Herman B. "Dutch" Leonard of Harvard University concluded that the organization operates based on values and faith, rather than planning.

This value-based economy revolves around inner convictions and differs from the traditional economy. Subsequently, we explore the differences in economic views and results between the two.

Another concept in Christian economics is hospitality and altruistic caregiving to one's neighbors and humanity.

This thinking is the main teaching in the gospel of Christ. Giving selflessly seems quite strange compared to modern economic theory which is based on competition, self-interest, fulfilling desires without limits, and disregarding spirituality and love. Even worse, this is widely accepted as good and as a public value. Whoever takes more is seen as successful, not whoever gives more. This goes against Christian economic thought.

Christ's economic thought is to accept, give, and selflessly aid all in need.

The Bible teaches us to invite the poor, the crippled, and the widowed to our homes, to give to our neighbors, and to all people, in an effort to bring our society to abundance. However, slavery—whether ancient and cruel or modern and commercial—runs contrary to the economic teachings of Christ. In contrast, the economic justice of equal wealth is the highest form of goodness within the Christian economy.

Christ's economic teaching is rooted in mercy for all humans, including family, brethren, neighbors, Gentiles, and even enemies.

Can we be merciful to our business competitors?

This is a common practice in economic activity today; finding legal or illegal ways to beat competitors.

If we show mercy to consumers, we won't permit products that can cause harm to be manufactured.

If we can show mercy to our employees, we will form a family in our workplace rather than exploiting human nature.

If we are merciful to our shareholders, we can use their capital responsibly and conscientiously, fulfilling their trust.

If we show mercy to our competitors, we won't monopolize, undercut prices, or slander them for business gain.

If we show mercy to all God-given things, we will not pollute the environment nor exhaust the earth's resources, but strive to make the earth sustainable.

The acquisition of one's own survival and well-being, with compassion benefiting others, is the Christian economy that unites material and mental.

To achieve equal wealth, free everyone from material worries, and share with others from a place of mutual love is Christ's greatest economic kindness.

Section 3: Economic Thought of Islamic Civilization

The Prophet Muhammad was initially a trader. He traversed the Middle East, taking his family with him on extended trips of forty or fifty days for vacation, where he would spend time in prayer and in silence.

One year, He went on holiday as usual and during days of prayerful silence, He received a revelation from Allah, telling Him to write down His words. Muhammad initially felt conflicted, confused, and his heart ached, but after days of contemplation, He accepted Allah's call and chose to preach.

Muhammad embarked on his mission with great effort. The Arab tribes did not trust him and even sought to capture him; only his wife and nephew Ali had faith in him. The Quran, composed according to divine revelation, was the first written work in classical Arabic. Throughout his life, Muhammad was involved in religion, politics, and warfare. His business acumen focused on God's compassion.

Such business thinking advocated loving one's brothers and helping the vulnerable by Allah's grace, so that nobody would suffer hunger and persecution.

Muslim commercial activity relied on their nomadic lifestyle, with animal husbandry and trade as the dominant activities. Islam advocates integrity in trading, forbidding deceit and profiting from price discrepancies.

Muslims see trading places as holy places of devotion, and everyone had to be truthful when engaging in a transaction. Muslims highly regard the intangible atmosphere of honesty which can be felt immediately. In the eyes of Allah, Muslims must be honest and totally truthful in all their dealings.

Muslim trade is based on mutual agreement between comrades-in-arms. By the sixteenth century, Ottoman sultans offered this "comrades-in-arms covenant" to Christians, Jews, and all foreign peoples. Vienna, Venice, France, and so on were included in the "Ottoman trade comrades-in-arms letter."

Such a covenant was not expressed in a fixed written form, but upheld through an unspoken pact guaranteeing honesty and mutual advantage, which proved more stable than a human agreement.

In addition to honesty and mutual trust, Muslim economic thinking reflects the teachings of the Koran, which emphasize that Muslims should not pursue their own greatest interests, but take into account the needs of the disadvantaged.

According to the Koran, Muslims must share their wealth and provide warmth and sustenance to the needy. In its glory days during the sixteenth century, when Western Capitalism was emerging, the Ottoman Empire maintained that the Muslim economy must not chase profits indiscriminately, but should be primarily focused on farming and ensuring stability for their people. All economic activities must be tied to a system where Islamic teachings take precedence.

M. al Mabarak, a Muslim sage, asserted that the Muslim economy is an objective, not a means. Its aim is to sustain the destitute and those in hardship, and engender contentment for future generations.

The Ottoman Turkish Empire in the sixteenth century was more economically powerful than the West. Western societies mobilized several forces for expeditions in pursuit of economic benefits worldwide. Despite the risks of financial loss and casualties, the reward was great. Capital provided substantial support and profit for these seafaring ventures, preceding the birth of Capitalism.

At this juncture, the Ottoman economy was reoriented toward agriculture instead of capital growth, refusing to partake in capital transactions. This adherence resulted in Muslim countries being supplanted by the West in terms of future world economy and politics.

Despite this, the Ottoman economy continued to grow and the difference between rich and poor remained minimal. Charitable institutions maintained the subsistence of the less fortunate, and Muslims, such as Mabarak, believed charity was pleasing to Allah, as it was expected of His followers.

The Ottoman Empire's economic power stemmed from the Sultan and his regime, who were responsible for redistributing agricultural harvests.

When Western Capitalism was in its infancy, autonomous commercial forces began to assert themselves and even organized chambers of commerce to negotiate taxes with kings. For example, King John of England worked out the Magna Carta with commercial bodies regarding taxation in war. While Western commerce spread rapidly across the world, the Muslim Ottoman Empire remained devoted to the Koran's teachings of not only pursuing one's own interests but also ensuring social order and harmony. The kingship governing commerce answered this holy mandate.

At that time, the market, salaries, and profits held a religious significance since the Sultan, who was in charge of both religion and politics, determined economic distribution. This economy was not based on free trade, as in the West, but was instead based on religious and governmental justice.

The supreme idea of a successful Muslim economy was to return all to the worship of Allah, making the world a unified place and eliminating inequality between the wealthy and the destitute.

The Muslim economy, at its peak in Istanbul, remained largely in the hands of the monarchy and government. As religion was nationalized, so too was business.

The Koran's teachings forbid Muslims to charge interest on loans, so that in the Middle Ages—when commerce was booming—no banking or lending institutions existed in Muslim regions. Instead, loans with interest were common among acquainted relatives or friends, being mainly short-term and in small amounts, intended for consumption rather than business investments.

Court records from the fourteenth to sixteenth centuries show that Muslim courts handled disputes over loans.

The ban on private loans for business investment impeded the global expansion of Muslim businesses. In the fifteenth century, maritime trade flourished in Venice and other Western lowlands, becoming widespread in Europe; however, trade investment in Muslim areas was uncommon.

From the fifteenth to sixteenth centuries, the Ottoman imperial government sourced money from private tycoons for military needs, under the guise of tax cuts. Muslim businesspeople were not as wealthy as their Western European counterparts, so they were unable to exert or temper government policies or bargain for lower taxes. The growth of the Chamber of Commerce saw the birth of Capitalism in the West, but the Muslim Ottoman Empire did not have a similar driving force in commerce.

Muslim businesses extended to countries in the Ottoman Empire, such as Egypt, Syria, Iran, and Turkey. Compared to the corporate system in Western European nations, Muslim businesses enabled free private partnerships (corporations) to trade internationally. These partnerships disregarded national borders and became a major driving force in the growth of Capitalism.

It is noteworthy that before the Middle Ages, Muslim countries were economically stronger than European countries and merchants were commonly involved in public and governmental affairs. However, in the ninth century, the governing elite began to focus on cultivating military talent, giving it increasing influence over cities. This resulted in the concentration of power among military and urban elite and commercial forces had to continue to operate without the same capacity to participate in politics as before.

In losing its commercial power, the Ottoman Empire disregarded the burgeoning Capitalism of Western European countries, which expanded their military power globally. This ultimately resulted in the fall of the Ottoman Empire.

From the sixteenth to the early nineteenth centuries, the Ottoman Empire's commercial power was eclipsed by the booming capitalist expansion in the West.

I don't claim that the rise of Capitalism brings goodness, nor do I think it was of no benefit for Muslim countries that didn't develop it or traditional farming at the turn of the eighteenth century.

Rather, before the Industrial Revolution, Muslim areas were stable and affluent, with people enjoying a high standard of living and social harmony. This was due to their rejecting usury and prohibiting lending, which suppressed economic exploitation. People didn't speculate, instead focusing on production and trade.

This is a return to the essence of commerce. A balance of manufacturing and consumption prevents the proliferation of vain financial wants and averts commercial domination that can lead to extreme poverty.

Charity, aiding the suffering, banning loans with interests, and reducing economic disparities all contributed to ensuring fairness and prosperity in Muslim communities.

Compared to modern times, Muslim societies from the Middle Ages to the end of the nineteenth century were largely stable without significant political and social upheavals. Trade was still flourishing at this time.

Muslim areas would have been in harmony and justice, had it not been for the spread of Western Capitalism worldwide.

SECTION 4: ECONOMIC THOUGHT AND PRACTICE OF CONFUCIANISM IN CHINA

The Economy of Goodness Is Consistent with the Way of Heaven

The exploration of Confucian economic thought should start with the concept of the Way of Heaven in Confucianism.

The Confucian Way of Heaven denotes the supreme truth of the universe, and its embodiment in the world is benevolence, implemented through propriety.[2]

Duke Lu of Lu State asked Confucius, "I venture to ask what it is that the superior man values in the way of Heaven." Confucius replied:

> He values its unceasingness. There is, for instance, the succession and sequence of the sun and moon from the east and west - that is the way of Heaven. There is the long continuance of its progress without interruption - that is the way of Heaven. There is its making (all) things complete without doing anything - that is the way of Heaven. There is their brilliancy when they have been completed - that is the way of Heaven.[3]

In the eyes of Confucius, the Way of Heaven is the eternal truth by which all things in the universe operate, without ceasing or pausing, generation upon generation. Confucius said, "Does Heaven speak? The four seasons pursue their courses, and all things are continually being produced, but does Heaven say anything?"[4] The Way of Heaven has no words, no forms, but it gives birth to all things and the same virtue should be true of the gentleman. "The superior man does not, even for the space of a single

---

[2] Propriety in Chinese, pronounced Li (禮); its definition denotes treating with respect and courtesy.

[3] Confucius. (2013). *The Book of Rites (Li Ji): English-Chinese Version* (D. Sheng, Ed., J. Legge, Trans.). CreateSpace Independent Publishing Platform. p. 242.

[4] Legge, J. (1971). *Confucian Analects: The Great Learning, and The Doctrine of the Mean*. New York: Dover Publications. p. 326.

meal, act contrary to virtue. In moments of haste, he cleaves to it. In seasons of danger, he cleaves to it."[5]

The gentleman always lives in truth and aligns with the way of Heaven.

The Way of Heaven is like the sun and moon's alternating from east to west; it implies that everyone should do their part and mutually respect each other. Monarchs, courtiers, fathers, and sons must all respect and assist one another.

The enduring progress of Heaven shows it does not hinder the development of any being. Rather, it fosters their growth, so gentlemen should be indefatigable in instruction.

An emperor should take the Way of Heaven to educate their people tirelessly. An emperor is a leader, so is the head of a company, an institute, or an NGO. They could all love and enlighten their colleagues, so the latter will devote themselves to their organization. To learn the Way of Heaven, one must know the long continuance of its progress without interruption.

The Way of Heaven looks after people silently and invisibly, with nothing required of them to achieve completion.[6]

The Way of Heaven in the economy of goodness reveals life's potential. The countless creations in economic life must remain unceasing. People should therefore live and labor peacefully and joyfully with the right forces invisibly creating suitable conditions for the same. This is the art of making all things complete without action.

The implementation of Confucius' Way of Heaven shaped a peaceful agrarian lifestyle in ancient China. During the chaotic Warring Period, when Confucius lived, all people yearned for was tranquility and a carefree life, with authorities far away.

In today's society, Confucius' Way of Heaven implies an Economy of Goodness where nothing needs to be done in order for things to be completed. Leaders must nurture creativity and responsibility in their peers, learning and developing without any sense of suppression, while working toward organizational and social ideals.

---

[5] Legge, J. (1971). *Confucian Analects: The Great Learning, and The Doctrine of the Mean*. New York: Dover Publications. p. 166.

[6] In both Taoism and Confucianism, it is believed that true leaders should not overpower and dominate people, but rather support and nurture them to enable self-sufficiency. This is the wisdom of attaining everything by doing nothing.

What it has achieved will be made known. Heaven's Way nurtures all creatures and leads to completion. This is the manifestation of Heaven's Way.

When gentlemen achieved their goal in governing the country and ensuring a peaceful, prosperous life for all, they set great causes and role models for future generations.

The Justification of Personal Desire

Confucius considered Guan Zhong[7] an exceptionally capable ruler of the country in the Spring and Autumn Period (770 to 403 BCE). He once said, "But for Guan Zhong, we should now be wearing our hair unbound, and the lappets of our coats buttoning on the left side."[8] Had it not been for Guan Zhong, barbarians would have ruled the Central Plains and there would have been no continuation of the Central Plains civilizations. Guan Zhong had extensive experience in both business and politics; he was successful in both.

Guan Zhong's economic philosophy is akin to Lao Tzu's "Do nothing (of purpose), and the people will be transformed of themselves"[9] and Confucius' "Without any effort, it accomplishes its ends."[10] Its premise is to lead the people with benefits, without disturbance or vexation, enabling the populace to be self-sufficient and create a wonderful way of life.

Guan Zhong observed that the inclination of ordinary individuals is to gravitate toward profit and avoid harm whenever possible. Merchants, adept at trade, traverse various paths tirelessly, even through the night, covering vast distances without fatigue, driven by the prospect of profit. Similarly, fishermen brave the perilous depths of the ocean, navigating contrary currents and enduring hazardous conditions, because the potential for profit lies within the water. Thus, wherever there is opportunity for gain, be it atop towering mountains or in the deepest abysses, people

---

[7] Guan Zhong was a great prime minister for the Qi State in the Spring and Autumn Periods of ancient China. (725–645 BCE).

[8] Legge, J. (1971). *Confucian Analects: The Great Learning, and The Doctrine of the Mean.* New York: Dover Publications. p. 282.

[9] Tzu, L. (Eds.). (2021). *Tao Te Ching* (J. Legge, Trans.). Standard Ebooks. Retrieved from https://standardebooks.org/ebooks/laozi/tao-te-ching/james-legge.

[10] Confucius. (2013). *The Book of Rites (Li Ji): English-Chinese Version* (D. Sheng, Ed., J. Legge, Trans.). CreateSpace Independent Publishing Platform. p. 262.

will pursue it relentlessly. Consequently, those who possess skill naturally seek out avenues for profit, leading to a sense of security and contentment among the populace. People are not coerced or compelled but willingly engage, undisturbed and untroubled, resulting in their prosperity. This can be likened to a bird hatching its eggs, and without too much stirring, the fledglings could emerge.[11]

Guan Zhong advocated creating favorable conditions to guide people in pursuing their own interests. He saw the best policy for governors as one of non-interference.

This implies deregulation of policy-making, allowing private sectors to develop independently. Additionally, entrepreneurs should grant more freedom to employees, leading to individual and collective satisfaction derived from self-realization.

Over two thousand years ago, Guan Zhong painted a vision of abundant, stable, and free living—an ideal model of the Economy of Goodness.

Erasing any signs of selfishness and self-interest, Guan Zhong sought ways to use people's self-interest for the good of both individuals and societies, creating a peaceful existence.

Confucius agreed with personal desire but stressed wealth combined with propriety. Confucius said, "Riches and Noble are what men desire. If it cannot be obtained in the proper way, they should not be held."[12]

The industrialist should start as a gentleman who can cultivate his desires in harmony with Tao, which follows the rules of "beginning with desires and yet complying with Propriety," first as a gentleman and then as a businessman of wealth.

Xunzi (316–235 BCE) asserts that while wealth and status are desirable, they must be acquired through ethical means. His ultimate vision of wealth is to possess abundance without causing resentment through its acquisition, and to generously distribute wealth without fearing impoverishment.[13]

---

[11] Tang, X. C. (1995). *Xin yi guanzi duben (xia)* [New Translation of The Book of Zhuangzi (Vol. 2)]. Taipei: Sanmin shuju. p. 894.

[12] Legge, J. (1971). *Confucian Analects: The Great Learning, and The Doctrine of the Mean.* New York: Dover Publications. p. 166.

[13] Wang, X. Q. (1994). *Xunzi ji jie* [Collected Annotations of Xunzi]. Shandong: Shandong Friendship Publishing House. pp. 853–854.

It is a sign of benevolence that there is wealth in the world, and all rejoice in it. Giving to the world with no loss is an expression of justice. The more altruistic one is, the more they gain self-interest. So, there is no need to fear aiding others.

The Enterprise Rooted in Virtues

Confucius expected the wealthy and powerful to behave like gentlemen, adhering to etiquette, while also weighing the good and bad of the family and nation.

Confucius said, "When a country is well governed, poverty and a mean condition are things to be ashamed of. When a country is ill governed, riches and noble are things to be ashamed of."[14]

The wealthy should take the state's growth as their own duty; otherwise, it is disgraceful to recline in riches.

Confucianism maintains that successful businessmen should be concerned with the prosperity of their nation, not just their personal ambitions. Thus, it is considered unjust and dishonorable to be wealthy when the nation and its people are suffering.

It can be seen that in Confucianism, businessmen are expected to carry out enterprises with virtues. Confucius said, "The superior man, in the world, does not set his mind either for anything, or against anything; what is right he will follow."[15]

It is a Confucian ideal for men of virtue to choose justice over profit.

In Confucianism, a man of virtue will maintain justice despite external changes. Confucius subscribed to the affluence of individuals and nations. "Ran You asked Confucius, 'Since they are thus numerous, what more shall be done for them?' 'Enrich them,' was the reply. 'And when they have been enriched, what more shall be done?' The Master said, 'Teach them.'"[16]

Confucius did not only expect everyone to be well-fed, but to also be well-off. After abundance comes teaching propriety and righteousness.

---

[14] Legge, J. (1971). *Confucian Analects: The Great Learning, and The Doctrine of the Mean*. New York: Dover Publications. p. 212.

[15] Legge, J. (1971). *Confucian Analects: The Great Learning, and The Doctrine of the Mean*. New York: Dover Publications. p. 168.

[16] Confucius. & Legge, J. (2010). *Chinese Classics: Confucian Analects*. General Books (Original work published 1861).

Merchants who abide by "rituals and righteousness" is the Confucian economy ideal.

The Economic Thought of the King's Way

After Dong Zhongshu in the Han Dynasty established Confucianism as the ruling ideology, it became the most influential value and regime in Chinese history. Confucian classics were used as criteria for scholar evaluations, while rulers and state officials exercised power according to Confucian principles.

Confucianism, after being politicized, gives priority to Confucian scholars and farming to build a state. Despite merchants possessing considerable clout in the social order, they are not given any real esteem. The ranking system puts scholars, farmers, industry, and merchants at the bottom.

The primary characteristic of Confucian political rule is how it ensures the stability and prosperity of a dynasty. According to Confucianism, "Heaven sees according as my people see; Heaven hears according as my people hear."[17] The continuation of royal governance relies on the prosperity of the people's lives. Since the people's livelihoods are primarily based on agriculture, the vitality of agriculture depends on both the land and the weather. While land represents a fundamental and controllable economic resource, the unpredictability of weather necessitates that the ruler adheres to the King's Way (王道 Wangdao refers to the way of a benevolent and just ruler), which is in accordance with the Way of Heaven. Hence, both the monarch and his court officials must show reverence, fear, and perform ceremonies to honor Heaven.[18]

The Economy of Goodness and China's Historical Cycle of Governing Social Chaos

In ancient China, commercial prosperity, and especially the acquisition of land and charging interest, had an impact on agrarian society. During times of famine, farmers would have to borrow money and be charged

---

[17] M. & Legge, J. (2011). *The Works of Mencius*. New York: Dover Publications. p. 357.

[18] Qu. W. L. (1983). *Shangshu ji shi* [The Collected Commentaries of the Shang Shu]. Taiwan: Linking Publishing Co., Ltd. p. 320.

interest by businessmen, officials, and wealthy peasants. Interest was a major factor in poverty, so China prioritized agriculture and tried to minimize commercial activities, seeing money transactions as a threat.

The dynasties did not obstruct trade, however, expansion of land and money interests usually caused people to be displaced, thereby disrupting social stability.

In reality, Confucian politics held that, once Confucian scholars became officials and were granted land, they would become landlords and collect rents, having farmers produce for them. When production dropped, farmers could no longer pay rent or bring harvests on time, so they had to borrow money, often leading to poverty due to interest payments.

The proportion of land owned by farmers was fixed; the harvest stayed the same. A father would divide his land among several sons, each receiving a much smaller share than what their father had. Production was still the same for each "mu"[19] of land, meaning without any revolutionary advances in agriculture, the farmers' incomes would unavoidably decrease from one generation to the next. This was an inevitability.[20]

A study by Roman H. Myers of Harvard University revealed that a triangular relationship between farmers, merchants, and the government had a long-term impact on the deprivation and marginalization of Chinese farmers in traditional societies.

Myers noted that farmers without a spring harvest would have to borrow from affluent entrepreneurs, leading to substantial debt if they failed to yield a satisfactory autumn crop.

Despite agricultural technology remaining largely stagnant for millennia, it was still hard to enhance agricultural production. Compounded by heavy taxation and interest on land, farmers suffered under crushing economic pressures and were often forced to sell their land to landlords or wealthy businessmen and instead become tenants. As land in the early years of the dynasty was continually annexed, stability and sustainability were steadily eroded. Peasants, who had been reduced to tenants, earned even lower incomes, with harvest demand going first to the landlords. Economic crises triggered by such events as illness,

---

[19] Mu is equal to 666.6667 m².

[20] Ash, R. (1989). Kang Chao: Man and Land in Chinese History: An Economic Analysis, xii. Stanford: Stanford University Press, 1986. p. 268. *Bulletin of the School of Oriental and African Studies*, 52(2), 386–387.

weddings, and funerals meant these farmers were increasingly plunged into debt and teetered on the edge of destitution.[21]

In a vicious cycle, the inefficiency of tax collection by officials and imperfect taxation mechanisms have caused a rise in the number of officials, termed a tax increase. This has caused taxes to rise and led to structural exploitation of farmers.

In this structural economic cycle, Confucian officials didn't take up farming nor contribute to the development of agricultural technology. Consequently, due to the limited farmland, high taxation and interest rates, Chinese farmers faced a slim chance of improving their situation.

When the emperor of the dynasty gave land to officials, wealthy merchants soon accumulated vast acreages, which they rented out to tenant farmers in return for rent or fixed grain parcels. This situation caused farmers to become lifelong laborers of the rich merchants and officials.

In the Han Dynasty, the burden of corvee labor and taxes often induced bankruptcy in peasants. In turn, wealthy landlords and businessmen seized the opportunity to purchase the land and tenants became their slaves. Over time, the destitute population increased, exposing the dynasty to disintegration.[22]

At the end of the Eastern Han Dynasty, Cao Cao (155–220 CE)[23] seized the remaining Western Han regime and implemented military farming, under which soldiers across the country were ordered to till land when wars were suspended. Cao Cao also controlled land annexation by wealthy businessmen and landlords' power. Xuchang, which was then the capital of Cao Cao's regime, became prosperous. This shows that land and agricultural policies were the key to China's traditional agricultural economy.[24]

[21] Myers, R. H. (1970). *The Chinese Peasant Economy: Agricultural Development in Hopei and Shantung, 1890–1949.* Taiwan: Harvard University Press. pp. 288–289.

[22] Rawson, J. (1984). Han Civilization. By Wang Zhongshu, translated by K. C. Chang and collaborators (Early Chinese Civilization.

[23] Cao was one of the rulers during the Three Kingdoms Era, 184–280 CE.

[24] Rawson, J. (1984). Han Civilization. By Wang Zhongshu, translated by K. C. Chang and collaborators (Early Chinese Civilization.). New Haven and London: Yale University Press, 1982. *The Antiquaries Journal*, 64(2), 430–431.

Before the Tang Dynasty, despite commercial progress, traditional Chinese society did not spur agricultural technology, resulting in no increase in agricultural output. This contributed to the growing divide between the wealthy and the impoverished, due to high taxes and interest rates causing peasants to be forced into labor or extreme poverty.

Many scholars believe that after the tenth century, the development of dry farmland in rural China and the irrigation system of terraced fields brought great innovations to China's agricultural technology and increased agricultural output. From about the eighth century to the twelfth century, during the Southern and Northern Song Dynasties, China's agriculture did make great progress.[25]

However, Wang Anshi's (1021–1086) reforms in the Southern Song Dynasty aimed to tackle shortages of tax revenue in the country and the burden of high taxes on farmers. We may ask: Who benefited from this situation?[26]

In explaining why Capitalism did not emerge in Chinese society, Max Weber theorized that unlike in modern Western countries, ancient China's administration was a parish system, or Prebendal Bureaucracy. Officials had the power to tax people within their own territories, often through monopolizing salt production, levying land taxes, and collecting business taxes, with no set standard for taxation. This made it difficult for the central government to determine the amount of tax income actually received from local governments, leading to an increase in taxation as the number of local officials rose, impoverishing the people in the process.

During Song Shenzong's reign (1048–1085 CE), Wang Anshi's political reform focused on raising government revenue without increasing taxes on the populace. Specific tax collectors were appointed, yet this policy directly contradicted the rights and interests of local governments. In the context of Chinese Confucian societal ties, such a professional taxation system was hard to put into effect.

This is Weber's point that Chinese society's culture impeded Capitalism's growth. Western Capitalism relies on individuals and the rule

---

[25] Smith, P. (2009). Shen-tsung's Reign and the New Policies of Wang An-shih, 1067–1085. D. Twitchett & P. J. Smith (Eds.). *The Cambridge History of China* (pp. 347–483). Cambridge: Cambridge University Press. p. 390.

[26] Smith, P. (2009). Shen-tsung's Reign and the New Policies of Wang An-shih, 1067–1085. D. Twitchett & P. J. Smith (Eds.). *The Cambridge History of China* (pp. 347–483). Cambridge: Cambridge University Press. p. 384.

of law, while Chinese culture is patrilineal. Local officials were termed "father-and-mother" since they acted like parents. Like filial children, people paid taxes to them. Confucian officials had to both protect the common people from distress and be moral role models for them.

However, in reality, more detailed governmental wisdom was required, and this necessitated more officials. Frequently, when officials rose and the financial performance was unsatisfactory, taxes increased but wouldn't be necessarily transmitted to the central government; instead, they wound up in private hands or local governments. Consequently, local governments gradually distanced themselves from the central government. Business-people and local officials for their own benefit amassed taxes and interest, which resulted in more suffering for the common people and eliminated any chances of having a larger capital market economy.

In the seventeenth and eighteenth centuries, China's output and commerce were comparable to the entirety of Europe. Why could China not establish a lasting market economy?

The Confucian system attaches importance to interpersonal relations, such as teacher and student, master and apprentice, clan, and family members, and is key to social stability. Could these be impediments?

Scholars' views differ on this topic. Family and clan, being the engine of Chinese businessmen, have the benefit of not eliciting individual cravings, yet flaws in establishing a large-scale, flexible, and cooperative market economy.

Weber believed that the distinguishing feature of a market economy was that people had the freedom to transact and create firms to engage in international trade, while governments would manage private enterprise according to the law.

Although powerful during the Song and Ming Dynasties in Ancient China, the Chamber of Commerce lacked the strength to withstand imperial power. Some sought family welfare, others pursued land expansion; some collected rents and interest. However, compared to the Confucian bureaucratic system in China, which allowed individuals to attain official positions through the imperial examination system, Chinese merchants throughout the fifteenth and sixteenth centuries were unable to amass sufficient capital or wield political influence as their Western counterparts did. Western merchants during that period were capable of accumulating substantial capital, influencing political power, and extending their economic strength beyond the seas.

In contrast, Western capital markets created individualism and the rule of law that checked and balanced monarchical power. Eventually, a vast global capital market formed; however, this also spurred individual wants, leading to disparity in wealth between the rich and poor and social upheaval.

Rather, this book investigates the economic tenets of Confucian Governance in historical China, in light of its one-of-a-kind geographical, historical, and cultural features, and how the highest moral standard was theorized and implemented in this thought.

The Economy of Goodness Is Rooted in Prosperity and Harmony and the Shared Responsibility of Government and the Public

An economic system focused on family prosperity should function best under the Confucian system.

Wealth in line with benevolence is what Confucianism holds in highest esteem. The writings of Mencius documented his ideas on benevolence and wealth.

"Yang Hu said that he who seeks to be rich will not be benevolent. He who wishes to be benevolent will not be rich."[27] Yang Hu, and Yang Huo, were a vassal of the Ji Family in the Lu State. Seeing natural laws incompatible with human desires, Yang Hu expressed his concern that being humane might harm being wealthy.

Mencius quoted Yang Hu, expressing his worry that wealth could hinder being moral. The man of virtue and the one of malice always embody divergence.

The sovereign of the Xia dynasty (2010–1600 BCE) enacted the fifty mu[28] allotment, and the payment of a tax. The founder of the Yin Dynasty (1600–1046 BCE) enacted the seventy mu allotment, and the system of mutual aid. The founder of the Zhou Dynasty (1047–771 BCE) enacted the hundred mu allotment and the share system. What was paid in all these was a tithe. The share system means mutual division. The aid system means mutual dependence.[29]

---

[27] M. & Legge, J. (2011). *The Works of Mencius*. New York: Dover Publications. p. 240.

[28] A mu was a measure of land in ancient China, equal to 666.7 square meters or 1/15 of a hectare.

[29] M. & Legge, J. (2011). *The Works of Mencius*. New York: Dover Publications. pp. 240–241.

The three dynasties levied a 10% tax. Government officials could not lower this during hard times, which would provoke public anger.

Therefore, Mencius lamented that the government's taxes were so oppressive that people could not provide for their parents.

> In good years, when the grain lies about in abundance, much might be taken without its being oppressive, and the actual exaction would be small. But in bad years, the produce being not sufficient to repay the manuring of the fields, this system still requires the taking of the full amount. When the parent of the people causes the people to wear looks of distress, and, after the whole year's toil, yet not to be able to nourish their parents, so that they proceed to borrowing to increase their means, till the old people and children are found lying in the ditches and water-channels: —— where, *in such a case*, is his parental relation to the people?[30]

Mencius viewed the well-field system of the Xia, Shang, and Zhou Dynasties favorably, wherein eight hundred acres were allotted to individuals and one hundred acres devoted to land held in common by joint efforts.

The well-field system in ancient China represented an economy of goodness that emphasized balance and harmony between individuals and groups.

> A square li covers nine squares of land, which nine squares contain nine hundred mu. The central square is the public field, and eight families, each having its private hundred mu, cultivate in common the public field. And not till the public work is finished, may they presume to attend to their private affairs. This is the way by which country-men are distinguished from those of a superior grade. Those are the great outlines of the system. Happily to modify and adapt it depends on the king and you.[31]

Mencius believed that emperors were obligated to explicitly define the boundaries of land and property to avoid officials taking advantage and causing public discontent. Mencius said:

> Since your king, wishing to put in practice a benevolent government, has made choice of you and put you into this employment, you must

---

[30] M. & Legge, J. (2011). *The Works of Mencius.* New York: Dover Publications. pp. 241–242.

[31] M. & Legge, J. (2011). *The Works of Mencius.* New York: Dover Publications. p. 245.

exert yourself to the utmost. Now, the first thing towards a benevolent government must be to lay down the boundaries. If the boundaries be not defined correctly, the division of land into squares will not be equal, and the produce available for salaries will not be evenly distributed. On this account, oppressive rulers and impure ministers are sure to neglect this defining of the boundaries. When the boundaries have been defined correctly, the division of the fields and the regulation of allowances may be determined by you, sitting at your ease. Although the territory of Teng is narrow and small, yet there must be in it men of a superior grade, and there must be in it country-men. If there were not men of a superior grade, there would be none to rule the country-men. If there were not country-men, there would be none to support the men of superior grade. I would ask you, in the remoter districts, observing the nine-squares division, to reserve one division to be cultivated on the system of mutual aid, and in the more central parts of the kingdom, to make the people pay for themselves a tenth part of their produce.[32]

Mencius believed officials, aside from their salaries, should get a maximum of fifty mu, similar to the quantity regular people held.

From the highest officers down to the lowest, each one must have his holy field, consisting of fifty mu. Let the supernumerary males have their twenty-five mu. On occasions of death, or removal from one dwelling to another, there will be no quitting the district. In the fields of a district, those who belong to the same nine squares render all friendly offices to one another in their going out and coming in, aid one another in keeping watch and ward, and sustain one another in sickness. Thus, the people are brought to live in affection and harmony.[33]

In the well-field system, people could lead a life of joy and unity, supporting each other. This was an ideal agricultural life in ancient China.

In this system, the well-being of ordinary people and the peaks of officials were secured, and the needs of the regime were fulfilled as well.

This is a central expression of the Confucian economic ideal: people equally participate in public and private life, officials and the masses are interdependent, and neighbors help each other. All this creates an ideal world of economic goodness and harmony.

---

[32] M. & Legge, J. (2011). *The Works of Mencius*. New York: Dover Publications. pp. 243–244.

[33] M. & Legge, J. (2011). *The Works of Mencius*. New York: Dover Publications. p. 245.

The Economy of Goodness with Virtue-Based Governance

By today's standards, Mencius' stance on business and technology reveals he was against professionalism.

In response to Chen Xiang's view of Xu Xing, Mencius thought that the agriculturalist and thinker—who cultivated his land, wove his own clothes, and had many followers—was not a suitable model for Confucian scholars.

Chen Shan concurred with Xu Xing's opinion on kingship; that a king must be accomplished in both leadership and cooking to lead the nation. A dialogue between Mencius and Xu Xing was recorded as follows:

> Having an interview with Mencius, Chen Shan related to him with approbation the words of Xu Xing to the following effect: The prince of Teng is indeed a worthy king. He has not yet heard, however, the real doctrines of antiquity. Now, wise and able kings should cultivate the ground equally and along with their people, and eat the fruit of their labor. They should prepare their own meals, morning and evening, while at the same time they carry on their government. But now, the king of Tang has his granaries, treasuries, and arsenals, which is an oppressing of the people to nourish himself. How can he be deemed a real worthy king?[34]

Mencius: "I suppose that Xu Xing sows grain and eats the produce. Is it not so?"
Chen: "It is so."
Mencius: "I suppose also he weaves cloth and wears his own manufacture. Is it not so?"
Chen: "No. Xu wears clothes of haircloth."
Mencius: "Does he wear a cap?"
Chen: "He wears a cap."
Mencius: "What kind of cap?"
Chen: "A plain cap."
Mencius: "Is it woven by himself?"
Chen: "No. He gets it in exchange for grain."
Mencius: "Why does Xu not weave it himself?"
Chen: "That would injure his husbandry."
Mencius: "Does Xu cook his food in boilers and earthenware pans, and does he plough with an iron share?"

[34] M. & Legge, J. (2011). *The Works of Mencius*. New York: Dover Publications. p. 247.

Chen: "Yes."
Mencius: "Does he make those articles himself?"
Chen: "No. He gets them in exchange for grain."[35]

Mencius refuted Xu Xing's life philosophy of self-farming and self-reliance by arguing that Xu could not weave his own clothes or make his own utensils. Mencius then stated:

> The getting those various articles in exchange for grain, is not oppressive to the potter and the founder, and the potter and the founder in their turn, in exchanging their various articles for grain, are not oppressive to the husbandman. How should such a thing be supposed? And moreover, why does not Xu act the potter and founder, supplying himself with the articles which he uses solely from his establishment? Why does he go confusedly dealing and exchanging with the handicraftsmen? Why does he not spare himself so much trouble?[36]

> Chen Xiang replied, "The business of the handicraftsman can by no means be carried on along with the business of husbandry."[37]

Mencius resumed:

> Then, is it the government of the kingdom which alone can be carried on along with the practice of husbandry? Great men have their proper business, and little men have their proper business. Moreover, in the case of any single individual, whatever articles he can require are ready to his hand, being produced by the various handicraftsmen. If he must first make them for his own use, this way of doing would keep all the people running about upon the roads. Hence, there is the saying, Some labor with their minds, and some labor with their strength. Those who labor with their minds govern others; those who labor with their strength are governed by others. Those who are governed by others support them; those who govern others are supported by them. This is a universally recognized principle.[38]

[35] M. & Legge, J. (2011). *The Works of Mencius*. New York: Dover Publications. pp. 247–248.

[36] M. & Legge, J. (2011). *The Works of Mencius*. New York: Dover Publications. pp. 248–249.

[37] M. & Legge, J. (2011). *The Works of Mencius*. New York: Dover Publications. p. 249.

[38] M. & Legge, J. (2011). *The Works of Mencius*. New York: Dover Publications. pp. 249–250.

Mencius argued that a Confucian should govern others, not do everything themselves. Cultivating professional skill, wisdom, and virtue in leadership was how one could best be a king or Confucian. Mental or physical labor distinguishes social status and determines who is governing and being governed.

This prevented Confucians from giving significant importance to pioneering technology in ancient China. In comparison to today's professional attitude where technology has the foremost priority, Mencius underscored the need for virtue and wisdom in government affairs, whereas professional expertise was second to that. He further added:

In the time of Yao, when the world had not yet been perfectly reduced to order, the vast waters, flowing out of their channels made a universal inundation. Vegetation was luxuriant, and birds and beasts swarmed. The various kinds of grain could not be grown. The birds and beasts pressed upon men. The Paths marked by the feet of beasts and prints of birds crossed one another throughout the Middle Kingdom. To Yao alone, this caused anxious sorrow.[39]

He raised Shun to office, and measures to regulate the disorder were set forth. Shun committed to Yi the direction of the fire to be employed, and Yi set fire to and consumed, the forests and vegetation in the mountains and in the marshes so that the birds and beasts fled away to hide themselves.[40]

"Yu separated the nine streams, cleared the courses of the Ji and Ta, and led them all to the sea. He also opened a vent for the Ru and Han and regulated the system of the Huai and Si so they all flowed into the Jiang. When this was done, it became possible for the people of the Middle Kingdom to cultivate the ground and get food for themselves. During that time, Yu was eight years away from his home, and though he thrice passed the door, he did not enter. Although he had wished to cultivate the ground, could he have done so?"[41]

The Minister of Agriculture taught the people to sow and reap, cultivating the five kinds of grain. When the five types of grain were brought to maturity, the people all obtained subsistence. But men possess a moral

[39] M. & Legge, J. (2011). *The Works of Mencius*. New York: Dover Publications. p. 250.

[40] M. & Legge, J. (2011). *The Works of Mencius*. New York: Dover Publications. p. 250.

[41] M. & Legge, J. (2011). *The Works of Mencius*. New York: Dover Publications. pp. 250–251.

nature, and if they are well-fed, warmly clad, and comfortably lodged, without being taught at the same time, they become almost like the beasts. This was a subject of anxious solicitude to the sage Shun, and he appointed Xie to be the Minister of Instruction to teach the relations of humanity: how, between father and son, there should be affection; between sovereign and minister, righteousness; between husband and wife, attention to their separate functions; between old and young, a proper order; and between friends, fidelity. The highly meritorious sovereign said to him, encourage them; lead them on; rectify them; straighten them; help them; give them wings—thus causing them to become possessors of themselves. Then follow this up by stimulating them, and conferring benefits on them. When the sages were exercising their solicitude for the people in this way, had they leisure to cultivate the ground?[42]

What Yao felt giving him anxiety was not appointing Shun. What Shun felt giving him anxiety about was not appointing Yu and Gao Yao. But he whose anxiety is about his hundred mu not being properly cultivated is a mere husbandman. The imparting by a man to others of his wealth is called kindness. The teaching others what is good, is called the exercise of fidelity. The finding of a man who shall benefit the kingdom, is called benevolence. Hence to give the throne to another man would be easy; to find a man who shall benefit the kingdom is difficult.[43]

A governor should know how to place people in proper positions. For instance, Emperor Yao abdicated his kingship and handed it over to Shun, who handed it over again to Yu. Yu did not enter his home for eight years in order to control the flood. Farming and labor were small things for the king; the most important was to teach people virtue and propriety and equip them with ethics as depicted between father and son; there should be affection; between sovereign and minister, righteousness; between husband and wife, attention to their separate functions; between old and young, a proper order; and between friends, fidelity.[44]

The sage directs their attention to the people's knowledge and ceremony; so, how can they find time to cultivate?

[42] M. & Legge, J. (2011). *The Works of Mencius*. New York: Dover Publications. pp. 251–252.

[43] M. & Legge, J. (2011). *The Works of Mencius*. New York: Dover Publications. pp. 252–253.

[44] M. & Legge, J. (2011). *The Works of Mencius*. New York: Dover Publications. pp. 251–252.

Before the Qin Dynasty, Confucianism emphasized saintly and royal governance over technology, agriculture, and commerce. During this period, virtue was given priority over techniques, and Confucian education was considered ahead of agriculture and commerce.

In today's terms, a person who governs a country or a business should do so according to virtue, delegating technical and management tasks to experts. A governor ought to prioritize justice and ethics in order to effectively understand people and achieve meaningful goals, ultimately aiming for the ideal of an Economy of Goodness.

Mencius valued the ways of kings and the virtues and wisdom of their leaders. He spoke not to the common person, but to kings and their leadership.

After all, Mencius did not discriminate against wealth; he said, "The imparting by a man to others of his wealth is called kindness, but the teaching others what is good, is called the exercise of fidelity."[45]

A leader teaches his people that goodness is the practice of loyalty. True, devoted love is loyalty itself.

Mencius believed leaders should possess talent for the betterment of society, not for their own gain. This is referred to as benevolence, and he stated: "The finding a man who shall benefit the kingdom is called 'benevolence.'"[46]

From an economic perspective, business leaders should originate from corporate cultures such as Yao and Shun, and educate their co-workers through principles of beneficence, filial piety, righteousness, and fidelity.

It is kind to give money to your colleagues, but to teach them loyalty is what goodness is.

An employer should be loyal and loving toward their colleagues, while colleagues should likewise be loyal and loving toward their employers. Moreover, leaders ought to show deep concern for the spiritual and moral development of those they lead. Yao and Shun exemplified this care through provision of sustenance. Mencius advocated this as a fundamental approach to business and leadership.

---

[45] M. & Legge, J. (2011). *The Works of Mencius*. New York: Dover Publications. p. 253.

[46] M. & Legge, J. (2011). *The Works of Mencius*. New York: Dover Publications. p. 253.

Entrepreneurs of Internal Sage and External King

It was not until Wang Yangming (1472–1529 CE) in the Ming Dynasty that Confucianism incorporated the concept of Study Things to Acquire Knowledge. Wang Yangming was strongly influenced by Buddhism, as well as by Western technology brought to China by Catholic priests by the end of the seventeenth century. Wang Yangming's, "to Study Things, to Acquire Knowledge, to Be Sincere, to Have a Rightful Mind, to Cultivate Oneself, to Raise One's Family, to Govern the Country and to Harmonize the World," signified not only knowledge and understanding of things, but also the Confucian quest for sainthood. This could be seen as an early form of professionalism.

Wang Yangming revolutionized the traditional Chinese mindset by challenging the notion that scholars were superior to merchants. He asserted that individuals across all societal roles, whether scholars, farmers, artisans, or merchants, could adhere to the moral principles of Confucian merchants. Wang Yangming emphasized the shared moral foundation among different social classes, stating that despite their diverse occupations, they all followed the same righteous path. He argued that engaging in commerce did not compromise one's moral and intellectual integrity; instead, a virtuous merchant upheld ethical conduct in their business dealings. Wang Yangming extended the concept of "internal sagehood and external kingliness" to encompass merchants, underlining their capacity to embody these ethical ideals.[47]

Wang Yangming applied the philosophy of Internal Sage and External King to business, maintaining that businesspersons could be both Internal Sage and External King—roles traditionally assigned only to government officers and emperors.

The goodness in traditional Chinese economic thought culminated in perfection in Wang Yangming's philosophy.

Wang Yangming advocated thorough knowledge of the world and cultivation of one's own mind, in order to contribute to society, from family to country governance.

Wang Yangming's economic thought could be summed up as:

Studying and acquiring knowledge points to the importance of expertise.

---

[47] Wang, S. R. (Eds.). (2011). *Wang yangming quanji* [A Complete Collection of Works by Wang Yangming]. Shanghai Century Publishing Co., Ltd. p. 986.

To be sincere and to have a rightful mind signifies spiritual and moral growth.

While caring for family welfare and prosperity, we should distribute wealth equitably to the society and thus make the country prosperous and tranquil; this is known as Governance of country.

Finally, we should strive for a peaceful, prosperous, and harmonious world for all people, called "Harmonize the World."

This is the ultimate ideal of the traditional Chinese economy of goodness.

Section 5: Economic Thought in Early Buddhist Civilization

Economic Life During the Time of the Buddha

Ancient India, where the Buddha lived, was a time of material wealth. As it was transitioning from the Bronze to the Iron Age, people were able to plow their fields with cast iron. During this period when Brahmins were dominant, cows were mostly used for sacrifices, thus making it difficult for the common person to acquire them even if they had plows.

The Buddha taught abstinence from killing and traveled to Northern India to promote compassion. This led to animals no longer being sacrificed, but instead used for farming, aiding the flourishing agricultural industry.

Brahminism had forbidden trade for other castes. However, via the Buddha's notion of all beings being equal, the king granted the right of all to trade, resulting in trade booming in ancient India. Moreover, the Buddha's impact on the kings which contributed to the economic glory of ancient India.

Despite their success, the Buddha and His disciples kept a pure intent while they practiced. Everywhere they traveled, they were supported with great generosity by merchants and noblemen. The literature shows that providing for the Buddha and His 1,200 disciples took a considerable amount of money. Yet merchants and businessmen still sought the opportunity to make offerings to the Buddha and receive His teachings.

Indian scholars noted that donations to the Buddha were more for social status than merit. Literature portrayed a wealthy society during this period. The Longley Elder's building for the Buddha, highlighting its luxurious interiors and offerings, was remarkable.

The Buddha, however, never accepted money Himself. His residence always belonged to lay Buddhist donors and was not the property of the Sangha. The Buddha was ever at peace with Himself, whether He lived in a high mansion, under a tree, or in a valley. This was the Buddha's practice of rejecting no abundance or humbleness of living conditions. The Buddha flatly objected to high beds, ornate architecture, and gastronomic offerings for the bhikkhus.[48] Sarvastivada-vinaya recorded his warning to bhikkhus as follows:

There are three practices called great wickedness that could lead to great retributions when prolonged for lay practitioners. They can hardly be removed shortly. They are practicing wild fabrication, practicing dangerous dishonesty and possessing an undue number of properties.

The former two kinds of wickedness are as mentioned earlier. What does it mean by possessing an undue number of properties? It means that a person has farming lands, workers and properties and thinks of giving the assets to those who can teach me something. Hence the name. The above three practices on the long run produce great retributions and lay practitioners cannot remove them quickly.

Likewise, there are also three evil practices that could lead to great retributions for monks and they would not be able to remove them quickly, either. They are practicing wild fabrication, practicing dangerous dishonesty and being attached to alms like clothing from people. The former two are the same. What does it mean by being attached to alms like clothing from people? It means that it will be better for me to gain more clothing, quilts, sleeping items and medicine and I will give it to those who can teach me something. These three practices on the long run produce great retributions and monks cannot remove them quickly.[49]

Greg Bailey and Ian Mabbett attempted to illustrate how the travel of the Buddha's monks indirectly led to local economic and trade growth. Their monastic community consisted of thousands, and wherever they went their need for resources enabled local commerce.

The building of Jetavana for the Buddha was costly, fueling local economic development.

[48] Bailey, G., Mabbett, I. (2003). *The Sociology of Early Buddhism*. Cambridge University Press. p. 65.

[49] *Shi song lu* [Sarvastivada-vinaya (Sect. 49)]. *Dazheng xinxiu dazang jing* [Taishō Tripiṭaka (Vol. 2)]. No. 1435.

This was proof of economic success in the Buddha's time. Monastic groups brought prosperity to local trade, and the Buddha's teachings influenced social elites to understand the Dharmas, aiding the establishment of more compassionate and peaceful localities.

Those who donated to the Buddha and his followers encompassed not only wealthy business people, but also lower-class laborers.

A master barber told his two sons to go to the village upon the Buddha's arrival to raise offerings for Him and His 1,200 disciples. Accordingly, the two sons followed their father's directions, taking with them their barber's tools in order to announce the impending arrival of the Buddha. Not long after, the villagers' contributions, through generous donations, had collected sufficient supplies to support the entire monastic group. The Buddha, displaying an equal benevolent compassion, accepted the donations from both the rich and the humbler households.[50]

The Buddha's Views on Worldly Possessions

As previously mentioned, the Buddha did not oppose materialism or reject the Five Aggregates. He declared that all the Five Aggregates are empty in the sense of being impermanent instead of non-existent.

The Buddha believed that the world is impermanent and ultimately empty,[51] but did not deny the existence of the material world. The Five Aggregates are suffering precisely because they exist. Early Buddhism advocated that the mind is not affected by the Five Aggregates, and that the mind is pure. The spirit of the early *Agama Sutras* is that the world exists but is impermanent. Impermanence causes suffering, and by understanding suffering and its causes, we can achieve enlightenment.

Buddhist disciples eliminate afflictions and karmic obstacles one by one through the "Thirty-Seven Aids to Enlightenment" and achieve pure nirvana.

---

[50] Bailey, G., Mabbett, I. (2003). *The Sociology of Early Buddhism*. Cambridge University Press. pp. 72–73.

[51] Emptiness in the Buddhist context does not mean nothingness but that all existing beings are impermanent. Another meaning of Emptiness is the ability to accommodate everything. Emptiness is like the sky having the capacity to hold countless stars, and like a bottle having the potential to contain water. The endless use and arising is Emptiness.

The Five Aggregates comprise a physical world of formation, existence, decay, and disappearance; a physiological world of birth, aging, sickness, and death; and a mental world of arising, abiding, changing, and extinction of all existences.

The Buddha's teachings did not deny the existence of these three realms. He asserted that all of the Five Aggregates are impermanent, suffering, and empty, coming into being through karma and ceasing with karma. Thus, the mind and the Five Aggregates depend on each other due to interdependent arising.

When a mind is subject to the Five Aggregates, it cannot escape the cycle of birth and death. When the mind is no longer subject to the Five Aggregates, Right Wisdom arises and the mind becomes immortal. As Samyukta-agama states:

> At that time, the Blessed One said to the monks: There are five aggregates of clinging. What are the five? They are the bodily form aggregate of clinging, the feeling, the perception, the formations, and the consciousness aggregate of clinging.

> It would be well, monks, if you do not delight in bodily form, do not commend bodily form, do not cling to bodily form, do not attach to bodily form. It would be well, monks, if you do not delight in feeling... perception... formations... consciousness, do not commend consciousness, do not cling to consciousness, do not attach to consciousness. Why is that?

> If a monk does not delight in bodily form, does not commend bodily form, does not cling to bodily form, does not attach to bodily form, then by not delighting in bodily form his mind attains liberation. In the same way [if he] does not delight in feeling ... perception... formations... does not delight in consciousness, does not commend consciousness, does not cling to consciousness, does not attach to consciousness, then by not delighting in consciousness his mind attains liberation.

> If a monk does not delight in bodily form and his mind has attained liberation... in the same way [if he] does not delight in feeling... perception... formations... consciousness and his mind has attained liberation, [for him] there is no perishing and no [re-]arising, he is established in balanced equanimity, with right mindfulness and right comprehension.[52]

---

[52] Anālayo, B. (2013). *On the Five Aggregates (3)—A Translation of Saṃyukta-āgama Discourses 59 to 87.* Dharma Drum Journal of Buddhist Studies. New Taipei City: Dharma Drum Buddhist College. pp. 5–6.

By not being subject to birth and death and can equally abandon the greed for all things and have right thoughts and wisdom, the Buddha does not deny the Five Aggregates in the real world, but puts forward the concept of right thoughts and wisdom, which leads to Tao.

Likewise, according to the *Agama Sutra*, the Buddha did not repudiate worldly wealth but advocated that it should be obtained rightfully.

It is the right way to have a mind not bound by wealth.

The Buddha had very clear expressions regarding worldly livelihood, finances, and economic life. It can be divided into two aspects: "wisdom in livelihood" and "adherence to principles" or "self-regulation of precepts."

The Buddha believed that the only way to be blessed is to live by wisdom.

In other words, economic life is not just about monetary gain, but about fostering wisdom. When wealth is acquired through knowledge, contentment follows.

In modern economic life, many earn money yet cannot attain happiness. Rather, after becoming affluent, the balance between work and family life is thrown off-kilter. This type of making money is not consistent with the Buddha's ideal model of economic activity.

The Bodhisattva of Wealth, Purity, and Tranquility

The Buddha emphasized integrating economic activity with Buddhist practice. In the *Great Skillful Means Sutra on the Buddha's Repayment of Kindness*, he explained how Bodhisattvas cultivate purity over time, gaining wisdom, skills, wealth, and pleasure. Yet, their hearts remain unblemished and focused on helping others.

The Buddha described Bodhisattvas as possessing pure conduct and various skills, including art, mathematics, science, and physical prowess. They acquire wealth ethically and live in splendid homes adorned with gems and pearls. However, they remain untainted by these possessions and free from desires for entertainment.[53]

This doctrine emphasizes that Bodhisattvas' ongoing and pure Buddhist practice grants them mastery of worldly skills, arts, and wealth. However, their hearts remain uncorrupted and unattached to these possessions.

---

[53] *Dafangbian fo bao'en jing* [Great Skillful Means Sutra on the Buddha's Repayment of Kindness (Sect. 2)]. *Dazheng xinxiu dazang jing* [Taishō Tripiṭaka (Vol. 3)]. No. 0156.

Therefore, Bodhisattvas should diligently hone diverse skills like music, entertainment, calendar keeping, measurement, arithmetic, even cursing spells and elixirs, alongside elephant and horse riding, archery, military strategy, and martial arts. By acquiring such wide-ranging expertise, Bodhisattvas command respect and obedience from ministers and ordinary people alike.[54]

This illustrates the high regard in which Bodhisattva was held by worldly kings and courtiers.

The Buddha described Bodhisattvas as possessing immense wealth—luxurious clothing, jewels, grand palaces, and devoted servants. Yet, despite such abundance, their hearts remained untouched by worldly desires. They found true joy in the stillness of meditation, seeking peace and tranquility amidst nature.[55]

Even when engaging in everyday activities, their minds stayed focused on compassion and wisdom. Living among others, they generously utilized their possessions to benefit all, shunning any harmful behavior. The suffering and needy found solace in their support, turning to them as beacons of hope and unwavering generosity.[56]

A Bodhisattva was not only wise, skillful, pleasurable, and wealthy, but also had a pure, unselfish heart. They strove to benefit all sentient beings, utilizing their property to create karma and advantage for others. They provided aid to the destitute and the suffering, and addressed every need. Great Bodhisattvas were eminent exemplars.

The Buddha's Views on Business Development

In the Samyukta-Agama, the Buddha gave a young man in Jetavana a response which outlined the wisdom that should be employed by lay Buddhists when engaging in business and the ideal of economic activities.

The Buddha expounded business wisdom through the Four Sufficiencies:

---

[54] *Dafangbian fo bao'en jing* [Great Skillful Means Sutra on the Buddha's Repayment of Kindness (Sect. 2)]. *Dazheng xinxiu dazang jing* [Taishō Tripiṭaka (Vol. 3)]. No. 0156.

[55] *Dafangbian fo bao'en jing* [Great Skillful Means Sutra on the Buddha's Repayment of Kindness (Sect. 2)]. *Dazheng xinxiu dazang jing* [Taishō Tripiṭaka (Vol. 3)]. No. 0156.

[56] *Dafangbian fo bao'en jing* [Great Skillful Means Sutra on the Buddha's Repayment of Kindness (Sect. 2)]. *Dazheng xinxiu dazang jing* [Taishō Tripiṭaka (Vol. 3)]. No. 0156.

1. Professional competence in business skills, which are Expedient Sufficiency.
2. Protection Sufficiency in safeguarding economic property.
3. Good Knowledge Advisor Sufficiency to ensure a joyful life materially and spiritually.
4. Right Livelihood Sufficiency to live reasonably within our means, and maintain mindfulness and well-being.

These Four Sufficiencies covers all the ways to wealth and happiness for the EOG and Good Enterprises.

According to a conversation recorded in the Samyukta-Agama, the Buddha offered four paths to prosperity and well-being. A young Brahman named Yuduja inquired about how laypeople could attain peace and happiness. The Buddha responded by outlining the Four Sufficiencies: Expedient Sufficiency, Protection Sufficiency, Good Knowledge Advisor Sufficiency, and Right Livelihood Sufficiency. He elaborated on the first aspect, Expedient Sufficiency, explaining that individuals can earn a living through various respectable skills, like farming, trading, serving in government, or engaging in arts like calligraphy or painting. The Buddha emphasized that diligently practicing these skills is the key to achieving Expedient Sufficiency.[57]

The Buddha's Four Sufficiencies, presented in response to the young man's question, align with the core principles of the Economy of Goodness.

Business activities must rely on expertise to determine profitability. The key to success is the Buddha's Expedient Sufficiency.

The Buddha advised his disciples to be diligent, not only in their spiritual practice, but also in their work and careers—this is the path to wealth, known as Expedient Sufficiency.

Only when ordinary people are industrious and officials diligent in governing and stimulating economic growth, can a nation's wealth accumulate. The Buddha meant that not only enterprises but even the king of a country must practice diligently to realize Expedient Sufficiency.

---

[57] *Za'a han jing* [Samyukta-agama (Sect. 6.4)]. *Dazheng xinxiu dazang jing* [Taishō Tripiṭaka (Vol. 2)]. No. 0099. p. 23.

Companies tend to neglect customers' needs and focus on what their competitors are doing, which results in a loss of ideals rather than Right Effort.

By diligence, the Buddha meant Right Effort in both professional and inner cultivation; combining one's internal and external worlds to achieve Expedient Sufficiency.

In short, the Buddha sought merchants and rulers to cultivate both internally and externally. Internal values must be the starting point to be a real practitioner. This applies to running a business or governing a country, in line with the Buddha's teachings on proper values. External practices and creativity combined with internal cultivation make up the fundamentals for enterprise growth and continual national progression.

The Buddha then elaborated on the concept of Protection Sufficiency. This principle stresses the responsible management of wealth. Just as ethically acquired wealth fosters long-term security, individuals have a duty to safeguard their possessions from various threats, including theft, natural disasters, and misuse. Failing to do so puts their resources at risk. Those who manage their belongings with care, ensuring their continued well-being, embody the practice of Protection Sufficiency.[58]

This concept resonates with the importance of responsible resource management for business growth and national development.

In modern economic terms, "Protection Sufficiency" means creating new sources of income and reducing costs. Yung-ching Wang (王永慶), one of the wealthiest Taiwanese entrepreneurs of his time, stated that it is harder to earn a dollar than to save one. Therefore, it is essential to safeguard your property as earning it is so challenging, which is why adhering to the principle of Protection Sufficiency is so important for entrepreneurs.

How do we secure national economic fruits systematically? The Buddha pointed out that wealth could only be kept when it had been acquired rightfully. Otherwise, it could not be preserved for long. Wealth acquired rightfully lasts a long time.

Rightfully obtained wealth must still be carefully maintained. The Buddha used the word cherish for securing one's property. Those who do not cherish economic fruits will lose them to natural and man-made disasters. So does a country without effective systems to secure its economy.

---

[58] *Za'a han jing* [Samyukta-agama (Sect. 6.4)]. *Dazheng xinxiu dazang jing* [Taishō Tripiṭaka (Vol. 2)]. No. 0099. p. 23.

When officials do not cherish economic fruits with factions, corruption, dereliction of duty and carelessness, a country will suffer great losses. Without Protection Sufficiency, the fruits of development are bound to be lost.

The Buddha had a profound idea on how to guard against corruption and calamities. He supported the economic well-being of laypeople and taught them ways to protect their possessions and keep them safe.

If a man acquires wealth rightfully and cherishes it, then he is a good man capable of protecting it, thus achieving Protection Sufficiency.

The Buddha then elaborated on Good Knowledge Advisor Sufficiency. This concept emphasizes the qualities of individuals who can offer valuable guidance. It highlights the ability to utilize knowledge proactively to: anticipate and prevent suffering, offer guidance to those facing challenges, uplift those who have found joy, and help them sustain their happiness. Those who possess these qualities and use their knowledge to guide others toward well-being are said to embody Good Knowledge Advisor Sufficiency.[59]

The Buddha's Good Knowledge Advisor Sufficiency is the third level in His view of wealth.

The first level is advancing expertise, the second is protecting property, and the third is achieving true happiness.

Though they live in material wealth, many modern entrepreneurs experience spiritual emptiness, misery, and stress.

After economic success, business owners and national leaders must have no self-degradation, no self-indulgence, no dishonesty, and no danger to themselves, become good knowledge advisors for others, and be able to comfort those in distress. Such a state means not just a successful entrepreneur or leader, but a spiritual guide for others. To be a Good Knowledge Advisor entails providing others with true happiness and joy. This state is not just about being a successful entrepreneur or leader, but about being a spiritual mentor for others. To be able to bring genuine joy and happiness to others is to have good knowledge.

Franky Oesman Widjaja, a long-time volunteer of Tzu Chi Foundation, is one of the leading entrepreneurs in Indonesia. He has been contributing to charity for over two decades and was deeply involved in helping those affected by the 2004 Aceh Earthquake and the 2004

---

[59] *Za'a han jing* [Samyukta-agama (Sect. 6.4)]. *Dazheng xinxiu dazang jing* [Taishō Tripiṭaka (Vol. 2)]. No. 0099. p. 23.

Indian ocean earthquake and tsunami, acting as one of the co-organizers to provide five million households with rice. His example even spread to his 400,000 employees and their families, as they too followed his lead to become Tzu Chi volunteers or donors. Especially Muslim employees, who took it upon themselves to care for low-income families in the five kilometers surrounding his company farms. Franky Widjaja achieved Good Knowledge Advisor Sufficiency and thus advanced to Right Livelihood Sufficiency.

Finally, the Buddha addressed Right Livelihood Sufficiency. This principle focuses on striking a balance between income and expenditure, similar to a skilled weigher adjusting weights for accurate measurement. It emphasizes responsible financial management, avoiding wasteful spending or excessive frugality. The Buddha compares uncontrolled spending to an individual mindlessly consuming figs, demonstrating a lack of foresight for the future. Conversely, excessive stinginess is likened to a dog starving itself. Ultimately, achieving financial balance is identified as Right Livelihood Sufficiency. By practicing these Four Sufficiencies, the Buddha assures the young Brahman, one can attain peace and happiness.[60]

One's material achievements must be accompanied by inner strength of mind and culture to be a true entrepreneur and, beyond that, a mentor guiding others in spiritual matters, happiness, and Right Livelihood Sufficiency.

The Buddha's philosophy straddles the Confucian view of the Internal Sage and External King. Chinese traditional Tao states that a king must be a sage and a sage must be a king. Wang Yangming in the Ming Dynasty argued that a businessman could also aspire to the Internal Sage and External King title, not just kings.

Wang Yangming, a renowned philosopher of the Ming Dynasty, made a breakthrough in the traditional, heavily scholastic Chinese mindset. He believed that scholars, peasants, craftsmen, and merchants were all on the same path of Confucianism. Wang Yangming stated: The four sorts of people are of different professions and are on the same path; people who do business all day long could still be saints or virtuous persons; a good businessman who is in the field of wealth and goods could still cultivate his wise virtues. Wang Yangming thought that a businessman could also be an Internal Sage and External King.

---

[60] *Za'a han jing* [Samyukta-agama (Sect. 6.4)]. *Dazheng xinxiu dazang jing* [Taishō Tripiṭaka (Vol. 2)]. No. 0099. p. 23.

Yu Ying-shih thought that the Ming first Emperor Zhu Yuanzhang's lack of respect for Confucian scholars led to many of them in the fifteenth and sixth centuries flocking to do business, which was called abandoning Confucianism for business, the spirit of a scholar and talent of merchants.[61]

This social phenomenon shows that the meanings of Internal Sage and External King were enlarged during the Ming Dynasty, with Internal Sage still indispensable but an External King referring to any activity that benefits society.

The Kingship of the External King was no longer exclusive to the state ruler: it was no longer the only expected quality for a scholar-official. However, the External King must derive from the Internal Sage which necessitates engaging in the Right Way of Heaven and self-development in order to benefit the public, regardless of vocation. The idea of sage and king in Confucianism and previous to the Qin Dynasty evolved greatly.

The Buddha was advocating this two thousand years before Wang Yangming.

Yet the Buddha did not specify the stages of such thought. He believed merchants and kings had the ability to impart profound wisdom to other living beings through their actions, thus illustrating their Skill Sufficiency.

The Buddha's views on business and economic governance can be seen as a refinement of professionalism, adherence to principles, emphasis on good character, and the benefit of society as the highest goal in sustaining and growing businesses. As he said, the fourth fold is Right Livelihood Sufficiency.

The Buddha advocated for financial responsibility, condemning both excessive accumulation and wasteful spending. He emphasized the importance of managing finances wisely, comparing a balanced approach to a skilled professional ensuring accurate measurements. He believed this balanced approach, termed "Right Livelihood Sufficiency," contributed to overall well-being.[62]

As property is taken from society, it should be spent for society's benefit. It is wrong to waste money, and it is just as wrong to hoard

[61] Yu, Y. S. (2010). *Jinshi zhongguo rujia lunli yu shangren jingshen* [Confucian Ethics and Merchant Spirit in Modern China]. *Zhongguo wenhua shi tong shi* [Chinese History and Culture]. Hongkong: Oxford University Press. pp. 43–58.

[62] *Za'a han jing* [Samyukta-agama (Sect. 6.4)]. *Dazheng xinxiu dazang jing* [Taishō Tripiṭaka (Vol. 2)]. No. 0099. p. 23.

it. Neither becoming a money worshipper nor a miser is ideal. This applies to entrepreneurship and national economic development too, as Buddha taught. This is the ideal of economic development and good entrepreneurs.

In the Buddha's eyes, only a balance between income and expenditure can be labeled as "right livelihood sufficiency." Ultimately, his ideal of wealth and economy centers on serving society and all beings, seeking not just material wealth, but to create happiness.

Professional leadership, wealth protection, being a source of good knowledge guidance, and creating social well-being align with the Buddha's Four Sufficiencies of Skill Sufficiency, Protection Sufficiency, Good Knowledge Guidance Sufficiency, and Right Livelihood Sufficiency.

By contrast, Protestant ethics and Christian entrepreneurship emphasize the divine mission in entrepreneurship to observe God's laws and grow their business to demonstrate they are of God's chosen people.

The Buddha didn't promote an unending buildup of wealth. His suggestion was professional accomplishment, growth in one's career, and a balance of income and outgoings. The point is not amassing riches, but the social worth of the riches produced. The Buddha lauded entrepreneurs as originators of collective joy and repositories of valuable knowledge for others.

The Buddha's economic philosophy unites the generation of wealth, its safeguard, the judicious application of it, and the contentment of all living beings. It envisions a prosperous society where material wealth and compassionate wisdom are balanced; all creatures are enriched physically and mentally; the nation is abundant and the populace ecstatic.

The Buddha's Teachings on Wealth Management

The Buddha advised laypeople on how to generate wealth and how to handle it.

Samyukta-Agama records that, one night, the Buddha, while residing in Jetavana, proposed a four-part wealth management strategy in a conversation with a celestial visitor.

The Buddha indicated that one should distribute one part of wealth for one's own use, two parts for business development, and one part stored away for future use. The reason for such management could not be inferred from literature, but the Buddha stipulated that wealth should be used for maintaining the family, developing one's career, and positive saving for the future.

According to the *Samyukta-Agama*, the Buddha, while residing in Jetavana, was approached by a celestial being seeking guidance on accumulating and managing wealth. The Buddha advised a four-part approach: firstly, developing skills to earn, then dividing the earnings into four portions. One portion for everyday expenses, two for business investment, and the final portion reserved for unforeseen circumstances.[63]

This method of saving and investing, emphasizing responsible allocation for daily needs, business growth, and future security, demonstrates a surprisingly sophisticated economic concept present in India over 2,500 years ago.

The daily portion should be used sparingly. Two parts should be allocated for business growth, as entrepreneurship requires adequate funding. A portion put away could be vital for a company to ride out crises.

The sudden collapse of many large businesses in our time are mostly attributable to excessive credit lending. Bill Gates surmised that the sudden downfall of a large business is often related to a dearth of cash flow, so he promotes a satisfactory stash of cash for a company to weather economic downturns.

The Buddha's four-part wealth management could give businesses today something to mull over. A man from Heaven visited the Buddha at night, his noble stature was unmistakable.

It was said that the person emitted light, a symbol of wealth. Rich and powerful, he approached the Buddha seeking advice not on asceticism, but how to use his wealth wisely—showing the Buddha to be a great saint knowledgeable in worldly matters, willing to discuss any topic.

Beyond advising on wealth allocation, the Buddha also offered guidance on acquiring it.

He identified various sectors with potential for prosperity, including agriculture, finance, trade, animal husbandry, real estate, and construction. By engaging in these industries with wisdom and diligence, one could accumulate wealth steadily, akin to a sea enriched by rivers and bees diligently building their honeycombs.[64] These six sectors, encompassing

---

[63] *Za'a han jing* [Samyukta-agama (Sect. 48)]. *Dazheng xinxiu dazang jing* [Taishō Tripiṭaka (Vol. 2)]. No. 0099. p. 353.

[64] *Za'a han jing* [Samyukta-agama (Sect. 48)]. *Dazheng xinxiu dazang jing* [Taishō Tripiṭaka (Vol. 2)]. No. 0099. p. 353.

"planting agriculture," "currency business," "trade relations," "livestock husbandry," "real estate value preservation," and the "building furniture industry," were presented as avenues for leading a prosperous and fulfilling life.

From Buddha's words to the wealthy divine being, it can be seen that India of that period was a highly developed urban economy and a prosperous agrarian state. According to Indian scholars Greg Bailey and Ian Mabbett, it was a commercially booming and well-supplied era in northern and eastern India with such cities as Kusinārā and Rajagaha at that time.[65]

The wisdom of the Buddha touches on the right way of doing business and financial management, so those of wealth and high-standing come to him for advice. At night, those who arrive are likely feeling very confused or anxious. The Buddha listens to their concerns and offers suggestions, from how to allocate funds to the type of industry and even the right business structure and partners. He answered each one completely.

The Buddha further emphasized the pursuit of wealth through wisdom, comparing it to a stream naturally flowing back to the ocean. Just as bees gather nectar and ants diligently build their piles, wealth acquired through wise efforts accumulates naturally and steadily.[66] This resonates with modern business concepts, where entrepreneurs are encouraged to focus on creating value through intelligence rather than solely chasing after profits. By prioritizing wisdom, wealth becomes a natural consequence rather than the sole objective.

As long as you start a business wisely, wealth will flow like the tide and accumulate like bees gathering honey and ants storing food. This is the Buddha's suggested wisdom for economic and commercial growth. In modern terms, it means choosing the right industry and creating an efficient business operation; consequently, prosperity flows naturally.

The proverb, "Don't chase money, let money chase you" aligns with the Buddha's teachings. Instead of relentlessly pursuing wealth, the Buddha advocated for choosing the right industry and establishing a sound business model. By doing so, success and prosperity become

---

[65] Bailey, G., Mabbett, I. (2003). *The Sociology of Early Buddhism.* (n.p.): Cambridge University Press. pp. 66–67.

[66] *Za'a han jing* [Samyukta-agama (Sect. 48)]. *Dazheng xinxiu dazang jing* [Taishō Tripiṭaka (Vol. 2)]. No. 0099. p. 353.

natural outcomes of wise choices and diligent effort, attracting wealth like a stream flowing back to the sea.

The Buddha explained to the celestial being who to conduct business with, and whom to steer away from. Like a wise fire, having the right business partner, surrounded by true friends, high-ranking officials, fellow practitioners, associates and helpful reminders are the keys to success for entrepreneurs in choosing business partners.

The Samyukta-Agama offers further guidance on managing wealth wisely. The Buddha advised against entrusting resources to the elderly, disadvantaged, or unreliable individuals. Instead, fostering relationships with capable and like-minded people is crucial, as they can collaborate and support each other's endeavors. Additionally, valuing family and friends, sharing resources with relatives, and living a harmonious life are emphasized as key contributors to well-being. The celestial being, deeply moved by the Buddha's teachings, expressed his gratitude and departed, acknowledging the Buddha's wisdom in both achieving enlightenment and offering practical guidance on financial management and wealth creation.[67]

The Buddha's words not only addressed the celestial being's financial concerns but also provided broader insights that fostered his understanding and inner peace.

Samyukta-Agama offers future generations a glimpse of the Buddha's economic and commercial acumen.

The Buddha explained the most important aspects of modern economy and commerce, such as industry situating, business strategies, wealth oversight, asset governance, and partner formation, etc. He also laid down precepts in economic and economic dealings.

According to the Madhyama Āgama, the Buddha expounded His views on business principles using Six Non-Tao.

The Buddha's Views on Business Principles

After explaining the enthusiasm and usefulness of wealth in the previous section, let us now discuss the Buddha's views on principles and precepts for business and economic activity. It is clear that any economic activity

---

[67] *Za'a han jing* [Samyukta-agama (Sect. 48)]. *Dazheng xinxiu dazang jing* [Taishō Tripiṭaka (Vol. 2)]. No. 0099. p. 353.

can only be sustained and successful if it's governed by certain principles and disciplines.

Jews are renowned for their business acumen. They're involved in all types of diamond, banking, film and watch industries worldwide. Jewish belief holds that God favors them in this life and this world; thus, inspiring them to aim for success in those realms. According to economists, this is a major motivation for the Jewish community's economic successes.

However, Jews have strict discipline, such as the prohibition of any economic activity on the Sabbath. From sunset on Friday, there is no cooking or lighting, only rest. Activities do not resume until after sunset on Saturday.

Economic conditions are restricted, resources are scarce, and labor must be restricted. This discipline not only encourages the Jewish practice of following the Commandments from a young age, but also encourages their habit of working with limited resources.

I visited Israel in January 2018. Israel and Jordan have the same original geographical environment, yet Jordan is still mainly desert whereas Israel has become an oasis due to recycling 70% of its used water. Tel Aviv, the capital, is now a thriving metropolis.

In Jerusalem, I saw many adherents of Orthodox Jewish sects clad in black robes and hats, sporting long braids on men and boys. Over 30% of Jews in Jerusalem are Orthodox believers. Despite their conservative and traditional beliefs, they have created an impressive economy.

Tel Aviv, situated 66 km from Jerusalem, is a sophisticated modern city, topped by an arch with Jewish sages etched in. This arch symbolizes the desert-to-metropolis transformation in Tel Aviv and serves as a reminder of God's promise of abundance and prosperity.

Israel's economic success was intertwined with their adherence to laws that glorified God.

On the contrary, after my journey to Israel in January 2018, I visited the Buddha's Vulture Peak, Jetavana, and Nalanda University, which still radiate their grandeur through mottled ancient buildings. Nevertheless, the beggars around these places indicate an economic decline in later generations, despite the Buddha's teachings.

The Buddha did not just accept wealth, but called on people to use it for society's benefit. Similar to Judaism, he still emphasized the importance of guidelines and principles in economic affairs.

The *Madh Yamagama-sutra* offers guidance to laypeople seeking wealth through the "Six Non-Tao." These principles emphasize ethical and sustainable practices: firstly, avoiding dishonest means of acquiring wealth. Secondly, seeking opportunities at appropriate times, avoiding impulsive decisions. Thirdly, abstaining from excessive indulgence, which can hinder sound judgment. Fourthly, choosing trustworthy associates who share ethical values. Fifthly, maintaining self-control and avoiding excessive desires, which can lead to poor financial decisions. Lastly, remaining diligent and innovative to adapt to changing circumstances.[68]

The Six Non-Taos refer to the six principles that businessmen should adhere to when acquiring property.

First, no cheating or speculation and no acquiring wealth through illicit means.

Secondly, it is non-Tao to seek wealth at inappropriate times. For instance, hoarding goods and obtaining wealth when there is a scarcity of supplies in the community.

Third, no drinking of alcohol or bribing to gain business or wealth.

Fourth, do not associate with wicked people for the sake of wealth.

Fifth, no fraternizing, revelry, and gratifying of wants upon acquiring wealth.

Sixth, no slothfulness in endeavor or innovation when seeking wealth.

The *Madh Yamagama-sutra* warns of potential consequences for engaging in the "Six Non-Virtuous Actions." These actions can lead to a series of unfortunate outcomes: firstly, generating resentment from others. Secondly, suffering financial losses and facing the associated humiliation. Thirdly, experiencing restless sleep due to anxieties and worries. Fourthly, bringing satisfaction to one's competitors who may exploit one's downfall. Fifthly, causing concern and disappointment among family and friends. Sixthly, potentially damaging one's reputation and creditworthiness. The sutra emphasizes that carelessness in business practices, fueled by these non-virtuous actions, hinders career achievements and hinders the accumulation of sustainable wealth. Even wealth gained through speculative means is likely to be short-lived.[69]

Business gambling refers to speculation and deception that can lead to resentful feelings and humiliation. It may also cause insomnia, worry for

[68] *Zong'a han jing* [Madhyama-agama]. *Dazheng xinxiu dazang jing* [Taishō Tripiṭaka (Vol. 1)]. No. 0026. p. 639.

[69] *Zong'a han jing* [Madhyama-agama (Sect. 33)]. *Dazheng xinxiu dazang jing* [Taishō Tripiṭaka (Vol. 1)]. No. 0026. p. 639.

friends and families and delight for one's opponents. Furthermore, it can harm one's reputation and result in the loss of property.

The Buddha referred to businessmen as Bodhisattvas, and disapproved of any unlawful appropriation of others' property, or being swindled.

He illustrated this concept through an analogy: imagine possessing various forms of wealth and comforts, yet still fearing harm from others. Recognizing this universal desire for security, the Buddha stated that true Bodhisattvas would rather sacrifice themselves than exploit others for their resources, including clothing, food, and wealth.[70]

This ethical approach stands in stark contrast to "economic aggression," which the Buddha condemned as incompatible with the principles of a Bodhisattva. Such businesses would avoid exploiting individuals or manipulating prices for personal gain, ensuring their conduct aligns with broader societal well-being.

The Buddha detailed the morality and legitimacy of commerce in Six Non-Tao and cautioned that doing business at the wrong time could bring social scorn and serious repercussions.

He warned laypeople against pursuing wealth at inappropriate times, highlighting the potential consequences: firstly, jeopardizing one's own safety. Secondly, risking the security of one's possessions. Thirdly, exposing one's family to potential harm. Fourthly, damaging one's reputation and creditworthiness. Fifthly, attracting further suffering. Sixthly, facing public criticism and blame.

The Buddha further explained that such ventures, driven by poor timing, hinder focus and impede career progress, ultimately leading to a lack of sustainable wealth accumulation. Even wealth obtained through these means is likely to be short-lived and volatile.[71]

Hoarding food, inflating prices, and charging exorbitant interest are all forms of exploiting disadvantaged people. The Buddha had enlightened views on equitable and fair trade.

In addition, the Buddha advised that businesspeople take care of their lives, as indulgence can result in ill health, disordered living, and business failure. These words are still pertinent to the world of business today.

[70] *Dafangbian fo bao'en jing* [Great Skillful Means Sutra on the Buddha's Repayment of Kindness (Sect. 2)]. *Dazheng xinxiu dazang jing* [Taishō Tripiṭaka (Vol. 3)]. No. 0156. p. 131.

[71] *Zong'a han jing* [Madhyama-agama]. *Dazheng xinxiu dazang jing* [Taishō Tripiṭaka (Vol. 1)]. No. 0026.

In his teachings to laypeople, the Buddha warned against the dangers of heavy drinking, outlining six potential consequences: firstly, it can lead to the loss of existing wealth. Secondly, it increases susceptibility to illnesses. Thirdly, it can fuel conflicts and arguments. Fourthly, it hinders self-reflection and prevents admitting mistakes. Fifthly, it damages one's reputation. Sixthly, it can impair wisdom and lead to poor decision-making.

The Buddha further emphasized that excessive drinking disrupts focus and hinders effective business practices, ultimately hindering career achievements and hindering the accumulation of sustainable wealth. He highlighted that individuals who prioritize indulgence over responsible management are unlikely to achieve success or acquire lasting prosperity.[72]

In business, it is crucial to be close to good friends, stay clear of thieves, and guard against unscrupulous people. The deceiver, the drunkard, the arrogant, and the playful should be all kept at bay.

Those who are close to the wicked would keep no property.

The Buddha, addressing laypeople, cautioned against associating with individuals who engage in unethical conduct, outlining six potential pitfalls: firstly, increased risk of encountering thieves and dishonest individuals. Secondly, exposure to deceitful and untruthful behavior. Thirdly, associating with those who are reckless or intoxicated. Fourthly, being influenced toward excessive indulgence and pleasure-seeking. Fifthly, prioritizing frivolous entertainment over responsibilities. Sixthly, forming partnerships or friendships with individuals known for unethical practices. The Buddha emphasized that such associations can lead to a lack of focus on sound business practices, ultimately hindering career achievements and hindering the accumulation of sustainable wealth.[73]

He highlighted that success in business often requires surrounding oneself with individuals who exemplify virtue and avoiding those who lack integrity, echoing the perspective of Confucius who similarly saw this as a key to achieving business success.

---

[72] *Zong'a han jing* [Madhyama-agama (Sect. 33)]. *Dazheng xinxiu dazang jing* [Taishō Tripiṭaka (Vol. 1)]. No. 0026. p. 639.

[73] *Zong'a han jing* [Madhyama-agama (Sect. 33)]. *Dazheng xinxiu dazang jing* [Taishō Tripiṭaka (Vol. 1)]. No. 0026. p. 639.

The Buddha, emphasizing the importance of frugality in business, taught laypeople to avoid becoming preoccupied with frivolous music and dancing, lest they hinder their achievements in life.

He warned against excessive indulgence in frivolous entertainment, such as music, dancing, and elaborate festivities, outlining six potential consequences: firstly, becoming captivated by musical performances. Secondly, developing an attachment to dance presentations. Thirdly, falling into a habit of excessive indulgence in merriment. Fourthly, seeking amusement through the sound of bells. Fifthly, deriving pleasure from hand clapping. Sixthly, gravitating toward extravagant celebrations.

The Buddha stressed that such distractions can lead to a lack of focus on responsible business practices, ultimately hindering career achievements and hindering the accumulation of sustainable wealth. He emphasized that even wealth obtained through fleeting pleasures is likely to be short-lived and unsustainable.[74]

The Buddha further emphasized the value of consistent effort in business, urging laypeople to avoid idleness. He advised against allowing external factors, such as time of day, weather, or hunger, to dictate one's work ethic. Instead, he encouraged them to maintain a diligent and consistent work ethic regardless of these circumstances.

The Buddha outlined six potential consequences of slothfulness: firstly, squandering valuable mornings. Secondly, wasting the potential of nighttime hours. Thirdly, neglecting opportunities for personal growth during cold weather. Fourthly, failing to capitalize on opportunities during hot weather. Fifthly, neglecting responsibilities when well-fed. Sixthly, being unable to work effectively when hungry.

The Buddha concluded by reiterating that such a lack of diligence can hinder focus on essential business practices, ultimately leading to difficulties in achieving career success and accumulating sustainable wealth. Even wealth acquired through sporadic efforts, he warned, is likely to be short-lived.[75]

The Buddha's forward-thinking mindset was essential for those aspiring to succeed. Nowadays, people often discuss comfort, well-being, and rest periods related to work. However, the Buddha believed

---

[74] *Zong'a han jing* [Madhyama-agama (Sect. 33)]. *Dazheng xinxiu dazang jing* [Taishō Tripiṭaka (Vol. 1)]. No. 0026. p. 639.

[75] *Zong'a han jing* [Madhyama-agama (Sect. 33)]. *Dazheng xinxiu dazang jing* [Taishō Tripiṭaka (Vol. 1)]. No. 0026. p. 639.

entrepreneurship called for continual effort, no matter the situation. If everything became too accessible, business opportunities would be missed. Challenging conditions help cultivate the growth of enterprises.

Crises in today's enterprise management are seen as a test for enterprises. Those that can successfully ride out crises are the soundest ones.

As Mencius of Confucianism said, "When Heaven is about to confer a great office on any man, it first exercises his mind with suffering, and his sinews and bones with toil. It exposes his body to hunger, and subjects him to extreme poverty. It confounds his undertakings. All these methods stimulate his mind, harden his nature, and supply his incompetencies."[76] Great achievements are carved out of rough conditions.

The US President Franklin D. Roosevelt was born into a noble family and was handsome and talented. He graduated from Harvard and, in his thirties, became a New York senator. At 40, however, he was struck by poliomyelitis and resigned. After four years of perseverance, he was able to recover, though he was unable to walk normally.

The time of illness strengthened Roosevelt. After his recovery, he was elected Governor of New York, and later President of the US.

Over the next decade, President Roosevelt guided the US out of economic distress, defeated German and Japanese imperialists and won WWII, restoring peace. This may have been the greatest challenge of his life.

Master Cheng Yen asked Tzu Chi volunteers to not rest for two days a week, but instead focus on self-cultivation on those days. On weekends, volunteers would continue their charitable work as usual and never experience "Monday blues" from being worn out.

The Buddha encouraged entrepreneurs to strive despite any adverse conditions, just as the monks' practice of zeal.

Judaism teaches Jews from young to overcome hardships. Since the sixth century they have been displaced, having no land of their own or protection from their homeland. Thus, they developed symbolic economies instead of relying on land, farming, and production. This allowed them to roam the world with activities such as banking, clock-making, and trade.

---

[76] M. & Legge, J. (2011). *The Works of Mencius*. New York: Dover Publications. p. 75.

This enabled Jews to become a formidable economic force in spite of harsh conditions. Their persistent diligence was also how the Buddha taught laypeople to conduct business.

While not intended as a rigid moral code, the Buddha's "Six Non-Tao" offers guidance for laypeople seeking financial prosperity.

The Buddha emphasized the importance of acquiring skills and utilizing them to generate wealth. He recommended a four-part approach to managing wealth allocation: one part for daily needs, one for investment in agriculture, one for emergencies, and one for business ventures. Additionally, a portion could be used for marriage and another for housing. Fulfilling these six aspects, the Buddha suggested, would lead to a fulfilling life. He further compared wealth accumulation to the natural processes of a sea receiving rivers and bees collecting pollen, emphasizing a steady and sustainable approach. The Buddha offered advice on lending as well, cautioning against lending too freely and avoiding untrustworthy borrowers, including those known for dishonest behavior. He offered an analogy comparing different societal groups to compass directions: east representing parents, south representing teachers and elders, west representing wife and north representing servants. He encouraged individuals to show respect and share their wealth with both laypeople and monastics, believing such acts could contribute to a positive future and even spiritual progress.[77]

The Buddha summarized His views on commerce; it requires proficiency to acquire and manage property, implementing a four-part method: one part for household use, one part for industrial development, one part to earn interest, and one part to save. He did not object to earning interest, which was in contrast to Christian churches since the Middle Ages who declared interest to be evil and frowned especially upon usury. The Buddha opposed unreasonable usury and supported the Six Non-Tao, which forbid cheating, speculation and acquisition of property at inappropriate moments, as well as taking advantage of people in distress and harshly collecting usury from the poor. Nonetheless, the Buddha seemed to believe that taking interest was reasonable in some cases, possibly reflecting the very sophisticated commercialization of that period.

---

[77] *Zong'a han jing* [Madhyama-agama (Sect. 33)]. *Dazheng xinxiu dazang jing* [Taishō Tripiṭaka (Vol. 1)]. No. 0026. p. 639.

The Buddha on Economic Responsibility

The Buddha advised both laypeople and nobility that managing wealth judiciously is a matter of wise consideration. He offered three key principles: avoid taking out loans for excessively long terms to ensure repayment, refrain from frequent borrowing to minimize risk, and never do business with criminals or swindlers to protect your assets.

One must use wealth to provide for parents, respect mentors, and take care of their wives, relatives and friends, colleagues (servants in ancient times), and spiritual practitioners to cultivate their virtues. To be so courteous to all parties, one would be in a paradise of riches and honor. This is the outlook of commercial responsibility in the Economy of Goodness.

A business owner is like a parent, not making money for self-indulgence but to care for all people around them, such as their relatives and all those in need.

In the *Mahayana Sutra on the Contemplation of the Mind-Ground of Essential Nature*, the Buddha offers a perspective on wealth through the analogy of a wealthy elder. This elder, known for his good deeds, divides his wealth into four parts: one for generating income, one for daily needs, one for helping the less fortunate, and one for supporting family and guests. This practice of responsible financial management is passed down through generations, fostering family prosperity.[78]

The Buddha, through this parable, outlines a complete approach to financial well-being. It emphasizes the pursuit of happiness through wise management and mindful use of resources. The Buddha presented this approach to laypeople as a path to prosperity and fulfillment, similar to the path leading to enlightenment. Earning money should be done thoughtfully, adhering to ethical principles, and using it wisely to support loved ones and contribute to the well-being of all. This balanced approach to wealth creation and utilization forms the core of the Buddha's teachings on economic life.

True happiness should not be mere Hedonic pleasure. Aristotle believed a fulfilled life could be achieved through self-awareness and adhering to morality, providing one had enough material resources. This notion is echoed in what the Buddha said to laypeople.

---

[78] *Dacheng ben sheng xindi guan jing* [Mahayana Sutra on the Contemplation of the Mind-Ground of Essential Nature (Sect. 6.4)]. *Dazheng xinxiu dazang jing* [Taishō Tripiṭaka (Vol. 3)]. No. 0159. p. 310.

The Buddha required laypeople to be diligent in their professions to accumulate wealth and avoid speculation and swindling in business. They should also abstain from indulging in everyday life and avoid the Six Non-Tao. Having accumulated wealth, people should learn to balance income and expenditure and manage them accordingly. Adhering to moral principles is part of this business path and its rewards include happiness.

More importantly, the Buddha showed that attending to parents, teachers, spouses, kin, friends, associates, spiritual practitioners and even all those in pain leads to true, great joy and paradise.

The Buddha stressed the need for combining wisdom and morality in business for achieving economic contentment and utilizing wealth to create positive interpersonal relationships.

Confucius advocated combining wealth and propriety,[79] emphasizing that one should always look after their relationships with others, as well as emphasizing the importance of harmony in ethics.

Take care of one's family, teachers, relatives, friends, colleagues, and good people for the consummation of propriety, as contentment is born from harmonious and loving relationships with people.

Confucianism has extended the love based on propriety to tribes, neighbors, countries, and the world. Therefore, it is said that there must be righteousness between ruler and subject; a proper order between husband and wife; respect between the old and young; and loyalty between friends.[80] This demonstrates great compassion and love.

The Buddha highlighted compassion as the foundation of life. Compassion is the driver of joy in life. Great contentment in one's economic life comes from compassion, love, and morality.[81]

Like passing clouds, hedonistic pleasure leads to sorrow and worthlessness. The Buddha taught that in order to find happiness with wealth, one must show compassion and take care of others, even extending to the masses.

---

[79] Propriety in Chinese, pronounced Li (禮), denotes treating others with respect and courtesy.

[80] M. & Legge, J. (2011). *The Works of Mencius.* New York: Dover Publications. pp. 251–252.

[81] Brown, C. (2003). *Buddhist Economics: An Enlightenment Approach to the Dismal Science.* United States: Bloomsbury Publishing. p. 45.

The Buddha's Ideal Bodhisattva Businessmen

Master Cheng Yen, began by using the Buddha's compassion to persuade the affluent to assist the underprivileged. In Tzu Chi, the well-off embrace hardships as their teacher, understanding the joy of helping out the needy and the value of recognizing and treasuring their own happiness while creating happiness for others. Through Tzu Chi, numerous wealthy individuals have given up smoking, drinking, and gambling. Additionally, their family ties have grown stronger, and their commercial management style has become gentler.

Entrepreneur Tzu Chi volunteers, after experiencing charity work, have a greater appreciation for their employees, families, and society for all that they have given them. Master Cheng Yen refers to these wealthy individuals as "the rich among the rich."

There are also "the poor among the rich"; those with successful careers, who indulge too much, leading to estrangement from their families, conflict in their businesses, and social notoriety. Insufficient compassion is to blame.

"Compassionate heart" should start with "compassionate actions," learning from doing and realizing in action. In practicing compassion, we can inspire our inherent compassion and establish a life value of compassionately helping the world.

Cultivating compassion and accumulating blessings is key to the success of enterprises and individuals.

The Buddha taught His disciples that the sustainable wealth of enterprises lies, as previously quoted, in the four-part management of wealth: one portion for daily use, one for assisting the lonely and bereaved, taking the practice of doing good as joy; one for helping relatives and visitors. The four parts are to be maintained by the father and sons for family advancement.

The Buddha wanted people to not only purify their minds from wealth after obtaining it, but to also use wisdom to manage it so that they may take care responsibly of their families, friends, comrades, and sentient beings.

Master Cheng Yen believes that one should keep their mind untainted while using compassion to benefit all sentient beings, not only through material relief but also with a perfectly pure mind and great love.

According to the *Great Skillful Means Sutra on the Buddha's Repayment of Kindness*, the ideal entrepreneur embodies the qualities of both a Bodhisattva and a Wheel-Turning Sage King.

The seventy Great Bodhisattvas with pure practices have tirelessly offered alms to countless myriads of Buddhas in past countless eons; they cultivated themselves with mercy and protected dharma with goodness; they also harbored great compassion and benefited all parties. These Bodhisattva in the past countless eons have consistently displayed unwavering devotion to learning, unwavering commitment to all beings, and boundless compassion and impartiality. They have been Wheel-Turning Sage Kings, teaching all sentient beings with ten good deeds. With my permission, they followed me happily and finally ascended to the heavens at the end of their lives. They then enjoy the subtle joys of five desires and enjoy a stately luxurious and comfortable lives. They lives in splendid palaces and travel in sedan-chairs and on saddled horses. They entertain themselves in various gardens with music and dancing and they enjoy food copiously.[82]

From the chapter, The Parable of Medicinal Plants in the *Lotus Sutra,* Master Cheng Yen quoted that the Buddha expected everyone to become a rich, compassionate, and beneficent Wheel-Turning Sage King. Master Cheng Yen said:

> The Wheel-turning sage kings have four kinds of blessings. The first is great fortune, treasures, property, and land, making them the richest in the world. The second is a beautiful and dignified appearance, possessing thirty-two physical characteristics. The third is good health and peace, free from sickness and full of happiness. The fourth is a long life, the longest in the world. When the Wheel-turning sage kings appears, the world is at peace, people are kind, happy, and there are no natural disasters or human disasters. These kings all see benefiting the world as their path of practice.[83]

---

[82] *Dafangbian fo bao'en jing* [Great Skillful Means Sutra on the Buddha's Repayment of Kindness (Sect. 2)]. *Dazheng xinxiu dazang jing* [Taishō Tripiṭaka (Vol. 3)]. No. 0156. pp. 131–132.

[83] Shih, Cheng Yen. [Tzu Chi Culture and Communication Foundation]. (2021, Jul 26). *Wisdom at Dawn E913—Realizations Differ According to Capabilities* [Video]. YouTube. https://www.youtube.com/watch?v=vP_wyW1uhUA.

Buddhism held that industrialists should strive to be Wheel-Turning Sage Kings, meaning, when wealthy, they could care for those near them and take into consideration the welfare of all living creatures.

This mindset should be ingrained from the outset of a career. All careers and endeavors should be for the benefit of all living things, rather than for personal ambition and gratification.

Individuals in contemporary Capitalism generally begin with self-interest: striving for higher grades and universities, then better income and careers. After attaining success, people often indulge in entertainment and desires, resulting in harm to society.

Professor Clair Brown, who studies Buddhist economics at the University of California, Berkeley, commented on an American survey of 150 large companies, which found that their operations deteriorated in relation to the salaries of their CEOs.[84] Conversely, when these salaries were lowered, the company's performance improved—a phenomenon perhaps attributable to a lack of responsibility and compassion by business owners.

Altruistic Bodhisattva entrepreneurs are Buddhism's highest expectation for economic and commercial endeavors.

Bodhisattva entrepreneurs, should be industrious and acquire wealth using their wisdom and profession. They should remain pure and free from material taints, seeking to benefit family and friends as well as all sentient beings with compassion. As well as enriching all sentient beings, they should also work to equip them with wisdom and purified minds. This is the practice of Buddhism altruism in a Bodhisattva entrepreneur.

The Lonely Elder: A Good Business Model

Anathapindika, also known as Sudatta, was a renowned lay follower of the Buddha, known for his devotion and generosity. He earned the nickname "Anathapindika," which translates to "The Lonely Elder Who Gives," due to his compassion for the elderly.

Upon meeting the Buddha, Sudatta, who had already attained the spiritual stage of Non-Returner (Anāgāmi), expressed his desire to host the Buddha and his disciples in his city, Sravasti, offering to provide for their needs with everything from food and clothing to housing and medicine. The Buddha, seeking a suitable place for the monks to reside, requested

---

[84] Brown, C. (2003). *Buddhist Economics: An Enlightenment Approach to the Dismal Science*. United States: Bloomsbury Publishing. pp. 40–42.

an appropriate dwelling, prompting Sudatta to eagerly commit to building a monastery as long as the Buddha agreed to visit.[85]

Sudatta vowed to build an abode in Sravasti for the Buddha and His disciples to preach. He searched for land and saw a place owned by Prince Giotto of Persia. No matter how much he pleaded, the prince refused to sell. After numerous negotiations, the prince eventually agreed to sell the land—provided Sudatta paved the Praying Garden with gold.

Sudatta was overjoyed by the response. He was ready to purchase the land whatever the cost, and, with the prince having no other option, managed to achieve his goal. But the prince brought up a problem—the garden's trees were encased in gold, so they would have to be moved out. How could that be possible? For without the trees, the garden wouldn't be as beautiful. Sudatta proposed that he would be willing to donate the land to construct the abode, and the trees could be viewed as the prince's contribution. To this, the prince agreed and thereafter, the two joined forces to support the Buddha. The abode in Sravasti was hence named Jetavana, which loosely translates to donating trees to the Lonely Park.

Sudatta was a great Bodhisattva, perfect in Buddhist practice and wealthy in Buddha's time. But what made him so rich?

The *Sutra of Various Parables* records that Sudatta had been in poverty seven times, due to wrongdoings from his past life. He was so poverty-stricken that he couldn't even have a daily meal.

One day, Sudatta found a sandalwood bucket and sold it for four buckets of rice. With joy, he and his wife brought it home, eager to prepare and eat the much-missed grain. When the delicious flavor hit their taste buds, both shed tears of happiness. But just as they were about to eat, Sariputta came begging for food and, respectfully bowing, Sudatta and his wife offered all their rice.

The next day, Sudatta and his wife cooked another bucket of rice, and this time Mahamaudgalyayana came to seek alms. As before, the couple gave him what they had.

On the third day, the couple cheerfully cooked the third bucket of rice, yet Mahakassapa appeared. The couple remained happy and respectful, offering Mahakassapa their third bucket of rice.

---

[85] Shih, Cheng Yen. (2000). *Si shi er zhang jing jiangshu* [Commentary on The Sutra of Forty-Two Chapters: Spoken by the Buddha]. Taipei: Jing Si Publishing Co., Ltd. p. 75.

On the fourth day, they believed they'd eat rice, but the Buddha appeared. With extreme respect and joy, they offered the fourth bucket of rice in respect.

The Buddha took the rice, and, in an instant, Sudatta found himself in lavish grandeur. His clothing was of splendid silks and satins, and he enjoyed music and dance performances without end. He and his spouse became millionaires, overflowing with innumerable riches.

Why is he so meritorious? His great charity achieved this distinction in one lifetime.

This story demonstrates how following the Buddha's teaching of giving can lead to wealth.

Giving to the poor and virtuous practitioners are all great virtues. As *The Sutra in Forty-Two Sections Spoken by the Buddha* said:

> The Buddha said, "Giving food to a hundred bad people is not as good as giving food to a single good person. Giving food to a thousand good people is not as good as giving food to one person who holds the Five Precepts. Giving food to ten thousand people who hold the Five Precepts is not as good as giving food to a single Srotaapanna.[86] Giving food to a million Srotaapannas is not as good as giving food to a single Sakridagamin. Giving food to ten million Sakridagamins is not as good as giving food to a single Anagamin. Giving food to a hundred million Anagamins is not as good as giving food to a single Arhat. Giving food to one billion Arhats is not as good as giving food to a single Pratyekabuddha. Giving food to ten billion Pratyekabuddhas is not as good as giving food to a Buddha of the three periods of time. Giving food to a hundred billion Buddhas of the three periods of time is not as good as giving food to a single person who is without thoughts, without dwelling, without cultivation, and without accomplishment."[87]

[86] Srotaapanna is the first state of a pure practitioner on the path to becoming an Arhat. There are four states of practice to Arhat: Srotaapanna, Sakridagamin, Anagamin, and Arhat. It is through the state of Arhat, the purity of all sentiments, that one continues to practice the way of the Bodhisattva and can eventually reach the state of Buddha's enlightenment.

[87] Hua, H. (Eds.). (2008). *The Sutra in Forty-Two Sections Spoken by the Buddha: A Simple Explanation by the Venerable Master Hsuan Hua*. United States: Buddhist Text Translation Society. p. 129.

The greatest merit of charity is not only to give to the poor, the virtuous, or to the Buddha, but to impart a mindset that seeks nothing in return when helping others.

Giving without expecting anything in return is true merit. It is not about giving material goods, but imparting a respectful, Buddha-like mindset to those without cultivation or accomplishment.

This giving without asking for anything in return holds the highest merit. This merit brings riches to Sudatta in a single lifetime, making for a great cause and practice.

In conclusion, the Buddha's economic philosophy is to give without expectation of gain, thus preserving all that is given. This is the concept of the Economy of Goodness, which involves providing material and spiritual benefits, as well as developing oneself internally and externally.

Section 6: Economic Thought and Practice in Traditional Chinese Buddhism

The Entry Period of Buddhism in China

There was profound interaction, impact, integration, and reconstruction between Confucianism and Buddhism in history.

Introduced to China during the late Eastern Han Dynasty, Buddhism developed in Wei, Jin, the Southern and Northern Dynasties. Confucianism's declining status in these troubled times played a part in Buddhism becoming a part of all facets of Chinese life. Arthur Wright (1913–1976) argued that it was during the disorganized politics of the Wei, Jin, the Southern and Northern Dynasties period when Buddhism took hold and became the belief of the people.

First of all, Arthur Wright advocated that kings who invaded the Central Plains were unwilling to base their countries on the Confucian ideology of the Han people. So Buddhism became the ideological basis of rule. Wright said:

> First of all, it was a religion alien to China. When the barbarian chiefs learned enough to know that their own tribal ways would not long sustain them in control of North China, they were reluctant to adopt the Confucian principles urged on them by wily Chinese advisers; this course might well mean the loss of cultural identity, the cession of a fatal amount of power to the subject Chinese. Buddhism provided an attractive alternative,

and its monks, many of them foreigners, seemed, in their total dependence on the rulers favor and their lack of family networks, to be useful and trustworthy servants. A further point in favor of Buddhism was that its ethic was universalistic, applicable to men of all races, times, and cultures; it thus seemed the very thing to close some of the social fissures that plagued these regimes and contribute to the building of a unified and pliable body social.[88]

Wright pointed out that the chaos of the Wei and Jin period (220–589 CE) gave Buddhism an opportunity to spread in various states. Buddhism provided a foundation for people of all backgrounds to settle down with. Some of the gentry moved south during the wars, causing the traditional gentry class and religions to decline. Buddhists took the chance to disseminate the idea of charity to the wealthy, making them feel essential. The Wheel-Turning Sage King in Buddhism blessed Hu people (Barbarians) leaders from the north with a holy dynastic basis. Ordinary people struggling with the constant warfare were eased by the concept of the Buddhist Pure Land in the afterlife to alleviate their current sufferings.

Each class saw its role in Buddhist doctrine, and Buddhism became the predominant belief in Chinese society at the time. White referred to this as the domestication of Buddhism in China.

Buddhism in China began to localize from then on. In the early days, foreign monks translated scriptures, and the Tang Dynasty was a period of growth due to Xuanzang, a Chinese monk who traveled to India and brought back scriptures. After that, Buddhism and monk practices were entirely localized, and the temple system was too.

The development of Buddhism was spurred on by the generous donations of its believers, the leadership of exemplary practitioners, and the expertise of the most gifted artists and architects of the time. Chinese Buddhism incorporated Chinese thoughts and culture, leading to a period of creative development spanning hundreds of years.

Buddhist rituals provided a backbone for national and royal ceremonies, such as new emperors ascending the throne, the births of princes, and memorializing royal ancestors. These and other occasions incorporated Buddhist chants and incantations, vegetarian feasts, and offerings to temples.

---

[88] Wright, A. F. (1959). *Buddhism in Chinese History*. Stanford University Press. p. 57.

The emperors of Sui (581–619 CE) and Tang Dynasties (619–907 CE) dynasties re-established them as the center of a unified empire, but these emperors differed from their predecessors in the Han Dynasty. The traditional rationalization of the emperor's power in the Han Dynasty used to depend on local traditions, but now emperors relied heavily on foreign religions to reinforce their credibility and stateliness.[89]

During the Sui and Tang Dynasties, the Han people regained their power and Confucianism was gradually restored to its former position. The simultaneous existence of Buddhism and Confucianism during this period created the conditions for their eventual integration.

At the very beginning, the Buddha founded the Sangha in an egalitarian, uninvolved, and informal manner. No firmer organizational structure was established, and everything was for spiritual cultivation. The monks were nomadic, sustained on minimal food provisions with no hoarding or temple holdings.

Into Perfect Extinction, the Buddha left with no successors or a strict hierarchy of monk groups, precepts, and disciplines. All practice returned to cause and effect. Making mistakes has its own cause and effect, so there was no need for external punishment. When one had attained personal cultivation to its fullest, they could reach Enlightenment. In the early days of Buddhism in India, the spiritual practice organization was focused around a group of monks and the collection of precepts.

In China, Buddhism established a temple system, which was not readily accepted by Chinese people who strongly value family life, especially because of the cold winters of northern China, which made it difficult to beg and travel far. During the Five Dynasties and Ten States era (902–979 CE), the construction of temples increased due to their support from the local gentry, and when rulers converted to Buddhism, constructing temples became seen as an act of merit. In addition, many monks in temples led to the emergence of a management hierarchy system for temple-related economic affairs.

Exploring Buddhist Economics at the Dunhuang Grottoes

The first peak of the Buddhist economy in China may be attributed to the Dunhuang Grottoes. During the Northern and Southern Dynasties,

---

[89] Wright, A. F. (1959). *Buddhism in Chinese History*. Stanford University Press. p. 70.

Dunhuang was a major point of passage on the Silk Road and saw many travelers coming and going between West Asia, Central Asia, India, and Arabia. Central and West Asia were subject to Buddhist influence at this time. Notable Chinese translator of Buddhist sutras, the monk Kumarajiva, was born in Western Asia, before coming to China and translating many classics.

At the time, though the travel industry had flourished, the risks were still high. Across the desert, travelers ran the risk of facing danger due to war, thieving, and robbery. In the face of this, wealthy merchants donated funds to construct temples and statues of Buddha in Dunhuang in the hope of securing peace and prosperity. Over several dynasties, Dunhuang was developed 30 miles outside of the city and became a remarkable, affluent piece of art and religion in human history. Stretching over multiple kilometers were Buddhist caves, representing and honoring the devoted faith of rulers, aristocrats, and merchants through the generations, seeking their blessing.

Apart from praying for safe travels and smooth trade, businessmen also prayed for their families and parents. Furthermore, kings prayed before Buddhas and Bodhisattvas to promote peace in their nation and among the people.

The Buddhist economy of that period was based on trading. The introduction of craftspeople and the designing and embellishment of Buddha statues by merchants and monks necessitated a sizable economic entity. Dunhuang's location facilitated its commerce and travel, while Buddhist faith fostered its economic well-being. For the fabrication of Buddha statues, businessmen had to reside, and sometimes even reside there for an extended period. The rise of those traveling to and through Dunhuang contributed to its prosperity.

An Inexhaustible Store of Teaching Across Three Levels and an Altruistic Economy

The teaching of the "Three Levels Sect of Buddhism" in the Sui and Tang Dynasties demonstrated the economic thought and practice of Buddhism. Dharma Master Xin Xing (540–594 CE), founder of Teaching of the Three Levels Sect, taught his disciples with *The Lotus Sutra* that all living beings should be regarded as future Buddhas and should be respectful to all living beings. The followers of Teaching of the Three Levels Sect bowed down to everyone and regarded all living beings as future Buddhas. They engaged in charitable relief, medical treatment and drug administration, and relief for countless suffering people and the poor. Dharma Master Xin Xing also proposed Inexhaustible Storehouse where the temple received donations and loans, and poor people could borrow money from temples. There was no need for receipts, nor was there any stipulation on how much loans must be repaid. All depended on one's own conscience.

As a result, most borrowers paid back with interest. This economic activity, steered by compassion and love, was distinct from today's capitalist economy, where banks and pawnshops both demand mortgages and contracts.

This inexhaustible storehouse, based on good will and trust, was a success. It brought great wealth to the Teaching of the Three Levels Sect, thereby thriving Buddhism.

The concept of the Inexhaustible Storehouse began in India during the Buddha's era and was used as a reserve to expand Buddhist groups. To avoid criticism, the Buddha adopted an expedient means to transport these alms to those in need and repair temples.

The earliest implementation of the Inexhaustible Storehouse in China dates back to Emperor Wu of the Liang State (464–549 AC.) during the Southern and Northern Dynasties. It was used to transfer alms from believers to the poor; similar to how second-hand clothes are now donated in modern times.

Tzu Chi Foundation has established recycling centers worldwide for the preservation of natural resources. Over 8,000 of these recycling stations exist in Taiwan alone, manned by 200,000 volunteers. Several of the larger centers have sections for second-hand clothes, which can be had without charge and any donations are sent to charities. It is an excellent way to show appreciation for material goods and care for all living beings.

The charity of the Buddha's teaching has always been highly esteemed. During the Sui Dynasty, the Teaching of the Three Levels Sect maximized the efficacy of the Inexhaustible Storehouse.

The land and assets of the Teaching of Three Levels Sect grew until they posed a threat to state power, sparking envy from kings. Emperor Wu (543–578 AC.) of the Northern Zhou Dynasty initiated a massive effort to suppress the Teaching of the Three Levels, confiscating temple property, culminating in the Extinction of Buddhism. Nonetheless, the religion endured for another 300 years until the Song Dynasty.

Master Xin Xing, emphasizing the practical application of the "Inexhaustible Storehouse" teachings, encouraged monks to not only spread these principles but also actively embody them. In his will, he outlined sixteen specific practices associated with the concepts of Permanence, Bliss, Self, and Purity. These practices included acts of devotion such as paying tribute to Buddhas, chanting scriptures, and offering various forms of material support to all living beings. Additionally, they emphasized ethical conduct by encouraging monks to abstain from harmful actions and adhere to twelve specific ascetic practices. The list further encompassed acts of generosity, ranging from offering food and utensils to providing shelter and essential supplies. Finally, Master Xin Xing included practices related to creating an environment conducive to spiritual development, such as lighting candles, ringing bells, offering incense, and preparing charcoal for offerings.[90]

Master Xin Xing demanded his followers to practice the Inexhaustible Storehouse relentlessly daily, wishing that all living beings would employ it to nurture the kind intent of benefactors and beneficiaries, and in turn attain Enlightenment.

The economic thought of the Three Levels Sect embodies the Buddha's spirit of kindness and compassion for all. Everyone was seen as a being who could give back to the temple and all living things.

After Master Xinxing's death, Inexhaustible Storehouse was better organized with expanded funding and lending. It is said many gave money which was loaned to the destitute, and for monastery use. Emperor Taizong (598–649 CE) of the Tang Dynasty even bestowed honors on Dharma Master Huiliao as a Monk of The Country.

The Three Levels Sect's teaching aided those in distress and destitution with aid and loans without interest, leading to higher economic profits. Further, it fostered kindness and communal assistance. This exemplifies the Economy of Goodness where through unselfish generosity, one reaps greater monetary gains.

Zen Master Baizhang's Temple Economic Reform

Ancient China's economy and Buddhism flourished during the Tang Dynasty. Under the reign of Emperor Wu Zetiang (624–705 CE),

---

[90] Fang, G. C. (ed.). *Dacheng wujin cang fa* [Mahayana Infinite Collection of Dharma (Vol. 2)]. CBETA Electronic Buddhist Texts Integration (Vol. 4). No. 0042.

Buddhist culture and the economy peaked. However, Confucian scholars' suppression of Buddhism in later Tang Dynasty impels changes in Buddhism: monks had to survive without offerings from generous followers, and this occurred to satisfy the needs of Buddhist practice, as well as to improve Buddhism's social image.

Zen Master Baizhang's (749–814 CE) monetary pure rules, which laid the groundwork for China's Buddhist agricultural economy. His motto, "A day without work is a day without food," became his lifelong belief.

Baizhang, along with his disciples, engaged in farming and shared teachings with them in the fields. Master Taixu (1890–1947)[91] admired Baizhang's unique system of Zen agriculture, remarking that during the Tang Dynasty, Baizhang seamlessly integrated Zen with farming, blurring the lines between inner spiritual cultivation and outer agricultural labor, thus fostering a new form of monastic life that required no dependence on others. Departing from traditional monastic practices, Baizhang established rural communities where he and his followers embraced a daily routine of labor and abstained from food on days when they did not work. They also engaged in agricultural activities to sustain themselves. Baizhang's teachings were not merely theoretical but were lived out through personal example, encouraging everyone to develop wisdom independently. He often emphasized that while he preached to the assembly, they should each seek their own livelihood. However, over time, some monastic communities drifted from Baizhang's original vision, becoming complacent with existing resources or commercializing Buddhist teachings without embodying the principles of wisdom and compassion. As a result, they faced criticism and stagnation, failing to uphold the transformative spirit of Buddhism.[92]

Zen Master Baizhang corrected the corruption of Temple monks, which had flourished during the Tang Dynasty due to the excessive support of believers and the real estate owned by temples. His advocacy of self-reliance helped improve the internal practice of Buddhism and purify

---

[91] Dharma Master Taixu was a great Buddhist reformer in early twentieth-century China. He emphasized that Buddhism should pay attention to the secular world and transform it into a pure land. He advocated that "Buddhism is about life, not only about death." This changed the traditional perspectives of Chinese Buddhism, in which monks and nuns sought self-enlightenment instead of engaging in social reformation. Master Taixu is perceived as the initiator of contemporary Humanistic Buddhism.

[92] Shi, Taixu (1998). *Tai xu dashi quanshu* [Corpus of Venerable Tai Xu's Buddhist Studies]. Taipei: Pu dao si fojing liutong chu yinxing. p. 163.

it of money and worldly ties, enhancing its social image among Confucian scholars.

Baizhang's monastic regulations successfully combined the spirit of Confucianism and Buddhism, resulting in a syncretic organizational structure. Confucian influences could be seen everywhere, from the appointment of abbots to the behavior of monks. Economically, Baizhang's monks engaged in both permissible and impermissible activities. Master Taixu described Baizhang's labor practices as follows: Human needs such as clothing, food, shelter, and medicine were met through activities such as digging wells, making pottery, mining, farming various crops and medicinal herbs, constructing roads, bridges, buildings, utensils, tools, agricultural implements, as well as manufacturing clothing and medicines. The use of money, precious treasures, silk, leather, tobacco, alcohol, fish, meat, boats, carts, idols, and various other useless items was prohibited.[93]

Zen Master Baizhang set a model for himself, insisting on working with his disciples even when old. When his disciples hid his hoe, he refused to eat as a sign of his commitment, so they had to give it back and let him continue farming. Master Taixu suggested taking Baizhang as a model of frugality and diligence.

Instead of calling it "agricultural Zen," it should be seen as the integration of human labor and Buddhist study. In this perspective, agriculture represents one aspect of human labor, while Zen represents one aspect of Buddhist study. By elaborating on Baizhang's agricultural Zen, it emphasizes the essence of this practice. Prioritizing human labor promotes simplicity and frugality for physical well-being, while the cultivation of Buddhist study emphasizes strict adherence to the teachings for spiritual refinement. Therefore, its essence lies not in the ascetic practices of begging monks but in the balanced pursuit of both human labor and Buddhist study.[94]

Zen Master Baizhang established an agricultural model for Zen temples that persisted for thousands of years. Buddhism was then re-associated with farming, and it was usual for temples to own farmland. During the Ming (1368–1644) and Qing (1644–1911) dynasties periods, there were many temple-owned farmlands, yet with the monks not really working

[93] Shi, Taixu (1998). *Tai xu dashi quanshu* [Corpus of Venerable Tai Xu's Buddhist Studies]. Taipei: Pu dao si fojing liutong chu yinxing. p. 164.

[94] Shi, Taixu (1998). *Tai xu dashi quanshu* [Corpus of Venerable Tai Xu's Buddhist Studies]. Taipei: Pu dao si fojing liutong chu yinxing. p. 165.

them; the task was typically given to a monk-supervisor, with believers and employees hired to do the labor.

Buddhism's agrarian economy supported the independence of monks from secular society. Thus, interaction between givers and monks diminished, leading to a focus on the monks' own practice. Laypeople were then able to practice the expedient means and read scriptures from home. Consequently, economic involvement decreased, causing a decline in the depth and width of the interaction between temples and laypeople.

The Good Economic Ideal of Chinese Buddhism

Professor Jinhua Chen of the University of British Columbia argued that in the early days, the Buddhist economy was largely driven by trade, particularly under Emperor Wu Zetian. Through trade trips to and from Central and West Asia, Buddhism experienced a high point. The Dunhuang economy had a Buddhist trading network. However, with the fall of Buddhism in the mid-Tang Dynasty, it became associated with farmers and lower classes, thus hindering its potential in doctrine and wider society.

Chen's view has historical roots: In the Buddha's era, notable businessmen, rather than craftsmen and farmers, provided clear support to the Buddha and His disciples. The Buddha welcomed offerings from those in less advantageous positions, but the monk economy was mainly mandated by the business society. This relationship with economics governed the strength and direction of Buddhism's growth, allowing it to progress among tycoons who experienced economic interaction with it.

The Buddhist economy in Dunhuang was also a commercial one. Business enabled the prosperity of Buddhism which in turn acted as a spiritual backbone for commerce. It was a profound synergy between Buddhism and economics.

Business must be bolstered by spiritual values. The greater the spiritual vigor, the more profitable the business can be, despite the fluctuations and uncertainties in business. This is the knowledge gleaned from Dunhuang's Buddhist economy.

The mutual causal relationship and combination between spiritual beliefs and economic prosperity is the ideal of the Buddhist Economy of Goodness.

Section 7: A Modern Look at Confucian and Buddhist Views on the Economy of Goodness

According to Xunzi (旬子 A great philosopher of Confucianism in ancient time of China), the essence of Confucian Li, or propriety, is to address people's fundamental desires and meet their basic needs.[95] Mencius adds that what is desirable aligns with what is morally good, "A man who commands our liking is what is called a good man."[96] This underscores Confucianism's focus on ensuring satisfaction and prosperity in daily life, reflecting its economic perspective.

Contemporary Humanistic Buddhism has absorbed the spirit of Confucianism to assist all living beings; this was a major breakthrough in Buddhist history. As opposed to traditional Buddhism, it focuses on disseminating Buddhist teachings for the salvation of all creatures.

The integrated philosophical system that merges Confucianism and Buddhism seeks to provide all beings with completeness in body, mind, and environment. The revival and amalgamation of Confucian and Buddhist ideologies lay the foundation for contemporary economic and practical life philosophies and practices.

Master Taixu's Reform of Temple Teaching and Property Management

In terms of religious assets, Master Taixu opposed the transformation of the assets belonging to the masses into temple assets, ultimately becoming the property of the abbots.[97]

He stated that nearly ninety-nine percent of current Buddhist controversies revolve around temple assets. Originally, the role of a Buddhist monastic leader was to inherit the teachings of the Buddha's wisdom. However, nowadays, it has morphed into inheriting temple assets and livelihood, which has deteriorated over time. Even efforts to maintain the crumbling temple economy have proven futile. The evident outcome is that monks are burdened by property, sinking into worldly

---

[95] Wang, X. Q. (1994). *Xunzi ji jie* [Collected Annotations of Xunzi]. Shandong: Shandong Friendship Publishing House. p. 593.

[96] M. & Legge, J. (2011). *The Works of Mencius*. New York: Dover Publications. p. 490.

[97] Lou, Y. L. (2013). *Zongjiao yanjiu fangfa jiang ji—jicheng yu pipan* [Lecture Notes on Religious Research Methods: Inheritance and Criticism]. Beijing: Peking University Press. p. 183.

affairs, while the assets themselves become neglected burdens upon the monks. Both people and wealth become unusable for Buddhism and become hindrances to its advancement. The fundamental reason lies in the inability to uphold the precepts by refraining from grasping onto wealth to maintain the pure appearance of possessing no property, and in the unwillingness to contribute temple assets to the entire religious community, instead allowing them to be controlled as private possessions by a small number of individuals in a clan-like manner. If this continues, as monks become increasingly burdened by temple assets and livelihood, they will become more ignorant, eventually lacking the strength to sustain the crumbling temple economy. Consequently, they will completely detach from monastic life.[98]

Indian Buddhism has no problem associated with temples accumulating wealth, as monks in the Buddhist era do not accumulate property but rather carry alms bowls while they travel. However, in Chinese Buddhism, concerns exist regarding temple economy, where communal temple assets may become personal property of the abbots.[99]

Mr. Yulie Lou, an Emeritus professor of Peking University, elaborated on Master Taixu's reforms regarding temple assets, stating that the aim is to transform Buddhist assets into communal property shared among monks from all directions. These assets are to be used to support venerable elders with virtue, nurture young monastic communities, and establish various Buddhist endeavors. This reflects Master Taixu's views on reforming Buddhist temple assets.[100]

Master Taixu identified a crucial reform direction for Buddhism in modern China.

[98] Shi, Taixu (1998). *Tai xu dashi quanshu* [Corpus of Venerable Tai Xu's Buddhist Studies]. Taipei: Pu dao si fojing liutong chu yinxing. p. 305.

[99] Lou, Y. L. (2013). *Zongjiao yanjiu fangfa jiang ji—jicheng yu pipan* [Lecture Notes on Religious Research Methods: Inheritance and Criticism]. Beijing: Peking University Press. p. 182.

[100] Lou, Y. L. (2013). *Zongjiao yanjiu fangfa jiang ji—jicheng yu pipan* [Lecture Notes on Religious Research Methods: Inheritance and Criticism]. Beijing: Peking University Press. p. 182.

Jing Si Abode's Self-Reliance Through Independent Farming

The Jing Si Abode, the home and birthplace of Tzu Chi Foundation, does not accept offerings like most monasteries and is instead self-sustaining. All donations go to the foundation for helping those in need. Tzu Chi's branch offices around the globe serve as public spaces for the community together; these are managed solely by Tzu Chi volunteers with no residing monastics. This is a continuation of Master Taixu's educational reforms of the 1940s. Although the way Tzu Chi functions may differ from the reforming teachings of Master Taixu, the same core spiritual values remain, adhering to the original Buddhist dictum of observing the precept of monetary purity without accepting material items as alms.

Master Taixu once said that his three reforms had failed, yet as Mr. Yulie Lou stated, Life Buddhism evolved into Humanistic Buddhism. Taixu's ideal did not fail but illuminated a new direction of growth for Buddhism.

Practicing Monetary Purity

Monastics at the Jing Si Abode adhere to the precept of monetary purity and possess no possessions; all belong to the Jing Si Abode. This is the essential guideline of the Buddha for monastics.

In ancient times, the Buddha and monks could accept food and shelter, while money was not accepted. One hundred years after the Buddha's death, bhikkhus in the East believed they could receive alms of gold and silver, causing divisions among monk groups. Master Cheng Yen's Jing Si Abode, however, follows the Buddha's teachings and doesn't accept money and upholds the Zen Master Baizhang of the Tang Dynasty's philosophy of self-sufficiency: "A day without work is a day without food."

The monastics at the Jing Si Abode have calloused hands from hard work, and talking to them brings peace and joy. In discourse with them, we feel the wisdom of love and tolerance.

As Confucius said, "Where the solid qualities are in excess of accomplishments, we have rusticity; where the accomplishments are in excess of the solid qualities, we have the manners of a clerk. When the accomplishments and solid qualities are equally blended, we then have the man of virtue."[101] Besides planting things like rice and fruit trees initially, masters at Jing Si Abode had to read Buddhist and Confucian classics. This endeavor was designed to create a complete personality. Working on the fields enabled one to get close to nature and form character. This plain and self-regulated character is the unshakeable source of functioning in the ordinary.

The Jing Si Abode is as simple as monasteries come. The semi-Tang-style main building measures less than 30 square meters, and has been used for chanting, charity meetings, meals, and sleep. Despite having had more than ten additions, the structures remain three stories high. Nevertheless, it is the spiritual home of Tzu Chi volunteers worldwide.

Senior monastics have described how four people would sleep shoulder to shoulder back when they were still living in the small wooden hut. Master Cheng Yen would ask her disciples to walk "like the wind," stand "like a pine," sit "like a bell," and lie "like a bow." Walking, standing, and sitting as required is relatively easier to do, but maintaining such sleeping postures is quite challenging. This strictness has been embraced as a spirit of self-restraint and morality by Tzu Chi volunteers in more than 68 countries worldwide. For an organization to grow, its values and beliefs must remain firm and its ceremonial requirements become ever more important and pressing.

There is a candle room at the back of Jing Si Abode, usually filled with monastics and volunteers who make candles on weekdays. The Dharma masters will melt the wax, pour it into the mold, wait for it to set, and then finish by placing an incense stick as the wick in the middle. The "candle without tears" is an original design, reminding people to treasure their material lives.

In her early years, Master Cheng Yen enjoyed watching the flicker of candlelight in the dark, finding it an aid in her meditations. Uneasy with the wasteful drippings of wax, she made use of discarded beverage bottles, pouring wax into them so the wax remained contained when the candle burned. The candlelight thus metaphorically lacked tears, meaning helping others does not injure oneself.

At the Abode, meals are served on round tables, creating a warm family-like atmosphere. Public chopsticks and spoons are used for hygiene and also allows for leftovers to be collected and shared for the next group

---

[101] Legge, J. (1971). *Confucian Analects: The Great Learning, and The Doctrine of the Mean*. New York: Dover Publications. p. 190.

of diners. One should only take what one can eat, and eat everything that has been taken. A small pot of hot water is provided on the table. After finishing a meal, any remaining food scraps on one's plate should be rinsed with a bit of hot water and consumed, leaving no waste at all.

This simple lifestyle has been maintained for over 50 years. Not only do the monastics follow this dining etiquette, but the over 200 Tzu Chi Foundation staff members who work at the monastery also adhere to it. All of the hundreds of thousands of certified Tzu Chi volunteers and their families have adopted this habit in their own homes. This is how the Jing Si Abode has brought forth a new way of life for Tzu Chi members.

Diligence, Self-Restraint, and Extending to All People

Self-restraint and frugality are embodied in the working environment of the Abode where more than 400 people practice daily. Until 2019, offices were fitted with ceiling fans but lacked air conditioning, despite summer temperatures of up to 33 °C.

The guest dormitories and offices at the Jing Si Abode are adorned with simple, wooden furniture, wooden gatehouses and latticed windows, reminiscent of an ancient academy. Upon first glance, it is hard to imagine this place to be the headquarters of one of the largest global charities.

Volunteers and visitors from everywhere stream in endlessly, and it is the masters' duty to greet these travelers returning to their spiritual homes. All day long, the kitchen is busy providing sustenance for over 400 people. All the expenditures in the Abode are covered by the masters' through the hard work of their own earnings: their love for Tzu Chi members and aid to the Tzu Chi Foundation without any remuneration.

The masters of the Jing Si Abode have pioneered Tzu Chi's volunteering practices for over 50 years, contributing generously and participating in emergency relief. Master Cheng Yen, Tzu Chi's first volunteer, does not accept personal offerings, is self-reliant, and dedicates herself to relieving those in suffering.

All Tzu Chi volunteers embody her spirit, traveling to various parts of the world to provide disaster relief at their own expense. "Self-reliance, self-discipline, self-purification, saving all beings, and selfless giving" are some of the spiritual teachings that have been passed on from masters of the Jing Si Abode passed down to all Tzu Chi members.

Such a legacy demonstrates Tzu Chi's presence during various disasters, as well as its support for the most impoverished around the world.

It illustrates that leading a simple life helps keep one away from calamities and that self-control is essential to preserving a sustainable lifestyle on our planet.

I refer to Tzu Chi's model as the Economy of Goodness. Its Four Missions and Eight Footprints encompass Charity, Medicine, Education, Humanistic Culture, Environmental Protection, Bone Marrow Donation, International Relief, and Community Volunteerism. These missions greatly benefit social justice and equitable distribution.

In addition to helping tens of millions of suffering people yearly, Tzu Chi has proposed new values for numerous professional fields: In Charity, one gives with gratitude; in Medicine, patients are seen as teachers; in Education, the core teaching is altruism; and in Humanistic Culture, reports should be truthful and positive.

These values have a far-reaching effect on constructing the goodness of the era.

While guiding volunteers to contribute to society, Tzu Chi has inspired many entrepreneurs to become volunteers. Their dedication to charity has improved their business practices, transforming companies into sources of altruism and goodness.

The charity's economic contribution is explained in detail in Chapter 7. It is essential that charitable organizations rooted in goodness and love can provide relief and new value, demonstrating that altruism and charity can create more economic resources while also creating an equitable economic system.

Beginning with charity, entrepreneurs should be encouraged to recognize the satisfaction derived from alleviating suffering and to shift from a self-centered outlook to an altruistic one. They should practice kindness and manage with love, taking altruism as the foundation to achieve the Economy of Goodness in society.

CHAPTER 7

Economic Goodness Before the Industrial Revolution

Section 1: Economic Mutual Trust Structure in Medieval Commercial Society

The Ascension of Medieval Towns

In the ninth century AD, as the Roman Empire declined, towns began to appear, signaling the ascent of a mercantile society in Western countries, such as Britain, the Netherlands, Germany, and France in place of an agrarian one.

In medieval Germany, especially in the west, the countryside was divided into small units that could be traversed on foot in five or six hours. This meant that farmers could bring their produce to market and return home in the evening.[1]

In the Middle Ages, these towns were usually military bases from Roman times, with high stone walls built to resist foreign invasions or fend off bandits. Initially, the town was not solely commercial but a blend of agriculture and commerce.

In France, between the tenth and twelfth centuries, towns acted as hubs of commerce, agriculture, and universities. In Western Europe,

---

[1] Postan, M. M., Rich, E. E., & Miller, E. (Eds.). (1963). *The Cambridge Economic History of Europe: Economic Organization and Policies in The Middle Ages.* Cambridge: Cambridge University Press. p. 5.

following the collapse of the Roman Empire, some fledgling towns lacked proper fortifications, so the German term Burgus was utilized to describe their undefended inhabitants. This then evolved into Cititas, which referred to urban dwellers in Medieval Germany and signified early citizens.

The rise of commerce can be attributed to the commercial groups formed by Jews in the Middle Ages. They functioned as commercial negotiators, mainly in Eastern Europe. In the late Middle Ages, they were involved in currency and commodity transactions, especially with the Arab world, Western Europe, and Asia.

In medieval Europe, Christians devoted to business were known as Frisians. Similarly, to Jews, they conducted trade between East and West. Initially, their profits were limited, yet by the late Middle Ages, their commercial presence could be seen in every city. Due to their faith, they had access to vast resources, whereas the activities of Jews were marginal.

By the ninth century, Dorstad was the first commercial town on the European continent and the Frisians' primary city for trade. Businesspeople grew a new commercial frontier in Rhine and Mainz, Germany, which became the dominant commercial cities on the continent. Commercial cities developed in low-lying lands and England influenced by the Roman-built castles.

Pirenne's research demonstrates that castles in England and Holland differed from Burgs in Germany, which were known as Faubiurgs, deriving from the Roman Empire-era fortified castles that were reconfigured for commercial purposes. Between the twelfth and thirteenth centuries, German cities grew exponentially, and walls were even erected for the protection of commercial activity. This period marked the beginning of a commercially oriented Europe.

The Origin of Capital

From the sixth to the seventh century, Jews held a significant amount of land in Spain, Italy, Germany, and Gaul. However, when Rome enforced laws to compel them to part with their lands, they had to take to trade.

Between the sixth and eighth centuries, commercial trading brought considerable capital to the Jews, constituting an indispensable social force in the Middle Ages.

Many records show that in the early 1200s, it was common to trade land as capital for profit or to acquire land to gain capital.

At that time, capital was universally used even among the Christian clergy. The priest Gordic, referred to as a saint later on, embezzled the holy grail with the agreement of his peers and gained a substantial profit before returning it to the church.

The Catholic Church in the thirteenth century owned a multitude of land and capital which priests managed through negotiation. The Cistercian Order sought to manage husbandry, primarily wool, which became a crucial asset and source of income at the time. Priests ran ranches, and the wool was sold across Europe.[2]

When monks dedicated themselves to wool trading, bishops amassed church wealth through pilgrimage as a commercial endeavor.[3] As not all believers had the resources to go on pilgrimages to sacred sites, regional churches became pilgrimage destinations, where wealthy landlords sought religious salvation, while ordinary people sought refuge from the plague and some provided medical care.

The way for an entrepreneur bishop to raise funds for church renovation was to encourage believers to make pilgrimages. This pilgrimage was often accompanied by holy miracles, bringing more pilgrims and wealth to the church. Circa 1230, monks in Worcester Cathedral Priory in England recorded that Thomas, who lived in Elderfield, had lost his male organ and eyes in a duel; yet, thanks to St. Wolfstan's miraculous intervention, his eyes were restored and the male organ regrew. This story inspired countless Christians to make pilgrimages to Worcester Cathedral.[4]

Factors that contributed to the rise of capital in the Middle Ages were the Black Death, which caused a population plunge in Europe, and the Hundred Years' War, which led to new taxes, enabling capital accumulation. The death toll from the plague meant that landlords had to negotiate with fewer tenants or serfs, who then had free time to work as craftsmen in cities to gain more money.

On the other hand, the Hundred Years' War (1337–1453) necessitated Britain and Edward III to take out loans to pay off debts incurred by the war. So, they issued bonds to settle the debts. William De La

---

[2] Casson, M., & Casson, C. (2014). *The History of Entrepreneurship: Medieval Origins of a Modern Phenomenon.* Business History, 56(4), 1223–1242. p. 1231.

[3] Casson, M., & Casson, C. (2014). *The History of Entrepreneurship: Medieval Origins of a Modern Phenomenon.* Business History, 56(4), 1223–1242. p. 1231.

[4] Casson, M., & Casson, C. (2014). *The History of Entrepreneurship: Medieval Origins of a Modern Phenomenon.* Business History, 56(4), 1223–1242. p. 1232.

Pole, an English businessman, convinced the king to create the English Wool Company, and he was paid in advance in return for the wool market monopoly. Multiple shareholders of the company held the king's debts, and they monopolized wool trading to make a mammoth profit, which directly impacted the financial resources of the royal family. These commercial forces eventually led to the emergence of individuals as citizens.[5]

The Rise of Free People

Economic historians such as Pirenne believe that liberty is a necessary and universal attribute of city dwellers. As commerce developed, the number of free people increased.

In medieval Europe, most people were serfs belonging to the Church, which protected their work. Business People could move about and stay in cities as long as each claimed to be serving a specific host.

The church's demand that serfs weren't allowed to be freed, as per the law at that time, was overturned after the Middle Ages. Farmers associated with the church were free to move about and disassociate from their identity as serfs; the church rarely intervened in such emancipations. The labor of a free man could generate considerable income; according to literature in 1293 CE, 93% of city dwellers earned over 30 Li, the legitimate currency of the period, equivalent to one pound of silver (240 Li).

In 1122 CE, a group of businessmen demanded to serve Saint Vaast in France of today. They provided administrative help to the church in exchange for tax exemptions in the city's commercial activities. These city businessmen, with similar noble standing were the earliest middle class before Capitalism arose.

The Establishment of the Medieval Chamber of Commerce

The establishment of the Chamber of Commerce was key to the former Capitalism's rise. During Europe's so-called dark period, most wealth was held by property owners. Although commercial trading continued to develop then, the breakthrough came in the eleventh century when

---

[5] Casson, M., & Casson, C. (2014). *The History of Entrepreneurship: Medieval Origins of a Modern Phenomenon*. Business History, 56(4), 1223–1242. p. 1233.

the Normans invaded, causing the feudal dynasty to decline and fall. The Crusades also enabled the expansion of continental and sea routes, notably the Italian businessmen increased their trading from land to sea.

From the twelfth to the thirteenth century, trade was focused in Louis Champagne's significant trade fairs. These garnered many caravans from Italy, Flanders, Germany, France, and countries at sea level, like the Netherlands. International commodities trading was wholly manifested in this form of trade fair but eventually had to give way to long-term business representatives. Italian traders were notably prominent at the time.

At the end of the thirteenth century, Italian business people replaced their single-trip visits to trade fairs with permanent representatives and offices. They started establishing these reps' offices in different parts of Europe, then reading the financial reports from the reps and providing direction. This caused trade fairs to become less relevant. The creation of these permanent cross-regional commercial organizations also contributed to the decline of the Champagne Fairs.

In today's trade, people book goods in specific quantities and then transport them by land or sea. During Medieval times, merchants were expected to bring domestic goods to other lands, sell them in bulk and purchase foreign goods not available in their own country, to be brought back. Trade disputes arose and were sometimes taken to court, however local businessmen received favoritism from the judges, providing limited protection to foreign merchants.

The Church's clergy were prohibited from trading, since they kept to their residence whereas mercantile merchants were continually traveling. The Church's doctrines, such as honesty, abstention from usury, and mutual help, were still having an effect on commercial activities then.

The Formation of the Joint Stock Company

Trade in the maritime era had significant risks; robbery, war, and the perils of the sea could easily render goods and endanger crew lives. To mitigate this, Italian business people sought out additional investors for maritime trading.

The joint-stock partnership system began emerging.

Their profits were apportioned according to their capital contributions. This free association, involving innumerable investors, infused commerce with great vigor at the time.

According to Venetian literature, Genoese trade contracts of the medieval period were of two types: Commenda and Societasmaris. Contracts in Venice at this time were based not on the length of a year, but on a single expeditionary trade. This expedition traded with Africa, Spain, and later America. Investment businesspeople with capital, and navigators knowledgeable in sailing, could join in the shareholding.

In Commenda's joint-stock contract, the investor and the contributor held shares jointly. The investor who stayed on land and did not embark on an expedition was referred to as "stan," while the contributor venturing out to sea was known as "tractor." Ordinarily, stans would receive 3/4 of the profits, while the captain tractor was allocated only 1/4. Human life was not highly valued then, but capital was scarce. If the captain tractor contributed a quarter, he and Stan, the investor, would divide the profits equally.[6]

A Business System of Fraternity and Mutual Aid

For the sake of safety and profit, Italian chambers of commerce and sailors conceived the notion of fraternity. They promised to ensure caravans protected and looked after each other while they traveled or sailed, and faithfully safeguarded the interests of each investor.

The risk of sailing and expeditions in caravans was high, with expertise being essential. An anonymous author's book called *King's Mirror*, detailed sailing knowledge and showed the crew how to work together onboard and practice discipline on land, avoiding indulgence. This book furthered navigational knowledge and ethics post-Middle Ages.

We can see that an embryonic modern economic society, characterized by professional skills and ethics, had gradually taken shape.

Due to a shareholding system, massive capital was generated to promote European commerce both then and afterward.

Apart from trading, by the start of the thirteenth century, banking had taken the form it would adopt. Traders could be provided with currencies from abroad and even barter foreign currencies, which had become an ordinary practice, either through oral commitment or written accord.

---

[6] Postan, M. M., Rich, E. E., & Miller, E. (Eds.). (1963). *The Cambridge Economic History of Europe: Economic Organization and Policies in The Middle Ages*. Cambridge: Cambridge University Press. p. 5.

Loans to merchants engaged in maritime trade were commonplace in thirteenth-century Europe. Interest rates spiked to 25%, due to the risks associated with oceanic trade. Yet, providing investors with an opportunity to secure windfall profits upon their ventures' safe return from the seas.

Businesspeople who had profited from sea trade also turned to land-based operations with fewer risks. In 1285, 25 merchants from Douai formed a caravan to trade in Syria and Egypt, guarded by 36 armed soldiers. They also employed troops to create permanent fortifications in the colonies, rewarding each military commander with a house, land, a highway, and even a town.

As investment grew, business people had to rely on their foreign representatives to handle trade. Bookkeeping became a must for business. Literature shows that from 1296 to 1305, double-entry bookkeeping was fully formed.

Various professional modes of contemporary commercial society had taken shape in the thirteenth and early fourteenth centuries, marking the start of capitalism's pioneer period.

The early development of Capitalism occurred in the oft-called Dark Middle Ages, which weren't actually dark. Risk-taking and business development grew in an environment where royal power declined. Ambitious interests were harnessed by means of cooperation and mutual aid; such as organizing caravans to protect against bandits, forming joint-stock companies to decrease risks, and utilizing contracts and fraternalism to foster success in maritime trading.

The altruistic spirit beneath self-interest paved the way for the dynamic growth of modern commerce.

The Rise of Citizen Economy and the Establishment of Mutual Aid

The great success of ocean trade from the thirteenth to the fifteenth centuries was due to the mutual support between businesses and sailing crews. Without it, no system of citizen economy could have been established.

Italy, from the fifteenth to seventeenth centuries, gave rise to the Renaissance. It broke free from feudalism and the Church, offering citizens the chance to improve their social welfare through trade.

In this period, Italy saw the introduction of the Civic Economy, which contrasted with the Feudal Economy, wherein the wealthy hereditary class benefited the most. The Civic Economy, however, brought advantages to businessmen and cooperative professionals.

Italian philosophers Genovesi and Dragonetti expressed their ethical and philosophical views on economic development, believing that policies and laws should award virtue rather than power. Dragonetti argued that criminal justice alone could not display social goodness—which arose from rewarding virtue instead. He asserted that commerce fostered the cultivation and refinement of citizens' virtue, as well as that of others, through trade, favoring both parties and promoting the common good of society.[7]

Genovesi viewed Mutual Assistance, not Mutual Gain, as the driving force behind commerce.

Mutual Assistance denotes good virtues. Genovesi, a philosopher during Adam Smith's era, proposed Mutual Assistance, emphasizing creating mutual benefit, instead of Smith's Mutual Advantage advocating for the pursuit of individual interests through offering gains to others. "This slight difference may generate a thousand miles apart," as an old Chinese proverb says.

Mutual benefit is concerned with protecting one's own interests.

Mutual assistance poses the question: what can I do for others?

Mutual benefit is based on the logical premise that, as the other party can give something to me, I choose to benefit them in return.

Mutual assistance shows that even though I won't gain from it, I still want to give assistance.

Mutual assistance is an altruistic practice.[8] Genovesi and Dragonetti, two philosophers in Naples, Italy, held the opinion that commerce would offer the most effectiveness when it comes to embodying civil virtue. According to Dragonetti, people could be rewarded for their goodness and virtue just by aiding one another. Genovesi, in turn, saw business as a successful example of mutual assistance.

From the thirteenth to eighteenth centuries, the citizen economy was based on mutual aid, the thought and practice of the Economy of Goodness prior to the Industrial Revolution.

---

[7] Bruni, L., & Zamagni, S. (2014). *Economics and Theology in Italy Since the Eighteenth Century*. The Oxford Handbook of Christianity and Economics. pp. 64–76.

[8] Bruni, L., & Zamagni, S. (2014). *Economics and Theology in Italy Since the Eighteenth Century*. The Oxford Handbook of Christianity and Economics. pp. 58–63.

Until the twentieth century, this ideal of a citizen's economy had not waned, but persevered like a perpetual stream underneath Capitalism. To date, several Italian economists have discussed the economic philosophy of Genovesi and Dragonetti, differing greatly from Adam Smith's.

The Civil Economy places more importance on collective interests than individual ones, and its goal is to cultivate public prosperity, not state strength. It envisions a system of collective welfare, not centralism or individual welfare.

SECTION 2: HISTORICAL DIALECTIC OF ALTRUISM AND EGOISM IN COMMERCE DEVELOPMENT

Around the fourteenth and fifteenth centuries, as maritime trade flourished, commercial loans became a major driving force. This raised tensions between religious teachings and economic progress, as the Church opposed loans. Thomas Aquinas did not object to maritime commerce, but Catholics and Protestants such as Martin Luther were strongly against collecting interest. In particular, they viewed pure money chasing as a sin.

Since the Enlightenment in the seventeenth and eighteenth centuries, intellectuals had divided views on monetary commerce. On one hand, the struggles, civil wars, and entanglements between Catholicism and Protestantism from the fifteenth to seventeenth centuries had caused Western people to reflect deeply on the relevance of religion.

After traditional Christian business ethics waned due to religious disputes, intellectuals began lauding commercial pursuits.

Illustrating Voltaire, a French philosopher of the Enlightenment, as an example, he was the first to receive publishing royalties. In the seventeenth century, intellectuals usually wrote and published books under the patronage of nobles or wealthy businessmen, with no concept of royalties. However, Voltaire eventually became wealthy due to this concept. He observed that commerce was often the only means for allowing religious and ethnic groups to live in peaceful harmony. He described how commerce promotes this harmony.

Come into the London Exchange, a place more respectable than many a court. You will see assembled representatives of every nation for the benefit of mankind. Here the Jew, the Mohametan and the Christian deal with one another as if they were of the same religion, and reserve the name "infidel" for those who go bankrupt. Here the Presbyterian puts his trust in the Anabaptist, and the Anglican accepts the Quaker's promissory note. Upon leaving these peaceful and free assemblies, one goes to the synagogue, the other for a drink; yet another goes to have himself baptized in a large tub in the name of the Father through the Son to the Holy Ghost; another has his son's foreskin cut off, and over the infant he has muttered some Hebrew words that he doesn't understand at all: Some others go to their church to await divine inspiration with their hat on their head. And all are content.[9]

Voltaire portrayed commerce as a form of justice in a time of political and religious strife. It allowed for mutual exchanges, thus teaching people to tolerate each other's differences. This likely explains why Adam Smith praised personal interests as fostering social good.

In an era of strife and accusations of paganism, trade invited people of various faiths to gather in the stock exchange to form a peaceful, free, and mutually beneficial group, with the aim of accumulating wealth.

Although all religions then declared that pagans would go to hell, the pursuit of wealth became a widely accepted norm.

Jerry Muller wrote: "Here Voltaire is the prophet of the profit motive: compared to the competitive quest for salvation, the quest for wealth is more likely to make men 'peaceful' and 'content.' Compared to the altruistic crusade of forcibly saving one's neighbor's soul, even if it leaves his body in ruins, the pursuit of wealth is a potentially more peaceable pursuit, and one that leaves one's neighbor content."[10]

As the Renaissance and Enlightenment continued, religious imprisonment was brought to an end. Beforehand, centuries of religious clashes between Christians and Muslims and between Catholics and Protestants had caused immense persecution of pagans in Western society.

The intellectuals of the Enlightenment were disgusted by the relentless search for truth. When the power of the sea opened up the globe, business exchange and the mutual enrichment of wealth became the prized values of the new society.

At the time, wealth appeared to bring more joy than religion. Trade embodied economic freedom and equal opportunity, thus benefiting more people as a great stride forward in human society.

---

[9] Muller, J. Z. (2007). *The Mind and the Market: Capitalism in Western Thought.* United Kingdom: Knopf Doubleday Publishing Group. p. 29.

[10] Muller, J. Z. (2007). *The Mind and the Market: Capitalism in Western Thought.* United Kingdom: Knopf Doubleday Publishing Group. p. 30.

The commercial economy after the Renaissance broke the stronghold of religion and economic monopolies of aristocrats, kings and elite classes. City businesspeople acquired the influential power of wealth, and traditional nobles and kings—no longer able to depend on hereditary lands and tenants for sustenance or taxes to fund the state—had to deal with businesspeople to levy taxes. The Magna Carta in England was the result of this. By negotiating taxes with the king, business people also achieved more political sway.

Section 3: Historical Dialectics of Self-Interested and Altruistic Economy

Voltaire praised self-interest for both personal happiness and the greater good of society, countering Pascal's view that the social order should rest on altruism. He argued that society would not fall apart if everyone took care of their own interests, whether politically or economically.

Voltaire advocated the advantages of self-interest. His view influenced or echoed Adam Smith and the later day of Hayek (1899–1992 CE) and claimed that self-interest was the driving force for promoting social and economic well-being.

Voltaire stated in *Le Mondain* that wealth was the root of artistic creation and material wealth a necessity for a higher civilization.

Voltaire defended self-interest, believing that only those who love themselves could love others more. To love ourselves is the nature that God endowed us. Voltaire said:

It is impossible for a society to be formed and to persist without self-esteem - just as it is impossible to create children without desire, to think of feeding oneself without appetite, and so on. Self-esteem is what allows us to love others; it is through our common needs that we are useful to humanity; and this is the fundamental basis of all commerce, an unbreakable bond between people. Without love, no form of art can be created and neither man nor community can be built. It is nature that has given us the instinct of self-respect, reminding us to respect the self-respect of others. Law has restrained us, but religiousism has perfected us. When God created human beings, He may have been considering that people should take those of others into account. This is of course true - merchants would not have gone to India for charity, and stonemasons would not have carved stone just to please their neighbors. Therefore, let us stop condemning our God-given instincts and use them as God intends us to.[11]

As a pioneering figure of the Western Enlightenment, Voltaire's thought concurred with that of the ancient Chinese philosopher Xunzi. Xunzi's depiction of propriety encouraged nurturing people's basic needs, so as to satisfy their desires in the name of justice and morality. The Confucian thought of "putting oneself in another's place" reflected the expansive and compassionate love, which begins with oneself and radiates outward to others. However, Confucianism also held that people's desires were limitless; these should be reined in through propriety. On the other hand, Voltaire did not suggest any way to limit the proliferation of desires.

He commended the liberty brought by commercial capital, such as the people's freedom anchored in the Magna Carta. The burgeoning of commercial capital endowed citizens with the capacity to challenge the monarch and struggle for freedom.

However, citizens who had attained freedom were likely to exploit others in return. This was an issue Voltaire did not address.

Voltaire was an accomplished scholar and a savvy businessman, renowned for his financial prowess. At a time when loans were still frowned upon by the government and the church, social lending flourished, and Voltaire particularly benefited, having lent hundreds of thousands of gold coins to the royal family and receiving enormous profits in return.

Over the next 20 years, he acquired a remote farm and converted it into a new town. Till the end, he was one of Europe's most renowned authors and wealthiest citizens.

Despite praising interests and commercial wealth, Voltaire perceived a new world wherein all people could share wealth and prosperity—the same ideal as Adam Smith put forth in his "Wealth of Nations," advocating for the construction of a world of great harmony wherein trade between countries would be advantageous to all.

Economic Exploitation and Fair Distribution

While Voltaire praised commerce and became wealthy, his contemporary philosopher Justus Moser (1720–1794 CE) worried that pursuing

---

[11] Steiner, P. L. (2007). *Voltaire: Philosophical Letters: Or, Letters Regarding the English Nation*. United States: Hackett Publishing Company. p. 107.

commercial interests, particularly the expansion of global trade, would devastate local cultures and economies.

Justus Moser ought to be the first philosopher to oppose globalization. He thought the growth of the market would displace citizens' values. Farmers reliant on the land for their subsistence felt the impact of burgeoning commercial cities. Traditional craftwork was unable to compete with urban manufacturing of mass-produced goods. Consequently, farmers lacked an income, came to cities in search of sustenance and became laborers striving to survive. Once they lost their occupations, they became destitute.

Peasants in rural areas engaged in agricultural activities to eke out a living. Small retailers sold leather gloves, silk handkerchiefs, cotton hats, and metal buttons directly to farmers. This expenditure and luxury goods from other parts of the country exploited their peaceful, agricultural lifestyles that only addressed their basic needs and enticed people's greed.

Justus Moser's hometown was a small, agricultural-dominated town, unlike Voltaire's. He witnessed the breakdown of locally valued handicrafts under industrial capital, with farmers becoming workers and the local culture declining. Consequently, he held the view that urban industry ruined culture and civic virtue.

Therefore, capital commerce caused an exchange of cultures, faiths, and peoples in the world, and a greater exploitation of the working class and marginalized people. This resulted in a significant imbalance in wealth distribution that became the main focus of economic life.

Self-Interest Leading to Structural Global Exploitation

This exploitation of economic outcomes was not only seen in Europe during its commercial peak but occurred also in areas colonized by European countries, such as South America, Asia, and Africa, where it was even more severe. The aid of citizens' economy was between commerce, while exploitation happened between consumption and colonized territories. This was a matter of economic injustice in the early days of Capitalism.

British philosopher Edmund Burke (1729–1797 CE) thought that the East India Company wielded political and economic power, exploiting Indian resources without any regard for ethics. This was an inhumane and blatant plunder by Western Capitalist pre-commercialism. Burke, however, did not put the blame on commercialism but on the political power vested in the East India Company, thus leading to its cruel exploitation.

The East India Company used political clout to extract taxes from Indian citizens, then purchased goods in India and shipped them to the UK. Their cargo to India was not for the natives but for politicians, soldiers, and Europeans in India.[12]

Britain conquered India through war and exploited its resources via the East India Company. This system was firmly opposed by Burke, as the symbiosis of politics, the military, and the economy was a problem common outside Europe in the early stage of Capitalism.

After all, should Capitalism or political hegemony be blamed? Perhaps both.

Capitalism spurred on unmitigated production and consumption, driving the demand for commodities and prompting European armies to incessantly pillage the world.

It is because commercial capital enabled the modernization of armies, which allowed European countries to loot Asia, America, and Africa between the seventeenth and nineteenth centuries.

Those who benefited from capital commended it, whereas those who were exploited were pushed to a social class more anguishing than Europe and Asia in times of agriculture and wildness in America and Africa.

Regardless, the new class created by business and capital civilization was tired of the hereditary bureaucracy and the Church. The eighteenth-century French Revolution highlighted the emerging capitalists, financiers, and liberal intellectuals, who joined forces to overthrow the existing social order and embrace a new one.

It is not easy to fully grasp the history of Capitalism's overall development, yet its commercial prowess had an effect on religious doctrine, freeing people from the Church's control. Plus, commercial capital weakened hereditary royal power and conferred people with citizenship and political authority. It was seen as a sign of the justice and efficacy of commercial capital.

---

[12] Muller, J. Z. (2007). *The Mind and the Market: Capitalism in Western Thought*. United Kingdom: Knopf Doubleday Publishing Group.

Section 4: Deviation from Mutual Assistance in Commerce

Commercial capital's subsequent exploitation at home and abroad deviated from the mutual benefit concept of the fourteenth and fifteenth centuries. After the Renaissance and Enlightenment, Western foreign expansion and aggression saw commercial capital wield political and military power to plunder worldwide, disregarding commercial parity and mutual aid.

While treating domestic people equally, commercial capital perceived those in countries without industry as inferior, contrary to Voltaire's message of harmony and respect for all.

Any power, be it commercial or cultural, would be seized and controlled by politics. It was the combination of politics and commerce that caused Capitalism to invade various countries in the eighteenth and nineteenth centuries, as observed by Burke of England.

After all, the joint-stock commercial model developed in the thirteenth and fourteenth centuries was successful. The issue lies in human values; whether they are self-interested or altruistic.

While treating domestic people equally, commercial capital viewed people in countries with no industry as inferior, deviating from Voltaire's narrative of harmony and respect for all.

In an altruistic era, everyone could invest in maritime trade and share both risks and profits. People embraced their self-interests as well as altruism.

However, once the capital was highly developed, the wealthy class became more independent. The pursuit of greater commercial gain, be it for the glory of God or personal gain, became a beast in conjunction with politics and the military, ruthlessly consuming the economically disadvantaged—countries, people, families, and nations.

The goodness of mutual benefit, mutual aid, and inclusiveness in the economy was forgotten, leading to more human conflicts and wars around the turn of the nineteenth and twentieth centuries.

Voltaire saw in his time a peaceful, commercial society no longer fighting about faith. Yet, he didn't anticipate the next two centuries would bring an unfair, unjust, and disrespectful human society, motivated by desires to fight for benefit and exploitation.

Regarding economic philosophy and ethics, the goodness of business should be inclusiveness, equality, and respect for business and civic virtues, as Voltaire saw at the end of the eighteenth century. Yet the pursuit of self-interest he'd defended was responsible for consuming such goodness and virtues.

Voltaire and Adam Smith rationalized the pursuit of self-interest that indirectly created numerous business groups and individuals to plunder, fight, and expand endlessly all over the world, dragging humankind into unprecedented conflicts. One colonial revolutionary war after another, World War I, World War II, and struggles for freedom in the name of communism and Capitalism all brought countless precious lives and happiness was ruined under the wheel of self-interest.

CHAPTER 8

The Evolution of Self-Interested and Altruistic Economic Thought

SECTION 1: THE BEGINNING OF SELF-INTERESTED ECONOMY

Self-interest is the driving force behind modern economic lifestyles. It fosters the economy's flourishing development and deepens the gap between rich and poor. This gap occurs between individuals and between nations. The notion of a laissez-faire economy is no doubt a reaction to the monopolization of economic resources by small groups, the new affluent class (which corresponds to the aristocrats in feudal society), or a government dictatorship. However, it still cannot solve the problem of economic inequality. The emergence of an Economy of Goodness began with public welfare organizations, expanding to social enterprises, impact investment, and the universal good of all economic activities. This chapter discusses the origins of the Economy of Goodness to solve the dilemma of the historical legacy of economic inequality and economic freedom left behind.

Adam Smith said: "It is not from the benevolence of the butcher, the brewer, or the baker that we expect our dinner, but from their regard to their interest." Under Adam Smith's understanding of economic activities, benevolence and morality are derived from the voluntary creation of positive output for society within individual interests. The invisible hand of the market can reshape personal interest into a public good. Under the

R.-S. Her, *The Economy of Goodness*, https://doi.org/10.1007/978-981-97-6363-4_8

working of the invisible hand, the sin of privatization will automatically and inadvertently bring about the common interests of the entire society.[1]

So, what do good intentions and morality have to do with economic activities?

Indeed, modern economists strenuously avoid distinguishing between good and evil. Economics hopes to draw a dividing line between good and evil and strives to seek empirical evidence and neutral value. Socio-economics researchers, whether classical or modern economists, all seem to exclude personal morality and good intentions from the discussion of capitalism or for establishing a fair, orderly commodity marketplace. More often, socio-economists spend time investigating the structure and operating mechanisms of the economy and their impact on a market order, mode of transaction, and interests of capitalists and workers. Economic sociologists are concerned about structures but not individuals' ethical attitudes. These individuals should include capitalists, consumers, workers, and professionals.

Economists stress neutral value. Under such Capitalist commercial activities, research on people's goodness and morality should be addressed. This has led to a substantial structural blind spot in the development of Capitalism. Marx believed that structural exploitation of the labor force by the capital market does not come from the malicious intent of a single capitalist but the entirety of capitalists. On the other hand, Adam Smith believed that seeking personal gain helps maximize public interest. Weber held that charismatic leadership[2] is the crucial key to social change. Hence, he proposed the Calvinist ethical doctrine of calling to foster a capitalist with a clear conscience and a diligent worker to eliminate the internal conflict between capitalists and laborers. Weber foresaw that a Capitalist society would be made up of an abundant bourgeoisie class and not an exploited worker class.[3]

Schumpeter believed that during the process of the development of Capitalism, the emergence of bureaucracy was inevitable. Bureaucrats are a new social class that allocates production. It comes from the need for

[1] Smith, A. (1960). *The Wealth of Nations*. United Kingdom: J.M. Dent & Sons, Limited. p. 15.

[2] Weber, M. (1978). *Economy and Society: An Outline of Interpretive Sociology*. United Kingdom: University of California Press.

[3] Weber, M. (2003). *The Protestant Ethic and the Spirit of Capitalism* (T. Parsons, Trans.). United States: Dover Publications.

management after the maximizing of Capitalism. He believed that the bureaucratic class would expel capitalists and the bourgeoisie to become true leaders in the Capitalist market. In the US, Steve Jobs founded Apple, Inc., but the board of directors had once expelled him that he had established. The founder of Yahoo almost had the same fate. Schumpeter believed that the bureaucratic class' sense of responsibility and team was the unavoidable leading force in Capitalism. In today's terms, outstanding professionals will dominate economic development.[4]

However, the irony in historical development shows that these bureaucratic leaders and elites were neither responsible for defending the worker's interests nor for protecting the interests of the capitalists. All they did was safeguard their interests with their specialized knowledge. The collapse of large Wall Street finance companies in the US is an example.

Up to now, socio-economists are still seeking a good socio-economic order. They wish to find the problems within it, analyze its structure, and establish a better mode. However, these economic modes rarely stress the importance of inner morality and good intentions.

This chapter wishes to discuss the possibility of actualizing an Economy of Goodness in contemporary times and the future by looking at one's goodness and morality, especially from the perspective of one's sense of morality. This actualization's outcome may differ from the expectations of specific socio-economists. For instance, Marx predicted that the last phase of Capitalism would be socialism. The existence and expansion of the Economy of Goodness would significantly make up for the bias and lack within a country's contemporary Capitalism or Capitalism. Economy of Goodness stresses economic activities' benevolent motives and altruistic morality even more. One's goodness refers to not seeking personal interest, and character refers to not seeking the maximization of individual or organizational benefits. Instead, it is to solve social problems or to bring about social equality and justice.

This article argues that this economic activity is based on good motives and moral objectives. An Economy of Goodness would construct a fair and just social life that better conforms to the expectations of humankind.

---

[4] Schumpeter, J. A. (2010). *Capitalism, Socialism and Democracy*. United Kingdom: Taylor & Francis.

SECTION 2: FREE MARKET AND OVERALL INTERESTS

In *The Wealth of Nations*, Adam Smith argued that maximizing individual interest would inevitably lead to maximizing public interest.

He gave an example of a hunter proficiently making bows and arrows. In the early stage, this dexterous hunter made them out of personal interest. His craftsmanship was gradually appreciated and recognized among the hunter community. Sometimes, he would give some bows and arrows he made to his hunter friends, and they would thank him by giving him some venison. Over time, he found that he could, in this manner, get more venison easier than if he went to the field to hunt deer. Hence, making bows and arrows became his chief business, and he became a fletcher. According to Adam Smith, this is how the division of labor begins.[5] As a pioneering theorist of Capitalism, Adam Smith's theory presented the division of labor in Capitalism. Everyone in society does what they can, and they and the entire community will ultimately obtain the maximum benefits. When seeking individual interest, the interests of the people are also achieved.

This is the fundamental view in *The Wealth of Nations*, namely that public interest comes from the maximization of personal welfare, which significantly impacted the structure of Capitalism. The wise utilization of individual interests benefits both oneself and the masses simultaneously. However, in reality, under a Capitalist environment, the development of maximizing personal interest does not necessarily create the result of public interest. Instead, it makes what Marx criticized as the unjust distribution of surplus value and infinite exploitation of social classes.

The Free Market and Exploitation of Workers

Free competition under Capitalism cannot bring maximum benefit to consumers as a whole, and it is also unfair exploitation of the producers.

In Capital, Marx mentioned that in the process of Capitalism becoming highly developed, workers belong to the exploited class. Workers face alienation of labor not only in terms of their income proportion compared to capitalists; their low income means they cannot afford necessities. According to Marx, Workers exchange their commodities, namely their

---

[5] Smith, A. (1960). *The Wealth of Nations*. United Kingdom: J.M. Dent & Sons, Limited. p. 16.

labor, for capitalists' commodities, namely money. These transactions are done under set rates. Workers are trading their commodities and work for various other kinds of commodities.[6]

Workers, under the mechanism of exploitation of distribution of surplus value, may work 12 hours a day, then they smoke, eat, and sleep. For workers, the commodities they obtain from their labor based on their flesh and blood are just like a capitalist's horse that complies with the exchange mechanism of labor for reward. Marx even gave an example that a wage worker is like a silkworm spinning for a living.

Marx harshly pointed out that the working class' labor commodities do not belong to a particular capitalist; instead, they belong to the entire Capitalist class.[7] In other words, the problem of exploiting the working class is not limited to a single capitalist alone. Still, it belongs to the inherent structure of all capitalists and Capitalism.

Could an increase in wages help to save the working class? Is reducing working hours helpful in protecting the working class from exploitation? Marx believed that an increase in the price of labor commodities would not solve the structural problem of exploitation. Even if capitalists increased wages, they would also raise the market price of commodities to make up for the cost. A rise in workers' salaries would be a rise in the prices of items. Either the workers purchase products they do not need, or, as profits increase, the capitalists become rich and require more workers for production. As the labor force increases, capitalists have more workers under their control, so workers' labor is more easily replaceable.

Furthermore, the increase in production relies on a finer division of labor. The deeper the engagement of the division of labor, the harder it is for the working class to change jobs. In other words, the speed of the rise of commodity prices corresponds to the rate at which the working class is being replaced. This is a structural exploitation in Capitalism.

Marx believed that profit from capital surplus not only causes the status of workers to disappear; it also causes small and medium-sized capitalists to disappear. During the rapid increase and concentration of profit through mergers, large enterprises are causing many other enterprises to shut down. Marx noted that at a particular time, the number of

[6] Marx, K. (Eds.). (1993). *Capital: A Critique of Political Economy* (Vol. 3). United Kingdom: Penguin Publishing Group.

[7] Marx, K. (Eds.). (1993). *Capital: A Critique of Political Economy* (Vol. 3). United Kingdom: Penguin Publishing Group.

these entrepreneurs would decrease to the point where it is impossible to maintain dominance.[8]

During Marx's time in the nineteenth century, the Capitalist environment was characterized by a concentration of profits and exploitation of surplus value. Even to the present, Marx's theory and observation on the tensions between capitalists, workers' labor, and commodity prices still exist to a certain extent. The difference is this unjust distribution of surplus value is dealt with in contemporary society by the marketization of capital circulation (stock transactions), capital redistribution through government intervention, and the working class with stock options. These are methods leading to a fairer distribution of surplus value.

In terms of the essence of Capitalism, from Adam Smith's perspective individual interest means public welfare; it is unnecessary to criticize capitalists' greed and endless seeking of commodity profits because self-benefit would induce maximum public welfare. On the other hand, Marx pointed out that structurally even the most generous capitalist would have to seek profits to survive. This means they have to lower wages, seek a greater market share, increase production, and improve people's purchasing power. That was why Henry Ford let workers work five days a week, so they would have time to buy the commodities they had produced.

However, Marx argued that workers are the most disposable group under capitalists seeking maximum profit. A rise in wages means an increase in working hours or the prices of merchandise sold by capitalists. This leads to the exploitation of the working class' labor or the power to consume. For Marx, the notion of good intentions was not a fundamental problem. It is because people's way of life depends upon the method of production. Social structure determines the people's mode of existence, but the people's mode of reality does not determine society's mode of existence. People's subjective values are often sacrificed under the larger structure. Hence, Marx did not criticize problems concerning humanity's morality in Capitalism. In the same way, but with a different perspective, Adam Smith did not criticize people's selfishness and greed.

Adam Smith and Marx envisioned a good, impartial, and just economic lifestyle, namely a social-economic structure that conforms to morality. In other words, although they both wished for the outcome of constructing

---

[8] Marx, K. (Eds.). (1993). *Capital: A Critique of Political Economy* (Vol. 3). United Kingdom: Penguin Publishing Group.

an ideal economic environment that also served morality, they did not believe that achieving this vision and outcome was related to the sense of morality and goodness of individuals or groups engaging in economic activities.

The End of the Free Market Is Freedom

Marx predicted the crisis of Capitalism from the perspective of class struggle. The problem was that profit margins would drop under continuous expansion in production, with excess production and monopolistic Capitalism, thus creating even more unemployment and proletariat. The relationship between exploiter and exploited would continue to deepen class conflict, leading to a proletariat revolution. The proletariat would seize the capitalists' capital, converting capitalists' assets to public assets. This would lead to the inevitable demise of Capitalism and finally create a communist society where all private properties would be removed. By then, the working class would replace capitalists to become the government and distributors of entrepreneurial production to implement new social and economic fairness and justice. However, Marx did not specify the social operation after the emergence of communism.[9]

Marx employed class struggle and proletariat revolution to achieve a fair and just outcome, and he was using evil to achieve good. For Marxists, revolution is a process, a necessary evil and evil can be used to achieve good. Such a rationale is similar to what Adam Smith believed, under the working of the invisible hand, various private evils in society would lead to good for the entire society. The difference is, the invisible hand in Adam Smith's theory became the proletariat workers' hands that hold the gun in a revolution.

The key to Capitalism is free competition. Competition is good for Adam Smith, but to Marx, it means class exploitation and conflict. Only by eliminating competition in the free market can ultimate freedom be brought to the proletariat workers. However, looking at the outcome of implementing communism in Russia, it did not bring about the hegemony of the proletariat; rather, it only created a new group of bureaucrats controlling the order and distribution of production.

---

[9] Marx, K. & Engel, F. (2002). *The Communist Manifesto*. London: Penguin Books (Original work published in 1848).

Hence, Trotsky wrote *The Revolution Betrayed*, where his view was that Stalin's bureaucracy was not the communist ideal of Marx and Engels. In Marx's communism, the nation-state is not a prerequisite for fairness and justice. Communism cannot come about under the rule of the nation-state governmental bureaucratic system. Trotsky believed that the proletariat's hegemony would not mean the formation of control by a new class or governmental bureaucracy.[10] Therefore, the rise and fall of Stalin's bureaucratic government was not the rise and fall of Marx's and Engels's communism.

In seeking a solution to avoid the emergence of class conflict between exploiters and the exploited in a free market, Max Weber proposed that the bourgeoisie would play an important role in the distribution in a Capitalist economy. He also brought Protestant ethics to amend Capitalism and laid an ethical basis for capitalists and workers. In contrast to Weber's amendment to Capitalism, Joseph Alois Schumpeter also amended Marx's theory. He proposed that the rise of the new bureaucratic class was an inevitable development for the Capitalist market and predicted the end of Capitalism.[11]

In General Economic History, Weber first affirmed capitalists' status, saying, Capitalism is present wherever the industrial provision for the needs of a human group is carried out by the method of enterprise, irrespective of what condition is involved.[12] Weber believed that capitalists are the core force of innovation, large-scale entrepreneurs who are pioneers in creating a modern economic climate.[13] Furthermore, he adopted the Calvinist religious doctrine of calling to describe the process in which large-scale entrepreneurs fulfill their calling from God when they construct rational Capitalism.[14]

---

[10] Trotsky, L. (1991). *The Revolution Betrayed: What Is the Soviet Union and Where Is It Going?* United States: Labor Publications (Original work published in 1936).

[11] Schumpeter, J. A. (2006). *History of Economic Analysis*. United Kingdom: Taylor & Francis.

[12] Weber, M. (1978). *Economy and Society: An Outline of Interpretive Sociology*. United Kingdom: University of California Press.

[13] Weber, M. (1978). *Economy and Society: An Outline of Interpretive Sociology*. United Kingdom: University of California Press.

[14] Weber, M. (1958). *The Protestant Ethics and the Spirit of Capitalism* (T. Parsons, Trans.). New York: Scribner.

In The Protestant Ethic and the Spirit of Capitalism, Weber deeply analyzed how Protestant ethics influenced Western large-scale entrepreneurs' view of life. This group of Protestant entrepreneurs aligned themselves with Christian commandments and expanded their work externally. Calvinists firmly believe that only God can decide who His chosen people are. Hence, Protestants believe that obeying commandments and mundane achievements prove they're God's chosen people. They expanded their corporations around the world and became imperial transnational corporations, and at the same time, constantly confirmed that they received God's grace and favor.[15]

Weber did not criticize the capitalists' constant expansion of imperial corporations and their impact on class exploitation. On the contrary, he believed that the development of corporations would lead to the expansion of the bourgeoisie class. Unlike Marx's prediction, Weber did not think that the exploitation of the working class would constantly increase and that the growth of the proletariat class would necessarily overturn Capitalism. Weber saw the rise of the middle class, contributing to the emergence of civil society. This was one of the bases for the rationalization of a Capitalist society. Weber also emphasized the role of the nation-state, whereby state power was used to reduce class conflict, formulate policies to prevent unfair exploitation, and so on, which are the keys to establishing rational Capitalism.

Weber was opposed to socialism and believed it would lead to civil servants' hegemony, not the proletariat. He said that eliminating private property in Capitalism would lead to the hegemony of nation-state bureaucracy. At the same time, Weber was also concerned that the continuous expansion of rationalization and bureaucracy would create a new slave class. In contrast to Marx's criticism of capitalists, Weber relied on those large-scale entrepreneurs who saw their corporations' expansion as their sacred calling to change the fate of Capitalism. He claimed that these entrepreneurs with religious missions had charismatic leadership. To Weber, entrepreneurs with charismatic leadership were the only ones who possessed creative revolutionary power throughout history. He believed that in the age of unprecedented bureaucracy, charismatic leaders were the only ones who could change these detrimental developments. Weber

[15] Weber, M. (2003). The Protestant Ethic and the Spirit of Capitalism (T. Parsons, Trans.). United States: Dover Publications.

was also concerned that any creation would ultimately enter a state of reutilization, making Capitalism a heartless industrial development.[16]

Unlike Weber, who was concerned about the extreme development of new bureaucratization, Schumpeter argued in his work, *Capitalism, Socialism, and Democracy*, that emergence of the bureaucracy as a new class was inevitable under Capitalism. In his view, under Capitalism, as production and division of labor continue to increase, a new group of bureaus is bound to appear. Within a maximized Capitalist society, capitalists would lose their position, namely the so-called degeneration of an entrepreneur's function. Schumpeter believed that as economic growth became increasingly depersonalized and automatic, the team power of bureaucrats and committees would replace individuals' action and knowledge.[17]

Schumpeter criticized that entrepreneurs have no divine charisma when managing people and things. However, he agreed with Weber's rational Capitalism, though he did not think rational Capitalism would result in a mechanical and rigid operation, but the decline in Capitalism and the arrival of a socialist economic system. In the later phases of Capitalism, where science, technology, and Capitalism are highly developed and complex, innovation and the spirit of enterprise no longer originate from capitalists but are gradually replaced by rational and bureaucratic management. In other words, capitalists are replaced by groups of bureaucratic control. Furthermore, as the number of intellectuals increases, a sensible and critical attitude would steer confrontation toward the social order of Capitalism. A kind of socialism that places even more emphasis on fairness, justice, specialization, and rational governance, with a reduction in class benefits, would rise, signaling the end of Capitalism.

Weber and Schumpeter constructed an ideal social-economic order by defending the historical dominance of Capitalism and socialism, respectively. Their positions were both empirically observant and value-oriented. Weber hoped that capitalists would embrace religious ethics, to some extent, and he was hoping to inject goodness and morality into economic activities. Also, the rise of the bourgeoisie class meant the weakening of class exploitation. It was a reflection and response to Marx's criticism

---

[16] Weber, M. (2003). *The Protestant Ethic and the Spirit of Capitalism* (T. Parsons, Trans.). United States: Dover Publications.

[17] Schumpeter, J. A. (2006). *History of Economic Analysis*. United Kingdom: Taylor & Francis.

of the malady of Capitalism. In Schumpeter's view, rational bureaucratic management meant the development of rational Capitalism, which could inhibit capitalists' domination of capital and surplus value. This allows rational distribution through elite bureaucratic management and the elimination of unfair distribution of profit. Schumpeter's economic thought finally ended with a rational and fair socialist mode of living.

SECTION 3: BUREAUCRATIC MORALITY AND GOOD AND EVIL ECONOMY

Schumpeter's successor, Keynes, emphasized the importance of strengthening the government's economic plans. Keynes proposed strengthening state intervention in economic activities and that the government should play an essential role in economic plans. Governments needed to resist economic decline and depression through financial and currency policies. Government public infrastructure expenses were one of Keynes' methods to fight economic depression. This depended upon a group of specialized bureaucratic management and required the joint enterprise management by specialized bureaucrats and government bureaucrats. Such an economic form was still the ideal modification to Capitalism or socialism for many Eastern European and Northern European countries.[18]

Opposite to Keynes's economic thought was Hayek's laissez-faire economic concept. To some extent, Hayek saw the economic malady under Stalin's bureaucratic management in Eastern Europe and proposed an approach of minimal government intervention. Hayek's proposition was not based on financial interest; instead, he believed that there was a close relationship between a free market and individual freedom. In his view, personal freedom in the economic environment was the highest good.

Hayek opposed government intervention in economic activities from at least two standpoints. He believed that during economic operations in free markets, there is often an unfair distribution of capital. The government's unreasonable monetary policy causes this.

In *Prices and Production*, a 1931 work, he suggested that the business cycle is created when the central bank has policies, like deliberately

---

[18] Keynes, J. M. (2018). *The General Theory of Employment, Interest, and Money.* Germany: Springer International Publishing.

lowering interest rates and so on, through inflation and the over-expansion of credit. This results in an inadequate distribution of capital in the market. Hayek proposed that the instabilities of the market economy were due to the most critical self-regulatory element, currency, being controlled by the government rather than by the market mechanism.[19]

Hayek opposed the planned economy because such systems would eventually lead to the exploitation of individual freedoms. In his master-piece, *The Road to Serfdom*, he explained that under socialism, there is bound to be a centralized economic plan. Also, such a planned economy would eventually lead to totalitarianism because once the government was given great power in economic control, it would inevitably possess the power to control individuals' lives in society. Only then would the planner be able to centralize information from various levels to make decisions.[20]

Keynes's and Hayek's theories were two extreme economic value systems debated by many Capitalist countries and communist countries transitioning to revised socialism for the past half a century. At the same time, Professor Daniel Bell of Harvard University proposed the End of Ideology. He asserted that government policies were no longer the domi-nant element for the economy and social problems. Social and cultural elites were going to address the various issues faced in the more significant structures of the economy from the nineteenth to twentieth centuries, one by one, through the power of technological development.

Adjustment, rather than overthrowing, was the essential thinking of Daniel Bell's social reform. His hope for this power of change came neither from a big government nor the bureaucratic elite community of commercial enterprise but from idealistic social and cultural entrepreneurs dedicated to social, economic, and cultural reform.

Daniel Bell believed that 41 politics, economics, and social culture were classified as three distinct fields in the post-industrial era. They were not subordinate to one another. The creation of multidisciplinary areas to solve social problems was a characteristic of the post-industrial era. (Bell, 1976) The social enterprise was a new field independent of polit-ical and commercial mechanisms, which set up new models for social and economic order.

[19] Hayek, F. A. (1967). *Prices and Production*. New York: Augustus M. Kelley Publisher.
[20] Hayek, F. A. (1994). *The Road to Serfdom*. Chicago: University of Chicago Press.

One contemporary to Daniel Bell was a renowned British social entrepreneur, Michael Young, a proponent of social entrepreneurship. He spent his whole life establishing over 60 non-profit enterprises, advocating the social entrepreneur concept. Bell acclaimed him to be the greatest proponent of social enterprise of the century. From the very beginning, the concept of social enterprise incorporated the motivation of making the world a better place, namely goodness and morality, into social enterprise activities. Hence, social enterprises missions became the critical force in promoting the public interest.

SECTION 4: GOODNESS AND MORALITY OF SOCIAL ENTERPRISE

In the Coming of Post-Industrial Society, Daniel Bell stressed that the crucial elements of post-industrial civilization are information-led and service. The shift from manufacturing to service is a characteristic of post-industrial civil society, and service is the mission of social entrepreneurs.

Unlike entrepreneurs of Protestant ethics, social entrepreneurs do not believe in God, while increasing production and consumption at the same time. Entrepreneurs of Protestant ethics care about God's grace and favor. Their interest in obtaining enterprise achievements was not beneficial to fair and just social distribution.

The social enterprise aims at fairness and justice from the very beginning. This fairness and justice can be environmental, like the Intergovernmental Panel on Climate Change, or about consumers' rights protection, such as the Public Citizens, founded by Ralph Nader.

These social enterprises neither have the goal of making money for themselves nor are they driven by motives for religious salvation. They base themselves on striving to achieve a particular social or economic justice, stepping up to fight without hesitation. They do not fight by engaging in revolution or military force, but do it under the rule of law and through public opinion and legislation to promote a new social and economic order.

Social entrepreneurs are not a group of entrepreneurs with an abundance of capital in society. Many of them should be categorized as proletariat. Basing themselves on their mission, they seek goodness and morality as a goal, attracting numerous donors and unpaid volunteers to join their causes. It is just as stated by Peter Drucker, the greatest management scholar of the twentieth century: non-profit organizations, namely social enterprises, are proponents of values, as well as beneficiaries of values. Being led by values rather than by proles is the philosophy of social enterprise.

Presently, individuals and groups engaging in social enterprise come from both religious and secular domains. These include non-profit organizations, for-profit organizations (with income injected back into social welfare and not to individuals), and hybrid for-profit–non-profit organizations.

Leading the Historical Development of Economic Fairness and Justice

Since the nineteenth century, Marx's observations of the Capitalist malady have been mainly focused on criticizing Capitalists' enjoyment of the surplus value created by laborers. This resulted in exploitation of the labor class, creating conflict and opposition. Marx predicted that power to dictate capital would shift from capitalists to the proletariat dictatorship. Then, for Weber, distribution power was on the rise of the bourgeoisie and the sacred calling of the entrepreneur. When it comes to Schumpeter, it was well-trained bureaucratic management. For Keynes, it became the shrewd policy-making bureaucrat. For Daniel Bell and Michael Young, it became social entrepreneurs dedicated to promoting public welfare.

We can see that Marx spent his whole life embracing the noble idea of constructing a fair social order, the idea of harmony and prosperity. However, this prosperity and harmony must be achieved through battle or military force. Marx emphasized the goodness of the end, but neglected goodness in terms of motive and method. Such a viewpoint could be the product of unfairness during that time.

On the other hand, Weber employed the religious ethics of the calling to rationalize capitalists' expansion of enterprises. However, this could not solve the Capitalist problems of overproduction of material goods, over-consumption, and considerable class exploitation. Weber hoped for appropriate intervention by the government to moderate the injustice brought about by the expansion of Capitalism. On the other hand, Schumpeter saw that the rational ability of bureaucratic management could bring an end to Capitalism and the advent of socialism.

So now, who should distribute capital? Is it the capitalist class? Is it the bourgeoisie? Is it the Protestant entrepreneurs with their sacred calling? Is it a Stalinist bureaucratic dictatorship? Is it the Proletariat? Is it the teams of bureaucrats? Or is it professional government officials?

When discussing a rational structure for capital wealth distribution in society, economists stress structure and outcome. However, under the so-called rational economic structure, its outcomes are still disappointing. Schumpeter anticipated that bureaucratic management teams could distribute capital rationally. However, the financial crisis of 2010, spreading from Wall Street to the whole world, revealed the bureaucratic professional management teams' true colors of greed. CEOs and management of giant financial enterprises like the Lehman Brothers, AIG and others were earning hundreds of millions of US dollars, while allowing their investors to lose everything. These bureaucratic managers caricatured as living off selling out investors not only included the management personnel of enterprises, but government officials and economists, too. They were all embedded in this structure of collective self-interest and greed.

Neglecting individual goodness and morality resulted in what Schumpeter anticipated, rational management by bureaucratic teams. They coldly planned to take over and even sold a huge number of investors' financial capital.

When economists sought to construct a rational and fair economic model, social enterprises placed their emphasis on the motive and mission of the good. They took goodness and morality as the motive, attitude, and goal for economic development and activities. Such an economy of goodness works as for-profit or non-profit organizations striving to promote consumer sovereignty, defend environmental rights, assist the poor, and prevent and cure infectious diseases. The motive and mentality for all of the above are not for personal gain, but the welfare of the entire society.

These social entrepreneurs are not government officials, nor do they need to be rich and powerful with large corporations (though they do not exclude them, like Bill Gates, for example.) They are idealistic people with good motives. With tangible capital or intangible value, they aim to benefit specific groups or communities or even humanity.

Micro-Credit and Social Enterprise

Social entrepreneur Muhammad Yunus was awarded the Nobel Peace Prize in 2006. Yunus is an economist and the founder and representative of micro-finance. In 1976, he loaned US$27 (about NT$900) to 42 impoverished Bangladeshi women, which allowed them to start up their businesses or to work so they could support their families.

Today, the Grameen Bank founded by Yunus has given out loans totaling more than six billion US dollars to more than six million debtors. Yunus required his staff to actively go to villages and visit impoverished people who needed funds.

The Grameen Bank has never signed any loan contract with its debtors, most of whom are illiterate women. The Grameen Bank collects simple interest at a fixed rate from the debtors, much lower than the compound interest loan put out by Bangladeshi commercial banks. Even though the debtors are mostly impoverished people without any property, Yunus noticed that the loans were more guaranteed when lending money to these women, who have no social status in Bangladesh. These women use their micro-credit to engage in small businesses or work, which usually benefits their families tremendously. Their average repayment rate is 98%.[21]

Yunus strictly requires loan applicants to understand how the Grameen Bank operates fully, and only then would the loan be approved. Knowing how the bank operates, they are more likely to cherish the loans they receive and repay on time. To reduce the stress of repayments, Yunus required the debtors to begin making repayments in the second week. Ostensibly, such a practice seems to create huge stress on the debtors, but this mechanism eases the stress of paying a large sum of money for debtors at the year's end.

The Grameen Bank utilizes the social connections in villages, and six to eight debtors must form a group and supervise one another in making repayments. If one person in the group cannot repay on time, the whole group may face blame. Loaning and repayments are conducted publicly at the weekly center meetings. The Grameen Bank has received extensive praise in Bangladesh for its open and transparent operation.

Twenty-three countries in the world that promote micro-credit and over 8.5 million people around the globe have received micro-loans from Paupers Banks. Yunus' efforts in promoting micro-credit have helped at least 66 million people out of poverty and created over eight million jobs. That is why, in 2006, the Grameen Bank and its founder, Muhammad Yunus, were awarded the Nobel Peace Prize.

---

[21] Yunus, M. (2007). *Creating a World Without Poverty: Social Business and the Future of Capitalism*. United Kingdom: Public Affairs.

Yunus' success came from his belief in goodness and moral value as a social entrepreneur. His Grameen Bank was to accumulate personal wealth and solve the long-standing social poverty. Yunus said: "One day, our children will have to visit a museum to see poverty."

As micro-credit became widespread, many commercial banks also adopted the model. The commercial bank Compartamos Banco in Mexico began engaging in micro-finance. Micro-credit became very well-known after Yunus received the Nobel Peace Prize. The Mexican bank, Compartamos Banco, was listed in 2007, with its stock price worth more than one billion US dollars. Local critics denounced it as a blood-sucking loan shark, and its annual loan interest rate was as high as 79%. Compartamos Banco was shamed for squeezing impoverished debtors to obtain profits.

With the same micro-credit scheme, Yunus maintained a benevolent motive, and his micro-credit scheme has helped innumerable people be alleviated from poverty. However, Compartamos Banco in Mexico adopted the same micro-credit model, but chances are that they became a new large financial capital, oppressing the underprivileged, due to its selfish core.

This article hopes to convey that seeking a good economy alone cannot save humanity because individuals' goodness and morality are essential in constructing a fair, just and orderly economy.

The Actualization and Case Example of Economy of Goodness and Public Welfare

The concepts of public welfare and social enterprise were roughly initiated in the late 1970s and only became popular in the 1980s and 1990s. However, in 1966, a Buddhist nun name Master Cheng Yen founded the Tzu Chi Merit Association in Hualien, on the east coast of Taiwan. In the 1960s, Taiwan's economy was just taking off, and poverty was common. Against this background, Tzu Chi began its charity work.

Tzu Chi engages in public welfare through its Four Missions and Eight Footprints of charity, medicine, education, humanistic culture, environmental protection, international relief; bone marrow donation, and community volunteerism. Through charity, Tzu Chi strives for all people's hearts to be purified, all societies to be in harmony, and the world to be free of disasters. This is an archetype of the Western social enterprise, which Master Cheng Yen refers to as missions.

Tzu Chi was founded on a simple thought of compassion. In March 1966, in Hualien, on the east coast of Taiwan, Master Cheng Yen saw a pool of blood outside a clinic. After inquiring, she found that the blood came from an indigenous woman experiencing a difficult labor. Her people had brought her out from the mountains on foot for eight hours to arrive at the clinic, but she was denied treatment because she could not afford a deposit of TWD 8,000 (approx. USD 200). The men could only carry her back home, leaving behind a pool of blood. Learning of this, Master Cheng Yen felt pained by the cold realities of this world. Hence, she vowed to establish Tzu Chi, beginning the path of relieving the impoverished.

At the time, Master Cheng Yen and her five disciples sustained themselves by doing handicrafts. They began making one more pair of baby shoes each day in order to help the poor. Each pair of baby shoes earned them four New Taiwan dollars (approx. USD 10 cents), and they could thus save 8,000 New Taiwan dollars a year, which was the amount needed to save the pregnant woman who could not pay the hospital deposit.[22]

Master Cheng Yen and her disciples lived a simple lifestyle of religious cultivation and have insisted on maintaining a life of self-reliance and not accepting offerings. Even though they lived a hard life, they continued to exchange their labor for a small amount of money to engage in relief work.

Later, Master Cheng Yen called on 30 housewives to contribute TWD 50 cents (approx. USD 2 cents) into a bamboo coin bank each day before grocery shopping. In doing so, each of them could save TWD 15 (approx. 60 cents) a month for people in need. Kindness begins with a small step, and charity is not only for the rich. Everyone can expand great love and kindness. The combined strength of individuals can lift people out of suffering and poverty.

Tzu Chi refers to this time period as the Bamboo Bank Era. At that time, someone approached Master Cheng Yen and expressed their desire to donate fifteen dollars once a month rather than 50 cents every day. However, Master Cheng Yen emphasized the importance of donating 50

---

[22] Shih, Cheng Yen. (1996). *Huigui xinling de guxiang* [Return to the Spiritual Hometown]. Taipei: Tzu Chi Publishing co. pp. 173–201.

cents a day, as one would give rise to a kind thought each day as fostering a compassionate heart is more important than raising funds.[23]

Master Cheng Yen guides Tzu Chi volunteers to donate money and personally engage in relief work. She teaches us to realize our own blessings upon seeing suffering and to take suffering as our teacher. Master Cheng Yen guides the wealthy to give love, reflecting the notion of educating the rich through relieving the poor. Master Cheng Yen inspires the rich not only to give without asking anything in return, but to also be grateful for the opportunity to give.

Master Cheng Yen proposes to teach the rich to help the poor and guide the poor to realize their riches. This means that in helping the impoverished, we should inspire them to also do what they can to help others in need. Many people in South Africa, Haiti, Indonesia, the Philippines, and Sichuan, China, who have received help from Tzu Chi have joined Tzu Chi as volunteers. This is the cycle of love and goodness.

In 1978, Master Cheng Yen vowed to establish a patient-centered hospital in the remote eastern region of Hualien, Taiwan. At that time, charitable activities were not widespread in Taiwan, making fundraising extremely challenging. A Japanese entrepreneur offered to support Master Cheng Yen's compassionate aspiration by donating 200 million US dollars, enough to complete the construction of the hospital and sustain its operation for ten years. However, Master Cheng Yen graciously declined the offer. She hoped for broader support from the Taiwanese society to build a hospital founded on goodness, rather than relying on a wealthy individual's donation. She emphasized that compassion is not the exclusive domain of the wealthy but the right of anyone with a loving heart.[24]

Today, Tzu Chi has eight hospitals in Taiwan. Tzu Chi also established the volunteer-based Tzu Chi International Medical Association (TIMA), with over 14,000 medical personnel and volunteers. It has provided free medical services in over 50 countries around the world.

---

[23] Shih, Cheng Yen. (1998). Shan men yi kai [The Gate of Goodness Has Opened]. *Tzu Chi Monthly*, Issue 378 (May 25, 1998). Tzu Chi Culture & Communication Foundation. pp. 11–15.

[24] Shih, Cheng Yen. (1991). Xinshi rensheng chengjiu gongde [Faith and Integrity Make Life Virtues]. *Tzu Chi Monthly*, Issue 292 (April 25, 1991). Tzu Chi Culture & Communication Foundation. pp. 10–18.

Since its establishment in 1966, Tzu Chi has come a long way from the Bamboo Bank Era of saving 50 cents (approx. 0.02 USD) a day in rural Hualien, Taiwan, to now having over ten million donating members worldwide and over two million volunteers. Each year, Tzu Chi's work helps around 20 million people with 136 countries and regions having received relief.

Tzu Chi draws its strength from the belief that each person has the capacity to express genuine kindness and love. Their conviction is that eradicating evil entails fostering goodness rather than engaging in conflict, and addressing poverty involves promoting great love rather than targeting wealth.[25]

The basic operating rule of Capitalism is freedom of competition. It stresses freedom in the Capitalist market and allows all individuals and enterprises to develop fully. However, freedom does not necessarily bring balance and equitable development. The growing wealth gap and poverty are common problems in the current world.

The way to remove poverty is neither by removing competition nor eliminating freedom; it is by expanding great love and goodness. Tzu Chi has been dedicated to developing great love and goodness for over half a century to eliminate material and mental poverty and conflicts caused by economic development.

The most prominent symptom of Capitalism is inequality. Contemporary political philosopher John Rawls theory of justice discusses the meaning of equality and justice in contemporary times. There are two principles of justice in Rawls' *A Theory of Justice*: The first is the principle of equal opportunity, and the second is to give the greatest benefit to the weakest.[26]

Rawls published the true meaning of equality at Harvard University in the 1980s. He expressed the most penetrating thoughts on the freedom of highly capitalized countries and the loss of equality—however, Tzu Chi volunteers led by Master Cheng Yen has quietly practiced this concept of equality for decades.

Tzu Chi has crossed boundaries between races, nations, religions, and cultures to help all those suffering worldwide. This is why people often

---

[25] Her, R. S. (2008). *Ci ji shijian meixue xia: qingjing meixue* [The Philosophy of Practices of Buddhist Tzu Chi, Part 2]. Taipei: New Century Publishing Co., Ltd. pp. 75–141.

[26] Rawls, J. (1999). *A Theory of Justice*. United Kingdom: Oxford University Press.

say, where there is a disaster Tzu Chi volunteers will be there. Tzu Chi gives with goodness and love to the most disadvantaged individuals or groups in the poorest, most urgent, and most rural regions. It truly demonstrates John Rawls' viewpoints on justice and equality. Capitalism advocates free markets; however, equality and justice are values and concepts capitalism needs the most.

Non-profit Social Enterprise with Revenue

A social enterprise's goal is to have a goodness as its motive (not seeking personal gain) and a moral concept (not seeking to expand the organization) to compensate for the neglected inequality and injustice in society. A social enterprise is an organization that utilizes an enterprise model to solve a particular social problem. These entities can exist in the form of for-profit companies or non-profit organizations. They can have revenues and profits, but these profits are mainly used for their missions as social enterprises to solve specific social problems rather than for investors' or proprietors' gain.

Tzu Chi is currently the largest charitable organization in the Chinese world. In the 1990s, it started an environmental initiative, which led to the establishment of Taiwan's first not-for-profit company specializing in environmental protection.

In 1991, the international media named Taiwan the most expensive trash island. In a public lecture, Master Cheng Yen called on the audience to use their applauding hands to protect the environment. Therefore, Tzu Chi volunteers began setting up recycling points in many communities with the purpose of educating surrounding neighbors to join in recycling work and environmental protection. By 2019, Tzu Chi had more than 200,000 volunteers in Taiwan who devoted their time and energy to maintaining community cleanliness and environmental protection in more than 6,000 recycling stations. Inspired by Tzu Chi volunteers, thousands of families began to recycle resources at home and donate the income from resource recycling to Tzu Chi's charity. Resource recycling is indeed social entrepreneurship for public welfare.

Tzu Chi's recycling stations attract volunteers of various ages and social statuses, ranging from 3 to 104 years old, including doctoral students, entrepreneurs, police officers, housewives, and diplomats. Taiwan recycles more than 200 million bottles annually, and it is estimated that Tzu Chi volunteers recycle one-third of them. Tzu Chi's environmental protection efforts have also spread across the world.

A recycling station is also a place for spiritual healing and to receive encouragement and support from one another. Through participating in recycling, people with chronic conditions and mental illness discover that they can find spiritual comfort, hence improving their conditions. Studies show that recycling has psychological implications for restoring confidence. When an old person picks up an empty plastic bottle, they may think, "There is still use for this abandoned plastic bottle." It can be made into a blanket for emergency relief. Like this bottle, the aging body could still be useful. From recycling, we can learn to cherish material life. Recycling can help protect the earth and restore volunteers' self-esteem and life value.

In addition, certain interviewees with depression, psychological disorders, drug addiction, gambling, or alcoholics have personally recovered from their negative habitual tendencies through Tzu Chi's recycling work. These interviewees even specifically pointed out that by focusing on sorting recyclables, they have learned to reorganize their lives and reduce the impact of worries and uncertainties in their lives. The promotion of Tzu Chi's environmental volunteer initiatives has transformed relationships between individuals and the Earth, individuals and communities, individuals and others, and individuals with themselves. This represents one of the powers of social enterprises.[27]

In 2008, Tzu Chi founded DA.AI Technology Co. Ltd. and pushed the mission of environmental protection to another new level. DA.AI Technology is a social enterprise founded by five social entrepreneurs. The company's core objective is environmental protection through upcycling waste materials. It turns recycled plastic bottles into blankets and clothing. Over 450,000 blankets made by the company have been sent worldwide in disaster relief. Textiles made of recycled plastic have also entered the market. All profits made by the company are fed back to Tzu Chi Foundation for public welfare. Tzu Chi volunteers transform plastic bottles regarded as trash into disaster relief blankets, clothes, scarves, and handbags. This has become a new form of urban mineral resource.

---

[27] Her, R. S. (2008). *Ci ji shijian meixue xia: qingjing meixue* [The Philosophy of Practices of Buddhist Tzu Chi, Part 2]. Taipei: New Century Publishing Co., Ltd. pp. 75–141.

DA.AI Technology's five founders are Tzu Chi volunteers and volunteers of this social enterprise. DA.AI Technology became the first social enterprise for environmental protection in Taiwan.

Concrete Contributions of Social Enterprises to the Economy

What influence do social enterprises emphasizing goodness and moral values have on the economy?

In September 2007, through the collaboration of the Centre for Civil Society Studies at Johns Hopkins University, United Nations Volunteers, and the United Nations Statistics Division, the International Conference on Non-Governmental Organization Studies was held in Bonn, Germany. At the conference, Professor Lester M. Salamon presented social enterprises in eight countries: Australia, Belgium, Canada, Czech, France, Japan, New Zealand, and the US. Statistics indicated that social enterprises contributed to the total economic yield in these countries. It was shown that non-profit organizations of social enterprises possess massive economic strength. On average, they contribute 5% of the nation's GDP. Social enterprises contribute far more to the GDP in some of these countries than major industries. For instance, the energy industry (gas, water, electricity), the construction industry, and the financial intermediation industry.[28]

Many countries gathered information on social enterprises using the internationally recognized System of National Accounts (SNA). However, the SNA system used only to include non-profit organizations that provided services to families in its statistics. Most of the non-profit organizations that had a significant impact on the economy were categorized as government or regular company sectors, and hence, this resulted in incomplete statistical findings. Furthermore, many countries should have included non-profit organizations' economic contributions in the statistics.

Given this, the United Nations Statistics Division issued the Handbook on Non-profit Institutions in the System of National Accounts in 2003. The handbook was put together jointly by UN consultants and scholars from Johns Hopkins University and redefined statistical criteria

---

[28] Salamon, L. M. (2010). Putting The Civil Society Sector on The Economic Map of the world. *Annals of Public and Cooperative Economics*, 81(2), 167–210. https://doi.org/10.1111/j.1467-8292.2010.00409.x.

for non-profit organizations of social enterprise. Up to now, 32 countries have adopted the statistical method from the handbook. At the 2007 conference, Johns Hopkins University presented research data indicating that social enterprises' economic contributions could have been more recognized. The research institute concluded as follows:

1. Non-profit organizations of social enterprises possess huge economic strength. They accounted for 5% of the surveyed countries' GDP.
2. In the US and Japan, non-profit organizations' contributions were 7%, far more than some major industries: the energy industry (gas, water, electricity) was 2.4% of GDP, the construction industry was 5.1%, and the financial intermediation industry was 5.6%.
3. Non-profit organizations primarily engaged in sectors like medicine, education, and social services. All of these were critical accomplishments of the United Nations Millennium Development Goals.
4. Non-profit organizations' economic growth rate (average 8.1% annually) was higher than the total growth rate (average 4.1% annually.)

It is not difficult to see.

The economic growth of social enterprises is faster than total economic growth. Non-profit organizations of social enterprises, which take goodness economics as their core value, are slowly becoming an important force in economic production.

SECTION 5: A CAPITALIST MARKET WITH THE MOTIVES OF GOODNESS AND MORALITY

Just as Daniel Bell proposed the end of ideology, it is clear that be it a Capitalist society or a socialist society, both are heading toward integration and blending. When these global economic orders are integrated to a certain degree, their common directions include the government is required to play a suitable role in economic activities to maintain fair market order, the participation of professional bureaucrats in market order brings equilibrium to the past situation of capitalists dictating and monopolizing market interests, giving benefits and considerations or even the right to choose to have shares to the working class, and so on. All of these are attempts to rectify Marx's criticisms of capitalist malpractices of the time, bringing fairness and impartiality to Capitalist markets.

However, suppose the Capitalist market still seeks personal gain as the primary motive and still seeks the expansion of enterprises or even maximization of interest as a goal. In that case, we will not be able to break free from the problem of unfair distribution of Capitalist surplus value, as criticized by Marx.

Looking back in history, humans have put in much effort in making profit distribution fair: the outcome of Adam Smith's proposition to maximize self-interest became public welfare in the end, which led to severe exploitation of the classes; Stalinist communism asserted that government should control distribution, which resulted in a bureaucratic dictatorship; Weber's calling of the sage hero, the entrepreneur, the actualization of which has caused many imperialist expansions of Capitalist enterprises; Hayek's laissez-faire system, which resulted in Austria's economic depression and high unemployment rate; and Schumpeter's bureaucratic specialized management, where we see senior management gobbling up huge amounts of investors' capital on Wall Street. Can Marx's ideal of the proletariat's dictatorship in a highly Capitalist society ever be fulfilled?

A social entrepreneur who does not take the accumulation of personal assets as their goal gives up seeking material abundance; instead, they invest themselves in solving social problems, which makes them the new proletariat. This newly risen proletariat creates wealth for numerous people, including both the proletariat and bourgeoisie, as well as brings about social justice. As an economist who studied in the US, Yunus did not seek the dream of becoming the prime minister of impoverished Bangladesh. Instead, he created livelihoods and necessities for thousands of impoverished people as a common citizen.

Ralph Nader, who established the world's first consumer protection organization, did not become a lawyer making lots of money after graduating from Harvard Law School. Instead, he used the five hundred thousand US dollars he won in a lawsuit against the Ford Motor Company to set up a consumer protection foundation called Public Citizens. Master Cheng Yen maintained a simple monastic lifestyle and founded the Tzu Chi Foundation, benefiting countless people worldwide. Both of the above individuals have benevolent motives and moral goals and have created outcomes of impartiality and justice, which traditional economic forms could not achieve.

Participation and achievement in the social enterprise depend not on capital but on the idea. Only when there is an idea will there then be capital. People who devote themselves to social enterprises are close to being proletariats. They might be under a financial strain, but this does not hinder them from seeking benefits for others in the world. Social enterprises' key to success is to seek benefit for others instead of oneself.

We are not saying that social enterprise does not bring any negative impact to society or that all those who are engaging in it are doing it out of benevolent attitudes and moral ideals. We have also seen new reports of situations where social enterprises engaging in public welfare have financial malpractices. Furthermore, this article is not implying that all Capitalist enterprises or commercial corporations do not possess benevolent motivations and moral concepts. Kōnosuke Matsushita, who had a considerable sense of morality, once said, "An enterprise is not an expansion of the entrepreneur's personal gain; it needs to be in accordance with the needs of the entire society." This article wishes to emphasize the importance of benevolent motivation and moral concepts for the development of the economy, and social enterprise is such an enterprise that bases itself on goodness and morality. If one asks, how do they foster their goodness and morality? The answer is the passing down of a model of character.

Daniel Bell stressed in his theory about the end of ideology because we could not simply depend on governmental action to solve economic problems. On the other hand, Weber's pursuit of a large structural reform of contemporary socio-economic systems could have been more realistic. Many aspects of socio-economic reform relied on a group of elites, namely the character model. Gradually, rationally, and step by step, they made adjustments and resolutions.

Hundreds and thousands of social entrepreneurs are now dedicated to solving social problems. They do this based on benevolent motivations (not seeking personal gain) and moral goals (not seeking individual or organizational expansion). What they embody is significantly different from conventionally Capitalist enterprises, which pursue the maximization of individual or enterprise interests. Social enterprise is only the beginning of an Economy of Goodness and morality, not the end. If more commercial corporations and for-profit enterprises could base their operational philosophy on goodness and morality, it would have a historically profound and far-reaching impact on socio-economic impartiality and justice.

CHAPTER 9

Goodness as the Foundation: The Motivation of Goodness in Economic Activities

SECTION 1: ALTRUISTIC MOTIVATION AND ECONOMIC ACTIVITIES

When it comes to motivating economic activities, from production to consumption, how should we foster a positive mindset and selfless motivation to realize economic prosperity and people's contentment?

In capitalism, production and consumption are driven by self-interest and self-desire.

I believe production and consumption can still be altruistic, even within Capitalism, for the benefit of all humanity.

The economic thought and practice derived from altruism is known as the Economy of Goodness. It encompasses not just charity-based activities, but all economic and commercial endeavors that are altruistically driven to generate beneficial social outcomes.

The EOG encompasses the motivation of goodness, process of goodness, and outcome of goodness which are essential.

This chapter will discuss the concept and practice of the Economy of Goodness. This new economic thinking combines the motivation, method, and purpose of the economy.

R.-S. Her, *The Economy of Goodness*, https://doi.org/10.1007/978-981-97-6363-4_9

I believe an altruistic economy will be more beneficial for society's economic development than self-interest. The EOG could forestall negative impacts of economic development on the environment, disadvantaged groups and human morality and will guide humankind to pursue economic success without causing major conflicts or devastation.

Altruistic goodness is beneficial not only to individual well-being but also the long-term success of businesses. It safeguards the sustainability of the environment and overall harmony of human society.

Motivation and Objectives in the Economy

Aristotle believed that any activity has its ultimate goal, namely Summum Bonum, which is peace and happiness. This means that for any activity, the ends should not contradict the means—for example, the goal of a war should be peace and the goal of seeing a doctor should be health and happiness.

Motivation must be aligned with a purpose, which is of greater importance than the means. Means should not be the objective, just as war should not be the objective. Motivation must be in line with the goals. The means should not be the aim, and war should not be sought.

Since goals are more important than means, the latter cannot replace the former. Motivation should be directed toward goals, not toward means. What is the purpose of obtaining money in economic activities? Earning money is not an end goal; instead, the aim is the joy and satisfaction from life after money is earned. Therefore, the aim of economic motivation should be in accordance with the goal.

What should be the economic goal? Not just making money, which is merely a means that should not replace real goals. Those who strive to amass riches will eventually forfeit their joy. Those who strive to make money as their end goal are not only misguided in their motivation, but they also distort their objectives.

Making money does not equate to happiness, and spending freely does not equate to freedom.

This is precisely what Aristotle pointed out: that human life needs a supreme goal, lest they regard the means as the goal.

However, modern philosophers have denied Aristotle's notion of supreme goodness; Enlightenment scholars such as Hobbes and Locke argued there was no such ideal and that individuals have different standards of goodness. This cast uncertainty on aiming for the supreme good, and people's goals for goodness became vague and diverse, satisfactory desires were taken as the ultimate objective.

As a consequence, the ethics of economic activities became the standardization of all methods, which was viewed as the financial goal.

For example, what value does an accountant provide? Rather than engaging in tax-avoidance, their responsibilities should focus on doing a job that benefits the company in the long run. The fraudulent activities of Enron Corporation came to light, with Arthur Andersen, the firm responsible for their reports, being charged with information falsification, tax evasion, and destroying accounting data. As a result, Anderson had his license revoked and was prosecuted by the US Department of Justice. The collapse of these two major organizations caused a global economic shockwave.

What is the goodness of law? If there is no supreme goodness but only professional standardization, what would be the basis of law? Is it the enactment and compliance of those laws, regardless of justice?

Can justice be realized through litigation? Or does litigation merely foster enduring antagonisms? The assumptions underlying existing professionalism are commonly accepted without much consideration.

Legal justice is typically used by people to battle each other. Criminals can even get full protection as respect for human rights. Lawyers will do their best to protect criminals instead of encouraging them to confess. The existing legal system calls for defense lawyers to safeguard defendants rather than guide them to admit and fix errors. This shows individual dominance instead of showing care and helping others.

This assumption, as per Aristotle, lacks the notion of a supreme good. Everyone perceives self-interest as good, thus all professional norms become a shelter for one's desires.

In recent years, the non-violent communication developed by the American legal scene focuses on the reflections of criminals instead of helping them evade punishment or accept punishment, which helps little for their repentance, and they may even feel bullied by the legal system. The goodness of the law lies in the awakening of criminals. It is supreme goodness indeed. Material and physical punishment means only instrumental justice, while true justice is to let all people realize justice and be willing to follow it. In other words, the goodness of economy and law considers not merely individual interests but communal interests and spiritual purity and growth that brings supreme goodness and happiness.

To Aristotle, supreme goodness is not based on emotion but on behavior. It entails good morals, civic involvement, and loving relationships.

The pursuit of desires and self-interests leads to the loss of souls.

If we make goodness the aim of our life, we won't chase after self-interests, but instead put others' interests first. We will empathize with them and consider the consequences of our actions, since it's spiritual perfection, not deceiving, avoiding, and disrespecting, that we strive for.

Just as in Buddhism, karma is a concept that one cannot escape even if they avoid a legal penalty, meaning one must repent and save their soul. This is leading an honest life.

Buddhism hides no sins or wrongs in its generations-long pursuit of perfection for its soul. Desire and self-interest, however, are antithetical to the supreme goodness of wisdom in life.

This is Aristotle's view that humans must be motivated to strive for the highest good, avoiding desires and interests which bring no genuine joy. Spiritual fulfillment is contrary to the pursuit of desires.

Confucianism pursues the realm of sages. Confucius said, "Now the man of perfect virtue, wishing to be established himself, seeks also to establish others; wishing to be enlarged himself, he seeks also to enlarge others."[1] He also said, "The noble man does not, even for the space of a single meal, act contrary to virtue. In moments of haste, he cleaves to it. In seasons of danger, he cleaves to it."[2]

Those who could keep their ideal and observe moralities and those who follow the way of justice instead of interests could be called people of virtues. Those who could benefit and give to the masses are saints. People of benevolence could find people around them in need and help them. The ultimate goal of the Confucian way of life is to consider the interests of others and provide service to them.

Surely, motivation through money and desire produces no supreme goodness of life. Confucianism seeks to benefit the country and people— not individual desire for fame and wealth. This requires the pursuit of Tao which excludes the satisfaction of wealth and desire. Without an ultimate goal, there is no motivation for goodness.

---

[1] Legge, J. (1971). *Confucian Analects: The Great Learning, and The Doctrine of the Mean*. New York: Dover Publications. p. 194.

[2] Legge, J. (1971). *Confucian Analects: The Great Learning, and The Doctrine of the Mean*. New York: Dover Publications. p. 166.

Through many civilizations, one can conclude that life should not be about satisfying material desires but about striving for higher moral ideals and helping others. This is likely due to humans' innate inclination to pursue the infinite.

The Human Pursuit of Infinity

Once humans have a goal, they often seek to extend it without limits. Pursuing infinity is part of human nature, and an inescapable driving force.

The human pursuit of infinity is evident in the quest for political power, eternal life, business growth and maximum gain, and unrestrained consumption. Wanting and getting it all results in loss for others. Resources are finite, power balances out, money is limited, and though life may be long it still has an end.

Making money the primary motivator in life will not result in true happiness or contentment. Consumption will never bring joy.

People must focus their endless striving on giving, rather than seeking to acquire. Otherwise, their tireless pursuit will only bring endless emptiness.

The more you give, the happier you will be.

This statement is the practical experience as demonstrated by Tzu Chi volunteer entrepreneurs, not merely an ethical code.

However, the logic of gaining happiness is that the more you gain, the harder it is to be happy.

You'll need two after one, three after two, then ten, and even more.

The wealthy have a greater craving for money than anyone else, but cannot be appeased. With their first ten million, they find joy, yet, the second fails to bring satisfaction. To achieve the joy of the initial ten million, they must now earn significantly more; and to receive the same happiness, they must now earn 100 million. This endless quest encourages the insatiable need for more and, eventually, their own economy cannot bear the strain.

Marshall's Law of Marginal Diminishing Utility[3] states that further consumption of a good or service will not bring greater satisfaction, but instead make it more challenging to be fulfilled. The idea that money and

---

[3] Lu, M. R. (1995). *Jingji xue gailun* [Introduction to Economics]. Taipei: San min shu ju. pp. 72–76.

material goods cannot evade this law is echoed throughout; the initial joy and contentment from making money can hardly be replicated in future, ephemeral earnings, or it may need far greater wealth to capture the same satisfaction of the first.

On the other hand, could the joy of giving evade the law mentioned? Will giving again bring the same joy as initially?

Think of someone giving to others to find more joy while helping the community. Even utilitarians would agree with this act.

Why doesn't the joy of giving to others decrease, but instead abide by a rule that the more you give, the happier you become?

That is because the energy of inner love increases when giving. When you seek to gain, your inner emptiness will only grow. Jiddu Krishnamurti (1895–1986) said, "Seeking means lacking within, and the more you seek, the more you lack."[4] Thus, the more you yearn, the more heartache you will endure, and the more difficult it is to feel content.

The More You Ask for, The Less You Receive.

People who prioritize giving and altruism as economic objectives will find more happiness as they help others, creating a bond of trust and love. Trust yields wealth, and love brings joy.

The goal of the economy should be happiness, and altruistic pursuits are more beneficial than self-serving ones, leading to true happiness.

Only in love can one be free. Giving love brings freedom.

Therefore, good economic motives lead humankind to ultimate happiness and freedom.

Altruistic Practices in the Economy

In the West, between the fifteenth and eighteenth centuries, there were fierce conflicts between Christianity and Catholicism, and Christianity and Islamism; as well as political clashes between kings, nobility, and emerging citizens. Despite this, there was a relatively peaceful, equitable, and mutually beneficial arena for the various classes and religions, and that was business.

As Voltaire saw in the eighteenth century, Jews, Protestants, Catholics, Muslims, and Hindus met in business and discussed mutual advantages—everyone excluding the bankrupt was on equal footing and could

---

[4] Krishnamurti, J. (1969). *Freedom from the Known*. India: HarperCollins.

cooperate. Once trading had concluded, some would baptize their children as Christians, others circumcise their children in accordance with Jewish custom and others worship Allah. Nonetheless, this did not restrict working together in trade—there was no other field like business where tolerance, acceptance, trust, and benefit were as evident.

Therefore, in Europe, where religious and political conflicts had long been a cause of suffering, commerce was a major contributor to civilization, integration, and unity.

Business is based on mutual trust and mutual benefit for all involved; every person has their interests at heart, but we understand that to gain our own benefit, we must ensure others thrive. Thus, business is the law of self-interest obtained through altruism.

Although capitalist society regards self-interest as its standard, the driving force behind economic and commercial activities is the desire to benefit others and oneself. To help oneself, one must prioritize helping others.

As previously noted, humans evolved to display altruism, enabling them to prevail over natural trials. Darwinists have also consistently demonstrated that altruistic groups could survive in the law of natural selection. Altruism is ingrained in the human genome and motivates the Economy of Goodness.

However, I do not believe that self-interest should be absent from a commercial society. While it exists, overly selfish economic and commercial dealings will not last long. An economy based on altruism will bring lasting success and social advancement, as well as prosperity.

Max Weber (1864–1920) tried to explain the spirit of Western entrepreneurs through Protestant ethics, believing it was the duty of an entrepreneur to conduct business in accordance with God's commandments.

Weber endowed entrepreneurs with a sacred mission and founded businesses based on goodness, taking Franklin as a model for achieving glory for God. He insisted on keeping the commandments to be God's good people. Rockefeller, Warren Buffett, and Franklin, were all frugal, independent, and thriving, accumulating huge wealth and showing active charity. They epitomize good Christian-based businesses. While there have been cases of greedy Christian entrepreneurs, Weber believed that motives of goodness and good enterprises helped Christian entrepreneurs succeed.

What caused the great divide between wealthy entrepreneurs and struggling employees in eighteenth and nineteenth-century Western business? The achievement of success should be attributed to God, and a business that is able to expand its territory is evidence of this divine grace. God's favor is not equally distributed, as only those who adhere to His principles may be selected. Ultimately, it is impossible for humans to comprehend God's will, so it is impossible to know who is truly His favor until the results of His blessings are seen.

The gap between the rich and the poor in this chosen group of people was foreseeable. In the last two centuries, wars and suffering caused a much greater disparity between those with wealth and those without, than it had in thousands of years prior. Personal economic success does not guarantee societal economic success, and a failure to do so is certain to bring about a depression and the ruin of individual wealth.

Here, we are discussing the motivation of goodness in the Economy of Goodness, which concentrates on altruism rather than individual benefit. Confucianism emphasizes that individual successes are essential for the prosperity of the clan and nation, while Buddhism asserts that personal fulfillment is acquired via altruism. Taoism suggests that the ruler should not impose their acknowledged values on the public, but should instead offer conditions for people to be self-sufficient, live and work peacefully and contentedly, and remain in harmony with nature; emphasizing the broad masses, rather than oneself. To summarize, Confucianism, Buddhism, and Taoism all prioritize the collective contentment of the entire human race.

Karl Marx (1818–1883) hoped to bring people common happiness through political power. The altruistic Economy of Goodness that I advocate should start with voluntary individuals, and altruism should be spontaneous and joyful. When we recognize that all human activity is interconnected, and selflessness is in our own interest, people will be more inclined to engage in economic activities with generosity.

Admittedly, desire often prevails over reason. Still, both Aristotle and Kant argued that rationality is a choice humans can make. Nevertheless, when faced with desire, reason is often overcome.

Eastern philosophy often emphasizes emotion. Mencius said that everyone had compassion; and the Buddha believed all beings had a nature of compassion, mercy, generosity, and joy. For creating an Economy of Goodness, emotional inspiration is just as necessary as rational cognition. Economically minded people should understand that altruism is more effective and allows greater rewards than self-interest. Emotionally, the wealthy should have empathy towards those less fortunate to nurture altruism.

Adam Smith suggested that, in the market, everyone starts with self-interest, and an invisible hand will lead to the equilibrium of public interests. This invisible hand is the desire within us, ultimately leading to the distribution of production, consumption, and capital gains reverting to said desire. This desire, acting as the invisible hand, is what controls the market and capital. As a consequence, the gap between rich and poor keeps widening, social problems arise, and the environment is deteriorating.

In Weber's view, an "invisible hand" is God's will, making those whom God has chosen to be rich. According to Marx, it is the governance of the proletariat. Schumpeter held it was professional bureaucracy while Keynes argued that it is through government regulation.

From this invisible hand to the manifest hand of the state, all are working to achieve just distribution of resources and capital to limit the boundless proliferation of individual wants.

Nevertheless, this invisible hand for the Economy of Goodness should not be one of governments, the proletariat, professional bureaucrats, or desires of the heart, but instead everyone's spontaneous compassion and inherent goodness.

Government regulations and controls will not stop entrepreneurs from wanting to expand their business territory by any means, or from trying to acquire wealth endlessly.

To eliminate desires and greed, we must start by fostering the inner compassion of entrepreneurs.

Using the global development of Tzu Chi Charity Foundation as an example, Tzu Chi inspires many entrepreneurs to devote themselves to charitable relief work. Entrepreneurs "find blessings in seeing suffering" and "are inspired by their innate compassion through their experiences with suffering." This changes the business model from one of greed to one that is not engaged in harmful or unethical economic practices. It embodies honest business practices based on sincerity, righteousness and trustworthiness.

This transformation stems from the love and compassion present in human beings. It allows entrepreneurs to recognize and abolish suffering, shifting their mindsets from greed to charity and from self-centeredness to self-improvement. This is a way to nurture their inner kindness.

Cultivating motivation for benevolent economics can begin with inspiration and refinement through charitable work. Engaging in philanthropic activities can nurture the altruistic spirit of entrepreneurs, enabling them to empathize with the hardships of the less fortunate. This approach, compared to the distribution justice within the system, is more effective in achieving fair allocation of capital.

SECTION 2: NATURE OF PRODUCTION AND CONSUMPTION

The Source of Product Creation Is Altruism

How to establish motivation based on goodness? Motivation has rarely been explored in social sciences influenced by Western scientism, as it is hard to discern a person's true motivation.

The law's fair judgment emphasizes motivation as an important factor in determining whether a person's behavior is in accordance with statutes.

Can good and altruistic motivation spur people to engage actively in economic activities?

Adam Smith hypothesized that a baker or brewer wasn't considering the consumer in their production but the cost of his own life and that of his children's dinners. Yet, how could a baker or brewer who disregarded consumer tastes make wine and bread?

Behind commercial self-interest lies altruism. Businesses can only thrive when considering goodness.

Chinese entrepreneur Jack Ma expressed his motivation for doing business in the early years in a speech at Tel Aviv University in Israel. He said he had never expected to achieve the results he did. He sacrificed teaching in order to put his words into action, intending to practice business for ten years and then prove to students he had kept his promise. However, he needed help finding a job in America and observed there were no Chinese products available on the Internet when he learned to use it. Ma pondered how marvelous it would be if he could bring the goods of housewives and small business owners to the web. Back in China, he established Alibaba, believing that it would succeed if it could help these people become successful.

Many people attribute Jack Ma's success to luck and his choice of industry. At the start, he sought help from several prominent entrepreneurs, but was often rebuffed. Not only did he pick the right industry, but Ma also showed altruism His skill in business, employment of talent, timing, and efficient use of capital were all essential to his achievements.

In referencing altruism within the Economy of Goodness, we don't anticipate entrepreneurs to be Christian missionaries or Buddhist masters who would sacrifice themselves for others. We don't expect Jack Ma to become a saint and permanently discard his self-interests. It's of little consequence if he accumulates wealth, what matters is that his success begins with altruism.

We argue that altruism is more conducive to economic success than self-interest.

The Motive of Production Should Be for Human Welfare

Steve Jobs, the co-founder of Apple, was driven by the idea of empowering humanity to control machines with their bodies, and the development of the iPhone exemplifies this vision. Jobs believed that the environment we inhabit is constructed by others, and he encouraged individuals not to believe that others are smarter than them. Instead, he emphasized the power of creating something new, influencing others, and allowing them to enjoy one's creations. Jobs was one of the most creative individuals of his era, and his motivational force remained centered on creating innovative things to impact others. Altruism continued to be the core of his life.

Jobs believed that the excellence of Silicon Valley is largely due to the powerful people who come from universities like Stanford and Berkeley. Also, Hewlett and Packer, founders of HP Computer, served as great examples. For Jobs, the key to success was not gaining wealth, but providing worth. As engineers, the inventors of HP were cognizant of what their peers wanted, hence their computers met their needs. Through this, HP achieved triumph.

Jobs earned $1 M at 23, $10 M at 24, and $100 M at 25. But he said money isn't crucial; it's about customers and products. An old friend noted Jobs didn't care about money, just product innovation. After his cancer diagnosis in 2017, Jobs stated that customers were foremost, that Apple wanted to make great products to gain consumers' approval, which was the key to success.

Democratization and publicization of technologies brought him great success, earning him tremendous recognition by the whole world.

Jobs said computer engineers always sought faster computers; however, Apple's aim was not computing, but people's needs. Apple sought music, movies, aesthetically pleasing artwork, and communication—not computers—to fulfill people's desires. Crafting to people's needs is the groundwork of successful businesses and fundamental to creating goodness.

Steve Jobs said that we should not release new tech directly in the market but must understand them and create the greatest benefit for them to be a successful business.

Creation Comes from the Individual's Pure Nature

But how does one truly understand consumers? Steve Jobs' experience was to return to one's natural self.

Steve Jobs was the most brilliant and great inventor and entrepreneur of the twenty-first century. He pursued both a successful career and a spiritual life, embracing meditation. By tapping into his intuition, he developed many of his creations, knowing what customers wanted better than they did themselves. He saw in 1970 that IBM's computers weren't the right product, feeling that IBM was on the wrong track and that their computers should not be so large and cumbersome. Because of this, his signature MacBook was produced to be small, stylish, and user-friendly, with a visually appealing design and a user-friendly interface. His instincts told him that the computer he created would change people's lives, and this was proven with the monumental success of the iPhone when it was released in 2007.

Intuition leads us away from the usual human lifestyle and Apple is a brave innovator determined to give people an improved lifestyle, not defeat rivals.

This innovation combines altruism with a fundamental force in human imagination. The great German philosopher, Hegel (1770–1831 AD), said that true product creation arose from people's imagination, not market needs. Imagination and culture are the prime movers of economic innovation. According to Hegel, most of human need stems not from natural desire, but rather from imagination. Imagination is the thing that separates us from animals. Necessities are not given by nature, but rather a product of second nature, arising out of historical change. Civilization creates a variety of needs, a ceaseless process.

Material creation is not driven by desire, but by the evolution of civilization. Humans' evolving needs lead to innovation. Steve Jobs' contributions were not based on personal or customer desires, but on improving human life, getting humans closer to themselves and enabling them to integrate with technology and master machines, rather than being subjected to them.

Meditation drew Jobs nearer to his true nature, allowing him to understand himself and take others' perspectives into account. Commonly held humanity makes this possible. Becoming aware of oneself lets one gain greater comprehension of others. Buddhism's open-mindedness and the elimination of impurities that bring inner and outer clarity, allows people to gain insight into the lives of others. Meditation, plus Western analytical thinking, broke Jobs away from the usual standards of the world, launching him into a state of higher insight.

Choosing Does Not Equal Freedom

Capitalism is premised on self-interest; entrepreneurs' endeavor to make money and consumers seek to purchase to fulfill selfish desires—all being deviant economic practices. The Economy of Goodness, by contrast, is created with the aim of elevating humanity and human life and consumption is aimed at increasing the value of life.

Consumption driven by desire and manufacture catering to that desire are, according to Herbert Marcuse (1898–1979 CE), the ways a capitalist society exerts control, causing them to forget their exploitation in the capital market while satisfying their desires. This consumption, however, only earns them an identity that won't bring true joy. Wealthy people may don designer outfits to signify their social status, but this won't lead to true contentment.

Marcuse concurred with Hegel's opinion that the decision to buy does not generate genuine liberation. Folks simply elect among disparate items, incurring the cost of labor and the trepidation of toil.

Making money isn't equal to happiness, and consuming isn't equal to freedom; this is a critique and self-reflection on Capitalism.

Marcuse thought that Capitalism was not replaced due to its incapability of providing commodities, but because it failed to deliver them in a richer form. Consequently, our ideal Economy of Goodness does not only consist of offering novel goods, but of goods that are able to give life meaning and enhance its quality.

John Keynes (1883–1946 CE) stressed the importance of artistic activities beyond the economy, emphasizing that economic life must bring people the setting of the value of life and the enhancement of the quality of life. Aside from consuming and striving for commodities and social prestige, people should strive to create a tranquil, peaceful, and stimulating material environment.

Capitalism urges people to strive to make money and consume until individuals become fixated on production and gratification.

Money Cannot Buy Happiness

As Aristotle said, the accumulation of wealth does not bring true happiness; it is the ability to benefit society, participate in public affairs, live by virtue, and contribute to the community that brings it. Buddhism teaches that true happiness is found through the awareness of oneself and compassion for others.

Aristotle said that true happiness comes from forming loving relationships, taking part in public affairs, and living ethically. Money doesn't result in happiness, instead leading to servitude; genuine happiness stems from freedom, kindness, and morality.

Master Cheng Yen, stresses all-encompassing great love, creating loving connections between all people and things, demonstrating ultimate altruism.

Goodness in economic life is not the pursuit of money but forming loving relationships with people, serving the community and giving to others. Participating in charity has been known to regenerate life and bring fulfillment, not just riches.

Sugianto Kusuma, Indonesia's second-largest real estate developer, had a difficult upbringing. He used to take on any endeavor with profit potential. Despite achieving great wealth, he found no fulfillment or joy.

In 2002, Sugianto Kusuma (also known as Aguan) joined Tzu Chi and assisted in relocating thousands of people living on the banks of the Angke River, the dirtiest river in Jakarta, to the newly constructed thousand-family Great Love Village and Tzu Chi Great Love School (Sekolah Cinta Kasih Tzu Chi). He was involved in the distribution of 50,000 tons of rice to 5 million low-income families, and relentlessly worked on the aid effort after the 2003 South Asian Tsunami—surveying disaster scenes with the Indonesian President until the completion of the 4,000-home Great Love Village for the tsunami survivors. As a result, Sugianto Kusuma's life, family, and career were greatly transformed. He ceased to be involved in any questionable business but gained even greater wealth. His bond with his children and wife has grown stronger and he has been given meritorious recognition from the Indonesian government and society. He is now living a much happier life.

Happiness does not lie in chasing wealth, but in dedicating oneself to public causes—that is a fulfilling life that comes from selflessness.

A Global Organization Built with Goodness

As the biggest religious charity in the Chinese-speaking world, Tzu Chi Foundation is involved in activities such as charity, education, medicine, humanistic culture, and environmental protection among other efforts. Its work has reached 136 countries and regions worldwide, with presence in 68 countries and regions. In total, there are more than 10 million donating members and 2 million volunteers. The vast tangible and intangible assets accumulated by Tzu Chi are a result of compassion and values. Indeed, these assets of Tzu Chi are not owned by any individual but are shared by the love of over 10 million supporters.

Tzu Chi's successes have come from altruism. Master Cheng Yen began with the making of baby shoes and urged housewives to save TWD 50 cents (approx. USD 2 cents) a day to save lives. And after half a century, Tzu Chi has evolved into one of the world's most prominent NGOs, a result of altruism.

The more we dedicate ourselves to customers' interests and the greater good, the more innovative we will be.

Indeed, it is easy to find instances when self-interest leads to success. However, such success might be rejected by society if it is not driven by altruism.

Bill Gates faced a trying time when Microsoft was boycotted, criticized by customers and held under an antitrust investigation by the government. His embrace of corporate incentives kept him in a stalemate. Businesses that were too absorbed in their own gain risked missing the newly arising wants and transforming trends. Though Google and Facebook had already taken off, Microsoft was slow to turn to a platform business model, but still, Gates delved into philanthropy.

The Bill & Melinda Gates Foundation, which he founded, is devoted to researching and developing vaccines for major infectious diseases worldwide, including polio, malaria, AIDS, etc. He has concentrated on clean water resources in underdeveloped regions and committed himself to educating children there, all of which have had remarkable accomplishments. Bill Gates eventually stepped away from Microsoft after turning to philanthropy. In 2018, Forbes designated him the richest person in the world. His involvement in altruistic activities intensified his commercial clout, which was converted into concrete commercial capital, making him again the wealthiest person in the world, and his wealth continues to expand.

Warren Buffett donated 90% of his fortune to the Bill & Melinda Gates Foundation, appointing Bill Gates to oversee its use. Gates, a man of considerable wealth and renown, shifted from a focus on profit to an altruistic purpose, beginning an impressive commercial and philanthropic journey.

Bill Gates' altruistic outlook enabled him to fully realize his ambitions and wealth. In contrast to Microsoft's prior dominance, Gates is now seen as an exemplar of both wealth and virtue in the modern world. He has attained greater success through his concern for others; championing the Economy of Goodness.

Altruism Not for Self-Gain

If you dedicate yourself to altruism out of self-interest, it will not be considered evil, but it will not be perceived as good either.

A business owner who only looks after their own interests must create economically successful outcomes that are widely recognized. People's behavior and outlook shape the path of their professional life. Business ventures which act with concern for consumers, shareholders, families, and the nation have a greater chance of succeeding.

Those who pursue their interests may succeed initially, but they'll soon confront conflicts of interest. If business owners only care about their own interests, others will undoubtedly do the same. This could lead to reaching a consensus by negotiation, or worse—having to stand in court, which would be a waste of time and money. When compared to those who opt to simply avoid these issues by creating their own causes, it's evident which is the wise choice.

The start of prioritizing self-interest foretells a decrease in creativity. We don't support sacrificing personal interests; however, we should always consider altruism in financial matters, and our interests will be properly looked after. But why?

When considering the advantages for others, it helps us to comprehend market demand.

Mark Zuckerberg, the founder of Facebook, had a vision to connect people in a virtual community. His altruistic concept was uncertain but has since become an immense success in the Internet Age. If he opts to expand his career at the cost of altruism, Facebook will likely suffer more from rumors and anonymous attacks. Although they can't be held responsible for every negative piece of information, they would not let all come to pass if they maintain their altruistic standard; this being key to the long-term success of the enterprise.

When we consider ways to benefit others, we can reduce costs and make prudent use of shareholders' funds.

At the Tzu Chi Foundation headquarters, all the staff are taught by Master Cheng Yen to cherish the love of all living beings, so managers can trust that there will be no corruption and wasteful practices among their employees.

During my 20 plus years at Tzu Chi, this is indeed the case. Internal expenses are basically carried out based on trust. Although the staff receive a lower salary than average, many do not apply for overtime pay and see their extra hours during holidays or weekends as volunteer work. Everyone values and cherishes every bit of love donated from society. This how they embody the spirit of altruism.

When considering the interests of others, we should not suppress their voices but instead allow for everyone to have a say in the decision-making process.

As Ingvar Kamprad stated, we should not be apprehensive of making mistakes, but rather permit all to engage in decision-making, for it is only those who sleep who never err. Allowing staff involvement in decision-making is critical to IKEA's prosperity. It was a colleague's suggestion of being able to take furniture away in a car that made IKEA an exceptional furniture empire.

When considering others' interests, we won't exploit the peril of others to push up interest rates, thereby keeping financial stability.

The 2008 financial crisis was caused by too much credit being extended. Banks allowed for increased credit availability and insurance firms provided assurance. This fueled bubbles that brought short-term benefits to consumers, yet all the while, banks desired higher rates of interest. Purchasing power accelerated, leading to an increased cost of living, but salaries remained stagnant. When too many people couldn't meet their interest payments, the banks had to declare bankruptcy and the related insurance sector folded. The danger of prioritizing selfish gain was never clearer.

When we consider others' interests, we will not seek to increase prices by taking advantage of a need. This would keep prices stable and balanced relative to costs, supply, and demand, thereby benefiting all.

Real estate in China was overly-inflated, prompting President Xi Jinping to caution that homes are meant for habitation, not speculation, thus curbing house prices. When people passively rely on a substantial rise in the value of real estate, and a great deal of funds are invested in such commodification ventures, the cost of goods will increase, and both low-income and middle-income earners will suffer further.

Educate People with Goodness After Enriching Them

When China's GDP has become the second largest in the world, a Confucian story still rings in many people's ears. When Ran You, a disciple, asked Confucius what the next step for politicians is when people can earn a basic living, The *Analects of Confucius* recorded this:

> You said, 'Since they are thus numerous, what more shall be done for them?' 'Enrich them,' was the reply. 'And when they have been enriched, what more shall be done?' The Master said, 'Teach them.'[5]

In recent years, the government of China has aimed to eliminate speculative investment on housing as their way to "instruct" (or traditional context of educate) wealthy people to be benevolent and refrain from speculation. Commercial speculation has been a recurring problem for all dynasties in China's history, increasing the wealth disparity and ultimately causing social unrest. Keeping house prices steady, then, is a genuinely beneficent action which maintains social stability. As Mencius expressed:

> Now, the first thing to being a benevolent government must be to lay down the farm boundaries. If the boundaries are not defined correctly, the

---

[5] Legge, J. (1971). *Confucian Analects: The Great Learning, and The Doctrine of the Mean*. New York: Dover Publications. pp. 266–267.

division of land into squares will not be equal, and the products available for profits will not be evenly distributed.[6]

The housing prices are the economic boundaries within a city. If ordinary citizens cannot afford housing, it is akin to the unequal distribution of fertile land in an agrarian society, leading to disparities in grain harvests. Unequal distribution of properties results in price imbalances. The wisdom imparted by Mencius remains relevant to this day. Therefore, the intervention of state power is the path of benevolent governance. However, at its core, it still revolves around education. There is no time in China's history that is in greater need of advocating for a virtuous economy than the present.

Engaging in economic activities with goodness and altruism is the path to family harmony and social governance. Now, Chinese business plays an important role in the world, making the establishment of economic culture critical. It would be advantageous if Chinese entrepreneurs could create valuable career paths with altruism, make innovative commercial products, and generate wealth for families and society at large. This is possible within China's special economic system (as opposed to the Anglo-American system led by individualism). Therefore, constructing an Economy of Goodness through altruism is a distinguishing feature of China.

In recent years, Chinese have been speculating on housing prices while Japanese enterprises have ventured into organic, non-toxic clothing and food industries. South Korea is rapidly gaining a foothold in the Asian cultural market. Uncontrolled commodity prices, along with collective self-interest, can result in greater losses for individuals and society as a whole.

The financial misuse of excessive loans in the US has been the prime cause of economic recession in recent years. President Trump's conservatism and insularity have been increasing steadily. He was blindly defending the vanishing traditional manufacturing industry and his own interests. Without an altruistic or self-interested motive, it's hard for the US economy to restore its past greatness.

Altruism keeps creativity alive; Japan's UNIQLO and MUJI have become world lifestyle leaders, offering quality clothing and supplies from an altruistic stance.

---

[6] M. & Legge, J. (2011). *The Works of Mencius*. New York: Dover Publications. p. 244.

How can Chinese enterprises innovate in a global economy, especially if they expect to be an economic model for other countries? The key factor is Altruism.

China's current development and characteristics preclude the adoption of an "American supremacy" and isolationist approach like that taken by President Trump. Rather, China should blend into the global economy while still showcasing the goodness of Chinese culture, which derives from Confucianism, Taoism, Buddhism, and Western scientific thought.

Businessmen Can Be Sages

The Economy of Goodness recognizes Confucian benevolence and wealth, as well as the spirit and practice of compassion advocated by Buddhism.

Ren (仁 in Chinese, meaning benevolence) is two characters that embody caring for others. Mencius said, "Benevolence is the distinguishing characteristic of man."[7] "He is affectionate to his parents, and lovingly disposed to people generally. He is lovingly disposed to people generally, and kind to creatures."[8]

Being able to love others and things is an act of altruism. Doing business with a love for others equals an Economy of Goodness.

The motivation of goodness is characterized by benevolence before wealth, not wealth before benevolence. While it might be admirable to be wealthy before being benevolent, this does not constitute goodness. Therefore, we must prioritize benevolence over wealth.

Wang Yangming's philosophy of the mind highlights the significance of righteous intentions. Most importantly, one must possess sincerity and an earnest heart to grow in morality, regulate one's family, administer the state, and create a harmonious world. Regarding sincerity, Wang Yangming said:

> It is only he who is possessed of the complete sincerity that can exist under heaven, who can give its full development to his nature... assist the transforming and nourishing powers of heaven and earth.[9]

[7] M. & Legge, J. (2011). *The Works of Mencius*. New York: Dover Publications. p. 485.

[8] M. & Legge, J. (2011). *The Works of Mencius*. New York: Dover Publications. p. 476.

[9] Legge, J. (1971). *Confucian Analects: The Great Learning, and The Doctrine of the Mean*. New York: Dover Publications. pp. 389–399.

Sincerity is the foremost of the saints' teachings for self-cultivation.

The essence of the Great Learning is sincerity. When sincerity is fully developed, it becomes supreme goodness.[10]

In Wang Yangming's view, studying things, obtaining knowledge, having sincerity, and having a rightful mindset are all interlinked; the material is inseparable from consciousness—this is akin to the Buddhist notion of "the mind creating all things." Studying things requires the deepest understanding, and only those who are sincere are capable of this.

To acquire knowledge does not mean simply accumulating all the current scientific knowledge available, but rather understanding all things derived from our appreciation of our nature. Wang Yangming emphasized that the key to unlocking our full potential and comprehending the universe's mysteries lies within our minds.[11] Through introspection and by making the best use of our inherent nature, guided by our conscience, we can unlock our potential and gain profound insights.

Chinese Confucianism espouses sincerity and a righteous mindset. It asserts that one should be devoted to caring for all living creatures selflessly.

Contemporary science matters more than the mind; however, ancient Chinese sages would begin with a sincere and righteous mindset and attain all things in the world.

John Rawls mentioned the veil of ignorance for understanding knowledge in *A Theory of Justice*.[12] One must enter the veil of ignorance and abandon their social status and pre-existing opinion to determine justice. The veil of ignorance refers to the impartiality one is born with; as Buddhism teaches, all beings have sufficient nature for compassionate judgment.

This aligns with Wang Yangming's concept of Sincerity. It was about more than gaining knowledge; it also emphasized empathy and care for all in the universe. Rather than a mere scientific realization, this was an enlightened human wisdom.

---

[10] Wang, Y. M., & Deng, A. M. (2000). *Chuanxi lu zhushu* [The Annotations of Chuan Xi Lu]. Fa yan chuban she. p. 31.

[11] Wang, Y. M., & Deng, A. M. (2000). *Chuanxi lu zhushu* [The Annotations of Chuan Xi Lu]. Fa yan chuban she. p. 31.

[12] Rawls, J. (1999). *A Theory of Justice*. United Kingdom: Oxford University Press.

The Economy of Goodness: Rooted in Compassionate Giving

Businesses can engage in commerce with a compassionate heart rooted in Buddhist principles. The term "慈" (ci) encompasses both the material and spiritual realms, representing the embodiment of both compassion and wisdom. "悲" (bei) refers to the absence of self-centeredness, extending empathy and understanding beyond one's own ego to embrace the perspectives of others. This selfless motivation, driven by a genuine desire to benefit others, forms the cornerstone of a benevolent economy.

Compassion propels the virtuous cycle of the Economy of Goodness. Businesses that operate with compassion can create products and foster a work environment that benefits everyone—employees, consumers, shareholders, and society as a whole. Compassion allows for love and respect toward others, while empathy fosters understanding of their needs. By approaching both employees and consumers with empathy, respecting their rights, businesses can build a foundation for the Economy of Goodness. This involves cherishing resources and protecting the environment, demonstrating compassion for all aspects of society.

The practice of loving-kindness and compassion must be based on joyful giving. Thomas Alva Edison (1847–1931 AD), one of the greatest inventors in history, found joy in his creations. His invention of the lightbulb changed life as we know it, while the phonograph revolutionized human writing. As Edison worked, he took delight in his craft, experiencing pure joy. These inventions have been great boons to humankind and altruistic endeavors.

Benefiting others with a joyful heart is the foundation of EOG.

The captivating typography of Apple computers and iPhones owes its genesis to Steve Jobs' decision to continue auditing calligraphy classes at university after dropping out. His deep appreciation for the elegance of letters, coupled with his vision of human–machine interaction, culminated in the revolutionary inventions that transformed the modern industrial era. The introduction of touchscreen smartphones dramatically increased our reliance on and demand for these devices, establishing them as indispensable hubs for information, communication, and entertainment.

Doing things for the benefit of others with a simple and joyful heart is the driving force behind creating great things.

The concept of giving (捨 shè), is either to "give up" or to "give alms" holds profound significance in the pursuit of personal growth and societal well-being. To truly understand the essence of giving is to grasp the key to unlocking abundance and fulfillment. As Master Cheng Yen eloquently stated, "To gain, one must first give." This profound wisdom encapsulates the transformative power of selflessness. True giving manifests not only in the willingness to give to others but to also give without expecting anything in return. It is the embodiment of a magnanimous heart that embraces what others may find unacceptable or intolerable.

Giving is also a reflection of wisdom, the understanding that giving up on somethings is not a sign of weakness but rather a path to true prosperity. This concept is beautifully illustrated by the actions of Zeng Guofan, a renowned Chinese statesman, who voluntarily demobilized his army after defeating the Taiping Rebellion,[13] demonstrating his humility and selflessness. As an old Chinese saying goes, "When the birds are gone, the good bow is put away." Lao Tzu said, "The work is accomplished, and there is no resting in it (as an achievement). The work is done, but how no one can see; 'Tis this that makes the power not cease to be."[14] This is great wisdom.

For businesses, the act of giving or giving up is also crucial. Expansion in success can be a crisis. As management gurus Peter Drucker and Peter Senge point out, blind expansion often leads to corporate collapse.

Firstly, markets change. Products that once thrived may not be what the market needs. Mindlessly repeating past successes can lead to a miserable defeat when the market shifts. Nokia, for example, failed to see the rise of smartphones and couldn't keep up, falling from a mobile phone leader to a quick sale. Giving up is vital. Without the ability to transcend past achievements, businesses and the entire economic landscape can decline.

Another example of failing to give and practice restraint after success is Zhao Cheng, a company that expanded and pursued excessive profits without control. This led to an overwhelming number of orders that

[13] From the end of 1850 to the beginning of 1851, a group led by Hong Xiuquan launched an armed uprising against the Qing Dynasty in Jintian Village, Guangxi. Later, the "Taiping Heavenly Kingdom" was established, and Jiangning (now Nanjing) was captured in March 1853. The capital was established there, and the name was changed to Tianjing. In August 1864, Tianjing, the capital of the Taiping Heavenly Kingdom, was captured by the Hunan army, and Hong Tianguifu, the son of Hong Xiuquan and the young king of heaven, was captured. In 1872, Li Wencai, the last Taiping army leader, was defeated in Guizhou.

[14] Tzu, L. (Eds.). (2021). *Tao Te Ching* (J. Legge, Trans.). Standard Ebooks. Retrieved from https://standardebooks.org/ebooks/laozi/tao-te-ching/james-legge.

exceeded their internal management capabilities, resulting in delays in meeting customer demands and a decline in product quality. Consequently, Zhao Cheng gradually lost its market share. This is why Lamborghini limits its annual production of sports cars to 6,000 units. This decision serves two purposes: maintaining quality and preserving the exclusivity that makes the brand so desirable. It exemplifies the principle of giving in order to gain.

Giving ultimately means letting go of desires and negativity. A heart overflowing with desires hinders rational decision-making, leading to tragedy. Letting go of control allows colleagues and partners to participate more, creating the high-efficiency of collective wisdom, just like Ingvar Kamprad of IKEA's "Let's decide together!" philosophy.

Loving-kindness, compassion, joy, and giving are prerequisites for business success and sustainable economic development. Loving-kindness attracts good outcomes. Compassion fosters good connections. Joy sparks endless creativity. Equanimity cultivates endless wisdom.

Business leaders who manage with these in mind contribute not just to their companies, but to society and the nation—the core ideal of EOG. Building an economy of goodness driven by altruism is the challenge and mission for today's entrepreneurs.

Section 3: Cultivation of the Motivation of Goodness

How Can We Foster a Rising Spirit of Altruism?

The prerequisite for the EOG is altruism, but how can it be cultivated?

It is generally accepted that people are self-interested, yet how can they become altruistic?

Whether human nature is evil or good has long been debated. Xunzi, an ancient Chinese philosopher, asserted that human nature should be governed by laws and nurtured with virtues. Mencius argued that all have compassion. Socrates maintained people have a rational character, while Kant contended, they possess transcendental rationality.

Eastern philosophy values the exploration of temperaments and emotions, whereas Western philosophy gives importance to reason. Buddhism and Taoism have a similar viewpoint that humans have the capacity for both good and bad, and the ultimate goal for self-refinement is to transcend these two. Lao Tzu mentioned that everyone knows that beauty is beautiful, because of the existence of ugliness and that everyone knows that good is good because evil exists.[15] Wise people recognize that good and evil are on opposite sides, but they can turn evil to good, taking good as a mentor and evil as a lesson. He also continued by saying that a skilled person is a master (to be looked up to) by those who are not skilled; and the unskilled is the helper of (the reputation of) the person who has the skill.[16]

The Buddha taught that "good and evil are not fixed." Both good and evil are worldly phenomena, and both should be transcended. Buddhism emphasizes that the human mind has eight consciousnesses. The eighth consciousness, the Alaya Consciousness, is where the seeds of good and evil from countless lifetimes are stored. When these seeds meet with the right conditions, they will sprout into evil or good actions. Therefore, practitioners must transform evil seeds into good actions in every circumstance. When faced with any situation, we should practice love not hate, praise not jealousy, and giving not possessiveness. Do not criticize, but be tolerant. Every moment is an opportunity to turn evil into good.

Therefore, enlightenment lies in a single thought in the present moment. Every circumstance is an opportunity for practice, an opportunity to transform the seeds of evil from countless lifetimes into seeds of good. When all thoughts are turned to good, it is enlightenment, it is the transformation of consciousness into wisdom and Bodhi.

Good and evil are both possible, rooted in human nature. Circumstance and self-creation are the keys.

A moment of good thought can transform evil into good, just as a single candle can dispel eons of darkness in one room.

Therefore, everyone has both a self-serving mind and an altruistic mind. How we can expand altruism and shrink the self-serving mind is a crucial question in exploring the good intentions of EOG.

Enhancing altruism begins with reaching out to suffering people.

Those who are generally well-off or still struggling to make ends meet are often preoccupied with self-interest and how to achieve their own happiness. However, this pursuit of happiness rarely leads to true fulfillment and joy. Life is a long and arduous journey. Even those who

---

[15] Tzu, L. (Eds.). (2021). *Tao Te Ching* (J. Legge, Trans.). Standard Ebooks. Retrieved from https://standardebooks.org/ebooks/laozi/tao-te-ching/james-legge.

[16] Tzu, L. (Eds.). (2021). *Tao Te Ching* (J. Legge, Trans.). Standard Ebooks. Retrieved from https://standardebooks.org/ebooks/laozi/tao-te-ching/james-legge.

have achieved wealth often find that their material possessions no longer hold much meaning. However, when people encounter those who are suffering, their inherent compassion is often awakened. They recognize their own abundance, feel grateful for their blessings, and find the capacity to help others. In doing so, they experience a joy that material possessions cannot provide.

At Tzu Chi Foundation, I observed many entrepreneurs engaging in disaster relief, offering aid to the less fortunate, and experiencing genuine happiness. Offering help without expectation of reward brings a profound sense of joy and happiness.

Helping the afflicted is the key step in converting self-interest into altruism.

In 1949, Pitirim Alexandrovitch Sorokin established the Altruism Research Center at Harvard University. In *"The Ways of Power and Love: Types, Factors,"* Sorokin categorized the process of transforming the individual self into altruism into three types, namely, the early lucky type, the late worrying type or late forming type, and the intermediate type between the two.[17]

For the first type, Sorokin listed Catholic Father Damian (Saint Damien of Molokai 1840–1889) who treated leprosy patients in Hawaii in the nineteenth century, Dr. Albert Schweitzer (1875–1965) who practiced medicine in Africa, Catholicism's Saint Francis (1181–1226), and Benjamin Franklin (1706–1790), a pioneer of the American revolution. These people recognized transcendental consciousness in their early formative ages. When they grew up, they could devote themselves to altruism without hesitation as soon as the chance came.

For the second type, Sorokin cited people such as Prince Siddhartha in Buddhism. These people had either struggled to fully connect with groups or incorrectly associated individualism with specific values at an early point in their lives. With a disruptive transformation, they then re-built the relationship between themselves and groups, and realized a selfless identity beyond themselves. Sorokin also named Buddha, Saint Paul (3–67 CE) and Saint Ignatius Loyola (1491–1556), founder of the Jesuits.

The third intermediary type lacks self-group integration in early life and does not develop mature transcendence consciousness. However, when

---

[17] Sorokin, P. A. (1954). *The Ways and Power of Love: Types, Factors, and Techniques of Moral Transformation.* United States: Beacon Press. p. 147.

presented with the chance, this type can seamlessly join groups and transform life with altruism at its core. According to Sorokin, Gandhi and Mother Teresa belonged to this type.[18]

Heuristic Altruistic Practices

In addition to the types mentioned above, I shall include type 4 heuristic and type 5 introspective.

The three types proposed by Sorokin all exhibit a strong self-awareness. Such sages as Saint Ignatius Loyola, Gandhi, Apostle Paul, Mother Teresa, and Tzu Chi founder Master Cheng Yen, all demonstrate an extremely high level of self-awareness. In contrast, ordinary people lack this level of self-awareness, thus, requiring external guidance and environment for inspiration. I call this type 4 heuristic altruism.

Take Tzu Chi as an example, Master Cheng Yen teaches the wealthy to help the poor, guiding them to learn from the suffering they witness. In seeing suffering, they come to realize their own blessings, cherish what they have, and further reach out to help others in need. Many entrepreneurs do not initially set out to do charity, just agreeing to take part out of politeness. But after engaging in relief work, they discover their own compassion within, transforming their life focus from self-interest to altruism.

Michael Pan (潘明水), a Tzu Chi volunteer and successful Taiwanese entrepreneur in South Africa, was not initially interested in doing charity work. It was only through the persistent invitation of his neighbor, a Tzu Chi volunteer, that he agreed to help drive a car and take part in a relief distribution. After participating in the distribution, he found that volunteer work actually brought him much joy, and the work was very meaningful. He then noticed during many of the charity distributions that men in South Africa had no work and women had nothing to do. So, with scrap fabric donations from Taiwanese-owned factories, he established sewing classes in rural communities.

Pan recycled old sewing machines from his friends' textile factory and sent them to Zulu villages to teach women sewing. Through this program, many Zulu women have been able to sell their products and earn a living. After the success of the first class, the second and third

[18] Sorokin, P. A. (1954). *The Ways and Power of Love: Types, Factors, and Techniques of Moral Transformation*. United States: Beacon Press. p. 148.

followed. The machines were only lent, not given, so they could be moved to another village if not continually used. Therefore, the women worked hard and were taught over and over until they excelled at the craft.

Although the process was laborious, the compassion of these Zulu women in South Africa was inspired by Michael Pan. They sold their clothing in the market and earned some money, yet instead of spending it all, they took 5% of their earnings to open another sewing class in the next village. After more than 10 years, Durban now has more than 600 sewing classes with 25,000 Zulu women participating. Around 7,000 of them have joined Tzu Chi as volunteers. During holidays, dressed in Tzu Chi's blue and white uniform, they visit and care for poor and sick families, along with offering assistance to the elderly living alone

In South Africa, around 22% of the adult population lives with HIV/ AIDS. Tzu Chi's Zulu volunteers from Durban visit them regularly, providing care both mentally and physically. This is how the Zulu volunteers though poor themselves have come to realize their own riches, giving them the opportunity to help others. This embodies the spirit of "helping others before liberating oneself" found in the *Sutra of Infinite Meanings*.

Helping the suffering inspired Michael Pan and transformed the impoverished South African volunteers, shifting their focus from self-interest to altruism; an example of heuristic altruism.

Today, Pan Ming-shui and Zulu volunteers in South Africa have expanded their charitable efforts across ten Southern African nations, empowering local communities and inspiring more non-affluent individuals to engage in relief work and shift from self-interest to altruism.

Introspective Transformation into Altruism

The fifth type of transformation into altruism is "introspective."

Many successful entrepreneurs and professionals feel emptiness and meaninglessness in mid-life and turn to philosophy or art for spiritual strength. They find that the world is ultimately immaterial and that things like desire, consumption, money, reputation, and power are all ultimately meaningless. The essence of life, they discover, lies in the integration of self into a greater, collective life, thereby granting them the premise of altruism. People then realize the insignificance of their own selves and recognize the existence of realities beyond them like Tao, Heaven, the

Buddha-mind, God, Truth, or the collective unconscious. This recognition leads them away from focusing on self-interests and toward altruism, symbolized by drops of water returning to the sea, understanding that the essence of altruism is the recognition of the world as one.

Introspective people are mentally ready yet remain in their emotions. As they practice and sense the completeness of self and others, they view all with more love.

The best way for this person to become more altruistic is to join groups. These could be religious, spiritual, philosophical, philanthropic, educational, or artistic. Groups are better than cultivating one's character alone, as they can transform it more effectively, by guiding them from being externally to internally focused, and from self-interest to altruism. Furthermore, C. G. Jung's "Collective Unconscious" also strengthens individuals in the group.

Why are young people so passionate at rock concerts, and why do collective religious or political ceremonies so deeply imprint beliefs in individuals? This is because they are able to access collective unconsciousness, good or bad. Therefore, when someone experiences a positive collective unconscious, its power to alter their personality for the better is far greater than that of individual reflection.

Richard M. T. Chen (陳明澤) is the Chairman of Chang Ho Fiber Corporation. In the past, he dreamed of rewarding himself for his hard work with gourmet food and exotic cars.

Chen owned seven luxury cars. He rose before dawn to take advantage of the empty highway and enjoyed high-speed rides, pushing his cars to their limit of 240 kilometers per hour (149 mph), relishing the engine's smooth sound.

However, in 2011, at Justin Wei's (魏良旭) invitation, Richard Chen and his wife Ethel Lee (李瑞璧) took part in Tzu Chi's *Compassionate Samadhi Water Repentance* sutra adaptation performance. In order to participate, one had to adhere to a vegetarian diet for 100 days, learn the sutras, and rehearse with the group. All of this focused on abandoning the self: rehearsing with other people, abstaining from eating meat, understanding the scriptures, and embracing the sincere piety of the team.

Tzu Chi volunteer Justin Wei recalled the difficulty of getting Chen to attend the event. He made over 20 calls before Chen said yes. Chen admitted that at first, they were just going through the motions.

However, once he immersed himself in the performance, things started to click for Chen. As he delved deeper into the meaning of the scriptures and adopted the vegetarian diet, he gained a deeper understanding and introspection of life.

The solemn music, scriptures, and sincere piety of the participants profoundly affected Chen. He heard the wails of animals on screen while interpreting the scriptures and was reminded not to consume meat. He played the part of a shark whose fin was to be removed in the performance, feeling the pain of the fin being cut off over 100 times during rehearsals. Shark fin soup had been his favorite delicacy, but through the performance he came to deeply feel the pain of the shark.

After the sutra performance, he decided to live life as a vegetarian. Chen remarked: "As a gourmet, vegetarian fare is a real test for me. It's quite hard to quell my craving for delicious food, yet I have been able to do so." His wife was astounded at the transformation in him.

Furthermore, he decided to donate six of his beloved cars to charity. All the cars being luxury imports from Europe and the US, he gave them all away. His wife said, "This decision is a good start. To give up the cars is to give up the trouble!".

Now, as a Tzu Chi volunteer, Richard Chen is constantly involved in charity and relief work around the world, truly embodying a life of altruism. He not only promotes Master Cheng Yen's *Jing Si Aphorisms* to every employee, giving them spiritual strength, but also promotes vegetarianism, humanistic care, and environmental protection to his factories around the world.

Chen's transformation was not due to introspection, but was instead guided by outside forces and blended into a collective sense of goodness and mindfulness.

His first encounter with Tzu Chi wasn't through disaster relief, but an interpretation of scriptures. Venerable Wu Da's (811–883 CE) *Water Repentance Sutra*, adapted from the China Tang Dynasty, was turned into a sutra adaptation performance. Through the healing music, Chen conveyed the scripture's meaning through body and mind, and found harmony in a collective consciousness within the team. This connection transformed his attitude toward food and cars, and shifted his motive from self-interest to altruism.

Synchronized dances, congregational ceremonies, chanting of classics, group prayers, and choral music can all induce spiritual transformations through collective unconsciousness.

Carl Jung's *Collective Unconscious* can transform a person, as individual unconsciousness is connected to it; however, it can be dangerous as it may overwhelm an individual. Thus, studying the classics, such as rational training and practice, are key to mastering the positive use of collective unconsciousness.

SECTION 4: THE CONSTRUCTION OF AN ALTRUISTIC SYSTEM

In addition to personal efforts, how can we establish a structural mechanism for transitioning people from self-interest to altruism?

I believe enterprises should promote charity to motivate employees to participate, and nurture and stimulate their altruistic mindset. Patagonia, for example, allows its employees to take two months of paid leave annually so they can volunteer for environmental protection projects. Altruism is not a concept, it's a mentality that must be instilled through practice. From my two decades of involvement in charity, I'm confident volunteering is the ideal way to cultivate such an outlook.

Enterprises can set up long-term charitable activities to bestow both owners and employees with love, compassion, and thankfulness. Gratitude can also foster harmony between business owners and employees. Doing charitable work can lead to mutual equality, esteem, and affection between business owners and employees.

The cultivation of altruism at the governmental level doesn't enforce economic altruism, but instead rewards it. Hospitals in Taiwan are not for-profit, yet the hospital housing tax still applies. However, if the charity expenditure of a hospital surpasses a certain ratio, the government will waive the tax. It will also reward businesses that invest in charity by providing them with certain tax exemptions. Donating to non-profit organizations is exempt from taxation, though using them for taxation evasion does not encourage altruistic entrepreneurship or economic altruism. Therefore, the government should reward companies for engaging in specific charitable activities, permit a certain degree of tax-exemption, and encourage them to participate in charity rather than financially supporting it with donations.

Charity is a creator and catalyst of a corporate culture of goodness. Enterprises engaged in public welfare foster core values that prioritize the public good and economic activity. Practicing changes the way one thinks and feels, thus shaping one's character.

Furthermore, tax breaks should be granted to self-employed individuals or professionals based on the time they dedicate to establishing charitable organizations, in order to encourage citizens to engage in public welfare and philanthropy.

Aristotle said that true happiness lies not in amassing wealth, but in participating in public affairs, leading a moral life, and cultivating loving relationships. Precisely, charity and public welfare meet these criteria.

Investing in charity and public welfare allows business owners to consider their corporate culture and core values, encouraging employees to love others and strengthen their collective unity. Externally, enterprises can help decrease the wealth disparity or promote artistic, cultural, social, leisure, and spiritual values, which are essential for social prosperity.

CHAPTER 10

Goodness in Use: The Means of the Economy of Goodness

Under the laws of cause and effect, evil cannot bring about genuinely good outcomes. There is no such thing as necessary evil, only necessary good. This chapter examines goodness as the route to secure good economic returns.

EOG emphasizes the use of good methods; however, from an ethical and practical standpoint, good methods can be met with dilemmas, such as the relativity of values, the notion of maximizing benefits at the expense of a few, and the balance between individual and collective good—which this chapter hones in on.

Section 1: The Method of Goodness, Its Value and Significance to Human Beings

We tend to think that we often have to take measures we consider "necessary evil" to achieve something. But the Economy of Goodness sticks to necessary "good." It follows approaches of goodness, and adheres to processes of goodness.

If the method is not virtuous, our minds will not be good-natured and honest, and the reason for righteousness will disappear. An evil mind draws the cause of wickedness—this is what Buddhism refers to as the law of karma.

R.-S. Her, *The Economy of Goodness*, https://doi.org/10.1007/978-981-97-6363-4_10

Is there a situation wherein my mood is good yet needs to be done using some evil way to get good results? Every war is fought with this in mind, and the war for peace can often result in a greater loss of life.

However, can we face Hitler with goodness? Should Winston Churchill negotiate with him, as Chamberlain suggested, instead of refusing to cave until Hitler fell? Churchill believed peace was impossible with a tyrant. Would a war against slavery be a necessary evil?

Buddhism has a discussion that if a Bodhisattva has to kill one person to save 500 people, should the Bodhisattva do it? Venerable Yin Shun (1906–2005), a major figure in modern Buddhist philosophy, replied that a Bodhisattva has no desire to kill but that sacrificing one to save many is permissible. According to Ven. Master Yin Shun, from the perspective of the precept against killing, sacrificing one life to save many is permissible, yet it hinges on the bodhisattva's intentions. If the bodhisattva acts with a compassionate heart to save the majority of sentient beings and eliminates one wicked being, it is considered blameless.[1]

However, if we subtracted this, could we justify killing ten to save a thousand, a thousand to save ten thousand, or ten thousand to save a million? This has become an unresolvable moral conundrum.

In Tzu Chi Hospital, some doctors had to experiment on animals for research, so they asked for guidance from Master Cheng Yen, the spiritual mentor of Tzu Chi and chairman of Tzu Chi Medical Foundation. In response to the query, Venerable Cheng Yen declared, "This karmic burden will be on me." This signified that although killing animals wasn't good and would incur karmic repercussions, Venerable Cheng Yen was prepared to take them on.

The karma of killing cannot be escaped, particularly when it is done deliberately. Those who don't kill or act in self-defense may have their reasons for justifying their actions. War, oppression, or racial strife often begin with seemingly valid causes. People often use immoral means to pursue the greater good.

Fundamentally, Hitler couldn't have formed the Nazis on his own. Countless Germans who believed in racial superiority led a war in the name of creating a just society, believing killing was a necessary evil. It was this same belief that enabled people like Hitler to take power and enact

---

[1] Shi, Yin Shun (2003). *She dacheng lun jiang ji* [Commentary on the Compendium of the Great Vehicle]. Taiwan: Zhengwen Publishing House. p. 409.

war and religious persecution. Many Germans then mistakenly thought that they were doing good by fighting evil through evil.

But why could we not use good methods to expand goodness?

Expand Necessary Goodness

If everyone rejected permitting evil through a necessary evil, evil could be prevented and Hitler would not have had a chance. Hence, there would be no need for Churchill to eliminate Nazism through war, a necessary evil.

Thus, we must not accept evil; instead, when we observe it, we should contemplate good and work to extend it promptly. By growing goodness, evil will eventually diminish.

Not just destruction or killing, but the evil of lust. Greed for wealth and the fulfillment of desires. Running businesses cheaply and believing that, even after amassing money and helping others, some karma has already been set in motion.

We gain power through immoral and unlawful acts thinking only when we have power can we act and only when we are influential can we help others. Thus, we climb to the summit, but our spirits are tarnished in the process.

The power to bring light to others does not originate from darkness. It is impossible for one's darkness to give illumination to society.

Confucius said of politics, "Is he not a man of complete virtue, who feels no discomposure though men may take no note of him?"[2] People of virtue aim not at becoming high-ranking officials or acquiring wealth, but at refining their character to make their lives complete. Confucius also said, "When good government prevails in his state, he is to be found in office. When bad government prevails, he can roll his principles up, and keep them in his breast."[3] This serves as a warning for people of virtue to not to be ensnared in a den of iniquity. Yet, we may ask, who in this case will restore the world's order from chaos?

In fact, every person who incites turmoil believes that they are establishing order. Different individuals advocate for various political,

[2] Legge, J. (1971). *Confucian Analects: The Great Learning, and The Doctrine of the Mean.* New York: Dover Publications. p. 137.

[3] Legge, J. (1971). *Confucian Analects: The Great Learning, and The Doctrine of the Mean.* New York: Dover Publications. p. 296.

economic, and social orders, leading to numerous conflicts. While differing opinions are harmless in themselves, however, regardless driven by power-driven self-interest or by selfless and just ideals, employing attack and destruction as means results in inevitable conflicts and chaos.

If there is no way for a nation, people of virtue will retreat; Confucius suggests avoiding further chaos. Not creating chaos can prevent the world from becoming chaotic. Although Confucius' outlook may appear passive, it can actually help lessen social unrest.

Seeing more thoroughly, Lao Tzu said that everyone knows that beauty is beautiful because of the existence of ugliness and everyone knows that good is good because evil exists.[4] It is not good to distinguish good from evil and then fight against evil.

Buddhism teaches us that good and bad are indeterminate, transcending both good and evil and cultivating compassion for everybody while abiding by moral laws. To think that good and evil are relative and can be acted upon impudently would be a mistake.

Expanding Good Is Not Fighting the Evil

Fighting evil for a long time will drive goodness away.

In history, most dynastic founders have claimed that they are fighting for justice and an ideal society when they rally people to overthrow existing evil forces. Once people join them enthusiastically, the existing evil force is quickly eliminated. However, under the banner of justice, a new oppressive class and evil force emerges.

In 1910, Lenin guided the Bolsheviks in launching the Russian Revolution, with the goal of overthrowing Tsarism's corruption and brutality. Lenin's brother was put to death by the Tsar for being part of the revolution. Upon the Tsar's ouster, the formerly loyal navy concluded that the Bolshevik government had not fulfilled the revolution's original intention, after which they rebelled against it only to be brutally suppressed by Trotsky (1879–1940 CE), the Bolsheviks' second leader.

However, Trotsky was purged by Stalin, after Lenin's death, and exiled to Mexico, and then assassinated by secret agents sent by Stalin during World War II. Trotsky wrote *The Revolution Betrayed*, accusing Stalin's

---

[4] Tzu, L. (Eds.). (2021). *Tao Te Ching* (J. Legge, Trans.). Standard Ebooks. Retrieved from https://standardebooks.org/ebooks/laozi/tao-te-ching/james-legge.

communist party of abandoning Lenin's ideals.[5] Trotsky accused Stalin of exactly what the navy, which he had wiped out, had been accused of. Those who obtain justice through force will eventually be engulfed by force. We tend to think that means are only processes and good results require evil means, yet in the end, we realize that means not only determine results, but become results themselves.

Fighting evil will keep one away from good, so what attitude should we take toward it?

The foremost issue should be how to define evil. Good and evil are often relative, without any objectivity to differentiate them.

Lao Tzu's idea that everyone knows that good is good because evil exists[6] has two meanings. One is the relativity of good and evil, and the other is that true goodness is the return to the natural state of mind, where everyone is good and forgets that there is good or evil. This is the ultimate level of social excellence.

People produce good and evil or distinguish between them because they leave the whole Tao. Therefore, Lao Tzu stated that when the Tao was lost, its virtues appeared; when its virtues were lost, benevolence appeared; when benevolence was lost, righteousness appeared; and when righteousness was lost, the proprieties appeared.[7] If everyone understood the Tao, the world would be a harmonious unity. Then, altruism and self-interest would have no difference, and supreme goodness would be attained.

However, the distinction between good and evil still exists, so how to rid evil and embrace good is an issue that must be tackled.

What is evil? When you say that another person is evil, that person is perhaps saying the same of you. Evil is relative, not absolute. Evil is often a minority, but the suppression of the majority of good by a minority of evil is especially intolerable. That is why evil is evil.

However, ironically, when most are evil, they are often seen as good. Evil typically denotes confrontation, destruction, addiction, darkness, and a negative power.

[5] Trotsky, L. (1991). *The Revolution Betrayed: What Is the Soviet Union and Where Is It Going?* United States: Labor Publications. (Original work published in 1936).

[6] Tzu, L. (Eds.). (2021). *Tao Te Ching* (J. Legge, Trans.). Standard Ebooks. Retrieved from https://standardebooks.org/ebooks/laozi/tao-te-ching/james-legge.

[7] Tzu, L. (Eds.). (2021). *Tao Te Ching* (J. Legge, Trans.). Standard Ebooks. Retrieved from https://standardebooks.org/ebooks/laozi/tao-te-ching/james-legge.

To eradicate the relativity between good and evil, good must rise above confrontation, attack, and destruction.

Learning not to fight evil is the key to attaining good, and wisdom is needed to expand goodness.

Many may not agree with this view, thinking, "Are we just going to let evil be?" In fact, not engaging evil doesn't mean allowing it to exist forever, but rather, bolstering goodness to challenge the foundation of evil.

Gandhi utilized non-violence to demonstrate the injustice of the British rule that oppressed Indians with violence.

If violence is met with violence, the world will be in perpetual conflict.

Goodness means fulfillment, love, tolerance, giving, light, and positive power, so one must fend off negative energy.

Expanding goodness and love is an effective way to eradicate evil.

Master Cheng Yen stated: "When our heart is filled with seeds of goodness, evil has no place to grow." As long as you are still fighting against your own evil thoughts, this very act of fighting is a negative force that will eventually lead to the growth of evil.

The sacred state in religions is often depicted with halos. The Buddha's halo radiates infinite purity. God's manifestation is also illuminated with faultless light. Light and dark are relative yet distinct. If light is present, darkness is absent; yet light does not dispel darkness, merely illuminating it.

Good does not fight against evil; it simply reveals and expands its own power. This is the message that Master Cheng Yen has strived to impart to the world throughout her life.

Therefore, in the face of evil, we must act quickly to spread goodness. Even a tiny glimmer of light can dispel the darkness. No matter how small our goodness is, it will overpower wickedness.

Section 2: The Means and Results of Goodness

Only good means can bring good results.

We have discussed the motivation of goodness and the concern of using evil unintentionally earlier. Yet, without wisdom, even the right motivation and means can bring no good result.

The means of goodness requires not only subjective integrity but also wisdom in practice, regardless of any social, economic, political, or cultural undertakings. Lao Tzu explained this in detail.

Lao Tzu also said, "The excellence of a residence is in (the suitability of) the place; that of the mind is in abysmal stillness; that of associations is in their being with the virtuous; that of words is in their trustworthiness; that of government is in its securing good order; that of (the conduct of) affairs is in its ability; and that of (the initiation of) any movement is in its timeliness."[8]

These attributes or abilities refer to wisdom when choosing suitable measures to implement.

Being good means having wisdom, being good at choosing a place to live with benevolence and righteousness. As Confucius said, "If a man, in selecting a residence, does not fix on one where such prevail, how can he be wise?"[9] Living in a place with benevolence and righteousness, and being surrounded by benevolent people, is called wisdom and goodness.

Goodness in terms of governance, capability, and the timing of action is key to success in politics, one's career, and business ventures. They necessitate the ability to seize the moment. This kind of wisdom is what constitutes goodness.

The means of goodness are important; they require not only morality but wisdom. The result of goodness is determined by these means.

The motivation of goodness will not generate the required evil. Western political science stresses not evaluating political personalities by their motivations.

The virtue of means in Western culture is considered as checks and balances. Western culture believes that it is difficult to judge the goodness of motives, so it relies on the virtue of checks and balances, and auditing methods to prevent human wrongdoing.

Is the outcome of these checks and balances beneficial?

Checks and balances produce endless conflicts, both politically and in other arenas. Although these can help fix biases, but without emphasis on motivation, they prioritize interests, both economically and politically. This causes strife in politics and competition and exploitation in commerce. To promote goodness, motivation and method must be emphasized.

---

[8] Tzu, L. (Eds.). (2021). *Tao Te Ching* (J. Legge, Trans.). Standard Ebooks. Retrieved from https://standardebooks.org/ebooks/laozi/tao-te-ching/james-legge.

[9] Legge, J. (1971). *Confucian Analects: The Great Learning, and The Doctrine of the Mean*. New York: Dover Publications. p. 165.

Pure compassion can be seen as a motivating force and a means of good, requiring wisdom.

What Are the Paths to Goodness?

No striking, destroying, suppressing, doubting, blindly checking, or balancing are the basic conditions for the Means of Goodness.

The means of goodness is to help others succeed, support, trust, and respect them.

To support the needs of others substantially is goodness; it requires both means and wisdom.

The Chinese value harmonious inclusivity. Alibaba's success serves as an example. Dragon is a symbol of all nationalities coming together in ancient China. The dragon totem is an emblem of tribal integration. Fish scales grew when the snake tribe amalgamated. It developed the ability to soar after joining forces with the bird tribe. Finally, it grew antlers due to its partnership with the moose tribe. Thus, China is a symbol of clans coming together and living in unity.

Alibaba at its triumph, had combined large, medium, and small enterprises horizontally, and upstream, middle, and downstream enterprises vertically, once forming the world's largest shopping platform. Finance has enabled Alipay to be created. Constraining forces have been converted into cooperation and assistance, creating an inclusive, all-sharing, and mutual prosperity.

In the Internet era, commodities have become more individualized to facilitate shared prosperity. This is an approach of benevolence which advocates cooperation, rather than competition, as a means of achieving a sound economy.

Therefore, how to best highlight goodness? Through confrontation or cooperation? Conflict or peace?

On the porch of the entrance to the New York Museum of History hangs a famous quote by President Theodore Roosevelt, who served in the US presidency from 1901 to 1909 and was the uncle of President Franklin Delano Roosevelt, victor of WWII.

The quote is: "We wish peace, but we wish the peace of justice, the peace of righteousness. We wish it because we think it is right and not because we are afraid." In other words, we prioritize righteousness over peace if brought to make a choice.

Western thinking tends to prioritize justice; war may be waged to punish the wicked if necessary.

Professor Jye-siung Fang is a Christian and an important elder in the eastern region of the Presbyterian Church in Taiwan. However, he served as former president of Tzu Chi University. One day, President Fang told me that Christians always spoke of justice while Buddhists always spoke of peace.

It is hard to reach peace while seeking justice, as many human conflicts don't come from a downfall of fairness but too many interpretations of it. Each party often declares itself blameless. Russia claimed that annexing Crimea was just since most Crimeans opted to be Russian. Meanwhile, the US saw this as unjust, as Russia had invaded before carrying out a referendum that contradicted Ukraine's constitution. Thus, with both claiming justice, mutual animosity was sparked.

Conflict may lead to social chaos and economic recession, or even worse, a nation divided by war, like Syria is today. Former US President George W. Bush famously stated when attacking Afghanistan in 2001: "Whether we bring our enemies to justice, or bring justice to our enemies, justice will be done."[10]

The slogan of justice is only a facade for the strong to exploit. As Tolstoy remarked, justice throughout history has been like a snow shovel in front of a locomotive; clearing the way for the powerful to resort to force.

True justice should safeguard human dignity and life, not take them away. When an executioner claimed justice with a human head, justice was being suffocated.

Today, many conflicts among humanity are caused in the name of justice, leading to strife.

Buddhism believes attachment to one view of justice is wrong; acting out of it is sinful, and thinking oneself just is a delusion.

Those obsessions, prejudices, stereotypes, and delusional views are the source of disaster for humankind. They stem partly from desire and partly from bias. How can we rectify them and foster proper mindfulness? The Buddha's teaching emphasizes the removal of greed as the starting point.

How can we apply a greed-free mindset to a political leader with the power to ignite conflict? Their greater power can incite a stronger

---

[10] The White House. (2001, September 20). *President Declares "Freedom at War with Fear"* [Press release]. https://georgewbush-whitehouse.archives.gov/news/releases/2001/09/20010920-8.html.

desire within them, resulting in deeper levels of self-importance and self-justification. Those who oppose them may be seen as unjust, leading to an urge to eradicate them. The Buddha warned of greed, resentment, and ignorance, therefore the first step in spiritual practice is to eliminate greed.

SECTION 3: GOODNESS IN TRADE

Adam Smith argued that, contrary to what was thought in the Middle Ages, pursuing personal interests through trade distinguished humans from animals, as the market could self-adjust production and keep prices at a natural level.

Natural price refers to the lowest profitable selling price, with costs deducted. This is beneficial to both consumers and producers, creating the largest market, which is an inevitable result of the law of supply and demand.

The market price refers to the price at which goods are sold. In the context of supply and demand, when the market price is much lower than the natural price, producers will turn to other products for more profits, as Adam Smith said. With a higher market price than the natural price, manufacturers will manufacture more of a given product. An increase in the product's market output will lead to a drop in price, to the benefit of target consumers. Consequently, a free supply-and-demand market naturally balances the price and quantity of products. Self-interest is the key factor here.

What Adam Smith did not observe is that conversion of production is not easy; it requires new capital, hence producers will not switch production immediately, but reduce prices. Or producers with more capital may deliberately lower prices in self-interest, eliminating competitors and leading to the emergence of a monopoly.

A natural monopoly exists where, in the absence of intervention, the largest capital holder will always be the largest. Those with abundant capital can use prices lower than market prices to force competitors out of the market. This market dominance allows them to raise prices, resulting in consumers having to purchase goods for much higher prices than usual.

American newspapers have formed an industrial landscape of one region-one newspaper since 1950, which communication economists call a Natural Monopoly. In 1950, there were 99 independent newspapers competing in 38 regional markets, but by 1980 that number had decreased to 66 and, by 1987, only 15 metropolitan newspapers remained. This Natural Monopoly demonstrates that if operators have sufficient funds, a large enterprise can offer low prices and attract top journalists with high salaries in order to increase its market share and push out smaller, less capitalized competitors.

The free market, driven by self-interest, has seen large-scale enterprises monopolizing since the late eighteenth and early nineteenth centuries. This was why Marx strongly criticized capitalist systems that concentrate power among the few, drive wages down, and raise prices. Entrepreneurs saw large profits, but workers couldn't afford the goods they manufactured. Consequently, the majority of people could not buy commodities, resulting in capitalists no longer making a profit and henceforth the masses rallied against them, fulfilling Marx's prophecy of Capitalism's collapse.

Adam Smith might argue that when workers cannot afford the goods they make, capitalists will reduce prices. For instance, Henry Ford permitted workers to work for five days so that they could afford the products they produced. It is an inescapable rule for free markets to pursue self-interest, which means that only when capitalists start to benefit the public can they thrive. Otherwise, capitalists will get nothing.

The free market's longevity is not due to self-interest as Adam Smith believed, but to altruism driving the invisible hand, which determines social supply and demand.

Self-interest ultimately leads to the domination of enterprises, which is disadvantageous to workers who can't afford products, resulting in the disintegration of both enterprises and society.

Adam Smith believed that people have a rational capacity to pursue their interests. However, these interests are driven by desires, not rationality, and hence, cannot result in the maximum public interest that he anticipated.

It is due to altruism that reason is empowered. Altruism is also an emotional force. Altruism signifies compassion, not craving.

Only altruism based on rationality and compassion can justify market transactions.

When a product's price is too high, an altruistic producer will reduce it so consumers can purchase it and producers can still profit. Altruism can provide producers with more rewards than self-interest.

In a market, producers caring more for consumer needs will yield beneficial products. Consumers do not always know what they need, so producers must use their imagination to create products that had not previously been thought of, as Steve Jobs did with the iPhone. The key is to think for customers: Jobs himself said that from MacBooks to smartphones, he was focused on the product and people's needs, not money.

If Adam Smith were still alive, he might say that Jobs sought to fulfill his ambitions and interests in designing this pioneering product. Jobs must have had the drive to fulfill his goals. What we propose is that everyone has their aspirations, but if they don't consider the requirements of others, they won't realize their potential.

It is by benefiting others that one can realize the self.

The self is not erased, but instead recognized through beneficence toward others in the altruistic Economy of Goodness.

Self-interest stems solely from altruism; this applies to individual accomplishment and national wealth alike. Through altruism, a nation is able to increase its power in a beneficial way. Economies based on altruism will not foster exploitative groups, meaning countries can remain balanced and affluent.

Section 4: Financial Goodness

In economic activities, besides commodity transactions, financial transactions are paramount.

Finance is a purely monetary transaction. Earning money through money trading has been viewed as immoral since ancient Greece. Aristotle thought that if one's wealth derived from money, not from producing goods, it contradicted natural commercial forms.

The medieval Christian Church opposed interest on loans, while as early as the *Old Testament*, Moses objected to Hebrews charging interest to their own people. Jews would not charge interest among each other, but would carry out usury on foreigners—Deuteronomy (23:19) stating that "Thou that shall not lend usury to thy brother; usury of money, usury of victuals, usury of anything that is lent upon usury."[11] Jews in Europe and Germany at the end of the nineteenth century had an infamous reputation for their usury endeavors.

---

[11] Bible. (2017). *The Holy Bible: Chinese Union Version* (Deuteronomy 23:19). In Old Testament (p. 245).

Christianity expands brotherhood to all peoples in the world, therefore the Church firmly opposes usury, deeming the making of money from money evil. From the twelfth to eighteenth centuries, Popes issued several decrees prohibiting usury. Despite Capitalism flourishing in the eighteenth century, loans were still used as a source of capital for urgent money needs in the market. Because the Church was unable to restrain the capital market, Capitalism swept away the social order of Europe for over ten centuries.

Even in the eighteenth century, the Islamic world banned interest on financial transactions, as seen in the Ottoman Empire. Although there were still loans available, those were only used for daily purchases, while loans for business and investment were forbidden. When Western Capitalism began to expand its overseas territories in the seventeenth and eighteenth centuries, the Islamic empire remained focused on narrowing the wealth gap and curbing capital expansion. Islamic countries didn't decline economically during the eighteenth century, but they were relatively behind Western Capitalism in terms of growth. Nevertheless, the economic thought of brotherhood and aid for the poor kept the empire's ruling foundation strong.

The Buddha appeared to be unopposed to interest, but opposed speculation and capitalizing on people's misfortune to garner interest.

The Financial market was pivotal in promoting early Capitalism. Loans and investments were made in the fifteenth and sixteenth centuries to fund seafaring expeditions in search of spices, fabrics, gold, and more. Capitalists emerged with unrestricted financial trade. Capital accumulation spawned the urban class, which set up chambers of commerce to restrain nobles and kings and leverage commercial prowess to obtain political influence and eventually install a parliamentary democracy.

The financial system is a boon for entrepreneurs with expertise but without capital. Ancient sages often revealed usury and interest as blatant expressions of greed. They viewed gaining vast wealth without engaging in production as a sin. Today's banks secure profits by leveraging money, and the system aids with people's needs, both economic and otherwise.

People deposit their money in banks to earn interest, then banks lend it to industries and collect interest to pay depositors and turn a profit. This is commonplace in the current financial market. Similarly, in the stock market, investors with additional capital can earn extra money for their family's benefit. Business owners gather funds to create businesses and owe responsibility to their investors. This is a helpful financial cycle.

The evil of financial transactions is speculation and usury done improperly, especially taking advantage of others. Speculating in stocks instead of investing based on business operations is wrong.

On the other hand, easy access to bank loans allows the wealthy to become steadily wealthier. Utilizing their assets as security, they use bank money—the money of ordinary depositors—to accrue more wealth, expanding the disparity between rich and poor and destabilizing the middle class. Certain real estate developers exploit bank loans to acquire land and afterward take out mortgages to build houses for inflated profits. The predicament isn't just caused by house builders, but also by banks that lend to those with assets.

Economists say that banks are like pawnshops. Without assets, there would be no loans.

Muhammad Yunus, in Bangladesh, has created financial justice and benefits through micro-loans; lending money to those who need it, rather than those with assets, embodying the goodness of financial transactions.

In 1976, Yunus established Grameen Bank. Grameen means rural, village-like. It has since lent over $6 billion to over 6 million poor Bangladeshis.

To ensure repayment of loans, Grameen Bank has adopted a system of group guarantees. Members of the group provide a joint guarantee, supporting one another in achieving financial stability. Facts have proven that 98% of women repaid their debts. Using micro-loans to purchase the necessary materials for their businesses, they managed to pay off their debts within a year.

The bank founded by Yunus, Grameen Bank, is revolutionary compared to traditional banks. It lacks telephones, computers and lavish furnishings. Yunus' employees go out to rural villages to meet with poor borrowers, and they don't need contracts as most borrowers are illiterate.

Although their clients are all impoverished with no assets, Grameen Bank experiences no losses, but instead produces a surplus. Grameen sets a fixed interest rate for borrowers, normally 20% each year, which is lower than the 15% cumulative interest of other business loans in Bangladesh. The surplus has enabled Grameen Bank to have funds to lend to more people.

So far, over 80 million people have received benefits from Yunus' Grameen Bank's micro-loans.

More than 96% of Grameen loans are lent to women with a low social status in Bangladesh. Despite their poverty, they pay more than men in the family and provide family needs through handicrafts or small businesses. Yunus hopes that one day poverty will only be seen in museums by our children and grandchildren.

Yunus' model has been rolled out in over 50 countries, such as the US, Philippines, India, and Nepal, resulting in major improvements in the lives of impoverished borrowers.

Ironically, a Mexican bank whose investments were in micro-finance and that was listed in 2007, worth more than a billion US dollars, turned out to be a vampire taking huge profits off of poor people.

Without altruism, any good financial or economic model could be detrimental.

Altruism Made Micro-Banks Successful

Yunus' bank demonstrates that lenders should be judged on their capacity and ingenuity, not just assets. As a result, financial dealings could be beneficial exchanges of goodness.

Likewise, stock investment should be based on the operation of the enterprise, rather than speculation or hyped publicity.

Warren Buffett specialized in investing in companies that performed well but were undervalued by the market. He would carefully study an enterprise before investing. This is a financial transaction of goodness.

Warren Buffett refuses to invest in companies with personnel issues, like those that plan to lay off staff, those subject to labor-capital disputes, or whose shareholders fight among themselves. He instead puts his capital into well-managed enterprises. Warren Buffett is a prime example of good finance.

Since the start of the twenty-first century, the concept of public welfare combined with profit has arisen. Enterprises are motivating managers to invest in charity while fulfilling social obligations; not just to gain funds without care and then compensate by addressing social accountability, but to contemplate ways of linking the stock market with public benefit and corporate profits from the outset, giving balanced attention to fairness and earnings. This is called Impact Investing, something financial pundits have been pushing for recently.

Ping An Insurance (Group) Company of China, Ltd. has crafted a compassionate, innovative model for poverty alleviation.

Ping An, a global Fortune 29 enterprise and No. 1 in the insurance industry, has transitioned from traditional "Blood Transfusion Charity" to "Innovative Hematopoiesis Charity" for poverty relief, focusing on wisdom-guided assistance. It has implemented "Industrial Hematopoiesis, Health Protection, Education and Public Welfare" programs, with the launch of major projects, "Village Officials, Village Doctors and Village Education" in early 2018, to mark its 30th anniversary.

From Poverty Alleviation to Local Economic Incubator

Ping An has initiated the Hematopoiesis Poverty Alleviation program, which is becoming increasingly mature. Of the 832 poor counties in the country, over 700 have abundant water resources. Through cooperation with 6 hydropower projects, in the Yangtze River and Pearl River areas with a capital investment of 2.8 billion yuan, more than 100,000 documented poor households have benefited. Infrastructure, energy supply, and empowerment have been established,[12] and hydropower construction provides energy for local secondary and tertiary industries. This enables villagers to have access to funds and sale channels for agricultural products, and to gain a steady stream of dividends and sales income through constant upgrading of production techniques, thereby fully realizing their role as engines of rural development.

Zhaoheng Hydropower Co., Ltd. has over 100 small hydropower stations in China. Ping An provides Zhaoheng with loans at favorable rates, allowing the company to use the funds to build hydropower stations in rural areas and compensate relocated households. The average loan interest rate is higher than 7%, yet Ping An only charges about 2 or 3 per thousand. The gap in interest rates is then transformed into shares for poor households in the hydro power plant, ensuring a subsidy of over 4,000 yuan each year for at least 15 years.[13]

China's poor farmers have lifted themselves out of poverty by earning more than 4,000 yuan a year. Yao Pinggui, ex-VP of Ping An and current chairman of Ping An Trust, beamed proudly when describing the

---

[12] Sohu. (2019, June 14). *Ping'an yinhang shuidian fupin moshi, lianheguo dianming biaoyang!* [The United Nations Named and Praised Ping An Bank Hydropower Poverty Alleviation Model!]. Retrieved from https://www.sohu.com/a/320684329_100049995.

[13] Generally speaking, a monthly income higher than the local minimum wage level is considered outside of poverty. According to the China Central Poverty Alleviation and Development Work Conference and the requirements of the goal of comprehensively building a well-off society by 2020 in China, the per capita net income of farmers should reach 2,300 yuan.

story: Initially, over 100 websites reported the news and the UN organized forums highlighting this model. Furthermore, the UN published an annual book compiled with this case.

Intelligent Poverty Alleviation Through Production and Marketing

Notably, poverty alleviation projects need not be mortgaged or guaranteed; they are run by local industries utilizing advanced technology to help poor peasants in production and marketing. In the past, poverty alleviation was done by merely giving money to farmers, which did not solve the problem fundamentally. Ignorance was a main cause of poverty and so inspiring wisdom has become of utmost importance in poverty alleviation, according to Yao Pinggui.

Giving chicken raising as an example, the loan is not offered to farmers, but to the feed factory. Daily feed rations for each chicken is calculated and the money remitted to the factory to provide it accordingly.

In addition, Ping An will install electricity, water and intelligent cameras in chicken houses to track water and electricity consumption levels. The chickens' growth data will be uploaded to a Silicon Valley company for multi-dimensional analysis. This analysis will enable details, such as how many steps the chickens have taken, which chickens are ill and what medicine is needed, to be processed at specific intervals. Accordingly, suitable improvement measures will be proposed. Big data enables fine monitoring and control of chicken growth and pricing.

The sales pipeline is integrally contained in the full-service offering. Poor cultivators are selling chickens to the processing plant, which deducts feed costs and then reimburses the surplus to the feed factory. The whole production and marketing cycle is a sealed process. Farmers don't need to disburse any of their own funds, yet they can still gain steady profits in the end. Every chicken yields a profit of around 2 or 3 Chinese yuan, so 10,000 chickens bring an income of 20,000 or 30,000 Chinese yuan.[14]

---

[14] The content of Yao Pinggui's talk about Ping An's poverty alleviation came from the author's personal interview with him on August 2, 2019.

A Harmonious Symbiosis of Commercial Revenue, Poverty Alleviation, and Public Welfare

From multiple reports, we know that Ping An has used a combined production and marketing model with the use of the Internet, big data, and AI in many poverty alleviation cases. An example is Yinshan Oats in Ulanqab, Mongolia Province, China, which benefited from 30 million interest-free loans and was obligated to support the raw material growth of 1,087 poor households, and guaranteed their purchases, resulting in a 3,700 yuan per capita income improvement for those households.

Impact Investing for Public Welfare and Good Enterprises

The benefit of finance is the benefit of an investment. A good investment should be based on the enterprise's performance as the investment yardstick, not speculation and exaggeration.

We usually think public welfare serves public interest, not personal interest, so it's deemed "good"; whereas business is for individual benefit, so it is usually labeled "non-good." But this distinction is unnecessary. Both public welfare and enterprise can be good. It all depends on how business and public welfare organizations create positive social values.

The past decade of "impact investment" proposed by Western society aims to profitably tackle social issues. This investment departs from the usual distinction between business and public welfare, meaningfully inserting the business landscape into public concern. In doing so, it yields profit while tackling social problems.

Impact Investing, first proposed by the Rockefeller Foundation in 2008, blends public welfare and business purposes to solve social problems while rewarding shareholders.

The profit here means investors make profits and the business achieves sustainable development to solve social issues.

In 2013, the British Prime Minister highlighted the significance of impact investing at the G8 Summit; a joining of public welfare organizations and firms to tackle large-scale regional or international matters, including climate changes, inexpensive housing, renewable energy, healthcare for elderly people, and banking services for the poor.

Impact investing combines public welfare and commerce, along with government and private sectors. According to the OECD (Organization for Economic Co-operation and Development), the economic scope of impact investing is predicted to reach 40 trillion euros in the next 50 years.[15]

Traditionally, governments and NGOs tackle social difficulties. Enterprises or banks rarely engage in welfare endeavors. However, commercial capital is far larger than public welfare capital and impact investing can mobilize commercial capital to tackle important social issues and generate profit.

Principles of Responsible Investment (PRI) has been adopted by many charitable organizations and funds in recent years to tackle social issues. The Rockefeller family in the US, the Bertelsmann Foundation in Germany and the Bill & Melinda Gates Foundation have all achieved great successes through PRI, including preventing and treating infectious diseases, facilitating remote education, and providing clean energy sources for a sustainable environment.

Business is more innovative than government or NGO, and more flexible and effective in meeting market needs. Bill Gates' PRI has surpassed US$1.6 billion since 2009.

Such a mix of business and public welfare illustrates humanity is stepping toward an epoch of Good Enterprises and the Economy of Goodness since the creation of Social Enterprises in 1999.

This does not imply that enterprises utilize welfare for self-promotion or that NGOs generate income via commercial methods, deviating from their initial purpose. Social Enterprises are not defined as NGOs or public philanthropic organizations legally, but they can help tackle social issues together with the government and NGOs while generating profits. For instance, an agency could deliver care services to the elderly and make commercial gains at the same time.

Social enterprises and impact investing are financially supported by business revenue and donations from NGOs, such as PRI and online crowdfunding, that used to be considered the specialty of NGOs.

Indeed, investors, public organizations such as the Bill & Melinda Gates Foundation, and crowdfunding donors, will eventually assess the extent to which an organization has solved social issues. It is akin to shareholders of listed companies evaluating business operations, but the focus is on how much the organization has contributed to society.

---

[15] Wilson, K. E., Silva, F., & Ricardson, D. (2015). *Social Impact Investment: Building the Evidence Base*. The Organization for Economic Cooperation and Development. p. 23.

Impact Investing in China

Mr. Ma Weihua, a leading proponent of China's impact investing, is the former president of China Merchants Bank. Ma is one of the most innovative bankers in the country and, under his leadership, created many firsts for the bank. China Merchants Bank was the first international bank in China and its transition was due to Mr. Ma's work—he revitalized it from a small bank with substantial financial risks in a decade, to achieving first-class status. Ma's vision is to benefit the public and disadvantaged enterprises, helping them reach levels similar to those of giants such as Huawei, Tencent, and Alibaba.

Under Ma Weihua, China Merchants Bank was the first bank in China to move from wholesale to retail. Initially, with just 200 billion yuan in capital, Ma Weihua steered it to become an international bank with 3 trillion yuan.

When state-level banks including Bank of China, Construction Bank and Agricultural Bank were offering wholesale and lending services to big state-owned and state-backed organizations, Ma Weihua focused on credit to small-capital entrepreneurs. He told me that Merchants Bank would lend to them, like Tencent, Alibaba and Huawei, as long as their business objectives and plans were clear. Emphasizing on emerging industries and young entrepreneurs was what made China Merchants Bank successful.

As we may recall when Henry Ford pledged to make owning a car accessible to all, and eventually became the auto leader in the US and the globe. Jobs endeavored to make computers that had been restricted to large research centers available to individuals. Aiming to help more people is the key to success.

Ma Weihua, born in June 1949 in Jinzhou, Liaoning Province, China, graduated from high school before staying in the countryside for four years in the educated youth going to and working in the countryside campaign. Afterward, he was accepted into the Jinzhou Railway Bureau after the entrance exam. In 1978, he was admitted to Jilin University's Department of Economics and, upon graduation, was assigned to the Liaoning Province's Planning Commission where he was rapidly promoted to deputy director and deputy secretary-general.

In 1988, Ma Weihua was transferred to the Central Bank's Deputy Director of the General Office and Deputy Director of the Planning and Capital Department in Beijing.

During his tenure at the Central Bank, Ma Weihua took part in China's macroeconomic operations and observed numerous crucial transformations in China's banking sector.

At that time, China had no concept of a commercial bank; instead, economic reform focused on enterprises, with banks offering merely supportive services. But when the 1984 reforms began to pay off, a financial system to support the new form of economy was required and so four specialized banks were created: the Industrial & Commercial Bank of China, Agricultural Bank of China, Bank of China, and China Construction Bank. After 1986, commercial banks started to emerge, with the State Council approving the reopening of the Bank of Communications, and the setting up of the Shenzhen Development Bank, Everbright Bank, and more. Subsequently, commercial banks developed across cities.

The Shutdown of Hainan Development Bank

At the end of 1992, Ma Weihua was transferred to the Hainan Branch of the Central Bank and made Director of the State Administration of Foreign Exchange until he left in 1999. In this term, he shifted from supervision to operation, and presided over China's first successful bank closure. He also earned his Ph.D. in economics from Southwest University of Finance and Economics.

In 1995, to tackle the real estate crisis in Hainan and ensure the stability of the financial system, the Hainan provincial government founded the Hainan Development Bank, which absorbed five trust and investment companies, some of which had varying levels of debt problems. Nevertheless, the Hainan Development Bank managed to clear the bad debts, thus stimulating the banking industry.

At the end of 1997, Hainan Province had many credit cooperatives with insufficient assets to repay their debts. As a result, 28 of these credit cooperatives were merged into Hainan Development Bank. However, due to the large scale of debt, a bank run could not be prevented. On June 21, 1998, Hainan Development Bank had to be shut down. With the support of the Central Bank, Ma Weihua oversaw the bank's closure.[16]

---

[16] Lin, H. (2014). *Jinrong jigou tuichu yu jinrong xiaofeizhe baozhang—hainan fazhan yinhang daobi fengbo jian xi* [The Exit of Financial Institutions and Financial Consumer Protection—A Brief Analysis of the Collapse of Hainan Development Bank.]. Zhongguo shangmao, 2014 Issue 4.

Ma's Dealing with Two Major Crises upon Entering China Merchants Bank

On March 17, 1999, Ma Weihua was appointed by the Board of Directors of China Merchants Bank as President and Chief Executive Officer. On taking up the role, he was immediately confronted by two major crises. Firstly, due to the Asian financial turmoil, the rate of non-performing loans had risen, resulting in the China Central Bank suspending offshore banking services. With China Merchants Bank's offshore business standing at US$1.5 billion, the possibility of a run on the bank should the news be made public was imminent. To avert this, Ma Weihua asked the Central Bank not to release official documents and wrote the contents down by hand and committed to make improvements, thereby raising foreign exchange reserves. After six months, the crisis was resolved.

The second crisis occurred on the day Ma Weihua was appointed President of China Merchants Bank. A large bank run took place at their Shenyang Branch. Ma informed the staff that an early withdrawal would result in a loss of interest. He explained that customers could take out whatever sum they desired. Encouraging the staff to be friendly, Ma advised that cash should be piled up visibly to provide assurance to the customers. Gradually, the assurance that the bank wouldn't fail began to ease their doubt, so the crisis was resolved.

Development of Internet Banking and Electronic Commerce

The development of Internet Banking and Electronic Commerce has enabled customers to do business and banking operations from anywhere at any time.

Upon establishing Merchants Bank, resources were insufficient, but the Board of Directors decided that money for computerization and employee training could not be spared. This prompted Merchants Bank to construct a computer center instead of an office building.

Merchants Bank became the first bank in China to provide interconnected, nationwide service, with unified distribution, planning, equipment, and management. Other banks had been computerized prior, but couldn't unify service nationally. Despite its small scale, Merchants Bank achieved better standardization, and launched the first all-in-one card in China, allowing a customer to have multiple accounts under one name.

In today's view, an all-in-one card is commonplace. Most banks offer it. Nevertheless, at that time, it was a huge innovation to have all personal accounts on one card, Ma Weihua said.

Merchants Bank pioneered the provision of comprehensive online financial services for businesses and individuals in China. To drive forward this novel venture, Ma Weihua targeted college students, who are more likely to quickly embrace change.

The first stop of Merchants Bank's new business venture was Peking University. After the speech, a student from Peking University made history by purchasing a bouquet of roses for his girlfriend online, marking the first online banking transaction for China Merchants Bank.

In 1999, there was also the "72-Hour Internet Survival Experiment," in which contestants were confined to small rooms and could only communicate with the outside world through the Internet. One participant successfully completed the challenge by purchasing food with a China Merchants Bank debit card. This event caused a significant stir in China, especially since the Internet was not yet widely available, resulting in a significant increase in e-commerce. Ma Weihua's promotion of internet information technology within the most traditional and stable industries enabled people to access financial services from the comfort of their own homes, strengthening China Merchants Bank's position as a leading bank in the Internet age.[17]

Strengthening the Bank's System and Accumulating Funds

Now an industry leader in its home market, Ma Weihua sought to drive internationalization through a public offering, increasing reserve funds and bolstering the bank's strength.

In 2002, CMB made public a 1.5 billion A-share offering in China, raising 10.769 billion yuan and establishing three records: the most extensive total equity of a listed bank, the highest total capital raised and

---

[17] China Youth Daily. (2010, September 7). *Zhaoshang yinhang: weiyou kuihua xiang ri qing* [China Merchants Bank: Only sunflowers lean towards the sun]. Retrieved from https://zqb.cyol.com/content/2010-09/07/content_3407711.htm.

circulated in the nation then, and the first Chinese entity listed to implement international accounting standards. Additionally, CMB made bad
debt allowances and bolstered its reserves, reinforcing its structure.[18]

In 2003, CMB released a dual-currency credit card with the international standard to the Chinese market. In under a year, it issued over one
million cards, setting a new industry record.[19]

In 2004, CMB issued 6.5 billion yuan of convertible bonds to the
public, and it was a success. Transactions 164 times the amount of issued
bonds, made it a record-breaking event in China's stock market.

In 2006, CMB issued 2.42 billion shares on the Hong Kong Stock
Exchange, raising HK$20.337 billion. International investors were highly
enthusiastic, with public offerings and international placements both
oversubscribed by 266 and 51 times respectively.

The following fundraising was greatly acknowledged by the capital
market, which reinvigorated CMB in its successful internationalization.[20]

Taking Hong Kong as a Pilot to Move Toward Internationalization

With financial globalization accelerating, China's banks have been moving
toward internationalization. In 2002, CMB took the lead by establishing
the first Hong Kong branch among China's joint-stock banks.

On September 30, 2008, Ma Weihua acquired Wing Lung Bank, which
had a 75-year history and was ranked fourth among Hong Kong's banks.
This acquisition enabled CMB to become more international.

Ma Weihua's expectation of CMB's internationalization can be seen
from his reply to United Commercial Bank in Los Angeles. The latter
had approached Ma Weihua before its bankruptcy, hoping CMB could
purchase its shares. Yet Ma Weihua conveyed to them that their destina-
tion was Wall Street, not Chinatown.

[18] China Youth Daily. (2010, September 7). *Zhaoshang yinhang: weiyou kuihua xiang ri qing* [China Merchants Bank: Only sunflowers lean towards the sun]. Retrieved from https://zqb.cyol.com/content/2010-09/07/content_3407711.htm.

[19] Shen, M. (2010). "Yinhang xintu" Ma WeiHua ["The Bank Believer" Ma WeiHua]. In *Licai* [Financial Management]. China: Hai yan chubanshe. pp. 120–127.

[20] China Youth Daily. (2010, September 7). *Zhaoshang yinhang: weiyou kuihua xiang ri qing* [China Merchants Bank: Only sunflowers lean towards the sun]. Retrieved from https://zqb.cyol.com/content/2010-09/07/content_3407711.htm.

On October 8, 2008, Ma Weihua's wish came true as CMB New York Branch opened—the first Chinese bank branch to be approved in the US since 1991 when The Foreign Bank Supervision Enhancement Act was put in place.[21]

The China Banking Regulatory Commission has assessed CMB as the top on the list for many years. Financial Times rated CMB as the world's largest bank, in terms of price-to-book ratio, and its brand value saw an increase. Additionally, Forbes listed CMB as number 24 of the world's most prestigious, 600 top companies. Moreover, The Wall Street Journal Asia also recognized it as one of China's most respected companies.

All these extraordinary achievements can be attributed to Ma Weihua's core idea of taking the masses' interest as the bank's operational strategy, and his sagacity of empathy and leadership.[22]

Capital to Goodness

Ma Weihua has dedicated recent years to impact investing, aiming to direct capital toward noble causes while ensuring business operations remain profitable. This approach enables companies to achieve sustainable growth while addressing various societal challenges. He has delivered speeches globally, urging entrepreneurs to prioritize societal issues and engage in impact investing. Over the past twenty years, technological advancements, financial innovations, and globalization have spurred rapid economic growth worldwide, resulting in a significant accumulation of wealth. Despite this, persistent challenges such as poverty, inadequate healthcare, and educational disparities persist, affecting billions globally. To address these issues, the United Nations established the Sustainable Development Goals (SDGs), aiming to comprehensively tackle societal, economic, and environmental issues. However, bridging the funding gap to achieve these goals remains a challenge. Ma Weihua emphasizes the

---

[21] China Youth Daily. (2010, September 7). *Zhaoshang yinhang: weiyou kuihua xiang ri qing* [China Merchants Bank: Only sunflowers lean towards the sun]. Retrieved from https://zqb.cyol.com/content/2010-09/07/content_3407711.htm.

[22] China Youth Daily. (2010, September 7). *Zhaoshang yinhang: weiyou kuihua xiang ri qing* [China Merchants Bank: Only sunflowers lean towards the sun]. Retrieved from https://zqb.cyol.com/content/2010-09/07/content_3407711.htm.

importance of considering societal impact alongside financial returns in all economic activities, promoting a concept known as impact investing.[23]

As the founder and chairman of the China Global Philanthropy Institute, Ma Weihua has dedicated almost five years to philanthropic education, nurturing numerous global-minded leaders in this field. With previous experience as the chairman of the One Foundation, he deeply understands philanthropy's role in advancing social welfare and addressing wealth disparities. However, he stresses that philanthropy alone cannot fully tackle societal issues. Instead, he advocates for promoting philanthropy and corporate social responsibility to mobilize corporate capital for addressing social problems, which is his vision for impact investing. He highlights a philanthropic organization that successfully transitioned into a social enterprise through impact investing.

In Zhejiang, there existed a nursing home that operated as a private non-enterprise for over a decade due to financial limitations, having only 500 beds. Subsequently, an impactful investment from a Shanghai-based enterprise facilitated its rapid expansion to ten thousand beds within three years, making it the largest medical and elderly care chain in Asia. This illustrates how issues related to disability and semi-disability can be addressed with affordable care solutions. The high return on investment was attributed to favorable government policies in the sector, lowering operational costs. Similarly, in Sichuan, another nursing home specialized in providing intelligent elderly care solutions for families. An investment from a fund company led to a fourfold increase in six months, addressing its need for funding and impact investment. With numerous societal issues that cannot be solved solely by government or charity, Ma Weihua echoes Peter Drucker's sentiment that "all social problems can only be fundamentally solved when they are turned into profitable business opportunities." Therefore, he believes that combining social enterprises with impact investing can provide solutions to many of the social problems we face.[24]

---

[23] Sohu. (2019, April 28). *Maweihua: Yingxiang li touzi shi yige biran de qushi* [Maweihua: Impact Investing is an Unstoppable Trend]. Retrieved from https://www.sohu.com/a/310848199_99947734.

[24] Sohu. (2019, April 28). *Maweihua: Yingxiang li touzi shi yige biran de qushi* [Maweihua: Impact Investing is an Unstoppable Trend]. Retrieved from https://www.sohu.com/a/310848199_99947734.

Ma Weihua hopes that his endeavors will help China become the most influential country in impact investing, directing its financial capital and businesses toward the Economy of Goodness.

SECTION 5: PRODUCTION OF GOODNESS

The Industrial Revolution led to large-scale, mechanized production replacing traditional manual production. Mechanized production could produce large quantities of the same quality, but it also mechanized workers. In the early nineteenth century, many of Charles Chaplin's films satirized people's alienation from mechanized production.

Division of labor is key to maximum productivity, but finer divisions reduce the sense of accomplishment for the workers. Chaplin's movie Modern Times showed a man with his hands mechanically rotating every day for eight hours and still going at it when he returned home. Though it is an exaggeration, it captures the reality of low pay and job insecurity experienced by those in mechanized production.

As Max said, the finer the division of labor, the more difficult it is for workers to transition to other job roles. Moreover, with the low-skill level of their work, they can be quickly replaced. If a worker has been doing the same job for years, it is due to an absence of other abilities. This makes it more advantageous for capitalists as replacement is effortless and they don't have to worry about employee welfare and wages.

This was the production mode at the onset of industrial civilization. Capitalists plundered the profits. Even in the midst of capitalism, when the service industry was booming and white-collar workers were afforded decent living standards, they still had to adhere to the division of labor—even in companies like IBM and Ford where employees were confined to their same job for life. Today, this is called a profession.

Professional division of labor was what Capitalism continued to follow in the middle and later stages, standardizing both manufacturing and the service industry. It also standardizes humans.

Confucius said, "The accomplished scholar is not a utensil."[25] What modern capitalism and industrial civilization have created is the objectification of people. Focusing solely on one task certainly creates many

[25] Legge, J. (1971). *Confucian Analects: The Great Learning, and The Doctrine of the Mean*. New York: Dover Publications. p. 150.

outstanding professionals, but it also imprisons people in a limited area, not allowing their full potential of talent and personality to be realized.

A Chinese Confucian scholar must have knowledge of rituals, music, archery, charioteering, written characters, and mathematics. In Chinese history, the imperial system of exams caused mathematics to be neglected. Now, however, modern Capitalism favors professional abilities above all else, leading to a tedious existence in which people seek only consumption for self-fulfillment. This has caused an unbalancing, wiping out the spirituality tapped into for joy. Ultimately, this is a systemic crisis.

The emerging network economy places greater importance on creativity, allowing employees greater flexibility and freedom. Companies like Google, Facebook, and Amazon have taken the lead by providing employees with features such as sneaker-friendly workplaces, open working spaces, sports fields, free coffee, and high-quality refreshments. However, pressure and competition are still strong challenges to be addressed. To meet these challenges, improved working conditions are a must.

Competition among businesses is commonplace, be it from outside sources or from within. It can even take the form of power struggles, which take a toll on people. This pressure will not dissipate simply because a particular project has been completed; projects go on until one is worn out and vanquished, at which point new creative minds are brought in. This can lead to individuals retiring early, but with generous remuneration.

Can we have another way of working? One which is not solely driven by competition and profit, but rather by love and compassion. Such compassion can help us truly identify needs and opportunities for innovative production. As Steve Jobs stated, "consumers do not know what they need until it is brought to them." The founding of Apple Inc. is a fantastic example of this. Before its existence, computers were giant machines, as big as a room. Then, personal computers revolutionized our intelligence and enabled us to gain access to greater potential. Such creations do not merely serve as competition or sources of wealth—they make far greater contributions to the masses.

Jobs said he believed they could transform the world with their enthusiasm, so Apple still holds this same core belief.

Creation arises from deep compassion and love for humans, driving production. The production system should be based on love and compassion.

When Jenn Weng Chu (朱振榮), founder of ViTrox, Malaysia's second-largest technology company, was at university, his mother worked in a restaurant. She saw a second-hand camera being used by one of the diners and thought her son would like one, so she bought it for him. Chu took pictures everywhere with this camera, a symbol of his mother's love and hard work supporting his education. During his junior year internship at HP, he discovered factories were using high-tech optical cameras to look for defects in products. This piqued his curiosity and he made it the focus of his graduation thesis. After he graduated, Chu entered HP where he had the chance to visit Silicon Valley. This spurred him on and a few years later, he and his colleagues established their own business producing instruments to detect chip surface defects using optical cameras.

Cameras are a love of his. In 2011, Chu stumbled across Tzu Chi Foundation, and attended a Jing Si Retreat for entrepreneurs in Hualien, Taiwan. There, he was impressed by how Tzu Chi's spirit of humanism motivated hundreds of thousands of volunteers to cover their own expenses to travel the world to help in times of disaster. The key to all this is love.

After returning to Malaysia, he began sharing with his partners on his wish to establish Tzu Chi's humanistic culture and compassion within the company. His wife drew up a model to introduce the Jing Si Café, providing books, tea, coffee, chats, and items made from recyclable eco-friendly materials. Employees could escape from their work whenever they wanted to contemplate and discuss plans in this space. Chu had in mind to construct a home-like setting for his staff, believing a company should feel like home and be filled with love.

Chu encourages his employees to volunteer for charity. During the Penang flood of 2017, his 300 engineers took turns to do disaster relief and at least 150 employees volunteered in the flooded area daily. Upon completing the said duties, they would return to the factory without requesting overtime pay. As Tzu Chi's culture was implemented, Chu's company saw its market value soar from 300 million to 3.3 billion US dollars by 2018. His Catholic partner claimed the key to success was rooted in Tzu Chi's culture.

Japan's large enterprises have a lifelong employment system that treats employees like family. Equally, Chu's enterprises view employees as family, while also training them to extend this level of care to the wider society.

Indonesia's second-largest entrepreneur, Franky Widjaja, has inspired his 2,000,000 employees and their families to become Tzu Chi members.

To date, more 10 thousand people at Sinar Mas Group have become certified Tzu Chi volunteers who look after the poor within three kilometers of the company's farm. Key to employee mobilization is instilling love.

Tzu Chi's volunteer entrepreneurs not only treat their employees as family, but also encourage them to love more people. Work powered by love is the most effective way of working.

There is no perfect system for production or service. Nor is there an unalterable efficient system. However, as long as love is embedded within the system, employees can strive for achievement according to their life values. Businesses with love encourage growth rather than exploit people or impede creativity. Love is essential to the efficient functioning of production and service, making people feel accepted and allowing them to be creative and support one another, rather than being repressed or competing for dominance.

Zhiyong Xi, head of China's largest elderly care institution, retired from his role as regional leader in Shanghai at a young age in order to pursue business. He'd often heard stories on his business trips of a friend's father being hospitalized or what happened to a friend's mother when they had accidents, leaving their children at work feeling helpless. So he was determined to build an elderly care center that could provide lifetime support for parents. Qinheyuan (Care and Harmony Houses) has since built high-quality centers in ten cities in China. The old people residing in the centers look vibrant. When asked how he made it happen, Xi's answer was simply: "love."

Creating a loving environment for the elderly is the key to business success. Each elderly person has two secretaries: a life secretary and an administrative secretary. There are various sports, leisure, and public welfare activities available, so the elderly can gain value and love here.

Xi drew inspiration from Tzu Chi's charity. Many of Tzu Chi's environmental volunteers are elderly, laboring under harsh conditions to recycle resources in their communities. The satisfaction found in this work unifies them—70 year olds, 80 year olds, and even 90 year olds work daily for the community and earth. Recycling stations offer daily meals and they ask nothing in return. By working in such places, the elderly finds value and love.

Home is where there is love.

Where there's love in production and service, people gain a sense of belonging and accomplishment; when value is seen, suppression, exploitation, and alienation are ousted.

The Economy of Goodness that Cherishes Material Life

Maximizing production is the essence of Capitalism. It seems an iron law of economic development that new products are continuously produced for profit and to maximize the market. Yet, individuals don't need so many products; how many pairs of shoes can one person wear? Nonetheless, shoe-making companies create new products and attempt to encourage people to keep buying. Smartphone brands produce new models each year to increase purchasing. Computers are now also having shorter battery lives, meaning people don't use them for long before replacing them with newer models.

What is the significance and logic behind this manufacturing? Is it for the benefit of consumers or to promote economic development? Or is the business simply trying to maximize profits?

Compared to pre-twentieth-century humans, our generation has consumed far more products. Do these products bring human happiness?

Production is essential for human life and joy, but excessive production and consumption could deplete the Earth and hinder human bliss. Instead, excessive consumption materializes people, going against the quest for happiness.

Maximum production and consumption can lead to standardization and the division of labor, which reduces workers to tools in mechanical systems, destroying respect for human nature and creativity. This was true in the early and middle stages of the industrial revolution; however, in the late stage, demand for humane working conditions increased. Nowadays, Internet giants like Amazon, Facebook, and Google offer their employees a great deal of freedom to create.

In the era of the manufacturing system, it followed control and dominance. In contrast, in the era of knowledge economy, the norm shall be empowerment and innovation. However, the pressure on working individuals persists. Enterprises seek creative products with market potential in a highly competitive environment, making personal happiness more of a challenge.

Both business owners and employees are caught up in this endless and tremendous work pressure. Many business executives in China and the West either indulge in entertainment or suffer from physical and mental diseases.

People stay busy creating but forget how to live. Producing goodness must depend on improving the whole human community. Chasing after profiteering is a Capitalist prejudice based on isolated individualism.

Buddhism perceives the world as interconnected; nothing can exist separately. This is what the Buddha referred to as Interdependent Arising. The mass production of items causes havoc to the earth's resources.

All production and manufacturing should take into account their impact on human health and other living things.

We should cherish every manufactured commodity as a unique part of life.

Buddhism states that all material has a life, and all things and beings possess the Buddha nature.

Excessive manufacturing and rapid discarding will harm the environment and are a waste of resources.

A cornerstone for spiritual joy and strength, people seek fine material products; a beautiful cottage, landscaped gardens, ornate yet simple decor, intricately woven carpets, and elegant wooden furniture offer comfort and inspire creativity.

Switzerland has a beautiful, clean environment that promotes healthy, creative, and happy living.

Happiness and freedom are inseparable from matter; the physical environment affects our attitude toward it. If we consider matter only as a tool, it will not bring true positive results for the human mind.

French sociologist Pierre Bourdieu echoed this view. He said that when we came into contact with something, whether material or social, we would acquire a certain temperament.[26]

Pierre Bourdieu believed that a link between mind and matter exists, but matter only has a beneficial effect on our minds when it has value.

A product can be beneficial as long as its manufacturing takes sustainable development into consideration.

In manufacturing, the Economy of Goodness considers:

First, what is the genuine worth of commodities to consumers?

Second, what is the impact of commodities on sustainable development of the Earth?

Third, what is the value of commodities in a circular economy?

---

[26] Fromm, E. (1995). *Ai de yishu* [The Art of Loving] (M. Xiang, Trans.). Taipei: Zhiwen chuban she. p. 25.

Are these three points indicative of a product's ability to be recycled and reused after being discarded? This not only extends the life of the product but also safeguards environmental resources, thus allowing enterprises to save costs.

Commodities have not only transactional value, but also those of use, life, and social well-being. Hence, commodity production should factor in market requirements and maximize benefits, while exploring the possibility of enhancing social joy.

Commodity manufacturing should factor in the life span of the commodity and conserving earth's resources for the long term.

We can assert that producing real goods depends on treating commodities like life, nurturing them in the same way we nurture our children.

We will not allow children to injure other lives and will not view this life as a way to generate wealth, nor will we discard them like trash in a landfill and damage the Earth, our source of all life.

Thus, cherishing material life should be the essence of commodity production.

In the Hollywood movie, a robot boy spoke and appeared like a human. Significantly, he had emotions, acted endearingly, and desired to be hugged. Ultimately, his foster parents got a real son, making the robot boy battle for approval and endure heartache from his "mom's" rejection. In the end, the parents chose to let go of the robot.

The movie "Artificial Intelligence: AI" was directed by Steven Spielberg. The sentimental little robot boy was sent to the robot dump, where we saw how miserable a world of material life forgotten by humankind was. From time to time, there would be large machines and tools to hunt down the robots that had not been destroyed. Robots were either missing arms or legs or had their faces mangled. They did not know the future or where they were from.

Spielberg demonstrates that matters can be alive or emotionally meaningful. Life is esteemed, not only by living creatures, but material life too, which is essential for successful Capitalism today.

All creatures and all things are equal, and should be embraced in the human realm. Thus, we should love and respect them all equally.

SECTION 6: THE CONSUMPTION OF GOODNESS

The greatest revelation of Capitalism to modern people is that we don't need Heaven—Heaven is here and now, as long as we have wealth.

There is nothing wrong with this. Buddhist scriptures, such as the *Lotus Sutra*, that constantly refer to gold as the rope and colored glaze as flooring. The Buddhist state shown by the Buddha could indeed be built in the Saha world (Means Secular World) free from material contamination. However, in a Capitalist society, people fill their minds with materials in the absence of faith. However, matter only satisfies temporary desires, and people will become more and more spiritually empty.

As faith is cast aside, modern people are misled to think that material possessions bring happiness. However, it is not possible to be happy without possessions, and having them is not enough for genuine happiness. Only spiritual fulfillment will bring true joy.

Erich Fromm thought that contemporary people define themselves by what they have.[27] When the value of life is lost, people try to fill the void with material possessions. This is the greatest exploitation of the human soul by capitalism—pushing people toward alienation through endless consumption.

Lao Tzu said:

> Color's five hues from the eyes their sight will take;
> Music's five notes the ears as deaf can make;
> The flavors five deprive the mouth of taste;
> The chariot course, and the wild hunting waste
> Make mad the mind.[28]

Desire only leads to more confusion and is difficult to control. If consumption is driven solely by desire, it is endless and can never be satisfied.

Henry Ford enabled workers to labor five days a week, thereby allowing them to purchase the goods they manufactured. This sparked a period of mass production and mass consumption within the economy. Several economists believe this consumption stimulates a cycle of economic prosperity. This idea is shared in many economic theories.

Undeniably, it is beneficial to engage in business and stimulate an economy. Still, it is uncertain whether perpetual consumption can boost

[27] Fromm, E. (1995). *Ai de yishu* [The Art of Loving] (M. Xiang, Trans.). Taipei: Zhiwen chuban she. p. 25.

[28] Tzu, L. (Eds.). (2021). *Tao Te Ching* (J. Legge, Trans.). Standard Ebooks. Retrieved from https://standardebooks.org/ebooks/laozi/tao-te-ching/james-legge.

the economy. In fact, overindulgence in consumption has slowly forced people into a materialistic lifestyle. As E. F. Schumacher, the pioneer of contemporary Buddhist economics said, the Capitalist economy pursues the maximization of production and consumption,[29] while a Buddhist economy focuses on moderate production and consumption. In Capitalism, material possessions equate to human worth, and considerable consumption is often a sign of one's social status. As such, human values are traded off for material gains.

True happiness does not lie in material satisfaction, but in spiritual joy. To attain such joy, lead a moral life, be devoted to others, and form loving relationships. People may become wealthy yet isolated from loved ones. They experience anxiety due to crippling workloads and interpersonal stress. When facing stress, people often attempt to fill it with consumption.

The fundamental principle of Buddhism is for humans to be free from the bondage of desire, so Buddhism talks about "samadhi"; samadhi is the freedom from being bound by desire. To be the master of oneself, one must be able to resist the urging of internal desires and external temptations, and be constantly in a state of tranquility. Although Confucianism advocates cultivating people's desires and meeting their needs, it requires moderation. Only by controlling desires can one achieve true happiness and joy.

Consumption in Cognition of Material Life

Buddhism offers an alternate perspective on consumption, as opposed to the aimless consumerism of today.

In her early years, Master Cheng Yen would cherish the paper she used. She would first write with a pencil, then two ballpoint pens, first blue and then red. When the front side was full, she would turn it over and continue writing on the back—a way of cherishing material life, not mere frugality.

To cherish material life, we should not buy new items until the old ones are unusable. At Tzu Chi's recycling stations, I saw many intact discarded clothes and items; if we value the life of material goods, we shouldn't so readily let go of our old stuff and purchase new ones.

[29] Schumacher, E. F. (2011). *Small Is Beautiful: A Study of Economics as If People Mattered*. United Kingdom: Random House.

All things contain life. Buddhism professes that all things and beings possess Buddha-nature. Every object symbolizes life. Respect for material life can greatly improve our existence and soul. Volunteers working in recycling centers have seen so much waste. In contemplating their own way of living, they become aware that they, too, have been profligate and wasteful. Thus, in reducing their consumption and living a simple life, they discover the spiritual joy of frugal living.

Consumption that Cares for One's Mind

Reducing consumption goes beyond just cherishing material possessions; it's also about rediscovering one's intrinsic value and autonomy. According to the teachings of Xunzi, humans shouldn't be enslaved by material desires. When desires are kept in check, they won't be endlessly chasing material wealth, and material wealth won't succumb to excessive desires.[30] As materialistic desires diminish, inner spiritual resilience grows stronger. Consumption, unless fulfilling essential life needs, risks diminishing our self-awareness and inner purity.

In the pursuit of high consumption and wealth, one's inner pressure rises. Trust and love are scarcely found in business. With a lack of love, material items are used to meet desires, creating a vicious cycle of endless consumption and money-making in today's capitalist society.

We need not spend so much time chasing money. Many professionals in high-tech industries work day and night, compromising their health. A healthy life is one where a suitable job provides enough time for family, art, public welfare, spiritual beliefs and communing with nature—all of which are beneficial to the mind.

Only by balancing material and mental needs, life and work, and emotional and intellectual cultivation can we attain true happiness.

Seeking outwardly leaves the heart lacking, and a life of emptiness can never find satisfaction. Unfulfilled desires often result in numerous conflicts. According to Xunzi's teachings, humans are born with desires, and when these desires are unmet, they continue seeking without restraint, leading to disputes and chaos. The wise of ancient times

---

[30] Wang, X. Q. (1994). *Xunzi ji jie* [Collected Annotations of Xunzi]. Shandong: Shandong Friendship Publishing House. p. 318.

abhorred chaos and thus established rituals and ethics to establish boundaries.[31]

Less desire, fewer conflicts. Schumacher's research showed that those living in isolated communities and being more self-reliant were less likely to have wars or revolutions than those who depended on others for resources in large urban areas.

All sentient beings could coexist peacefully, leading lives of joy and tranquility if not for their relentless pursuit of more. This insatiable quest often leads to inner turmoil and the accumulation of negative actions. Consequently, the adage "the more one seeks, the more one loses" holds true. Excessive desires not only bring social conflicts, but on an individual level, many products are fundamentally harmful to our bodies and souls.[32]

Consumption in the Economy of Goodness should cause no physical or spiritual harm. People are living longer, but at greater cost for medical bills. Unhealthy foods full of chemicals and artificial ingredients have resulted in various types of cancers and heart problems in modern society.

The premise of consumption should be health. We buy too much that is not only useless but also damaging. Many of the clothes we purchase are made of chemical fibers with negative health effects. Many cleaning items in our buildings can harm our respiratory systems. Cars we buy can lead to air pollution and put public health at risk.

The Netherlands encourages cycling, serving the travel requirements of most Dutch citizens. Together with their mass transit network, they have far fewer cars than America, where multiple vehicles per family are not uncommon. Now, China's cities are experiencing an increase in cars, causing the government to implement buying limits. Still, it has led to more car purchases, worsening air pollution.

The premise of consumption should be to love oneself, avoid harms, and opt for products beneficial to our minds. Take computers, for instance: over 50 years, they've gone from giant machines only professionals knew how to use, to PCs for all, and now smartphones, smaller computers. This gradual democratization of the product shows the Economy of Goodness.

---

[31] Wang, X. Q. (1994). *Xunzi ji jie* [Collected Annotations of Xunzi]. Shandong: Shandong Friendship Publishing House. p. 593.

[32] Shih, Cheng Yen. (Eds.). (1989). *Jing si yu* [Jing Si Aphorisms]. Taipei: Chiu Ko Publishing Co., Ltd.

For consumers, over-use of electronic items such as smartphones and computers can harm both their bodies and minds. Children hooked on video games are a considerable source of worry for many parents. Should children be forbidden from using smartphones, or should phones be less capable or lacking gaming features?

Naturally, we must use computers or mobile phones. Yet, when people keep buying newer versions with improved functions, human cognition may suffer.

Consumption, not being beneficial for the human mind, cannot be a method for the Economy of Goodness.

Master Cheng Yen once conversed with a group of high-tech leaders from computer, phone, and silicon wafer manufacturers in Taiwan. She hopes that they will utilize technology only for good, and prevent technology from being used for harm or the dissemination of harmful content.

Bewildered, the business leaders didn't know how to respond. They had always believed technology to be neutral, not differentiating between good and evil.

Internet technology can help accumulate knowledge and propagate truth, but it can also be utilized by terrorists to teach their adherents how to make bombs or for other nefarious intentions.

Can science and technology be used for good? In other words, if science and technology are not used for good, mankind will be destroyed by them.

Stephen Hawking warned that artificial intelligence (AI) could be humanity's greatest yet most perilous creation. Could humans be dominated by AI? If technology disregards morality, then the AI-ruled scenarios often seen in movies could become a reality.

Consumption for the Protection of Lives

If customers reject dangerous goods, manufacturers won't make them. Conversely, if people buy items which are beneficial for their health, mental well-being, and the environment, such as environmentally friendly clothing, they'll gain from it and promote businesses which are doing good.

Patagonia Outdoor Clothing & Gear promotes the use of organic cotton to make non-toxic clothes. Now, manufacturers are also cultivating customers' sense of purpose in environmental protection while selling their products. If consumption can awaken people's conscience and morality, it can be considered a form of ethical consumption.

Japan's MUJI introduced organic, non-chemical products ranging from clothing to items for everyday use, reducing damage to the Earth. By providing quality and safe products, they can encourage customers to be environmentally conscious. Only consumption that is beneficial to people's physical and mental health can be seen as a role model of the EOG.

Each cup of organic coffee in a customer's hands helps coffee growers, as organic coffee beans are hard to grow. To preserve the environment, however, coffee farmers stay true to their convictions. Moreover, consuming organic coffee is akin to guarding the planet from the use of chemical fertilizers and the extermination of many insects. This consumption safeguards lives and provides goodness.

I once visited Song Yan Resort an organic farm in Malaysia. Jessie Lee (李權英), the co-founder of Song Yan told us that her belief is to let all those who come to Song Yan for vacation better understand the importance of protecting nature. Here, visitors can work with the soil and be surrounded by forests on 16 acres of land. Song Yan only offers vegetarian food because vegetarian food can better protect the environment and the earth.

A carnivore's diet emits twenty times the carbon of a vegetarian one. Humans slaughter tens of billions of chickens annually; transport them, as well as opening up forests for husbandry, all contribute to environmental detriment. The founder holds that practicing environmental education in leisure is essential.

DA.AI Technology Inc. in Taiwan makes blankets from PET bottles recycled by Tzu Chi volunteers. These blankets are distributed for disaster relief around the world. Through developing thousands of products, they promote the significance of environmental preservation to customers.

These are all good enterprises. Consumers who support them are consuming goodness and protecting lives.

CHAPTER 11

Goodness as Reality: The Result of Economy of Goodness

SECTION 1: ACHIEVING EQUAL WEALTH THROUGH LOVE

Classical Utilitarianism seeks to maximize the interests of all in society and hopes that economic activities generate well-being and happiness for all. This must be based on maximizing materials and equal distribution.

The Exquisite Happiness of the Majority

In 1776, Jeremy Bentham proposed in *A Fragment on Government* that the best interests of the majority should be pursued.[1] Critics argue that moral life rather than happiness or interests should be the chief principle, and that the definition of happiness and benefit is difficult to pin down: when we prioritize a large population's benefit, we run the risk of neglecting the minority's. Nonetheless, Bentham's utilitarianism remains the favored orthodoxy of governments.

This principle necessitates exact calculation, however, outcome theorists view this as overly stressing the quantification of benefit maximization and disregarding the fact that human joy can't be quantified.

---

[1] Bentham, J., Burns, J. H., & Hart, H. L. A. (1988). *Bentham: A Fragment on Government*. United Kingdom: Cambridge University Press.

For example, we would not know for sure which yields the most happiness: providing more subsidies to the elderly living alone or having volunteers visit them regularly.

Figures cannot quantify the needs of the human mind or make accurate moral judgments.

For example, is it necessary to sacrifice eight people in order to save Private Ryan, as portrayed in the movie *Saving Private Ryan*? It is at least unacceptable from the standpoint of the principle of maximum benefit. Humanitarian concerns must take precedence over the principle of maximum benefit with regard to quantity or happiness.

What does equal wealth signify as a consequence of the EOG?

Equal Wealth Should Be Both Material and Spiritual

Equal wealth in the EOG refers to material abundance and a mentally purified state. Wealth should stem not from greed, but from the rational acquisition and use of resources. Material enrichment and moral living should go hand in hand.

Equal Wealth emphasizes both material and spiritual prosperity.

Utilitarianism is prone to gauging maximum happiness through material means. However, in ancient China, equal prosperity was both spiritual and material. The concept of equitable wealth, as outlined in *Luxuriant Dew of the Spring and Autumn Annals*, advocates for ensuring that the rich have sufficient means to demonstrate their nobility without descending into arrogance, while the poor have enough resources to maintain their livelihoods without succumbing to despair. By using this principle as a measure to balance wealth distribution, ensuring that wealth is abundant, and fostering peace between social classes, governance becomes more manageable.[2]

In other words, *Luxuriant Dew of the Spring and Autumn Annals* and utilitarianism both hope that everyone is rich. However, the former advocates no equally distributed wealth for everyone, but that all live and work in peace and contentment and have their place. There is still a wealth difference between rich and poor, but the rich are not arrogant and even help the poor, so that they are free of worries about livelihood. That is

---

[2] Dong, Z. (Eds.). (2012). *Xin yi chunqiu fan lu (xia)* [Luxuriant Dew of the Spring and Autumn Annals (vol. 2)] (Z. Y. Jia & W. Z. Chang, Trans.). Taipei: San min shu ju. p. 626.

what equal wealth means in *Luxuriant Dew of the Spring and Autumn Annals*.

Mencius believed that people's talent and wealth varied and to force universal equality would bring chaos. Equal wealth in ancient China was to ensure a basic standard of living for all and the well-field system reflected Confucius' thought. Confucius said:

> I have heard that rulers of States and chiefs of families are not troubled lest their people should be few, but are troubled lest they should not keep their several places; that they are not troubled with fears of poverty, but are troubled with fears of a want of contented repose among the people in their several places.[3]

Traditional Chinese society was based on a natural economy dominated by small-scale agriculture, and land was the main source of social wealth. "Equal wealth" to some extent meant equal land, and the concept of equal land has become an eternal topic of Confucianism, gradually forming several models such as the "well-field system," "limited land system," and "equal land system."

During the Warring States Period, Mencius, who observed people's war-ravaged lives, proposed a return to the well-field system. Dong Zhongshu, a great Confucian scholar in the Western Han Dynasty, denounced the disparity between rich and poor and presented the limiting farmland system, rooted in Mencius' well-field system, to secure basic living conditions for people.

Wang Mang usurped the Han Dynasty to establish a new dynasty, while politicians like Su Chuo in the Northern Zhou Dynasty, Li Gou, Wang Anshi, and Zhang Zai in the Northern Song Dynasty all recommended the Rites of the Zhou Dynasty, a Confucian classic, to introduce the concept of equal land shares.

Hai Rui (1514–1587 CE), a famous Ming Dynasty official renowned for his incorruptibility, pursued radically different land policies, even turning a blind eye to the poor snatching the land of the rich. This extreme approach was taken against a backdrop of widespread disregard for social justice and morality. However, the root of the disparity between the rich and the poor does not lie in land policies, but rather in the loss of social propriety (禮 li) and love.

China's equal land system aimed to create equal wealth. In prosperous and politically intact dynasties, this was reflected. However, when dynasties neared their end, corrupt and ineffective officials let merchants seize land. As the land was inherited through generations, later descendants held less and less of it. Wealthy merchants' lands outweighed those of small farmers. In famine years, these small farmers had to get loans and ended up with their lands taken by merchants or large landowners.

That was why ancient China, founded on agriculture, experienced an endless cycle of social unrest. This was due to faulty land policies; initially, the intention was to make wealth equal, however, it failed due to the lack of guidance and structure in managing the farmers' skills. In contrast, in the late feudal period of Europe, many farmers went into handcrafts and moved to cities, becoming a prime source of civil society.

Love as the Key to Achieving Equal Wealth

Equal wealth in ancient China was a concept which held that wealth could not be totally equal, but all must recognize the moral value of equal wealth. The rich should not be arrogant; instead, they should seek spiritual enlightenment for the sake of morality. The poor should be free of financial worries and pursue a virtuous, contented life. Ultimately, equal wealth means having riches of both a material and spiritual nature.

In the words of Master Cheng Yen, there are four types of wealth: "the rich among the rich," "the poor among the rich," "the rich among the poor," and "the poor among the poor."

To have an abundance of love is to be the rich among the rich. Possessing great wealth but still longing for more is the poor among the rich. Being poor but loving others is the rich among the poor, and to be poor and bitter is the poor among the poor.

Love is the key to achieving equal wealth.

If people from all social classes were full of love, and ready to be selfless and aid those in need, there would be no land taking and capital looting.

Utilitarianism aims to attain the greatest happiness for the greatest number of people, yet it can sacrifice the happiness of a few, and fail to bring about material satisfaction.

Altruism and love are more fundamental paths to equal wealth. While it may sound morally obligatory, it is the most fundamental and best requirement.

Only through the practice of altruism and love can society naturally achieve mutual supplementation and avoid both individual and structural exploitation.

Altruism and love will prevent sacrificing and exploiting underprivileged talents or disadvantaged strata in the capital market.

John Rawls believed that justice should entail equal opportunity and benefit the most vulnerable. He was spot on, yet if this is only advocacy of policy without love being put into practice, it will be hard for society to achieve full justice and fairness.

In pursuit of fairness and justice, or equality of wealth, we must understand that fairness does not mean that all people have the same income, salary, or treatment. Human intelligence and fortune differ and equality should mean opportunity equality, a basic living standard, and developing love and altruism. With love shared by both the rich and the poor, true equality can be realized.

Angus Deaton, a Nobel laureate in economics at the University of Cambridge, said of wealth and happiness that the wealthy could eradicate poverty by donating one dollar each. It's a straightforward notion, yet tough to execute. Deaton noted that it was hard to distribute these funds.

Certainly, the wealthy are not always eager to part with that one dollar. Even if the well-off are inclined to do so, the funds have to pass through intermediary organizations such as the government, which in impoverished countries, tends to be inefficient or corrupt.

Deaton noted that, by providing international aid, poor countries would find it increasingly difficult to develop. These subsidies could sustain corrupt governments and exploit the poverty of their population for personal gain. The only way a country can prevail is when its economy grows and people's livelihoods improve; therefore they will no longer need global aid. This is why many struggling states that have received assistance do not progress.

The dearth of love is the cause of poverty. If the affluent would donate a dollar, and if governmental personnel managed the funds with honesty and efficiency, poverty worldwide could be tackled.

Love is the key to equal wealth. Rich and poor alike can experience spiritual and material abundance when love is present. It brings about a connection between those in need and those who are able to help, thus achieving true equality.

If the poor had love, corruption by government officials in poorer countries would not arise. With love, the poor would be able to aid the even more destitute, even if they themselves are impoverished.

In 2008 when floods affected Myanmar, Tzu Chi volunteers brought aid to those affected, distributing rice and other essentials, as well as rice seeds. The farmers who sowed the seeds soon reaped a bountiful harvest. Expressing their gratitude, they stored a portion of their daily harvest in pots for use by those less fortunate. This reflects the spirit of the Bamboo Bank Era when Master Cheng Yen first founded Tzu Chi, where she encouraged 30 housewives to donate TWD 50 cents (approx. USD 2 cents) every day into bamboo coin banks to help those in need. Though the sum was negligible to them, it might save a life. The farmers in Myanmar are not wealthy, but still they committed to setting aside a handful of rice into a rice bank every day to help those less fortunate than them. The actions of one person soon inspired more to join, and now there are thousands of households across the country practicing this act of kindness every day. Now, there is about 8,000 families taking part in this relief effort on a daily basis. This is what it means to be the rich among the poor.

Contentment brings abundance, and love is the greatest wealth. Even the poor can be as rich as the wealthy, lacking nothing in material goods and possessing a rich inner life. This is true common prosperity.

There Is No Competition in EOG

Equal wealth has been an ideal of Chinese Confucianism, upon which communism and capitalism could agree. However, as long as competition remains the dominant force in society, equal wealth is unlikely to be achieved.

Competition drives today's capitalism, but it also fuels exploitation and widens the gap between the wealthy and the impoverished. The dwindling of the middle class in many developed countries is a result of concentrated capital in the hands of a few. Big data and financial resources ensure the continuous growth of large companies. Greater equity in wealth distribution can only be achieved by making information more open and providing more equal education.

If competition leads to innovation, it also creates social inequality. On the contrary, love and compassion can be the foundations for social innovation and justice.

Can love and compassion be the foundation of the economy?

An entrepreneur with love and compassion comprehends social needs. Meeting them ensures success. Jack Ma mentioned he taught for seven years and had to execute what he taught before returning to school.

Seeing no products made in China on the Internet in the US, he envisioned a blueprint for selling small business owners' and women's products from China via the web. Out of compassion and love grew a distinguished generation of Chinese entrepreneurs.

Tzu Chi Foundation, the world's largest ethnically Chinese charitable organization, carries out its Four Missions of charity, medicine, education, and humanistic culture in 136 countries around the globe, with tangible and intangible assets. Tzu Chi maintains that these assets do not belong to any individual or organization, but to all citizens of the world; they are born of compassion and love for all living beings.

The Economy of Goodness does not prioritize self-interests; instead, it works to secure a shared, prosperous society for all. Production activities and their benefits are geared toward greater inclusion and mutual benefit.

Aristotle believed that pursuing business was damaging to political and personal morality. He didn't oppose wealth, but thought that a sound economy meant the wealthy should contribute to the public interest of the city, pursuing spiritual perfection.

Capitalist society places too much emphasis on consumption and wealth, seeing them as satisfaction and happiness. However, this can easily lead to an excessive burden on the human body, with excessive appetite, material desires, and lust impairing it. Having money but no life goal can result in spiritual emptiness, so it's important to check desires for health.

Material wealth should not be restricted to an individual level but extend to the whole society. Things such as ancient slavery and materializing people during the early stages of Capitalism need to be abolished in order to end collective economic exploitation. Contemporary information symmetry and transparency and equal access to intellectual training are effective ways to combat this exploitation.

In economic activity, improper exploitation among people should be avoided, such as unfair interest and salary arrangements. Excessive leisure can lead to a labor shortage and overall economic downturn. The EOG should strive for all-inclusive success to provide material abundance for everyone.

The EOG strives for a world where everyone is healthy and wealthy in both material and mental aspects.

SECTION 2: BENEVOLENCE AS HAPPINESS

The ideal life of Taoism speaks of a small country with few people outside the scope of the ruling powers. It was a political ideal in the Han Dynasty. Rule Through Non-Action was adopted as the national policy, allowing people to recuperate after the Qin Dynasty's autocracy and the Chu-Han War (207–202 BCE).[4] This resulted in the Han Dynasty becoming a marker of Chinese culture, seen in the distinct Han Chinese culture compared to other ethnic groups in China.

The emphasis on loosening government regulations in small countries with few people allows for autonomous living and creativity among the people. This is similar to Hayek's idea of free-market economics, where the government has minimal control but must maintain a diverse balance to prevent any one element from dominating or monopolizing societal resources. During the time of Dong Zhongshu (179–104 BCE), although Confucianism was revered, other governance models such as Huang-Lao, Yin-Yang, and Legalism were also incorporated. The book *"Luxuriant Dew of the Spring and Autumn Annals"* is a collection of Confucianism, Taoism, Legalism, Yin-Yang, and Five Elements.[5]

Economically, a small country with few people is self-sufficient, tranquil, and carefree, as Tao Yuanming delineated:

> I pluck chrysanthemums under the eastern hedge,
> And gaze afar towards the southern mountains.
> The mountain air is fine at evening of the day
> And flying birds return together homewards.
> Within these things there is a hint of Truth,
> But when I start to tell it, I cannot find the words.[6]

---

[4] A severe civil war in ancient China after the collapse of the Qin Dynasty.

[5] Dong, Z. (Eds.). (2012). *Xin yi chunqiu fan lu (xia)* [Luxuriant Dew of the Spring and Autumn Annals (vol. 2)] (Z. Y. Jia & W. Z. Chang, Trans.). Taipei: San min shu ju.

[6] Birch, C., & Keene, D. L. (1965). *Anthology of Chinese Literature.* United States: Grove Press. p.184.

The ideal life for a small country with few people is one harmonious and free of disputes, both among people and within nature. Lao Tzu believed that the less government intervention, the better. As he said:

> The government that seems the most unwise,
> Oft goodness to the people best supplies;
> That which is meddling, touching everything,
> Will work but ill, and disappointment bring.[7]
> I will do nothing (of purpose), and the people will be transformed of themselves; I will be fond of keeping still, and the people will of themselves become correct. I will take no trouble about it, and the people will of themselves become rich; I will manifest no ambition, and the people will of themselves attain to the primitive simplicity.[8]

In modern terms, deregulating governments means more room for creativity. Hayek believed that too much intervention by governments led to economic sluggishness.

Hayek criticized the Austrian government's rigid rent control, causing rents to remain excessively low. Homeowners had no extra money to invest, businesses lacked funds, and the low-income people chose not to move out of Vienna to take advantage of the lower rent. This meant workers in the suburbs had to pay more for commuting, which benefitted no one—not the wealthy or the poor. Hayek thus advocated for the government's adopting a laissez-faire approach and allow the free market to regulate itself.

Non-action in Lao Tzu's philosophy does not equate to doing nothing, but to establishing a reasonable social order to unleash people's creativity. Conversely, if a government believes it can control and regulate social wealth such as through heavy taxation for social welfare, it may provoke more social problems. Lao Tzu foresaw that taxing heavily would only lead to more distress for the common people.

> The people suffer from famine because of the multitude of taxes consumed by their superiors. It is through this that they suffer famine.

---

[7] Tzu, L. (Eds.). (2021). *Tao Te Ching* (J. Legge, Trans.). Standard Ebooks. Retrieved from https://standardebooks.org/ebooks/laozi/tao-te-ching/james-legge.

[8] Tzu, L. (Eds.). (2021). Tao Te Ching (J. Legge, Trans.). Standard Ebooks. Retrieved from https://standardebooks.org/ebooks/laozi/tao-te-ching/james-legge.

The people are difficult to govern because of the (excessive) agency of their superiors (in governing them). It is through this that they are difficult to govern.

The people make light of dying because of the greatness of their labors in seeking for the means of living. It is this which makes them think light of dying.[9]

In a little state with a small population, I would so order it, that, though there were individuals with the abilities of ten or a hundred men, there should be no employment of them; I would make the people, while looking on death as a grievous thing, yet not remove elsewhere (to avoid it). Though they had boats and carriages, they should have no occasion to ride in them; though they had buff coats and sharp weapons, they should have no occasion to don or use them. I would make the people return to the use of knotted cords (instead of the written characters). They should think their (coarse) food sweet; their (plain) clothes beautiful; their (poor) dwellings places of rest; and their common (simple) ways sources of enjoyment. There should be a neighboring state within sight, and the voices of the fowls and dogs should be heard all the way from it to us, but I would make the people to old age, even to death, not have any intercourse with it.[10]

Lao Tzu's ideal society is one without the suppression of powerful political forces, where people uphold their inherent goodness and simplicity, leading a pure life without conflicts or grievances with other communities. In this society of small nations and sparse populations, there is no military turmoil, heavy taxation, or oppressive labor. The society remains pure and untainted by the pollution of civilization, isolated from its influence.

People free from anxieties and fears, villages and communities economically self-sufficient—a perfect balance of well-being.

The Han Dynasty utilized Taoist principles to structure their economy, emphasizing balance between nature and humankind. *The Book of Fan Sheng*[11] detailed the farming methods in the Han Dynasty that stressed the harmony with the four seasons and laws of heaven and earth for great

---

[9] Tzu, L. (Eds.). (2021). Tao Te Ching (J. Legge, Trans.). Standard Ebooks. Retrieved from https://standardebooks.org/ebooks/laozi/tao-te-ching/james-legge.

[10] Tzu, L. (Eds.). (2021). Tao Te Ching (J. Legge, Trans.). Standard Ebooks. Retrieved from https://standardebooks.org/ebooks/laozi/tao-te-ching/james-legge.

[11] Shi, S. H. (1956). *Fan sheng zhi shu jin shi* [A Current Annotation of Works of Fan Shengzhi]. Beijing: Kexue chuban she.

economic results. Around 50% of China's land was reportedly farmland in Shanxi. Under state guidance, many poverty-stricken individuals traveled to Shanxi and Sichuan to start a new life. Additionally, rulers relocated around 700,000 people to create new farmland in the northwest of the country and the area to the north of the Huai River.

Therefore, the great economic and political achievements of ancient China during the Western Han dynasty were a result of its ability to foster vitality among the people rather than suppress it. Of course, the concerns about land annexation led the Han dynasty to establish a system that emphasized agriculture over commerce, aiming to maintain stability of the empire. This was an inevitable choice of the era.

Confucianism set propriety (禮 li) as the social base. Taoism provided the rulers with political insight into deregulating government. The Yellow Emperor's heritage was agricultural, following the laws of nature. Philosophies of Yin & Yang, alongside the 5 Elements, filled the Han people with awe for Heaven. The success of the Han's ruling came from their pluralistic use of philosophies, which created peace and contentment for 200 years—the strongest time of the Han Dynasty.

Based on the analysis, it can be concluded that a small country with few people can still achieve national prosperity.

The few people who live peacefully and contentedly are connected to their country through shared values. They live securely within the same value system.

In today's overpopulated world, population growth is causing a global crisis. Scientists and demographers are forecasting an upcoming war for water resources. The earth's resources can no longer sustain the increasing population. Once a disaster occurs, cities reliant on high energy consumption and remote sourced transportation, such as New York City which experienced a windstorm in 2013, will quickly face blackouts, water and food shortages.

Experts propose that a small country with few people should be self-sufficient. If possible, they could utilize solar energy, grow small crops and sustain their daily needs. Via the Internet, they can continue to connect and support each other, ultimately leading to an affluent, peaceful, and pleasant life while remaining informed with the rest of the world.

The communal governance of a small country with few people can reduce personality distortion and economic pressures to a great extent. It also brings people closer to nature and promotes environmental protection. The blueprint of economic development in the EOG should enable people to become self-sufficient and connected with society.

Confucianism strives for a world of harmony in which the elderly can provide for themselves, the prime of life put their skills to use, the young are nurtured, and widows, widowers, orphans, and the disabled always have a place. It hopes for a world without theft or poverty, where people can feel secure and without worry, leaving their houses unlocked.

Section 3: Altruistic Innovation

The third indicator of the EOG is continuous innovation for happiness and perfection of human life; which includes good health, plentiful material matters, and a tranquil psychological state. Perfection implies an inclusive, shared, and prosperous society.

Innovation is the measure of economic development. Competition usually drives it, and without competition, there would be no innovation. This assumption is inherent in Capitalism.

The EOG doesn't mean to do away with competition, but to have it based on altruism. It sees competition not as the goal but as a tool. Competition that leads to altruism and virtuousness is desirable.

If economic innovation is based on compassion, altruism, and love, can it lead to greater economic success for humans?

Drug research and development globally is mostly tailored to the markets of affluent countries. Few pharma firms are willing to invest in research and development for diseases prevalent in impoverished nations, where the populace cannot purchase pricey medicines. Consequently, drug companies allocate more medicines and medical technology to wealthy countries than necessitated.

Therefore, patients with special and rare diseases would lack access to proper medical care. In 1983, US legislation, the Orphan Drug Act, was passed to incentivize drug firms to invest in medicines for rare diseases. This included granting tax exemptions for research and development, and extended patent rights. Thus, the government promoted the market by being altruistic toward patients with rare diseases.

Can the EOG combine commodity transactions and altruistic practices? With altruism, innovation won't just be focused on wealthy nations but will provide treatments and technologies to those living in underdeveloped nations as well as rare patients in prosperous countries.

In 2015, I visited the earthquake zone in Nepal for disaster relief. It was heartbreaking to see children receiving skull surgeries with no painkillers in such underdeveloped countries; whereas in countries like the US, Germany, Japan, and Taiwan, minimally invasive operations, operated by automatic artificial arms worth several hundred million yuan, are painless and allow for quick recovery.

This is a dichotomy between rich and poor countries: Innovation targeting the wealthy can't be considered an Economy of Goodness. The challenge, however, lies in finding a way to account for the cost of this R&D innovation. Will altruistic EOG be undertaken at an economic loss?

Take orphan drugs as an example. These medicines refer to those for patients with less than 200,000 people. Could it be profitable to develop new drugs for such a small population? In 2015, the orphan drug market was worth 102 billion US dollars, representing 15.5% of the global medicine market. According to Evaluate Pharmacy, the orphan drug market has reached a value of 176 billion US dollars by 2020; twice the growth rate of generic drugs.

Some orphan drugs originally designed for one disease were found to be effective for other patients. For instance, an orphan drug for Carnitine Deficiency was later utilized effectively to aid fat loss and muscle building, making pharmaceutical companies very profitable.

This is the benefit based on altruistic innovation that the EOG pursues.

Too much economic output concentrated in select markets leads to excessive competition and narrower living space for businesses.

By innovating through altruism and compassion, economic production can fulfill social needs while avoiding oversupply. Drug development can bring not only social benefits but also build powerful businesses. This type of innovation balances both altruistic and self-interested goals.

I believe that innovation driven by altruism can sustain enterprise growth more enduringly than that driven by competition and profits.

First, altruistic motivation aims to address real social needs and problems. This economic model often produces the Long Tail Effect and more dedicated customers, who will consume with appreciation, thus protecting the best consumer loyalty.

Second, altruistic innovation can help transform corporate values to be more justice-oriented instead of solely profit-driven. This can motivate and bring staff together to promote sustained creativity.

Thirdly, enterprises with altruistic innovation will gain greater public recognition, potentially more investments in stock and increased market value.

Fourthly, altruistic innovation in economic production helps balance social wealth, leading to a society of equal wealth and well-being in which everyone can experience happiness and even minority groups can be supported. Only through altruism can the stability and happiness of society as a whole be achieved.

SECTION 4: SUSTAINABLE AND COMMON PROSPERITY

How can an economy attain sustainable and shared prosperity?

One indicator of common prosperity is that everyone lives and works in peace and contentment, with full employment being a modern interpretation.

Full Employment

Full employment was proposed by Keynes in The General Theory of Employment, Interest, and Money.[12] It denotes that, at a certain wage rate, there are employment opportunities for all those willing to work, even though there may still remain some amount of unemployment.

However, all unemployment is seasonal and only lasts a brief period. The natural unemployment rate is the sum of job-search and structural unemployment. Keynes believed full employment would be achieved when the unemployment rate equals the natural rate in society.

Temporary unemployment due to job changes aside, structural unemployment can cause more serious issues. Professionals may face structural unemployment when new technology is introduced.

Normally, governments are challenged by structural unemployment, which they try to address by subsidizing vulnerable industries or providing employment assistance. Typically, superior enterprises have little structural unemployment.

This section looks at how the EOG can deal with structural unemployment.

---

[12] Keynes, J. M. (2018). *The General Theory of Employment, Interest, and Money.* Germany: Springer International Publishing.

In a self-interested economic system, those structurally unemployed have the option of taking lower-level jobs or relying on government aid.

In an altruistic economy, can technical personnel ousted from their jobs be taken on by better-off companies? Can better-off companies help bring new life to struggling businesses?

Is the question revolving around whether dominant companies engage in such coaching and assistance purely based on altruistic moral values, or do these advantageous technological enterprises also benefit themselves by doing so?

The EOG opposes assisting others at one's own expense, yet it maintains that acting altruistically can bring even better rewards—a fact that certainly holds true when judged by the outcomes.

It would be commendable if superior businesses could assist disadvantaged ones through altruism. Yet, it is expected that such benevolence could even benefit those enterprises more. We hope this is not merely an expectation, but a realizable outcome.

After World War II, Germany and Japan, being defeated countries, suffered severe economic trauma and it was anticipated that it would take them a long time to recover. Astonishingly though, they had recovered their prosperity within just 15 years. Since then, Germany has been a leading economic force in the EU and Japan has been a major economic influence in Asia, with their people's cultivation and social stability being held up to the world as an example.

What lay behind Germany's and Japan's rapid recovery and ascent after the war? Theodore W. Schultz, Nobel Prize in Economics laureate of 1979, believed that a superior human capital that had endured the war played a significant role. Traditionally, both nations highly valued education, creating a prime workforce for economic growth.

Human capital is the key to economic success: this is a key point of human capital theory. Left unchecked, structural unemployment can lead to major social issues. Government intervention can provide direction for the temporarily unemployed during economic transition, or help them find work in other state-owned enterprises. How do free markets address such issues?

Adam Smith and his followers believed that a free market would regulate the supply and demand balance, of both material and human capital. In the US, unemployment levels are typically between 5 and 7%, more than that of Japan and China, which have government-aided market economies.

The free market, based on self-interest, has demonstrated it is impossible to achieve full employment. In an altruistic economic structure, unemployed individuals can be absorbed by advantaged enterprises, while fostering the transformation of disadvantaged ones.

Japan's six major consortia weathered the financial turmoil of 1997 with mutual and governmental aid. Faced with economic depression, businesses did not compete but worked together to dependently succeed. This cooperative culture enabled the six consortia and the many small businesses and people reliant on them to endure the crisis.

The system of lifelong employment set up by Konosuke Matsushita was essential to the economic success of Japan. Despite it being abolished following the 1997 financial crisis, the six Japanese corporations developed a dispatch system to address structural unemployment.

The mutual assistance of greater openness enabled personnel exchanges among enterprises and the re-employment of professionals.

This is not advocating economic collectivism, but rather a model of economic symbiosis that promotes mutual prosperity. The altruistic economic approach that emphasizes helping each other can result in job satisfaction, social wealth, and harmony.

In this digital age of the Internet and upcoming blockchain technology, technical professionals can be self-employed. We are likely to see high levels of talent mobility in the future. Blockchain and the Internet will enable talented individuals and businesses to freely match in their own best interests. This limitless form of employment offers a great opportunity for full employment.

To foster youth employment, the Japanese government, in conjunction with businesses, established Job Cafe and Hello Work in 2008 to better facilitate access to job-search information in leisure areas for young people. Consequently, their employment rate grew steadily.

New boundary-less careers and lifestyles are emerging. Young people aspire to work professionally and have the freedom to choose their working places and environment. To succeed in life, they must hone their skills and capabilities. Their connection with employers will rely on shared values.

Nowadays, artificial intelligence (AI) presents the most significant challenge to full employment. It is foreseeable that AI will eventually supersede plenty of technical roles, with the importance of work instead shifting toward interpersonal relationships—particularly spiritual connections—such as psychological counseling, philanthropy, religion, education, art, and literature.

What is the greatest enlightenment of AI to humanity? It could be that we no longer need to rely on manual labor for our livelihoods. Labor shapes our minds and thoughts.

In the long term, humans face not only the risk of job losses but, more alarmingly, the danger of being enslaved by AI, as shown in films, if we do not direct scientific and technological developments to the good and continue treating science as neutral whatever ethical issues arise. As Stephen Hawking put it, all the science created by human beings could eventually turn against us or get out of our control.

Work as Self-Cultivation

The most striking difference between humans and robots is that work can be self-cultivating for humans; for machines, it's mere work. People can give value to their work. Marx argued that the state and worth of human life is determined by labor. He viewed the exploitation of workers through the lens of labor structure. Nowadays, instead of their working conditions, it is labor's intrinsic value that is exploited.

To rediscover the intrinsic worth of labor is what the EOG promotes. Work is a way of self-cultivation.

This is a test of the beliefs and values of both employers and employees. What is the value of work? What is the value of a business? What is the worth of products?

Pierre Bordeaux, a famous French sociologist, thought that when people contact something, whether it is a person or an object, it will directly shape our personality.[13] Work will shape our personality, thoughts and values.

To cultivate value in work and practice it is self-development. When work is seen as self-development, it will no longer be a burden. When work is regarded as an enriching experience, it will be enjoyable.

In an industrial society, work and rest are distinct, yet if work feels as comforting as home, do people still require much rest? Nowadays, people usually rest for more than one hundred days annually. What is

---

[13] Bourdieu, P. (1977). *Outline of a Theory of Practice*. United Kingdom: Cambridge University Press.

the advantage of so much leisure time? Is it beneficial for physical and mental well-being?

Master Cheng Yen once expressed that switching tasks is essentially a form of rest.[14] Tzu Chi emphasizes the crucial spiritual principle of not distinguishing between work and rest, or between spiritual practice and rest.

Tzu Chi observes that people today are preoccupied with work and leisure, connecting and staying fit, which fragments them and deprives them of integrated well-being and control over their body, mind, spirit, and environment.

Tzu Chi volunteers believe that work itself can be restful. Master Cheng Yen often asks volunteers if they are tired, to which they always reply, "(We feel) very blessed!" Tzu Chi volunteers don't find volunteer work to be taxing.

Master Cheng Yen hopes that people will live to work, rather than work to live. In Tzu Chi, there is no concept of retirement. Master Cheng Yen once declared to the pure practitioners at the Jing Si Abode that Jing Si disciples do not retire. They should not send the elderly and senior Masters at the Jing Si Abode to nursing homes, but look after them instead. They ought to meditate and diligently cultivate themselves till their life's end, and continue to do their best to benefit the world and all beings after death.[15]

Taiwan's labor standards is to have two-day weekends ("周休二日" rest two days per week), while Master Cheng Yen encourages Tzu Chi volunteers to practice two days of self-cultivation each week ("周修二日" cultivate two days per week), distinguished by only a single word. Most of Tzu Chi's directors and volunteers do not rest at all during the year. Master Cheng Yen rises at 03:30 each morning to deliver talks. By 08:30, two talks will have been given. She does not take any respite throughout the year and her disciples similarly dare not allow themselves any slack but instead work tirelessly.

In my view, separating work from leisure breaks the cohesion of human existence.

Work should be our blessing and joy.

[14] Shih, Cheng Yen. (1989). *Jing Si Aphorisms*. Taipei: Chiu Ko Publishing Co., Ltd. p. 246.

[15] Shih, Cheng Yen. (2007). *Jing si jing she yu qing xiushi kai shi* [Jing Si Abode and Pure Practitioner].

When a person works diligently for all, desiring less and determining more, they reduce themselves to combine with a bigger self. This could be an aim in life worth everyone's striving.

Good economy comes from good work, and good work is built upon the establishment of the value of work.

To establish rightful values and beliefs means self-cultivation. This is not something others can bestow upon you; it must be self-given. Doing good starts from within oneself.

We are all being alienated at work, according to Marx's theory.

In today's society, we mostly work for money, power, social status, or reputation. We overlook the importance of embodying value in work, which is one of life's primary purposes.

Jobs without values drive us to desperately seek money. Greed and deception wreak havoc in economic activity. Without spiritual cultivation, we compete fiercely, trying to outdo others. Consequently, exploitation, control and oppression of individuals or society becomes the norm. Ultimately, we are alienated in our work.

If we strive to embody our values in our work and self-cultivation, we should not prioritize making money or defeating our opponents, but rather focus on creating and benefiting the public. This is the key to the EOG's growth.

The EOG stems from a good-natured effort that encapsulates value and self-improvement. This endeavor prompts us to foster joy to create strong ties with clients and maintain harmony with those around us, while simultaneously augmenting our mental well-being.

Live in Abundant Prosperity with All Beings

All human economic activities rely on the planet's resources. Damage to or depletion of the planet's resources is essentially self-sabotage for humans. The EOG for the future ought to encompass a symbiotic relationship with the earth and all its inhabitants for the long-term sustainability of growth.

In 1924, Dr. Rudolf Steiner suggested organic fertilizer, yet it wasn't until 1990 that organic agriculture became a new worldwide movement dedicated to safeguarding the environment and human health.[16] The

---

[16] O'Mahony, B., & Lobo, A. (2017). The Organic Industry in Australia: Current and Future Trends. *Land Use Policy* (66). p. 331.

IFOAM (International Federation of Organic Agricultural Movements) developed standards, certification processes, and professional instruction to extend organic farming around the world.

The production and consumption of organic agriculture shows humans that damaging the earth harms people.

The EOG seeks to sustain the earth and humanity, and organic agriculture is a leader in this effort. Organic farming is more expensive than conventional farming that relies on chemical fertilizers and pesticides. It must help to purify land polluted for centuries, control pests, and help to restore balance between insects in nature over time. Unfortunately, organic farming yields less than traditional farming, hindering its growth.

With altruism, however, countless promoters of organic agriculture have yielded outstanding economic rewards after decades of effort.

Take Australia as an example; it is a leader in the global organic agriculture industry. Italian anthropologist Ernesto Genoni visited to promote organic farming as early as the 1920s. The Australian Organic Farming and Gardening Society (AOFGS) was formed in 1944, and the following Australian Sustainable Agriculture Initiative is committed to promoting organic farming.

Up to this point, Australia's organic farms have reached 15.69 million hectares. Since 2010, the output value of the country's organic food industry has grown by double digits every year. Fewer than 1% of the general market is composed of organic agriculture and the food industry, though milk and nutrition products from organic farming make up 22.3%, organic meat 16.2%, and organic vegetables and fruits 11.9%.[17]

In 2012, the total production value of organic agriculture reached $240 million. This economic sector is steadily growing in size and impact.

Striving for the sustainability of the planet is now a social responsibility of modern businesses. The organization must focus on the sustainability of the Earth and people, pursuing the shared prosperity of all life.

The earth has seen the ethnic group extinction because of unreasonable economic development in human history. Near Chile in the South Pacific Ocean lies Easter Island; a desolate, barren isle with no trees yet thousands of immense towering humanoid statues, weighing dozens of tons and standing several meters high. Astonishingly, no rocks of this size exist on the island. How were the stones transported? How were

---

[17] O'Mahony, B., & Lobo, A. (2017). The Organic Industry in Australia: Current and Future Trends. *Land Use Policy* (66). p. 334.

they erected? How were they sculpted? This continues to be a mystery to archaeologists.

According to historians and geologists, the Polynesians settled here in 800 BCE, when the forest was thick and the land was fertile. They tilled the land and developed their culture, complete with frequent religious sacrifices, crafting a veritable earthly paradise.

From the soil collected on the island, it was found that fish accounted for only a quarter of the residents' food, with sweet potatoes and other crops comprising the majority. Evidence of the island's deposits and swamps showed that Polynesian agriculture was highly developed with dense woodlands and fertile soil. However, the land was gradually ruined due to generations of deforestation for arable farming. Worse, without the protection of trees, the land was highly vulnerable to flooding due to rain. As a result, the island's residents either left for other islands or fought each other to survive. Ultimately, this led to Easter Island being a short-lived civilization.

Two hundred years prior to the arrival of Captain Cook, an eighteenth-century British explorer, Easter Island had reached its peak of civilization with a population of about 20,000. Its stone statues were dedicated to religious sacrifice. However, over-exploitation of forests and land resulted in the island's downfall.

Economic life cannot be separated from the earth. The ancient Chinese teachings of respecting heaven and loving the earth are something that every individual engaged in economic activities today must keep in mind. How to make environmental sustainability and harmony with nature fundamental goals of economic development, much like organic agriculture, where economic progress promotes the enduring prosperity of both humanity and the Earth—this is the ideal economy of goodness.

CHAPTER 12

Thoughts and Practice of Good Enterprises

SECTION 1: FAITH AS THE CORE

Yvon Chouinard is the founder of Patagonia, the biggest outdoor mountaineering brand in America. In 2018, Forbes listed Yvon Chouinard as one of the world's billionaires. As a teenager, Chouinard was captivated by rock climbing. In 1953, at the age of 14, Chouinard and his friends attempted to train eagles and falcons to hunt in their natural habitat. An experienced rock climber instructed them in the art of reaching eagle and falcon nests. This is how Chouinard's rock climbing journey began.

At eighteen, along with Swiss rock climber John Salath, Chouinard tackled the challenging climbs of Yosemite in Yellowstone Park. Observing the necessity for numerous pitons in rock climbing and seeing John's reused hard nails, Chouinard decided to fashion his own pitons and mountaineering spikes in his garage.

His homemade chrome-molybdenum steel pitons quickly gained traction among like-minded friends, inadvertently kickstarting a business venture. Driving around with his toolbox, he would craft pitons on demand, selling them for $1.50 per pair, enough to make ends meet. As demand soared, Chouinard upgraded to mechanical tools for faster production. In 1965, he partnered with Tom Frost, an aerospace engineer and skilled climber, to establish a company. Their vision was clear: to create climbing tools that embodied perfection, stripped down to their essence, lightweight, and effortlessly efficient. This philosophy was

© The Author(s), under exclusive license to Springer Nature   351
Singapore Pte Ltd. 2024
R.-S. Her, *The Economy of Goodness*,
https://doi.org/10.1007/978-981-97-6363-4_12

inspired by Antoine de Saint Exupéry, the French aviator, who famously said, "In anything at all, perfection is finally attained not when there is no longer anything to add, but when there is no longer anything to take away, when a body has been stripped down to its nakedness."[1]

In 1970, Chouinard became the largest supplier of mountaineering tools in the US. But, with the growing number of rock climbers, damage to the rocks became increasingly criticized. Accordingly, Chouinard abandoned his range of pitons, forcing him to start afresh.

Sales of pitons accounted for 70% of the company's revenue. However, Chouinard maintained that people should climb rocks due to their affinity for nature, and not to damage them.

Though at risk of a shutdown, Chouinard halted the piton business.

In 1972, Yvon Chouinard introduced aluminum pitons that could be easily wedged by hand during climbing and easily removed without damaging the rock surface. This innovation allowed the next climber to experience the natural state of the rock without leaving any marks. In the product description accompanying the launch of this new product, Chouinard expressed his views on the importance of "Clean Climbing" across seventeen pages. He explained:

> There is a word for it, and that word is clean. Climbing with only nuts and runners for protection is clean climbing. Clean because the rock is left unaltered by the passing climber. Clean because nothing is hammered into the rock and then hammered back out, leaving the rock scarred and the next climber's experience less natural. Clean because the climber's protection leaves little trace of his ascension. Clean is climbing the rock without changing it, a step closer to organic climbing for the natural man.[2]

In the 1980s, Patagonia transitioned from mountaineering equipment to mountaineering clothing, and its coarse cotton apparel became popular among climbers. However, Chouinard soon found that the production of this coarse cotton was harming the environment and potentially endangering customers' health. He then shifted to manufacturing clothing with

---

[1] Saint-Exupéry, A. (1992). *Wind, Sand and Stars* (L. Galantière, Trans). United States: Harcourt Brace Jovanovich. (Original work published 1939). p. 42.

[2] Pesterfield, H. (2007). *Traditional Lead Climbing: A Rock Climber's Guide to Taking the Sharp End of the Rope*. Birmingham: Wilderness Press. p. 245.

pesticide-free cotton, which sparked the vigorous development of organic pesticide-free cotton production in California.

Whenever faced with the choice between profit and public interests, Chouinard returned to his original love for the environment in the climbers' best interests.

Sticking to faith is the way to success for Patagonia Outdoor Clothing & Gear.

In 1985, Patagonia Outdoor Clothing & Gear actively engaged in environmental and wildlife protection. Chouinard took part in purifying an industrially polluted river. Moreover, he decided to donate 10% of the company's revenue to safeguard wild animals. Additionally, there was a campaign to dismantle dams that prevented fish migration.

Patagonia Outdoor Clothing & Gear became the world's largest outdoor sports brand in 2014 due to Chouinard updating their mountaineering tools and clothing conscientiously, while continually seeking suggestions from consumers. For instance, Chouinard would require redesigning until some T-shirt button prone to fall off could be secure. Patagonia's mountaineering clothes are equipped with various pockets that are a bonus for climbers, although these pockets would ramp up the cost.

In 2013, Chouinard began manufacturing clothes made from recycled plastic bottles for environmental protection.

Patagonia Outdoor Clothing & Gear is an enterprise with faith at its core, despite market fluctuations. Yvon Chouinard's love for nature never wavered; he never put profit first, insisting that Patagonia be a contributor to the environment and society.

Nowadays, the number of people wearing Patagonia clothes far outnumbers mountaineers. When people wear Patagonia, they are advocates of nature. For a business to be successful, its brand needs to reflect its core values and operation philosophy.

Patagonia Outdoor Clothing & Gear realizes its love for nature top-down. Although a billion-dollar billionaire, Chouinard often does manual work and goes fishing in the wild, and employees can even wear diving suits to meetings! Globally, staff can play volleyball in the company's backyard beach and enjoy organic food, preceding Google's fancy staff treatment. Before any product goes public, it must first pass tests from the R&D team, both from employees and management personnel. Patagonia sells products they have confidence in and love, believing in loving consumers as much as loving oneself, and caring for the environment as if it is one's own life.

Faith Is Better than Strategy

In the case study of Tzu Chi, Professor Herman Leonard of Harvard University observed that Tzu Chi's success as one of the world's most effective charitable organization stems from its unwavering commitment to its core beliefs rather than its reliance on strategies. In the context of emergency disaster relief, planning and strategies often prove ineffective. Businesses typically develop their strategic plans well in advance, often for the coming year or even multiple years. However, disasters are unpredictable in nature. There is no way to foresee when they will occur, the extent of their impact, the scale of the damage, or the specific manner in which they will cause loss of life and property. In the aftermath of a disaster, governments often become paralyzed, and relief organizations face unforeseen challenges in terms of transportation, security, and logistics. As a result, strategies and plans are often ill-suited to the demands of disaster relief.

In 2013, Typhoon Haiyan (Yolanda) brought devastation to the Philippines, destroying over 90% of the buildings in the cities of Tacloban and Ormoc. Tzu Chi proposed the cash-for-work relief program, provided 500 Philippine pesos a day per person, calling on locals who had fled the city to help rebuild their own homes. The number of participants grew from 500, to 1,000 to 2,000 and eventually reached 15,000 locals joining in to help clean up their homes and streets every day. 19 days later, Tacloban City had been restored.

In Typhoon Morakot, which hit southern Taiwan in 2009, Pingtung, Kaohsiung and Tainan were greatly affected as municipal dysfunction set in due to flooding. Over ten thousand Tzu Chi volunteers traveled daily by high-speed train to clear sediment and urban trash. With over a million volunteer shifts, the southern cities were cleaned and order restored within two weeks.

The Philippines had few Tzu Chi volunteers compared to Taiwan, so they adopted a new method of gathering people to help with disaster relief.

In 2015, a major earthquake struck Nepal. Only three days later, volunteers from 8 countries arrived in the affected area. Local homes fashioned primarily of bricks and tiles were destroyed, making it impossible to determine ownership of the scattered material. Therefore, Tzu Chi distributed rice, blankets, tents and foldable beds to 25,000 households and quickly set up tent housing for thousands of families.

These three cases demonstrate that there is no panacea for disasters of various magnitudes and contexts. Frontline volunteers must rely on improvisation, trusting in their capacity to help people, rather than any predefined plan. Tzu Chi volunteers exhibit this commitment and dedication.

Professor Herman Leonard of Harvard University concluded that in the future, enterprises will face more drastic environmental changes, unknown technological challenges, cultural barriers, and various natural and man-made disasters, including terrorist attacks. Strategies and plans may fail; enterprises will gain greater strength and unity from their faith. Tzu Chi's effective and efficient management of disasters, due to the collaboration between frontline volunteers and the headquarters, is owed to their common faith of unconditionally assisting others, being appreciative for doing so. Compassion and gratitude are why Tzu Chi can face any challenge with composure.

Professor Leonard believes enterprises should not relinquish strategic management, rather, foster inner core values and faiths. Leaders as well as ordinary employees need to recognize and adopt them into their convictions. This may enable their employees to become proactive in tackling obstacles, much like Tzu Chi. Its volunteers are not only unsalaried but pay out of pocket for disaster relief trips. Their power and acumen are derived from the determination to assist.

Employees and directors in enterprises should establish shared core values. By doing so, they will be better equipped to withstand the pressure and make informed decisions when faced with difficult situations.

Fostering Corporate Culture for Exponential Growth

Jenn Weng Chu (朱振榮), a Tzu Chi volunteer, founded ViTrox Corporation Berhad, the second-largest technology manufacturer in Malaysia. In 2011, Chu was profoundly touched with his experience at Tzu Chi's Jing Si Retreat for entrepreneurs. Upon his return to Malaysia, he began to introduce Tzu Chi's values into his company, redefining ViTrox's values and establish "sincerity, integrity, faith, and steadfastness" as its core principles. ViTrox also created a humanistic space within the company, implementing a round organization that manages with love. Employees are allowed to leave their workstations at any time and work, think, and meet in a beautiful, quiet, and solemn space. It gives employees a humanistic and creative space, bringing love and compassion into the enterprise.

Chu informed me his business had suffered in the last two decades, yet since embracing the ideals of Tzu Chi and reconstructing the corporate culture, their market value has rocketed from US$ 300 million seven years ago to US$ 1 billion currently—making it the second-largest tech company in Malaysia.

The co-founder of ViTrox is a Christian. He reported a rise in orders after customers visited the company, experienced its humanistic space and interacted with them. The core values presented by the humanistic space earned customers' trust.

During the 2017 Penang flood, 300 engineers from ViTrox joined Tzu Chi every day for disaster relief, returning to the company to work overtime without complaints or pay demands. This sense of togetherness, due to shared values, permeated through all employees.

After joining Tzu Chi, Jenn Weng Chu took the four core values taught by Master Cheng Yen—sincerity, integrity, faith, and steadfastness—as the guidelines for serving customers in his company.

Sincerity is essential for businesses and is the foundation for long-term growth. Integrity engenders trust. Faith facilitates expansion. Steadfastness leads to success.

Faith cannot be transplanted, but must be nurtured. Business owners must nurture it in themselves and demonstrate it for their employees and customers, else it is just a slogan that will not inspire.

With re-established core values, Jenn Weng Chu shaped a more efficient and independent company. ViTrox won customers' recognition, leading to business growth.

Change the World with Faith

Steve Jobs, the most successful entrepreneur and inventor of our time, said that he earned one million at the age of twenty-one, ten million at the age of twenty-four, and hundreds of millions of dollars at the age of twenty-six. However, from Macbooks, Pixar, to iPhones, his inner belief remained unchanged. He said that with our Passion we can change the world and make it better.

The People who are crazy enough to think they can change the world are the ones who do.[3]

Steve Jobs is the greatest inventor in human history after Edison. He transformed computers from room-sized machines to personalized devices. From personal computers to iPhone, we have witnessed the democratization and personalization of computers. This has allowed people to enjoy such fast and intelligent tools.

iPhone successfully combines technology and humanity, art and engineering, creativity and machinery; revolutionizing the way science and technology are accessible to people. It has changed human life.

All this comes from Jobs' unchanging core beliefs. In a television interview in his fifties, Jobs said that he had many inventions in his life, but his core belief had never changed.

Practicing the New Wangdao[4]: Stan Shih, the Pioneer of Taiwan's IT Industry

Stan Shih co-founded Acer in 1976 alongside four partners. He then guided it through a successful restructuring in the early 1990s, resulting in it becoming the first renowned computer brand from Taiwan and one of seven major personal computer companies worldwide. In 1995, he unveiled the Aspire multimedia home computer, achieving worldwide popularity.

Stan Shih made extraordinary contributions to elevating Taiwan's image and computer production. He was selected as one of Taiwan's Top Ten Outstanding Youths and the 1st Ten Outstanding Young Persons of the World. His innovative, forward-thinking approach and commitment to social responsibility earned him recognition from Fortune Magazine in 1989 as one of the 25 People to Know for Business in Asia. Additionally, The World Executives Digest honored him in 1995 as one of the 15 Most Dynamic Entrepreneurs. Early in 1996, Business Weekly of the US officially named him as one of The 25 Top Managers of the Year.

---

[3] Apple's "Think Different" commercial, 1997.

[4] Wangdao refers to the saintly king who governs his state with benevolence and compassion. It exemplifies an organizational model in which the leader cares about the people and guides them into a peaceful, prosperous, and pure state of life.

After retiring in 2004, Stan Shih founded the iD SoftCapital Group and StanShih Foundation, striving to incubate projects. He believes that ethnic Chinese enterprises should follow the philosophy of Wangdao (the King's Way) to thrive in the global business arena of the twenty-first century, balancing interests and creating value to foster long-term success amid the shifting markets.

Tracing back Acer's history, we find Stan Shih to be a staunch adherent and beneficiary of the Wangdao philosophy.

The Key to Operating a Business of Goodness Is Subtlety, Invisibility, and Future

In his new take on Wangdao, it espouses three core beliefs: Value Creation, Balance of Interests, and Sustainable Development.

Stan Shih believes that an enterprise should contribute to society and create value, not just make money. He emphasizes their social responsibilities with all business activities. He stated that value could be expressed using the General Theory of Hexa-aspect Values, consisting of the visible values of tangible, direct, and present as well as the invisible values of intangible, indirect, and future.

Tangible, direct, and present are highly valued by ordinary enterprises. Both democratic politics and capitalist management prioritize direct values as the core. For example, key performance indicators are utilized in corporate management. Yet, goodness, in the end, is invisible and can't be fully comprehended. Excellent business operations include the invisible values of intangible, indirect, and future. In addition to creating values for society and living up to core beliefs, successful enterprises should also understand how to cultivate talent and provide a space for them to reach their full potential, and even invest in skill development for the enterprise or larger society. Corporate culture, meanwhile, is another important yet invisible corporate asset. Stan Shih believes that it is a framework for corporate growth and transformation, and is a practice of corporate values.

From the very beginning of his business, Stan Shih saw people as basically good, which he trusted and prioritized this belief as Acer's most integral corporate culture. Stan Shih proposed that, in order to go high up into the skies, the dragons must be leaderless and launched a long-term strategy to train a hundred general managers and empower their autonomy within the company. Taking inspiration from the Taiwanese proverb "I would rather be a leader among chickens than a straggler among cattle," he proposed a system of trading stocks to his employees and giving them a sense of being entrepreneurs. He also advocated for teaching others everything with no secrets and for encouraging employees to view their leaders as masters and themselves as apprentices. To combat short-sightedness and the seeking of quick profits, Shih proposed a relay marathon, wishing for all his colleagues to give their utmost in their posts and to be extra careful when changing their job roles for the sustainable development of the company.

Middle-level cadres play a key role in establishing corporate culture and should understand and bring this to fruition by enforcing it from the top-down each day. The employees' perspectives should be welcomed, and their capabilities should be maximized. Cadres should be ready to step in anywhere and work like shareholders for the company and their own benefit. This will help minimize those who take the path of least resistance and further corporate progress.

Customer-Oriented Branding

Wangdao should place equal emphasis on visible and invisible values. Stan Shih believes that a "Good" enterprise needs to be profitable to stay true to its values. Goodness is not a lofty idea, but an essential part of business. Business signifies a value exchange; when buying and selling, both sides create value. The seller gains money, while the buyer gains value.

Economically, enterprises must strike a balance between supply and demand, staying abreast of market trends. To provide products and services of value to society they must be customer-centric. Products without market demand won't have success. Competing solely for financial gain, instead of also considering their ecological footprint, could lead to product devaluation. Companies that lack forethought in this area won't survive in the long term.

Stan Shih has a well-known Smiling Curve Theory. It represents innovation and branding. Acer does not believe in being a follower or copying others. In the manufacturing industry, research and development, plus intellectual property innovation provide value to products, while branding and channel expansion aids sales. Creating value in a certain field, with corporate IP and profile branding, allows enterprises to craft an inimitable niche that is still irreplaceable.

Altruism: A Force that Promotes Harmonious Balance of Multi-Party Interests

Regarding the balancing of multiple parties' interests, Stan Shih stated that selflessness is the best form of self-interest. It's often thought that people are inherently selfish—the proverb "every man for himself" captures this belief. Businesses usually prioritize their own interests, followed by those of investors, followed finally by customers and employees. Stan Shih, however, established the "Acer One Two Three" philosophy, with a focus on customers first, followed by employees, and then shareholders. Leaders must understand that failure in the future can come from success in the present. Wangdao helps to create a balanced approach to interests. If the leader is willing to consider others, a concerted effort will result, making the pie bigger and allowing everyone to benefit. This is what Stan Shih conveyed.

Acer's Wangdao and altruism have been the unsung heroes in two major successful transformations of Acer. This enterprise must continually update itself to create new value. Over the past 40 years, Stan Shih has led Acer in three reforms and transformations, during the global financial highs and lows, while successfully creating new value.

At the beginning, Acer had $35,000 and developed through microprocessor technology. In 1987, it started to construct the brand. Into the twenty-first century, its worldwide operations and marketing had matured. A new geostrategic business strategy allowed it to shift from PC building to e-commerce and IT services, forming the Acer Enterprise Groups with subsidiaries like BenQ Group that specialized in IT products and Wistron Group, who specialized in OEM services, taking Acer to become the second-biggest computer manufacturer. When Acer stumbled in 2014, the already-retired Stan Shih was appointed chairman of the board, and in 8 months managed to accomplish the rollout of its cloud service with the hardware + software + service model.

In Stan Shih's view, the industrial chain relies on division of labor and cooperation, with vertical division and horizontal integration as the trend. Businesses should focus on a certain segment, streamlined for effective management. Integrated industries need sufficient economic scale. In today's cloud era, competition is fiercer and the division/integration of labor has made a more flattened world. Winners must approach the situation differently, innovating their business models to benefit a greater range of stakeholders. He believes that those who lead global resource integration, or the choicest integrator, will be the ultimate victors.

Run a Marathon with Chinese-Western Philosophy

The EOG advocates altruism, harmony and "Management with Love" in corporate operations, creating products for consumers with good faith, and cooperating with business partners harmoniously and inclusively. When faced with a conflict between business revenue and social good, companies should firmly prioritize the overall social interests for sustained development; echoing Stan Shih's philosophy of Wangdao.

Acer combines the Latin roots of "acute" and "sharp," symbolizing positivity and energy, as well as excellence and superiority. In Chinese, it can mean the game of Go and "great," implying that the company is playing an ongoing, grand game of Go.

Looking to the future, Stan Shih believes the biggest challenge may be finding a way to draw from the Western systematic management to create an accessible, practical, localized business methodology for use in ethnic Chinese contexts that can be globally promoted. He told me, "This is a relay marathon that cannot be finished by one person or one generation; we will do our best to do so."

One of the World's Largest Faith-Based Charity Organizations

Sustainable large businesses must acknowledge, retain, and transmit their core values.

Peter Drucker, a management scientist, once defined an NGO as an advocate, practitioner, and beneficiary of values.

The practice of valuing is the main driving force of NGOs. Can this impact profit-making enterprises' success or failure? Could these enterprises be value-driven during development? In Harvard Business School, a concept and framework on valuing practice since 2010 has been put in place. For-profit enterprises should take value-oriented leadership.

In 2010, I was invited to speak at Harvard Business School. Professor Herman B. Leonard, a senior professor there, said that he had invited me because the school had been focused on strategy and competition and he wished for the students to learn Tzu Chi's leadership approach, focusing on values and management with love.

During the two-hour speech, Professor Leonard and I both spoke about faith- and value-based leadership. Professor Leonard particularly noted that Tzu Chi followed no strategies, only beliefs and values. Some enquired: Didn't Tzu Chi consider disaster relief methods? Wasn't the method comparable to strategies?

Surely, disaster relief needs methods. However, due to the unpredictable location, scale, and local relief capacities, as well as governmental effectiveness, no fixed method can be adopted in advance.

Tzu Chi volunteers act with a sense of mission to bring relief to wherever disasters occurs. With such values and commitment, they develop numerous methods for disaster relief. Volunteers must lean on their own core beliefs to make decisions and modify their plans. When set techniques no longer work, values become their only means of judgment.

Tzu Chi volunteers live by the ideals of giving without expecting anything in return and expressing gratitude; they directly distribute relief items to those affected by disasters. Guided by this value, in over half a century, Tzu Chi has provided aid to 136 countries and regions across the globe, making Tzu Chi one of the leading charity organizations worldwide.

Tzu Chi has nearly 2 million volunteers around the world, radiating immense energy in disaster relief. These volunteers mostly work for their communities; when a major disaster hits, they often pay out of their own pockets to travel to affected areas. They uphold the value of kindness and compassion for all.

Section 2: Value-Oriented Leadership

Value-Oriented Leadership in Corporate Management

Ingvar Kamprad, founder of IKEA, wears second-hand clothes and flies economy class to stay on a level with his employees, who can't usually afford first-class fares. Forbes Magazine, once ranking him as the fourth richest man on Earth with $48 billion, attested to his commitment to IKEA's philosophy of high-quality at a low price by his leadership demonstrating "I'm like you all."

Ingvar Kamprad was born in a small Swedish town. His grandfather had taken his own life due to the farm loan he could not pay. His grandmother and father then ran the farm. His dad said to him one time: "You'll never make it." Determined to show otherwise, Ingvar Kamprad had a strong character.

At seventeen, his father rewarded him for his good grades with a small sum that would serve as his startup capital. He started by trading pencils and eventually shifted to logistics. One day, upon leaving a factory, Ingvar Kamprad noticed that a pair of socks that only cost one dollar was being sold for eight. This prompted him to offer consumers high-quality products at a low price.

His entrepreneurship and values are the key to IKEA's success; he is committed to producing excellent and affordable goods.

Value-oriented leadership applies to both employees and customers. Throughout his life, Ingvar Kamprad adhered to simplicity and moderation, setting a social example.

Ingvar Kamprad attaches great importance to employees, often embracing them and telling them that delivering excellent services to customers is the foundation of the company. He encourages them to support each other in their work and home lives, to foster a warm, homey atmosphere. His intention is to also make IKEA itself a home, providing products and furniture that create a warm, comfortable living space for customers. This is a value-driven form of leadership.

IKEA's furniture and decorations give the impression of being in a home. Small vases, pictures hung near the bed, and the courteousness of the staff all contribute to the customers' feeling of being at home. These practices embody IKEA's values, which Ingvar Kamprad emphasizes in all branches where they employ over 125,000 people in 48 countries.

Ingvar Kampla's diligence, simplicity, and treating his employees like family were not done to benefit business, but rather to cultivate his character, instilled in him since childhood. He constantly remembers his father's warning, "You will never make it," keeping him vigilant.

Ingvar Kamprad was a nostalgic person. His initials, "IK," were taken from his name; "E" for Elmtaryd (the farm where he grew up) and "A" for Agunnaryd (the name of his hometown). In 1945 he founded IKEA in Sweden, but due to the strict taxation system of the Swedish government he moved it to Copenhagen, Denmark in 1973. It is now headquartered in the Netherlands, however, Ingvar returned to Sweden to live out his last few years and died there aged 91.

Management based on character is the key to value-oriented leadership. Character is the core of value and the source of value creation.

Ingvar Kamprad insisted that IKEA would not be listed, refusing to let the capital market determine his career or compromise the values he stood for. To aid the less fortunate, he established the IKEA Foundation and invested substantially. He is an icon of entrepreneurial spirit and the value of creating beautiful homes.

Not only enterprises but all organizations and civilizations were formed and founded through the power of values.

Lend Life to Enterprises with Value

Red Bull is a beverage that rapidly restores physical energy and combats fatigue. It was introduced to the market in Austria in 1987. Austrian entrepreneur Dietrich Mateschitz discovered this drink in Thailand and saw it as a great business opportunity. He believed that if he could offer Red Bull to truck drivers, travelers dealing with jet lag, and tired office workers, it could tap into a vast market. When Dietrich Mateschitz initially founded the company, he not only saw a business opportunity but also cleverly imbued Red Bull with distinctive and meaningful values. Red Bull beverages quickly became associated with extreme physical activities. Mateschitz sponsored various extreme sports events including skiing competitions, surfing, breakdancing contests, and even skydiving competitions involving aerial acrobatics. This series of events was aimed at creating the mythical corporate image of "Red Bull - Gives You Wings," symbolizing extraordinary supernatural power.

In 2003, Red Bull sponsored Sadek Gesia, a bike race champion and developed products to increase physical fitness. This garnered them many consumers.

Red Bull sponsored Felix the adventurer to cross the English Channel. From 39,000 meters, Felix leapt from the stratosphere and glided thousands of meters before his safe arrival. This event was broadcast by over 200 TV channels worldwide and the Red Bull logo on Felix's suit was seen by tens of thousands of viewers.

There are over 600 athletes sponsored by Red Bull. Their fans, who watch the sponsored films on YouTube, outnumber those reached by ESPN. These athletes have brought a great deal of popularity to Red Bull, plus the values of health, transcendence, dreams, and boundless possibilities.

Red Bull spends billions of dollars on marketing, with only a few of those funds allocated to traditional media, such as TV and newspapers.

By supporting extreme sports, Red Bull has positioned itself as a symbol of human strength and perseverance. This energy drink has gained global recognition.

Red Bull transmits values through storytelling rather than propaganda.

Red Bull's slogan, "Red Bull Gives You Wings," implies superhuman abilities and realizing dreams.

This is an example of endowing an enterprise with value. Through storytelling, Red Bull gained widespread recognition. Although it is believed that Red Bull could help reduce fatigue, the notion that it can provide limitless energy is merely a myth—which nevertheless serves as the foundation of the brand's values.

Value-oriented leadership can come from internal beliefs or conscious construction. It can build trust, connection, involvement, and support for a mission, be it a business, organization, or nation.

Consolidate a Country's Culture with Value

The establishment of value is key to the origination and sustainable development of human civilization. It is because humans share the same values that they are able to form a large society and specialize in labor.

Anthropologists have concluded that among the origins of many human groups, Homo sapiens[5] have become the common ancestor, due to their ability to tell stories, the stories convey and form common values which enabled them to build a vast human organization.

It is storytelling that binds human society together, creating a powerful community.

Why does storytelling empower humans to organize large groups?

This is because storytelling serves as a powerful tool for uniting large groups of people, as it enables the transmission of shared values and the establishment of exemplary models.

How do humans unite feelings and beliefs without individual contact? Storytelling conveys shared beliefs and generates shared emotions.

Nearly every civilization has its own flood story. In Hebrew culture, there is the tale of Noah's Ark; in Chinese culture, the story of Nüwa mending the heavens; and in Mesopotamia, there is also a flood narrative. These stories convey to humanity, to different ethnic groups, the process of struggle and the spirit of perseverance exhibited by their ancestors. Through the narration of these stories, values, and emotions are transmitted from one person to another, from one tribe to another, and from one generation to the next.

[5] Harari, Y. N. (2018). *Homo Deus: A Brief History of Tomorrow* (Illustrated ed.). Harper Perennial.

The earliest Chinese poetry is, after all, history; a treasure trove of accrued national experience, transmitted through stories.

The Bible chronicles how humans broke away from nature and rose above other species in the story of Adam and Eve. As part of nature like other creatures, Adam and Eve were originally unclothed. After eating the forbidden fruit, they felt embarrassed, highlighting the emergence of individual consciousness. This enabled them to have discerning thoughts and morality, break from nature, differentiating them from animals, and thus commencing humanity's destiny.

Humans are anxious about this evolution, which is the root of Western original sin. Tales transmit value; in this Christian narrative, humans began their finite life as a civilized race subject to birth and death, and the dichotomy of femaleness and maleness, conscious of honor and disgrace.

The values conveyed behind the story bring humanity together, forming a nation and a collective of people.

Nevertheless, throughout history, many ethnic groups have appeared, developed, and disappeared. Arnold Toynbee noted that at least 5,000 nations and civilizations have been lost in the flow of history. Why do some ethnic groups succeed while others decline? The answer lies in their beliefs and values.

It can be said that the Chinese nation's lasting 5,000 years can be partly attributed to the cultural representation of the Chinese dragon.

The legend of the Chinese dragon is one of the oldest in China; blending reality and fantasy. It is a product of national integration, and not whether it is true or false that matters, but the value it conveys.

The dragon is a symbol of the fusion of various ancient Chinese ethnic groups. The totem of the dragon originated from the merging of the snake tribe, which swallowed the bird tribe, thus adding wings that could fly. Subsequently, it also merged with the fish tribe, giving the dragon its scales. It further incorporated the deer tribe, resulting in the dragon having antlers. The dragon symbolizes the repeated integration of different ethnicities. This symbolism represents a belief and value that the Chinese hold, which is that in the face of conflict and so-called assimilation, no one has truly eradicated another. Instead, it's about a great melting pot where "you are within me, and I am within you." Thus, the values of integration, harmony, mutual growth, interdependence, coexistence, and mutual prosperity are emphasized in Chinese culture. These values are ingrained in the nation's ethos, disseminated throughout every corner of the land and within the heart of every individual, conveyed through generations of dragon legends, expressing the Chinese emphasis on holistic unity and harmonious integration.

With the concept of great unity firmly held, Chinese people firmly believe that the world, long divided, must come together. This concept has been handed down from one generation to the next through totems and myths; it has been instrumental in creating a unified country. Without these values, China would surely have fragmented like European countries. Through totems and stories, this value of great unity has been transformed into a strong faith for the Chinese people.

This kind of unified ideology, which emerged after the Xia and Shang Dynasties, became the orthodoxy of China. No authoritarian ruler could shake this ideology; instead, they were assimilated and dissolved by it. Even the Yuan Dynasty, despite its vast reach across Eurasia, similarly dissolved within this extensive land. The Qing Dynasty, as well as the earlier Five Dynasties and Ten Kingdoms of the Sui and Tang Dynasties, also existed within this immense crucible of values. It is values that consolidate a nation's history and shape the strength of a community.

Value constructs national culture, shaping its existence and development.

Value shapes the destiny of a country.

In the same vein, value determines an organization's prosperity, sustainability, decline, and survival.

The establishment of value is essential for a nation, country, and organization.

Confucius' great contribution was the transformation of political unity into a shared ideological orthodoxy which formed the basis of the nation-state. This allowed China to maintain national unity and cultural completeness, even amid invasions of the Central Plains by various ethnic groups. His importance far outpaces that of any emperor or great businessman. This is why Zhuang Zi said, "The services of the Dis and Kings are but a surplusage of the work of the sages."[6]

This book does not discuss national governance, instead emphasizing the importance of establishing values for organizational development, prosperity, and sustainability, ranging from businesses to NGOs.

---

[6] Legge, J. (1962). *The Sacred Books of China: The Texts of Taoism* (Vol. 2). New York: Dover Publications. p. 154.

Value-Oriented and Spiritual Leadership

Improving one's mental strength is an essential part of becoming a leader.

Some Buddhist and contemporary spiritual teachers, such as Krishnamurti and David Hawkins, have concluded that this world is composed of souls, which determine the evil or good, bitterness, joy, or happiness of human society.

Only those strong in spirit can attain high-achievement careers and bring greater joy to many.

What is a Mind? Is it Consciousness, Thought, or Emotion?

A mind is an intangible yet powerful entity, which spawns and shapes our thoughts, feelings, and awareness.

A mind is a repository of consciousness, where emotions, desires, and thought are kept.

At the start of World War II, Hitler seized the Czech Republic and Poland through blitzkrieg attacks, then subjugated Belgium and invaded France. 300,000 British troops were trapped in Dunkirk. At a critical moment, the British Parliament called upon Churchill, the least popular First Secretary of the Navy, to lead the British Cabinet. Churchill jokingly stated that the job was a punishment, as he was to save a sinking ship. Churchill was elected Prime Minister, as only he could confront Hitler's growing strength and aggression.

Britain had little hope. Only 300,000 troops faced off against 1 million Germans, with the British only able to withdraw at most 10%. Fearful, Cabinet ministers Halifax and Chamberlain urged Churchill to negotiate a peaceful occupation of Britain by Hitler. Yet, Churchill remained convinced victory was near.

Churchill told the British they would prevail. He gestured a "V" to the press to encourage the British. Yet, cabinet ministers believed Churchill was misrepresenting the British. Churchill was steadfast in his stance and convinced members of parliament and the British people. He vowed to safeguard Britain and ensure neither Buckingham Palace nor Windsor Castle displayed Hitler's banner.

Churchill didn't have strong military, political or economic clout, but he had powerful spiritual strength. His faith in freedom and affection for England made his heart strong.

Churchill knew the free world could never be defeated by Hitler and the British Empire could never be enslaved by totalitarianism. Such conviction inspired his strong will, uniting the British and Americans against the European battlefront. This led to the eventual defeat of Hitler, demonstrating spiritual power's superiority over material might.

As for Mao Zhedong, there are many different views on him, not only from Western society but also from Eastern society. Nonetheless, when we look at his early years, he conveyed a strong spirit. We can see his inner strength through his poems. It was his strong determination and inner strength that allowed him to guide the communist movement and conquer all of China in 1949.

Mao Zedong worked as a librarian at Peking University. He had been driven out of the Communist Party because he advocated peasant revolution, conflicting with great professors such as Chen Duxiu and Li Dazhao, founders of the Communist Party. Mao returned to his hometown in Hunan and wrote the renowned poem Qinyuan Spring in Orange Isle, Changsha, Hunan Province. This poem presents Mao Zedong's lofty ambitions.

> With crystal blue, the river is pervaded,
> And hundreds of barges are vying with each other for it.
> The eagles are striking the vast sky,
> And to the shallow bottom the fishes glide,
> All creatures strive for freedom in the rimed world.
> Being melancholy over the immensity,
> I ask the boundless land,
> Who decides the descent and ascent?[7]

He reminisced about the past, recalling moments with friends boating on the river. He wrote:

> With a hundred companions I once visited this very resort.
> Upon my recall, many eventful years remain vivid.
> Verily juvenile schoolmates were we all,
> Elegant in bearing and brilliant in talent;
> With a scholar's spirit so fervent,
> Being vigorous and unshackled.
> Pointing to the mountains and rivers,
> We boosted the writings seething and critical,
> And deemed the then noble marquises muck and dirt.

---

[7] Zhang, C., & Vaughan, C. E. (2002). *Mao Zedong as Poet and Revolutionary Leader: Social and Historical Perspectives.* United Kingdom: Lexington Books. p. 33.

Remember or not,
How we dashed against the waters in the midstream,
And the flying boat cuts into the surges stirred?[8]

Each of Mao's poems is filled with a strong and vigorous spirit, even in
the darkest of times. Compared to Wang Jingwei's (1883–1944)[9] poetry,
which is always sad and melancholic, it is like night and day. A person's
poetry represents their fate because it is a reflection of their innermost
thoughts. A feeble spirit cannot carve out magnificent verses, nor can it
create a grand history.

Mao Zedong's spiritual strength remained robust even during his most
challenging times. His fortitude was rooted in his unwavering faith in
China's destiny and Communism.

Chased by Chiang Kai-shek's troops from Jinggangshan, Mao
temporarily retreated and settled in Yanan, which became a base for
communists. With only tens of thousands of Communist troops, Mao
Zedong wrote another famous poem:

The northern scene,
A thousand Li ice-sealed,
And in the myriad-Li air the snow wafts about.
Behold within and without the Great Wall,
Nothing remains save a vastness of white;
And up and down the great river,
The torrents are suddenly lost.
Like silvery snakes the mountain dance,
And as waxen elephants the lands prance,
All want to match the sky in height.
Wait until a sunny day,
And see the gay attire and white wraps.
What an extraordinarily enchanting sight.
So charming are the rivers and mountains
As to have attracted countless heroes to vie for bowing in respect.
It's pitiable that Qin Huang and Han Wu,

[8] Zhang, C., & Vaughan, C. E. (2002). *Mao Zedong as Poet and Revolutionary Leader: Social and Historical Perspectives*. United Kingdom: Lexington Books. p. 33.

[9] Wang Jingwei was one of the revolutionary leaders of the KMT in the early twentieth century. Later, he turned against General Chiang Kai-shek, the leader of the KMT, and collaborated with the Japanese government in the domination of the southern part of China.

A little less bred in cultural accomplishments;
And Tang Zong and Song Zu,
Sort of deficient in literary talent.
The favorite with heaven for a day,
Genghis Khan,
Knew only bending his bow at the vulture in the vast.
All have passed away,
Those that can be counted brilliant characters
Are still to be seen at the present.[10]

At their lowest point, Mao remained strong-willed. Despite having limited military, political, and economic power, he eventually overcame Chiang Kai-shek and founded the People's Republic of China.

Mind-power surpasses material power, creating it through faith and value.

Mind-Power Unleashes Material Power

The mind is an Origin of Capital.

Mind energy determines our physical world and our fortunes. Willpower, compassion, faith, and values are what fuels it.

The mind can be seen as an existential force beyond time and space.

Power vs. Force: The Hidden Determinants of Human Behavior[11] by David Hawkins, an American medical scientist, shows that all the world's components, including the existence of matter, are streams of energy consciousness. The soul can be imagined as a floating butterfly, constantly changing shape. The butterfly's two wings do not exist in the same time or space; they transcend time and space.

Our mind is like a butterfly in the field of consciousness, interacting with other butterflies. When it flutters its wings, it causes turbulence and combines with other currents, even forming a whirlwind.

Everyone's spiritual consciousness interacts with that of others, forming the world we inhabit.

David Hawkins developed the Map of Consciousness via Kinesiology. The energy index of Jesus and Buddha reached 1000, while Lincoln

---

[10] Zhang, C., & Vaughan, C. E. (2002). *Mao Zedong as Poet and Revolutionary Leader: Social and Historical Perspectives.* United Kingdom: Lexington Books. pp. 66–67.

[11] Hawkins, D. R. (2014). *Power vs. Force: The Hidden Determinants of Human Behavior.* Hay House Incorporated.

and Gandhi's were 500, noteworthy scientists 400 and entrepreneurs/ philanthropists 300. Below 100 is an existence filled with hatred, fear, and shame.

David Hawkins has obtained energy indexes from thousands of tests, showing people's varying levels. Greatness, he believes, is attainable through a high index. Subsequently, our attitude and worldview are simply reflections of our energy. Reversing the cause-and-effect dynamic, he sees the mind as a product of the energy field producing its own causes. Consequently, our thoughts and ideas are dictated by our level of consciousness, so to make changes in our lives, we must first improve our energy.

How can we improve our energy index?

Hawkins believes that it depends on value and meaning. If one can live in value and meaning, one's energy field will improve.

Compassion can increase our energy field. Compassionate people can have an energy index greater than 400 or 500. Living based on values and compassion is key to boosting one's energy field and transforming their fortunes.

Why should we develop our spiritual energy? Because it is the key to all career accomplishments.

Why did Gandhi defeat the British Empire? Hawkins believed that Gandhi possessed strong spiritual energy. According to studies on muscle dynamics, Gandhi's spiritual power was estimated at 700, while the British Empire's energy field was mainly composed of selfishness and desire, and only had 100. Gandhi's success was therefore certain.

Nelson Mandela's energy index exceeded 500, while those white people in South Africa responsible for apartheid had an energy index of less than 200. Mandela ultimately achieved the presidency, safeguarding his country with acceptance and empathy, unifying black and white. His spiritual strength prevailed.

Everything is from within. One must be qualified for owning or obtaining anything. Michael Roach, author of *The Diamond Cutter: The Buddha on Managing Your Business*,[12] teaches business with *The Diamond Sutra*, a Buddhist classic. He always emphasizes that implanting goodness, compassion, and magnanimity in the mind is the key to a business' long-term success. Being generous, compassionate, and kind to

---

[12] Roach, G. M., & McNally, L. C. (2009). *The Diamond Cutter: The Buddha on Managing Your Business and Your Life.* United States: Harmony.

others and helping them will create a cycle of goodness and cultivate one's spiritual power, leading to career achievements.

Why can being compassionate and adhering to values be so powerful? According to Hawkins, compassion and values are powerful energies in the universe—mobilizing more energy to meet them. The universe is an interconnected energy field and our minds, like giant magnets, are moved by planet-like materials such as the sun, with the earth and seven other planets revolving around it.

Universal gravitation is invisible, as is a mind energy field. High energy fields can affect lower ones and a person with strong spiritual energy can significantly impact individuals, as well as history and civilization.

Ancient Chinese sages discussed the concept of "Qi" (氣), which refers to an invisible energy field. A person's Qi influences their fortune, and this Qi is the convergence point of their spiritual consciousness energy field. Hawking used chaos theory to explain the flow of the universe and human consciousness, which is composed of a series of unstable consciousness interactions. Within this chaotic flow of consciousness, what stabilizes a group of different interacting consciousness flows is something called an attractor.

Attractors constitute an energy field that, when our mind changes, gathers different consciousnesses to join our original stream of consciousness. As Hawkins always emphasizes, every stream of consciousness in the universe is interconnected and has the components that make up universal consciousness. When our compassion grows and we choose to be true to our beliefs and live in accordance with our values, we attract stronger consciousness to ourselves, creating attractors in the field of consciousness. As Mencius said, "I am skillful in nourishing my vast, flowing passion-nature."[13]

Wen Tianxiang, an ancient Chinese poet and politician, said, "Between Heaven and Earth, the positive Qi takes its shape in a variety of forms, and down here, it's in the rivers and mountains; up there, it's in the sun and the stars."[14] Ancient Chinese saints believed that heaven and man are united as one, in the sense of the Qi between heaven and earth that

[13] M. & Legge, J. (2011). *The Works of Mencius.* New York: Dover Publications. p. 189.

[14] Yang, Y. (2021). The Culture of Canonization: Reading Wen Tianxiang's "Song of the Noble Spirit". *Journal of East-West Thought September 2021.* California State Polytechnic University. p. 24. Retrieved from https://scholarworks.calstate.edu/downloads/r494vr33x.

interacts with that of people. As psychologist C. G. Jung noted, great achievers lead a small self to the collective subconscious of the universe. Wen Tianxiang distilled this into an idea of ever-changing things in the universe, each of which carries the spirit of righteousness.

Imagine a few hundred watts of electricity from a small bulb leading to several megawatts of electricity. When electricity leaves the light bulb, determined to lead to a power plant with several megawatts, it is not just a small light bulb that can shine, but the whole city that illuminates the Heavens.

It is no wonder that Christians want to live in the omnipotence of God and do not trust their own wisdom, but trust the Lord, because God will guide people. Through relinquishing attachment to one's own limited understanding, one gains more energy. This parallels the Indian philosophy of uniting Brahma and oneself. The power of Brahmas universe anticipates unification with the self and Brahma. The key to spiritual transcendence and success lies in the merging of one's body with the energy between heaven and earth.

The energy field we inhabit is based on the beliefs and values we hold that enable us to grow a stronger energy field. When someone remains true to their values, they will draw people of the same values to them. Helping others is highly regarded by everyone and altruism makes someone an attractive magnet to others. Altruism and aiding others combine energy fields.

The adherence to beliefs and values affects our energy and shapes our energy field. This theory is actually articulated very well by Mencius. Mencius said, "The will is the leader of the Qi. The positive Qi pervades and animates the body. The will is first and chief, and the Qi is subordinate to it."[15] Qi is determined and guided by the will, and it fills every part of our body.

In David Hawkins' experiment, the body can distinguish the authenticity of documents, poisonous substances and good and evil. Body muscles are full of consciousness that is determined by our beliefs and values.

Mencius continued to say, "Maintain firm the will, and do no obsolete the Qi …when it is the will alone which is active, it moves the positive Qi.

---

[15] M. & Legge, J. (2011). *The Works of Mencius*. New York: Dover Publications. p. 188.

When it is the positive Qi alone which is active, it moves the will."[16] If our beliefs are focused and unwavering, our energy field begins to change. No wonder Hawkins said that principle and focus on the present will change our field. When our energy field stabilizes in principle and concentration, our faith can exert enough strength. Faith upgrades our energy field and reconstructs and combines greater consciousness. This is what Mencius meant by aspiration affects emotions.

With a larger energy field, let us use faith to maintain it and draw out its full potential in an ascending spiral.

Faith and values determine the level of our energy field and success or failure. Gandhi and Mandela demonstrate the immense energy generated by beliefs and values which influences history.

Why might compassion lead to a larger energy field? Compassion holds a larger energy field due to its inherent openness and empathetic connection with others. This openness allows the energy of other consciousnesses to enter our own field. Conversely, emotions like hatred and selfishness create a self-imposed barrier, solidifying our energy field, halting its flow, and isolating it from other energy fields, thus diminishing its capacity to attract greater power.

At the core of Buddha's enlightenment lies the profound realization that the universe and all its elements are interconnected. Within the interdependent cosmic order, everything is interconnected and interdependent, with no single entity existing in isolation. This echoes Hawking's assertion that all energy fields in the universe are interconnected, forming a unified universal consciousness.

Just as Buddha perceived the oneness of the universe and all its beings, we too can recognize the inherent unity of all. This understanding eliminates the distinction between self and other, fostering the realization that benefiting others is akin to benefiting oneself. Through acts of altruism, we cultivate a more expansive and favorable environment for our own existence.

A leader who embodies the vastness of emptiness can encompass the universe within their embrace, as Master Huineng said, "The wondrous nature of people is originally empty; there is nothing that can be grasped.

---

[16] M. & Legge, J. (2011). *The Works of Mencius*. New York: Dover Publications. p. 189.

And the true emptiness of the essential nature is the same."[17] This emptiness signifies the expansion of the self to embrace others, and compassion serves as the foundation of this expansive heart.

From an energy field perspective, an empty heart signifies the connection of our individual consciousness to the universal consciousness. We transcend the confines of our personal energy field and merge with the collective consciousness, encompassing all energy fields. Within this dynamic and interconnected flow of consciousness, we harness compassion and altruism as unifying forces, cultivating a grand spirit and embodying a remarkable leader.

Values are Better at Creating Wisdom than Strategies

Beliefs and values may be more fundamental and accurate when making major decisions than strategies.

Strategy is always limited, boiling down to makeshift solutions that are short-lived and inadequate for long-term goals. Hence, enterprises seek new approaches instead of continuing with the old ones.

The strategy should not be discarded but rather take its foundations from core values. If a strategy fails, it should be revisited based on those values, and even adjustments at the practical level should be considered.

Good strategies help breakthrough obstacles and create new triumphs. All in all, strategies originate from a set of convictions and values. Someone with firm beliefs and values will explore every avenue to locate the best strategies.

In the Cuban missile crisis, then US President Kennedy's (1919–1963) advisers proposed two conflicting strategies: an airstrike to remove the nuclear warheads from Cuba, or diplomatic negotiations to persuade the Soviet Union to remove the missiles themselves. Faced with the prospect of a war, Kennedy tapped into his core values and beliefs, determined to bring peace and safety to the world. He had no intention to demonize the Soviets, instead seeking to avoid any situation that might lead to a conflict. With this as his motivation, he managed to restrain the US military while negotiating with the Soviets, ultimately bringing the 13-day Cuban missile crisis to an end.

---

[17] Huineng, D. (Eds.). (2014). *The Sixth Patriarch's Dharma Jewel Platform Sutra.* Buddhist Text Translation Society. p. xlv.

Strategies are essential for enterprises and organizations, but need to be grounded in their values and beliefs to avoid contradicting themselves in the future, which would otherwise put their survival at risk.

During the Warring States Period in ancient China, when Shangdang City in the Han State (403–230 BCE) was besieged by the military of the Qin State (822–305 BCE), Feng Ting, the chief of Shangdang City proposed to give the city away to the Zhao State (403–222 BCE). However, when the king of Zhao asked his ministers for advice, Zhao Bao, the Pingyang Duke argued that it was not feasible. Qin had been unable to take the city after long assaults, and would be extremely agitated if the Zhao State got hold of it. Nevertheless, the king of Zhao accepted the offer, as advised by Zhao Sheng, the Ping Yuan Duke. This situation made Qin very angry; it felt as if the piece of meat from its mouth had been snatched away by other wolves.

Qin attacked Zhao, and with their heavy troops, defeated Zhao's military at the Battle of Changping. Bai Qi (332–257 BCE), a Qin general, buried 400,000 surrendered soldiers alive. This battle gave Qin unstoppable momentum. Pingyang Duke had advised Zhao not to take the city to guard against Qin, but Ping Yuan Duke argued that Qin's attack was inevitable and the city could be used to bolster defenses.

Leaders often face two conflicting strategies, often focusing their decisions on tangible outcomes, which can lead to disaster. It is essential to take into account values and ideals when selecting a strategy; for instance, if Zhao had looked at both the advantages of taking the city, as well as the consequences in terms of justice, he would have realized that taking it would be unjust and could lead to negative results, and so would not have done so.

Values should take precedence over strategy, and self-awareness of one's values is critical to strategic success.

Psychology has demonstrated that although there are innumerable techniques to attain a goal, values and convictions remain fundamental. Teams and individuals with strong values and convictions will strive to create strategies for sustainable development. In contrast, they will either quit early or self-destruct due to internal disputes. Notably, when assistants present competing strategies, leaders should rely on their beliefs and values for decision-making.

Mobilize People with Value

Professor Herman Leonard of Harvard Business School visited Tzu Chi in 2009, and after meeting Master Cheng Yen, revealed to me privately that among the many political and social leaders he had encountered around the world, Master Cheng Yen and Nelson Mandela were two who led by values—Mandela being the former President of South Africa.

Mandela described the arduous struggle of the anti-apartheid movement in South Africa in his book *Long Walk to Freedom*.[18] Mandela held freedom and equality dear as his values and beliefs. After being imprisoned for 27 years, South African President Berta had asked him to sign a racial peace agreement in exchange for his release. However, Mandela refused, believing that only a free person could sign an agreement, and that an agreement signed by someone who was shackled would be both humiliating and invalid.

Mandela had a strong faith in the potency of love. He commented, "Forgiveness liberates the soul, it removes fear. That's why it's such a powerful weapon." With the value of peace and love, he forgave the prison guards who harshly treated him. In the end, he changed the ethnic relations in South Africa with peace and love instead of political struggle.[19]

In 1995, South Africa hosted the World Cup of football. Taking advantage of the game, Mandela, while president, was able to bridge the gap between black and white people in South Africa.

Before the game, President Mandela personally met the white captain, expressing the hope that the largely white-dominated team would win the championship and accept black players as main players. He also asked the teams to use the opportunity to teach football in country schools and help bring young people of different ethnic backgrounds together. During the match, blacks and whites were united in the fight for the South African team, and watched the game in solidarity, sharing both the disappointment of defeat and the joy of victory. The intense football competition brought out common feelings among South Africans, and eventually the team won their first championship. Through his efforts, Mandela had managed to create peaceable relations instead of resorting to tough legislation or confrontation.

---

[18] Mandela, N. (2013). *Long Walk to Freedom*. Hachette UK.

[19] Mandela, N. (2013). *Long Walk to Freedom*. Hachette UK.

A president with the greatest power in South Africa addressed racial inequality not by force, but through valuing praxis.

Universal Equality in Value Practice

Tzu Chi's mission exemplifies the concept of universal equality in value practice. While disparities may exist in wealth, ability, qualifications, and ethnicity, value can provide a common ground for equality among all individuals. Tzu Chi volunteers come from all walks of life—different social classes, races, and religions—and what unites them is a shared sense of value. Their motivation for volunteering stems not from a desire for salary or power, but from love—a profound and selfless love.

Despite their poverty, Tzu Chi's Zulu volunteers in South Africa dedicate themselves to volunteer work. Michael Pan, a Taiwanese volunteer entrepreneur who leads the Zulu volunteers, resides in a well-appointed residence; yet, his dedication to charity is no less than that of the Zulu volunteers who live in simple homes. The Zulu volunteers do not envy Pan's home because their love for service is equal. Pan's compassion serves as a model for the Zulu volunteers. Within the volunteer system, individuals from all social classes wear the same uniform, embodying the same values and demonstrating a powerful sense of equality.

Hierarchies exist within enterprises and organizations, and they serve a necessary purpose. Salary structures are not, and should not be, completely equal, as individuals contribute varying levels of ability, qualifications, and dedication. Recognizing these differences is a fundamental principle of equality. John Rawls emphasizes the importance of accepting inherent differences in individual abilities when discussing the true meaning of equality. Even with fair conditions and equal opportunities, people's abilities will lead to diverse outcomes. Rawls' concept of equality goes beyond equal opportunities; it also strives to ensure that the most vulnerable members of society receive the greatest support, with those who benefit most contributing the most.[20]

Another fundamental way of achieving equality is by embodying a shared set of values. Even if the most disadvantaged receive the greatest benefits, their desires will always be limitless. True equality lies in uniting people via a value system that promotes equality.

---

[20] Rawls, J. (1999). *A Theory of Justice*. United Kingdom: Oxford University Press.

Tzu Chi volunteers come from many races, incomes, and occupations. Yet, they unite in their shared desire to give selflessly with gratitude. They demonstrate equality and love, allowing givers and receivers, the wealthy and the destitute, to work together.

Employees in an enterprise or organization can never be equal; they possess different professions, different salaries, educational attainments, and qualifications. Blindly motivating them with salary, however, can lead to them demanding better treatment, becoming job-hoppers, or, worse, engaging in fraud and corruption. Such are potential outcomes of dealing with employees in materialistic terms.

Reasonable promotion and distribution of benefits in enterprises are necessary and this is a sign of enterprise wisdom. What is more crucial is creating and passing on values. Workers should not be treated equitably with business owners, and entry-level employees cannot expect the same pay as high-level executives yet still be united through shared beliefs and values. The key is for business owners to specify their beliefs and values and uphold them to guarantee a single-minded and highly motivated workforce.

The value established should not be based on slogans but rather on role models. Business leaders must genuinely and conscientiously practice their values in order to create role models among their staff.

A cleaner in a hospital is aware that their work is equally as important to that of a doctor when it comes to treating patients and both are of equal value. When a nurse recognizes themselves as an essential part of the medical field, understanding that saving lives is a sacred duty, they will not fixate on the disparity in compensation between themselves and the doctors. Despite the differing salaries of doctors and janitors, the distinctiveness of the nursing and medical professions, the value they embody is equal.

Only under shared values can people be united, equal, and harmonious, collaborating and loving one another.

Value in Work

In 2010, the Tzu Chi Foundation became officially registered in China. This was the first time the Chinese government had approved an overseas charity organization to establish a legal foundation in the country. For the past two decades, Tzu Chi volunteers from Taiwan and other parts of the world had been visiting remote areas of China to alleviate poverty.

Over the past half-century, Tzu Chi has attracted millions of volunteers to join its philanthropic endeavors. These individuals, at their own expense and with their own time, travel across the globe to provide disaster relief. What inspires them to dedicate their efforts so selflessly and without seeking any reward? The answer lies in value—the value of life, which finds expression through their involvement in charitable work.

In 2010, a Taiwanese-owned mega factory in China experienced a succession of employee suicides. Unpaid volunteers were doing charity work happily, yet paid workers were committing suicide in succession. Why?

The reason lies in the embodiment of value. Work must embody value. Tzu Chi volunteers find their life's worth through their charitable efforts. That's why they do it with joy, even without pay, even if they have to cover their own expenses and travel costs. Factory workers, on the other hand, receive a decent salary and have a good work environment with basketball courts, swimming pools, nice restaurants, and dorms. So why did a dozen or so suicides happen in a row? The reason is simple: they did not find their life's value.

Why is there a lack of value in their work? Because there's no belief in their work, only labor and material rewards. Because there's no love in their work. Love creates value, not being loved, but loving others. By loving more people, one can find their value in life.

Kahlil Gibran said, "All knowledge is vain save when there is work, and all work is empty save when there is love."[21]

We don't have to change our jobs frequently for a meaningful life; we can find it where we are. Why do we have these jobs? What is their purpose? It is unreasonable to turn our work into an ordeal just for money. Imagine how an assembly line worker would work if they saw their consumers as family. How would they be motivated to make quality and safe products then?

As a rule, enterprises are overly attached to income when motivating employees. In reality, true motivation derives from the love one feels in their work; that their work holds value. Not only should a boss love their employees, but employees should love the products and consumers they serve, so that their whole working process is fueled by love, making their lives all the more meaningful.

However, enterprises often strive to exhaust employees to their maximum potential for maximum production, where systems and outputs

---

[21] Gibran, K., & Bushrui, S. B. (2012). *The Prophet: A New Annotated Edition*. Simon and Schuster.

take precedence over individuals. Those subjected to an emotionless system won't develop an affinity for products and consumers. It is with love and care that an individual ultimately bonds with products and consumers; their eagerness and motivation are noticeably increased.

After Taiwan's 921 Earthquake in 1999, Tzu Chi helped reconstruct fifty schools in the affected regions, all of which were created by renowned architects and constructed with steel-reinforced concrete structures. Amazingly, the task was achieved within only two and a half years. Government Reconstruction officials remembered that anyone collaborating with Tzu Chi was just like a family member and would try to minimize costs and upgrade quality. Nonetheless, those who worked with the government had to be closely inspected to guarantee standards were met. What caused this disparity? It was because Tzu Chi's selfless love and principles of reconstruction made it clear to all its agents that Master Cheng Yen's mandate was to construct schools that would last for thousands of years.

Master Cheng Yen believes that during a disaster, schools and hospitals must remain standing. These facilities are vital for saving lives, with schools able to act as temporary shelters. This importance was tragically demonstrated during the devastating Wenchuan earthquake in China which was close to the proportions of Taiwan's 921 Earthquake in 1999, during which thousands of school buildings collapsed and tens of thousands of children perished. It is the responsibility of architects and builders to ensure that future generations are protected, by creating secure and reliable structures. Seeing this as a priority they should not regard this as a business but rather as an opportunity to express love through quality and cost-efficient construction.

The Hospital of Love Built with Love

Tzu Chi promoted construction site etiquette, believing that a building of love can only be built with love. I witnessed the construction of Taipei Tzu Chi Hospital, beginning in 2003. The construction workers became vegetarian and stopped smoking, drinking and chewing betel nuts, creating a clean construction site.

During the construction, the workers naturally changed their habits due to the sincere companionship and care provided by the volunteers. When the workers start their day and feel fatigue setting in after an hour or two, their usual remedy is to smoke a cigarette to relieve tiredness.

However, at this point, volunteers would bring fruits with warm and friendly greetings, saying, "Bodhisattva, you've worked hard, please have some fruits." The workers happily accepted the fruits, finding relief from fatigue and forgetting about the need to smoke. After a while, when the workers felt tired again and wanted to have a drink, the volunteers promptly brought iced tea. As the workers drank the iced tea, feeling refreshed and cooled down, they once again forgot about their usual desire for alcohol to alleviate fatigue.

In the beginning, the workers would go outside to buy pork chop meals for lunch, at TWD 100 (approx. USD 3.00) each. However, volunteers would provide nearly twenty vegetarian dishes at the construction site, all selflessly prepared and supplied by volunteers. Regardless of cost, each meal was priced at only TWD 20 (approx. USD 0.60), featuring delicious and diverse vegetarian options. Before the meal, the volunteers arrange the hand washing area in a clean and elegant manner. After washing their hands, the workers are respectfully greeted by volunteers who bow and offer towels, expressing gratitude. The workers had never experienced such treatment at any other worksite. Touched by this gesture, they not only savor the deliciousness of the vegetarian food but also brought their families to Tzu Chi's construction site to enjoy vegetarian meals, even on holidays when they are not working.

As a result, the construction site was free of cigarette butts, beer bottles, and betel nut residues. The hospital of love was built with love and its workers were ecstatic, feeling their work was making a difference. Forty-plus construction workers and supervisors became certified Tzu Chi volunteers during this project. The hospital was completed on schedule within two years, with the largest number of sky gardens in Taiwan.

It was love that motivated workers with value.

It is not only workers but also professionals and successful individuals who can find a sense of belonging and value in love.

Sanmao, the renowned traveling novelist; Leslie Cheung, the famous Hong Kong singer and actor; and Ni Min-jan, the noted Taiwan actor and comedian, all committed suicide. Throughout my career as a journalist, I've heard of many successful people taking their own lives. Why?

There could be many factors, but the primary reason for this is often the inability to find one's own intrinsic values. External achievements, after all, can be hollow unless we discover the inherent value within them.

People's values are liable to change. The emptiness felt after career achievements may drive individuals to seek love. However, when love brings disappointment, some may feel hopeless, ultimately leading to suicide. The act of suicide is not caused by love itself but rather by a profound sense of meaninglessness in life.

Emptiness drives many successful individuals who have achieved great heights in their careers toward drugs, sex, gambling, or even the pursuit of greater achievements. The consequences vary—some face legal penalties due to excessive greed, while others find themselves trapped in the quagmire of an unmanageable business scale. Some experience a decline in their well-being due to indulgence in luxury and excess, while others suffer physical deterioration from the overwhelming pursuit of accomplishments. There are those who, in their pursuit of wealth, end up in legal disputes with their children over inheritance. With desires boundless and values empty, countless successful individuals ultimately find themselves on a path toward decline.

Manifesting value is the core of work and the core of building a career. Steve Jobs pursued the idea of integrating technology with humanities, successfully transforming Apple computers and iPhones to change the course of human life.

Warren Buffett was the most successful investor in history. When his stocks rose, he kept food costs to just $6 a day, and just $3 when they didn't. Instead of luxury, he sought value. He created a wisdom in investment that allowed well-managed companies to access significant capital, thereby contributing to societal well-being. Assisting businesses in creating welfare is the value he firmly believes in, which is why he does not experience emptiness. He doesn't need to resort to vices like alcohol, sex, drugs, or gambling, nor does he risk losing the prosperous empire he has built due to excessive greed.

The value in work brings joy and energy to an individual, spreads happiness to those around them, ensures high-quality products, provides consumers with reliable goods, brings harmony to organizations, and offers entrepreneurs a sense of well-being and purpose.

SECTION 3: MANAGEMENT WITH LOVE

Kahlil Gibran's Poem on Work:

Life is indeed darkness save when there is the urge, and all urge is blind save when there is knowledge, and all knowledge is vain save when there is work, and all work is empty save when there is love.[22]

In 2002, when I began working at the Jing Si Abode, Tzu Chi Foundation's headquarters and a spiritual home lovingly treasured by Tzu Chi volunteers, I was struck with a newfound appreciation for working and management with love.

I left Taiwan's media industry and made my way to Hualien to join Tzu Chi. My office is at the Jing Si Abode, home to Master Cheng Yen, and where over 200 monastics live, farm, and support Tzu Chi's charity work around the world. In addition, Tzu Chi Charity Foundation employs over a thousand people with several hundred located at the Jing Si Abode.

Behind the Abode stands the towering Central Mountain Range. The verdant mountain skylines are even more striking against the azure sky. Jing Si Abode is surrounded by lush grass and farmland scattered with lush trees, with sunlight transforming into mottled halos. My office back then was located on the ground floor of a three-story building at the back of the Abode.

One time, when I walked out of the office and headed to the guest reception area, as I walked through the corridors, taking in my surroundings, it hit me that this was my home. A great joy filled my heart.

I believe that very few felt love in the workplace. Neither did I in the past. But then, I encountered Master Cheng Yen's way of management with love. When Tzu Chi members come to the Jing Si Abode, they all say that they are returning home. The Jing Si Abode is the home of all global Tzu Chi members.

When it comes to management, people tend to talk about systems and institutionalization. We often talk about managing a company, an organization and a government, but we do not talk about managing a home. Home is not to be managed, but to be loved.

Home is caring, tolerant, considerate, and willing to give without expecting anything in return. It won't cast out people for the mistakes they have made.

---

[22] Gibran, K., & Bushrui, S. B. (2012). *The Prophet: A New Annotated Edition*. Simon and Schuster.

Home makes us feel comfortable, safe, and warm. These indelible emotions in human life aren't attained by control. What do they stem from? Love!

Love in a home makes us feel safe, comfortable, warm, and comfortable. Why are they not a result of management?

Management means efficiency, duty, responsibility, and accomplishment—seemingly having nothing to do with love.

Business management does not rely on love; instead, it emphasizes efficiency, getting rid of those who lack competence, and making sure people accept that they come and go. A home, though, can remain a person's forever.

What if we treated a company like a home and our colleagues as family?

In Tzu Chi, we often witness volunteers traveling from overseas to report about their charitable work to Master Cheng Yen. After a meaningful dialogue, volunteers share pictures of their grandchildren, discussing their private lives. This demonstrates that Tzu Chi is a place where one can open up about personal matters. As a caring, parent-like figure, Master Cheng Yen treats everyone with the same amount of attention.

A home should be based on love, not interest. In Tzu Chi, volunteers hold value as the foundation and have dedication as their goal, not chasing after interest. Value pulls them to Tzu Chi; love keeps them devoted. They donate their money and dedicate themselves to disaster relief. Business managers often question how Tzu Chi can do all this; the answer is always value and love.

Especially, the power of love makes Tzu Chi a big family, where everyone feels at home. Those who have experienced hard times gain warmth from the love there. Employees are modestly paid; however, many professionals chose to significantly reduce their salaries to join Tzu Chi and be happy in their role. This is why; values and, especially, love come into it. Whether it be volunteers or admirers, anyone working with Tzu Chi every day knows that love is the key.

With lower incomes and heavier workloads, Tzu Chi's staff still devote decades to charity out of love. Love increases security and creativity.

By managing with love rather than interest, people will feel more secure, content, and inspired. Home is a person-oriented approach, paying attention to people, not just abilities. If we pick those with the right abilities and treat them with love in a pleasant atmosphere, their creativity will grow far more than in a tense setting.

Management with love means taking a people-oriented approach, tailoring tasks to individuals' talents, and providing the necessary resources.

In a management system of rules and regulations, humans must restrict themselves to conform to the system. In an overly structured system, the potential and creativity of individuals is stifled, resulting in mediocrity or oppression. Depression and various psychological diseases of modern people are mostly related to institutional pressure.

By contrast, in a people-oriented system, talents can reach their creative potential with the right resources.

Love makes people be themselves, rather than a tool of institutions.

However, individuals in modern society are institutionalized, leading to the relinquishing of individuality and the substitution of human emotion with institutional ones, resulting in a complete reliance on the will of the institution.

Management with love focuses on personal development, taking people as the starting point so that members of an organization can find resources and connect with their partners.

People-Centered Polycentric System

Holacracy, developed in Philadelphia, USA, is a polycentric system geared toward people; individuals are free to join teams, set market goals, and become centers of initiative. Everyone may draw on resources within and outside the organization, provided they comply with certain shared values and principles.

The practice of Tzu Chi volunteers adheres to this concept. There are more than 30 different sub-groups focusing on different aspects of Tzu Chi's missions, including groups focused on charity home visits, environmental protection, medical care, documenting, education, parent–child relations, entrepreneurs, etc. These sub-groups adhere to defined principles, allowing volunteers to design different plans to meet community demands. This is the people-centered approach that has enabled Tzu Chi to bring relief aid to 136 countries and regions.

In this people-centric, polycentric Holacracy, everyone is a free creator.

Nevertheless, management with love does not mean that individuals can neglect the organization's overall goals and principles. On the contrary, success in such a people-oriented organization is determined by its strong appreciation of values.

The organization permits individuals the freedom to devise their own contributions, but they must adhere to the core values. There is regular and ongoing training organized for Tzu Chi volunteers, so that volunteers understand the core value of giving without expecting anything in return. This is one of the important factors that make Tzu Chi's volunteer system so successful.

Family-Like Management

Management with Love means caring for employees' family life, as it impacts their job performance. Good leaders stay informed about employees' living conditions, offering suitable aid and support. Employees are viewed as both business friends and family members, who, when treated as such, are more likely to perform diligently.

In the year 2000, Dalin Tzu Chi Hospital (located in a rural area of western Taiwan) was established, with Dr. Chin-Lon Lin as its director. He embodied the humanitarian medical spirit of Tzu Chi, bringing it to life in this rural hospital located in a rice field. To attract excellent doctors to Dalin, a rural area in Chiayi, Dr. Lin knew that the love and idealism of Tzu Chi's medical care would be key. He led by example, getting up at six in the morning, inspecting the hospital grounds, and picking up any trash he saw, which deeply moved the younger doctors. Dr. Lin also established the Great Love Vegetable Garden at the hospital, where doctors and patients could garden in their spare time. He worked there himself every week. As Master Cheng Yen said, "Changing the work you do is a form of rest." Doctors enjoyed gardening in their free time, a different kind of labor that allowed them to be close to nature and relieve the stress of their medical duties.

Mrs. Lin, Dr. Lin's wife, known to everyone as "Mother Lin," was like a mother to everyone at Dalin Tzu Chi Hospital. She would make daily rounds at the hospital, caring for the well-being and emotions of the doctors and nursing staff. She was well-acquainted with the families of the doctors. She knew every detail about the families, including any happy news and the situations of their children at school. The leadership style of Mother Lin and Dr. Lin fulfilled Master Cheng Yen's vision— turning the hospital into a home, a big, loving, and warm family. Patients, families, doctors, nurses, and volunteers were all members of this large family, caring for each other without distinction. This familial atmosphere was a key reason doctors stayed in this remote area.

The establishment and operation of Dalin Tzu Chi Hospital not only created a large family within but also integrated love into the community, making the surrounding areas of Chiayi a large community family through selfless love, which in turn inspired more selfless love.

Dr. Lin, seen as a father figure by the hospital staff, would often organize outings on weekends for doctors to help clean homes in rural areas, particularly for elderly or disabled individuals who were amazed to see them cleaning their homes. This community involvement was another practical application of the hospital's work, and it let doctors experience the harsh realities of life, embodying Master Cheng Yen's hope that doctors learn from suffering and from patients.

In 2005, under Dr. Lin's leadership, doctors at Dalin Tzu Chi Hospital purchased farmland near the hospital and became farmers, establishing the Great Love Farm. Doctors personally farmed twice a year, sowing, transplanting, weeding, and harvesting. This farming experience let them feel the hard work of their patients, who were local farmers, deepening their appreciation for the difficulty of growing each grain of rice. The doctors, taking off their white coats to farm, learned humility and empathy, which touched and impressed the local community of Chiayi Dalin, who were moved by the doctors' willingness to share in their hardships.

The harvested rice was donated by the doctors, allowing volunteers at Tzu Chi to use the rice stalks during the annual end-of-year blessings, attaching them to red envelopes funded by Master Cheng Yen's book royalties, as a thank you to volunteers and committee members for their selfless service throughout the year, and as a blessing to Tzu Chi members worldwide. The rice symbolizes fullness and humility, the fruit of the sweat and love offered by the doctors and staff of Dalin Tzu Chi Hospital. The Great Love Farm also serves as a place to learn how to love.

The leaders' love is crucial for staff cohesion.

In ancient China, the renowned general Wu Qi (440–381 CE) once used his mouth to suck the wounds of a soldier. When the mother of this soldier heard about it, she shed tears. A neighbor asked her why she cried when General Wu Qi seemed to care so much for her son. The mother replied, "My husband was once also a subordinate of Wu Qi. Back then, Wu Qi also sucked the wounds of my husband. My husband was a fearless warrior, valiant in battles, willing to sacrifice his life without turning back. Eventually, he fell in battle." Now, seeing Wu Qi treat her son in a similar way, she knows that her son won't come back. That's why she is crying.

When a general genuinely loves his soldiers, the soldiers will go through fire and water, unyielding until death. This can be said with the old Chinese proverb, "A man of honor will lay down his life for one who understands him."

Zeng Guofan (1811–1872), a prestigious official in the late Qing Dynasty, also fostered solidarity and cohesion among soldiers with such general-soldier bonds. In Zeng Guofan's Hunan Army, Zeng would be appointed the corps commander, who would appoint division commanders who appoint brigade commanders, all the way down to platoon leaders, squad leaders, and soldiers. All appointed commanders and troops could find their relatives or neighbors in the army, so the troops are on a strong emotional chain. In this army, if a division commander died, then the division would be canceled. This was the same for all the units. Therefore, all soldiers would fight relentlessly to protect their leaders.

These bonds of love formed an invincible and unified Hunan Army.

Many soldiers who participated in World War I, World War II, and even the Vietnam War, when asked why they fought bravely, would not only mention it was for their country but also for their comrades. It was the love among comrades that compelled them to serve on the battlefield. In the main character of "All Quiet on the Western Front," even after many comrades had died, he felt like a stranger when returning to his hometown. His heart remained on the battlefield because his comrades were still there. Consequently, he willingly returned to the battlefield and died there. Love, in this context, deeply influences a soldier's soul, making them willing to sacrifice their lives.

Love is so powerful that people could die for it, let alone work hard for an organization or enterprise that only requires their ability and dedication.

Love is capable of eliciting the most devoted dedication from members of an organization.

In the shogunate era of lifelong employment, Japanese enterprises transformed employment into family-like ties. The employers used to be the duke of a traditional city-state shogunate, and the employees are the retainers. Employers are not only concerned about their employees' work performance, but their family life. They are familiar with each other and interact with each other frequently, which forms clan-like bonds. It is an employer's responsibility to take good care of the welfare of his employees. Employees should work for their employer and enterprise, which is like a big family, a big city-state or a big shogunate.

This practice is certainly the cultural legacy of the Japanese shogunate era. However, from 1980 to 1990, this lifelong loyalty foundation created the world's largest production capacity. During this period, the cohesion of Japanese employees was almost absolute, and the stable relationship between employers and employees made the production creativity and quality of Japanese automobiles far superior to those of American manufacturers. That is why American management scholars once shouted Japan as number one.

The love of human connections spawned the legendary Japanese entrepreneurship, and also formed Zeng Guofan's Hunan Army to revive the nation.

If the head of an institution shows love to their colleagues, the institution will become a loving family.

If the leader of an enterprise loves their partners, their enterprise will be a team of love.

If business owners can show their love for their customers, their field will be one of affection.

Loving Employees Means Guiding Them to Love Others

Franky Oesman Widjaja (黃榮年), from the Sinar Mas Group, Indonesia's second-largest enterprise, has been a volunteer for Tzu Chi since 1996. He generously donated his office to serve as Tzu Chi's first Jakarta branch. During the peak of the 1998 Indonesian riots, countless Chinese people were subjected to horrific incidents of death, rape and theft. Meanwhile, Tzu Chi volunteers in Indonesia, guided and encouraged by Master Cheng Yen, responded to hatred with love and continued the planned distribution of relief supplies and medicine. While many Chinese Indonesians were fleeing, Tzu Chi volunteers ventured further into the heart of Jakarta. In that year, Tzu Chi signed an agreement with the military to distribute aid to 130,000 households, including the poor and the families of 40,000 military and police personnel who had not received their salaries for several months and became beneficiaries of Tzu Chi's assistance.

Franky Widjaja's family business faced a huge crisis during the Asian financial crisis. Indonesia's inflation rate skyrocketed to dozens of times higher than before, four presidents changed in two years, and bank interest skyrocketed tenfold. Sinar Mas Group instantly became the world's largest debt-ridden company, with total debts of nearly USD

40 billion. Despite this adversity, Franky Widjaja and his father stayed honest and faithful, paying their interest as usual. Fortunately, their main management personnel didn't leave the company, sticking together to negotiate the postponement of repayments. Franky Widjaja also remained committed to his charity work with Tzu Chi.

More than a decade later, Franky Widjaja's own businesses (excluding those of his brothers) have grown to an asset value of USD 30 billion. He owns seventy times more land than of Singapore, and his over 400,000 employees have become Tzu Chi's donating members or volunteers, despite the fact that most of them are Muslims.

Drawing inspiration from his father's integrity and the teachings of Master Cheng Yen, Franky Widjaja was able to revive his enterprise. In 2002, he and his father led a team of entrepreneurs to Jakarta, to restore Angke River and resettle thousands of impoverished people in the newly-built Tzu Chi Great Love Village. Franky Widjaja was actively involved in the entire process, from cleaning up the river and distributing aid to supporting the free medical clinics and counseling residents during their temporary relocation to their eventual move into the Great Love Village.

In 2003, Franky Widjaja and Sugianto Kusuma (郭再源), along with other volunteer entrepreneurs, distributed 50,000 tons of rice to 5 million Indonesian poor households. He organized his employees into over 40 task forces, and they moved quickly. The Indonesian Muslim employees were deeply moved; their boss carried rice bags for several years and distributed them to the elderly while holding their hands as a greeting. Franky.

Widjaja and other entrepreneurs told me that, in the past, they had organized donations but Indonesians thought they were simply seeking forgiveness. Master Cheng Yen, however, required them to distribute necessities in person, which deeply moved Indonesians.

In 2016, Franky Widjaja made a pledge to find one million Tzu Chi donating members in Indonesia. He inspired his employees' love for helping others and encouraged more employees to become donating members. He first used incentives, giving each employee a raise and donating a portion of the raise to Tzu Chi in their name, which was met with enthusiastic approval from the employees. He encouraged employees to form charity teams to care for all the poor and disabled people within a five-kilometer radius of the plantations. By 2018, Sinar Mas had mobilized 1.2 million donating members, including employees and their families. These employees are all Muslims, and many have also participated in Tzu Chi's volunteer training to become certified Tzu Chi volunteers.

Sinar Mas' initiative to encourage everyone to do good has inspired its employees to cultivate compassion and gratitude, fostering a harmonious and appreciative atmosphere throughout the organization. This is a family of love, where it is not just about the employer loving the employees, but rather about empowering each employee to embody love for others and extend a helping hand. This truly exemplifies the essence of great love.

Franky Widjaja's goal was to have two million donating members by 2019, intending to call on more people to join charity, create jobs, and save fifty million Indonesians from poverty. He believes that with stable politics and society, Indonesia will become the fourth largest economy and population by 2040. He deems goodness to be the key to Indonesia's stability.

Franky Widjaja believes an enterprise without ideals, beliefs, and principles will become an Economy Animal. He strongly values honesty and trustworthiness for commercial and economic growth. He agrees that creating positive social value is paramount. As the CEO of Tzu Chi Indonesia Education Foundation, the Tzu Chi schools in Indonesia teach in Chinese, Indonesian, and English, aiming to nurture children's character and global vision and act as the breeding ground for future Indonesian leaders.

Charity creates a bond between business owners and employees, equal in value and grateful to each other. This book has long encouraged enterprises to prioritize values and beliefs rather than profit and money. Otherwise, ties between employees and business owners will be severed as they are connected only by self-interest and exploitation.

Advocating and practicing values and beliefs will make employees and business owners partners, striving for a common ideal and cherishing each other like family members. This is a case of management with love.

How to Love an Unfit Employee

Dr. Amartya Sen, a Nobel-winning economist, posed the question: what criteria should the employer use to select suitable employees?

A single mother needing income and liking a job might be inefficient and, at times, inebriated when at home. This is the type of candidate the enterprise should exclude.

A fit employee should be diligent, responsible, positive, enterprising, and productive. Will slothful employees in the enterprise that practices Management with Love be eliminated? Of course! But before that the enterprise could suggest to the employee to abstain from alcohol and concentrate on her work. After all, she is a single mother responsible for her family.

Management with Love is to unleash employees' potential; it does not imply insincerity or laxness when managing.

At the Tzu Chi Foundation where I work, every employee is conscientious and diligent. As they are aware they are working to help those in need, they remain productive and have no time for idleness. With everyone taking on a proactive approach, there is no place for slothfulness.

Why can a non-profit be more active and conscientious than a for-profit organization?

For NPO employees, no matter how hard-working they are, their remuneration will not see much improvement. Their industry is spurred not by the external rewards, but by the faith and perspective they have toward life.

Admittedly, remuneration is necessary, as are promotion and performance appraisal. Nonetheless, compared to enterprises with a strong material incentive, employees at NPOs are more driven by their love for people in need and for their co-workers and leaders. Since love motivates people to stay diligent, they would never slack off.

I have been with Tzu Chi for more than 20 years but have taken few vacations. In my tenth year, my family joined me in America as I was due to give a speech at Harvard Business School. We seized the opportunity to travel around New York, Boston, and Washington, and the entire trip was taken on private leave and at my own cost. This is how one's private life can benefit one's work.

For work, I went to the Harvard Business School to give a speech on Tzu Chi's disaster relief model and concept; for personal reasons, I took my family to tour the East Coast of the US. As it was a private trip, I took personal leave at my own expense. Tzu Chi does not take advantage of public funds, since it receives donations from various sources, and dedication is part of its values. I have been more active and demanding of myself in Tzu Chi than in any commercial organization. You cannot measure what you give and get in return, as life values and beliefs cannot be quantified and one always feels that they have not done enough.

This is especially the case with Master Cheng Yen as an example. She wakes up at 03:30 every day to lead morning classes for practitioners. At 05:15, she begins a one-hour lecture. Within ten minutes of finishing breakfast, she is preparing for her next lecture at 07:00, then listens to volunteers and directors until 08:25. At 08:45, meetings continue. Following a one-hour nap at noon, she then continues with more meetings all afternoon. In the evening, Master Cheng Yen responds to phone calls and reports from overseas branches. Whenever there is time, she will prepare for the following days' lectures on sutras, and watch programs on the Da Ai TV. Day after day, the routine remains unchanged. The diligence of her disciples and managers cannot compare to Master Cheng Yen's busy schedule. If she were a CEO of a company, she would be the most hard-working one out there. She is the most stalwart member of Tzu Chi.

Under the leadership of Master Cheng Yen, no one would want to rest more and do less, nor would they want to lead life aimlessly. Master Cheng Yen cares deeply for all beings, not just herself. She was the first, and forever, Tzu Chi volunteer—a shining example of character and endeavor. With such guidance, how could anyone think they have a license to slack?

Master Cheng Yen's diligence, sincerity, and love have inspired the hard-working staff of Tzu Chi. Her example has been followed by managers, who in turn set an example for the rest of the staff.

Think of business owners who become rich through diligence. If the owner still perseveres after success, the employees will naturally follow suit. However, if the business owner opts for a luxurious lifestyle, his staff may feel less motivated. It is hard to switch from extravagance to thriftiness. The luxurious lives of business owners and higher-ups can give the idea to grassroots workers that their efforts result in only a select few living lavishly. This will greatly reduce corporate cohesion, and they may choose other opportunities that offer better remuneration.

Surely, few grassroots employees would think their talent or fortune is equal to that of business owners, nor their income. Nonetheless, the luxury enjoyed by business owners may give employees the notion that work is only for self-indulgence, inciting them to find a more comfortable work life and, in turn, slack off.

Business owners must demonstrate that a business is to manifest an ideal and motivate their employees to work hard.

The Power of Leading by Example

Zeng Guofan stated in his correspondence from home that the only way to manage a household is through diligence and frugality, which is also paramount for any enterprise. No matter how successful, companies must be diligent and prudent, inspiring the same of their staff. If an entrepreneur and their family become excessively indulgent with success, the enterprise may soon be spiritually devastated, despite giving employees generous pay and incentives.

Management with Love does not mean being lax or effusive in management, but rather managing based on values, hard work, and thrift.

Warren Buffett lives a frugal life, eating McDonald's and drinking Coke. He makes his money not for pleasure but for self-fulfillment. His wealth and success are not to fulfill his own wants but to practice life values.

The founder of IKEA lives a simple life and is known as the poorest millionaire. He upholds his values by offering his global consumers a simple, independent, frugal, yet elegant lifestyle.

Warren Buffett's accomplishments demonstrate that it is beneficial for individuals to utilize market trends to benefit businesses and society through their financial acumen.

They all lead diligent and frugal lives.

Once when I was in conversation with Master Cheng Yen, one of the Abode masters brought me a bowl of dessert. When I finished, there was still a small amount of residue left in the bowl. Looking at me, Master Cheng Yen reminded me to finish every drop, teaching me a lesson on frugality. According to the Abode masters, the room in which Master Cheng Yen receives guests is never fully lit as it would waste electricity. This is what they have learned through her example.

Additionally, Management with Love must be rooted in self-improvement. Individuals must comply with the standards and principles of any organization; otherwise, chaos and dissolution could result. Principles are fundamental to keeping the organization loving and people-focused.

There is a Tzu Chi volunteer and entrepreneur from Sichuan who has thousands of employees. After joining Tzu Chi, he noticed his workers were discarding a vast amount of leftovers. However, his message of frugality didn't always get across. One time, he saw an employee throwing away food that had barely been touched. Rather than reprimand him, he gave him a gentle smile and said, "It looks delicious! If you no longer want it, I'd be happy to help you finish it." He then sat down and ate the leftovers.

Conceivably, the employee would have feared that he would be reprimanded. But in the end, their boss had just taken the leftovers. Embarrassed beyond measure in front of so many onlookers, the employee wanted to disappear and vanish. No one has had leftovers since then.

This is the virtue of frugality and management with love that leads through example, not admonishment.

Employees' Autonomy and Entrepreneurship

Traditionally, companies are not governed democratically like governments; they usually follow elite governance and authoritative governance models. However, there is a large Spanish corporation called Mondragon Corporation (M.C.) that has successfully achieved a significant level of employee governance and autonomous entrepreneurship.

The Mondragon Corporation has a market value of 20 billion euros with a history of 60 years. It is hard to imagine that this large company was founded by a Basque[23] priest named Jose Maria Arizmendiarrieta. The Mondragon Corporation is a world-class cooperative, and what makes it especially unique is that 80% of the company's shares are owned by all employees.

After the Spanish Civil War of 1941, Jose Maria Arizmendiarrieta arrived in the parish of Mondragon as a priest. He found the area struggling with poverty, depression, and high unemployment; in response, he set up a company where all could support one another. He first established a training college for the local youth, which had its inaugural cohort of five graduates in 1956. This group created a business producing cookware and stoves. This venture soon became the largest industry in Basque and the seventh largest in all of Spain.[24]

---

[23] The Basques may be descended from the residents of the Paleolithic period in Europe. Their main language is Basque, which has essentially no connection with the Indo-European language family. This suggests that the Basques have been present in present-day France and Spain since before the Indo-European nations entered Europe.

[24] Ricard, M. (2015). *Altruism: The Science and Psychology of Kindness*. United Kingdom: Atlantic Books.

José María Arizmendiarrieta's concept guided the creation and growth of the company. In 1959, several entrepreneurs founded the Financial Assistance Alliance, "Caja Laboral Popular Corporation de Credito," geared toward helping their employees establish new companies independently. By 2010, the Alliance's assets were worth 20 billion euros.

The Mondragon Corporation now has over 250 businesses, half of which are cooperatives. In 2010, 85,000 employees were employed, with 43% being women, and the annual revenue exceeded €30 billion. Between 80 and 85% of the workforce owns the firm's equity or a role in running it.

Every year, at the shareholders and employees meeting, shareholders and employees democratically elect, appoint, or lay off managers. The one chosen has the authority to decide the company's running and financial usage.

More importantly, the salary gap is limited to a maximum of 600%. 25% of the surplus revenue is invested in R&D for highly innovative products. The company has established a university with 4,000 students.

When Gardien, a British journalist, visited the company, a staff member said, "This is a home, not a paradise. We are still striving for its survival and advancement."

Although the efficacy of staff governance needs to be proven over a longer period, the British journalist concluded that while in Spain unemployment was as high as 25%, economic mismanagement outside of government control, and the banking system's collapse, the company's operations were like an oasis in the desert.

To love employees as family requires both faith and welfare. Moreover, Management with Love encourages employees to love others.

SECTION 4: GOVERNANCE WITH PRINCIPLES

Kazuo Inamori founded the Kyocera Group at twenty-eight. He said that, due to his inexperience, he always applied the principles of fairness and proper social norms whenever he had to make decisions. He consulted his conscience for guidance, trusting his instincts over strategies, abilities, and quick fixes. In other words, Inamori's early choices were guided by values and principles. This approach bore fruit as he eventually created an enterprise worth trillions of yen, earning him the nickname of the "God of Japanese Business" for saving Japan Airlines.

Returning to values and principles, Kazuo Inamori has created a Kyocera company with outstanding achievements.

Value, not strategy, is the key to sustained growth for businesses.

1994 was one of the tensest years in cross-strait relations between China and Taiwan. The Qiandao Lake (Thousand Islands Lake) incident, where a group of Taiwanese tourists were robbed and killed on a boat, causing deep dismay in Taiwan. Lee Teng-hui, then the President of Taiwan, R.O.C., denounced the Chinese mainland and stirred up the people's emotions. Nonetheless, Tzu Chi still continued to provide charity and disaster relief in China. As a consequence, some Taiwanese people with extreme statements refused to donate to Tzu Chi and threatened to rent a tour bus to Hualien to besiege the Jing Si Abode, its headquarters.

Some newspapers harshly criticized Tzu Chi's disaster relief in China. Public pressure was intense, yet many senior Tzu Chi leaders and even closest aides were unable to convince Master Cheng Yen to halt the relief. She implored, "Alright! If Tzu Chi doesn't want to help, I, Master Cheng Yen, will go and help alone! We are helping people abroad; why wouldn't we help our compatriots on the China, who share the same language and culture?".

This is how the Tzu Chi founder made decisions by values: to always aid the needy, regardless of opinion. This unwavering determination led Tzu Chi to become the first non-profit organization to be legally registered in China, carrying out charitable work in its 30 provinces. And the same determination, is why Tzu Chi has grown to be one of the largest NGOs in the world.

Chairman Lim Wee Chai (林偉才), a Tzu Chi volunteer and entrepreneur in Malaysia, founded Top Glove in 1991—now the world's largest glove manufacturer, with a global market share of over 25% and annual revenue in 2023 of MYR 2.257 billion (around USD 473 million). His success is attributed to his commitment to principles.

At Top Glove, every employee, including Lim himself, must wear a badge stating "No Bribery, No Corruption, Bribery is a Crime." There is no room for kickbacks at Top Glove. Lim informed me that his and his employees' adherence to these principles was instrumental in his success. Additionally, no smoking is allowed in or out of the company by its 22,000 employees as Lim believes healthy employees are pivotal for a business' longevity. Notably, Lim values and upholds cleanliness, health, and protection for the manufacture of surgical gloves, thereby fostering a substantial amount of good will from the public.

Lim told me that a great enterprise must have a strong foundation. I asked what this foundation was, and he said "principles." He is known for adhering to these principles.

He stated that, due to the badges worn by members of staff, only a few producers had the courage to request kickbacks. He requested for his employees to abide by the Five Healthy Wells: Clean Well, Eat Well, Work Well, Exercise Well, and Sleep Well. He firmly prohibits smoking on the premises of both public and private establishments, as it is a hazard to their health. He recommends meeting with a nutritionist regularly to ensure that the employees' diet is balanced. At Top Glove, there is a policy in place that requires employees to get seven to eight hours of sleep per day, exercise for at least half an hour, and show a positive and proactive mindset while on the job. He also emphasized the importance of being punctual and enforced this by posting a board outside the meeting room with the note: "Say sorry when you are late to the meeting."

The key to Top Glove's success is adhering to values and principles in providing customers with protective, clean, and hygienic gloves. Hence, all staff must be physically and mentally pure and healthy.

Lim Wee Chai practices principles not through words, but by example. After all, people judge based on others' actions, not words.

Integrity-Based Business

Sugianto Kusuma (郭再源), a Tzu Chi volunteer and entrepreneur in Indonesia, was conducting any form of business for gain prior to joining Tzu Chi. Since then, he has taken on the teachings of Master Cheng Yen, abstaining from all activities that would be detrimental to society. As a consequence, his business has grown substantially over the last decade, and his wealth has multiplied by dozens-fold.

The reason is that after he devoted himself to charity, he decided to stop all detrimental undertakings, and as a result, he attracted more good enterprises, setting a better social reputation. People trust him more and many resources proactively seek him out.

After joining Tzu Chi and learning Buddhism, his goal shifted from chasing wealth to facing wealth with principles. Kusuma mentioned that he adopts a view of wealth based on conditions. He doesn't pursue earnings that shouldn't be made, cannot be made, or don't have the right conditions. This non-insistence, not chasing money based on desires, is a principle for accumulating wealth. This principle has not only prevented his wealth from decreasing but has actually made him even more prosperous.

Kusuma's principles of life are not only evident in his views on wealth but also in his attitude toward life. He mentioned facing five major challenges, including illnesses, some of which were potentially life-threatening. In 2016, he experienced widespread misunderstanding and criticism from the public, even facing legal proceedings, but the court later confirmed his innocence. Kusuma shared that when facing challenges, he does not blame the heavens or others; instead, he sees it as his own karmic obstacles, bravely facing and dealing with them, hoping to eliminate negative karma. Master Cheng Yen brought wisdom to his life and gave him her blessings, helping him overcome the five major challenges in his life.

With the principle of not making any undeserved money, Kusuma accumulated even more wealth, enabling him to safely ride out life's crises and enjoy a broader life. A notable Indonesian philanthropist, he has accompanied the President of Indonesia on multiple visits to disaster sites, and, through his efforts, Tzu Chi has entered into a partnership with the military to aid in disaster relief. For instance, following the 2015 earthquake in Nepal, Tzu Chi in Indonesia worked with the Indonesian military to quickly transport materials and personnel by special plane. Additionally, Kusuma facilitated Tzu Chi's cooperation with the largest Islamic group to pursue educational and charitable projects in harmony and cooperation with other religions.

Kusuma began a small enterprise with his father from a young age. His father's last words prior to his demise were that he left no possessions but rather his good name and credibility as his greatest inheritance. Kusuma remarked that foreign credit and mutual aid would help Chinese entrepreneurs abroad to stand and succeed.

Sugianto Kusuma's father showed him by example the importance of conducting business with integrity and faithfulness, instilling lessons that he would then pass on to future generations. This echoes the teachings of Master Cheng Yen, who emphasizes the importance of leading by example. In business, one must adhere to the principles of "sincerity, integrity, trustworthiness, and practicality."

Kusuma's outlook on life is that as long as his business principles and orientation are correct, he won't be afraid of making rectifiable mistakes. Most importantly, he must maintain the principle and orientation.

Sugianto Kusuma is true to his word to Master Cheng Yen and always answers her requests with "No problem!" He was thus nicknamed Mr. No Problem. He practices what he preaches. From keeping his word in dealing with various people in the past to keeping principles in Tzu Chi where he became a convert to Buddhism, his life value has grown into a new realm. In Master Cheng Yen's eyes, he is the rich among the rich (both materially and spiritually wealthy).

Faithfulness must be rooted in integrity and sincerity. Master Cheng Yen encourages entrepreneurs to act with sincerity, integrity, trustworthiness, and practicality, to be trustworthy, and to demonstrate their values through tangible actions—just as Lim Wee Chai and Sugianto Kusuma do.

After joining Tzu Chi, Sugianto Kusuma managed his company with goodness, leading to increased endorsement from employees and their families, as well as greater social recognition.

Goodness is essential for enterprises to develop sustainably. Sugianto Kusuma noted it exists in practice. What impact can charity have on society? The answer lies in inspiring more entrepreneurs to embrace goodness through their actions.

This stands true for companies as well. Practices must be put in place to encourage goodness within an enterprise.

Thanks to the efforts of Sugianto Kusuma and other Indonesian volunteers and entrepreneurs, Tzu Chi greatly improved the social standing of the Chinese in Indonesia within a few decades. Tzu Chi provided an avenue for the Chinese to positively contribute to Indonesian society. Charity became a hallmark of the Chinese in Indonesia, thus granting further security of life and business. Over the past ten years, the anti-Chinese riots have steadily declined due to the acts of Chinese philanthropy. In 2007, the Indonesian National Assembly passed an equality law that enabled the Chinese to learn Chinese again. Congress members informed me this was a result of the Chinese's charitable work in Indonesia.

Responding to hatred with love is the only way to put an end to hatred. Doing good only returns good, which is an undeniable truth.

Tzu Chi's charity work has broken down three barriers in Indonesian society: racial, economic, and religious. They supported the Al Ashriyyah

Nurul Iman Islamic Boarding School, reshaping its teaching philosophy and revising students' outlook on life. Changing their original idea of jihad as a means to combat enemies to a concept of jihad as a spiritual combat against inner evil, the students now learn not only the Koran but also Master Cheng Yen's Jing Si Aphorisms. These efforts have led to the dissolution of social divides, with entrepreneurs such as Sugianto Kusuma and Franky Oesman Widjaja determined to help alleviate poverty for 50 million Indonesians. This is the power of goodness, transforming Indonesian as well as Chinese people's fortunes.

Goodness is the foundation of business growth, social harmony, and national prosperity.

Section 5: Innovation with Compassion

Capitalism drives creativity with profit and competition. Can compassion be a driving force behind creation? Yvon Chouinard, founder of Patagonia, innovated pitons that didn't harm the mountain, driven by his empathy and love of nature. He also created organic and pesticide-free cotton clothes, due to the potential harms of conventional clothing, which provided a new business peak and helped California's organic cotton growers prosper.

Compassion is the source of creation. As Steve Jobs said, consumers may not know what they want, and enterprises bear the responsibility to bring them the best products and the greatest benefits.

If profit is prioritized, producing low-cost products that buyers accept is all that enterprises need. However, successful large enterprises last the longest if they create benefits for the consumer. Steve Jobs' dream was to give people the convenience of science and technology, best symbolized in the smooth sliding of their fingers on an iPhone screen. After seeing his daughter download music on her computer, he developed an iPod so consumers could download thousands of songs simultaneously. Thanks to the iPod, songwriters made huge profits. Caring for public interest is compassion and a path to success for companies of moral standing.

Innovate with Compassion

Tzu Chi's missions of charity, medicine, education, humanistic culture, environmental protection, bone marrow donation, international relief, and community volunteerism have all been founded out of love. DA.AI

Technology Co., Ltd., which specializes in making eco-blankets from PET bottles began as an act of love and devotion to the earth and disaster survivors.

The Jing Si multipurpose foldable bed and chairs were created in 2009 during Tzu Chi's disaster relief in Pakistan. Master Cheng Yen could not bear to see a photo of a newborn baby lying on the ground at minus two degrees and urged the Tzu Chi International Humanitarian Aid Association to develop a portable and folding bed for refugees. Subsequently, it won the Red Dot Award in Germany and Gold Label Awards at the Pittsburgh International Invention Exhibition. This development was not driven by profits or competition; it was an act of great love for humanity and the earth.

During the rainy season in 2015, after the earthquake in Nepal, Tzu Chi's foldable bed enabled refugees to avoid sleeping on muddy ground. Now, both Taiwan's firefighters and disaster relief police have adopted them, and they have also become a form of income for the Jing Si Abode. Compassion not only facilitates charity but also generates economic advantages.

James Lee (李鼎銘), one of the founders of DA.AI Technology Co. Ltd. associated with Tzu Chi, told me he was inspired by Master Cheng Yen's altruistic empathy to dedicate himself to DA.AI Technology. This non-profit social enterprise had an annual income of about NT$150 million and is now the biggest of its kind in Taiwan.

DA.AI Technology uses recycled PET bottles to make blankets, clothes, handbags, windbreakers, and suits. Its research and development of over 1,000 products arose out of compassion for the environment and a sense of responsibility in promoting environmental protection through social education. All earnings are donated to Tzu Chi for disaster relief and cultural education. James Lee is a Tzu Chi volunteer, providing unpaid service, and his family has joined him in this charitable endeavor as well.

In 2015, a water park dust fire explosion in Taipei severely burned over 500 college students, causing them to experience skin-peeling-like pain during treatment. To protect healing skin, the team from DA.AI Technology developed a pressure suit that provided adequate ventilation and the right amount of tension. Now, DA.AI Technology's pressure suit is a global leader in its industry.

This is how compassion is the source of an enterprise's creativity.

The Practice of Compassion

The Compassion and Altruism Research Center at Stanford University held an 8-week meditation experiment, wherein participants showed much-improved compassion for others and communal recognition. It can be seen that compassion is innate and can be heightened and strengthened through meditative practice.[25]

Fundamentally, an effective way to cultivate compassion and altruism is by engaging people in charitable activities.

In Tzu Chi, many entrepreneurs may initially take part in charity due to their social connections. Nevertheless, once in charity, their compassion is likely to be awakened.

Michael Pan (潘明水), a successful Taiwanese entrepreneur in South Africa, initially did not take part in charity willingly, but only reluctantly assisted his Tzu Chi volunteer neighbor in taking and handing out necessities to the needy. After finishing the distribution, he felt happy and fulfilled, realizing that being a volunteer was so rewarding. Following that, he dedicated his life to charity and became a devoted Tzu Chi volunteer.

It is evident that even if one's initial mind is not compassionate, it can be enlightened through altruistic acts.

Michael Pan discovered later that the men in South Africa had no work, and women had no employment. He began gathering scrap fabric from Taiwanese factories and established sewing classes in local tribes.

Inspired by Michael Pan's love, Zulu women sold their clothes to earn money and donated 5% of their income to set up a sewing class in a neighboring village. With this self-reliance, over 10 years later, there were more than 600 sewing classes with 25,000 Zulu women learners in Durban, and nearly 7,000 of them became members of Tzu Chi as volunteers.

During holidays, dressed in Tzu Chi's blue and white uniforms, they visit and support the elderly living alone. In South Africa, 22% of the population suffers from AIDS. These Zulu volunteers also regularly visit and assist AIDS sufferers, although they themselves remain in poverty. Nevertheless, their generous spirit enables them to aid those more in need than themselves.

---

[25] Ricard, M. (2015). *Altruism: The Science and Psychology of Kindness.* United Kingdom: Atlantic Books.

Michael Pan and the impoverished Zulu women both demonstrated their inner compassion in action, demonstrating enlightenment in practice.

To enlighten one's compassion through charity and philanthropic action carries the greatest strength.

Similarly, encouraging employees to take part in charity builds their compassion and altruism.

Innovation with Concentration

Steve Jobs was the most outstanding inventor of the twenty-first century. Behind his great endeavor, he pursued a spiritual life and enjoyed meditation. Much of his creation came from the intuition of his inner life.[26]

His intuition drove him to go beyond existing life patterns, be enterprising and creative, aiming not to defeat competitors but to improve people's lives.

Job's innovation combined altruism and intuitive imagination; a fundamental driving force of human nature.

Hegel once said that creation stems from people's imagination. Through imagination, they can break away from reality and explore unexplored realms. Imagination is not mere fantasy; it requires one to have a well-cultivated culture. Personal cultural caliber plays an integral role in economic innovation.

After dropping out of college, Steve Jobs didn't idle but took a calligraphy course, learning much about the past blended with art and aesthetics. This impacted how he blended art with tech later.

The biographer of Steve Jobs, who also wrote biographies of American founding father Benjamin Franklin and inventor Thomas Edison, highlights a significant key to Steve Jobs' success related to his meditation practice.[27] Jobs had studied Buddhist meditation in India and practiced Zen meditation in Japanese monasteries. He immersed himself in the elegance, dynamism, and liberated nature of Zen, appreciating the

---

[26] Isaacson, W. S. (2012). *The Real Leadership Lessons of Steve Jobs, Harvard Business Review* (April 2012 Issue). Massachusetts: Harvard Business Publishing.

[27] Isaacson, W. S. (2012). *The Real Leadership Lessons of Steve Jobs, Harvard Business Review* (April 2012 Issue). Massachusetts: Harvard Business Publishing.

beauty of Japanese Zen monasteries. This interdisciplinary learning and cultivation laid the foundation for Steve Jobs' innovation.

Steve Jobs learnt the value of focus through meditation. Having returned to Apple in 1997, he convened 100 key staff members at a meditation retreat to talk about the most important objectives of the company. On the final day, Steve Jobs wrote out ten goals on a blackboard based on everyone's thoughts. Eventually, he crossed off the last seven objectives, leaving only the top 3.

Innovation requires focused concentration, which can be attained through meditation. Conversely, blindly chasing all will yield no innovative results.

When Jobs rejoined Apple, he reoriented the company from its focus on marketing to one on product innovation. This was a direct contrast to the approach of former president Sculley, who Jobs had recruited from PepsiCo. Differences of opinion led to Jobs' dismissal by the board of directors, while Sculley had put too much emphasis on making profits, marketing, and new product functions, raising product prices. This allowed new competitors with equally good but cheaper products to gain market share and put Apple in a difficult situation. When this happened, Apple had no choice but to plead for Jobs' return to save them.

Jobs launched the Mac Air, iPod, iPad, and revolutionary iPhone. He changed his focus from marketing to innovation, and the MacBook became a leader in tech development.

Focusing on innovation rather than profit was the key to Steve Jobs' successful entrepreneurship.

Particularly, the development of innovations that benefit all humanity is crucial to the success of a business. This is the most valuable legacy of Steve Jobs to entrepreneurs of future generations.

Innovation with Equality

In a case study of contemporary commercial organizations, Harvard University proposed the term "Agile," meaning small-unit operations to better serve consumer needs. Frontline staff innovation can better reflect market demands.

The recent issue of Harvard Business Review mentions that large organizations are breaking apart their giant systems into hundreds of small Agile units, leaving it to the members of the small unit to do research and manage quality on their own. In such scenarios, the Agile management model succeeds only if the staff has consistent ideologies with the managerial layers, otherwise, the quality of the product is hard to control.[28]

This concept of consistency should be viewed not as profit-driven, but with compassion and altruism for consumers. If driven by profit, product deficiencies will be more obvious. However, beginning with compassion and altruism for consumers, Agile will be much less likely to produce faulty products that could have been avoided.

Companies that adopt Agile or Holacracy currently aim for leadership in small units to increase creative efficiency and foster better communication.

The big companies' innovation models may involve cultivating compassion, which Harvard Business Review had never discussed. This will ensure members strive to create and not harm business, and prioritize consumer and environmental interests. Cultivating compassion among members should be a priority for horizontal, decentralizing organizations.

Section 6: Round Organization

The concept of pyramid organizations and societies has dominated humankind for centuries, with elites holding decision-making power as an unspoken rule. This inequality and class opposition created by such structures have continued to plague human society for centuries. Could a round organization, which does away with top-down and bottom-up control, and instead allows people to flow up and down based on skills beyond rigid distinctions, be feasible in practice?

In 2003, Master Cheng Yen created a volunteer system that divided certified Committee members into four teams: Unity, Harmony, Mutual Love, and Joint Effort. The Unity team consists of the most experienced volunteers while those within the Harmony team are responsible for event planning and organizing events. They serves as the driving behind volunteers. The Mutual Love teams manage small units in a district and is in charge of concrete work arrangement and execution, while the Joint Effort team looks after frontline voluntary work in the neighborhood.

---

[28] Rigby, D., Sutherland, J., & Noble, A. (2018). *Agile at Scale, Harvard Business Review* (May–June 2018 Issue). Massachusetts: Harvard Business Publishing.

However, Master Cheng Yen hoped that the volunteers in the Unity team, while working on planning and organizing, would also go to the frontline and do the job themselves.

Only in the frontline can senior volunteers pass on the Dharma to the less-experienced frontline volunteers. On the frontlines, senior volunteers can also cultivate their modesty and avoid arrogance due to their positions and qualifications. Senior volunteers also have the opportunity to nurture and express their compassion and gratitude. Moreover, the world of Tzu Chi is able to instill a sense of equality without regard to status or superiority.

Always on the Frontline

Mr. Eugene Duh (杜俊元), was the Chairman of the Board of Tzu Chi Da Ai TV Station, a successful entrepreneur, and senior certified volunteer in Unity team who sponsored the Tzu Chi branch in Kaohsiung. Despite his generous donations and efforts, he still worked on the frontline, took shifts to direct traffic and sweep the streets. This is the Buddhist concept of equality, which does not necessitate the same work for everyone, but instead encourages everyone to contribute their skills to a common goal in the spirit of equality.

In 2008, Nokia was the biggest mobile phone maker globally. By 2013, its market share had dwindled to 3%, prompting Microsoft to acquire it for a mere $7 billion. Nokia failed to respond to the interface design and App market trends popularized by iPhone and Android, mostly due to its management being composed of people with engineering backgrounds who neglected software development and overlooked market feedback. They mistakenly thought that introducing their own operating systems instead of following the iPhone would bring them success.

Nokia even ignored competition from Huawei and HTC in the low-end market, ultimately resulting in the loss of their leading position in the mobile phone market and difficulty in remaining afloat.

It is a blind spot for decision makers to view themselves and the market demand through existing successful models when they are far from the frontline.

Engineering and a lack of market orientation should take the main blame for Nokia's downfall. There is nothing wrong with engineering orientation; however, frontline experience should not be overlooked.

Horizontal and multi-circle management in Internet companies can promote innovation among various departments while keeping up with social needs, which is also essential for organization growth.

However, responding to frontline demands for large organizations is not easy. Multiple departments and the need for coordination tend to slow decision-making and reduce consensus.

Holacratic Organizational Model

Holacracy, developed in Pennsylvania, USA, revolves around the members of an organization, enabling employees to take on different roles and make decisions independently. It is a big circle made up of small circles composed of group members. Each small circle is an autonomous unit with the capability to respond autonomously to the market. The small circles coordinate with each other and the larger circle convenes meetings of the smaller circles, providing them with necessary resources.[29]

When disagreements arise, the large group must respect the small ones. When representatives of the large group play a part in a small group, they must show respect for it.

Holacracy is characterized by frontline employees making decisions. Members in the small circle hold different roles, and each one's specialty has the final authority on pertinent subjects. Here, everyone is both leading and being led.

Members of Holacracy can independently join any creative team, thus optimizing organizational creativity. Holacracy is role-based, so members can occupy multiple roles and draw on their creativity. Brian Robertson, founder of Holacracy, underscored that Holacracy is not static; rather, it is continuously developing.

Holacracy is not a traditional hierarchical system; rather, it resembles the cells of the human body, with each belonging to an organ. In this manner, every layer is interlinked and adaptable to accommodate the varied needs of data, services, and goods from the outside world.

---

[29] Rigby, D., Sutherland, J., & Noble, A. (2018). *Agile at Scale, Harvard Business Review* (May–June 2018 Issue). Massachusetts: Harvard Business Publishing.

Pluralistic and Round Organizational Structure

Professor Richard Madsen from the University of California, San Diego, once gave a lecture at Tzu Chi Foundation. In his speech, besides acknowledging and praising Tzu Chi's significant contributions to global charity, he consistently expressed his hope that Tzu Chi not become overly institutionalized or professionalized. He emphasized the importance of maintaining the touching spirit of always being on the frontlines of service.[30]

This is also true for businesses and organizations, who should stay up-to-date with their customers' needs.

The round organization does not rely on the directives of upper management, but adheres to shared values and is judged on first-hand data. It is similar to Skype or the Internet, all of which are accessible and have standard protocols, yet the grasping and implementation of values necessitates subjective evaluation. In a round organization, all Tzu Chi volunteers, be they senior or junior, must take their place at the frontline. The round organization of Tzu Chi is what master Cheng Yen refers to as the Four-in-One teams that consist of Unity, Harmony, Mutual Love, and Joint Effort. They are not hierarchical but in parallel, which allows access to frontline work.

Tzu Chi also follows the principle of localization. When local volunteers encounter disasters in their communities, they can immediately initiate disaster relief without needing to seek approval from headquarters. Instead, they act in accordance with Tzu Chi's values and beliefs, directly launching emergency relief efforts. This does not diminish the importance of Tzu Chi's headquarters but emphasizes the urgency of disaster relief. The spontaneous initiation by local communities ensures immediate rescue operations, followed by informing the headquarters for assistance and support. This mechanism, as explained by Professor Herman Leonard of Harvard University, is both centralized and decentralized, combining centralized power with decentralized authority.

Community volunteers can take part in Tzu Chi's services and voluntary projects, such as charity, medicine, education, humanistic culture, environmental protection, and bone marrow donation. As long as their

---

[30] Lou, Y. L., & Leonard, H. D. (2017). *Ci ji zongmen de pu shi jiazhi* [The Universal Value of Buddhism & the Dharma Path of Tzu Chi]. Tzu Chi Culture & Communication Foundation. pp. 125–140.

contributions align with Tzu Chi's core values, volunteers are empowered to create new services and organize various initiatives. This embodies the concept of a liquid organization, akin to water, flowing wherever there is a need and Tzu Chi volunteers are present.

This liquid organization concept enables Tzu Chi to have various organizational forms worldwide. The American, Indonesian and Malaysian branches have charity, medicine, education, and humanistic culture institutions, each with an executive head in charge of work done locally.

Tzu Chi has more loosely organized branches in South Africa and Mozambique, where the family, friends, and neighborhood join together to carry out the charity work.

These organizations have no executive heads or management hierarchy, just senior volunteers with outstanding character guiding or joining them. Michael Pan of Tzu Chi, based in South Africa, helps thousands of local volunteers. He said, "I'm not leading them, I'm merely accompanying them; allowing them to consider what they can do for the community on their own initiative." The initiatives in South Africa, such as caring for AIDS orphans, were conceived by local volunteers themselves. It is the only region that Tzu Chi operates globally where the volunteer mission is specifically dedicated to caring for AIDS orphans.

The blockchain advocates for decentralization; in fact, one could call this poly-centralization. People with the same values can use this to further their mission in either public welfare or business, all the while upholding environmental protection. Decentralization reflects the efficiency and speed of point-to-point commodity transactions, while poly-centralization represents how members with the same ideals can work in separate capacities. This fluid organization can provide unlimited creative power for society.

Section 7: Altruism as a System

Any successful organization pays close attention to the needs of their target groups from the outset, seeking to provide the best services to them at the most economical cost in an altruistic manner.

Wealth Through a System of Benefiting the Public

Henry Ford wasn't the creator of the automobile, yet he was the first to make it popular. At the start of the twentieth century, cars were exclusively purchased by the wealthy. Henry Ford, however, used standardized production lines to manufacture more affordable cars for the middle class. Previously cars were only black, but he developed Model T cars with various color choices. By 1927, his car sales rose to 15 million at its highest point.

However, by the year 2003, Toyota Motor Corporation had surpassed Ford Motor Company, becoming the second-largest automaker in the US, trailing only General Motors. In 2008, Ford announced its first quarterly loss in 105 years, amounting to a staggering $8.7 billion. Ford also planned to discontinue fuel-consuming SUVs, which, despite their high unit prices, were experiencing poor sales.[31]

Why did Ford, once the richest man in the US and popularized for cars, fall behind Toyota?

After a century of glory, Ford shifted to targeting higher end customers, prioritizing profitability over design and value. Just as Jobs had accused his former CEO of getting caught up in marketing, the same pattern appeared with Ford, releasing more and more models with greater costs. This contradicted the original founding purpose of Ford, which was to make cars accessible for all. Meanwhile, Toyota, a Japanese brand, made its American debut with the Corona, a cheap and reliable option.

Ford was caught in a quandary, deciding between competing with Toyota in the low-end market or staying in the high-end one.

As a century-old brand, Ford Motor Company paid little attention to the newly-arrived Japanese cars and persisted with their high-price strategy, introducing a luxurious SUV accompanied with segmented cars for customers to choose from as an alternative to recreation vehicles. Consequently, Toyota Motor gained the upper hand in middle- and lower-end markets within a few decades.

Ford suffered an immense loss in 2008, prompting them to invite the retired president of Toyota Motor, James Farley, to save them. In this moment of life and death, Toyota too was in a similar predicament.

---

[31] Kiley, D. (2008). *Fute jiuwang zhao shang fengtian laojiang* [Ford Turns to Toyota Veteran for Help]. Taiwan: Business Today. Retrieved from https://www.businesstoday.com.tw/article/category/80393/post/200808070015/.

After becoming the 2nd largest auto industry in the US, Toyota launched Lexus in 1992. Taking a cue from Ford, they shifted toward higher end markets. At this point, Hyundai Motor entered. Should Toyota go down to the mass market and compete with Hyundai Motor? Toyota made the same call as Ford and got the same results. Hyundai Motor snatched away the low-end market that was dominated by Toyota.

This structural decline must be addressed through systematic analysis. Enterprises and institutions must undergo change for a new path forward.

In view of the inter-industry replacement cycle, Professor Clayton Christensen of Harvard School of Management proposed a systematic change mode, known as Disruptive Innovation. Crayton argued that enterprises must find new models and make changes when facing such cycles.

He believes that successful enterprises can preserve their wealth by leveraging efficient innovation to maximize profits, instead of popularizing their products. To expand profits, they must move beyond their comfort zone and embrace disruptive innovation. Rather than settling for high-profit markets that rely on high-priced strategies, enterprises should instead focus on how they can enter the market of the masses.

This theory inspired Andy Grove, the former CEO of Intel who was content with its high profit. Following Crayton's theory, Grove created an R&D team to produce cheaper products for the public market. Equally, two small chip companies were shifting Intel's market. Grove's systematic analysis and redefining, however, enabled Intel to maintain its dominant position.

Regarding Henry Ford, the greatness and success of his products lie in the benefits they have provided to more people. Previously, computers cost millions of dollars and required a year of training to use, something only possible for large organizations and top universities. Apple revolutionized this, and the iPhone shortly followed, returning technology to the masses.

Benefiting more people brought greater wealth and fame to Ford and Apple.

By contrast, their successors were profit and marketing-driven. There is a contrast between altruism and self-interest; the success of the enterprise is contingent upon which one they prioritize. Once it focused on self-interest, it declined.

Enterprises should always consider how to benefit others and the public. They should devise altruistic systems to promote sustained prosperity.

Whether an enterprise is altruistic or self-interested can be gauged by the degree to which its products are beneficial to many.

Structural Altruism and the Refresh of Microsoft

On December 29, 1999, Microsoft's stock price reached a historic high, and at that time, Microsoft was the world's highest-valued company. In 2008, after Bill Gates retired, Steve Ballmer took over as Microsoft's president, and Microsoft's stock began to fall sharply and then struggled to recover. By early 2013–2014, Microsoft's market value had dropped $300 billion. Internally, the company was fraught with internal divisions and struggles, reducing efficiency, and many executives left for companies like Amazon and Facebook. Faced with this crisis, Satya Nadella was tasked with turning the company around.

A year after taking the helm at Microsoft, in 2015, Nadella introduced a new mission for Microsoft: "To empower every person and every organization on the planet to achieve more." Accordingly, he proposed strategies such as "cloud first, mobile first, AI first," empowering every individual and organization globally to achieve extraordinary things. In other words, putting others first by fostering a sense of mission and pride in work rather than surpassing competitors through envy or aggressiveness, and surpassing one's colleagues. Moreover, he aimed to create impressive partnerships both inside and outside the company, reflecting a spirit of harmony. Nadella successfully redefined Microsoft's culture, shifting from a genius-driven culture to one focused on self-improvement. Following the cultural transformation, Nadella continued with three major goals.

The first goal, customer first. Addressing customer needs, some of which are not yet known, with innovative technology solutions. The second goal, diversity and inclusion. More than just diversity, but also embracing each other. Consensus is not the most important; inclusiveness is, and the pursuit of consensus can also be a form of centralization. The third goal, one Microsoft. Both Bill Gates and Steve Ballmer were very intelligent leaders who crafted the company's strategic plans, with others following. Nadella's approach involves everyone in raising issues, advocating for expression, stimulating curiosity, and collaboratively solving problems, turning the culture of altruism and harmony into a system.

In Microsoft's evaluation system, three dimensions are emphasized: "What have you done yourself?", "What have you done for others?", and "What have you done with others?".

"What have you done for others?" represents altruism. "What have you done with others?" represents harmony.

Before 2014, Microsoft faced a severe "innovator's dilemma" and was declining as a PC-era giant. By 2019, less than five years after Nadella became Microsoft's CEO, he had transformed the culture, and Microsoft's market value exceeded one trillion dollars, reaching a historic high and surpassing both Amazon and Apple, achieving remarkable success and becoming the highest-valued company in the world at that time. Leading Microsoft from a valuation of one trillion to two trillion dollars took Nadella only two years. Nadella is a wise and altruistic entrepreneur who institutionalized the culture of altruism and harmony, not just as a slogan. He showed the entire company the power of goodness and love, leading by example and witnessing the power of goodness and love with his colleagues.

In the "economy of goodness" that I advocate, "goodness" means altruism and harmony. The "economy of goodness" starts from compassion, benefits all beings, and ultimately achieves the goal of harmony.

Systematic and Structural Thinking and Altruism

In 2012, Mexico's fishing industry saw a record drop in its fish catch. Is this caused by the greenhouse effect, pollution, or other factors?

The Mexican fishing industry, in a state of perplexity and with fishermen facing extreme hardships, sought help. They reached out to Professor Peter Senge, a renowned figure from the MIT Sloan School of Management. In response to this, he, along with several faculty members and students from management schools, established the Academy for Systemic Change. This academy was specifically dedicated to researching structural blind spots in organizational growth.

In 2009, Peter M. Senge assisted Starbucks Coffee Company in forming a system team which included vital executives and suppliers from Starbucks worldwide. This team successfully recycled more than 4 billion coffee paper cups in a year for environmental preservation.

The challenges faced by the Mexican fishing industry prompted the involvement of Peter Senge's team. Professor Joe Shu of Harvard University, who co-founded the Academy for Systemic Change with Peter Senge, took on this task. Over a period of two weeks, Professor Shu and the change management team, along with members of the Mexican fishing industry, systematically mapped out the potential factors impacting the industry, referred to as a "Change Map."

The Change Map provided a detailed listing of various factors and their interrelationships. Subsequently, the team engaged in a thorough discussion and filtration process, addressing each factor one by one.

They attempted to identify structural factors that caused the decrease in catches.

Finally, they concluded that it wasn't climate change or marine litter, but illegal fishing that had diminished the whole catch.

The structural relationship is that when the illegal fishing catch increases in the black market, the market price of fish decreases. Legitimate fishermen are compelled to catch more fish to maintain their original income. In order to sustain their previous earnings, legitimate fishermen are forced to catch more fish, resulting in the creation of smaller mesh sizes in fishing nets. This leads to the capture of even the juvenile fish that would have grown in the following years, causing a gradual decline in the fish population.

The Mexican fishing industry set up autonomous defense teams to prohibit illegal fishing and assist illegal fishermen in joining formal fishing associations with negotiated catch standards, enabling all fishermen to thrive with mutual aid, rather than competing covertly and participating in unlawful fishing, resulting in mutual detriment.

This systematic analysis aids a slow-growing institution, snowballing one, or emerging group/enterprise to better comprehend its situation, identify structuring factors for transformation, and find a route to maintain success.

The case of the Mexican Fisheries Association illustrates how mutual benefit and aid can lead to collective prosperity. Indeed, altruism is a path to lasting growth.

Section 8: Establishing Role Models
for Sustainable Development

In the history of human organization studies, it can be concluded that no organization can outlast those of a religious nature. While dynasties, businesses, and clans have been known to endure for centuries, religious organizations have remained for thousands of years.

The reason is that religious organizations are rooted in ideologies and values, not kinship, interests, or other material connections. It is only a system of thought and values that can sustain an organization over time.

Commands, ideas, power and interests are all prone to fluctuation, but beliefs and values are everlasting. The more a company is grounded in beliefs and values, the more sustainable it will be.

Commercial Sustainability with Role Models

Since 2002, when I was appointed spokesperson for Tzu Chi, I've been asked constantly who would be Master Cheng Yen's successor.

I will reply as Master Cheng Yen advised me: Every Tzu Chi member should be a successor, each inheriting and carrying on the spirit of Tzu Chi.

In February 2009, Venerable Master Sheng Yen of Dharma Drum Mountain passed away. Many media outlets inquired about the issue of succession for Tzu Chi. When I consulted with Master Cheng Yen, her response was, "I am on the side of Master Sheng Yen. Tell them that in Tzu Chi, everyone is a successor, and everyone should carry on the legacy."

Over the past decades, Master Cheng Yen has been physically weak. Since the founding of Hualien Tzu Chi Hospital in the 1980s, she has been asked who her successor as leader of Tzu Chi might be. She always responds that there is no need to designate a single successor; rather, the mission should be carried on by all.

In fact, before Perfect Extinction of the Buddha, the same question had been raised in the monk group. According to *Ekottaragama Sutra*, when the Buddha was about eighty years old, Venerable Ananda came back with water and saw that the Buddha was ill. Venerable Ananda felt uneasy. He knew that the Buddha would soon leave the world. After the Buddha finished his grooming, Venerable Ananda asked the Buddha: The

Buddha, who will be your successor after your Perfect Extinction? Could you like to explain to the sangha (monastic community) in advance?

The Buddha replied: Ananda, I have taught my Dharma to each of you openly without discrimination for decades. What do I have to tell the sangha? If any of you think he can lead the sangha, he should tell you. I am but an old man who is about to die. What shall I say to you? "Oh, Ananda," Buddha continued, "be enlighten by yourself not by others, be illuminated by yourself, not by others."

The Buddha having left no successor, his disciples fanned out in all directions to spread the Dharma after his passing. Venerable Upaniṣad, first in precepts, and Venerable Mahakala, sent precepts to the west; Venerable Ananda and Venerable Subhuti, among others, imparted the Dharma to the east. Through their combined labors, Buddhism has flourished for over 2,500 years.

The collection of scriptures after the Buddha's parinirvana was not only compiled by the assembly of five hundred monks led by Venerable Mahākāśyapa and Venerable Ananda. According to tradition, Venerable Ananda, one of the original five bhikkhus who first heard the Buddha's teachings in Deer Park, also gathered more than fifteen thousand people outside the assembly to compile the Buddha's teachings. This became a partial source for the profound doctrines of Mahayana Buddhism that emerged later.

Without an appointed successor, everyone will be an inheritor so that the faith will be passed on.

The Sustainability of Commandments Over Time

The founder of Christianity, Jesus Christ, preached for only three years before being martyred. After the crucifixion of Jesus, the disciples hesitated about whether to disband and return to their hometowns. Peter, who was originally a fisherman, also contemplated going back home. However, through collective prayers of the disciples and some of them witnessing the resurrected Jesus, they regained confidence and decided to stay in Galilee to continue spreading the teachings. Peter, along with other disciples such as Simon, Matthew, Mark, and the rest of the twelve apostles, went on to propagate the deeds and the Gospel of Jesus.

In the early days, preaching Christianity was not fixed in one way, allowing the spirit of Christ to better adapt to various cultures and people.

Peter and Mary, the mother of Jesus, founded the Church that has endured for 2,000 years. The Catholic Church of St. Peter is based on the teachings of St. Peter.

If Peter is said to have spread the Gospel of Jesus among the Jewish people, Paul, on the other hand, is known for propagating the Gospel to the Gentiles. Six years after the crucifixion of Jesus, Paul, a Jewish Pharisee who had been persecuting Christians, had a transformative experience on his way to Damascus. Jesus appeared to him and questioned why he was persecuting His disciples. Paul was temporarily blinded during this encounter but was later healed by a disciple appointed by Jesus, although he retained weak eyesight in one eye.

Whenever Paul thought about his weak eyesight, he would recall the Lord Jesus. He understood that in his weaknesses, Jesus could make him strong. Paul realized that relying on Jesus was more important than relying on himself in all things.

Jesus chose Paul, leading him to repentance and becoming a faithful believer. Paul, in turn, preached in non-Jewish regions, making a vow to bring the Gospel of Jesus to the ends of the earth. He fulfilled this vow by extensively traveling through present-day Western Asia and Europe. Many, including the Greeks and Macedonians, embraced Christianity through his efforts. Paul played a crucial role in Christianity becoming a global religion. Today, Christianity has a following of around 2.4 billion people, and much of the spiritual foundation of Western civilization is rooted in Christian principles.

Every disciple is an inheritor of the Gospel of Jesus, a pivotal foundation for Christianity becoming a world religion.

All Are Successors

Muhammad, the founder of Islam, had his cousin Ali as his first disciple. When aged fourteen, Ali followed Muhammad, eventually becoming his most prominent follower. As his years drew to a close, Muhammad raised Ali's hands to his disciples and declared that whoever supported him should also support Ali, his most loyal devotee. His command was met with cheers. However, Muhammad did not officially assign Ali as his successor until his death, leaving his wishes unspoken and ambiguous.

Muhammad's youngest wife, Aisha, was the daughter of an important leader from a prominent Arab tribe and held a special place in Muhammad's affections. During Muhammad's lifetime, Aisha had disagreements with Ali. Those who later followed Ali became the Shia (meaning "followers of Ali"), while Aisha's followers eventually became the Sunni, the two major branches in Islam.

Muhammad did not explicitly designate a successor. On one hand, the founder of a religion must stand in a position of authority, supporting and caring for everyone who follows him. On the other hand, once a successor is explicitly appointed, there is a risk of immediate division within the community.

Today, despite the ongoing differences and occasional reconciliations between Sunni and Shia branches, both unanimously hold profound reverence for the Prophet Muhammad. They also share common ground in accepting the fundamental doctrines and spiritual principles of Islam.

Regarding the succession of leaders, whether in matters of saints or global organizations, it is often seen as a collective endeavor rather than an individual one. Succession involves multiple individuals rather than a single person, and this collective nature is a crucial factor in the enduring continuity of religious communities.

Allowing disciples to express the founder's spirit in a diverse way is key to the formation of a global religion.

With diverse doctrines, a religion can attract followers from many cultures, ethnicities, and countries, and still allow them to follow the teachings of the founders while maintaining their own cultural identities.

It is precisely why everyone must be a successor that saints stay silent on their succession.

The true faith is an inheritance of ideas, not administration.

An organization that is sustainable relies on value inheritance rather than system inheritance.

The essence of management should be role-modeling, rather than talent inheritance.

This is the secret for any great thought and organization to sustain for thousands of years.

Today's question is: How can non-religious organizations, such as enterprises, endure through role model inheritance?

Role Model in Enterprises

John Davison Rockefeller lived to be 94. He founded Standard Oil, which once accounted for 90% of the US oil market. At its peak in 1914, his wealth represented 2.4% of America's GDP. The US then passed antitrust laws, after which Standard Oil was split into 34 companies. ExxonMobil, which emerged from the splitting, is now the second-largest company in the US.

Rockefeller was driven to make, save, and donate money desperately. He was the wealthiest and greatest philanthropist of the twentieth century. Through The Rockefeller Foundation, he played a key role in establishing Johns Hopkins University, Harvard University's Public Health School, the University of Chicago, Rockefeller University, and Peking Union Medical College Hospital.

Rockefeller led a humble existence with no smoking or alcohol, devoting himself to philanthropy. He provided a model for later entrepreneurs like Bill Gates and Warren Buffett to follow. According to Weber's theory, he represented an entrepreneurial spirit expressing Protestant ethics. In his career he glorified God and adhered to religious rules through self-sacrifice, setting an inspiring example of charity for posterity.

Every descendant of Rockefeller, down to the 6th generation, adheres to the family's motto, showing dedication to charity, public welfare, and a frugal lifestyle.

Rockefeller may not have been a saintly figure, with plenty of questionable business practices. Yet, his commitment to hard work, austere living, and charity provide exemplary credentials for a successful entrepreneur. His legacy still lives on in the Rockefeller family.

Steve Rockefeller, a descendant of the fifth generation of the Rockefeller family, visited Tzu Chi in Taiwan in May 2011. With a Buddhist background, he was friendly and humble, attending the Buddha Day ceremony and taking photos and videos with his own camera. Upon meeting Master Cheng Yen, he showed the highest respect by bowing in the Buddhist tradition, praising Master Cheng Yen as an exemplary figure in charity. Steve Rockefeller later met with Shu-chu Chen, a famous vegetable vendor and philanthropic figure in Taiwan. During a photo session, he even bent down to balance the height difference between himself and Shu-chu Chen. This reflects the humble and down-to-earth family values.

Therefore, the sustainability of enterprises should rely on role models of character. The Rockefeller family has produced two governors, one vice president, one senator, and numerous CEOs of major corporations.

At 86 years of age, Rockefeller wrote a short poem capturing his life:

I was early taught to work as well as play,
My life has been one long, happy holiday;
Full of work and full of play
I dropped the worry on the way
And God was good to me every day.[32]

SECTION 9: COEXIST WITH PLANET EARTH

The world, as a whole, represents the shared understanding of global civilizations. Whether viewed through the lens of Confucianism, Buddhism, Taoism, or the achievements of ancient Greek, and Christian civilizations, and modern scientific development, it is evident that every part of this world is interconnected. This concept aligns with the Buddhist principle of interdependent arising, where all phenomena are interrelated, and nothing can exist in isolation. Therefore, any production and consumption activities on Earth are linked to the Earth's lifespan, as well as the continuity and survival of humanity. Depleting Earth's resources ultimately leads humanity toward the path of extinction.

Earth's resources are not limitless. To ensure economic success and a healthy environment, producers and consumers must take measures to minimize harm to the environment during production and consumption.

Cherish the Material Life

Coca-Cola, a carbonated beverage containing caffeine, is produced by the Coca-Cola Company. In most countries, it takes the lead in the beverage market, with sales far exceeding its competitors.

The Coca-Cola Company has been taking active steps to protect the environment and manage water resources in recent years. For the beverage industry, water is the key ingredient, and is needed in production stages such as cooling, cleaning, and rinsing. To conserve water resources, the Coca-Cola Foundation created a Water Resources Management Center in the US in 1984, and teamed up with WWF to devise an evaluation system for assessing water use efficiency. This system efficiently

---

[32] Winkler, J. K. (2007). *John D. Rockefeller: A Portrait in Oils.* United States: Cosimo Classics.

analyzes and reduces water consumption in production lines, thus saving on water.

With this system, Coca-Cola's water consumption decreased by 4% compared to 2010, and by 16% compared to 2004.

Coca-Cola not only conserves water resources, but dedicates itself to recycling them. In Israel, where water resources are scarce, people extract potable fresh water from the sea. 70% of utilized water is recycled and recycled again.

Coca-Cola is committed to setting up systems for recycling water resources. They've constructed factories worldwide, many in places lacking proper sanitation, where people don't have access to clean water. Consequently, Coca-Cola has partnered with local authorities to construct water purification plants for local people.

Coca-Cola was successful in three ways. Firstly, it conserved water resources; secondly, it created a more efficient use of water by recycling it; and finally, it provided improved water health, to the benefit of local people. This is a model of a business and economy that serves the common good: generating profits while protecting both people and the planet.

Likewise, Nike, the world's largest supplier of sneakers, promotes resource recycling comprehensively. With their aim to reach zero waste, they ensure that recycled plastic materials are used in all their sneaker factories. This helps them limit the wastage of the earth's limited resources.

It is yet to be determined if this zero-waste measure can be successfully implemented. To date, Nike Grind sneakers have recycled 71% of old shoe materials for stronger, longer lasting products.

Major electronics manufacturers such as Sony and Xexos are also committed to recycling and reusing materials from their electronic products in the production of new items. On September 28, 2006, Sony launched the Lithium Battery Voluntary Replacement Program globally, aiming to extensively collect lithium batteries used in laptop computers produced by various brands worldwide and providing free replacement services. Sony's Road to Zero environmental initiative aims to achieve a goal of zero environmental impact.

These electronics manufacturers are proactively taking responsibility in practicing Recycling and Reuse. However, the most crucial step for the earth is Reduce. These business giants have accomplished the first two steps. Reduction, however, goes against their interests.

At the core of environmental protection, the three Rs are indispensable: Reduce, Reuse, and Recycle.

Dedicated to Environmental Protection and Love for the Earth.

Tzu Chi has over 200,000 volunteers across Taiwan, involved in more than 8,000 recycling stations in various communities. They dedicate their time and efforts to maintaining cleanliness in neighborhoods and promoting environmental protection. Inspired by Tzu Chi volunteers, thousands of families have also started practicing resource sorting and recycling at home, with the income generated from recycling donated to Tzu Chi's charitable causes. Recycling has become a social enterprise with a public welfare focus.

Tzu Chi's recycling stations draw volunteers from all ages and backgrounds, from 3 to 104 years old. This includes doctoral students, entrepreneurs, police officers, housewives, and diplomats. Taiwan is estimated to recycle over 200 million PET bottles annually, with Tzu Chi volunteers contributing a third of them. Additionally, Tzu Chi's environmental protection influence extends to the Philippines, Malaysia, Haiti, Indonesia, Southwest China, and several South American nations.

In resource recycling, Tzu Chi volunteers are taught to cherish material life, espousing the concept of equality of all living beings with utmost compassion—the belief that everyone possesses Buddha-nature. By recycling and simplifying material usage, we can lessen our dependence on materials.

An eighty-year-old grandmother, rising at four o'clock in the morning, plus the blind and the limb-disabled volunteers, directors of financial companies, foreign ambassadors and their spouses, entrepreneurs, and homemakers; all of them have become aware of the environmental and social cost of their modern lifestyles. They've understood that materials possess a life of their own, and must be respected. Similar to chanting and meditation, resource recycling holds the same, or even greater, profundity of wisdom and spiritual understanding for the soul.

Recycling stations are sites of spiritual and interpersonal restoration. Through recycling processes, individuals with chronic or mental ailments can find relief. Research indicates a mental link between resource recuperation and self-reconstruction. An elderly person picking up a discarded plastic bottle, believing it could still be practical in formulating an emergency blanket, discovers that his supposedly outworn physical being still has value. The material world's worth manifests in recycled items, and The Doctrine of the Mean demonstrates the worth of oneself. Not only does resource recycling guard the environment, it also reinstates volunteers' self-respect and value.

In addition, people with depression, psychological disorders, drug addiction, gambling, and alcoholism have experienced success in getting rid of bad habits through participation in Tzu Chi's environmental recycling. Its environmental protection works to build relationships between people and the earth, communities, and themselves, displaying the strength of social enterprises. By classifying resources, people have reorganized their lives and reduced worries and insecurity.

In 2008, Tzu Chi established DA.AI Technology Co., Ltd., taking their environmental protection efforts to the next level. This company was founded by five volunteer industrialists and specializes in making blankets and apparel from recycled plastic bottles. To date, more than one million blankets from DA.AI Technology have been sent to 38 disaster-stricken countries. The five initiators of DA.AI Technology are all long-time volunteers of Tzu Chi, along with volunteers of the company with all profits channeled back to Tzu Chi. This enterprise serves as an epitome of volunteer entrepreneurship, being the first of its kind to focus on environmental protection in Taiwan.

The purpose of such a social enterprise like DA.AI Technology is not only to produce eco-friendly products, but to also promote the concept of environmental protection. PET bottles that were once considered garbage, are transformed into disaster relief blankets and clothes, scarves, and handbags in the hands of Tzu Chi volunteers. These products, which would have otherwise required continued reliance on oil extraction, are transformed into new forms of urban minerals through resource recycling.

DA.AI Technology hopes that these upcycled products can also bring greater awareness toward the dangerous effects of global warming and encourage more people to adopt sustainable lifestyles. From resource recycling to technological reproduction and environmental protection, DA.AI Technology looks to conserve our planet by reducing consumption. Their aspiration is to bring about a pollution-free lifestyle, reclaim the earth's cleanliness, and achieve symbiosis between humans and the Earth.

The Earth Is Our Home

Patagonia positions its corporate culture as "Earth first, profit second," and has developed a range of outdoor products. Since the 1970s, Patagonia has been committed to environmental conservation. In the early 1980s, they pledged 2% of pre-tax profits to non-profit environmental organizations. In 1985, this donation amount increased to 10% of company profits. By 1996, they committed to donating 1% of sales to focus on climate, food, land, pollution, water, and wildlife issues.

Founder Yvon Chouinard sees this not as charity, but as a tax—an Earth usage tax. On a dead planet, no business can be done. This is an important concept for Patagonia; they aim not only to make Patagonia the best example of an environmental conservation business but also to influence other entrepreneurs to participate in environmental conservation.

To protect the environment, Patagonia never stops; they hope to support more businesses in developing new environmental improvement technologies with their funding.

Patagonia's success lies in the fact that they truly embed the belief "The Earth is our home, the company is our employees' home" deep within their employees' hearts. Yvon Chouinard is fully confident about the future of the business: "Patagonia and its thousands of employees have the means and the will to prove to the entire business system that doing the right thing can successfully create a conscientious enterprise while being profitable and leading to wealth through goodness."

In building their corporate culture, Patagonia integrates the concept of environmental protection into their business, persistently fighting any environmentally unfriendly actions and continuously reducing energy and carbon footprints. All this stems from their philosophy: build the best product, cause no unnecessary harm, and use business to inspire and implement solutions to the environmental crisis.

In 1999, Patagonia became the first company in California to fully use recycled or green energy. That year, Time magazine named Yvon Chouinard an environmental hero.

While others pursue profits, Patagonia always focuses on the environment and responsibility. Chouinard states, "Our mission is to save our home planet; we care about every name, every life, and every landscape on Earth. Only in this way can we truly bring about change."

On September 14, 2022, Patagonia's official website published a letter from Chouinard titled "Earth is Now Our Only Shareholder." The letter stated that although Earth's resources are vast, they are not infinite, and it is clear that humanity has exceeded Earth's limits. However, the Earth is resilient, and if we are determined, we can save our planet.

Patagonia understands that their impact on the world comes from commerce, which is inseparable from purpose and profit. However, they can decide where the profit is used: they will not extract value from nature and transform it into wealth for investors; instead, they use the wealth created by Patagonia to protect the source of all wealth.

Wealth comes from the Earth and belongs to the Earth, "Earth is Now Our Only Shareholder."

SECTION 10: CO-PROSPERITY FOR ALL THINGS

Good Enterprises with a Philosophy of All Things Connected

The supreme aim of economic activities should be to create a symbiotic and shared prosperity for all.

For contemporary society, which holds individualism in high esteem, the concept of symbiosis and shared prosperity may sound elusive and insubstantial. However, whether we look to Chinese Confucianism, Buddhism and Taoism, or Western Greek philosophy, Christianity and contemporary science, they all acknowledge that the world is an organic unit. Only by recognizing that all things are connected, that all things can thrive due to human endeavor, can our practical successes and lives continue to flourish.

All things are an organic whole, yet many developments of human civilization have displaced us from that colossal collective energy.

Modern civilization teaches us that the root of humans is self, signifying isolation and loneliness.

According to the *Bible*, when Adam and Eve ate from the forbidden fruit and gained the knowledge of their own selves, they started to differentiate between themselves and others, between what is you and me, as well as between themselves and nature. This awareness marked the beginning of self-isolation and served as the root cause of original sin.[33]

---

[33] Fromm, E. (1995). *Ai de yishu* [The Art of Loving] (M. Xiang, Trans.). Taipei: Zhiwen chuban she. pp. 21–22.

Throughout history, we have continuously disconnected from the all-encompassing energy. With language, humans established distance from the essences of all entities; science created a divergence from the interconnecting power of religion; industrialization separated us from family; television generated estrangement from learning; and poverty alleviation eradicated the restraints of governance.

Have you ever heard that money can lead to freedom? Though it does not liberate many, the intelligent seek value, expertise, and personality. However, just as individuality begins to take shape, people discover that, in the end, they must stand alone, facing a world full of loneliness, confusion, and perilous uncertainty.

Not limited to this, in the contemporary emphasis on individualism, people employ various means to escape from themselves. Longing to abandon the self in the endless pursuit of desire, they seek a fusion of mind and body in the pursuit of pleasure. Intensely desiring to cast off the self in the intoxication of alcohol, they indulge in the frenzy of drug use to break free from the self. Some even bury themselves in the hurried pace of work, forgetting the self in the process.

Even if you consider yourself conventional, saying, "I don't use these indulgences to escape from myself," when we open the newspaper or turn on the television, we become connected to the societal collective. When we use a credit card to consume products advertised on television, we cease to be a distinct self and individual. Everything is shaped within the constraints of the collective. No one can exist as a solitary individual in this world.

Ironically, under the banner of liberalism, individuals vigorously advocate for the realization of the self and freedom as ultimate values, asserting the possession of self and independent individuality. However, at the same time, people employ various means to escape the predicament of self and isolation. After the failure in the pursuit of individual development, contemporary individuals attempt to replace the orderly, value-driven, and harmonious group model of the past with a scattered, disorderly, and trivial collective atmosphere.

Before the Industrial Revolution and rationalism, people belonged to group societies. In the West, medieval people were part of churches and families. In China prior to the eighteenth century, it was difficult for individuals to imagine who they would be after leaving their clans.

Even someone as carefree and unrestrained as Li Bai would say, "Let me sing you a song! Please lend me your ear." Drinking should not be done alone but is much better enjoyed with friends and nature.

So, that's why Li Bai finally says, "Together with you, dispelling the sorrows of all ages." No matter how troubled, he still seeks solace with friends. Because in that era, individuals were not seen as isolated entities; the individual and the collective were inseparable.

In the East, over 2,500 years ago, Prince Siddhartha in India practiced self-cultivation beneath a bodhi tree. One night, while looking at the star-strewn sky, he attained enlightenment and awakened to the laws of the universe. He realized that everything was originally one and that incredible karma separated and unified them all.

The ancient wisdom from both the East and the West continually reminds us of the inseparability and mutual dependence of the individual and the collective. Western psychologist Carl Jung said that for each person to attain the completeness of life or access greater energy, one must allow consciousness to connect with the collective unconscious.

On one occasion, Master Cheng Yen said to a group of media and arts professionals, "You only pursue the surging waves on the surface of the ocean, but in fact, the depths of the ocean are infinitely calm. The nature of the mind is also like this. Calmness is the most beautiful." No matter how grand the waves may be, eventually, they must subside back to the sea floor after reaching the shore. Yet, people entice themselves regarding the waves and remain stuck in the sludge on the shore. This represents the indulgence and obscuration of one's inherent purity.

Even the clearest water becomes obscured when trapped in mud, its purity compromised. Similarly, the Buddha, in the *Sutra of Forty-Two Sections*, highlights how desires and attachments can cloud the mind, hindering our ability to see the path forward. He presents the analogy of a clear pond, where stirring the water distorts its reflection, symbolizing how our desires can muddy our perception of the Way.[34]

Just like stirring and scooping muddy water only makes it dirtier, clinging to desires and attachments muddies the mind and hinders spiritual progress. As Master Cheng Yen teaches, letting go of these desires and finding the source of the true self is like returning the muddy water

---

[34] Shih, Cheng Yen. (2000). *Si shi er zhang jing jiangshu* [Commentary on The Sutra of Forty-Two Chapters: Spoken by the Buddha]. Taipei: Jing Si Publishing Co., Ltd.

to the vast, serene ocean.[35] It's akin to the saying, "A single drop of water remains undried because it merges with the vast ocean." This signifies the importance of letting go of worldly attachments to achieve true serenity.

Because the human heart is fragile, it is challenging to break free on one's own. Those who inherently understand are ultimately limited. Those who learn to understand are already considered precious. What do they rely on to learn? It is the environment. Environmental teaching is the greatest force. The influence inherited from the environment can either immerse people or uplift them.

Throughout history, whether it be the royal courts, churches, ancient Chinese academies of sacred philosophy, or contemporary organizations like the Tzu Chi Foundation established by Master Cheng Yen, all serve as a tranquil ocean. They provide a space for individuals to return to the collective and benevolent energy, allowing hearts tainted by influences to find the power of tranquility.

Christianity has a saying, "With men this is impossible; but with God all things are possible." (*King James Bible*, 1769/2017, Matthew 19:26) That is why people pray to God and rely on God for salvation.[36]

For Tzu Chi members, what's impossible to others is possible for Tzu Chi. Tzu Chi represents a collective and benevolent force, a pure and powerful energy that helps the water trapped in mud find its way back to the clean ocean.

This vast ocean explained through the collective unconscious perspective proposed by psychologist Carl Jung, is said to exist in the universe and within the individual's psyche. Jung posits that the human mind can connect to a greater cosmic power, a force referred to as God in Christianity, "consciousness" in Buddhism (where all things are created by the mind), Allah in Islam, and Brahman in Hinduism.

Jung said every great individual can access the collective unconscious. However, it can be a risk since the sheer power of it can overwhelm and shatter the psyche of those not prepared. It can be chaotic, disorderly, and difficult to handle.

---

[35] Shih, Cheng Yen. (2000). *Si shi er zhang jing jiangshu* [Commentary on The Sutra of Forty-Two Chapters: Spoken by the Buddha]. Taipei: Jing Si Publishing Co., Ltd.

[36] King James Bible. (2017). *King James Bible Online.* https://www.kingjamesbibleo nline.org/ (Original work published 1769).

Therefore, the question of how to guide the collective unconscious requires wisdom. In Christianity, the Holy Spirit is experienced through the church and the *Bible*. Religious rituals and scriptures aid mortals in attaining the energy of the vast unconscious.

The Enterprise of Goodness, Compassion, and Equality

The Buddha teaches "unconditional loving-kindness, universal compassion." We should love those we do not know, and for those we interact with daily, we should extend even more care.

Universal compassion requires delving into the essence of every life, understanding the impermanent nature of life, and exerting all efforts to give care and comfort. When the Buddha speaks of loving all sentient beings, it goes beyond humans and includes not only sentient beings in physical form but also those who have passed away and all material forms of life. All things, whether it's a piece of paper, a leaf, or a plastic bottle, are rich with life, and we must equally cherish and love them.

The Economy of Goodness grows and thrives on the basis of loving all sentient beings.

Master Huineng said, "The wondrous nature of people is originally empty; there is nothing that can be grasped. And the true emptiness of the essential nature is the same."[37]

The human mind is a void that holds all. This is how businessmen become both Internal Sage and External King. This is what it means to cultivate a merchant as a Wheel-Turning Sage King in Buddhism.

Chinese Zen Buddhism expresses the true meaning of entering the mundane world to practice self-cultivation by emphasizing that the empty cosmos can contain all manifestations, So is the emptiness of the human mind.[38] It is just like what Confucius said, "Does Heaven speak? The four seasons pursue their courses, and all things are continually being produced, but does Heaven say anything?".[39]

[37] Huineng, D. (Eds.). (2014). *The Sixth Patriarch's Dharma Jewel Platform Sutra*. Buddhist Text Translation Society. p. xlv.

[38] Huineng, D. (Eds.). (2014). *The Sixth Patriarch's Dharma Jewel Platform Sutra*. Buddhist Text Translation Society. p. xlv.

[39] Legge, J. (1971). *Confucian Analects: The Great Learning, and The Doctrine of the Mean*. New York: Dover Publications. p. 326.

Heaven is silent, hence it is not a personal god or deity, but rather a vast generative force capable of creating all things. That's why it's said, "When the Grand course was pursued, a public and common spirit ruled all under the sky."[40] Heaven remains aligned with the Tao. This Tao is the unceasing law governing the operation of nature. And humans must learn this law, which is why it is said, "Heaven, in its motion, (gives the idea of) strength. The superior man, in accordance with this, nerves himself to ceaseless activity."[41]

It requires someone of virtue to embark on an enterprise of goodness.

Following the laws of Heaven makes one virtuous. It is for humans to learn humility through the laws of Heaven.

As Mencius said, "That which is done without man's doing is from Heaven. That which happens without man's causing is from the ordinance of Heaven."[42] Heaven's mandate refers to a decision made by the mysterious workings of nature, not by any human or deity. This force beyond human control also includes the power of human agency.

This natural force is the totality of all life, and the energy of this totality is not random but rational. Therefore, people must follow the principles of nature and consider human desires. As *The Doctrine of the Mean* says, "Able to give its full development to the nature of other men, he can give their full development to the natures of animals and things. Able to give their full development to the natures of creatures and things, he can assist the transforming and nourishing powers of Heaven and Earth. Able to assist the transforming and nourishing powers of Heaven and Earth, he may with Heaven and Earth form a ternion."[43]

It signifies that both humans and the natural world adhere to specific rules, known as the Way of Heaven. The ultimate purpose for humans is to harmonize with this Way of Heaven, embodying the spirit of unity between Heaven and humanity.

The Qian Hexagram in *The I Ching* said, "The great man is he who is in harmony in his attributes with heaven and earth; in his brightness with

---

[40] Confucius. (2013). *The Book of Rites (Li Ji): English-Chinese Version* (D. Sheng, Ed., J. Legge, Trans.). CreateSpace Independent Publishing Platform. p. 100.

[41] Legge, J. (1963). *The I Ching: The Book of Changes.* United Kingdom: Dover Publications. p. 267.

[42] M. & Legge, J. (2011). *The Works of Mencius.* New York: Dover Publications. p. 359.

[43] Legge, J. (1971). *Confucian Analects: The Great Learning, and The Doctrine of the Mean.* New York: Dover Publications. p. 416.

the sun and moon; in his orderly procedure with the four seasons; and in his relation to what is fortunate and what is calamitous with the spiritual agents. He may precede Heaven, and Heaven will not act in opposition to him; he may follow Heaven but will act only as Heaven at the time would do. If Heaven will not act in opposition to him, how much less will men!".[44]

Confucianism emphasizes the unity between man, Heaven, Earth, and all beings. Man.

Humanism is a characteristic of Confucianism, as Mencius said, "All things are already complete in us."[45] This may mean that I am the spirit of all things, and all things are complete within me, which is the meaning of the great self. Although all things are within me, "There is no greater delight than to be conscious of sincerity on self-examination."[46] Being sincere to oneself has the connotation of humility and the idea that my heart is the heart of heaven and earth and all things.

Likewise, Buddhism emphasizes that all laws are only in the mind and that all beings are equal. Buddhism teaches that everyone can become a Buddha and that there is no distinction between mind, Buddhahood, and sentient beings.

Buddha's nature refers to being enlightened to the truth that all things are one, with no distinction between Buddha's nature and every other thing.

Comparatively, Buddhism puts more emphasis on the oneness of all things than Confucianism. Its objective is the same: no distinction between human beings and all other things, and no distinction between human beings and Buddha.

Zhuang Zi said, "Heaven, Earth, and I were produced together, and all things and I are one."[47] This statement seems to be closer to Buddhism's equality without distinction.

[44] Legge, J. (1963). *The I Ching: The Book of Changes*. United Kingdom: Dover Publications. p. 47.

[45] M. & Legge, J. (2011). *The Works of Mencius*. New York: Dover Publications. p. 450.

[46] M. & Legge, J. (2011). *The Works of Mencius*. New York: Dover Publications. p. 451.

[47] Legge, J. (1962). *The Sacred books of China: The texts of Taoism* (Vol. 1). New York: Dover Publications. p. 188.

Good Enterprises that Benefit All Things

Taoism recognizes the birth and existence of all things but believes that the force that has bred all things does not claim its name and control things.

Lao Tzu said, "All-pervading is the Great Tao! It may be found on the left hand and the right. All things depend on it for their production, which it gives to them, not one refusing obedience to it. When its work is accomplished, it does not claim the name of having done it. It clothes all things as with a garment, and makes no assumption of being their lord."[48]

As Lao Tzu said, "Man takes his law from the Earth; the Earth takes its law from Heaven; Heaven takes its law from the Tao. The law of the Tao is its being what it is."[49] Here, the term "law" conveys both the idea of following and being in harmony with. Ultimately, the Tao returns to nature, as it is an integral part of the natural order.

Humans should also walk the path of the Tao. Nature has two meanings: one is the grand nature, as advocated by scholars like Qian Mu and Ji Xianlin, which emphasizes the unity and harmony between humans and the universe and all things. The other is the inherent nature of oneself. All of these start from one's inherent self and return to one's inherent self.

The Chinese concept of Tian Tao (Way of Heaven) does not separate from the life of the individual self. This aligns with the Buddhist idea of "enlightenment inseparable from the mind," both representing a profound awareness that returns to the intrinsic nature of life.

In the philosophy of life, Confucianism emphasizes that a gentleman is one who aligns with the Tao. Confucius said, "The nobleman does not, even for the space of a single meal, act contrary to virtue. In moments of haste, he cleaves to it. In seasons of danger, he cleaves to it."[50] On the

---

[48] Legge, J. (1962). *The Sacred books of China: The Texts of Taoism* (Vol. 1). New York: Dover Publications. p. 76.

[49] Tzu, L. (Eds.). (2021). *Tao Te Ching* (J. Legge, Trans.). Standard Ebooks. Retrieved from https://standardebooks.org/ebooks/laozi/tao-te-ching/james-legge.

[50] Legge, J. (1971). *Confucian Analects: The Great Learning, and The Doctrine of the Mean*. New York: Dover Publications. p. 166.

other hand, Buddhism believes that one should cultivate a heart without dwelling anywhere.[51]

Confucius once said, "There is Heaven - that knows me!"[52] Heaven comprehends the hearts of the virtuous, aligning their intentions with the cosmic harmony of heaven and earth. This alignment enables virtuous individuals to resonate with the natural order of the universe. Therefore, Guan Zhong stated that a gentleman who remains steadfast in his purpose without faltering will be able to lead all things. He will shine as brightly as the sun and the moon, aligning himself with heaven and earth.[53]

What is the relationship between Buddha and Heaven and Earth? Buddha's heart is awakened to all truths, Buddha's heart is not eager to be known by heaven, but is immaculate, clear, and bright, uniting all laws in an omniscient holiness beyond humanity, and reaching the sacred realm.

The fusion of Buddhism, Confucianism, and Taoism marks the second significant synthesis of Chinese philosophy. Confucianism makes an assertion that Heaven and man are unified in harmony, which corresponds to the Buddhist concept of nirvana.

The encounter between Lao Tzu's Non-Action and All-Action meets Conditioned Dharma (samskrta) and Unconditioned Dharma (asamskrta) of Buddhism marks a significant leap forward in human thought. Chinese people do not favor nothingness or emptiness, so Chinese Zen Buddhism emphasizes that "emptiness" is like the space of the universe, containing the emptiness of myriad colors and myriad things.

The *Sixth Patriarch's Dharma Jewel Platform Sutra* says, "The wondrous nature of people is originally empty; there is nothing that can be grasped. And the true emptiness of the essential nature is the same."[54] In early Mahayana Prajna sutras, emptiness is discussed as being separate from the view of permanence and cessation. In Madhyamaka, it is discussed as the emptiness of the eightfold negations. In Yogacara, it

[51] Hua, H. (Eds.). (1974). *The Diamond Sutra*. San Francisco: Sino-American Buddhist Association. https://www.buddhanet.net/pdf_file/prajparagen2.pdf.

[52] Legge, J. (1971). *Confucian Analects: The Great Learning, and The Doctrine of the Mean*. New York: Dover Publications. p. 289.

[53] Tang, X. C. (1995). *Xin yi guanzi duben (xia)* [New Translation of The Book of Zhuangzi (Vol. 2)]. Taipei: Sanmin shuju. p. 680.

[54] Huineng, D. (Eds.). (2014). *The Sixth Patriarch's Dharma Jewel Platform Sutra*. Buddhist Text Translation Society. p. xlv.

is discussed as the emptiness of the middle way between existence and non-existence.

Nirvana's non-being and non-nothingness, merging with Heaven and Man, united as One, became Buddhist Master Huineng's emptiness that contains everything. Master Du Shun's Buddha-nature is from affinity, their Dharma Nature is from affinity, and their Realm of Reality is from dependent arising. This signified the unification and accommodation of all laws and things in a unified and great virtual entity that accommodates all laws and things—the integration and transformation of Heaven and Man as One. The Tiantai Buddhism also believed in three thousand worlds immanent in a single conscious-instant, which seemed to embody the saint's heart in harmonious unification with all other things and beings between Heaven and Earth.

Master Cheng Yen explained the connection between the enlightened state and the truth. She describes the enlightened realm of the Buddha as the "Hua-yan world," a pure and majestic spiritual realm like a lotus flower. This state of enlightenment encompasses all universal laws and recognizes the inherent Buddha-nature within all beings. Therefore, the aim is to guide individuals toward rediscovering their own inherent purity.[55]

Drawing on both Buddhist thought and the Chinese philosophy of unity between heaven and humanity, Master Cheng Yen offers a unique interpretation of the Buddha's famous declaration, recorded in the *Dirhagama-sutra*, "I am the chief in the world."

She explains that the Buddha wasn't claiming personal superiority, but rather expressing his oneness with the ultimate truth,[56] which itself is unique and worthy of reverence. This perspective, she suggests, offers a fresh perspective for contemporary rational thinkers.

Mahayana Buddhism emphasizes that Buddhas and Bodhisattvas should return to the human world in endless cycles to save all living beings. The Buddha's "Perfect Extinction" is not extinction in actuality; the Buddha's physical body is both existent and non-existent. His Dharma body, on the other hand, is eternal and can take on infinite forms in the human world to free suffering beings. This echoes Taoism's belief

---

[55] Shi, De Fan (2015). *Zheng yan shang ren na lu zuji* [Footprints of Master Cheng Yen]. Taipei: Tzu Chi Publishing Co. p. 138.

[56] Shih, Cheng Yen. (2014). *Wisdom at Dawn*. Hualien: Jing Si Abode.

that Being and Non-Being share the same lineage, and that Being and Non-Being will eternally cycle out of one another.[57]

Lao Tzu said, "(Conceived of as) having no name, it is the Originator of heaven and earth; (conceived of as) having a name, it is the Mother of all things."[58] This is comparable to Buddhism's Inaction and Action. Chinese ideology coalesces people with all other elements and entities between heaven and earth. Buddhism promotes All-Inclusive Cognition, realizing a realm of non-duality in which self-nature is unified with all things and laws.

Confucianism, Buddhism, and Taoism all believe in the harmonious and indiscriminate unification of all things and beings as one. They espouse that there is no difference between self and others, thus showing that loving others is the same as loving oneself, and altruism is a path to self-enlightenment.

Altruism is not for self-gain. It is about altruism itself. In life's depths, the fundamental principles of universal truth remain the same. The spiritual worlds of Buddhism, Confucianism, and Taoism all point to altruism.

Spiritual Cultivation for Good Enterprises

The ultimate goal of the Economy of Goodness is to lead entrepreneurs to be sages in Confucianism, Wheel-Turning Sage King in Buddhism, and the chosen people in Christianity.

Enterprises create materials that shape human civilization, while entrepreneurs create wealth that secures national happiness and prosperity. They demonstrate saintly traits by knowing people well and making the best use of them.

In the thirty-first chapter of Doctrine of the Mean, there are several sentences that can best depict the cultivation of entrepreneurs of goodness:

> It is only he who is possessed of the most complete sincerity that can exist under heaven, who can give its full development to his nature. Able to give

[57] Wang, B. X. (2010). *Laozi daodejing zhu de xiandai jiedu* [Modern Interpretation of Laozi's Dao De Jing]. Yuan-Liou Publishing Co., Ltd. p. 14.

[58] Legge, J. (1962). *The Sacred Books of China: The Texts of Taoism* (Vol. 1). New York: Dover Publications. p. 47.

its full development to his own nature, he can do the same to the nature of other men. Able to give its full development to the nature of other men, he can give their full development to the nature of animals and things. Able to give their full development to the natures of creatures and things, he can assist the transforming and nourishing powers of Heaven and Earth. Able to assist the transforming and nourishing powers of Heaven and Earth, he may with Heaven and Earth form a ternion.[59]

Great entrepreneurs can bring out the best of human nature and use it to work with nature. If they can bring out the fullest potential of the natural world, they can be part of creating a better world. This is their highest life goal.

Sincerity should be the premise. It entails combining purity, compassion, and wisdom. Cultivating sincerity starts with purity, and purity requires overcoming greed, with generosity as its foundation. By giving more to others, one can gradually overcome greed. Sincerely giving to others can inspire one's own compassion. When one can give to others, and others can joyfully receive, it can develop wisdom.

Therefore, in the act of giving to others, one should overcome greed and cultivate purity. Through continual selfless giving to others, compassion is nurtured. In all acts of giving, wisdom is honed.

The practice of Good Enterprises relies on the cultivation of personal character and the development of inner strength.

How to achieve spiritual and physical coexistence and co-prosperity of all beings, and even partake of the nourishing powers of Heaven and Earth, should be the goal of individuals and Good Enterprises.

Six Practices of Good Enterprises

For the spiritual cultivation of practitioners of Good Enterprises, I suggest the Six Practices.

They are from the six Paramitas in Buddhism: Generosity, Ethics, Forbearance, Diligence, Concentration, and Wisdom.

Generosity Should Be Rooted in Altruism;
Ethics should be based on principles;
Forbearance should be rooted in the understanding;

[59] Legge, J. (1971). *Confucian Analects: The Great Learning, and The Doctrine of the Mean*. New York: Dover Publications. pp. 389–399.

Diligence should be based on inclusivity;
Concentration should be based on non-attachment;
Wisdom should be grounded in harmonious unification.

The first step of the Six Paramitas is generosity, which embodies the true essence of benefiting others, which involves overcoming greed. The more capable a person is in practicing generosity, the less they are driven by greed. Because one is not greedy, one will not be poor.

Tzu Chi praises South African Tzu Chi volunteers for their simple life, noting that though they lack wealth, they are not greedy either, so they remain abundant in other ways. It is concluded that the greedier a person is, the poorer they will be; the more they desire, the more aggressive they will be.

Why do some aggressive countries who own vast territory invade other countries? Greed is the cause! Why do political leaders who are wealthier than anyone else extort and demand more wealth recklessly? Once more, greed is to blame! Greed makes people never feel satisfied.

If a country's prosperity is founded on the growth of desires, how can it avoid invading other nations when it gains strength? If a person's accomplishments spring from greed and the gratification of self-indulgence, then how can one not take advantage of others? Greed is in force.

Master Cheng Yen commends South African local volunteers for not being acquisitive, meaning they are not poor because they give without asking for anything in return. The more one can allot, the less rapacious they will be.

Today's society promotes consumption, personal desire, and self-pursuit, leading to inevitable conflicts. A culture focused on desire and self-gratification will breed conflict and discord.

Peace and justice have no opposite, only greed. Greed cannot coexist with peace, as it leads to attempts to seize and compete. This creates conflict, in the words of Master Cheng Yen.

Greed not only stirs up trouble and discord, but injustice too. Does the strong oppress the weak, the wealthy manipulate the destitute, supervisors intimidate their workers, subordinates rebel against their leaders, citizens defy authorities, and officials oppress the masses—are not these acts of injustice stemming from greed? The clash between justice and peace arises from greed.

Those who strive for peace are not avaricious, and those who seek justice do not take. True justice requires courageous generosity.

A society that encourages selfless contributions will be freed from greed and suffused with peace and justice.

Today's international conflicts and accusations in the name of justice are mostly driven by greed and a desire for personal gain. The only resolution is to eradicate greed and foster altruism.

It is better to promote charity and nurture people's willingness to donate than to depend on laws to curtail corruption and wrongdoing. When people understand the suffering of others and appreciate their own contentment, how can they not spare a thought for others? Those who are free from avarice will not compete, but give.

It is better to practice ethical actions beginning with oneself rather than fighting injustice.

We must not underestimate the influence of charity on society. Through charity, one can transform from doing good temporarily to making good decisions consistently, freeing oneself from avarice in charity. If one refrains from being greedy, they will not be destitute and will not compete or acquire.

When everyone contributes, justice will permeate society. Encouraging fair actions ensures an environment of calmness.

Ridding greed in charity is the only prescription for today's social conflicts.

Ridding oneself of greed is somewhat passive, whereas being proactively generous, with compassion and altruism, to others is more effective. True giving lies in not expecting anything in return; this is the Buddha's idea of donating without a focus on the form.

True joy comes from giving. When one gives joyfully, the recipient is likely to receive with joy, and they may even join in the act of giving. This is the true meaning of a joyful heart. Tzu Chi emphasizes the concept of "teaching the rich to help the poor" and also "guiding the poor to realize their riches." This is to give with joy, receive with joy, and further transform the receiver into a giver.

Giving doesn't just mean material things. Sharing knowledge, offering emotional support, and giving wisdom is called "Dharma dana." It helps others understand and overcome difficulties. This requires empathy, letting go of control, truly listening, and offering wise guidance. To give wisdom, one must have it. A strong mind is needed. Dharma dana is a high level of giving.

The third level of giving is fearless giving. Fearless giving means having the courage and strength to give compassionately and selflessly in any situation, without seeking anything in return. Fearlessness signifies wisdom and freedom from obstacles. Because of their abundant wisdom, they can provide enlightenment and inspiration to anyone in any situation, bringing joy to others. With no desire, there are no obstacles.

After giving comes upholding precepts, which is to adhere to principles. When we follow precepts we are shrinking ourselves. If one can shrink oneself, adhere to principles, and control desires, then one can truly strengthen the power of the mind. Because if the power of the mind is bound by desires or external forces, it cannot exert its strength.

Although desires are internal, they are easily drawn by external things. Anything that can be drawn by any external force will affect the strength of the inner mind. To possess the strength of the mind, one must refuse to be bound by desires.

Upholding precepts is followed by forbearance. Forbearance means having empathy and being able to understand others. Even when we are insulted, criticized unfairly, or misunderstood, we should use empathy to observe and understand those who criticize and revile us. Therefore, the first step in forbearance is understanding. If we can understand others well, we will not be provoked by them. Therefore, forbearance is not about enduring everything silently until we cannot bear it anymore and finally explode. All this does is destroy everything that we worked for.

Therefore, if forbearance is based on understanding, then it is possible not to be affected by great misunderstandings, criticisms, insults, distortions, and even grievances. Even those who insult us can still be loved and transformed, and in the end, we can even form good karma with them and even inspire them to work together for all beings. This is the true essence of forbearance.

After forbearance, the fourth cultivation of the mind is "diligence." Diligence means being able to continuously advance to a higher level of the mind. The mind can contain the void and can accommodate everything. This is the meaning of diligence.

In the ten grounds of the Bodhisattva, there are the Difficult to Conquer Ground, the Far-Reaching Ground, and then the Immovable Ground. The Immovable Ground is to reach the fifth cultivation of samadhi (meditative concentration).

Samadhi is to truly not be disturbed by external conditions, not to be drawn by the outside world, and to be able to firmly establish one's own nature internally. This is true samadhi.

Samadhi also refers to the state of "being at ease in any situation." In any situation, one can be still in the midst of movement, and in any environment, one can "generate a state of mind without attachments." This is to generate a joyful mind, a compassionate mind, a wise mind, a fearless mind, and a tranquil mind.

The sixth cultivation of the mind is wisdom. The realm of wisdom is that in any situation, with anyone, practitioners can solve confusion, enlighten, and give energy to others. This is wisdom.

In Buddhism, wisdom also includes understanding all the laws of the universe and the world, understanding all laws, and upholding all goodness. This is called wisdom.

The *Sutra of Infinite Meanings* refers to the aspiration of attaining great wisdom and comprehending all phenomena.[60] This is the state that everyone strives for. Everyone hopes to gain all wisdom and solve all worldly problems. But how can this be done?

The Buddha is to be able to reach such great wisdom through selfless giving in everything.

In fact, it is not about gaining all wisdom to save all people, but about gaining all wisdom in the process of saving all people. It is about gaining all wisdom in all our endeavors and cultivating all compassion in helping all people.

The center of economic activity is people, to benefit people and make them happy. To benefit people, but not to fuel their desires; to make them happy, but also to make them willing to give happiness to others. This is a good method in business economics.

---

[60] Liu, Q. *Wuliang yi jing* [The Sutra of Innumerable Meanings (Sect. 12.1)]. *Dazheng xinxiu dazang jing* [Taishō Tripiṭaka (Vol. 9)]. No. 0276.

Economic System for Common Goodness

The aim of the Economy of Goodness is to bring about a society that is abundant and in harmony across the physical, mental, and spiritual aspects. This is the Confucian ideal of balance and harmony between humanity and nature, and now it is time to bring it to life in modern society by means of the Economy of Goodness.

In Taoism, the highest virtue is like water, benefiting all things without contention, thus maintaining its own glory without striving. This is known as "Highest Goodness."

In Confucianism, goodness is found in the harmonious and appropriate fulfillment of relationships between individuals, as well as between humans and all elements of the natural world. Therefore, it is known as "Harmonious Goodness."

Buddhism advocates the concept that all phenomena are interconnected, and thus encourages living, sharing, and flourishing together with all beings. This is known as "Common Goodness."

In Western civilization, the emphasis lies on leading a morally guided life based on reason, aiming to create happiness in the present world. This is known as the "Utmost Goodness."

Economy of Goodness, while aiming for material abundance, also provides a path to inner purity. It seeks to pursue universal prosperity for humanity while promoting the sustainable life of the Earth.

It wishes that business, material, and mind could all be of goodness in the world.

445

THE ECONOMY OF GOODNESS
THAT BENEFITS BOTH OTHERS AND SELVES

"The highest excellence is like (that of) water. The goodness of water appears in its benefiting all things."[1] To benefit all things without attachment is the concept of highest goodness. Lao Tzu's fundamental philosophy is achieving an absolute transcendence of the mind after accomplishing all things.

Lao Tzu's philosophy is expressed in the statement, "They grow, and there is no claim made for their ownership; they go through their processes, and there is no expectation (of a reward for the results). The work is accomplished, and there is no resting in it (as an achievement). The work is done, but how no one can see; it is this that makes the power not cease to be."[2] The idea is to first generate, create, or achieve, and then transcend. The more one can transcend, the more enduring the results will be.

Lao Tzu's philosophy involves achieving positive outcomes through actions that appear contrary. He advocates advancing through retreat, esteeming humility, and having abundance through emptiness. In economic thinking, the idea is to give before acquiring, emphasizing the priority of benefiting others before oneself. The more one can benefit others, the more one can benefit oneself.

The spirit of altruism does not necessitate harming oneself. Self-harming altruism is neither ultimate nor sustainable. If we believe that every life is equally important, how can sacrificing one person to save another be justified?

Altruism without harming oneself is the only sustainable form of altruism, preventing it from devolving into morally questionable actions done out of a sense of obligation. Achieving this requires a higher level of wisdom.

Lao Tzu emphasized a small country with few people in economic life, as mentioned before. He was not advocating giving up the mundane world, but rather spiritual freedom for people, as derived from the way of nature. As Lao Tzu said, "Man takes his law from the Earth; the Earth

---

[1] Tzu, L. (Eds.). (2021). *Tao Te Ching* (J. Legge, Trans.). Standard Ebooks. Retrieved from https://standardebooks.org/ebooks/laozi/tao-te-ching/james-legge.

[2] Tzu, L. (Eds.). (2021). *Tao Te Ching* (J. Legge, Trans.). Standard Ebooks. Retrieved from https://standardebooks.org/ebooks/laozi/tao-te-ching/james-legge.

takes its law from Heaven; Heaven takes its law from the Tao. The law of the Tao is its being what it is."[3]

The virtue of Earth bears all things while seeking nothing in return. This also holds true for humans, meaning those who strive for success yet remain unattached. By being unencumbered, one can live a life of freedom. Lao Tzu believed that the less attached one is, the longer they can sustain something.

Earth follows Heaven. The way of Heaven is not to self-generate, so it can bring about the generation of all things. Lao Tzu said, "Heaven is long-enduring and earth continues long. The reason why heaven and earth are able to endure and continue thus long is because they do not live of, or for, themselves. This is how they are able to continue and endure."[4] They live for the needs of all beings and all things. Heaven and earth do not act from (the impulse of) any wish to be benevolent; they deal with all things as the dogs of grass are dealt with.[5] Straw dogs are the pole in sacrifice rituals in ancient China and by this Lao Tzu meant that heaven and earth take all beings and things as their returning point. Heaven does not foster its own life. Likewise, with non-self-interest, one profits; with a self-interested mind, one cannot profit.

Humans follow Heaven and Earth. Saints should not decide what the world needs by themselves, but rather consider what people need. Heaven and Earth generate for the needs of all things and do not define any standards; thus, allowing all things to form their categories and thrive.

This is the virtue of Heaven and Earth in benefiting all beings and things: the Way of Heaven is to benefit rather than harm people. Sages help others without competing or seeking anything in return, thus gaining their virtuous merit. Through selfless aid and expecting nothing in return, one reaps greater rewards.

This is the philosophy of helping both others and ourselves. The Economy of Goodness follows the Way of Heaven and Earth in benefiting both others and selves.

---

[3] Tzu, L. (Eds.). (2021). *Tao Te Ching* (J. Legge, Trans.). Standard Ebooks. Retrieved from https://standardebooks.org/ebooks/laozi/tao-te-ching/james-legge.

[4] Legge, J. (1962). *The Sacred Books of China: The Texts of Taoism* (Vol. 1). New York: Dover Publications. p. 52.

[5] Legge, J. (1962). *The Sacred Books of China: The Texts of Taoism* (Vol. 1). New York: Dover Publications. p. 50.

THE ECONOMY OF GOODNESS
WITH HAPPINESS AND RATIONALITY

From Socrates onward, Western civilization began stressing human reason and attributed evil to ignorance. Goodness comes from knowledge and reason. Plato, on the other hand, separated the supreme goodness of the ideal from the material, thinking that the ideal represents the supreme goodness while materials are subject to birth, death, and vicissitudes. Aristotle revised Plato's opinion, holding that ideas and materials coexist and the former cannot be separated from the latter, just as the idea of an apple cannot be separated from a physical apple.

Kant thought that the supreme goodness is the good will that follows reason.

Good will stands independently from all non-good outcomes; it is pure, existing on its own, based on innate reason and the innate moral laws of humanity. Acting in accordance with these laws is considered good. The happiness created by acting in accordance with this innate moral reason and the laws of good will is termed supreme goodness.

Therefore, following the rational moral order of Western traditional philanthropy to create human happiness is the ultimate good. In terms of a virtuous economy, the happiness generated by adhering to the moral principles inherent in human rationality is the goal of an economy of goodness.

It must be noted that people have innate reason as the origin of good will. The economic life of joy formed by innate human logic is referred to as the Economy of Goodness.

Therefore, from a Western viewpoint, the Economy of Goodness must adhere to reason and morality and bring about happiness.

This sets the EOG apart from economies driven by appetite, irrationality, and immorality, dubbed economies of evil.

Happiness created by reason and good will will endure. Otherwise, it will be fleeting and hollow. Socrates claimed that due to lack of knowledge, people strive for their wants, but those do not bring happiness.

Happiness in Western civilization is associated with spiritual wealth arising from material gratification, joys of life, appreciation of beauty, and family affection. This is ultimately based on truth.

The economy of the West encompasses reason, truth, morality, beauty, and love.

The Economy of Goodness
Unites Heaven and Man as One

The Confucian economic system of unity between heaven and humanity seeks the harmonious and well-rounded fulfillment of all relationships. We refer to it as "Harmonious Goodness."

In Confucianism, Heaven and Man are United As One means that humans can understand the Way of Heaven and the essence of all things and practice the Way of Heaven and the laws in the human world. This must be done with a character of supreme sincerity.

Sincere people are pure, compassionate, and wise.

With a pure, compassionate, and wise mind, one can comprehend the essence of the universe and unleash one's full potential.

Then one can comprehend the essence of people and objects, and draw on them, thus participating in the production of Heaven and Earth, which encapsulates mankind's highest sincere nature, and unites the human, all things, and Heaven and Earth as one.

The Way of Heaven in Confucianism translates into benevolence and propriety in reality. Benevolence means "wishing to be established himself, seeks also to establish others; wishing to be enlarged himself, he seeks also to enlarge others,"[6] which embodies a spirit of altruism. This cultivation of benevolence is particularly worthy of promotion in contemporary society. As for propriety in Confucianism, it is placed within an ethical order, emphasizing harmonious relationships between ruler and subject, father and son, husband and wife, elder and younger siblings, and friends. Goodness, in the eyes of Confucianism, lies in the harmonious relationships between individuals. The Great Learning calls for studying, gaining knowledge, being authentic, having a correct outlook, self-cultivation, caring for one's family, governing one's country, and unifying the world. It is said that governing a country starts with personal refinement, which must begin with being filial and fraternal.

In the Economy of Goodness, establishing positive relationships with family, colleagues, partners, customers, and the environment implies benevolence and propriety. All economic production is beneficial to the neighborhood, community, country, world, and Earth is benevolence.

---

[6] Legge, J. (1971). *Confucian Analects: The Great Learning, and The Doctrine of the Mean*. New York: Dover Publications. p. 194.

The Book of Rites says, "The noble man observes these rules of propriety, so that all in a wider circle are harmonious with him, and those in his narrower circle have no dissatisfactions with him. Men acknowledge and are affected by his goodness, and spirits enjoy his virtue."[7] Those who follow propriety maintain external harmony and internal peace, leading all tangible beings to embrace a heart of benevolence, even ghosts and deities enjoying this virtue.

The premise of propriety is to act reasonably with people and things. In the modern context, propriety should not only emphasize vertical ethical orders but also be implemented horizontally. Bosses and employees shouldn't be compared to monarchs and ministers; instead, their relationship should be like that between a father and son. Good Enterprises should not only be like a home; colleagues should be like siblings. Customers should be viewed as friends and nature should be respected and cared for like a mother.

Rebuilding the ethical foundations of today's enterprises with Confucianism, from The Way of Heaven to benevolence and propriety, is still relevant and appropriate.

The ancestral temple of the past is akin to an enterprise of goodness; its patriarch is analogous to today's business owner. A closely knit web of clan relationships is efficiently managed through rationale and fairness. As the *Book of Rites* states:

(The idea of) right makes the distinction between things, and serves to regulate (the manifestation of) humanity. When it is found in anything and its relation to humanity has been discussed, the possessor of it will be strong. Humanity is the root of right, and the embodying of deferential consideration. The possessor of it is honored.[8]

The Book of Rites states that wisdom is essential to practice Justice correctly and that fair and reasonable distribution is necessary to create it. This should be based on benevolence. The leader distributing Justice must have the strength to do so and cultivate respect and love, ensuring harmonious human relations.

---

[7] Confucius. (2013). *The Book of Rites (Li Ji): English-Chinese Version* (D. Sheng, Ed., J. Legge, Trans.). CreateSpace Independent Publishing Platform. p. 167.

[8] Confucius. (2013). *The Book of Rites (Li Ji): English-Chinese Version* (D. Sheng, Ed., J. Legge, Trans.). CreateSpace Independent Publishing Platform. p. 106.

Justice refers to the harmonization and reconciliation of different parties' interests, guided by equity or compassion, rather than just selfish desires. Justice in the Economy of Goodness accommodates both interests and collaboration. It emphasizes individuals' feeling of gratification through a fair and just allocation of interests under varied circumstances. This also applies to corporations and national economies.

Governance through benevolence brings seamless harmony; distribution with Justice brings contentment among all and when people abide by propriety, it leads to unified cohesion.

The Way of Heaven denotes the forces and laws of the universe. People of benevolence join with the Way of Heaven; this depicts harmony between mankind and everything under Heaven. Justice indicates a fair and equitable distribution of rights and interests, and propriety denotes serenity among individuals. When these three unite, goodness is achieved.

The Economy of Goodness ensures healthy and positive relationships by incorporating the Way of Heaven, benevolence, propriety, and justice. These three elements form the core principles and laws of economic activities in Confucianism. Entrepreneurs should strive to cultivate personal virtues by benevolence, wisdom by Justice and harmony using propriety.

In the Economy of Goodness, enterprises will be in harmony with staff, customers, and shareholders, fostering peace and contentment for all. Workplace contentment reflects Justice; harmony among one another stands for propriety; and social peace constitutes great virtue.

THE ECONOMY OF GOODNESS WITH THE COMPLETE PERFECTION OF BODY, MIND, AND SPIRITUAL REALM

Buddhism wishes that all sentient beings would achieve Common Goodness with the complete perfection of body, mind, and spiritual realm.

Buddhism's ideal for the world is expounded in The *Bhaisajyaguru Sutra*. *The Twelve Great Vows of the Medicine Buddha* revealed by the Buddha, illustrate the blueprint of the Economy of Goodness.

In this blueprint, material is unusually abundant, with gold as the rope and colored glaze as flooring. Everyone is attractive, healthy and dignified, benefiting others with a pure mind. Moreover, all reside in communities, inspiring many to aid others, granting abundant and tranquil lives, guiding them along the Bodhisattva Path, and achieving the common goodness of humanity.

The First Great Vow of the Medicine Buddha:

> I vow that in a future life, when I have attained Supreme, Perfect Enlightenment, brilliant rays will shine forth from my body, illuminating infinite, countless boundless realms. This body will be adorned with the Thirty-Two Marks of Greatness and Eighty Auspicious Characteristics. Furthermore, I will enable all sentient beings to become just like me.[9]

Growing up in a peaceful world with a wealth of material and cultural resources, people will naturally be in good health, attractive, and regal. Health stems from the fostering of a healthy environment and material abundance. Beauty is also a result of cultural enrichment.

In the First Great Vow, the Medicine Buddha expected that all beings would be happy upon seeing him, that the handicapped could regain their health, and those with darkened minds could be enlightened.

This means that a practitioner can attain a state of Bodhisattva and Buddha, form wise and compassionate connections with all people, accompany everyone, and even enlighten them to become creators of "Common Goodness."

In the First Great Vow, the Medicine Buddha signifies enlightening all beings, as the sun shines on the earth, promoting flourishing and joy.

The Second Great Vow:

> I vow that in a future life, when I have attained Supreme Enlightenment, my body, inside and out, will radiate far and wide the clarity and flawless purity of lapis lazuli. This body will be adorned with superlative virtues and dwell peacefully in the midst of a web of light more magnificent than the sun or moon. The light will awaken the minds of all beings dwelling in darkness, enabling them to engage in their pursuits according to their wishes.[10]

The Second Vow calls for self-purification of body and mind so that one can boast an aura of power and opulence. Professional success grants

---

[9] Thành, M., & Leigh, P. D. (2001). *Sutra of the Medicine Buddha* (H. Jung, Trans.). North Hills: International Buddhist Monastic Institute. p. 19. https://www.buddhanet.net/pdf_file/medbudsutra.pdf.

[10] Thành, M., & Leigh, P. D. (2001). *Sutra of the Medicine Buddha* (H. Jung, Trans.). North Hills: International Buddhist Monastic Institute. p. 19. https://www.buddhanet.net/pdf_file/medbudsutra.pdf.

access to an abundance of material comforts and provides the opportunity to help those in darkness reach their goals according to their gifts and inclinations, thereby bringing great merit.

The Third Great Vow:

> I vow that in a future life, when I have attained Supreme Enlightenment, I will, with infinite wisdom and skillful means, provide all sentient beings with an inexhaustible quantity of goods to meet their material needs. They will never want for anything.[11]

This Vow presents a world of abundance, where all may satisfy their material wants as they please. This is akin to Xunzi's belief that people's desires should be cultivated and their needs met. Thus, Buddhism does not reject material needs but rather seeks to provide endless material goods to all creatures through unfathomable wisdom.

The Fourth Great Vow:

> I vow that in a future life, when I have attained Supreme Enlightenment, I will set all who follow heretical ways upon the path to Enlightenment. Likewise, I will set those who follow the Sravaka and Pratyeka-Buddha ways onto the Mahayana path.[12]

The Third Vow illustrates material wealth and the Fourth spiritual liberation. If one strays, the Medicine Buddha can enlighten and guide them back with bodhisattva wisdom. Not only would the Medicine Buddha save those that are lost, but also inspire those focused on cultivating themselves to go out in the world and enlighten and rescue all with their insight.

The realm of the Medicine Buddha in entrepreneurship and all good knowledge is to make a vow to create useful substances for all living beings, employing wisdom, and to guide them to Enlightenment.

---

[11] Thành, M., & Leigh, P. D. (2001). *Sutra of the Medicine Buddha* (H. Jung, Trans.). North Hills: International Buddhist Monastic Institute. p. 20. https://www.buddhanet. net/pdf_file/medbudsutra.pdf.

[12] Thành, M., & Leigh, P. D. (2001). *Sutra of the Medicine Buddha* (H. Jung, Trans.). North Hills: International Buddhist Monastic Institute. p. 20. https://www.buddhanet. net/pdf_file/medbudsutra.pdf.

The Fifth Great Vow:

I vow that in a future life, when I have attained Supreme Enlightenment, I will help all the countless sentient beings who cultivate the path of morality in accordance with my Dharma to observe the rules of conduct (Precepts) to perfection, in conformity with the Three Root Precepts. Even those guilty of disparaging or violating the Precepts will regain their purity upon hearing my name, and avoid descending upon the Evil Paths.[13]

The Sixth Great Vow:

I vow that in a future life, when I have attained Supreme Enlightenment, sentient beings with imperfect bodies whose senses are deficient, who are ugly, stupid, blind, deaf, mute, crippled, hunchbacked, leprous, insane or suffering from various other illnesses will, upon hearing my name, acquire well-formed bodies, endowed with intelligence, with all senses intact. They will be free of illness and suffering.[14]

The Medicine Buddha wished for all sentient beings born with disabilities to be cured.

The Seventh Great Vow:

I vow that in a future life, when I have attained Supreme Enlightenment, sentient beings afflicted with various illnesses, with no one to help them, nowhere to turn, no physicians, no medicine, no family, no home who are destitute and miserable will, as soon as my name passes through their ears, be relieved of all their illnesses. With mind and body peaceful and contented, they will enjoy home, family and property in abundance and eventually realize Unsurpassed Supreme Enlightenment.[15]

---

[13] Thành, M., & Leigh, P. D. (2001). *Sutra of the Medicine Buddha* (H. Jung, Trans.). North Hills: International Buddhist Monastic Institute. p. 20. https://www.buddhanet. net/pdf_file/medbudsutra.pdf.

[14] Thành, M., & Leigh, P. D. (2001). *Sutra of the Medicine Buddha* (H. Jung, Trans.). North Hills: International Buddhist Monastic Institute. p. 21. https://www.buddhanet. net/pdf_file/medbudsutra.pdf.

[15] Thành, M., & Leigh, P.D. (2001). *Sutra of the Medicine Buddha* (H. Jung, Trans.). North Hills: International Buddhist Monastic Institute. p. 21. https://www.buddhanet. net/pdf_file/medbudsutra.pdf.

The Medicine Buddha wished to grant all beings material wealth and physical wellness, and then nurture them to acquire pure wisdom.

The Eighth Great Vow:

> I vow that in a future life, when I have attained Supreme Enlightenment, those women who are extremely disgusted with the hundred afflictions that befall women' and wish to abandon their female form, will, upon hearing my name, all be reborn as men. They will be endowed with noble features and eventually realize Unsurpassed Supreme Enlightenment.[16]

In this Vow, the Medicine Buddha spoke for the women with the low social status who suffer under unreasonable social systems. This remains true even in many countries and regions today. The Medicine Buddha hoped that they would receive the same fair treatment as men and have opportunities to cultivate themselves and attain Bodhi.

Nowadays, many Buddhist nations still prohibit women from becoming nuns, and even if they do, they don't have the same cultivation possibilities. The Medicine Buddha vowed to emancipate women and give them the opportunity to fulfill their potential.

The Ninth Great Vow:

> I vow that in a future life, when I have attained Supreme Enlighten-ment, I will help all sentient beings escape from the demons' net and free themselves from the bonds of heretical paths. Should they be caught in the thicket of wrong views, I will lead them to correct views, gradually inducing them to cultivate the practices of Bodhisattvas and swiftly realize Supreme, Perfect Enlightenment.[17]

The Medicine Buddha vowed to guide all sentient beings away from impure beliefs and distorted thoughts unknowingly. He further promised to lead them to the Bodhisattva Path, helping them attain compassion and wisdom to aid others. This Vow for Goodness and Good Enterprises

[16] Thành, M., & Leigh, P.D. (2001). *Sutra of the Medicine Buddha* (H. Jung, Trans.). North Hills: International Buddhist Monastic Institute. pp. 21–22. https://www.buddha net.net/pdf_file/medbudsutra.pdf.

[17] Thành, M., & Leigh, P.D. (2001). *Sutra of the Medicine Buddha* (H. Jung, Trans.). North Hills: International Buddhist Monastic Institute. p. 22. https://www.buddhanet. net/pdf_file/medbudsutra.pdf.

is intended to guide those undertaking unscrupulous economic activities back to the right path. By doing so, they can reconcile their career and soul while benefiting society.

The Tenth Great Vow:

> The Tenth Great Vow: I vow that in a future life, when I have attained Supreme Enlightenment, those sentient beings who are shackled, beaten, imprisoned, condemned to death or otherwise subjected to countless miseries and humiliations by royal decree - and who are suffering in body and mind from this oppression - need only hear my name to be freed from all these afflictions, thanks to the awesome power of my merits and virtues.[18]

The Medicine Buddha will not forsake any sentient beings, including victims and those suffering physically and mentally. He even swore to save criminals, freeing them from imprisonment.

The Eleventh Great Vow:

> I vow that in a future life, when I have attained Supreme Enlightenment, if sentient beings who are tormented by hunger and thirst to the point of creating evil karma in their attempts to survive should succeed in hearing my name, recite it single-mindedly and hold fast to it, I will first satisfy them with the most exquisite food and drink. Ultimately, it is through the flavor of the Dharma that I will establish them in the realm of peace and happiness.[19]

For those who commit crimes due to poverty, the Medicine Buddha will furnish them with the best food and inspire them to find joy in the truth and take the right path to straighten out their lives.

---

[18] Thành, M., & Leigh, P. D. (2001). *Sutra of the Medicine Buddha* (H. Jung, Trans.). North Hills: International Buddhist Monastic Institute. p. 22. https://www.buddhanet. net/pdf_file/medbudsutra.pdf.

[19] Thành, M., & Leigh, P. D. (2001). *Sutra of the Medicine Buddha* (H. Jung, Trans.). North Hills: International Buddhist Monastic Institute. p. 23. https://www.buddhanet. net/pdf_file/medbudsutra.pdf.

The Twelfth Great Vow:

> I vow that in a future life, when I have attained Supreme Enlightenment, if sentient beings who are utterly destitute, lacking clothes to protect them from mosquitos and flies, heat and cold, and are suffering day and night should hear my name, recite it single-mindedly and hold fast to it, their wishes will be fulfilled. They will immediately receive all manner of exquisite clothing, precious adornments, flower garlands, and incense powder, and will enjoy music and entertainment to their heart's content.
>
> Manjusri, these are the Twelve Sublime Vows made by the World-Honored Medicine Buddha Lapis Lazuli Radiance Tathagata, Arhat, the Perfectly Enlightened, when he was cultivating the Bodhisattva path.[20]

The *Twelve Great Vows of the Medicine Buddha* include physical health, material abundance, and spiritual purity. He promises to cure all the handicapped and supply the most afflicted with the best quality of life, food, clothing, music, and plays.

This is giving the greatest benefit to the weakest as John Rawls advocates in *A Theory of Justice*, isn't it?

The First Great Vow of the Medicine Buddha portrayed a world of abundance, with gold used as rope and glazed tiles for flooring. People in this world experience carefree, prosperous, harmonious lives, rich in material wealth.

It is important that everyone walks on the Bodhisattva Path, which is key to physical health, material abundance, and spiritual purity, as stated in the Twelfth Great Vow. Without the Bodhisattva Path, all prosperity and the purity of human bodies and souls would not be possible.

This echoes Aristotle's moral life advocating for the establishment of relationships of love with people, as well as participating in public affairs.

The Medicine Buddha espouses the same approach: to love all sentient beings, meet their material needs, nurture a pure mind, and then follow the Bodhisattva Path to assist and liberate more people, culminating in Bodhi; the greatest joys of life.

---

[20] Thành, M., & Leigh, P. D. (2001). *Sutra of the Medicine Buddha* (H. Jung, Trans.). North Hills: International Buddhist Monastic Institute. p. 23. https://www.buddhanet.net/pdf_file/medbudsutra.pdf.

The Medicine Buddha represents a visible embodiment of Buddhism that promotes the well-being of humankind in a collective and prosperous society.

An Invisible Mind that Creates Society of Equal Wealth

Altruism is an invisible force that fosters a wealthy and tranquil society.

The great vow of the Medicine Buddha lies not in his divine power, but in the compassionate vow to benefit others. If everyone possesses such a vow and a heart dedicated to benefiting others, it will undoubtedly create the abundant, pure, and harmonious world that the Medicine Buddha aspires to.

The thought of self-interest has dominated humanity's economic development for centuries. On one hand, it has spawned social prosperity but, on the other, pushed about half the world's population to the brink of exploitation and poverty. The Prisoner's Dilemma has demonstrated that both self-interested parties can never achieve the most equitable distribution for maximum benefit, i.e., Pareto-optimality. Only altruism can bring about optimized distribution.

As mentioned by Nobel laureate economist Angus Deaton from the University of Cambridge, if the wealthiest ten percent of the world each donated one dollar, it could lift everyone on Earth out of poverty. The challenge lies in the willingness of each individual to contribute. However, altruism, an invisible heart, has the power to create a society that is equitable, prosperous, and harmonious.

Modern medical scientists have identified the altruistic brain region, known as the Posterior Superior Temporal Cortex (PSTC), which is present in both humans and animals.[21]

When we humans see suffering, our inner compassion will arise as PSTC amplifies. If we human beings can commonly develop and establish altruistic emotions, human beings will not have to worry about how to create a rich, clean, and peaceful society. Altruism is an invisible heart that can guide society to make the most reasonable distribution of wealth and create a rich and happy life for every individual, and will naturally lead

---

[21] Paccione, C. E. (2020). *The Giving Brain: A Look at the Neurology of Altruism.* Brain World Magazine. https://brainworldmagazine.com/giving-brain-look-neurology-altruism./.

people to approach those in need of help, gather crowd wisdom, find ways to help disadvantaged groups and other species to survive and thrive and care for the Earth for the sustainable development of humans.

References

A. & Ellis, W.A.M. (2015). Politics. CreateSpace Independent Publishing Platform.

Anālayo, B. (2013). On the Five Aggregates (3)—A Translation of Saṃyukta-āgama Discourses 59 to 87. Dharma Drum Journal of Buddhist Studies. New Taipei City: Dharma Drum Buddhist College.

Ash, R. (1989). Kang Chao: Man and Land in Chinese History: An Economic Analysis, xii. Stanford: Stanford University Press, 1986.

Bailey, G., Mabbett, I. (2003). The Sociology of Early Buddhism. Cambridge University Press.

Ban, G., & Yan, S. G. (1962). Han shu [Book of the Han Dynasty] (Vol. 12). Taipei: Chung hwa book co. ltd.

Bangxiong W. (2010). A Modern Interpretation of Dao De Jing. Taipei: Yuan-Liou Publishing Co., Ltd.

Batson, C. D. (2014). The Altruism Question: Toward A Social-Psychological Answer. United States: Taylor & Francis.

Bentham, J., Burns, J. H., & Hart, H. L. A. (1988). Bentham: A Fragment on Government. United Kingdom: Cambridge University Press.

Bible. (2017). The Holy Bible: Chinese Union Version (Deuteronomy 23:19).

Birch, C. & Keene, D. L. (1965). Anthology of Chinese Literature. United States: Grove Press. p.184.

Bourdieu, P. (1977). Outline of a Theory of Practice. United Kingdom: Cambridge University Press.

Brown, C. (2003). Buddhist Economics: An Enlightenment Approach to the Dismal Science. United States: Bloomsbury Publishing.

© The Editor(s) (if applicable) and The Author(s), under exclusive license to Springer Nature Singapore Pte Ltd. 2024
R.-S. Her, *The Economy of Goodness*,
https://doi.org/10.1007/978-981-97-6363-4

Bruni, L., & Zamagni, S. (2014). Economics and Theology in Italy Since the Eighteenth Century. The Oxford Handbook of Christianity and Economics.

Casson, M., & Casson, C. (2014). The History of Entrepreneurship: Medieval Origins of a Modern Phenomenon. Business History.

Chang, J. (2002). The Book of Changes: A New Translation (Guo Jianxun Trans & ed.). Taipei: San Min Books.

China Youth Daily. (2010, September 7). Zhaoshang yinhang: weiyou kuihua xiang ri qing [China Merchants Bank: Only sunflowers lean towards the sun]. Retrieved from https://zqb.cyol.com/content/2010-09/07/content_3407711.htm.

Confucius. (2013). The Book of Rites (Li Ji): English-Chinese Version (D. Sheng, Ed., J. Legge, Trans.). CreateSpace Independent Publishing Platform.

Confucius., & Legge, J. (2010). Chinese Classics: Confucian Analects. General Books (Original work published 1861).

Dacheng ben sheng xindi guan jing [Mahayana Sutra on the Contemplation of the Mind-Ground of Essential Nature (Sect. 4)]. Dazheng xinxiu dazang jing [Taishō Tripiṭaka (Vol. 3)]. No. 0159.

Dafangbian fo bao'en jing [Great Skillful Means Sutra on the Buddha's Repayment of Kindness (Sect. 2)]. Dazheng xinxiu dazang jing [Taishō Tripiṭaka (Vol. 3)]. No. 0156.

Dong, Z. (Eds.). (2012). Xin yi chunqiu fan lu (xia) [Luxuriant Dew of the Spring and Autumn Annals (vol. 2)] (Z. Y. Jia & W. Z. Chang, Trans.). Taipei: San min shu ju.

Fang, G. C. (ed.). Dacheng wujin cang fa [Mahayana Infinite Collection of Dharma (Vol. 2)]. CBETA Electronic Buddhist Texts Integration (Vol. 4). No. 0042.

Fromm, E. (1995). Ai de yishu [The Art of Loving] (M. Xiang, Trans.). Taipei: Zhiwen chuban she.

Gibran, K., & Bushrui, S. B. (2012). The Prophet: A New Annotated Edition. Simon and Schuster.

Guo, J. X. (2002). Xin yi jing duben [New Translation of the Book of Change]. Taipei: Sanmin shuju.

H. & Stallings, A. E. (2018). Works and Days (Reprint ed.). Penguin Classics.

Harari, Y. N. (2018). Homo Deus: A Brief History of Tomorrow (Illustrated ed.). Harper Perennial.

Hawkins, D. R. (2014). Power vs. Force: The Hidden Determinants of Human Behavior. Hay House Incorporated.

Hayek, F.A. (1967). Prices and Production. New York: Augustus M. Kelley Publisher.

Hayek, F.A. (1994). The Road to Serfdom. Chicago: University of Chicago Press.

Heidegger, M., & Macquarrie, J. (2008). Being and Time. United Kingdom: HarperCollins.

Her, R. S. (2008). Ci ji shijian meixue xia: qingjing meixue [The Philosophy of Practices of Buddhist Tzu Chi, Part 2]. Taipei: New Century Publishing Co., Ltd.

Her, R. S. (2016). Shan jingji—lun ziben shichang de shan xing yu daode [Economy of Goodness: On the Virtue and Ethics of Capital Markets]. Shandong: Shandong Normal University Journal, Vol. 3.

Her, R. S. (2022) Ciji xue gailun [The Essential Studies of Tzu Chi Buddhism], Linking Publishing Ltd.

Hick, J. (2005). An Interpretation of Religion: Human Responses to the Transcendent (Second ed.). United Kingdom: Yale University Press.

Hick, J. (2013). The Fifth Dimension: An Exploration of the Spiritual Realm (Second ed.). Oneworld Publications.

Hua, H. (Eds.). (1974). The Diamond Sutra. San Francisco: Sino-American Buddhist Association. https://www.buddhanet.net/pdf_file/prajparagen2.pdf.

Hua, H. (Eds.). (2008). The Sutra in Forty-Two Sections Spoken by the Buddha: A Simple Explanation by the Venerable Master Hsuan Hua. United States: Buddhist Text Translation Society.

Huineng, D. (Eds.). (2014). The Sixth Patriarch's Dharma Jewel Platform Sutra. Buddhist Text Translation Society.

Isaacson, W. S. (2012). The Real Leadership Lessons of Steve Jobs, Harvard Business Review (April 2012 Issue). Massachusetts: Harvard Business Publishing.

Jaspers, K. (1949). The Perennial Scope of Philosophy (R. Manbeim, Trans.). United Kingdom: Philosophical Library.

Jaspers, K. (1962). Kant: From the Great Philosophers (Vol. 1). United Kingdom: Harcourt, Brace & World.

Jung, C. G. (1969). The Archetypes and the Collective Unconscious Collected Works of C.G. Jung, Vol. 9 (Part 1) (R. F. C. Hull, Trans.). United Kingdom: Princeton University Press.

Kant, I. (1997). Groundwork of the Metaphysics of Morals (M. J. Gregor, Ed. & Trans.). Cambridge University Press (Original work published 1785).

Kant, I. (2012). Kant: Groundwork of the Metaphysics of Morals (M. J. Gregor & J. Timmermann, Ed. & Trans.). United Kingdom: Cambridge University Press. (Original work published 1785).

Kehoe, D. P. (1992). Management and Investment on Estates in Roman Egypt during the Early Empire (Papyrologische Texte und Abhandlungen 40). Bonn: R. Habelt.

Keynes, J. M. (2018). The General Theory of Employment, Interest, and Money. Germany: Springer International Publishing.

Kiley, D. (2008). Fute jiuwang zhao shang fengtian laojiang [Ford Turns to Toyota Veteran for Help]. Taiwan: Business Today. Retrieved from https://www.businesstoday.com.tw/article/category/80393/post/200808070015/.

King James Bible. (2017). King James Bible Online. https://www.kingjamesbibleonline.org/ (Original work published 1769) Note: Subsequent quotations of the Bible are all from this source.

King James Bible. (2017). King James Bible Online. https://www.kingjamesbibleonline.org/ (Original work published 1769).

Krishnamurti, J. (1969). Freedom from the Known. India: HarperCollins.

Legge, J. (1962). The Sacred books of China: The texts of Taoism (Vol. 1). New York: Dover Publications.

Legge, J. (1963). The I Ching: The Book of Changes. United Kingdom: Dover Publications.

Legge, J. (1967). The Book of Poetry (Vol. 1). Taiwan: Paragon Book Reprint Corporation.

Legge, J. (1971). Confucian Analects: The Great Learning, and The Doctrine of the Mean. New York: Dover Publications.

Li, Z. H. (1996). Mei de licheng [Beautiful Journey]. Taipei: Sanmin shuju.

Lin, H. (2013). Jiben lunli xue [The Basics of Ethics]. Taiwan: San Min Book Co.

Lin, H. (2014). Jinrong jigou tuichu yu jinrong xiaofeizhe baozhang—hainan fazhan yinhang daobi fengbo jian xi [The Exit of Financial Institutions and Financial Consumer Protection—A Brief Analysis of the Collapse of Hainan Development Bank.]. Zhongguo shangmao, 2014 Issue 4.

Liu, Q. Wuliang yi jing [The Sutra of Innumerable Meanings (Sect. 1)]. Dazheng xinxiu dazang jing [Taishō Tripiṭaka (Vol. 9)]. No. 0276.

Lou, Y. & Leonard, H. D. (2017). Ciji zong men de pushi jiazhi [The Universal Values of Tzu Chi]. Taipei: Tzu Chi Culture and Communication Foundation.

Lou, Y. L. (2013). Zongjiao yanjiu fangfa jiang ji—jicheng yu pipan [Lecture Notes on Religious Research Methods: Inheritance and Criticism]. Beijing: Peking University Press.

Lou, Y. L., & Leonard, H. D. (2017). Ci ji zongmen de pu shi jiazhi [The Universal Value of Buddhism & the Dharma Path of Tzu Chi]. Tzu Chi Culture & Communication Foundation. pp. 125–140.

Lu, C. (2000). Yindu foxue yuanliu lue lun [An Outline of the Origins of Indian Buddhism]. Taiwan: Darchen Publisher. p. 182.

Lu, M. R. (1995). Jingji xue gailun [Introduction to Economics]. Taipei: San min shu ju. pp. 72–76.

M. & Legge, J. (2011). The Works of Mencius. New York: Dover Publications.

Mandela, N. (2013). Long Walk to Freedom. Hachette UK.

Marx, K. (Eds.). (1993). Capital: A Critique of Political Economy (Vol. 3). United Kingdom: Penguin Publishing Group.

Marx, K., & Engel, F. (2002). The Communist Manifesto. London: Penguin Books (Original work published in 1848).

McAdams, D. (2014). Game-Changer: Game Theory and the Art of Transforming Strategic Situations. United States: W. W. Norton.

Mencius. (2019). The Works of Mencius (Sun Jiaqi ed.). New Taipei City: Jen Publishing Co., Ltd., p. 339

Muller, J. Z. (2007). The Mind and the Market: Capitalism in Western Thought. United Kingdom: Knopf Doubleday Publishing Group.

Myers, R. H. (1970). The Chinese Peasant Economy: Agricultural Development in Hopei and Shantung, 1890–1949. Taiwan: Harvard University Press. pp. 288–289.

Nagarjuna. Da zhi du lun [The Treatise on the Great Perfection of Wisdom]. Dazheng xinxiu dazang jing [Taishō Tripiṭaka (Vol. 25)]. No. 1509.

O'Mahony, B. & Lobo, A. (2017). The Organic Industry in Australia: Current and Future Trends. Land Use Policy (66).

Paccione, C. E. (2020). The Giving Brain: A Look at the Neurology of Altruism. Brain World Magazine. https://brainworldmagazine.com/giving-brain-look-neurology-altruism/.

Pearce, Colin D. (2013). Aristotle and Business: An Inescapable Tension, Handbook of the Philosophical Foundations of Business Ethics (Vol. 1). Springer Publishing.

Pesterfield, H. (2007). Traditional Lead Climbing: A Rock Climber's Guide to Taking the Sharp End of the Rope. Birmingham: Wilderness Press.

Plato. (2018). Lixiangguo [The Republic] (Wu, S. L. Trans.). Taipei: Huazhi wenhua chubanshe.

Postan, M. M., Rich, E. E., & Miller, E. (Eds.). (1963). The Cambridge Economic History of Europe: Economic Organization and Policies in The Middle Ages. Cambridge: Cambridge University Press.

Poundstone, W. (1993). Prisoner's Dilemma: John von Neumann, Game Theory, and the Puzzle of the Bomb (First Edition Thus ed.). Anchor.

Poznanski, K. Z. (2015). Confucian Economics: The World at Work. World Review of Political Economy.

Qu, W. L. (1983). Shangshu ji shi [The Collected Commentaries of the Shang Shu]. Taiwan: Linking Publishing Co., Ltd.

Rawls, J. (1999). A Theory of Justice. United Kingdom: Oxford University Press.

Rawson, J. (1984). Han Civilization. By Wang Zhongshu, translated by K. C. Chang and collaborators (Early Chinese Civilization.). New Haven and London: Yale University Press, 1982. The Antiquaries Journal.

Ricard, M. (2015). Altruism: The Science and Psychology of Kindness. United Kingdom: Atlantic Books.

Rigby, D., Sutherland, J., & Noble, A. (2018). Agile at Scale, Harvard Business Review (May–June 2018 Issue). Massachusetts: Harvard Business Publishing.

Roach, G. M. & McNally, L. C. (2009). The Diamond Cutter: The Buddha on Managing Your Business and Your Life. United States: Harmony.

Saint-Exupéry, A. (1992). Wind, Sand and Stars (L. Galantière, Trans). United States: Harcourt Brace Jovanovich (Original work published 1939).

Salamon, L. M. (2010). Putting The Civil Society Sector on The Economic Map of the world. Annals of Public and Cooperative Economics, 81(2), 167–210. https://doi.org/10.1111/j.1467-8292.2010.00409.x

Schumacher, E. F. (2011). Small Is Beautiful: A Study of Economics as If People Mattered. United Kingdom: Random House.

Schumpeter, J. A. (2006). History of Economic Analysis. United Kingdom: Taylor & Francis.

Schumpeter, J. A. (2010). Capitalism, Socialism and Democracy. United Kingdom: Taylor & Francis.

Scott-Phillips, T. C., Dickins, T. E., & West, S. A. (2011). Evolutionary Theory and the Ultimate–Proximate Distinction in the Human Behavioral Sciences. Perspectives on Psychological Science, 6(1), 38–47. https://doi.org/10.1177/1745691610393528.

Shen, M. (2010). "Yinhang xintu" Ma WeiHua ["The bank believer" Ma WeiHua]. In Licai [Financial Management]. China: Hai yan chubanshe.

Shi song lu [Sarvastivada-vinaya (Sect. 49)]. Dazheng xinxiu dazang jing [Taishō Tripiṭaka (Vol. 2)]. No. 1435.

Shi, De Fan (2015). Zheng yan shang ren na lu zuji [Footprints of Master Cheng Yen]. Taipei: Tzu Chi Publishing Co.

Shi, S. H. (1956). Fan sheng zhi shu jin shi [A Current Annotation of Works of Fan Shengzhi]. Beijing: Kexue chuban she.

Shi, Taixu. (1998). Tai xu dashi quanshu [Corpus of Venerable Tai Xu's Buddhist Studies]. Taipei: Pu dao si fojing liutong chu yinxing.

Shi, Yin Shun (2003). She dacheng lun jiang ji [Commentary on the Compendium of the Great Vehicle]. Taiwan: Zhengwen Publishing House.

Shih, Cheng Yen. (1989). Jing Si Aphorisms. Taipei: Chiu Ko Publishing Co., Ltd.

Shih, Cheng Yen. (1991). Xinshi rensheng chengjiu gongde [Faith and Integrity Make Life Virtues]. Tzu Chi Monthly, Issue 292 (April 25, 1991). Tzu Chi Culture & Communication Foundation.

Shih, Cheng Yen. (1996). Huigui xinling de guxiang [Return to the Spiritual Hometown]. Taipei: Tzu Chi Publishing Co.

Shih, Cheng Yen. (1998). Shan men yi kai [The Gate of Goodness Has Opened]. Tzu Chi Monthly, Issue 378 (May 25, 1998). Tzu Chi Culture & Communication Foundation.

Shih, Cheng Yen. (2000). Si shi er zhang jing jiangshu [Commentary on The Sutra of Forty-Two Chapters: Spoken by the Buddha]. Taipei: Jing Si Publishing Co., Ltd.

Shih, Cheng Yen. (2003). Tzu Chi Bimonthly: Issue 558. Taipei: Tzu Chi Culture & Communication Foundation. May 25, 2003.

Shih, Cheng Yen. (2007). Jing si jing she yu qing xiushi kai shi [Jing Si Abode and Pure Practitioner].

Shih, Cheng Yen. (2013). Jing Si Abode Morning Service. Hualien: Jing Si Abode. Dec. 20, 2013.

Shih, Cheng Yen. (2013). Wisdom at Dawn. Hualien: Jing Si Abode. July 3, 2013.

Shih, Cheng Yen. (2014). Jing Si Abode Morning Service. Hualien: Jing Si Abode. August 31, 2014.

Shih, Cheng Yen. (2014). Wisdom at Dawn. Hualien: Jing Si Abode.

Shih, Cheng Yen. (Eds.). (1989). Jing si yu [Jing Si Aphorisms]. Taipei: Chiu Ko Publishing Co., Ltd.

Shih, Cheng Yen. [Tzu Chi Culture and Communication Foundation]. (2021, Jul 26). Wisdom at Dawn E913—Realizations Differ According to Capabilities [Video]. YouTube. https://www.youtube.com/watch?v=vP_wyW1uhUA.

Shih, Yin Shun (1992). Weishi xue tan yuan [Exploring the Origins of the Consciousness-only Theory]. Taipei: Zhengwen Publishing House.

Smith, A. (1960). The Wealth of Nations. United Kingdom: J.M. Dent & sons, Limited.

Smith, P. (2009). Shen-tsung's Reign and the New Policies of Wang An-shih, 1067–1085. D. Twitchett & P. J. Smith (Eds.). The Cambridge History of China. Cambridge: Cambridge University Press. pp. 347–483

Sohu. (2019, April 28). Maweihua: Yingxiang li touzi shi yige biran de qushi [Maweihua: Impact Investing is an Unstoppable Trend]. Retrieved from https://www.sohu.com/a/310848199_99947734

Sohu. (2019, June 14). Ping'an yinhang shuidian fupin moshi, lianheguo dianming biaoyang! [The United Nations Named and Praised Ping An Bank Hydropower Poverty Alleviation Model!]. Retrieved from https://www.sohu.com/a/320684329_100049995.

Sorokin, P. A. (1954). The Ways and Power of Love: Types, Factors, and Techniques of Moral Transformation. United States: Beacon Press.

Stander, H. (2014). The Oxford handbook of Christianity and Economics: Economics in the Church fathers. Oxford: Oxford University Press.

Steiner, P. L. (2007). Voltaire: Philosophical Letters: Or, Letters Regarding the English Nation. United States: Hackett Publishing Company.

Sturgeon, D. (2019). Chinese Text Project: A Dynamic Digital Library of Premodern Chinese (J. Legge, Trans.). Digital Scholarship in the Humanities. Retrieved from https://ctext.org.

Tang, X. C. (1995). Xin yi guanzi duben (xia) [New Translation of The Book of Zhuangzi (Vol. 2)]. Taipei: Sanmin shuju.

Thành, M. & Leigh, P.D. (2001). Sutra of the Medicine Buddha (H. Jung, Trans.). North Hills: International Buddhist Monastic Institute. https://www.buddhanet.net/pdf_file/medbudsutra.pdf.

The White House. (2001, September 20). President Declares "Freedom at War with Fear" [Press release]. https://georgewbush-whitehouse.archives.gov/news/releases/2001/09/20010920-8.html.

Toynbee, A. J., & Somervell, D. C. (1987). A Study of History: Volume I: Abridgement of Volumes I–VI. United Kingdom: Oxford University Press.

Trotsky, L. (1991). The Revolution Betrayed: What Is the Soviet Union and Where Is It Going? United States: Labor Publications (Original work published in 1936).

Tzu, L. (Eds.). (2021). Tao Te Ching (J. Legge, Trans.). Standard Ebooks. Retrieved from https://standardebooks.org/ebooks/laozi/tao-te-ching/james-legge.

Tzu, L., & Legge, J. (2013). Tao Te Ching (Legge): A New Translation and Commentary. Start Publishing LLC.

Tzu, L., Lin, D., & Das, L. S. (2006). Tao Te Ching: Annotated & Explained (SkyLight Illuminations) (1st ed.). SkyLight Paths.

Vygotsky, L.S. & Davydov, V.V. (1992). Educational Psychology (S. Robert, Trans.). Florida: St. Lucie Press. (Original work published 1926).

Wang, B. X. (2010). Laozi daodejing zhu de xiandai jiedu [Modern Interpretation of Laozi's Dao De Jing]. Yuan-Liou Publishing Co., Ltd.

Wang, S. R. (Eds.). (2011). Wang yangming quanji [A Complete Collection of Works by Wang Yangming]. Shanghai Century Publishing Co., Ltd.

Wang, X. Q. (1994). Xunzi ji jie [Collected Annotations of Xunzi]. Shandong: Shandong Friendship Publishing House.

Wang, Y. M. & Deng, A. M. (2000). Chuanxi lu zhushu [The Annotations of Chuan Xi Lu]. Fa yan chuban she.

Weber, M. (1958). The Protestant Ethics and the Spirit of Capitalism (T. Parsons, Trans.). New York: Scribner.

Weber, M. (1978). Economy and Society: An Outline of Interpretive Sociology. United Kingdom: University of California Press.

Weber, M. (2003). The Protestant Ethic and the Spirit of Capitalism (T. Parsons, Trans.). United States: Dover Publications.

Wilson, K. E., Silva, F., & Ricardson, D. (2015). Social Impact Investment: Building the Evidence Base. The Organization for Economic Cooperation and Development.

Winkler, J. K. (2007). John D. Rockefeller: A Portrait in Oils. United States: Cosimo Classics.

Wright, A. F. (1959). Buddhism in Chinese History. Stanford University Press.

Xenophon, X., & Hayes, B.J. (2017). Oeconomicus. Andesite Press.

Xianqian W. (1994). Collected Annotations of Xunzi. Shandong: Shandong Friendship Publishing House.

Yang, Y. (2021). The Culture of Canonization: Reading Wen Tianxiang's "Song of the Noble Spirit". Journal of East-West Thought September 2021. California State Polytechnic University. p. 24. Retrieved from https://scholarwo rks.calstate.edu/downloads/r494vr33x.

Yu, Y. S. (2010). Jinshi zhongguo rujia lunli yu shangren jingshen [Confucian Ethics and Merchant Spirit in Modern China]. Zhongguo wenhua shi tong shi [Chinese History and Culture]. Hongkong: Oxford University Press.

Yunus, M. (2007). Creating a World Without Poverty: Social Business and the Future of Capitalism. United Kingdom: Public Affairs.

Za'a han jing [Samyukta-agama]. Dazheng xinxiu dazang jing [Taishō Tripiṭaka (Vol. 2)]. No. 0099.

Zhang, C., Vaughan, C. E. (2002). Mao Zedong as Poet and Revolutionary Leader: Social and Historical Perspectives. United Kingdom: Lexington Books.

Zong'a han jing [Madhyama-agama]. Dazheng xinxiu dazang jing [Taishō Tripiṭaka (Vol. 1)]. No. 0026.

Index

A

Abraham, 11, 131, 135, 136, 138
Acer, 357–361
Agama Sutra, 62, 73, 173, 175
Agile management model, 408
Alaya Consciousness, 281
Altruistic economic approach, 344
Altruistic economic structure, 34, 35, 344
Altruistic economic thought, 231–256
Altruistic economy, 75, 258, 343
Altruistic goodness, 258
Altruistic practice, 222, 340
The Analects, 31, 116, 274
The Analects of Confucius, 23, 274
Ananda, 418, 419
Anti-Chinese riots, 402
Apple, 35, 233, 267, 268, 278, 316, 384, 407, 414, 416
Aristotle, 6, 11, 20, 47, 68, 73, 74, 106, 108–111, 193, 258–260, 264, 270, 288, 300, 335, 448, 457
Asceticism, 46, 183

Avatamsaka Sutra, 97

B

Baizhang (Zen Master), 205–208, 211
Balance of Interests, 358
Bālapaṇḍitasutta Sutra, 94
Bamboo Bank Era, 248, 250, 334
Bamboo coin bank, 248, 334
Being, 96, 97
Bell, Daniel, 242–244, 254, 256
Benevolence (仁 ren), 6, 19, 22, 23, 30, 42, 48, 57, 58, 72, 91, 113, 117, 118, 152, 156, 162, 168, 169, 231, 260, 276, 293, 295, 296, 343, 357, 449–451
Bentham, Jeremy, 329
Berkeley Innovation Forum, 90
Bible, 56, 135, 139–142, 147, 366, 428, 432
Bodhisattva, 66, 67, 80, 81, 97, 98, 144, 175, 176, 188, 195–200, 203, 290, 383, 437, 442, 451, 452, 455, 457

Bodhisattva Ksitigarbha, 24
Bodhisattva Path, 12, 67, 451, 455, 457
Bone Marrow Registry, 93
The Book of Poetry, 17, 18
Book of Rites, 3, 22, 37, 40, 41, 450
Bourdieu, Pierre, 320
Buddha, 12, 24, 43, 45, 47, 49, 62–67, 69, 73, 74, 81, 84, 88, 93, 94–99, 144, 171–205, 208, 209, 211, 264, 281, 282, 285, 294, 297, 298, 301, 320, 322, 324, 371, 372, 375, 418, 419, 422, 430–438, 441, 443, 452, 453
Buddha-nature, 62, 69, 96, 97, 324, 425, 437
Buddhism, 6, 12, 20, 24, 29, 43, 45, 49, 57, 58, 62–67, 68–70, 73, 80, 81, 92–94, 97, 98, 116, 118, 138, 139, 170, 173, 197–211, 260, 264, 269, 270, 276, 277, 280–282, 289, 290, 292, 297, 320, 323, 324, 400, 402, 419, 423, 428, 431, 434–440, 443, 451–453, 445, 457
Buffett, Warren, 12, 144, 263, 272, 303, 384, 396, 422
Build-Operate-Transfer (BOT) Model, 123
Burke, Edmund, 227–229
Business of Goodness, 358

C
Caesar, Julius, 122, 123
Capitalism, 6, 32, 51–53, 55, 56, 62, 68, 113, 116, 118, 119, 121, 128, 149–152, 160, 197, 218, 221, 223, 227–230, 231–241, 244, 250, 251, 257, 269, 270, 299, 301, 315, 316, 319, 321, 323, 335, 340, 403

Capitalist economy, 51, 55, 65, 204
Capitalist enterprises, 255–256
Capitalist market, 233, 238, 250, 255
Capitalist society, 232, 239, 240, 254, 255, 322, 335
Cash-for-work relief program, 354
Catholic Church, 7, 53, 54, 124, 125, 128, 217, 420
Central Harmony, 10, 25–29, 41, 42
Chamber of Commerce, 151, 161, 218
Change Map, 417
Cherishing material life, 321, 323
China Merchants Bank, 308–313
Chinese Buddhism, 200, 201, 208
Chinese civilization, 111
Chinese economy, 73, 114, 116, 119, 171
Chinese philosophy, 17, 20, 31, 37, 40, 42, 44, 436, 437
Chinese Zen Buddhism, 432
Chouinard, Yvon, 351–353, 403, 427, 428
Christian civilizations, 53, 139, 423
Christian economic thought, 127, 140, 142, 143, 147
Christian economy, 146–148
Christian entrepreneurs, 144, 182, 263
Christianity, 12, 20, 24, 95, 108, 124, 124–128, 134, 139–146, 262, 301, 419, 420, 428, 431, 432, 438
Chu, Jenn Weng, 317, 331, 355, 356
Churchill, Winston, 290, 291
Citizen economy, 221, 222
Civic Economy, 221
Coca-Cola, 8, 423, 424
Collective consciousness, 99, 286, 376
Collective economy, 101
Collective interest, 50, 223

Collective unconscious, 285–287, 430, 431

Common Goodness, 6, 10, 49, 445, 451, 452

Common prosperity, 42, 43, 72, 334, 342

Compassion, 9, 12, 24, 43, 44, 47, 50, 66, 67, 81, 88, 91, 93, 94, 97, 98, 148, 171, 173, 176, 182, 194–197, 204–206, 226, 248, 249, 264, 265, 270, 271, 276–284, 287, 290, 292, 296, 299, 303, 316, 317, 335, 340, 341, 356, 357, 362, 371–376, 379, 393, 403–408, 416, 425, 439, 441–443, 451, 452, 455, 457, 458

Compassion and Altruism Research Center, 405

Confucian economic system, 449

Confucianism, 6, 12, 19, 22, 37, 57, 68, 70, 72, 96, 116, 118, 152, 153, 156, 157, 162, 169, 170, 180, 181, 191, 194, 200, 202, 207, 209, 226, 260, 264, 276, 277, 323, 331, 334, 336, 339, 340, 423, 428, 434–436, 438, 445, 449–451

Confucius, 2, 6, 19, 22–24, 31, 37, 41, 42, 57, 68, 84, 112, 116–118, 120, 152–157, 189, 194, 211, 260, 274, 291, 292, 295, 315, 331, 367, 432, 435, 436

Consumption of Goodness, 321

Core beliefs, 357

Core values, 35, 287, 288, 353–356, 361, 376, 388, 412

Corporate culture, 169, 287, 288, 356, 358, 359, 427

Corporate management, 358

Cuban missile crisis, 376

Cultivation of the mind, 442, 443

D

DA.AI Technology, 252, 253, 327, 404, 426

Da Ai TV, 395, 409

Dalin Tzu Chi Hospital, 388, 389

Darwin, Charles, 5, 77, 79, 263

Decentralization, 412

Democritus, 46

Dharma dana, 441

Diligence, 213, 439, 440, 442

Disaster relief (Tzu Chi), 15, 95, 213, 252, 282, 286, 317, 327, 341, 354–356, 362, 381, 386, 394, 399, 401, 404, 411, 426

Doctrine of the Mean, 25, 30, 40, 48, 433, 438

Dragonetti, Domenico, 222, 223

Drucker, Peter, 243, 279, 314, 361

E

Eastern goodness, 46

Eastern philosophers, 97

Eastern philosophy, 21, 67, 97, 264, 280

East India Company, 227, 228

Economic innovation, 268, 340, 406

Economic justice, 139

Economic prosperity, 70, 115–118, 121, 127, 208, 257, 322

Eightfold Path, 29

Eighth consciousness, 281

Emperor Huang, 26, 111

Emptiness, 13, 20, 61, 63, 64, 69, 97, 173, 179, 261, 262, 284, 324, 335, 375, 376, 383, 384, 432, 436, 437, 446

Energy field, 371–375

Enkidu, 102–104

Enlightenment, 43, 55, 69, 80, 95, 98, 139, 173, 185, 193, 199, 202, 205, 206, 229, 258, 281, 332, 345, 375, 406, 430, 435, 437, 438, 442, 451–457
Enlightenment (Western), 223–226
Enterprise of Goodness, 432, 433, 450
Environmental initiative, 251, 424
Environmental protection, 9, 247, 251–253, 271, 286, 287, 326, 340, 353, 387, 403, 404, 411, 412, 425–427
Environmental sustainability and harmony with nature, 349
The Epic of Gilgamesh, 6, 102–104
Epicurus, 46
Epigenetic process, 78, 79
Epimetheus, 105, 106
Equal wealth, 329, 330, 332, 457
Equal wealth distribution, 23
Evolution of altruism, 231–256
Evolution of civilization, 269
Expedient Sufficiency, 73, 177, 178
Exploitation, 4, 8, 62, 85, 109, 116, 117, 140, 151, 159, 227–229, 232–242, 244, 255, 269, 295, 318, 322, 333–336, 345, 347, 349, 393, 458

F
Faith, 14–16, 54, 56, 87, 89, 104, 124, 127–130, 132, 137, 142–144, 146–148, 203, 216, 224, 227, 229, 249, 322, 351–356, 361, 367, 368, 371, 375, 378, 394, 398, 419–421
Faith-and value-based leadership, 361
Fan Li, 24, 61, 62
Father Basil, 125, 126
Feudal Economy, 221
Filial piety, 22, 57, 113, 115, 169

Financial Goodness, 300
Five Aggregates, 64–67, 173–175
Forbearance, 59, 442
Ford, 255, 315, 413, 414
Ford, Henry, 12, 35, 236, 299, 308, 322, 413, 414
Four Immeasurable States of Mind, 84
Four-in-One teams, 411
Four Sufficiencies, 73, 176, 177, 180, 182
Fraternity and Mutual Aid, 220
Free competition, 32–34, 40, 62, 237
Frisians, 216
Fromm, Erich, 322

G
Game theory, 85
Gates, Bill, 12, 144, 183, 245, 271, 272, 307, 415, 422
General Theory of Hexa-aspect Values, 358
Genovesi, Antonio, 222, 223
Gibran, Kahlil, 381, 384
Gilgamesh, 6, 102–104
Globalization, 227, 312, 313
God, 6, 11, 12, 18, 20, 24, 28, 46, 55–58, 61, 68, 91, 92, 95–97, 109, 116, 124–148, 148, 182, 186, 225, 229, 238, 239, 243, 263–265, 285, 294, 374, 398, 422, 423, 431
Good Enterprises, 15, 73, 74, 177, 263, 306, 307, 327, 400, 428, 435, 438, 439, 450, 455
Good Knowledge Advisor Sufficiency, 74, 177, 179, 180
Goodness and morality, 232, 240, 243, 245, 247, 254, 256
Goodness in Trade, 298
Goodness of law, 259
Good will, 35, 36, 47, 94, 137
Greater self, 58, 59, 62–64, 97

Great love, 24, 28, 43, 49, 195, 248, 250, 270, 393, 404
Greek Civilization, 105
Greek philosophy, 46, 428

H
Hainan Development Bank, 309
Han Dynasty, 44, 112, 157, 159, 200, 202, 331, 336, 338, 339
Harmonious balance, 360
Harmonious Goodness, 6, 47, 445, 449
Harmonious unification, 10, 48, 437, 440
Harmony, 10, 25, 26, 37, 40–42, 162, 318, 408, 411
Harvard Business Review, 9, 407, 408
Harvard Business School, 14, 361, 378, 394
Harvard University, 14, 39, 82, 147, 158, 242, 250, 282, 354, 355, 407, 411, 417, 422
Hawking, Stephen, 57, 326, 345
Hawkins, David, 368, 371, 372, 374
Hedonism, 46
Heidegger, 96, 97
Hick, John, 47, 96, 97
Highest goodness, 21, 24, 71, 109, 445, 446
Historical Dialectic, 223, 225
Hitler, Adolf, 290, 291, 368
Holacracy, 387, 408, 410
HTC, 409
Huawei, 308, 409
Huineng, 64, 65, 375, 432, 437
Humanistic Buddhism, 209, 211
Humanistic space, 355, 356
Humbaba, 102, 103
Hyundai, 414

I
IBM, 268, 315
The I Ching (The Book of Changes), 19, 25, 27, 29, 30, 43, 44, 72, 120, 433
Idealism, 105
IKEA, 144, 273, 280, 362, 363, 396
Impermanence, 69, 173, 432
Indian Buddhism, 210
Individualism, 51–58, 62, 67–70, 91, 162, 275, 282, 320, 428, 429
Indonesia, 179, 249, 270, 317, 391–393, 396–403, 412, 425
Industrial Revolution, 151, 222, 315, 429
Inherent goodness, 137, 265, 338
Intel, 305, 414
Interdependent Arising, 43, 63, 69, 98, 320
Islam, 24, 52, 148, 149, 262, 301, 401, 403, 420, 421, 431

J
Jaspers, Karl, 95–97
Jesus, 68, 124, 127, 134, 140–147, 371, 419, 420
Jewish Economic Philosophy, 129
Jews, 6, 11, 53, 129–136, 138, 140, 141, 149, 186, 191, 192, 216, 262, 300
Jing Si Abode, 211–213, 346, 385, 399, 404
Jobs, Steve, 34, 35, 90, 233, 267–269, 278, 300, 316, 356, 357, 384, 403, 406, 407
Joint Stock Company, 219
Jung, Carl, 99, 285, 287, 374, 430, 431
Justice, 7, 26, 37, 38, 42, 48, 49, 51, 56–58, 68, 117, 134, 140–142, 145–147, 150, 152, 156, 169, 214, 222, 224, 226–228, 233,

237, 238, 240, 243, 244, 250,
251, 255, 256, 259–260, 266,
277, 292–294, 296, 297, 302,
331–335, 341, 377, 440, 441,
451

K
Kamprad, Ingvar, 273, 280, 362, 363
Kant, Emmanuel, 35, 36, 46–47, 94,
137, 264, 280, 448
Keynes, John, 2, 15, 241, 242, 244,
265, 270, 342
Key to achieving equal wealth, 332
King David, 11, 131
King's Way, 157, 358
King Wen, 17–19
Kusuma, Sugianto, 270, 392,
400–403

L
Lao Tzu, 3, 21, 24, 29, 30, 45,
58–60, 69, 71, 84, 96, 97, 112,
154, 279, 280, 292–295, 322,
337, 338, 435–438, 446, 447
Lee, James, 404
Leonard, Herman, 14, 15, 354, 355,
361, 378, 411
Li Bai, 430
Liberalism, 56, 429
Liberty, 32, 70, 141, 218, 226
rise of free people, 218
Life Buddhism, 211
Locke, John, 54, 258
Long Walk to Freedom, 378
Lotus Sutra, 66, 196, 203, 322
Lu Cheng, 45, 93, 98

M
Madsen, Richard, 411
Mahayana, 193, 419, 453

Mahayana Buddhism, 12, 436, 437
Ma, Jack, 35, 266, 267, 335
Malaysia, 317, 327, 355, 356, 399,
412, 425
Management with love, 14, 361, 384,
387, 388, 394, 396, 398
Mandela, Nelson, 372, 375, 378
Mao Zedong, 369, 370
Marcuse, Herbert, 269
Maritime trade, 52, 127, 150, 221,
223, 229
Marx, Karl, 15, 68, 79, 126,
232–241, 244, 255, 264, 265,
299, 345, 347
Master Cheng Yen, 9, 13, 14, 31, 44,
66, 67, 81, 92–94, 144, 191,
195, 196, 211–213, 247–251,
255, 270, 271, 273, 279, 283,
286, 290, 294, 323, 326, 332,
334, 346, 356, 378, 382,
385–396, 399–403, 404, 408,
409, 411, 418, 422, 430, 431,
437, 440
Master Yin Shun, 66, 290
Materialism, 105
Material wealth, 22, 51, 108, 131,
143, 171, 179, 182, 225, 324,
453, 454, 457
Ma, Weihua, 308–315
Means of goodness, 25, 29, 31, 72,
294–296
Medicine Buddha, 67, 451–457
Medieval Chamber of Commerce, 218
Medieval Church, 127, 128
Medieval Commercial Society, 215
Medieval Scholasticism, 46
Medieval Towns, 215
Meditation, 269
Mencius, 3, 22, 46, 162–169, 191,
209, 264, 274–276, 280, 331,
373, 374, 433, 434
Metaphysics of Morals, 35, 47

Mexican Fisheries Association, 417

Microsoft, 271, 272, 409, 415, 416

Middle Ages, 55, 57, 68, 121, 126–128, 150–152, 192, 215–218, 220, 221, 298

Middle class, 218, 239, 302, 334

Middle way, 25, 26, 93, 103, 104, 110, 437

Mind-power, 371

Moser, Justus, 226, 227

Moses, 11, 68, 130–133, 140, 141, 300

Motivation, 258, 266

Motivation of goodness, 25, 29, 31, 35, 70, 257–288, 294, 295

Muhammad, 138, 148, 245, 246, 302, 420, 421

Muslim, 28, 52–54, 148–152, 180, 224, 262, 392

Mutual aid, 78, 86, 87, 99, 162, 164, 221, 222, 229, 401, 417

Mutual assistance, 222, 229

Mutual benefit, 4, 8, 10, 21, 29, 32, 35, 50, 85, 86, 90, 222, 229, 263, 335, 417

N

Nadella, Satya, 415, 416

Natural Monopoly, 33, 298

New Testament, 134, 140, 141, 143

Nike, 424

Nirvana, 12, 45, 49, 69, 437

Nokia, 90, 279, 409

Non-Action (concept), 59, 336, 436

Non-Being, 60, 69, 97, 438

Non-profit organizations, 81, 254

No-self, 62

O

OECD (Organization for Economic Co-operation and Development), 306

Oeconomicus, 107

Oikonomike, 108

The Old Testament, 126, 132, 135, 136, 141, 145

Oligopoly or monopoly, 33–35

Open Innovation, 90

Organic farming, 348

Origin of Capital, 216

Outcome of goodness, 31, 35–37, 257

P

Pandora, 105, 106

Pan, Michael, 283, 284, 379, 405, 406, 412

Pareto optimality, 9, 89

Pareto, Vilfredo, 9, 88–91, 458

Patagonia, 287, 326, 351–353, 403, 427, 428

The Perennial Scope of Philosophy, 95

Philanthropy, 44, 81, 144, 271, 272, 288, 314, 345, 402, 422, 448

Planned economy, 2, 15, 242

Plato, 3, 11, 17, 20, 109, 110, 448

Poor among the poor, 332

Poor among the rich, 195, 332

Precepts, 74, 175, 185, 202, 210, 419, 442

Preserving Harmony, 10, 27–29, 44

Principles of Responsible Investment (PRI), 307

Prisoner's Dilemma, 8, 84, 85, 88, 90, 458

Production of Goodness, 315

Prometheus, 105, 106

Propriety (禮 li), 19, 22–24, 49, 57, 58, 117, 118, 152, 155, 156,

168, 194, 209, 226, 332, 339, 449–451
Protection Sufficiency, 73, 177–179, 182
Protestant, 7, 12, 15, 53–55, 116, 144, 182, 223, 224, 238, 239, 243, 244, 262, 263, 422
Protestant ethics, 12, 15, 55, 119, 182, 238, 239, 243, 263, 422
Proximate Mechanism, 77–80

Q

Qin Dynasty, 114, 169, 181, 336
Qinheyuan, 318

R

Rawls, John, 39, 40, 42, 47, 250, 251, 277, 333, 379, 457
Recycling, 252, 318, 424, 425
Recycling stations, 204, 251, 323, 425
Red Bull, 364, 365
The Republic, 17
Result of goodness, 25, 42, 70
Rich among the poor, 332, 334
Rich among the rich, 195, 332, 402
Right Action, 29
Right Concentration, 29
Right Effort, 29, 178
Righteousness (義 yi), 10, 21–24, 30, 38, 48, 57, 67, 156, 157, 168, 169, 194, 265, 289, 293, 295, 296, 374
Right Livelihood, 29
Right Livelihood Sufficiency, 73, 74, 177, 179–182
Right Mindfulness, 29, 139
Right Thinking, 29
Right View, 29
The Rites by Daide, 120
Robertson, Brian, 410

Rockefeller, John Davison, 12, 263, 306, 307, 421, 422
Roman Empire, 121–124, 128, 215, 216
Round Organization, 408, 411

S

Sabbath, 6, 11, 131, 132, 186
Saint Thomas Aquinas, 46
Samadhi, 285, 323, 442, 443
Sandel, Michael, 82, 83
Sanmao, 383
Schumpeter, Joseph, 15, 32, 33, 128, 232, 238, 240, 241, 244, 245, 255, 265
Sedrakic, Thomas, 102
Self-cultivation, 113
Self-interest, 4, 9, 13, 15, 31–35, 45, 50, 55, 63, 69, 70, 74, 75, 79–81, 84, 85, 92–93, 98, 110, 113, 147, 155, 156, 197, 221, 225–230, 245, 255, 257–260, 263, 264–272, 275, 280–287, 292, 293, 298–300, 335, 341–344, 360, 393, 414, 415, 447, 458
Self-interested economy, 231
Selfless love, 44
Self-nature, 65, 69
Shih, Stan, 357–361
Silent Mentors, 93
Sinar Mas Group, 318, 391–393
Six Non-Tao, 73, 185–188, 192, 194
Smiling Curve Theory, 359
Smith, Adam, 4, 9, 15, 28, 31, 55, 84, 222–237, 255, 265, 266, 298–300, 343
Social enterprise, 15, 242–247, 251–256, 307, 314, 404, 425, 426
Socialist society, 254
Social norms, 77, 398

Socrates, 11, 16, 17, 20, 107, 280, 448

Song Dynasty, 41, 118, 160, 204, 331

Sony, 424

South Africa, 28, 249, 283, 284, 372, 378, 379, 405, 412, 440

Spielberg, Steven, 321

Spiritual leadership, 368

Standard Oil, 421

Starbucks, 416

Starvation Dilemma, 85, 87, 88

Stimulus of Goodness, 36

Structural Global Exploitation, 227

Suffering, 4, 5, 12, 13, 62, 65–67, 94, 102, 108, 136, 138, 151, 156, 161, 173, 174, 176, 179, 187, 188, 191, 201, 204, 213, 214, 248–250, 262–265, 281–284, 389, 437, 441, 454, 456

Sumerian, 6, 101–104

Supreme Enlightenment, 451–457

Supreme goodness, 16, 17, 20, 24, 35, 37, 43, 44–47, 71, 258–261, 277, 293, 448

Supreme Harmony, 10, 26, 27, 35, 44

Sustainable development, 7, 306, 313, 320, 358, 359, 365, 377, 418, 458

Sutra of Forty-Two Sections, 430

Sutra of Infinite Meanings, 284, 443

T

Taipei Tzu Chi Hospital, 31, 382

Taiwan's 921 Earthquake, 382

Taixu, 206, 207, 209–211

Tao, 3, 21, 24, 27, 30, 45, 48, 59–62, 65, 69, 72, 96, 97, 112–114, 117, 155, 175, 180, 260, 284, 293, 336, 338, 433, 435, 447

Taoism, 24, 58–61, 68–70, 96, 116, 118, 153, 264, 276, 280, 336, 339, 423, 428, 435–438, 445

Tenth Great Vow, 455, 456

Theory of evolution, 77

Tiantai Buddhism, 437

Toyota, 413, 414

True happiness, 6, 57, 74, 104, 110, 179, 261, 262, 270, 288, 323, 324

Twelve Great Vows of the Medicine Buddha, 451

2003 South Asian Tsunami, 270

2017 Penang flood, 356

Tzu Chi Foundation, 2, 9, 13–15, 24, 28, 31, 44, 66, 67, 81, 93–95, 144, 147, 179, 191, 195, 204, 211–214, 247–253, 255, 261, 265, 270, 271, 273, 282–286, 290, 297, 317, 318, 323, 327, 334, 335, 346, 354–356, 378–406, 409–412, 418, 422, 425–426, 431, 440, 441

Tzu Chi Medical Foundation, 290

Tzu Chi School of Buddhism, 95

Tzu Chi volunteers, 9, 15, 28, 31, 93, 180, 191, 195, 211–213, 249–253, 318, 327, 334, 346, 354, 355, 362, 379–381, 383, 385, 387, 388, 391, 393, 411, 412, 425–426, 440

U

Ultimate goodness, 35, 95, 109, 137

Unconditional loving-kindness, 432

Universal compassion, 432

University of Cambridge, 1, 2, 4, 333, 458

Utilitarianism, 46, 72, 83, 111, 136, 329, 330, 332

Utmost goodness, 22

V

Value Creation, 358
Value-oriented leadership, 14, 361–363, 365
Virtue, 16, 17, 46, 47, 106, 222, 227, 270, 272, 295, 397
Virtue (德 de), 6, 12, 18, 19, 22–25, 31, 37, 41, 44, 48, 57, 58, 72, 73, 117, 120, 152, 153, 156, 162, 167–169, 180, 189, 199, 210, 212, 222, 260, 280, 291–293, 433, 435, 445–458
ViTrox Corporation, 317, 355, 356
Voltaire, 7, 53, 223–230, 262
Vygotsky, 78

W

Wangdao, 157, 357–361
Wang, Yangming, 170, 180, 181, 276, 277
Weber, Max, 160, 238, 263
Western civilization, 2, 46, 420, 445, 448
Western goodness, 46

Western individualism, 56
Western philosophers, 47, 97
Western philosophy, 3, 22, 280
Western society, 52, 68, 124, 224, 306
Widjaja, Franky Oesman, 179, 180, 317, 391–393, 403
Wool trading, 217, 218

X

Xenophon, 107
Xexos, 424
Xunzi, 22, 23, 38–40, 45, 49, 155, 209, 226, 280, 324, 453
Xu Zhimo, 1

Y

Yin and Yang, 27, 30, 44, 45, 72

Z

Zeus, 105, 106
Zhao State, 377
Zhiyong Xi, 318
Zhou Dynasty, 31, 112, 162, 204, 331